DEEP RIVER

The Life and Music of Robert Shaw

DEEP RIVER

The Life and Music of Robert Shaw

Keith C. Burris

GIA Publications, Inc.
Chicago

For my mother and father,
in memory

G-7814

GIA Publications, Inc.
7404 S. Mason Ave.
Chicago, IL 60638
www.giamusic.com

Photographs courtesy of the estate of Robert Shaw.
Cover design and layout by Martha Chlipala.

ISBN: 978-1-57999-975-9

I hear not the volumes of sound merely,
I am moved by the exquisite meanings.
—Walt Whitman

CONTENTS

PREFACE

Painting a Life

A now-departed friend of mine was raised in Mexico in the early years of the last century. She told me a story about her father. Her father said that after he had lived in Mexico for a year, he thought he would write a book about the place; and after he had been there 10 years, he felt qualified to brief the incoming U.S. ambassador; and after 20 years in Mexico, he knew enough to say nothing.

The biographer's journey is similarly humbling. If he has lived with the life long enough, he discovers how much he does not know, and can never know, about it. He discovers that he cannot, finally, "get to the bottom" of the subject's nature, though his job is to try. He knows he must be wary of broad claims and generalizations. And it is not a bad thing if, when a fact cannot truly be determined or an incident is in dispute, this is admitted.

Yet the biographer's ambition is audacious, absurdly so. He seeks to reassemble or, if his subject has passed on, to re-call a life—to wake the dead. This he does by a journey into the past and by means of empathy, but potentially at his, and his subject's, peril. If he is at all wise, the writer knows his memory and imagination exercises are only that—exercises. He cannot resurrect flesh and blood. He cannot reproduce his subject as the public saw him or as friends knew him.

So, the biographer paints a portrait. He can only paint from his own perspective and his portrait cannot be other than subjective. For no two people see another in the same way. No one sees, or admires, or loves another person in any other way but his own. The writer cannot, in fact, give us back the man, but he can perhaps convey something of his subject's singularity. And his life's enduring light.

This book is intended to be three things: First, it is the story of Robert Shaw's work. I do not mean a chronicle of his work, per se. Shaw simply did too much in sixty years of music making to document and retell it all, and I doubt, in any case, that an endless, existential laundry list of triumphs and occasional defeats would take us to the heart of the man or his accomplishment. The real story is how Shaw defined and created work that was uniquely his, and then constantly refined what he had done.

Second, *Deep River* is about Shaw's approach to music. I hope it will attract the interest of scholars and musicians to Shaw's methods of preparation, particularly in the choral and choral-orchestral repertoire, and encourage their own in-depth, academic, and practical analysis of Shaw's techniques. Even more, I hope that this book will move young musicians to listen to Shaw's recordings and watch video of his preparation and that, rather than trying to mimic certain Shaw practices (like count singing or wearing a blue shirt), they will be inspired by his devotion to the music and his belief in music's power to change lives.

Finally, *Deep River* is a portrait of an artist. What did it mean to be a musician in the times and places in which Robert Shaw lived? What did being an artist mean to Shaw? What did it cost?

A portrait, to touch the mind and the heart, seeks an essence. Thomas Eakins's painting of Walt Whitman seemed to the poet himself, "truth"—high praise indeed. But Eakins could have found no truth had he not painted everything he saw and felt in Whitman—all the shadows, the strength of will, all the pain. My hope is that this book is neither a sentimental nor a clinical portrait of Robert Shaw. My hope is that it conveys both his art and his humanity, for they were indivisible.

Music must be converted into moral power.

—Paul Hindemith

PROLOGUE

American Self-Invention

Robert Lawson Shaw was born in Red Bluff, California on April 30, 1916—another century, another America. He died 82 years and almost nine months later, on January 25, 1999. Shaw had become one of America's classical music icons—standing as tall as a California redwood alongside a very few other key figures: Theodore Thomas, Leopold Stokowski, Charles Ives, Aaron Copland, Marian Anderson, Samuel Barber, Virgil Thomson, Isaac Stern, and Leonard Bernstein, to name some but not all. These founders created a culture of classical music in the United States. When Shaw was a boy, there scarcely was such a culture outside of New York, Boston, Cincinnati, Cleveland, Philadelphia, Yale University, and a few other places. And a classical choral tradition? It existed, but its existence was neither broad nor deep. In the Southern California of Shaw's youth, there was a tradition. There were many fine choirs and choral directors, like Howard Swan. Shaw was a beneficiary of this legacy. But there was not a true musical culture. Depth of musical experience and knowledge was not widespread. Certainly fine choral singing existed in 1900 and 1920 and 1930, and choral singing in the service of great works was going on. Thomas was conducting in Chicago, Mahler had conducted in New York, the Bethlehem Choir was singing Bach in Pennsylvania. The Westminster and St. Olaf Choirs, of course, also pre-date Shaw, and both influenced him.

But a mature choral art—a choral discipline that was formal and rigorous and sustained by a national infrastructure of well-trained singers—did not exist. More than any other single person, Shaw was responsible for changing this. He was the principle re-inventor of the choral art in America. Shaw didn't transform choral music from a hobby or an academic pursuit to an art form by himself. But he was the driving force behind the transformation of American choral singing. He led the way. He made it important, artistic, and popular. And this was not a role someone handed to him or created for him. It was a role he invented. Indeed, Robert Shaw had to invent the idea of Robert Shaw—he had to invent himself.

Shaw is part of an American mythic tradition that encompasses Jay Gatsby, Ronald Reagan, "American Idol," and Barack Obama. Shaw was his own mold, an American prototype—like Dwight D. Eisenhower, Mohammad Ali, Ernest Hemingway, or Clint Eastwood.

Great American lives are self-inventions. Shaw re-imagined his chosen craft, and in the process he created his own place in it—a character named Robert Shaw who did what only Robert Shaw did. And just as there was no Robert Shaw before, there will be no "next" Robert Shaw. He made and broke the mold.

There will be no next Eugene O'Neill, William Faulkner, Duke Ellington, or John Ford, either. American originals reconfigure their disciplines and leave them forever changed when they go. And when the originals go, they are gone—like shooting stars. One thinks of Fred Astaire or Gene Kelly in American dance. Kelly came out of a modest upbringing. His family had a dance background and had given him some training in dance. Kelly was a good dancer. But, based on his training, one might have expected him to become a skilled performer and a leading vaudevillian of his era. One would not have expected him to remake the American film musical and the landscape of dance. But Gene Kelly somehow had an idea in his head—an idea of a new and uniquely American form of dance and, later, of film musicals. He imagined something different from what had previously existed. He remade a discipline. He made something utterly new. How did he come up with it?

Well, gradually. But the instinct to make something new was simply within him.

We are dealing with the American autodidact—the inner-directed man. Such people come out of nowhere and begin to write, not only a new page, but a whole new book. They use a new language all their own. Other examples might be Henry Ford, Thomas Edison, Orson Welles, Frank Lloyd Wright, Martin Luther King, Jane Addams, Eleanor Roosevelt, and Jane Jacobs.

The two great prototypes for the native, unexpected, and unrecognized (including to himself) American genius are Abraham Lincoln and Walt Whitman. Both lives are unique and unprecedented, and later American originals, like Teddy Roosevelt and Mark Twain, were possible because of them.

Robert Shaw's is the same kind of story. It is a great American story. It is part of this tradition of the American original—the inner-directed man who is a maker and re-maker of forms and traditions. If his life had turned out differently, he might just as well have been Robert Shaw the preacher, or Robert Shaw the politician, or Robert Shaw the academic, for he was drawn, in his early life, to all of those fields. And it is possible that he might have had as profound an impact on those disciplines as he did on American music.

But Shaw chose music. And he did things in American music that no one had any reason to expect him to do, based upon his training and background. He made the first American recording of the Brahms *German Requiem*, and gave some of the first performances of Handel and Bach choral masterworks to be pared down to something like the scale of their period of creation. He took major works on national and international tours—performing the Mozart *Requiem* some 65 times in large halls in mid-size towns in America. He took the Bach *Mass in B Minor* on tour in Russia, among other places. While doing this, he set a performance standard that only he could meet, and then exceeded it. Eventually, he raised the national performance standard for choral music in the United States. Finally, he educated a people in the classical choral and choral-orchestral repertoire, and built a national audience for it. Granted, Shaw had some training in music, mostly from his mother, and certainly the young Shaw had a good sense of the song form and of gospel and folk music, thanks to her. He'd done church singing and glee club singing. But his background was modest in all respects, and one would also have to say his obvious natural talents were modest. One would no more have expected Shaw to re-imagine and re-form choral music than one would have expected Kelly to re-make dance.

Yet Shaw had a vision. He imagined something new, something that had not existed before. Shaw imagined a peculiarly American form of classical music, especially choral music. It was a notion considerably bigger than himself, but he incorporated it into himself. And unlike Kelly, whose work was contingent upon the market in pop art and culture, as well as physical abilities that do not endure into middle and old age, Shaw was able to continue his creative growth into his 70s and early 80s. Indeed, much of his best work was done in his last years. Certainly, his greatest fame and honor came then. His work was cumulative, and he was lucky.

The self-invented American knows how to make an old thing new. The best of America's classical musicians all do this. Bernstein did it in his day, and Yo-Yo Ma does it today. At his best, in live performance, Shaw could do it, too. He made the music new—as if it were being heard and played for the first time. For him, each performance *was* new—a re-creation of a composer's dream and a chance for the performer to get it right. And because it was new, Shaw could open new ears and reach new listeners.

But how, exactly? Was it simply a matter of charisma? And what in the world is that, anyway? In Shaw's case, "charisma" begins with his musicality—a distinctive rhythmic quality and then a sound peculiar to him. It also has something to do with a force within Shaw. He had driving energy and a sense of urgency. Shaw was a communicator by nature when making music. Because he gave his all to the music and his devotion was infectious, because he stood emotionally naked before his fellow musicians, baring all his insecurities, because he moved musicians who played for him as well as listeners who came to hear him, he communicated. This directly penetrating emotional urgency is a quality that all of the greatest of great artists possess, whether Andrew Wyeth, Robert Frost, Johnny Cash, Billy Holiday, or Glenn Gould. Such artists possess a rawness that is at once vulnerable and commanding. It is very difficult to resist. It is, perhaps, the power of the art rather than the ego. This raises another related point. Shaw was, for many, a sort of spiritual figure—a kind of guru. People looked to him for wisdom and to his music making for intimations of truth and beauty. Music lovers were drawn to what they saw as Shaw's spirituality. (This view of Shaw as a spiritual master sometimes amused friends who knew the ribald Shaw.) They were not wrong, though this spirituality, like the man, was more complex than it appeared. In any case, from this spiritual aspect, or quasi-halo effect, came a sense of kinship with Shaw, perhaps somewhat illusory: We know this man. He is speaking personally to us. Fans felt connected to Shaw. One can only compare the intensity of feelings that Shaw generated in listeners and fans to the feelings Bernstein elicited from his fans. And such feelings toward Shaw may have been even more familial than those toward Bernstein. Like "Lenny," Shaw was a popularizer of classical music, a household name. But people came to *see* Lenny. They expected to be dazzled. He was a star. They came to *hear* Shaw. No one expected theater. Instead, they hoped to be moved, maybe even changed. One did not go to a Shaw concert for an exhibition of maestro power. One went to a Shaw concert, in a sense, seeking grace. That's a tricky and perhaps even more dangerous expectation than power and glory. But this was Shaw's hope—not that he could command grace, or even invoke it, but that he could make a space for it. The magnification of the conductor was the thing Shaw most deplored. He thought the conductor should prepare and then "get out of the way" so the music could happen. But in a sense, what he sought was really more daring and ambitious than conducting grandeur. He sought the composer's living spirit. He wanted the composer to inhabit, or re-inhabit, the piece performed. Shaw, as conductor, could then, having made the space, step aside and let the *composer* unfold the work. It is at once a deeply humble and shockingly ambitious aim—so ambitious, one might call it borderline delusional. Except that Shaw sometimes pulled it off.

This persona—the conductor as medium, as connector of listener and players to creator—was one of Shaw's self-inventions, perhaps his most important one. He believed that if he made himself enough of a servant of the music, if he studied and rehearsed and perfected musical form and matter adequately, he could become a sort of live transcriber of the music. One sees the ultimate product of Shaw's self-invention if one watches the film documentaries on Shaw commissioned by Carnegie Hall, and produced from Shaw's successive workshops in that venue in the 1990s. (A complete list of the Carnegie Hall Documentaries, all titled "Preparing a Masterpiece," may be found at the end of this book.) These films convey what Shaw wanted to convey at the end of his life: his methods and his devotion. There are seven of these rehearsal documentaries. The first two films were produced by Philip Byrd and Janet Shapiro; the last five were made by Nick Doob. One sees the *pater familias*. One sees a gentle, loving, rather contemplative teacher. And that Shaw was real. Especially so in his ninth decade. One sees also just a little of the Shaw edge (it is mostly hidden from the camera), and quite a lot of the drive in him. Recalling Shaw, Doob retained, above all else, the sheer physical power of the man. Despite the avuncular image of later years, anyone who knew, played for, worked for, or sang for Robert Shaw will tell you he could be more than a little scary. His temper, when aroused, could be ferocious. The critic Tim Page (who was the last journalist to interview Shaw, in Shaw's suite at the Watergate Hotel in Washington, where Shaw was rehearsing the National Symphony) said the conductor, by then elderly and quite ill, nonetheless seemed like a "caged lion." Shaw changed the energy level around him. When he entered a room, you sensed it even if your back was to the door. If his intense blue eyes fixed on you, you only hoped it was because you surprised him by playing in time or singing with good intonation.

Robert Shaw believed that if he got the music right it would change lives. After all, music changed *his* life. The young Robert Shaw was one kind of man and one kind of musician—rough, on fire, carnivorous. The middle-aged Shaw was another—obsessive, penitential, lonely, and plagued by self-doubt. The elderly Shaw was yet another—an old lion in tall grass. He was (mostly) at peace with himself and the world, but still powerful and capable of a mighty roar. (Of course, each age of the man bleeds into the next and each previous man is a ghost haunting the next.)

The struggles of Shaw's life were classically American. He wrestled with addiction and with guilt, and bounced between polarities of excess and Spartan discipline, popularity and art, fame and fidelity to his own private vision, depression and elation, doubt and clarity, mechanized perfection and spontaneous passion.

So what was he like, this one-of-a-kind creation of little Bobby Shaw from small-town California? Well, he worked all the time. Robert Shaw may have been the hardest-working musician of his century. He worked 10- and 12- and 14-hour days, even into old age. When not performing, he rehearsed. When not rehearsing, he studied scores—breaking down their structure, learning the composer's language, learning all the parts (usually singing them to himself), and then editing all the parts for all the instruments. When he didn't work, he entered a kind of no-man's land, collapsing into himself. As a young man he partied. As an old man he read mysteries, watched sports or televangelists, vegetated, rested.

He was not social. Indeed, he was doggedly anti-social. He was comfortable with any sort of pulpit or audience. He was comfortable with a few friends. He was extremely uncomfortable with small talk, with cocktail parties, and with receptions, which he called "deceptions." He found purely social engagements and obligations painful. In the early days, he simply got drunk. In later days, a walkthrough, or "drive-by" appearance was his coping mechanism. Even if the event was in his honor, he might not remove his raincoat, and his stay was a question of minutes, not hours. If children were present, he might go off and play with them. On the other hand, if he was seated next to Andrew Young at an Atlanta dinner party, or John Silber at a Boston University dinner party, Shaw might have an engaging and animated conversation. He needed substance, some sort of work that he could edit or perform, to feel at home in the world.

Though Shaw was born to be the leader of something, he lived, like many leaders, mostly in his own head. He was drawn to beautiful things, and people. But he was also rather withdrawn, progressively more so as he aged. He once left a Princeton University cocktail party by a window and walked several miles home to his hotel. The party was in his honor.

Shaw was athletic. Though not a large man, his presence suggested force. He once played 18 holes of golf in his bare feet, because he had no golf shoes. He played very well that day, and he had never played before. He loved to watch sports, especially professional football and college basketball.

He liked cars—big ones and powerful ones. He was a fast but good driver—bold but not reckless. He owned, in his time, BMWs, Jaguars, and several other luxury or sports models. In his later years, he drove an old, beat-up Mustang most of the time. But his prize possession was a Bentley he bought "for a song" in the early 1950s, which he used on at least one occasion to outrun the Alabama highway patrol. (He was on his way home after an Atlanta Symphony Orchestra concert.) He never sold the Bentley, but he lost interest in it after his second wife Caroline died. She had it restored for him, as a gift. The restoration was completed after her death and he didn't want to see it then just as, after her death, he no longer wanted to go to their beloved summer home in France, which Caroline had rebuilt and decorated.

He loved women. And for most of his life, this was not a distant or abstract affection. Shaw was quite the Lothario in his younger days. He was both ashamed and proud of this. (Although he didn't broadcast it, he was privately rather proud of his affair with an actress he thought the most beautiful "Jane" of the American Tarzan movies.) Nor was he a libido-less old man. A participant in a Shaw-led high-school honors chorus performance of the Mozart *Requiem* in Atlanta remembers Shaw, then nearly 80, looking over his reading glasses at a shapely young woman as she walked past and saying to the bass section, once she'd passed out of hearing range, "Gentleman, there is nothing like the smell of a beautiful woman." He was being deliberately provocative and the remark did rather discombobulate the young men. But it was also Shaw. An Atlanta Symphony Chorus member's favorite Shaw one-liner, from many years of one-liners and many years of rehearsal, was: "I'm old enough to remember when safe sex meant a headboard."

He loved the sun and the water. He always ran, never waded, into the Pacific Ocean when he visited it—as if being reunited with an old love.

He adored his second family—Caroline, Caroline's son Alex, whom he adopted and treated as his own, and their natural son Thomas. But his children from his first family—Johanna, Peter, and Thad—felt he'd walked away from them, and more or less forgotten them. The first indictment was true; the second was not. His first marriage was never right and neither he nor his wife, Maxine Farley Shaw, could fix it, though both tried. Shaw's failure as a father haunted him. He didn't kid himself that he'd done his best or that it was all the fault of Maxine. But he never really found a way back to these children.

Shaw was, in some ways, compulsive. He had manic-depressive tendencies. He was, for much of his life, a working, or so-called functional, alcoholic. He liked ribald jokes and could talk trash with the best of them. He once considered running for mayor of Atlanta. He never felt he'd truly mastered any piece of music.

His work was as multi-layered as his persona. He made thousands of converts to choral music with his arrangements of American folk melodies and hymns, with Alice Parker, but almost no one has heard his arrangement of a section of Bach's *Art of the Fugue*, which he never published, which he almost certainly labored over for many agonized hours, and which likely meant more to him than any other arrangement he'd ever done.

He was always in motion, always on to the next great thing. He seldom looked back, or reminisced, and he never boasted of past triumphs. He did keep track of the failures. But he barely paused when a performance was over, either to savor or to analyze. He always focused on the task before him, as if to say, "This one will be the one. This will be the time we'll really make a statement. This time we'll really get this piece." But, after a performance, he never felt he had. Eventually, he savored the feeling of getting closer each time, though he never believed he'd arrived.

Certain pieces lingered in his consciousness after a performance, especially the *St. Matthew Passion* of Bach. Bach was Shaw's evangelist. He told author and broadcaster Martin Goldsmith, "[one would be] a damn fool to deny the possibility of resurrection," once one had heard it depicted in the *B Minor Mass* of Bach. Shaw made this statement in the last months of his own life, and at a time when he surely suspected that he was conducting his last performance of the *B Minor Mass*. But when, after the death of his wife Caroline, his friend David Lowance said, "You'll be up there with her one day," Shaw said, "I don't believe in that shit and neither do you."

He watched the televangelists almost every Sunday when he was not working, and cursed them like a drunken sailor. This was a recreational activity for Shaw—watching televised religion, working himself into a lather about it, and damning not only its fraudulence, but its sacrilege.

He didn't do much serious reading in his middle and late years. In his early life, he read a great deal of poetry and every available biography of Lincoln, and he devoured musicological studies throughout his middle years and still, to a degree, in later life. But, like a surprising number of people of great stature and intellectual power, he was not a great reader. In his later years, he read mostly mysteries. He was particularly fond of Robert B. Parker's *Spencer* books.

He also didn't spend much time listening to music. He called this "a serious flaw of mine." When he did listen to music he usually listened to historic recordings, for two reasons: "because there is a tradition" and to check and compare the tempos of important conductors. He did this only after he had finished his own preparations for performance. (Shaw's obsession with all matters of rhythm and pace extended to cataloging these sorts of comparative statistics.) In later life, he began to listen to early music recordings. He was interested in the Dutch conductor Ton Koopman's work, in particular. He also had great respect for John Eliot Gardiner. The early music movement interested him, and he presaged it in his own work, but he was not a participant and once or twice debunked it. He wasn't exactly a cinema buff either. The last movie he saw, and the first he had seen in some years, was *Babe*—a child's tale about a talking pig. He loved it.

Robert Shaw wrote of George Szell that he was "an enigma, even to himself." That rings true. But every great elegy is partly autobiographical. Shaw was meditative and athletic, rational and childish, compassionate and ill-tempered (impatience almost always got the best of him). He was a man of passion who constantly tightened the screws of self-denial on his own psyche. He had a mean streak and a deeply spiritual one. He was ferocious and pastoral, selfish and sensitive. He lived much of his adult life upon the public stage, yet he was isolated and protected from the world. He didn't know how to write a check, for example. He lived so much in his work, and in his own head, that he probably missed a lot—the small, chance interactions that make day-to-day life sweet, for one thing, and most of the childhood experiences of his first three children, for another. Generally, he didn't feel he had *time* to chat with a waitress or play catch with his sons.

And at the end of his days, Shaw sought to simplify and to narrow his life all the more. What did he need? What did he care about? The music. The composers. His beloved Caroline, until she died. His golden son, Thomas. His stepson, Alex. And, to the very limited degree that he was involved in their lives, his grown children, Johanna, Peter, and Thad. A few close friends and colleagues. Not much else. And this list is in order of his attentions.

There were three great stages in Shaw's life. There was the young man on fire—the pop star. Think young John Lennon; think young Johnny Depp; think young Orson Welles—hot tempered, a bit entitled, and a libido that never faltered. There was the almost Falstaffian middle-aged man. This Shaw was unsure, insecure, on the run, conspicuously over-indulging in food and drink, conspicuously philandering, generally miserable. There was the sage old man. In his last years he became a sort of Old Testament figure—turn away from fame; put your ego in your hip pocket; get behind the composer, the creator, the music. For Shaw, music was prophecy: his final and abiding wish was to be its servant.

PART ONE

ROOTS

Returning some years later, after a life of professional music—and amateur sin—in New York to the West Coast, I wondered how mother's voice would sound to these more sophisticated ears and tougher heart. That Sunday she sang "The Ninety and Nine"—about the Master Shepherd and his one lost lamb—of an aesthetic order of merit which, if it had been formed in solid rather than sound could have appropriately adorned the Babyland of Forest Lawn Cemetery—And I wept.

—Robert Shaw on his mother's singing

CHAPTER 1

California Boy

"Robert Shaw is American as corn."

It's a good line.

And nobody seems to know who said it.

Was it Leonard Bernstein? Was it Virgil Thomson? Either man could have said it. It sounds like something Shaw's friend Thornton Wilder might have said about him. But the line remains unclaimed.

It's a true statement, too. Shaw was not an American alienated from his culture. He came from what was later to be named Middle America. He liked football, Ford Mustangs, and Jack Daniels. As he once put it, "I'm *a part* of the great unwashed." He was Main Street and Grover's Corners down to his toes. Shaw wasn't born in Boston, or Cambridge, or Manhattan, but in a town called Red Bluff, in northern California—the third largest town (population 13,000) in the Shasta Cascades. His formative years were spent in the southern California town of Eagle Rock, where he claimed sagebrush blew up and down the main drag, pretty much unperturbed. The small town living of Shaw's youth was part of hardscrabble Americana. It wasn't *The Grapes of Wrath,* but it was Steinbeck country.

Shaw's roots are there, in the California of so many years ago, and in American Protestantism. His father was a Protestant minister, or "preacher":

"Son of a preacher, and grandson too," Shaw would say of himself. His mother had a professional identity as well. She was a *preacher's wife*.

His youth was idyllic—almost Huck Finn-like. As a boy, he spent a lot of time outdoors. He remembered abundant sunshine. His family camped in the mountains and at the ocean on alternating summer vacations. He loved to swim in the Pacific. As a young man, he surfed. He was small for sports but he played anyway. He briefly played high school football, once contesting against a team that had Jackie Robinson as one of its members. (Shaw was proud of this, and of his claim that Robinson broke Shaw's nose in the one play in which they made contact.)

Shaw grew up in the America of Hoover, the Great Depression, the Temperance League (one of Shaw's grandfathers was active in it), and the early years of FDR's reign. He was raised with small-town values—the neighbors knew him and if someone else's mother told him to do or not to do something, he obeyed. But he was formed most profoundly by his parents. Two things mattered to them—Protestant Christianity and music. Most of the music Robert knew first and best was the music of the mainstream Protestant churches in America.

Because his father was a minister, and his mother was a minister's wife, church was, Shaw would often say, "a '24-hour-a-day, seven-day-a-week' experience" in his house. That is, perhaps, the experience you would expect for a minister's son growing up in the 1920s and 1930s. Nor is it surprising when at least one son in a minister's family rebels against church, "churchiness," and all manner of piety. And that son was Robert, called Bob or Bobby then.

The thing that was distinctive about the Shaws was that the whole family felt so deeply about music. Religion was 24/7, but music and religion were bound together. The Shaw children were taught, by example, that music was a means of evangelization—preaching and teaching the gospel message—and, indeed, a form of worship. Music was not about entertainment, and it was certainly not background noise. It wasn't even church background noise—a soundtrack for Sunday service. Music was a prayer form. Each

Sunday service at his father's church involved a segment called the "Lesson in Song." Music was worship in its own right.

Shaw came of age between the world wars. He was born in 1916 and in 1938 went to New York to seek his fortune. In between, of course, came the worst of the Great Depression. Shaw was entering early adolescence when Wall Street crashed. Franklin Roosevelt was elected president when Shaw was 16. Only 12 years later, Shaw was singing for FDR with one of his early choirs.

Shaw went, essentially, from college to fame. By the time the war came he was a staple on national radio, thanks to Fred Waring. By the end of the war, Shaw was conducting the premiere, and later the radio broadcast, of a major work by a major composer commemorating (in part) the death of that same president: Paul Hindemith's *When lilacs last in the dooryard bloom'd: A Requiem "For those we love."*

Shaw would sometimes say his family had been "poor" in California, which irritated both his wives and his siblings. The Shaw family was never in a state of dire poverty or destitution. But it never had much. At one point, the family had to sell the car, which had been given to them, to pay the milk bill.

Millions of American men and women came of age as Shaw did—one's own family and almost everyone one knew had little money, but they were not what we today would deem impoverished. They had no savings. They had little "cash flow" or pocket money. They lacked "stuff—an abundance of material things. This was before children in America had closets full of toys and gadgets." But they were not homeless or malnourished and few of them suffered acute social pathologies, as many of the poor do today. They simply lacked.

Shaw's family lived simply. They struggled. But Shaw's parents always had a freestanding home—a rental, for no parsonage was provided—often with a guest room and a second bath. The family had adequate food and decent clothing. Bedrooms were shared (two boys in one, two girls in another, the baby with the parents). But these were not unusual arrangements for most American families in the 1920s and 1930s. And a minister and his wife had certain advantages. The Shaws usually had a student helper—a live-in person who came via the church and became, in effect, a nanny and maid. (It was "Christian cynicism" said one family member, because these helpers were loved but utterly exploited.) The longest lasting live-in was Flora A. Adams, an orphan who was psychologically needy, and eventually became a spinster schoolteacher. Adams lived with the Shaws off and on for many years and became an ex-officio family member. She and her successors and predecessors did virtually all the housework and laundering, thus freeing Shaw's mother, Nelle, to be a minister's wife, church musician, and matriarch.

Certainly Shaw's parents did not consider themselves poor. They had a certain social standing and, more important, a reason to get out of bed every day—a mission.

It was a very different time. Lack of wealth was not thought the same as poverty. Social status was not based solely on wealth. A minister was an important man in a small town, for churches were lynchpins of local community. The family structure was tight. The children, in the Shaw family in particular, were clear about their responsibilities, monetary and moral, to the family as a whole. They also knew their father was a prominent and respected man.

Bob had to grow up, or pretend to, fast. He had to work to help support his family in high school and college and to help pay tuition. His "big break," financially and professionally, came even before he had a college degree.

In these years, millions of Americans struggled and went without, but were neither jobless nor disenfranchised. They maintained middle-class values and ambitions even as they were buffeted by the tides of economic depression and collected incomes barely above the subsistence level. The Shaw family was doing substantially better than that. Yet this is certain: The Great Depression and the lack of things made an impression on Shaw. So did the glitter of Manhattan, once he got there. The lack of wealth of his parents, perhaps combined with their Christian pietism and sense of service, sacrifice, and restraint, were stifling to him, and stood in stark contrast to the bright lights of the big city. As for the world wars that punctuated Shaw's life, and the lives of millions of other Americans, they, too, became personal. The world was to peel away the idyll of Shaw's boyhood in a rather sudden, even brutal way.

But Shaw's boyhood was a lucky one: relatively ordered, open, non-neurotic and unburdened, even with constant church talk and church going. Certainly "Bobby" was no musical prodigy. He was not encumbered or sheltered in that way. For one thing, his parents couldn't afford a prodigy. And, for another, no one thought Bobby Shaw was anything particularly special musically. He sang. All the Shaw kids sang. The whole family sang. But it was a church thing. Music was a part of family and church. He participated, but with no particular distinction. If he seemed to have a special talent as a young man, it was in elocution, speech making, and essay writing. He was an average, an active, and a slightly rebellious boy. His "talent," if he had a talent, was enthusiasm.

All the Shaw children received a few piano lessons. None took to the instrument, including Bob. He played drums in the school band.

All of the Shaw children conducted a church choir in their late teens and early twenties in Glendora, California—they passed the job down one to the next. Singing was simply a part of church life and family life. It had to do with their parents' work. It was an integral part of existence and taken for granted. The family was known, in church circles, as "the singing Shaws." Rev. Shaw led the Lesson in Song each Sunday. Mrs. Shaw usually sang a solo.

After high school, Bob worked full time for a year to save money for college. His first job was wrapping bread. Then he worked in a steel mill. And finally, he worked in a factory assembling electric irons. There he worked 48 hours a week, for which he was paid $12—a week. And there he witnessed a horrific accident in which a co-worker lost his arm. He hated being a laborer and in later life was proud of having been one.

One would not have predicted an important American musician based on any of this.

Yet somehow, with minimal musical education, even in college (where he concentrated on literature, philosophy, and religion), Shaw went on to become an American maestro, a fairly rare thing then, and not all that common now. It is perfectly clear where his affection for music came from, but where and how did the attraction to classical musical literature begin?

Southern California, in those days, had a strong choral tradition. There was quite decent choral instruction in its communities, churches, and schools, and there were choral competitions. Shaw may have heard some of the shorter works of Bach in his youth. Certainly he heard parts of them. Howard Swan, who became an important American choral educator, was teaching in the area at that time—in the public schools. And he and Shaw made a connection. Swan first encountered Bobby Shaw when Shaw was in grade school, and they kept meeting up again through Shaw's youth. Swan rose to become the choral guru of Southern California. He also became one of Shaw's first mentors. By high school and early college, Shaw was beginning to conduct church choirs and, by his junior year in college, the Glee Club at Pomona College.

But this early experience with the choral arts must not have fully captured him, because it was Shaw's choice not to major in music in college or even to take many music courses. He was a word man then—words and ideas. Philosophy, poetry, and the study of world religions were his passions. He later said that he was "a sort of campus liberal" in his college years.

In the early days of his fame and success, Shaw told interviewers he'd been destined for the ministry after college. But in later years he mostly denied this and said that before music took him he'd been aiming for college teaching, probably in comparative religion. Which is true? Perhaps both. Certainly he went to college thinking of the ministry. The ministry was expected of him. He was, at that time, occasionally preaching from the pulpit. It is also clear that other thoughts and doubts began to form during his years at Pomona. He may not have fully voiced his doubts to his parents at that time. But sometime during college a vocation to the ministry morphed into a desire to study and teach the religions of the world. Shaw found a new father figure and a different way to approach religion.

It's a very American story. American as corn. Only a few years after entering Pomona as a possible preacher, with precious little music education, Robert Shaw was thinking about conducting the great oratorios. And only a few years after that, he *was* conducting them. Shaw began to conduct major works by 1942. He was 26 and had been in New York three years. (One of the first was the Brahms *Requiem* in that year at All Angels Episcopal Church in New York.) Soon thereafter, he was conducting not only spirituals but also major classical works on national radio. Roughly a decade before, he had been wrapping bread.

CHAPTER 2

The Lawsons and the Shaws

He was christened Robert *Lawson* Shaw. Lawson was his mother Nelle's maiden name. The name meant something to him and to his family. In Southern California, the Lawsons were an established line of preachers in a church known in California as "the Christian church," which was a part of the Disciples of Christ. Nelle's father was a preacher and her grandfather was known for his part in the anti-temperance movement. They had a history. The Lawsons had a sense of place and purpose.

Robert's father, Shirley Richard Shaw, was a first-generation minister. But his father had never been anything so august or revered as Nelle's. Indeed Robert Shaw's paternal grandfather, John Kent Shaw, is something of a mystery. He took his family from Ohio to Minnesota (Shirley was born in Duluth) and, eventually, to California. He was thought to have made some money somewhere along the way, a semi-substantial amount, perhaps in banking. But apparently he lost it, and then he began a decline, eventually becoming a shadow figure and more or less abandoning his family. His sons cared for their mother and ran the household after that. Shirley was the youngest son but bore much of the burden. He did not go to college until he was 25.

When he did go, Shirley Shaw attended Pomona College, as all his children would, graduating in 1912 at the age of 29. He emerged as a minister but received no further degree beyond his Pomona baccalaureate. It was that same year that Shirley Shaw married Nelle Lawson. He was marrying not only the daughter of a senior and experienced preacher, but also an already well-known church singer in Southern California. After marriage, and in her subsequent career as a church musician, she was known as Nelle Lawson Shaw.

The Shaw family clung to the name of Lawson. Perhaps it represented respectability, or a little bit of history in a place of newness, rawness, and self-invention. Robert would name the music publishing business he founded with his friend and agent Walter Gould, Lawson-Gould, and he would name his son Thomas, Thomas Lawson Shaw.

Shirley Richard Shaw was born June 28, 1883. He lived just over 60 years.

Nelle Lawson Shaw was born April 6, 1888, and would live until 1971—a life as long as her famous son's. She was to live as a widow for almost three decades. Without necessarily articulating it, her husband and her children were always clear about the fact that Nelle was a person of substance and importance in her own right. She was not simply the wife of a minister, but a kind of co-minister in that time and place. And—even more important in a way—she was a choral musician. Certainly Mrs. Shaw was neither a wallflower nor a shy and submissive wife. She was a full partner. She had her own work, her own career, her own identity, her own mission. And she had standards—in music and human behavior. She was a person of rigor, and also of detachment. She was supportive of her children but not hovering. She was impressed with Robert's success, when it came, but also with Holly's, and Anne's, and Jim's, and John's.

Nelle Shaw was a serious musician. She was discriminating about the "better" and "lesser" hymns and she certainly looked upon singing in church as a kind of performance, and wanted it to be solemn and beautiful. At the same time, she was working within the tradition of Protestant hymnody, and a small corner of it, at that. In American society throughout much of the twentieth century, there was Ford and Plymouth Protestantism (Methodists and Baptists), and Cadillac and Buick Protestantism (Episcopalians and Presbyterians). Nelle did not have access, for example, to the beautiful prose of the old *Book of Common Prayer*. Since she was not a Lutheran, she probably knew little Bach. She'd probably not been exposed to Palestrina or Di Lasso. That was not the music of working-class Protestants in the 1920s and 1930s.

Robert would remember his father's church as, theologically, slightly to the left of a liberal Baptist and slightly to the right of a Congregationalist denomination. But he would also sometimes equate his father's church with evangelical Protestantism, for reasons that are unclear. For Shirley Shaw was evangelical only in the literal and historical sense of the word—he was an evangelist (a salesman, a missionary) for revealed Christianity. He was certainly not evangelical in the current popular, and often caricatured, understanding of evangelical churches and ministers. He was an emotional preacher, and perhaps that is part of what Robert meant. But he was not an intolerant man, by nature or by conviction. Quite the opposite. Shirley and Nelle were strict and devoted Christians—gravely so. But the substance of their belief must be noted as well as the style. The Shaws belonged to the liberal Protestant tradition in America—a tradition that embraced the personal nature and social message of Jesus: a tradition that affirmed the equal human dignity of all, social progress, and positive thinking.

Shirley and Nelle were not Cromwellians and they were not Falwellians. They were not zealots, and they did not go door to door seeking converts, nor did they denounce liberal politicians from the pulpit. They were a part of the historical tradition of mainstream American Evangelical Protestantism, which is not fundamentalism, but a form of Christianity that embraces a personal God and is rooted in scripture. (The Rev. Martin Luther King, Jr. was, in this classic sense of the word, "evangelical.") So Shirley and Nelle Shaw were not what most people today would think of as evangelicals, but partly this has to do with the changing nature of the word and the movement of both right and left wings of American Christianity to ever more distant ends of the spectrum. Indeed, Rev. Shaw thought of himself as part of the liberal wing of the American Protestant church, both theologically and politically. He was interested in biblical scholarship. He was no literalist. He was interested, to a point, in church and social reform. (Pomona became more progressive in his children's generation but was progressive for his day.) And he and his wife were certainly mindful of the have-nots, particularly those who needed help in their own flock. The Shaws abhorred the know-nothing, Bible-thumping reactionaries. They wanted nothing to do with that kind of church. For their time and place, the parents of Robert Shaw were progressives and intellectuals.

At the same time, their personal tolerance had limits. There was never any question, according to his son-in-law Harrison Price, that the Rev. Shaw felt that the way of Jesus was the *best* way, and a person who had not found that path, or had abandoned it, was to be pitied and, if possible, saved. Only Jesus Christ, Rev. Shaw felt, could lead human beings to brotherhood. And brotherhood was the true test of success for Christianity. Shirley Shaw believed deeply that the Golden Rule had to be lived, but he was also a man of his time.

The Reverend and Mrs. Shaw were demanding, exacting and, at least as Robert sometimes saw it, somewhat emotionally stilted and withholding.

Shirley and Nelle were, after all, two people born in the nineteenth century. They were a couple raising five children on little more than Gospel values, frugality, and gospel song. They were sober folk. The Shaw children were coming of age in a very different world—one forever changed by the holocaust and the detonation of the atomic bomb—seemingly the world's final refutations of innocence. It is not at all surprising that the music of Benjamin Britten spoke so powerfully to Robert Shaw in his adult years.

Rev. Shaw had a job to do—to preach and to teach the gospel. It was a serious and demanding vocation. He didn't have the time or disposition to kid around much.

Mrs. Shaw was equally sober. She had children to raise, a house to keep, a husband to bolster, and music to prepare and perform. She was a preacher's wife. She was a dedicated church musician. She had no time for coddling. Shirley and Nelle expected their children to know and choose the right path, to work hard, to seize opportunity when it presented itself, and to serve the church. Nelle Shaw, in particular, wanted them to know good music—and to be able to differentiate good music from bad. It was she who scrimped and saved for the piano instruction (which didn't take) and she who encouraged elocution and persuasive public speaking (their father was, of course, the prime example here). It was she who enshrined singing and the song.

Shirley Shaw was also a small-church man—a man of his congregation, not the wide, larger church in abstract. He lived for the message, the word, and for his flock, which was an extension of his own family. He liked a flock small enough that he might know, really know, everyone in it. And as he traveled his road of service and Christian teaching and preaching, he did so at a series of small churches from one end of California to the other.

People without a lot of money in the 1920s and 1930s moved a lot. Even, or maybe especially, ministers. Rev. Shaw was not an "itinerant preacher." He always had a church, an address, and a proper home. But he must have been a restless soul, for he relocated his family often—moving from pastorate to pastorate. His pastorates included churches in Fresno, Red Bluff, Santa Barbara, Stockton, Ontario, Eagle Rock, and San Diego. Always he stayed with smallish parishes. He had at least one opportunity to accept a large and prestigious church, but declined it. His daughter, Anne Shaw Price, believed her father felt called to the little platoons. "He just liked the small community."[1]

All five Shaw children—Holly, Robert, Jim, Anne, and John, were born in different towns and during different pastorates. Rev. Shaw's career as a pastor and preacher was interrupted only by five years of teaching at California Christian College—later named, and still today, Chapman College. There he taught "Old Testament History" and the "Life and Work of Jesus." Though he was a pastor from head to toe, and not by nature a scholar, he dearly loved his days as a college teacher. There was some family speculation that Rev. Shaw wanted to be president of California Christian College. But the greater consensus is that he felt called to return to parish work.

Robert Shaw was his father's son in some ways. Shirley was a driven man. He was nervous, high-strung, passionate, particular, and impatient. He was the absolute master of his flock.

In other ways, Robert was the anti-Shirley. For Shirley had, so far as anyone detected or can recall, few doubts or qualms or second thoughts. Certainly Rev. Shaw had no regrets about devoting his life to carrying the Christian message. It was from Shirley that Robert learned comfort and familiarity with biblical language and comfort in a pulpit, at a lectern, or on a podium, as well as feeling ease of command. And perhaps it was Shirley who passed on the charisma gene. Rev. Shaw moved people; he held them when he preached; and sometimes he intimidated them.

Shirley had the same steely blue eyes as Robert and the same intensity. He was, said Harrison Price, a force of nature. It would not have been Rev. Shaw's style to ask, "Are you saved?" But it *was* his style to ask, "What do you believe, and what are your intentions?" When Price courted Rev. Shaw's daughter Anne, he felt the hot light of Rev. Shaw's scrutiny. Rev. Shaw's disapproval of Price's attentions to his youngest daughter was, Price felt, almost tangible. Price was secular and half Jewish. Years later, his wife Anne would show him a letter from her mother, "We pray every day," Nelle Shaw wrote, "that you will come to your senses."

---

1 Burris–Anne Price interview.

Harrison Price remembered a conversation with Rev. Shaw about the Christian church. Price could not recall whether he had, by that time, asked for Anne Shaw's hand formally. But his intentions had become clear. He'd been hanging around the Shaw home a lot. And Harrison Price did not plan to convert to Christianity. Rev. Shaw thought he should. The two men had a clarifying backyard talk one night. Rev. Shaw was holding on to a clothesline and leaning in toward Price, who was backed up to a fence wall. "It's like the Lion's Club," Rev. Shaw said, "You have to *say* you want to join." The would-be Christian had to realize he needed Christ. He had to become aware, Rev. Shaw explained, and ask for help. Price felt he didn't have much to offer his future father-in-law along these lines—and he knew he could come up with nothing that would satisfy him at that moment. So Price mumbled something about how he hoped to live the rest of his life differently than he'd lived his first 20-odd years, that's all he knew, and he ducked out from under that clothesline—around, under and away from Rev. Shaw. Price said he could not forget that night in the yard of the Shaw home, and the piercing eyes of his future wife's father and "the old man bearing down on me." "Those blue eyes," said Price, "looked through not at you."[2]

"Do you *want* to join?" Shirley Shaw had asked. No, Price did not want to join. But he knew he could not give that answer. After he managed an escape that night, Price thought Rev. Shaw visibly deflated for the rest of the evening. "He sulked over his defeat." And they never spoke of religion again.

Later, on another night, Price became ill, and Anne Shaw had to minister to him and his 104-degree fever. Rev. Shaw walked in the hallway outside the small room where the patient suffered and the beloved nursed. Rev. Shaw paced all night. He sensed the non-believing interloper was not going to be eliminated, and he was right. Harrison ("Buzz") and Anne Price were married in New York by a decidedly liberal preacher a few years later. A handful of people attended, and Anne's parents were not among them. The reception was in Robert Shaw's apartment, hosted by his new young wife, Maxine. Anne and Buzz had withstood the polite but steely disapproval of

2 Burris–Harrison Price interview.

Shirley and Nelle. The Prices formed and held on to a storybook marriage. Anne's sister Holly was not as lucky or, in the face of parental opposition, as strong.

Rev. Shaw may have been a liberal theologian in the pulpit or the classroom, but as a human being, he was a man of his time, and rather tightly wound.

One curiosity is Shirley Shaw's lack of formal ministerial or theological training. In this, he presages his son Robert, who lacked much formal training for his profession. Rev. Shaw did attend Union Theological Seminary in New York for one semester—in the summer. But he had already been a pastor for many years by that time. The family stayed in California. He appears to have been largely self-taught as a minister. He learned his craft from practicing his craft, much as his son Robert would learn music.

Since he was not a Lawson and did not inherit the profession, it is germane to wonder why Shirley Shaw chose the ministry. What drew him? We do know that he was an idealist and an orator, and we can be fairly sure that he did not become a preacher for social prestige or upward mobility. No, Shirley Shaw seems to have decided at some point that the message and ethic of Jesus was what mankind needed to survive. And after that he never wavered. He never veered from that straight path. The trigger may have been some experience or trauma of youth, or perhaps it was the way his mother was abandoned by his father. His mother was devout, and Shirley had seen that she was supported in her time of need by her fellow churchgoers. Shirley Shaw looked around a broken world and concluded that it needed religion. It needed, specifically, Christ. He was going to do his part.

Some years later, when it came time to choose his vocation, Robert Shaw examined what he saw as a broken and heartless world and concluded that it needed music—and he would do his part to bring the medicine *he'd* found to as many people as possible.

Shirley Shaw also burned himself out—preaching, teaching, helping, pastoring. He worked full out at his job, his calling, and then some. He wore himself out, again and again. It was a pattern: manic devotion and activity; collapse; recovery; beginning again; over extending and overworking again; crashing again. He was that sort of man. He overdid. He was subject to highs and lows of mood and outlook. This was a result, not only of workload and work habits, and hypertension, which he had, but also of temperament. Robert, too, as an adult would go from very high to very low and occasionally take to his bed for days after a significant concert. But he was luckier in health and in the quality of medical care available to him. In any case, the 50-year-old Shirley Shaw looks, in pictures, like the essence of the robust male of his age. But by 60, he looks 75—gaunt and frail and approaching death.

Shirley Shaw was felled by a series of strokes. Gradually, they whittled down a strong man. After each of his strokes, Rev. Shaw backed off and took time to recuperate. But soon he would be back at it—101 percent. He did not have the benefit of medical science that could regulate his blood pressure and heart beat, as his son Robert would many years later.

Robert would live 22 years longer than his father, and though Robert lived hard for much of that time, Anne Price speculated that perhaps alcohol actually helped diffuse his hypertension. Neither man, she said, could easily relax. "If Father had taken a drink now and then, perhaps he might have lived longer, like Bob."[3]

Of course, a massive stroke, preceded by mini-strokes over many years, would one day take the life of Robert. Both men were uptight dynamos, obsessed by work, manic-depressive by nature if not by official diagnosis, and devoted to higher causes for which they were willing to give all. Shirley was perhaps more manic and more uncompromising than Robert, at least the elderly Robert. But then Robert had the extra 22 years.

3 Burris–Anne Price interview.

Nelle Shaw was a different matter—more rock-like than her husband or son. She was never as high or as low. She was more stoical and contained. She was a proud woman. Dignified. Remote. Mind you, the Shaw household was not devoid of a sense of fun. There were many sing-alongs, at home and at church, and there were the annual camping trips with the children to the mountains or the ocean. There is a picture, famous within the Shaw family, of Shirley Shaw hoisting the first Shaw baby in the air and laughing. Perhaps it is accurate to say that Shirley and Nelle had a sense of joy, but not necessarily an acute sense of humor. If the essence of humor is a sense of irreverence, irony, perhaps even of the absurd, that was not a great part of Shirley and Nelle. (It became a part of Robert, perhaps in reaction.) No, for Shirley and Nelle, life was purpose; and life was work. They existed to spread the good news of Jesus of Nazareth—the most important of all work. They existed to do good and to help those who needed help—and to raise their children. Music was a means of praise and thanksgiving. It was not an end in itself, just as humor was not an end in itself. Notes and intonation mattered in singing, but the words mattered most. Robert would actually reverse that formulation in the working out of his musical theology, but his parents, and their faith, help to explain why he, perhaps more than any choral musician before or since, so loved words and insisted that words must be clearly understood. For a Christian, the beginning is the word.

Still, in their way, and according to their means and priorities, Shirley and Nelle loved music. Nelle had some voice lessons in her early years and was careful about her own voice. Robert would compare her to George Beverly Shea, though on a California—not a national—scale. She was a white, Protestant, Gospel singer. She was a dignified purveyor of the popular gospel tune. She was perhaps also more musically sophisticated than Robert liked to remember her. Anne Shaw Price insisted that her mother preferred

Mendelssohn to "The Old Rugged Cross." Robert and Anne agreed that their mother deplored anything she thought cheap or falsely sentimental.

Certainly, Nelle herself sang mostly church hymns. But it is possible that Robert remembered his family's musicality as more primitive than it was and his own musical background as closer to totally vacant than it was.

Nelle Shaw might be fairly thought a Grande Dame. From somewhere in her gene pool, or experience, or the stars, she had acquired a regal bearing and a knack for giving commands and receiving service. She did not abuse this gift, but she commanded the household as she could an audience.

And just as people came from miles around to hear Nelle sing, they came to hear Shirley R. Shaw preach. He was a thinking preacher, and a dynamic one. He was a trusted pastor. He was widely seen as gifted and exceptional. (Good pastors who are also good preachers are rare today.) And he was also seen as something of a Biblical scholar because of his teaching background.

Shirley could be a doting father. This straight-laced and somber man was totally supportive of his daughter Holly's career in show business. Holly left California at a young age to go to New York and become what was then called a "show girl"—a very elegant if somewhat generic lady pop singer, mostly in radio. Far from being scandalized by her chosen work—as he was by Anne's and later Holly's beaus—Rev. Shaw wrote letters to his flock telling them to write to New York and help Holly win a talent contest that would make it possible for her to win a radio contract. (They did, and she did.) Interestingly, Rev. Shaw wrote regular letters to his flock, a practice Robert would take up with his choruses and then continue throughout his life. Rev. Shaw's letters were chatty and reportorial, as opposed to reflective and provocative like his son's famous ones. Still, they were literate, upbeat and passionate, as he was. He used the epistolary form to pastor, as his son would later do. Rev. Shaw's letters are also full of boasts and boosts for Holly. He was always a fan of Holly's success in show business. Later letters to parishioners, including one announcing that Rev. Shaw was going on a doctor-ordered sick leave, apprised those who were radio listeners of where to hear Holly's radio broadcasts.[4]

4 Burris–Anne Price interview.

CHAPTER 3

The Preaching Line

Robert Shaw must have liked his line about coming from "a long line of preachers," for he used it repeatedly for the better part of 40 years. In one of three lectures at Memorial Church at Harvard in 1981, he said: "So that you appreciate how far back it is possible for one man to have slid, you should know that for three generations the Shaws and Lawsons—both of whose names I bear—have been ministers, chaplains and missionaries, in the service of an evangelical denomination removed from Congregationalism chiefly by water rites and Welch's grape juice."

But it wasn't such a long line. Not unless you were looking for history—looking for roots. The line was his mother's father, Shaw's own father, and his brother—just two generations prior to his own. His younger brother Jim became an Army chaplain. And there was his mother, who was not a preacher but whose vocation was religious. It was her ministry that was the decisive one. Nelle didn't sing for money or fame. She did it for love. She did it to praise. She did it as witness to a higher power. Nelle's ministry was her identity. Her life.

So, too, Rev. Shaw's ministry was not only his work: it was his identity and his life. He didn't preach for his own glory, or to advance a career, but because he could not *not* preach.

Rev. Shaw's devotion to his work was, by nature, sacrificial. And he was probably not an easy man to live with. Dying too young, he was a father too soon gone and the process of reconciliation that naturally should occur between fathers and sons never had its time and place. But one behavior became Robert's: spending one's self in holy work. Robert simply had to find his own work.

Shaw would write that, "From infancy 'church' in our family was no sometime thing but a seven-day, twenty-four-hour shift." Robert was in the pulpit himself by his late teens. He preached as a substitute for his father when his father was away or ill, and also as training for what everyone in the family, including Bob, then expected—he, too, would become a minister.

But Shaw rebelled. The signs of his rebellion were visible early, and never ceased. He shared his parent's seriousness and severity. But there was a wildness in him. Part of this was conscious rebellion and had to do, eventually, with his questioning of and rejection of his parents' religion. Part of it was innate—simply a matter of energy. His sister Anne remembers him running around the house in circles as a little boy. 'Round and 'round until he'd calmed or exhausted himself.

He was the minister's son who got into trouble—the kind of kid who threw spitballs from the choir loft. Bob and his brother Jim once sang off-tune in choir practice as a practical joke—just to drive the boy next to them crazy. (Rev. Shaw made the brothers apologize to the choir director before permitting them to attend a football game they viewed as all-important.)

Obligations came early in life—paper routes and part-time jobs. The money was kicked back to the family. Once Bob's mother sent him to the grocery store with household change to buy some supplies for the family, and he spent all the money on miniature hot dogs. He sat down in an empty field on the way home and ate the whole bag—and spent the night throwing up. Shaw told that story about himself—often. To illustrate what, one wonders?

That, like many of us, he had a bit of larceny in his soul? That guilt was a frequent and longstanding companion? That the family's brush with poverty still stung? Maybe all of the above. But perhaps what the story reveals most of all is that his parents' conventional, structured, Protestant, and to him somewhat banal, goodness was something of a straightjacket. That "long line" of preachers that wasn't so long, Shaw felt as a yoke. The expectation that he would continue the line was a weight he must have begun to feel early on.

Bobby Shaw was perhaps never ministerial material. For this was a boy with fire inside. A man who grew up in his neighborhood told Robert's son Peter that, as a boy, Robert was always on his bike—pedaling like mad. In fact, he said, Robert Shaw pedaled going downhill.

Eventually, a collegiate Shaw decided he could not accept his father's theology. But, as a boy and as a very young man, part of what Bob did not like about being a minister's son was the combination of enforced virtue and lack of funds. There was never any fun money—any walking around cash. Shaw once said, "All the churches of my early growing up were, I suppose, poor churches, with Wednesday evening suppers and Friday evening movies. It seemed to me quite natural that a good deal of emphasis should be placed on Heaven, for certainly for a lot of people—of which we were not nearly the least blessed—there was precious little to be had hereabouts. I suppose I took it for granted that salvation was assuagement for poverty." The Shaw family was certainly *not* the least blessed. They had fairly roomy houses. They had summer jobs for the kids. They had access to transportation. The parents had time off in the summer. The Shaw children were exposed to the ideas of great speech and lofty deeds; they were exposed to critical Biblical study (if you can think critically about scripture—the most important thing—it must also be possible, and permissible, to think critically about all things); and they were exposed to the notions of music as craft and as worship.

People did things for the children of ministers then, as they do now, helping them to get jobs and access to the good things of life. And, of course, all of the Shaw children were able to attend a very fine college thanks to combinations of scholarships, help from each other (when an older child succeeded, he or she helped the next one in line), and their own jobs. Rev. Shaw could not write each child a fat check for college, or help directly, much at all, yet they all went to college. Indeed, they all went to the "Harvard of the West": Pomona College, where their father had gone. The ornery boy, Bobby, became the questioning young man—Bob. So, the preaching life was a pretty good life for the Shaw family, including Robert. But he found it, then and in memory, constricting.

The two greatest gifts all of the Shaw children took from their childhoods, however, may have been matters of sensibility and perception. They grew up with a sense of possibility. There was, having grown up in such an open and unspoiled atmosphere, no reason to assume a person could not be anything he or she wanted to be. There was no reason to fear going to New York City to work in music, for example, which four of the Shaw children did eventually, to varying degrees. The second sensibility was the notion of purpose and responsibility. Shaw never stopped being a "son of a preacher," in this sense, and maybe that's one reason why he liked the phrase. Indeed, when Robert spoke in public, he tended to preach. A pulpit or lectern was like an old shoe to him. And though he was always uncomfortable with being social, he was always *entirely comfortable* with preaching. One might even say the ministerial model was his model for relating to people. But had he not rebelled against being a minister, a minister's son, and another link in the "long line of preachers," he could not have invented a man who reinvented a part of American music.

CHAPTER 4

Sunlit Days and a Shadow

The physical and spiritual openness of Shaw's boyhood shaped him, too. The Shaws' pre-"Californicated" California was a land of beauty, space, and light. And Shaw's boyhood seems to have been remarkably innocent and unstructured. The California of his youth was still a place of small towns and farms. Indeed, if we could travel backward in a time machine, the California of 1920 and 1930 might seem like a different planet. In this Rockwellian idyll Nelle would organize her alternate family camping trips—the high ground one year, and the sea the next. Shaw's parents had rigged up homemade tents, sort of quasi teepees, in which the Shaw clan was housed at leisure. Rev. Shaw was an enthusiast by nature, and would wax rhapsodic about the redwoods or the open shore. But by the time Robert Shaw went to college, this California was beginning to change. Los Angeles was expanding. More and more people were coming from the East. Many of them had cars. Most were looking for better lives.

The Shaw children grew up in a California still abounding with sagebrush and orange groves. One actually knew, or one's parents did, prospectors and miners and cowboys. Boys rode bikes all day long and safely wandered far. Surfing—40 years before the surfer craze—was not yet cool or vaguely counter-cultural but something ordinary people did outdoors. Bob liked to surf.

Could there be tension or shadow in a world this unspoiled and easy? Well, yes. Rev. Shaw had a temper. His health problems increased with each year. There was the moving from town to town and church to church—the restlessness. There was Nelle's busyness and distance. There was a certain severity to these good people, as there was to the mature Shaw himself. As much as Robert looked back on his parents through a golden haze of nostalgia (calling their partnership "perfect" and "unique"), there was usually also a shudder in his retrospection.

There was also a searing moment in Bobby Shaw's childhood; one that foretold an even mightier sting; one that involved Rev. Shaw.

The hyper-kinetic little boy had done something wrong one day. It was an offense deemed worthy of physical punishment: "The belt." It was not the first time it had come to this. But this time, Shirley Shaw, instead of administering corporal punishment, turned the tables. He handed his belt to the boy and explained to his son Bobby that he, Shirley, had clearly failed as a father. The father told the boy to give the whipping to *him*. The boy, horrified, ran from the room.

Longer shadows would fall. The darkness that loomed in America between 1929 and 1946 eventually did reach Bobby Shaw's life of surf and gospel songs.

CHAPTER 5

Jim

The Shaw children were, in order: Holly, Robert, Jim, Anne, and John. Holly was the first to go to New York, where she became the radio and Broadway singer who made Rev. Shaw so proud. She was a minor star for a few years, or perhaps on the threshold of stardom.

Jim followed the preaching line Bob rejected, but only eventually and by a strange route.

Anne was also a singer, though in adult life she devoted herself primarily to being a wife and mother. She sang more classical material than Holly did and, indeed, sang with her brother Robert on several occasions in the 1950s. She did marry Harrison (Buzz) Price, the man her parents "prayed" she would not marry. Price became an engineer, businessman, raconteur, and audiophile. He would help to build Disneyland.

John pursued music and then teaching, until being slowed almost to a halt by health issues.

Jim, though musical like the others, was the only one who did not place music at the center of his life.

Jim, born in 1918, two years after Robert, became in one sense the "favorite son." He was the steady, solid one and the one from whom great things—as Nelle and Shirley defined great things—were expected. Jim was "sunny," as Holly was, even and predictable of temper. He was thoughtful but not so given to dreaming or brooding as his brother Robert. Jim, too, conducted the church choir at Glendora, California, as Holly and Robert had, and as Anne and John would. But Jim was different. Holly, Robert, John, and Anne were essentially artistic. Jim was, according to his sister Anne, a natural businessman. "It astonished us all," she said, "we had no idea where it came from." "It" was a talent for organization, fraternity, and marketing. If Robert was a "campus liberal," as he later dubbed himself, Jim was a sort of future Rotarian. That's not to imply that Jim was shallow, or that he was self-satisfied. But he was practical and upbeat and did not share Robert's attraction to existential angst.

Jim worked, while in high school and college, at Walker's Department Store in Los Angeles.[5] He started as a stock boy and quickly became a very young, and innovative, manager. Jim made friends easily and knew how to get things done. He was seemingly untroubled, un-neurotic, able to sell, and able to count. In a way, he was the most like his parents of the Shaw children, for though they were not particularly sunny, they were workers and doers.

James Shaw graduated from college in 1940 and soon entered the Army. He became a chaplain, training at the Chaplain's School in Indianapolis, Indiana. He served at the Santa Ana Air Base and later at Deming, New Mexico. He wound up in the South Pacific—in New Guinea. He brought all of his entrepreneurial and organizational gifts to military service.

Jim entered the military a callow youth. He was "gung-ho" in the early days. Initially, he may have even considered being a chaplain a bit of a dodge, albeit a legitimate one. To be a chaplain might be a religious "call," but it was also a cushy job, and a relatively fast path to becoming an officer. Jim was qualified to be a chaplain, not by training in any divinity school or academic work in theology, but from a sort of correspondence course he'd taken: "The Army Chaplain's Guide." And of course, there was his father's

5 Walker's was an important California institution, eventually expanding to eight stores, including one in San Diego, known as the Walker-Scott Department Store. It is said to have contained San Diego's first escalators.

example. But Jim was not the one headed for divinity school. That was, everyone assumed, Robert. Jim was headed for a career in business. He had high hopes, big dreams.

The war changed the lives of millions of Americans, the Shaw family among them. The war sobered and matured Jim. He went from being a boy chaplain—a chaplain in name, mostly—to being a pastor. And this happened because it had to. He was learning hard and fast.

By the summer of 1943, Jim Shaw was in a place called Tsili, New Guinea, on an island called Biak and then an island called Owi. He was attached to the 39th Fighter Squadron where he was 35th Group Chaplain. And things were *not* cushy. Or sunny. He was not in a Dale Carnegie world. Jim was, in the parlance of the Vietnam War, "in the shit." He arrived to find his camp under heavy bombardment and casualties high. Some of the dead bodies were not being buried. Jim built caskets, laid out a cemetery site, registered the graves, and buried the dead. Jim also set up a crude but effective postal system for the base on Biak, installed a public address system, and produced weekly homemade entertainment for the men. He organized variety shows and sing-ins, and repaired a motion picture projector, which allowed the men to see their first movie start to finish.

On Biak and Owi Islands, Jim Shaw became a true chaplain. Testimony emerged, in later years, about his ability to listen, comfort, and console. Tribute is paid to him in a novel about the 39th Fighter Squadron and the life of pilots and fighting men in New Guinea and the Philippines in 1943, 1944, and 1945. The book is called *Outcast Red*, written by William Brevard Rogers, who was a part of that outfit. Rogers says that the character of the chaplain in his book is based on Jim Shaw. Indeed, he says that "the story of one person is told in the clear . . . ," which one takes to mean that Jim Shaw was much as the chaplain, Paul, was portrayed. The narrator of the story speaks of the feelings of the novel's protagonist, Lee, after the chaplain's death: "Of all the losses he had known, Paul's was the most preposterous! The most meaningless! He did not fly. The chances of such a happening were minute."

Rogers, who flew 146 combat missions and received the Distinguished Flying Cross, became a Presbyterian minister after the war. He evidently had many heart-to-heart talks with Jim Shaw, and was inspired by him. The portrait of Jim Shaw in *Outcast Red* is of a man of fortitude, considerable natural leadership skill, and great pastoral sympathy. All three qualities developed at an accelerated pace. The extremities of war left him little choice and less time. Jim came to his chaplaincy with a church youth group, almost Chamber of Commerce, mentality. He knew little of death and nothing of despair. When stationed in New Mexico, he wrote home about low attendance at chapel and considered the sales and marketing devices he might employ to solve the problem. He didn't *stop* thinking that way. He didn't stop being Jim Shaw when he was in the heart of war's darkness, but eventually, the "pastor" subsumed this "public relations" side of him. He dug deep and honed all the skills he'd learned from his father. He also found a mentor in the service in August Gearhart—a senior chaplain and Catholic priest. Father Gearhart took Jim under his wing, and taught him what he could in a short time. Given Jim's background, a Catholic priest was a most unlikely tutor. (The thought might well have been horrifying to his parents.) But Jim was growing up. In the world in which he now found himself, there was little tolerance for veneer.

Jim was killed on Owi Island, New Guinea, on July 30, 1944. (For years family members thought he died on Biak.)

American forces had not easily secured these islands, and many American and Japanese died there. Jim had just conducted his last service—a farewell service for the men. He was to depart for Brisbane, Australia to become assistant to Fr. Gearhart. According to Shaw family memory, Jim was conducting a communion service on the beach and a lone Japanese plane strafed the island. Before Jim could get to the chapel he'd built—the nearest shelter from the attack—one of the bullets got him. William Brevard Rogers tells the story differently, though the two versions are not utterly incompatible. He writes: "The bomb was only a stray . . . The stray hit a shallow trench without sandbag cover, where three group staff officers, including Paul [Jim] were cowering. A burial detail could not even properly sort out their remains."

Capt. James Shaw was 26 when his life ended.[6]

James Shaw's death shattered his family. The singing Shaws, who had known so much light, had been visited by untimely death. The young star was suddenly, starkly, irreparably gone—no body to bury, no trace or remnant, only memories of his brief life.

Jim's mother Nelle was already reeling. She had lost her husband, Shirley, in December of the previous year. She had lost her mother a month before that.

Here is what Jim wrote to her after Shirley Shaw died. It shows the pastor, the man, Jim had become:

My Darling mother:

Word has just come of the passing of your precious husband, our beloved father. It is hard to know what to write at this moment of mutual bereavement.

Your loss has been harder than mine, for you saw him go and now find yourself alone, except for your memories. I, on the other hand, have had nothing but memories for the past seven months. I do, however, realize something of what an empty feeling I shall have when I return and he is "not at home." My consolation is that although I am thousands of miles from that home, I have somehow felt his presence and camaraderie more this past hour than in the past seven months. He is with me now—seeing the chapel I've built, experiencing the joys of viewing these new lands, attending my services, hearing my prayers. These thoughts must keep me going.

6 Neither interviews with family members, nor the Shaw papers, nor U.S. government records provide an absolutely clear and definitive version of the death of James Shaw. All that can be said with certainty is that Jim was killed by enemy fire on what was to have been his last day on the island.

The memories of the day spent with him last May at Luke Field, and in San Francisco before being shipped overseas, will live forever. I'm deeply grateful that we had such fun-filled loving hours together upon those two occasions. He seemed so tremendously happy and I was so very proud of him.

You, too, have your memories and you will be living with them and with him throughout the days to come. As he would wish, we will carry on most cheerfully the traditions of our family, and we will be faithful and constant in our love to Christ's church, which was his life.

With abiding love,
Your son,
Jim[7]

James Shaw's death also changed his brother Robert. Bob was already Hamlet to Jim's Henry V. Robert was the melancholy artist/poet. Jim was Robert's happy-go-lucky kid brother who wanted to go into business. But he was the one in a hurry to find his place in the world. As children, the brothers were constant companions and the best of friends. They were bound by close age, by being the same sex, by family ties, by music, and by the church. They were bound as well by a sense of irreverence. They both liked sports, games of all sorts, and practical jokes. But as they grew into young manhood, they went different ways. Robert was the searcher, the mystic, and the rebel. Jim was straight up and straight ahead. Maybe they were two sides of a coin, for Jim became, in a short period of testing, not just a churchman but a helper and consoler, and Robert certainly showed a talent for labor, organization, and order in later years. But as the college years approached, these two very close brothers came to see the world and their part in it quite differently. Jim was working long hours in retailing. Bob was more and more deeply involved in music at Pomona. The two brothers were both Pomona graduates but Jim majored in business and Bob majored in religion and literature. They had

7 Shaw papers.

grown up in a home in which judgments—sometimes rather harsh ones—were made, and they were not above judging each other. Jim didn't see music as a practical career choice, especially when the world seemed to be on fire. Bob, whose campus liberalism included a pacifism that was rather callow but in the course of lifetime would develop into a deep conviction, thought Jim had "sold out" by volunteering for service in the war. And he said so. His brother's death shattered Robert and became a cornerstone of his profound and very personal hatred of war—a belief and emotion that would inform his performances of at least two works that became a part of his core musical repertoire.

Included in the appendices of this book are two youthful sermons given by Robert Shaw. Just as it would be hard to imagine the young Bob writing the letter Jim wrote to his mother, it is impossible to imagine Jim giving such sermons. One is entitled "The Tragedy of Growth." At age 21, the oldest son would write: "The capacity for suffering is the difference between personalities which live and personalities which do not live." Moreover, the hero of the sermon is not Jesus, but Beethoven.

Bob was regarded by his parents and members of his church as a bit "dreamy" and impractical. To them a free thinker was slightly flakey—a bit too easily seduced by the latest ideas.

It was Jim, the second son, who saw his course and enlisted, after the war broke out. It was Jim, the second son, who followed the Rev. Shaw into the ministry. It was Jim who was the dutiful and attentive son, and happily so, to both his parents. Indeed, Robert himself shared some of the perception of himself as somehow less solid than Jim.

By the time Shirley Shaw died, Jim Shaw was in the South Pacific, building chapels out of grass and mud, dodging Japanese fighter planes, pushing Jeeps out of the muck, and writing letters of condolence to the parents of men barely younger than himself—all under the tutelage of a Catholic priest. He'd been transformed from a sort of glad handing minister's apprentice to a war chaplain with a certain Zen-like stoicism. Surely it occurred to him that he might not have much time to become the man he was destined to be.

Robert had another 55 years.

We have no record of what Robert wrote to his mother, or whether he wrote at all, after Shirley died.

We also do not know what consolation Robert attempted to offer his mother after Jim's death. But we do know what Nelle said to Robert about Jim's death—at least as Robert heard and remembered it. This, too, shattered him.

Jim was to become the family's martyr, just as sister Holly was the family saint.

And Bob? From 1939 to 1945, he was building the foundations of his musical career—learning from Fred Waring, who had brought him to New York in 1938 to form and train a men's glee club for his radio show. Bobby was beginning to become Bob, who became Robert. And Robert Shaw was already forming his ambitions and ideas about serious music.

CHAPTER 6

HOLLY

Hollace Shaw was a woman of great beauty—natural, luminous, and innocent. She possessed generosity, warmth, and talent. Hers was a lyric soprano voice. It was golden and honey-like. It seemed to float. It was never overly sharp or piercing. It was seldom below the pitch. It never scooped or wobbled. It was pure, and light, and clear. Hers was a *bel canto* voice. Totally natural. Simply a gift. In 1940, Holly appeared in two musicals on Broadway, one of which was *Very Warm for May*. The play was a flop, but it was in it that Holly introduced Jerome Kern's lovely song, "All the Things You Are."

The family was, and remained, intensely proud of this, and of the fact that Jerome Kern more than once singled out the musicianship of Hollace Shaw for praise.

Holly was as much an embodiment of California sunshine as her parents were the embodiment of Christian duty. She had blond hair and green eyes. She was a person of grace, of seemingly infinite kindness, and of compassion. She was elegant. She looked and dressed the part of an up-and-coming Broadway musical star. She was also the sibling who looked out for the others and, later, their children.

Holly's career apex was as "Vivian"—lead singer for Phil Spitalny's "All Girl Orchestra" on his "Hour of Charm" on the radio. Spitalny also made records and public appearances at venues like Radio City Music Hall. Holly was a part of those shows as well. Florence Kopleff recalled that Holly also shared, for a time, a weekly half-hour radio broadcast with Mack Harrell (sponsored by Pet Milk). Holly was already a success in New York when Robert went there to seek his fortune. Indeed, she had sung with the summer Cleveland Orchestra at a time when Robert barely knew what it was. But her heart was not in classical works, much to Robert's dismay. For he felt his sister had a splendid and unique voice. Holly's taste ran to light opera and show tunes.

Holly was an enormously loyal and devoted person—generous to family and friends, literally to a fault. Her open heart could be, and sometimes was, exploited. Robert was the oldest son, and Jim the shining son, but Holly was the first-born (1913). And she was a protective and loving big sister. She used her New York earnings to help put her younger siblings Anne and John through Pomona. If Jim was the golden boy, Holly was the golden girl—a New York singing sensation: a radio star. She was as glamorous and, seemingly, easily successful as Jim was driven and dutiful. And, ultimately, she led a tragic life.

Holly was unable to defy her parents and marry the love of her life, as her sister did. She came close, but could not do it. That man was Jacob Javits, later to become United States senator from the state of New York, indeed a giant of the United States Senate. The two were very much in love in the late 1930s and early 1940s, and at one point Javits bought her a diamond and ruby engagement ring. But by 1941 they hit a brick wall. Javits and Holly went to San Diego to seek the blessing of Shirley and Nelle. The reception was cordial but decidedly cool. Holly's parents did not think a religiously mixed marriage was a good idea. And, as Javits told the story in his autobiography, that was it. At first, Holly said she was determined to marry Javits anyway. She did not break off the engagement. But she was shaken and unraveled. She and Javits would separate and try again several times. But Holly found that she simply could not defy her parents. *His* parents were not happy about the marriage either, but apparently they were not as adamant, nor did they wield as much power over their son as Shirley and Nelle did over Holly.

Holly's siblings, Robert and Anne, were supportive. The family loved Jack Javits, and indeed Holly's siblings remained friendly with him through the years. But Holly's great love would marry another. And Holly would marry, disastrously, on the rebound.

Did Shirley and Nelle actually forbid the marriage, or threaten to disown Holly?

No. They simply could not bring themselves to say anything but what they thought: This is a bad idea. We cannot endorse it.

As Anne Shaw Price, Holly's sister, recalled it, Javits's parents wanted Holly to convert to Judaism, as was and is the Jewish rubric. When Javits was ready to defy his family, Holly would hesitate. When Holly was ready to take the plunge and defy *her* parents, Javits would get cold feet. It wasn't only Holly's parents standing in the way, but the two histories, and two traditions, and two people who could not make up their minds. Finally, Holly was exhausted by the whole drama and, almost as a way out, chose another suitor who'd emerged.

The man who was to become Holly's first husband was a very young colonel in the war. He looked like the film actor, Melvin Douglas. He had long sought after Holly. "The colonel" just kept coming around. His message, said Anne Price, was: "He's not the one, I'm the one." When the relationship with Javits finally fell apart, Holly relented. Hollace Shaw made a beautiful bride and both Holly and her family were ready for her to ride off into the sunset. She even quit show business for the colonel. They moved to Virginia where she was told he was to be a "publishing executive." But the job turned out to be that of an itinerant book salesman. And even that didn't last. The colonel could never find work in private industry commensurate with the importance he had known in the military. He was comfortable with military life. And he was not so much suited to civilian life. He could not find his place in the workaday world. Moreover, he possessed a second, related flaw. He was an incurable alcoholic and wished to remain so. Eventually, his addiction took his health, and his life.

Holly was a person who made the best of things and she became a Virginia lady—fairly easy, given her sunny disposition. She also became a fine chef. In her later Virginia years, she carved out a new career as the host of a local television cooking show.

After the death of the colonel, Holly was persuaded by two old friends from her New York days to come home to California and start a new life. There they introduced her to a man they felt was ideal for her. He was a physician.

The doctor was a well-regarded gynecologist in the Golden State, and a gentle, arts-loving soul. He was elegant, courtly, generous, and kind. But Holly was as unlucky with men as she was lucky in looks and talent. For the doctor had a deep, and for Holly devastating, secret—he was a closeted gay man. He had a long-term lover, a fact that Holly discovered only a short time before her death in 1976, at the young age of 63.

The final bit of tragic luck to befall a person who had brought so much light and kindness to her family, friends, and fans was death through medical misjudgment, if not neglect. Holly had Addison's disease and needed to take steroids to live. She caught the flu and, therefore, was rejecting her medications without replenishing them. She needed to be hospitalized for an extended period and receive transfusions. But this did not occur. Perhaps she did not understand the risk. Perhaps she hid the depth of her condition from her physicians and from her husband. But she was not given the simple treatment that would almost certainly have saved her life.

Holly was deeply devoted to her siblings and their children. She was greatly loved by them as well. She became the family conciliator, uniter, and historian.

But Holly had a complicated relationship with Robert. Robert would brag that Kern had written "All the Things You Are" for his sister. When he did pops concerts in Cleveland, and in the early days in Atlanta, he would often program the song. But there was always friction between Robert and Holly when both were alive, and they were not close. Holly was closer to Robert's first wife Maxine than to Robert. In part, the friction was a matter of temperament. Robert thought his sister was a Pollyanna. She thought him anti-social and a Scrooge. There may have been some competition, too. She was the oldest and he the second. Sibling rivalry between the first and second child is common enough. But their great source of tension was . . . repertoire. They differed about the songs to be sung. Holly favored the lighter, brighter side of music. Though she sang in a "straight" or classical manner, and did not sing jazz, or in the contemporary Broadway fashion (with head voice), the material she chose was closer to light opera or pops repertoire. Holly sang hymns at the close of her radio shows and often some Schubert, but people tuned in to hear her sing Rogers and Hart's "My Romance" or Cole Porter, and she was comfortable, indeed happy, with that. Robert thought that was a sell-out, just as he thought Jim had sold out. Holly was forever promising Bob (he was still Bob to friends and family then) that she was going to take some serious voice lessons and audition for the Metropolitan Opera. But she never did. And Robert actually held this against his sister. He believed she was cheating her talent, and perhaps her soul. And he told her so. The Shaws were a judgmental brood.

Though Shaw made his living in his early years in New York working in, substantially, the same music as Holly—for Waring and radio—and he learned from it, he was dissatisfied with popular music, almost from the start. He also thought most opera was lightweight and shallow. (Light opera, then, would be weightless.) With conspicuous exceptions, he never changed his mind much about any of that.

Robert gave Holly a hard time about her music when he saw her, which was rare. He looked down on her career, and she felt hurt.

They never worked together. And he was often not very nice to her—gruff and dismissive. No doubt he saw things differently in later years. Doubtless there was also guilt after her death. Perhaps he saw that he had failed to fully appreciate her; he certainly failed to support her. In later years, Robert recalled Jim and Holly with enormous affection and pride. But Holly did not live long enough to experience the relative mellowing of her brother.

A strange and touching thing was also true: Holly's voice became Robert's ideal of what a soprano should be—gravity-resistant; sunny, but not shiny; no hint of nasal sound; and feminine—caressing the notes and never smothering them. This is the sound Shaw always sought and seldom but occasionally found in sopranos—especially soprano soloists. One hears Holly in the recordings Sylvia McNair made with Shaw. His soprano ideal was Holly. Furthermore, her demeanor became Shaw's image of a female singer—all poise and warmth.

It is poignant and ironic that Robert Shaw, who came to be so closely associated with Christmas and who all his life was what we today call a "crossover" artist where Christmas music was concerned, had a sister named Holly, with whom he battled over crossover music.

After Holly's death, Robert grew increasingly sentimental about "All the Things You Are." That song's simple grace epitomized his beautiful sister who had been so ill-used by life. It epitomized all the things she might have been, and the gentle woman that she was.

CHAPTER 7

Anne

Holly and Jim were both "accentuate the positive" stiff-upper-lippers. They were both givers. They shared a basic optimism. Robert was a questioner. He felt sympathetic to Anne—child number four, born in 1923. She was a questioner, too. Anne shared Robert's skepticism about old-time and churched religion. Both came to believe that any humanism based upon Christ had to be rooted in *his humanity*, rather than the human sacrifice of Christ. Like Abelard, they could understand Christ's sacrificial death as an act of empathy, but not as recompense. Neither could see how Christ's death obliterated human sin. Both came to believe that Christ's divinity was problematic and beside the point. Anne also shared Robert's political liberalism. Most important, Anne was attracted to the same music he loved—so-called serious music. It was the music of the three Bs and of the classic tradition, and above all, it was choral music.

Holly and Jim shared a bond. So did Bob and Anne—his little sister could, in his eyes, do little wrong as Holly could, sometimes, do little right. And he and Anne did work together. Shaw hired her to sing with the San Diego Symphony when he conducted the orchestra and was its music director. She sang the soprano solo in the Beethoven *Missa Solemnis*, an accomplishment that she found quite unbelievable upon reflection decades later.

Unlike Holly, Anne was not a competitor. She was a *little* sister—nine years younger. Bob's attitude toward her was nurturing and protective rather than critical and judgmental.

Holly was drawn toward the light and the "lite." She loved radio and the popular song. Robert tolerated, and sometimes detested, both. Anne was drawn to sacred music as her brother was.

Anne, also a soprano, also became a radio star of sorts in South America, where she lived for several years while her husband worked there. But she was not singing pop. She was singing Schubert—exploring the *Lieder* tradition as her brother was simultaneously exploring the choral-orchestral one. Like Robert, Anne's nature was serious, scholarly, and critical, though her temperament was gentle like her sister's. She was drawn, as Robert was, to music of high purpose and seriousness. Though her primary vocation was as a wife and mother, she was active for decades in the California choral scene. She sang with Roger Wagner and the Los Angeles Master Chorale. Wagner was, of course, Shaw's rival from the late 1940s to the mid-1950s. The two men were, respectively, the East (Shaw) and West (Wagner) Coast choral gurus, though Shaw was actually a Californian and Wagner a Frenchman. They both made popular records and they both made and marketed choral arrangements. They both had apologists and acolytes. The two proceeded on parallel tracks for several years—until Shaw seemed to leap off his steed and board a jet. Wagner never could get out of the choral box, and perhaps did not want to. Shaw moved to the orchestra. Their rivalry, mostly amicable and respectful, though perhaps taken more seriously by Wagner, faded; in their old age the two men became affectionate friends. But together, Shaw and Wagner constituted the yin and yang of American choral music in the decade after World War II. Both men were competitive by nature and critical of each other. Each admired talents in the other. Wagner was, perhaps, more a "natural" than Shaw. Anne Price described his feel for the Catholic French line as second nature—like hand to glove. Only rhythm was second nature to Shaw. Anne Price not only sang under Wagner, she became a key supporter, confidant, and friend. This was no problem for Shaw, who admired Wagner and his sister.

Anne was also willing and able to stand up to her parents when she chose a husband, which Robert respected.

Anne was a fellow seeker—musically, religiously, and politically. Shaw saw his sister as possessing an anti-war, Quaker mentality, rather than an enlistment mentality (like Jim's). And even though Shaw would eventually enlist in the Navy near the end of the war, he shared the same pacifist views as his sister.

Bob and Anne both believed, eventually, that there were many ways to God, not just their father and mother's way. They both began with the humanity of Jesus. That is where Shirley Shaw ended. Unlike his father, Bob had concluded that divinity was unknowable and inexplicable, and anyhow, true humanity was perhaps more important than godliness. Julius Herford, the man who was to become Shaw's first mentor in formal music, used to say, when asked his religion, "I'm a Bach." (Not even, "I'm a Bachian," but "I'm a Bach.") This is something of the way Shaw felt from a rather early age and he only became more outspoken in his Christian agnosticism. Jesus the man was not an inconvenient, parenthetical reality to be looked past, but the central reality to be focused upon. Shaw saw Anne as a kindred spirit, musically and theologically, and she was. Shaw and his younger sister both found sacredness in Bach's Passions, Brahms's Motets, and Mozart's *Requiem*. For them, that was divinity enough. The sacredness was in the music and the musical expression of the text, not in the dogma expressed by the text. In his later years, Shaw would say that sacred texts were merely "the best texts available" to the great composers of masses and sacred cantatas. Perhaps this was projection or selective biographical scholarship. For Mozart almost certainly did not find Christ's divinity beside the point as Shaw did. Shaw did not deny the possibility of Christ's divinity. He simply thought Christ's human existence was the thing that mattered. Christ was, to him, a hero, a model, a guru with a way, not a speed pass. Was Jesus also, somehow, divine? For Robert, probably not. But it did not matter. Jesus was ideally human. That's what mattered. The formula that Christ redeemed living men and women by dying 2000 years ago seemed to both Shaws irrational and, ultimately, irreverent superstition.

So these two siblings moved, in the course of their lives, far away from the theology of their father. And it was a bond. But even for Anne, Robert was, until his later years when the two siblings and their spouses grew close, a rather distant brother. Except on the few occasions when they made music together. They lived on opposite coasts and, for a few years, Anne and Buzz were away in South America. Moreover, Robert was always a step removed from the family, partly for reasons we shall see. But the greater impediment to intimacy with Robert Shaw, including for his siblings, was that he was married to his music. He did little but his work. He *wished* to do little but his work. Almost everything else bored him. And human beings, outside the context of musical performance, musical education, or musical discussion—though in theory of infinite value—were not necessarily interesting to Shaw for extended periods of time. To him, a speech or an interview was a human interaction. A rehearsal was fellowship. He did not "hang out." Since he was usually working, or on his way to or from work, he could sometimes treat people as impediments. And even though he needed companionship and release, and good food and drink, at the end of the workday, this did not necessarily indicate any inherent interest in what other human beings had to say. He might sit across from you and look right through you—not out of malice, but because his mind was elsewhere, or because he was spent.

When Anne and Buzz Price's son, as a young man, stopped in Atlanta to visit his uncle, Robert spent the day working in his study, as usual. He was willing to have dinner with the nephew he'd not seen in some time, but that was it.

Anne was Robert's closest sibling and remained the closest. They shared a deep love of music, especially choral music, and they made music together. That was how you got close to Robert Shaw.

CHAPTER 8

Pomona

If church—thinking about, talking about, and going to church—was a "7-day-a-week, 24-hour thing," as Shaw so often said, and thus the single greatest force in the lives of the Shaw children, Pomona College was the second greatest influence. And it was a very different influence—a radical influence in the best sense for Anne and Bob. At Pomona, these two Shaws found the freedom to question the foundations of faith—the faith of their church and their father—and to formulate the basics of their own humanism. Pomona probably changed all of the Shaw children, but it especially changed Robert.

Located in the town of Claremont, east of Los Angeles, Pomona College is leafy, Eastern looking, and ivy covered. (It looks like a Platonic conception of a liberal arts college—more like Harvard than Harvard.) Today, it is an oasis from suburban sprawl and megalopolis. To be sure, there was far less sprawl in the 1930s. But even then it had the feeling of a sanctuary. Certainly, looking the part of a college was one reason a film that changed the direction of Robert Shaw's life was made there. Pomona was thought to be a liberal hotbed in the 1930s and 1940s, and it is considered, by some, the most liberal college within the seven-college consortium to which it belongs today.[8]

8 The other colleges are: Claremont Graduate University, established 1925; Scripps College, 1926; Claremont McKenna College, 1946; Harvey Mudd College, 1955; Pitzer College, 1963; and the Keck Graduate Institute for Applied Life Sciences, 1997.

Pomona, founded in 1887, had been Shirley Shaw's college. And all of the Shaw children—Holly, Robert, Jim, Anne, and John—followed him there. But when the Shaw siblings matriculated, Pomona was a different place from the one Rev. Shaw had known. It had always been relatively progressive, but in Shirley Shaw's time it was still affiliated with the Congregational Church. By the time Robert got to Pomona, the school had been fully secularized. It was no longer officially affiliated with the church, and it was becoming ecumenical and humanistic. It was now a part of a progressive academic tradition, not merely a liberal Protestant tradition. It is impossible to say when Shaw lost his father's faith, but it is certain that it was at Pomona that he began to form his own.[9]

Pomona introduced all of the Shaw children to a liberal Christianity more philosophical than doctrinal. It was academic, as opposed to apologetic or promulgating. It introduced the Shaws to the notion of an un-churched humanism. Such humanism, even if inspired by Jesus, might not be linked to a denomination. It might be viewed more as a philosophy of life.

Robert was greatly influenced by a Pomona professor named Hartley Burr Alexander, who wrote an important book called *God and Man's Destiny,* published in 1936. Alexander took special interest in Shaw as a bright young student who could defend his own views. And Shaw quickly adopted Alexander's Christian personalism. Throughout his life, Shaw found mentors, gurus, and teachers who spoke to an intuition already forming within. Of course, this is what most human beings do, to a point, particularly in familial relationships. But the tendency was particularly pronounced in Shaw. He was always pulled, as if by gravity, toward teachers who more fully articulated what he already felt. Alexander shaped Shaw's thought decisively, but in his own youthful sermons Shaw had already been attempting to say similar things. (See Appendix VII, Two Early Robert Shaw Sermons.) Alexander approached Christianity as a scholar—from the standpoint of comparative religion. For

9 Shaw went to Pomona at age 18, after a year of working as a laborer to earn money for school. He had completed high school in three years. He also left Pomona before his four years and all his course work were quite completed to go to New York. But he finished up with later short visits and correspondence, roughly a year after departing for New York.

him, faith had little to do with organizations or denominations. For Alexander, faith was the individual's response to the mystic impulse. Alexander also taught that modern thought—modern scholarship, and science—could not only be reconciled with Christianity, but could actually support Christianity in new ways. Science and progress could be the allies of faith, he said. All of this was very exciting to Robert. And it resonated with him. Alexander, a prophetic scholar and Christian believer, while skeptical about "the church," became Shaw's first great teacher. The pattern with all of Shaw's teachers and mentors was that Shaw found a guru, a rabbi, who lifted him far above the level of understanding he had heretofore known, but who also guided him on a path he had already somehow chosen. The teachers in Shaw's life are all enormously important because growth was, in a sense, the engine driving his life, and the roles of student and teacher (preacher) were the roles that defined him throughout his life. Though he was not personally close to him, as he was to other rabbis later, Shaw reread and quoted Hartley Burr Alexander's work until the end of his own life. In Alexander, Shaw had found the compassionate Christ that he felt he had not found in is own father. Shaw loved an image, borrowed from Alexander, of Jesus "bending over mankind as a child would bend down over a flower."

Some time in this period, influenced by the authors Alexander recommended and those Shaw found on his own, Shaw began to adopt a very different idea of Jesus than the one he had learned from his parents. He began to see Jesus as the greatest and best of any man who had walked the earth, but most importantly, as a man.

Though Shaw read widely in religion all his life—and became particularly fond of the Jewish theologian Martin Buber—his fundamental stance on religion and things of the spirit was formed at Pomona, in sync with Professor Alexander. Shaw's theology deepened and he poured his musical ethic into it, but it did not change essentially from those days.

Eventually Robert Shaw would conclude this: Jesus was the model of how to live a life—how to love, how to forgive. Jesus was the human ideal. But organized religion got in the way of the ideal. Organized religion obscured the life of Christ and obfuscated his message. The real question therefore became: What would open the hearts and minds of humanity to the humanity of Jesus? Shaw eventually came up with his own answer.

Pomona undermined the religion Rev. Shaw knew, loved, and had passed on (or so he assumed) to his children. This was not because there was malice toward religion at Pomona, but because of the spirit of free inquiry encouraged there, and the championing of the notion that religion and reason could co-exist. (Pope Benedict XVI has based his papacy on a similar assertion, so the idea is hardly unorthodox.) But thinking through religion—indeed the whole idea of a thinking religion—liberated Robert Shaw from both dogma and personal history. Shirley and Nelle Shaw, though liberal Protestants in their own minds, certainly could not accept the notion of Jesus as simply a very good man.

One wonders whether Shaw ever broached Alexander's ideas on Christ and organized churches with his mother and father. One wonders whether he ever contemplated discussing the development of his own theological thought with Rev. Shaw. We do not know. Shaw was, however, by 1938 almost intractably on a different path from that of his parents. This can be seen in his young sermons.

Shaw found at Pomona the near antithesis to the religion of his childhood—the religion of his father and mother and grandfather. He then built upon it and created a belief system of his own. In time, he added two key elements that were entirely his own, not Alexander's: an outright hostility toward organized Christianity, which Shaw came to feel had not only obscured, but cheapened, perverted, and commercialized Jesus; and a substitution of the arts for the church. For Shaw, the arts, especially music, and more specifically choral music, became the proper medium for religious contemplation and praise.

Robert and his siblings were astonishingly alike in their formative years. All of the Shaw children participated in parish church life, sang, conducted choirs, failed as instrumental artists, and went to Pomona. But in early adulthood they veered apart. Two of them reexamined, and rejected, the religion of their parents.

Again, the years of Robert's coming of age were 1935 to 1938—years of Franklin Roosevelt's consolidation of his presidency, and years when fascism and militarism were gripping Europe. Social justice, world peace, religious tolerance, and racial harmony were then considered by "campus liberals" like Robert to be achievable, and even inevitable, goals. This may seem tremendously naïve now, but it was not thought so then. Nor was free-thinking theology. This is what the liberal university was. This is what Pomona fostered.

When Shaw did become a working musician, he found that music could be cheapened, just as religion could be, and that most musicians felt they were performers, not mediums or priests.

Certainly the first great musical mentor in his life, Fred Waring, did not see music as "holy" or musicians as "called" men. He was as pragmatic and secular as Professor Alexander was ethereal. Alexander changed the way Shaw thought about God and faith. Waring changed the direction of Shaw's life.

CHAPTER 9

WARING

Shaw did not initiate his professional life in music with grand artistic ambition. Those ambitions came, and came soon enough. But in the very beginning he simply wanted to enjoy making music and pay off some college debts.

Indeed, he was unsure, at first, that music was his calling.

Shaw came to New York in 1938 to work in radio. He was 22 years old. His boss was bandleader and radio star Fred Waring. Shaw's job, under Waring's eye, was to form and direct the Fred Waring Glee Club. The group performed on the air, along with the band, doing mostly popular songs and Broadway material, as well as a few spirituals. Waring had, famously, "found" Shaw on the campus of Pomona College.

The lore, which is mostly true, runs as follows: As a college student, Shaw was leading the Pomona Glee Club, filling in for the absent and ailing director, Ralph Lyman, and earning a few dollars. It was the kind of thing Shaw and his siblings had always done. Waring, at that time at the peak of his popularity, came to campus to film his part of the movie *Varsity Show*—starring Rosemary Lane and Dick Powell—and while on campus, spotted Shaw. The college was being used as a set and the students as extras. But Waring *heard* the Glee Club and the sound the young Shaw could get out of a choir, and as a natural, untrained talent himself, Waring knew how to spot natural talent in others. This was 1937: pre-war. Waring offered the young man a job. Initially Shaw said "no"—as he would to several other important job offers in his life. Shaw was not thinking about a career in music at that time. He was still bouncing back and forth between the expectation that he would become a minister and the notion of a career in academia, perhaps in the study of comparative religion. It was not a question of religion or some other career, but which type of career in religion. He had not thought about music seriously. Music was fun and inspiring. But Shaw had not made an attempt to master a musical instrument, nor had he taken music theory. Music was more than a lark to him, but it was little more than an avocation. His heart was still in religion and literature—the word. It is hard to say when Shaw really began to take music seriously. Probably it was not until after he got to New York. In any case, approximately one year after Waring's offer, contemplating college debt and the needs of his family (Rev. Shaw had suffered one of his collapses and Shaw's mother Nelle needed whatever financial help the children could give), Shaw reversed himself, wrote to Waring, and took the job. It was a big job—an amazing opportunity for a green young kid. Waring was willing to trust Shaw to create a Glee Club that would bear Waring's name and appear on Waring's national radio show. Waring had long included singing on his show, but it was by his band—a sort of musical afterthought. Now he wanted professional voices. It would be Shaw's job to find them, mold them, and rehearse them. Waring would conduct, but occasionally "Bob Shaw" was to be afforded a moment in the sun (and on the air). Waring made good on this promise. Shaw would often conduct the spirituals on the air. An early signature tune of the Fred Waring Glee Club, as it was to be for the later Robert Shaw Chorale, was Shaw's "arrangement" of "Set Down, Servant." Actually, when he first came to New York, Shaw did not know enough about musical structure to create an arrangement of his own. But he learned from all the musicians around him, not least of whom was Waring, who insisted on his "own" arrangements of virtually every song he performed. Interestingly, Waring, too, lacked formal musical training and outsourced the actual task of writing arrangements to highly skilled musicians whom he hired. Waring told them what he wanted and critiqued or modified what they put on paper. In performing "Servant" in the early years, Shaw probably was guided by instinct, but by the time the Robert Shaw Chorale existed, there was an arrangement committed to paper and little variation from it was tolerated performance to performance.

But how did Shaw get from Pomona to Manhattan? Well, after some wrangling about salary, and the young Shaw impressively standing up for his contract requirements, Waring wired Shaw money for a train ticket to New York. Instead, Shaw took a train from Los Angeles to New Orleans and a freighter from there to New York in order to save money and pocket the difference. Now, like his sister Holly before him, he was going into radio.[10]

And he was a success.

In this period, Waring "farmed out" Shaw to Billy Rose for the Aquacades (synchronized swimming spectacles) and then to Rose and others for Broadway shows. Shaw was, for example, music director for *Carmen Jones*. Very soon, and still pre-war, Shaw and his sister Holly, as "Vivian" on the "Hour of Charm," were both making $25,000 a year[11]—a huge amount of money for the time, especially for a California preacher's kids. A man of more prosaic ambition might have pinched himself and counted his blessings, or at least his bankroll. Between 1938 and 1945, most of the rest of the country was still climbing, oh so tentatively, out of the Great Depression. Shaw was on the road to being rich and famous. Thanks to the exposure on Waring's show, he was a household name, or nearly so. He could have made a career of Broadway and radio had he desired it. But Shaw was not thinking about money or success on Broadway. He had already begun to dream of doing larger things: great sacred choral music with a special kind of choir. How did *this* come into his mind? It's something of a mystery. Shaw began to listen to serious music in New York at this time—we know that. And he knew some choral masterworks already, from his youth and college

10 Shaw papers.
11 Burris-Anne Shaw Price interview.

years. He knew just a bit about Beethoven, too, enough to know he loved his music. But he had not heard much of it until he came to New York. He did know, when he heard such music, that it was something nobler than the music he had previously known, and he wanted to be a part of it. The job with Waring began as an escape from religion. But very soon after he started to work in music, Shaw began to imagine it as a substitute for religion.

Eventually, two things happened. First, Shaw founded the Collegiate Chorale and second, as Shaw sometimes told the story, "Toscanini pulled me up out of popular music." But that's not exactly the truth. Toscanini certainly pulled Shaw up. He gave him his chance in classical music. But he didn't put the idea in Robert Shaw's head. He didn't pluck him out of the Aquacades. Shaw pulled *himself* out of radio and Broadway. Arturo Toscanini did not just stumble upon Shaw and introduce him to Verdi and Beethoven. Rather, Shaw knew, at a very early stage, that he wanted to be a part of the world of Verdi and Beethoven, and he went about putting himself in a position to learn from the masters.

In the Waring years (1938 to 1945) Shaw was a bright young star in New York City. Though he still had little formal music training—in composition or orchestration, for example, to say nothing of conducting—and he played no instrument, he was considered a hot ticket. Sometimes he sang with the choirs he formed. He was astonished at his own luck, especially at the number and quality of really great voices available to him. An abundance of fine singers showed up for every series of Waring choir auditions. And here was a very young Shaw picking and choosing from this wealth of professional New York singers, of which almost all were more naturally gifted and better educated musically than he was. Shaw concluded that there were scores of superb singers in New York who were essentially unchallenged musically. What if he did something about that? Shaw was thinking more and more about a special choir—not a glee club but a group of volunteers who would form a classical choral ensemble, and they would be as serious and disciplined as a classical orchestra. They would do challenging music—old and new. The result was the Collegiate Chorale.

Formed in 1941, the Collegiate Chorale was to be, Shaw said, "a mixed choir of 150 young singers, amateur and professional, to be selected by competitive auditions." "Its attention," he announced "will be very largely directed to the *a cappella* literature of the Christian tradition. But in addition there will be an emphasis on contemporary American music . . . ." Shaw also said the Chorale would have to meet "the general artistic demands of the field of professional entertainment." This choir would do the greatest music with the best available singers.[12]

Shaw also saw the Collegiate Chorale as a musical community—a sort of musical version of a lay religious order that would embody Whitmanesque and democratic principles. He said it would be "a melting pot that sings."

In 1944, Shaw wrote these words in a letter to members of the Collegiate Chorale:

"What they don't see—and what I'm afraid you don't see—and what you must see is that the Collegiate Chorale is not a glee club or a stock company. You don't join the Collegiate Chorale, you believe in it. It's very damn near a religion. It's a way of life. Either you feel the fellow next to you is an important human being, and you like him, and you try desperately to understand how he feels about what he sings about, and pool your creative passions to make something a damned sight bigger than either of you could make alone—or this isn't your kind of choir. Either the music you sing is torn out of you—or you ought not to be singing."[13]

Shaw ended the letter by repeating: "You don't join the Collegiate Chorale. You believe it. And if you don't believe it, please don't come next Monday night."[14]

No longer was there any doubt about his vocation.

Shaw began to make music his cause and his reason for being. This conviction only deepened over the next 57 years. But he was drawn, even in the early years, to works of great spirituality and great majesty. That was what drew him to the classical world even before he had fully formed musical

12 Shaw papers.
13 Ibid.
14 Ibid.

ideas or adequate experience for realizing the oratorio literature either in spirit or in scale. He loved the *idea* of the sacred and he loved the *idea* of a band of brethren bound by a common vow to music.

Shaw's grasp of sacred choral literature, however, especially the choral-orchestral masterworks, was still quite limited at this time. In 1941 he was, after all, 25 years old. He knew this was material he loved. He knew it was music he wanted to conduct. But he didn't really understand its depth or complexity. And he didn't know how to go after it. Except to begin. Knowing he would be in way over his head, and would feel that way for a long time, maybe forever, he began his journey. Forming the Collegiate Chorale was a leap of faith and courage. Shaw plunged into a vast rich literature whose internal rules and structures he was only beginning to comprehend. It excited him. It petrified him.

The million-dollar question, asked by an Atlanta chorister many years later, is: "Where in the world did he get the nerve?" Perhaps the partial answer lies in the preaching impulse. A preacher cannot help but preach. He feels a compulsion, whether he is knowledgeable or not, qualified or not. Shaw had found *his* mission (human brotherhood via the choir) and *his* gospel (music lifts and unites). He had to preach both.

Shaw knew the depths of his own ignorance all too well. He learned more of that ignorance as the years passed. It embarrassed him. But music had now become his life. Moreover, Shaw now had his first congregation—the Collegiate Chorale. Shaw suddenly found that he was famous and respected, yet felt that he deserved neither fame nor respect. Even before leaving Waring in 1945 and striking out on his own, Shaw was considered a star and guru. He was awarded the Outstanding American-born Conductor of the Year by the National Association of American Composers and Conductors in 1943. And in 1944 he was the first American conductor to be given a Guggenheim Fellowship. His plan was to go to Europe to study piano and composition—to better learn how to absorb scores more quickly than note by note. Also, he planned to write a book about the needs of the symphonic chorus. He tried. But Europe was not his cup of tea, and he did not know how to study without the context of an upcoming performance. He never did conquer the keyboard, though he struggled mightily and improved. He never accomplished the other goal, either. He talked about that book, or some variation of it, off and on for the next 55 years.

He was a famous choral conductor at age 28. He toured and taught. During the war years, he crisscrossed the United States teaching "choral techniques," but also preaching choral music as a means to democracy and brotherhood. Dr. John Silber of Boston University remembered meeting Shaw at a Choral Workshop at Northwestern University in Chicago in 1944. Shaw, as he did in those days, stripped down to his old-fashioned U-necked T-shirt during rehearsal. He kept time, Silber said, with his shoulders.[15]

But Shaw was not ready for fame and he knew it. He was not ready musically, intellectually, or emotionally. This is what sometimes happens to "rock stars." Success and fame precede proficiency and self-confidence, which then results in psychic pressure. Shaw began to drink more than socially, as both recreation and release. Still, he insisted that he wanted to do something with the nature of the chorus, something that he could not do with Waring or in commercial radio. Shaw's dreams began to form. They were of a different quality than those of the musicians and friends he knew in New York in 1941 or '42 or '43. He tried to articulate these dreams in a seemingly endless flow of letters to members of the Collegiate Chorale, but no one had ever talked or thought that way about choral singing before, and while many of the singers were moved by his letters, others wondered what to make of them.

Meanwhile, Shaw was still working for Fred Waring.

Waring's Glee Club, formed by Shaw, was the first professional radio choir in the United States. They did ten performances a week: two a day—at 7 and 11 p.m.

15 Burris–Silber interview.

Each Waring radio program was 15 minutes. But the performers also put on an hour-long stage show for the public, *after* each radio broadcast, and those were hard tickets to get.

The Waring show was broadcast from the Vanderbilt Theater in New York, which was Glenn Miller's theater on weekends. Waring had it on weekdays. The Hollywood actor Paul Douglas was the announcer.

Like Roger Wagner in his métier, Waring was a natural. He once boasted to Shaw that he could "not make a mistake," in arranging or performing the popular song, and years later, an amazed and amused Shaw would agree. Waring was also a master of the radio medium. He understood his audience. He understood time. He understood variety and pace. His tastes were not Shaw's, not even the young Shaw's, but he was the second great teacher-mentor in Shaw's life, and the first musical one. From Waring, Shaw learned how to command people and how to run a rehearsal. He also acquired some bad habits—like temper tantrums, cursing, and occasionally bullying people in rehearsal. Shaw learned how to mold musical phrases from Waring. But the most important lesson he learned was that music *must be communicated.* And to be communicated, music has to be *articulated.*

Thanks, in part, to Waring, Shaw's music making would forever embrace the value of clarity—getting all the words across to an audience when music and text were combined. Initially, this lesson was learned with the song form. A song has a text. It fails musically if the text cannot be understood, and felt. Shaw would later decide that the words in a folk or Broadway song were an entirely different musical problem than the words in a Mozart or Verdi requiem. In the first instance, Shaw said, the problem is in communicating the text and in making sure the musical values and time support the text. In the second instance, text must be made subordinate to musical values and time.

For Waring, and his apprentice, communicating the words meant communicating all the *parts* of all the words. It was necessary, therefore, to be responsible for each linguistic unit—each vowel and consonant of every word. Waring invented what he called "the tone syllable technique," in which "all the beauty, in all the sounds, of all the syllables, in all the words" (Shaw's definition) were sounded phonetically. And how could this be done? By breaking down the sounds, syllable by syllable. It is an approach that is easily abused and almost as easily parodied. Waring's tone syllable technique can become the sung version of speech during an elocution lesson—exaggerated and robotic. It can become the enemy of musicality. And Shaw refined what he learned from Waring. He felt Waring's approach worked very well in the popular song. The musical line can be bent to accommodate pronunciation of the words, or even to accommodate the artist's own stylized expression of the words. Individual interpretation is what makes the song new. (Listen to Nina Simone or Mel Tormé for examples.) But in classical choral music, Shaw believed, the message is not confined by the words. The music transcends the words. Shaw often said that the text was the best the composer could find, but if what the composer wanted to say had been limited to the text, he would never have begun to compose. Hence, in classical choral music, the musical line is predominant, or so Shaw believed, and felt Bach, Mozart, and Brahms demanded. The words must be subservient to the music and the musical line *cannot* be bent or broken. Musicality cannot be compromised for expressivity, or even clarity, for the composer's deeper meaning, even his deeper dramatic or lyric meaning, is beyond what words can say. The meaning can be expressed only in musical texture. Thus, what recreates a Passion or an oratorio is ensemble discipline—listening and playing in sync—so that the musical texture will flow logically and naturally.

One can see that Shaw and Waring were very soon up to different things. Nonetheless, Shaw never abandoned the basic Waring concept of clarity and precision of text—not only every word, but every sound of every part of every word. Indeed, one of the primary things that the Robert Shaw Chorale was known and admired for was that the words could be understood. But even though Shaw loved words, and came to music from words, in what became his musical habitat, words were not king—sound was. In a sense, Shaw took Waring to the next level by applying the tone syllable concept to the musical line rather than the narrative line and to each musical constituent rather than each linguistic one.

Shaw quickly outgrew Waring in matters of musical taste, understanding, and repertoire. But Waring had a lasting impact on Shaw in several ways, and the most important was making the words heard and understood.

Waring's needs for his Glee Club, and for radio, were as different from Shaw's needs for the Collegiate Chorale as were his tastes and chosen material. Waring required a good deal of legato (and not inconsiderable schmaltz) for love songs. And for radio, the explosive consonants had to be suppressed, not accentuated. But Shaw could learn something even from a negative situation. From these "necessities," to use a favorite Shaw word, Shaw learned that each performance had to be adjusted to its medium, its venue, and its audience.

The other thing Shaw learned, not so much from Waring, but through association with Waring—by working in radio—was the importance of time. Shaw was forever fascinated by the discipline, calculus, and mystery of time. In radio, time is of essential and precise importance. Radio helped to shape Shaw's musicianship because he learned how to fit the performance to the time allowed. He was constantly timing movements and comparing the times to previous performances and the recorded performances of others. He budgeted his rehearsal time down to the second, and not only according to musical movement and section, but also phrase. And, of course, his obsession with time was related to his sense of musical time, of rhythm and tempo. One might argue about the positives and negatives of Shaw's time obsession on his musicianship. (On the good side, ultra preparedness, no wasted energy, precision both in preparation and performance. On the bad side, a slight tendency toward rigidity.) But Shaw was also fixated on the management of time and often said this fixation began with his radio days. The medium required that he master time in order to make music. And he did. Music, he said, is a "time art"—it exists in a specific time and space—unlike art on a canvas or in marble.

The time limits of radio required editing, sometimes extensive editing. Shaw recalled conducting an abbreviated CBS radio performance of Mendelssohn's *Elijah* in the early 1950s that had to be done in 56 minutes of musical time. The entire piece needs more like 2 hours and 15 minutes. This was radio-enforced excision. Shaw had to edit as quickly and nonviolently as possible—a process he enjoyed. In retrospect, he saw this exercise as good for Shaw, and not necessarily as good for Mendelssohn. But thousands of Americans heard a substantial part of that oratorio for the first time because Shaw was allowed to conduct it on national radio.

Conducting abridged versions of classic pieces forced Shaw to edit those pieces drastically, and thus to familiarize himself with the work thoroughly, for a good editor must master the whole piece to be able to cut judiciously and not barbarically.

It was excellent discipline. In radio you could not start or finish late. If you finished late, the end of the piece went unheard.

Shaw was so well thought of by the radio networks that he got his own national radio program in the summer of 1948—a 30-minute, 9-week summer replacement program for comedian Edgar Bergen. And that is actually how the Robert Shaw Chorale was born. Heretofore it had been the NBC or CBS Chorale—whatever network they were on. Now, since it was *Shaw's* program, the choir had to be named after him. Replacing Charlie McCarthy and Mortimer Snerd, the choir, with 30 voices and pianist, did madrigals by Monteverdi, part songs by Brahms, and chorales by Bach. It also did contemporary works, spirituals, and a little Broadway. They signed off, in the tradition of Waring, with a singing commercial for Royal Pudding.

During that summer, Shaw commuted between New York and the Berkshires, where he was head of the choral music program at Tanglewood. He worked at Tanglewood during the week, and did the radio show during the weekend. He raced between two big jobs and two worlds: one commercial and one classical. But the Robert Shaw Chorale had been born. It was born on radio, out of practical necessity, not on tour or in Shaw's head.

Shaw learned to conduct classical music, and the orchestra, with the nation listening. Radio was his classroom. Shaw's first experience conducting a symphony orchestra, without chorus, was with the Naumburg Orchestra—a pickup festival orchestra in New York. But the next orchestral assignment, and the first important one, one that was reviewed in the *New York World Telegram*, was for radio—with the NBC Symphony. He conducted the Beethoven *Symphony No. 2*, among other works. His formative orchestral experience was in radio. This meant that Shaw was not able to hone his craft working quietly with students or small musical groups. He learned in a very public setting. He learned "on the air." And all of this happened because of Fred Waring.

Shaw did a great many "special" concerts for NBC and CBS. NBC was Toscanini's orchestra, and Shaw became Toscanini's fair-haired boy. CBS's orchestra was formed and run by Bernard Herrman, later famous for his film scores and orchestrations. He also thought highly of Shaw and used him often.

Radio, for Shaw, was like swimming because he had been thrown in the water and had to move forward or sink. To a great extent, Shaw always did things this way—he put himself in impossible situations so that, in the end, he *had* to perform.

As with all influences on Shaw, radio's deepest influence spoke to something already within him. He learned how to work with limits, under pressure, and with time. Thanks to radio, Shaw deeply internalized his time sense. If he budgeted 6 minutes for a particular problem in rehearsal, he usually ended that portion of the rehearsal in just 6 minutes, without needing to consult his watch. If he marked tempi in such a way that his Bach *Magnificat* should be performed in, say, 26-and-a-half minutes, then his recording would be 26:25, or maybe 26:28.

Of the conductors in his lifetime, Shaw was perhaps least wasteful and most anxious about time. He regarded it as precious and he regarded the time of professional musicians as sacred. He knew that, for him, there would never be *enough* time. He would always be "playing catch up."

Shaw's relationship with Waring was complicated from the start and only got more complicated. It was that of student and mentor, but also that of two strong-willed men with very different musical interests and aspirations. They didn't really hit it off personally either.

Indeed, in some ways, Shaw didn't like Fred Waring very much. He thought Waring was cheap. He thought Waring exploited those around him. (Shaw recalled that Waring virtually compelled his employees to loan him money for his inventions, but when the Waring Blender succeeded, and succeeded spectacularly, all the profit went to Fred. The involuntary investors were paid back, but without interest.) Also, Shaw told a very few people privately that he feared Waring was something of a racist.

But Shaw would never criticize Waring in public. Or even hint at it. For the record, throughout the years, Shaw said only the most glowing things about his mentor. Fred Waring brought Shaw to New York. He showed Shaw how to take command of musical forces. He encouraged Shaw to form the Collegiate Chorale and gave him access to good voices. Because Shaw was introduced to the public on Waring's show, Shaw was able to realize his dream of "a melting pot that sings." He knew he was deeply in Waring's debt. Arguably, without Waring, Shaw would never have stumbled into inventing the Robert Shaw Chorale. It came from radio, and it was Waring who first put Shaw on the radio. The Robert Shaw Chorale achieved a critical acclaim (five Grammy Awards for one thing) that far eclipsed Waring's musical accomplishments, but Shaw never felt superior. Shaw may not have liked Waring much, but he felt enormously grateful. Waring started it all. Moreover, musically, Shaw never ceased to admire Waring.

Waring's radio career ended, sooner than it should have, and Waring spent the rest of his life touring the same basic show he'd done in the 1940s. He and Shaw did at least two choral workshops together in subsequent years, at Waring's behest. Waring, said Shaw, was "a man of fascinating personal industry." Was the blender his idea? Well, who knew? "If he didn't have the original idea for the blender," said Shaw, "he could have . . . He kept elves working on technical and mechanical things—at another site, possibly New Jersey."[16] Waring's men were also working on a rotary engine at one point. All the bandleaders of that era, Shaw once noted wryly, were good businessmen, *and* "naturally acquisitive."

Shaw often said that "the popular song was truly Waring's native habitat." He knew how to milk it and how to sell it. He knew, intuitively, how to turn Broadway sounds into choral sounds, not an easy task.

Shaw credited much of his early choral technique to Waring.

For one thing, he noticed that Waring had the men in the band sing along with the Glee Club. It gave Shaw the idea of having singers sing in quartets for homophonic music.

But Shaw also allowed that the principle of enunciation—the importance of making every sound of every syllable, and of separating vowels and putting daylight between consonants—did not begin with Waring and his "tone syllable" approach. Shaw said, "John Finley Williamson at Westminster was doing substantially the same thing at the time ... it was in the groundswell."[17]

Still, musical speech, according to phonetics, not custom, was a radical idea in the 1940s and Waring certainly was the leading spokesman for it.

Since he didn't really read music, Waring relied on a method of solfège of his own devising to learn the score, even music he had nominally "written" or "arranged." But Shaw insisted that Waring was neither a front man nor a cipher. He knew the sounds he wanted and was able to convey them to those skilled in musical notation. Shaw said Waring had an "incredible musical memory." He claimed that Waring could hear a score once or twice and have it memorized—"including ballet scores."

In his late years, because neither he nor his show changed much, Waring became a kind of parody of himself, doing a sort of Nixonian "Up With People" turn with his standard program in high school after high school across the land. He never quite made the transition from radio to television. But Shaw stood by him—always praising and thanking him. Shaw was almost incapable of a bald-face lie, and when he could not praise someone he was

16 *Robert Shaw: Preparing a Masterpiece* series.
17 Shaw papers.

asked to laud, he demurred or changed the subject. He almost certainly did not believe Waring to be a great musician the way he thought Rudolf Serkin was a great musician. (Or even in the way that Shaw saw George Szell as a great musician.) But what Shaw did say about Waring was that he was a fine, natural, and instinctive musician, which he believed.

Still, the two men were oil and water in the years they worked together. Walt Disney is supposed to have said, "I sell corn. I *like* corn." Well, so did Waring. Shaw hated corn. He distrusted sentimentality of any kind, particularly in the arts. He distrusted any impulse of his own toward emotionalism in music. He came to believe that a chorus singing a love song was both absurd and vulgar. (The Robert Shaw Chorale recorded plenty.)

It is impossible to imagine the later Shaw rehearsing some of the material he made on the Chorale records—material that grew out of his Waring radio persona—just as it is impossible to imagine Waring pouring over a Beethoven biography, or becoming fascinated with the *Missa Solemnis*.

Shaw learned all he could from Waring. Waring knew Shaw was an original and he knew he could not hold him or, beyond a certain point, teach him. Fred Waring was nobody's fool; he understood what Shaw wanted and perhaps, to some degree, what he was to become. Shaw and Waring were often at odds, sometimes at war, but there was always a built-in respect. They were both impatient perfectionists, after all.

Yet perhaps there is something inevitable about the self-created man. Maybe if there had been no Fred Waring, Shaw would have found another first sponsor. Years after this association had ended, Waring would ask Walter Gould, Shaw's sometime agent, business partner, and longtime friend, "Do any of these young fellas from Europe think they can hold a candle to Bobby?" There can't have been many people, other than Waring or Shaw's siblings, who called him Bobby at that point in his life.

Shaw stayed with Waring for seven years (1938 to 1945). He used his brief service in the U.S. Navy (from April 30, 1945 to some time in July of that same year) as a crossroads, turning what was supposed to have been a semicolon into a period. Soon after he got out of the Navy, Shaw began to send Waring messages, through intermediaries, of his desire to move into other aspects of music. By January of 1946, he had made the separation from Waring. Shaw saw this pause in his life, for military service, as an opportunity to break away from commercial music and devote his time to the kind of music he truly loved. The desire to become involved with serious music had been percolating for a while, in fact virtually from the time he arrived in New York. Certainly, friendships with several classical musicians had been deepening for some time. The two key people who helped Shaw make the break, and leap, were Julius Herford and William Schuman—the new president of Juilliard who had taken Shaw under his wing. Schuman saw Shaw as a raw and unformed, but magnificent, natural talent. It was he who introduced Shaw to important classical maestros like George Szell and Serge Koussevitzky. Schuman may well have been Shaw's initial link to Toscanini. In a 1981 tribute to Shaw, Schuman wrote that during the Waring years Shaw "harbored secret inner yearnings for other music—so-called serious music." Schuman then went on to say, perhaps in jest, that though Shaw had not *heard* much symphonic music, he formed the Collegiate Chorale to do symphonic and classical music. Schuman wrote that in the early days of the Collegiate Chorale, "the sounds of his chorus were as magnificent as the musical innocence and scholarly ineptitude of its leader . . . " But he also said that Shaw studied constantly and that he "mastered the intricacies of the musical art with astonishing speed."[18]

It was to Schuman that Shaw wrote during basic training in the Navy, wondering aloud what would happen to him there (he hoped to form a Navy Chorus) and lamenting, "Incidentally, discipline and training here is a farce. You learn nothing and waste thousands of man-hours doing it." It was not Toscanini, as Shaw often said, but Schuman who first "pulled him up" into classical music, or rather, gave him his hand after Shaw put out his own.

18 Shaw papers.

Julius Herford was not only a leading player in Shaw's life, but also a profound influence. Indeed, *the* profound influence. It was not that he taught Shaw how to be a musician. This gift, Shaw had innately. Shaw was perhaps innately more musical than Herford himself. It was not even that Herford educated Shaw, though he did (until Shaw learned all he could from him). Shaw was a sponge and took instruction anywhere and everywhere he could find it—from Cozy Cole to Stravinsky. Herford's contribution was that he gave Shaw's musical seriousness—his longing for musical depth—a venue, a home, a place to be nurtured. Herford and Shaw set up a mutually advantageous and satisfying musical partnership. Herford would work on call and on the fly—and constantly—which enabled Shaw to learn while he worked and to be a student when he was already a maestro. Plus, no small thing, Herford knew the music Shaw wanted to know. With Herford, Shaw could, for example, immerse himself in the music of Bach.

Julius Herford was a German émigré, a refugee from Hitler, and had been a well-known pianist and choral master in Germany. He came to New York for a two-year appointment at Columbia and stayed. He became Shaw's first scholarly tutor and master, artistic consultant and guide, and for a time, partner in the planning of programs. During this period, they collaborated on writing program notes for concerts. And for the better part of ten years, they would do workshops together. Herford would lecture and Shaw would rehearse and conduct. Composer and conductor Lukas Foss introduced Herford to Shaw during rehearsals for Foss's composition, *The Prairie*, and they hit it off. Herford could, Shaw believed, help him "catch up." Shaw decided Herford would be his one-man conservatory and graduate school.

Very soon after they met, Shaw told Herford he wanted to hire him more or less full time, which was fine with Herford who was barely making ends meet at the time. Shaw said: "I want to begin at the beginning and learn everything—harmony, counterpoint, the piano." Shaw actually told a lot of people he wanted to take lessons from them through the years. But this time it happened. Both men were available. They liked and respected each other. They found they could work together. Most of all, they shared a high church–

high art concept of music. Like Schuman, Herford was astounded at Shaw's innate talent. Herford became the unofficial artistic and academic advisor to Shaw's choirs. The two became a team, which was strange, since one was the teacher and the other was both student and employer. But somehow, for a long time, it worked.

Herford had a particular method of score study and a theory of preparation. Each piece had its own "gestalt" that would be revealed by discovering the composer's particular musical language. Score analysis was a search for the musical grammar of the composer at hand. Shaw bought into it. He became an adherent of the notion that musical meaning is revealed by musical structure, which was a central Herfordism, though hardly unique to him.

But perhaps the greatest thing Herford did for Shaw was to steep him in the music of Bach and, later, to encourage Shaw to develop his own ideas of Baroque choral phrasing, which Shaw did. If you believe musical structure reveals meaning, Bach is a Gothic cathedral.

Herford was another mentor-father figure but a far greater influence than either Professor Alexander or Waring had been. Herford came into Shaw's life at the perfect time. He could impart to Shaw a graduate-level music education one on one, and Shaw could learn while doing. Julius Herford, along with George Szell and Toscanini, was one of the three great teachers in Shaw's life.

Eventually, Shaw outgrew Herford, just as he had outgrown Waring. Shaw began to emerge as the senior in the partnership, and to seek other advice, even on the Baroque and Classical German literature, and to trust his own judgment. Herford worked in a narrow part of choral music and along strict lines he himself had drawn. Shaw was an adventurer. Shaw wanted to do works by Britten, Berlioz, and Schoenberg, as well as by Bach and Brahms. He learned what he could from Herford and moved on. But certainly, it was Herford who most helped Shaw get on the path he wanted to follow and helped him to develop the skills to stay on it. Shaw always took great pains to give Herford that credit. Though they drifted in and out of each other's orbit and never rekindled the intensity of those five or six years of intimate association, and though there were periods of alienation, they remained loyal and affectionate and would collaborate once every few years until the end of Herford's life. Herford spent the later third or so of his life teaching at Indiana University, and consequently, Shaw performed there often and formed a bond with the school and many of its faculty and students.

Shaw was never satisfied with much of the material for which he was responsible when in Waring's employ. That wasn't Waring's fault. It was the material. For Shaw, pop music was thin gruel: It "didn't feed you back." He was already saying this kind of thing after two years in New York. And by the summer of 1945, when he was ready to make the final break, the Collegiate Chorale was doing an ambitious series of programs and was commissioning new works.

After making the separation from Waring, Shaw's classical career exploded. In September of 1945, he did his first work with Toscanini. Moreover, Toscanini contacted Shaw. Whether this had to do with Shaw's already growing reputation in New York, or a conversation with another musician with whom Shaw had worked, or both, we do not know. In February of 1946, Shaw would conduct his first Brahms *German Requiem* with full orchestra with the New York City Symphony. And by May of 1946, he would conduct the premiere of *When lilacs last in the dooryard bloom'd.* He then began to expand his classical choral work with the radio networks and their symphonies. Finally, he became Director of Choral Activities at Juilliard, at Schuman's bidding. Mind you, he had been pursuing his own musical education with Herford for less than two years at this point.

Shaw made his first Christmas album in 1945; he was working with various big-name conductors on radio and on recordings; and he had prepared the chorus—it was then called the Victor Chorus (for RCA Victor)—for his friend Leonard Bernstein's recording of *On the Town.* By

1948, when he formed the Robert Shaw Chorale, and only about two years after leaving Waring, he had made several recordings of Bach cantatas (one with Marian Anderson) and his first recording of the Bach *Mass in B Minor* as well as a recording of spirituals, the Brahms *Liebeslieder Waltzes*, and the first American recording of the Brahms *German Requiem.*

When he quit Waring, Shaw wrote him an extraordinary letter. In it he not only explained why pop music didn't feed him, but he articulated his artistic ambitions. He was writing to Waring asking for, or declaring, a divorce. But he was also writing to himself—figuring out what he wanted to do. He was 29. In this letter Shaw mapped out his course, the course for what he hoped would be his great transition from glee club leader to learned musician. In fact, he sketched the future path of his life. He explained, to himself as well as to Waring, why he had to try, why he had to attempt to become a classical musician, though he felt unworthy of it. He then sent a copy to his friend and sponsor, William Schuman. It was Schuman who kept it and, coming upon it many years later, sent it to Shaw, congratulating him for being that rarest of specimens among human beings—someone who realized his dream. I quote it here, almost in full.

Shaw wrote:

Dear Fred,
January 15, 1946

It was just four or five months ago that you and Ed and I had dinner together and discussed my interest in the symphonic orchestral field and plans for this year's study. And this letter is, I suppose, the logical sequel to that discussion, those decisions, and study (a very happy and profitable four to five hours per day). It is also the outgrowth of the development since in the life and progress of the Collegiate Chorale (not all of it good and successful) and of new conducting assignments (particularly with the CBS, Victor, and NYC Symphonies.)

I told Ed[19] a couple months ago that which he already surmised, namely that Bill Schuman had asked me to come to Juilliard next year as Director of Choral Activities, a new post in their conventional set-up. It seemed to me that both of you should know that I was seriously considering accepting, and that when I reached a decision you must be the first to know it and the reasons which prompted it . . . I have accepted and will begin my duties there next September.

Ours is a peculiar relation: part employer and employee, part teacher and protégé, part father and son (as is the case of many of your professional family), and part, Ed seems to feel, competitors.

And that relation has been subject to considerable strain in the past few years. You have thought me thoughtless and ungrateful, and I, though certainly fairly treated financially, and by Ed's work at your direction, helped career-wise, have felt musically and expressively ill-at-ease, insecure, and unhappy.

Now that discontent was very largely within me, and due to the limitations of my own musicianship; for at no time during those years was I ready—nor am I now ready—to step into the symphonic and concert field as a schooled and authoritative musician.

But while my study the past few months has been only enough to show how much is to be learned and how great is my lack, I feel I know the way I must go and the music with which I must work. It is a hard decision, for with the music I love and believe in most I am the greater child and novice.

My going to Juilliard, then, is largely a "musical" decision. There is, of course, an element of "career" in it, for I will be given opportunity to work with the school orchestra, which, according to plans, should be a first-rate symphonic ensemble. There is, too, a reasonable measure of economic security—though nothing like that which could be achieved through commercial exploitation—but the main decision is musical.

19 "Ed" probably refers to Waring's business manager of that time, and for many years—Ed Lee.

It seems to me there are three types of music in our present life: (1) That of entertainment, which is probably the most disciplined, most popular, and most successful . . . (2) That of art for art's sake, whose ideals are in-breeding, sophistication, aloofness, and intellectual snobbery, and (3) That of a vital people's music, which holds that certain masterworks speak with integrity and faith far beyond their own time, that America can develop in this time its own musical expression of dignity and purpose, and that both are within the understanding and heart of today's people.

I am not sure that these words convey that which I feel so strongly. God knows we need music for fun. All music must have the joy and enthusiasm of re-creation. But some music—as when we used to play marbles "for keeps" has the element of "for keeps" in it. Music asks for mind and heart in varying degrees. Sometimes it asks for great mind and great heart. And by various people these are variously understood. And the only thing a person can say is, "For me this is real, and this I must do."

It seems to me that by going to Juilliard, I will be working with music to which I am nearest kin. There will be commissions of new works, there will be courses to teach in Bach cantatas and early English motets, there will be association with conductors and composers, and there will be the opportunity to build a healthy and knowledgeable American musical life.[20]

There are two elements to this letter. First, it is both Shaw's "Martin Luther moment" and a key moment of self-definition in his life. He has found the type of music to which he wishes to devote himself. Second, he imagines a people's music "that is for keeps," and will help to build a "healthy and knowledgeable American musical life." Not a small dream.

Shaw goes on to thank Waring and to tell him he will be using his technique, especially his insistence on "rhythmic vitality" and "clarity of text

20 Shaw papers.

and story." And he lists other "influences," like Schuman, Bernard Herrman, Toscanini, with whom he had just begun to work, as well as composer Norman Dello Joio.

But it is all there: The view of commercial music as sometimes fun, sometimes vapid, and sometimes "exploitation," as well as awareness of its commercial possibilities. There is Shaw's disdain for classical music as a badge of snobbery and pretention. There is, finally, Shaw's dream of a people's classical music in which great works would be allowed to work their grace on unprivileged lives. There is also his dream of a mature culture of American classical music—not one that he would lead, necessarily, but one in which he would participate.

Shaw moved from glee club and church singing, to Fred Waring and the Aquacades, to the *Mass in B Minor* and the Brahms *Requiem* with rapid speed. He was seeking something he felt he was not prepared to achieve. It all came too soon, but the dream, and the responsibility, came to him nonetheless. Yes, Shaw had been exposed to some classical music by Ralph Lyman and by Howard Swan. But Shaw came to New York to work in a pop music radio job, and soon thereafter was dreaming of a "people's" classical music. Shaw had ambitions that no one could have predicted for him. They came from within. So he found the teachers who could help him at each stage of the way. He didn't know where he was going, but he had his instincts. He could intuit a direction and choose the right guides. These ambitions were not worldly ambitions, but artistic ones. Given his background, they might have been seen as laughable. (Shaw claimed Schuman used to say of him in the late 1930s to mid 1940s, "My god, Bob, you were dumb.") Yet somehow people did not laugh. Shaw had a certain force, though somewhat manic, slightly pompous, and hyperbolic, when he was young. But the force and the sincerity were hard to deny.

Even if he felt unworthy, unqualified, terrified—and he did—even if the climb was steep and rocky, he was going to make the climb.

CHAPTER 10

"It should have been you"

When Shaw took the job with Waring and went into radio, it was a significant family event, but there was too much going on in the family for Bob's move to New York to be *the* family event. Then came the death of Rev. Shaw and the death of Jim.

If Jim was a kind of budding Rotarian who, in the pressure cooker of war, had become a true pastor, Bob was the brooding rebel who was, at the time of Jim's death, just beginning to come to grips with what might be required of a man who hoped to become a serious artist.

When Jim died in 1944, his brother Bob was in New York, working hard, and caught up in his own dreams. He was beginning to tiptoe away from Waring and he had begun to do the type of classical work that he yearned to do: the Collegiate Chorale having been formed in 1941.

Though Shaw would later say he "wasn't doing much, goofing off, just bumming around," at the time of Jim's death, that wasn't true. Far from it. He was working for Waring full time, doing Broadway and radio work, and putting everything he had into the Collegiate Chorale. He was fully challenging himself musically and physically.

There had been times when the older son felt or seemed aimless, especially compared to Jim. But Robert had begun to blossom by 1944. Indeed, when

Jim was killed, Robert was 28 years old and amazingly successful for his age. It was in the spring of that year, just weeks before Jim's death, that he had hired musicians from the New York Philharmonic and NBC and CBS orchestras to premiere a new cantata by Lukas Foss—*The Prairie.* In what was to become typical Shaw fashion, he began his first rehearsal with a confession of his limitations. Shaw told the players they knew their instruments better than he did, but he knew the score and what he wanted, so "Let's work along. If you can help my beat, fine."[21] That concert was important for Shaw. He began to be taken seriously as a conductor. And it led to the Herford partnership.

But Shaw didn't see himself as particularly successful, either during that period or looking back on that period.

Perhaps all this accomplishment seemed trivial when laid next to Jim's war service and death.

Shaw was not indifferent to the war, or to the suffering caused by the war. And he wasn't opposed to supporting his country while it was at war, which he did by participation with various choirs in sundry bond rallies and patriotic programs put on to bolster public morale and affirm the sacrifice of the troops. But he was also strangely detached from the war—until Jim was killed. Shaw seemed to perceive the war, totalitarianism, fascism, and the economic crisis that had gripped the United States and Europe for most of his life rather vaguely. The crisis of the age, he told friends, and wrote to Collegiate Chorale members, was a "human crisis" that required an answer from the arts. That's a solid position, of course, and one Shaw held all his life. But the crisis of the moment was also a military one, coming from Germany and Japan. The immediate crisis was war on two fronts, not an abstraction. The mature Shaw—the Shaw who lived in Atlanta and was deeply involved in the affairs of the city during the time he directed its symphony—was engaged in his time and community in concrete ways. The mature Shaw had also come to grips with many of the practical requirements and constraints of his profession. But Shaw at 28 was caught in the thrall of a career taking off as

21 Mussulman, p. 52.

well as the mist of his own unfocused ideals. He was, well, a bit callow. His understanding of his time was simplistic. He was focused on his own dreams, platitudes, and power. And he was thinking, almost exclusively, about music. Shaw was preoccupied with learning all he could about the field he had fallen into. Until his partnership with Herford, he had been working with some very basic childhood and college musical training—a fair amount of singing experience, and slight exposure to some of the choral masterworks as a student. He was learning on the job. But he had little theoretical background. Given what he had already accomplished, that is rather astonishing. But it was so. In the intellectual, artistic, and *musical* firmament of New York City during the years of 1939 to 1946, Shaw found Oz—an endless candy store of talent, knowledge, and collaboration. But he was trying to figure out how best to utilize this bounty. He was like a man who had found a Stradivarius and could play but one simple song. Thanks to Herford, he'd found a way to truly learn from his doing. And that occupied him. Shaw was hardly an aimless hobo in 1944, but he was absorbed. And the tragedies of the world were a bit gauzy. There is something a little disquieting about being work-absorbed and self-absorbed when the Holocaust and World War are going on. Jim had not died in the crisis of humanism, he'd died in a war. Japanese warriors had killed him.

In 1944, Shaw won a Guggenheim Fellowship—the first conductor ever to win it. His plan was to properly educate himself musically, with Herford's help, and write a book. It was the year Jim died on Biak Island. Shaw could no longer keep the war at an emotional and intellectual distance.

Far from "goofing off," Shaw had been an obsessed man on the rise. Now his family was reeling. His father had died and his brother was killed. He may have felt survivor's guilt, and perhaps also a big brother's sense of responsibility—for not having somehow protected his younger sibling. He also had specific guilt. Shaw was a judgmental man and at times a harshly judgmental young man. He had been angry with Jim. He felt that Jim had gone along with something he didn't believe in when he became an Army chaplain. (It happened that this was not true.) But Shaw felt that serving

Jesus in war was hypocritical and he perhaps assumed Jim felt this same way in his heart of hearts. He rather disapproved of Jim's service, and then Jim got himself killed and hero-ized. Jim himself, of course, seemed to have no doubt whatsoever about what he was doing. On the contrary, as time went on, Jim became more and more committed.

So there were perhaps several layers of angst developing, and various melodies of remorse within Shaw and within his family.

Then, in the immediate aftermath of Jim's death there was an event, within the family, of great moment—one that would dwarf whatever alienation Shaw already felt about his brother, his family, his parents' religion, and patriotic service. Someone wounded him severely.

Jim Shaw's family did not know of his death immediately. It had to have been days, perhaps weeks, before Nelle learned of it. But after Jim's death, the family was gathered together and Nelle said something to Robert that seared his psyche.

At least he remembered it this way. And other family members who were there did, too.

Nelle allegedly turned to her son Robert and said, "*It should have been you.*"

He never got over those words. They still stung when he recalled them near the end of his life, five decades later.

"*It should have been you.*"

Shaw would return to those words many, many times in conversations with loved ones, especially in his drinking days. Sometimes he would simply shake his head. Sometimes he would dredge the line up and reexamine it, word by word, freshly aghast and mortified each time. Nelle's piercing sentence had created a lasting wound in Bob, just as the family had been forever wounded by Jim's death.

A caution: We don't *truly* know all that happened here. What was the actual setting? Who was really there? How soon was it after Nelle had learned that Jim was dead?

In Shaw's memory, all the surviving siblings and his mother were present and the news of Jim's death was fresh.

But it seems unlikely that this is so. The moment and the setting were surely more haphazard, less precise and dramatic than Shaw's recall. Who knows how fresh to grief Nelle was or exactly what her state of mind was? Immediate, deep grief is a form of madness. We see this in Shakespeare. We know this from our own lives. Nelle may have been mad with grief at the time. The rest of the family was reeling. Robert's own grief, and the power of those words, certainly must have made his memory of them an event in which time stopped.

But Anne and Buzz Price *were* there and they also remember the words, however uncertain the details and circumstance may be so many years later. Nelle's words were not Robert's fabrication or exaggeration.

Maybe if we imagine the context in a certain way, we can feel pity for Nelle and try to comprehend the depth of her sorrow.

And maybe more *was* said at the time. Maybe there was an attempt to soften the horrible words once they tumbled forth. But this is how Shaw remembered the event—those words alone, the starkness of the blow, nothing else. Whatever came after, it did not register.

The importance of the story, for our purposes, is perhaps not Nelle's intent or state of mind, which cannot be known, but Shaw's. His memory was of an attempted psychic deathblow. His mother wished to trade his death for Jim's. This is how he told and retold the story. This is how he saw it.

The memory was of such haunting power that it became a sort of ongoing indictment. Shaw *forgave* his mother. He intended to; he said he did. He treated her with respect, deference, and kindness for the rest of her life. But he could not *forget*. He placed Nelle in a kind of psychological limbo. She was to live almost three more decades (she died in 1971), and during that time, Robert kept his distance, in all respects. On one occasion she wrote, pleading for her son's attention: "Please write or call. Your wife does. But you do not." Shaw may have replied. There is no record that he did. While he was supportive financially, and in other practical ways, correspondence and birthday greetings were largely left to Maxine Shaw or one of Shaw's secretaries.[22]

Bob and Nelle had at least one very good moment together in subsequent years. In the late 1950s, Shaw conducted the Cleveland Orchestra on tour in California, including a well-received concert at Pomona College, which his mother attended. They were photographed together, after the performance, both looking happy—she beaming pride and he looking exhausted and relieved, but pleased. The hapless son had returned in triumph, at least for one night.

A second caution: At least one Shaw family member, Robert's son Peter, remembers the story a different way. He believes he recalls his father telling a version in which the son, Bob, says to his mother: "It should have been *me*."

That's quite different.

We are, all of us, self-mythologizers. And Shaw was a better mythmaker than most. Is it possible that he created a gross fiction? It's possible. But we have the witness of Anne and Buzz Price, Shaw's sister and brother-in-law. They recall the first version.[23]

And close associates in New York, Cleveland, and Atlanta never heard any but the first version.

Perhaps wisdom here begins with the realization that memory is not documentary. It is always reconstruction—by anyone who remembers or collects what others remember. Emotion, drama, fantasy, and self-delusion are all part of what memory is.

It may be that Peter Shaw's memory is faulty. Or it may be that Shaw told only his son this very different version. Or perhaps Shaw told Peter about his uncle's death and then *added*, "It *should* have been me." It may be that Nelle's words struck so brutally because their recipient, as least in part, agreed with the indictment.

22 Shaw papers.
23 Burris interview with Harrison and Anne Price.

We do know what Shaw believed. We know that what he believed he recalled was true and that it was momentous for him. And we know that the blow—which Shaw believed represented his mother's true feelings—was resounding.

The worst injuries do seem to come from, and to, those closest to us. Nelle was not cruel by nature, which is surely one reason her words stung as they did. The blow she dealt to her living son, and his subsequent years of alienation from her, call to mind Kant's devastating, but ultimately compassionate, phrase—the "crooked timber of humanity."

Jim's death and Nelle's reaction was, perhaps, the beginning of the end of the dreamy Bobby, and the beginning of the practical Bob and, eventually, highly disciplined Robert. Any hint of the dilettante in him faded quickly now. He was always a dreamer of big dreams. But he became a practical dreamer—focused on nuts and bolts. He became a sometimes skeptical, and even cynical, dreamer—divided and conflicted, but seldom paralyzed or detached from reality.

Shaw's story depicts a mother who lashes out in her grief and withholds love, compassion, and warmth when these qualities were needed most. Interestingly, Shaw's view of his first wife, Maxine, was not dissimilar. He saw her as cool and withholding. But Nelle's words were not just cold. They were aggressive.

When Shaw was wounded, he took it hard, and withdrew. He was a man who needed approval, warmth, and devotion, especially from women. He didn't feel he got that from Nelle or, as we shall see, from Maxine.

Robert always portrayed Maxine as a chill wind. He never said that about his mother, but he made it clear that her words still chilled him many decades after they were said.

Was his view of these two women entirely fair? Almost certainly it was not. His mother had lost her husband and her son within weeks of each other. Maxine was a different sort of case. She was rather chilly, both by temperament and for understandable reasons.

But this was the way Shaw saw things.

There is also something Robert didn't see, and could not possibly see: that his wound from Nelle may have helped his music. Shaw always had something to prove. Something was always chasing him. If Nelle and Shirley had been warmer, more approving parents, would Shaw have made it to Pomona with the Cleveland Orchestra? Shaw often heard an echo in his head saying, "It should have been you," and perhaps it was one of the things that propelled him to greatness.

Another strange chapter of Shaw's life is linked to this painful, pivotal moment in it: his brief three-month stint in the U.S. Navy.

Incredibly, Bob Shaw, the pacifist musician who had scolded his brother for serving the Lord as a military chaplain, *enlisted*.

This was a truly amazing thing for Shaw to do—because he was Shaw, and everyone knew what he felt about war. In the context of Jim's death, and Nelle's comment, it is astonishing—and chilling.

According to Shaw, he'd registered as a conscientious objector. Then, after Jim's death, he withdrew his CO status and joined the Navy. But that does not quite make sense. Shaw did enlist. But an individual does not have the power to change his own draft status unilaterally. If Shaw's draft number had been called, and he'd registered as a CO, there would have been a consequence—a draft board hearing, for one thing. Had a draft board heard his case and declined to give Shaw CO status, he would have been required to serve. Had he declined, he would have gone to prison. Most people who registered as COs during World War II and were granted that status were required to serve as medics or in other non-combatant roles. They were not simply excused from service.

It is possible that Shaw had a low draft number and had registered to be a CO, but that his number did not come up so his case was not heard and the status of his conscientious objection not ruled upon. It is also possible that he *meant* to register as a CO *if* and *when* called, but that he was not called. Certainly, pacifism was his position at the time. It is also possible that there was some retrospective self-mythologizing going on here. Once again, all we can be sure about is that this is how Shaw felt. In his heart and mind he had been a CO because he considered himself a pacifist, yet he enlisted after Jim's death. His pacifism was, perhaps, not very well thought out or deep at that time. (It *would* be well thought out in later years, which might explain some late-life editing of his story.)

We know that, for whatever reason, Shaw was not called to serve during most of the war. Maybe there had been some kind of deferment, so that he did not have to serve. But there is no record of such a deferment in his papers, or of registration as a conscientious objector.

And here is an even stranger thing: by the time Shaw served, the war was essentially over. (V-E Day was May 8, 1945 and V-J Day was August 14 of that same year. Shaw's brief time in the Navy begins just before the first date and ends just before the second.) It was very late indeed for enlistment.

This, too, is strange: Jim died in July of 1944 and Shaw went into the Navy in April of 1945—nine months later.

Shaw's transformation from pacifist to Navy seaman—from detached artist to stand-in for his slain brother—was not easy for him to assimilate or to reconcile. On the one hand, he hated war and hated it more after Jim died. On the other, Shaw felt he was not doing enough to serve and his brother had now given his life. In terms of Christian symbolism, and concepts of sacrificial love, so second nature in the Shaw family, maybe Shaw's enlistment is not so inexplicable. Jim had died for the nation, but also, if one thinks of him stepping into the older son's shoes, for Robert. Now Robert would have to offer *his* sacrifice. But offer it for whom? His country? His dead brother? His mother?

What did happen then only deepens the strangeness. Robert was never in combat. He was never in any danger. He never left the states. In fact, he was out of the Navy in roughly two months.

Again, the evidence is sketchy and the story clouded by myth and memory. But Shaw was apparently working on musical projects, with an eye on starting a Navy chorus. That was the goal apparently set or approved by the brass. But at some point, Shaw experienced a severe allergic reaction either to the material in his uniforms or to shots meant to combat the clothing allergy, or both, and was hospitalized. He spent much of his short time in the Navy in the hospital. This medical condition ostensibly lead to his discharge. But how many people were discharged for clothing or medical allergies during World War II? Or might this medical condition be the reason he was not drafted to the service in the first place?

Here is what we actually *know*: First, Shaw was discharged honorably. Second, he found military life inexplicable and almost intolerable. Third, at this point in the war effort, Shaw was not exactly needed in the Navy. He was more valuable doing band rallies in New York.

Shaw wrote to William Schuman during this time and indicated he was bored and restless and that he saw the Navy rather like Yosarian, the hero of *Catch 22*, saw the Army. One Shaw family friend said, "Personally I think Robert just totally freaked out in the Navy. He could not handle the regimentation." This is speculation. But it is reasonable. If Shaw was in the Navy because of his dead brother and contrary to his own convictions, there must have been considerable mental strain, and a breakdown of some kind might more plausibly result in a discharge than an allergy. It makes more sense, which does not make it true.

It is not impossible, given his wide circle of acquaintances at this time, that Shaw, or someone close to him, pulled strings to get him *into* the service, *out* of it, or both. In any event, he was out of the Navy by July.

All in all, a strange interlude.

Though Shaw often talked about being a pacifist and a conscientious objector, he didn't write about or talk about his actual Navy service. He never identified himself as a veteran.

Jim's death stayed with Shaw always. He brought his political, philosophical, and personal feelings about war to his reading of the Britten *War Requiem*—a piece he dearly loved—and to Paul Hindemith's *When lilacs last in the dooryard bloom'd,* a piece he was justly proud of commissioning. He would talk about war when he rehearsed those works, and on a rare occasion he would talk about Jim. Shaw's opposition to war hardened and deepened considerably through the years—especially after his son Peter went to Vietnam. Shaw was essentially an absentee father to Peter and his other two children from his first marriage, Johanna and Thad. But he loved his children, and having a son in Vietnam certainly ripened his anti-war feelings.

Hatred for war became a personal passion as well as a philosophical conviction for Shaw. This had to do with Jim and with Nelle, too. Shaw often said that the Britten *War Requiem* was about "innocence shattered." And certainly his own innocence had been shattered by his brother's death, though not as completely or as brutally as what Wilfred Owen and Walt Whitman describe.

By his later years—certainly once he had settled into his second marriage to Caroline Sauls Hitz—Shaw had, in his own words, "grown up." What he meant by that was that he could deal with his problems head on and not run from them. Despite his insecurities about his musical talents and training, he had come to know what he could do. He could at least acknowledge his own feelings about his parents, siblings, and children. Shaw's feelings and insecurities were pretty much always out there for all to see. He didn't hide them. Indeed, he was sometimes, embarrassingly, an open book. For example, he never attempted to hide that he had been, in his younger days, a functional (sometimes barely functional) alcoholic. He put all of who he was on the table, with startling honesty, and he wrapped everything about himself, his anxieties, past hurts, and many follies, into his music making, or rather, his preparation of the music—rehearsal was his therapy. An anti-war choral text was, for him, not about international relations, but about Jim. In the same way, Beethoven's highly individualized religiosity, as expressed in his *Missa,* was something Shaw felt personally—God cannot be confined to religious dogmas or institutions. *Part* of what Shaw felt about religion had to do with his parents. He knew that the narrow road was not his road. But it also had to do with music. In music he found a religious tabernacle in which mysticism could rest.

It is not possible to separate Shaw's emotional life from his musical life. His artistic humility and his personal insecurity are of one piece. He never stopped feeling ill prepared for the life that was his—the life he'd chosen when he left Fred Waring. Truth to tell, Shaw's insecurity was rational. He conducted the NBC Orchestra before he conducted a college orchestra. He was thrown into, or chose, many musically challenging situations before he was ready. It's not just that he felt he was not ready. He wasn't. His insecurity was just. Yet he was the ultimate author of his own unlikely narrative. No one made him mount the *Missa Solemnis* at Carnegie Hall or record the *Mass in B Minor* as a very young conductor. Those were *his* calls.

Shaw became famous for his humility (a joke in itself not lost on him). But his humility was not a pose. He was always humbled by the majesty and nobility of art of any kind, including the oratory of Lincoln, which he studied and loved all his life. He could not get enough of Lincoln—another ordinary, extraordinary, insecure, and driven man; another wounded man who never broke but remade himself instead. But Shaw was also humbled by reality. Music is, in reality, enormously difficult to do well. And Shaw was, in reality, in over his head for much of his early career.

For the public record, Shaw always spoke of his parents with fondness and affection. No critical utterances exist, on tape or in print.

But as soon as someone—Hartley Burr Alexander at Pomona was the first—presented Robert with an alternative father figure, and an alternative form of Christianity, Shaw grabbed it.

And once Shaw had found another faith—art and the creation of art—and his own mission—the remaking of choral music in America—

he clung to both fiercely. He never went back to that "old-time religion" of his mother and father.

Shaw's antipathy toward organized religion—with the exception of a serious flirtation with unorganized religion (Unitarianism) during his Cleveland years, was manifest, and at times aggressive. Like most of what he thought and felt, he wore his feelings for organized religion on his sleeve. His jokes to choristers in Atlanta about their church choirs were more than mild. They bordered on harassment. He would often insist that he was an agnostic, though his whole frame of reference for the arts was worship, and one of the speech/lectures he continually re-wrote and delivered was entitled "Worship and the Arts." Worship of whom, or what?

His mother may be thought of as a sort of ghost to Shaw, even as she lived. His father was ill when Shaw was a young man, and dead before Shaw was 30. Perhaps he seemed ghostly as well. If Shaw saw his mother as frighteningly chilly, he may have regarded his father as frighteningly emotional. There is a passage in one version of Shaw's standard speech on worship in which he says that "the minister" of his youth seldom failed to move *himself* to tears. That minister, of course, was his father.

Shaw's oft-repeated line, that with most organized religion "you have to check your intelligence at the door," and his attraction to the rationality and structure necessary to compose great music, may have also had to do with his revulsion at emotionalized faith. David Hume is supposed to have said that justice should be "the cool virtue." Shaw wanted the mechanics of art—*his* faith—to be rational and cool. He loathed cheap emotion and he distrusted a sermon, or a musical performance, that began in emotion. He felt a good sermon had to be built on a rational structure of sequential argument and inference, just as a good musical performance must be built on fundamental disciplines of rhythm, harmony, and phrasing. The last leap might be intuitive and emotional. It might necessarily be so. But nothing of value could be *built* on a purely emotional foundation. Not an argument. Not a work of art. Not even a relationship. Certainly not a faith. To Shaw, pure, unearned emotion was either self-indulgence or play-acting.

Shaw's relationship with his parents was unresolved, as all epic, tragic relationships are. He admired them, loved them, longed for an approval that could never be, and sought ways to escape them.

Shirley Shaw was a man of energy, force, and rigidity. So was Robert.

Rev. Shaw's life was the church. Even family life was not its own end.

Robert's life was music. Music was his obsession, or as Duke Ellington put it, his mistress. Even when he discovered fatherhood, in his second marriage, Shaw could not put the family before music.

Shirley Shaw's family was expected to serve the church. Robert Shaw's family was expected to serve music.

Nelle Shaw's work was to be a minister's wife. When Robert found a marriage that worked, and lasted, his wife's primary vocation was to allow him to work—to aid Shaw in his service to music. Caroline Shaw made keeping Robert healthy, rested, organized, contented, and productive her full-time job.

Shirley Shaw had no life outside of church and family. His "relationships" had to do with pastoring.

Robert Shaw's friendships were formed and sustained in music making. He had no life beyond his life in music and with his family, and no desire for one.

Shirley would go, go, go until he crashed, and then repeat the pattern. So did Robert. Bobby was the little boy who ran in circles until he fell down in exhaustion, and the grown man who sometimes took to his bed for two days after an important performance.

The church *was* Shirley Shaw's life. Music *was* Robert Shaw's life.

Both men were idealists with volcanic tempers and large hearts. Both had manic-depressive traits. Their temperaments mirrored each other, though Robert embraced complexity and ambiguity in a way that would have baffled Shirley. Drive and passion were what the father and son had in common, and in time it might have united them, rather than dividing them. But in the few years allotted them of overlapping adulthood, they could not meet.

Except in song.

Robert's parents came to New York together at least once to make music. During a rehearsal one night at All Saints Church, th blackout. While waiting for light, four Shaws (father, mother, brother John, and Robert) stood together in the candlelit shadows of an alcove and sang *Beautiful Savior*. They could not bridge the chasm between them in matters of faith, religion, or personal history, but they could sing.

Surely this is one reason Shaw believed so deeply in music. It provided the only place in life where separation and alienation, loneliness, anger, and hurt could be overcome, however fleetingly.

"It should have been you"?

"Give the belt to me"?

Hard medicine from good people.

The full quotation from Immanuel Kant reads: "Out of timber so crooked as that from which man is made nothing entirely straight can be built."

Robert Shaw's childhood was bathed in light. For one thing, there was the singing—at home, at church, in the mountains by the fire. There was Bobby walking to school with Jim—Bob counting two beats per step against Jim's three. There was the bike and the wide-open town. There was football and the surf.

But the shadows, which tormented and shaped and oddly blessed him, were there, too. Shaw associated the shadows with two things: organized religion and warfare. Light and love he associated with song.

CHAPTER 11

The Healing Incident

When his father was ill, or away, Bob would sometimes substitute for him in the pulpit. At that time, a small Protestant church of modest means would not hire a fill-in preacher. Instead, the elders of the church, or the minister's eldest son, might stand in. This may have begun as early as Robert's 16th year. Shaw was a de-facto minister at age 20, preaching not only to other college students, but to adults. He was considered "a natural" for the preaching line, and quite gifted at sermonizing, especially for one so young.

But Shaw's preaching life came to a sudden and dramatic climax—a moment that Shaw also defined as the end of his Christian ministry.

One evening, during a summer period in which he was pinch-hitting for his father, Shaw was notified that a young woman, a parishioner at his father's church, was gravely ill. Bob was told he should go and call upon her and her family and pray over her. In his father's role, he went to the local hospital, where the patient appeared to be critically ill. Everyone in that hospital room, including the young ersatz minister, feared for the girl's life and prayed with clarity, fervor, and lack of self-consciousness. They were all believers facing sudden darkness. The next day was Sunday and when the morning came, one of the vestrymen told young Bob that he would have to lead the parish in prayer and petition for the girl. Shaw felt awkward about it. He felt, he later said, that God was doing what he could do, and it was up to human beings to do their jobs—chiefly to get the young woman the medicine she needed, the care and rest she required, and perhaps to supply her family with food, money for treatment, and companionship. So that Sunday morning, instead of a petitioning prayer, Shaw said approximately this: God is doing his job; let's do ours. But the congregation took his words—his attempt to replace the petition with a reflection—as the prayer, and bowed their heads as the young man spoke. This was, let us say, at 10:25 a.m.

After the service, while Bob was greeting people on the steps as they filed out of church, a man came bounding up the steps. "She's better," he said. "She got better at 10:25 a.m."

The time is immaterial. Shaw did not claim to remember the exact hour. He remembered only the correspondence of the prayer and the change in the patient's condition.

This is another mythic Shaw story, told by the man himself. And honed. He told it in essentially the same way, scores of times, refining it ever so slightly.[24]

Shaw had a Greek chorus punch line, too. "At that moment," he said, "I decided I wanted no part of this." It scared him. And when he told the tale, Shaw sometimes added with a half chuckle that he had also decided, "I would not exploit my temporary success."

Shaw would have been 20 or 21 when this incident occurred, probably 21 if it really was close to the moment when he turned his back forever on the church.

The tale sounds fantastic. And for this one there is no witness. Only Shaw. Like all his stories, it sounds a bit *too* perfect, too polished—a criticism sometimes made of his performances. His sister Anne, who survived Shaw,

24 Many of Shaw's stories were rather like set theater pieces: he told this one to all the people he wanted to remember it, like his son Thomas, his son Peter, and Nola Frink. Almost everything he did was repeated with an eye toward perfection. The set-ness and sameness of his speeches was not a sign of laziness (that he did not want to write new speeches, for he did re-write them), and even less to manipulate his own history or legacy, but evidence of care. As with his music he wanted to get the product right—perfectly formed and perfectly clear.

had no recollection of it. But many, many friends and family members heard the story from him and none doubt it.

There are two interesting things about Shaw's reaction to his own fable, which I believe to be substantially true, but which perhaps may not be absolutely true. The first is that he did not dismiss "the miracle" as a fluke, the harvest of good medicine, or a mere coincidence. That's not how he was raised to think. Obviously, the child's fever might have broken by dawn, or penicillin might have kicked in by morning—just about the time the service began. A logical explanation is not at all out of reach. But Shaw did not particularly reach for it. *He did not deny the possibility that the girl was healed by prayer.* Interestingly, when his wife Caroline was dying of cancer roughly 60 years later, he accepted the prayers of believers (many of whom he had teased for years), not only out of courtesy, but real gratitude. He told several that he thought their prayers had strengthened his wife at key times and perhaps given her some of her good days. But if *he* prayed for Caroline, he never said so. He was not a Christian believer. Not from the day of the healing incident. So he maintained.

Second, Shaw saw the healing incident as a warning to him: a reason to run. This was not for him; just as the music of Bach *was* for him. He could not be the instrument of something he could not believe in completely.

Thus, it was possible to Shaw that he might have been an inadvertent instrument of the Divine. And his response was, "If that *is* you, Lord, you've got the wrong guy."

Shaw had a deep respect for faith, and a deep revulsion for counterfeit faith. He was by nature a believer, but by conviction a skeptic. The believer was stronger. That is one reason why he regarded all exploitation of belief, all plastic and shallow religion, all complacent faith and "cheap grace" (to borrow Bonhoeffer's term) with the most corrosive and withering scorn.

Shaw constructed, or reconstructed, the healing incident as a turning point in his life—a renunciation of his parents' faith and the final disavowal of the life he had known. We know that Shaw's turning away from the church did not happen in an instant, as a kind of reverse road to Damascus flash of light. He knew it, too. But his story of the healing incident allowed him to represent this great change within himself as definitive, final, and epic.

When he went to New York, away from his family, away from the little churches of his father, and the simple but sincere and profound faith of his father's parishioners, away from the comfortable academic cloister of Pomona, Shaw fully embraced the secular world. He became an athlete of the saloon—frequenting the White Horse Tavern in Greenwich Village until the wee hours with other artistic types. He could out-curse anyone he met in the Navy, Fred Waring, and most of the Broadway and Rockefeller Center people he knew. He embraced all he'd hoped to find out there, and all his parents feared he would find—"amateur sinning" he called it. But the believer would not budge. In time, he built his own belief structure—*his* credo of the arts; *his* theology of music; and his own musical chapels, cathedrals, and parishes. That took 60 years. But even when rejecting the belief of his childhood, he did not reject belief itself.

CHAPTER 12

"You should have seen New York then"

After the Second World War, Robert Shaw was a part of what might be called "the greatest generation" of musicians in the United States: musicians like Leonard Bernstein, George Szell, Lukas Foss, Virgil Thomson, Isaac Stern, and many others who did not become as nationally well known (such as Julius Herford and Louis Lane). This greatest generation established the American musical culture that Shaw imagined when he wrote his declaration of independence to Fred Waring. During their watch, our country's classical music matured. There were many fine orchestras in, say, 1950, but regional orchestras were not generally fine, as many are now. Similarly, students could major in music at any number of colleges and universities. Pomona offered a music concentration in Shaw's day. And there were four or five superb conservatories in the country. But music education was not broadly excellent as it now has become. In the last half of the last century, a handful of musicians transformed our nation's classical music from something spotty and ordinary to something generally outstanding—they created a musical force that had standards, staying power and, inevitably, a star system. Moreover, there was not necessarily, in the years just after the war, a loyal and sustaining audience for serious music. The greatest musical generation changed this. They built a concert-going and record-buying audience. This generation of men and women (like Helen Hosmer at the Crane School of Music and Shaw's associate Alice Parker) wanted to change our musicianship and our listenership. And they did. They wanted first-rate musical education and a plethora of top-notch orchestras available at all levels throughout the land. They wanted an *American* classical music, not just a European import for Americans to consume (which they had been doing only parenthetically). Shaw's dream was not his alone. It was the dream of a generation of great American musicians.

Some of these musicians were quite deliberate and self-conscious about all of this, as Shaw was in his letter to Waring. Some were not. In any case, they succeeded. In the early twenty-first century, the mature musical culture exists. Young musicians are extraordinarily well trained today, and many musical amateurs do not simply love music, they understand its structure. American orchestras are generally thought to be every bit the equal of European orchestras, and it is sometimes said that they are better disciplined. And there is a solid audience, though that fan base is now aging. Shaw's dream—the maturing of classical American music making, particularly choral music making, and the democratization of that music making—has been greatly, if not wholly, realized. Classical music in the United States does not belong to a privileged elite, but simply to the interested and committed.

Bernstein, perhaps the greatest American maestro—at least in terms of his variety of gifts, his impact on the audience, and recognition—might be thought the Thomas Jefferson of these founding mothers and fathers: the one who epitomized the coming of age, the popularization, and the deepening of American classical music. And "Lenny" became a pop star. He was known not only on the street in Manhattan and on TV, but internationally. Bernstein's televised "Young People's Concerts," his forays into Broadway, his emphasis on living composers at the New York Philharmonic Orchestra, educated and expanded the audience for serious music. Lenny himself became the gate to the classical world for many music lovers. In the middle of the Cold War, pianist Van Cliburn represented our country in competition with the Soviet Union—and America won. Cliburn drew new fans to classical listening. And among composers, there was Samuel Barber, whose voice was somehow quintessentially "new" and American. These young American maestros were able to appeal to a previously untouched demographic.

But not many American conductors became stars. Szell became an American resident, and enthusiast. So, too, did Toscanini. But Robert Shaw was one of the few homegrown conductors to achieve celebrity status during the 1950s and 1960s. Indeed, in the post-war period, Shaw and Bernstein were friends, allies, and collaborators. Though their musical styles and methods were dissimilar, and in time almost diametrically opposite, they shared a vision of an American culture of classical music. Both used the bully pulpit to educate. Both appealed to the young. Both championed the music of their time. The two collaborated on Blitzstein's *Airborne Symphony* (in 1946) and on a recording of *On the Town* (1945), for which Shaw organized and prepared a chorus. When Bernstein conducted the New York City Symphony (1945 to 1948), he recruited Shaw for both choral work and guest conducting. In those years, Shaw felt himself a junior partner when he worked with Bernstein. As the years passed, and as Shaw grew, he felt less that way. The two men saw little of each other after Shaw went to Cleveland, and then Atlanta. But Shaw never ceased to admire his friend's proficiency, or to enjoy his profligacy. Shaw was sometimes appalled by Bernstein's ego and histrionic behavior, but he was always moved by his melodies. Shaw championed and conducted Bernstein's works to the end, particularly the *Mass*, the *Chichester Psalms*, and the "Symphonic Dances" from *West Side Story*. Their early time together in New York was a bond of affection. A sense of creation and possibility was simply in the air in those days. America's band of founding brothers then was small and intertwined. Serge Koussevitzky, for example, mentored Bernstein and Shaw. Rudolf Serkin played with both men. Aaron Copland composed for both.

The greatest musical generation also fostered, incidentally and ironically, a generation of audiophiles—serious LP listeners, and serious "sound" buffs—persons much disdained by the likes of Paul Hindemith and Robert Shaw.

Shaw's own part in the burgeoning of American classical music concentrated primarily on choral music—raising the standard for vocal musicianship and establishing the audience for choral masterworks, both live and on record. But his role was also deeper than that. He was an integral part of a tradition that was creating itself. He was there at the creation. If Bernstein was Jefferson, Shaw was Adams. He was, after all, commissioning Hindemith, conducting new works by Copland, and introducing America to works by Bartók and Poulenc. He was in the thick of it. In time, Shaw built a repertoire and a discography—not so much for himself as for the choral arts: roughly 100 recordings for RCA and approximately 60 others after he went to Atlanta, most of which were for Telarc. He helped build the American musical culture as a music educator and popularizer, first with his choral arrangements in partnership with Parker, which were widely used in schools, and second with regular residencies at American universities over the course of his career. He commissioned new music from American classical composers from the time of the Collegiate Chorale through his tenure as music director in Atlanta. He also built an American symphony orchestra; he refashioned it from regional status to one of the nation's best.

The young Shaw's goal, at the time he wrote to Waring, was not to become a world-famous symphony conductor—nothing that august. He wanted only to be a part of the creation of a serious and healthy American classical music. His role turned out to be much larger than anything he imagined.

The arts in America were experiencing a rich harvest in the 1930s, 1940s, and early 1950s. A small number of people, all living and working near each other within a small radius in New York City, ranging from Langston Hughes to Bernstein, Martha Graham to Copland, were changing the nation's intellectual and artistic life. An astonishing variety of artists and intellectuals crossed each other's paths between roughly 1940 and 1960. Orson Welles and Duke Ellington knew and liked each other, and talked of doing some sustained work together. Elia Kazan and Marlon Brando seemed to be remaking the American theater. Gore Vidal and Tennessee Williams were social friends as well as writing colleagues. Shaw left New York in 1956 to go to Cleveland, but he too had befriended a wide variety of musicians, actors, writers, and wannabees—from Dylan Thomas to Ed Sullivan. Shaw ate, drank, and partied with them. In his later years, he would tell stories about some of the famous people he knew in the Manhattan of the 1940s and about the sense of excitement and purpose. Cultural and intellectual life in the United States was coming of age. "You should have seen New York then," Shaw said. "It was so clean! . . . You could see it."

Shaw was highly nostalgic about *his* New York. The city had changed his life—it and the richness and intermingling of artists. Indeed, even after he went to Cleveland, he kept his family residence in suburban Scarsdale and operated the Robert Shaw Chorale out of New York City for one-third of the year.

According to Shaw, his New York was a pleasant, safe, well-run, and well-kept town where people were extraordinarily friendly. He claimed he was able to get a good breakfast for 18 cents. And a decent lunch for 35 cents.

His rent was 35 dollars a week and he had no trouble paying it.

His first apartment was at 116th Street and Riverside Drive—"with a view of the river. You just couldn't beat it."

"We had a hunger," he said. "It wasn't just choral rehearsals for the Collegiate Chorale, we held lectures and seminars. People would come talk to us for two hours before rehearsal . . . Dmitri Mitropoulos . . . Martha Graham, and she'd demonstrate. It was a wonderful life."

Shaw said it was also "great fun to walk into NBC and hear everyone talking about that week's musical programming, or telling stories about Toscanini."

Shaw was a regular at the White Horse Tavern—one of Greenwich Village's storied saloons—where artists, writers, and journalists hung out. Indeed, Shaw claimed he had been in Dylan Thomas's company the night the poet drank himself to death. Thomas had agreed to collaborate on a project—to be determined—with the Collegiate Chorale.

Part of the excitement was the cross-pollenation of the arts in New York. When Mark Blitzstein wrote the *Airborne Symphony*, he asked his friend Bernstein to conduct it, and later record it, and his other friend, Bob Shaw, to narrate on the recording. (Orson Welles had narrated a live performance.) Shaw was on a first-name basis with many jazz musicians, like Cozy Cole and Cab Calloway; playwrights, like Lillian Hellman; dancers; impresarios, like Billy Rose; and sundry writers and poets. One of the closest friendships he formed was with the playwright Thornton Wilder. The two corresponded for some years, Wilder writing far more. Wilder considered himself to be a kind of big brother to Shaw.

Shaw married in 1939, and he and Maxine began having babies right away. They moved to Scarsdale. But Shaw was seldom there. He formed the habit of staying overnight in the city, where he generally had several projects on various burners at once. (The Collegiate Chorale had begun by 1941, and in 1942 and 1943, he was choral director for the Aquacades and Carmen Jones, in addition to his Waring duties.) Shaw had space at Waring's offices and, for a time, one of the artists' lofts at Carnegie Hall. And at another point he had space made available to him at Rockefeller Center. He could sleep in one of these places if he had to or at the homes of friends. He didn't care much about sleep or commuting to Scarsdale. Thus he began a pattern of separation from his wife and children. Shaw's music and suburban family life were not compatible. Moreover, his response to conflict (especially with Maxine) was to escape.

Shaw was stimulated by the company available to him in Manhattan. He knew he was a part of a unique moment in American cultural history. The whole city seemed to be flying high, fueled by passion and newness. There was boldness of art and for Shaw an admixture of energy, youth, sex, booze, and cigarettes. He sensed that it was a blessed moment in time, if not that it was fleeting. He loved it, both when it was going on and when he looked back on it.

This was Shaw's wild time. He was on fire. But his dreams and his fame were running well ahead of his knowledge and capacity. He went out late drinking, not just with famous poets and musicians but also with his chorus members, almost every night. He lamented his own limitations, as well as those of the chorus. Meanwhile, Maxine was having babies and raising their children. But Shaw would not go home for days at a time. And soon, after 1948, he would be touring, living life on the road with the Robert Shaw Chorale part of the year—all music, and movement, and late nights.

Shaw was also a high visibility contributor to the New York arts and cultural scene then. All his concerts were reviewed, usually favorably, often lovingly, which embarrassed him. He had two not particularly consistent feelings about most critics—they didn't know that much and they treated him more seriously than he deserved to be treated. Features were written about him. In its December 29, 1947 issue, *Time Magazine* wrote:

> *The busiest musician in Manhattan this week will be a shock-haired young man named Robert Shaw. When the last round tones of his RCA Victor Chorale conclude NBC's RCA Victor Show, Shaw will just about have time to gobble his dinner, struggle into his heavy blue overcoat and dash four blocks to CBS's studios to lead The Columbia Chorale and Symphony in Beethoven's* Mass in C. *Two days—and eight hours of rehearsal—later he will conduct his Collegiate Chorale at Carnegie Hall in Bach's three-hour-long* Christmas Oratorio; *next night Christmas carols for CBS's annual Christmas program. And on top of all that, he has a Christmas symphony concert at the Juilliard School of Music, where he is director of choral conducting—in his spare time.*

Shaw was considered a young and charismatic star, and cut quite a figure. But at times, Shaw told friends, he felt like a fraud—in too deep. By the early 1950s, he had begun to get invitations to conduct the major orchestras. Charles Munch—like his predecessor Serge Koussevitzky, who had brought Shaw to Tanglewood as director of choral music—was particularly fond of Shaw. Munch turned the baton over to Shaw to conduct the Boston Symphony

Orchestra in the Haydn *Creation* at Carnegie Hall, a generous act. For Shaw, it was another honor he had not yet earned but could not turn down. Munch believed in Shaw, as many renowned maestros did. But Shaw wasn't sure he believed in himself. He still faced orchestras with hands trembling. When an invitation came to conduct the Chicago Symphony Orchestra, he accepted, but the doubts set upon him and in due course he told his agent, Walter Gould, to cancel the engagement. "I can't do it, Walter, I just can't." (A few years later, he would conduct that orchestra for the first and last time. Fritz Reiner, the legendary Chicago Music Director, was scheduled to conduct the Brahms *German Requiem*, but had become gravely ill. Lore has it that Reiner said only one man other than himself could do the piece justice and that man was Shaw. This time, in deference to Reiner, Shaw accepted.)

When Shaw moved to Cleveland in 1956, there were at least two factors at work. One was pedagogical. Toscanini was no longer on the scene, no longer available to inspire and instruct, and Shaw had learned all he could from Julius Herford. There was no one left to teach him and no place he could grow in New York City. The other factor was his need to escape a life that had become too fast. It's not that Shaw was worried that excessive drink and smoking (for he smoked then) would kill him. He had not yet come to that point of self-examination and resolution. No, the problem was that life in the high-speed lane was getting in the way of the music. Shaw wanted more time to study, and his nightlife left little room for that. He wanted out of the limelight and off the fast track. He had to change his life to deepen his understanding. By going away from New York City, where the world was his oyster, to Cleveland, where he would apprentice to George Szell, he relinquished a rich and interesting, but a somewhat destructive and, he increasingly felt, potentially shallow, life. Shaw found that as his musicianship matured, he seemed to need more time than ever to study and prepare. Shaw loved New York City. He loved his life and work there. His departure from it was a renouncement. He needed to leave New York to grow as a musician.

CHAPTER 13

A Tale of Two Chorales

Robert Shaw remade a word, or bastardized it, depending on your point of view.

Before Shaw, the world "chorale" referred to a musical form—a chorale by Bach, for instance, or Britten's *Chorale after an Old French Carol.* Shaw expanded the word chorale to also mean a choir. Not able to write a chorale, he formed one. In fact, he formed two, each quite different from the other.

While still full-time with Waring, in 1941 Shaw, along with a choral conductor from Oklahoma named Gordon Berger, founded the Collegiate Chorale in New York City. Berger, who had moved to New York to join Waring's Pennsylvanians, had started a community choir at the Marble Collegiate Church in New York, and he invited Shaw to guest conduct it. But soon Shaw was *the* conductor and the choir was to be reborn as something new, larger, and grander—The Collegiate Chorale. The word "Collegiate" came from the church that meant to sponsor the venture. (Collegiate in the church name is supposed to denote a sort of group ministry.) "Chorale" they simply thought sounded good. The Collegiate Chorale's purpose was to perform "serious" choral music—sacred and profane, modern and Baroque as well as eighteenth- and nineteenth-century works. So Shaw announced at the time of its creation. In fact, the group was closely associated with Waring for its first four to five years of its existence and did popular ballads and patriotic tunes as often as not. Shaw claimed this was because of time constraints and because, mostly, they were invited to sing at bond rallies. But the Collegiate Chorale grew musically as Shaw grew—soon taking on more serious and complex music, and commissioning pieces and hiring its own orchestras.

Shaw had been restless almost from the time he arrived in New York. He knew he wanted something more, without knowing what. He had experimented with a small occasional choir of roughly 25 professional singers, sometimes including his sister Holly. This group sang part-songs by Brahms, some madrigals, and some Negro spirituals. But the Collegiate Chorale was a different animal. It would be a big choir with a big idea behind it. First, the Collegiate Chorale was to be a volunteer choir. Choir members were not paid. But it was not really an "amateur" group in the strict sense, since most members were musicians and Shaw had his pick of New York singers. It *was* an amateur group in Shaw's sense: they sang for love.

The Collegiate Chorale's original membership was 185. Some 500 auditioned the first year. Shaw said this choir was to be for human beings of all creeds and colors, ages and backgrounds—the "melting pot that sings." Shaw conducted the Collegiate Chorale until 1954, and during that time it was very much his passion, the agent of his idealism and aspirations, his church.

The "melting pot" became an important part of Shaw dogma and lore, but it was initially accidental, as were so many things in Shaw's life at that time. Shaw had long felt, vaguely, that some social and political battles could be fought through the arts. He had not initially thought of the Collegiate Chorale as a social or political entity. But the top pastor at the Marble Collegiate Church, Dr. Norman Vincent Peale, opened Shaw's eyes. The choir had only just begun to get organized and start rehearsing when Peale called Shaw into his office and laid down some rules: Cut the number of the group to 100. Make sure 50 are members of the Collegiate Church. And eliminate the blacks, the Catholics, and the Jews. And, oh yes, Shaw's cursing would have to stop. An incensed Shaw immediately moved the choir from the Collegiate Church. And as he did so often in his life, he found virtue in necessity. He had not really *noticed* that he had an integrated choir. But once Peale pointed it out to him, Shaw decided they had stumbled upon something great: *This* is the model for the modern chorus, he decided—true democracy: the brotherhood of sweat and art. This, he decided, is what the chorus brings to music—a public space much wider and deeper than a voting booth or a poll can provide.

Shaw fell absolutely in love with this idea of the chorus as the model of and means to community. Peale did Shaw a great favor. And to the day he died, Shaw never fell out of love with the notion of the chorus as a fraternity—a melting pot for the creation of art that no single member of the community could create alone. But originally, it was an accident, and one initiated by a seemingly bigoted minister. Shaw often represented his career as a series of happy accidents, though there was at least as much intention and discipline as luck. But this *was* a happy, or ironic, accident. (Many years later, Peale wrote to Shaw to apologize. Shaw accepted and graciously allowed as to how he had been rather wild and free with his cursing in those days.)

In the time Shaw led it, the Collegiate Chorale would ultimately do many programs of great variety: much Bach, many Christmas concerts, spirituals, and the first American performances of works by Aaron Copland, Paul Hindemith, and Béla Bartók. The Collegiate Chorale still exists today as one of New York City's premier choral groups.

It was in the Collegiate Chorale days that Shaw really began to preach his gospel and build his own church: Art is transcendence, music is spirit, the score is the holy text, and the performance the sacrament. Getting the music right, through development of and adherence to rigorous rehearsal techniques—this was his doctrine. The Collegiate Chorale was his first parish, as it were. Each choir Shaw founded became the new church he was building. In time, the musicians of each "church" became his flock.

Shaw quickly developed an idea into a mantra: The chorus is not only one possible approximation of the ideal of the human family—it might be the *only* legitimate one available in our time—for politics and the church are corrupted. In a choir, the end is not power but service (to beauty); and its means are not coercive but selfless and freeing. This was the gospel according to Shaw—first draft.

Shaw's "religification" of music was not necessarily complete or consistent. Shaw had a large capacity for contradiction. He felt art was a higher morality. And he always presented himself as a moralist. But he never clearly saw his moral obligation to his first wife and family, or the contradiction in his moralizing on the meaning of the human family while neglecting his own family. Like many artists, he could be blindly selfish. Interestingly, though, Shaw transferred the congregational approach (with himself as pastor), first applied to the Collegiate Chorale, to the Cleveland Orchestra Chorus, and later to the Atlanta Symphony Chorus. He treated the Robert Shaw Chorale, his professional choir, more like he treated the instrumentalists in the Cleveland Orchestra and the Atlanta Symphony. They were not his flock, but his colleagues and friends. Amateur musicians brought out the pastor. Professionals got a peer.

There were times when Shaw invested the Collegiate Chorale with almost utopian hopes. His letters to the group are sometimes embarrassing in their dreaminess and preachiness. When people of all races, backgrounds, and talent levels (though none at the level of no talent) come together to make serious music, he said, there is almost no limit to what can be done. How many believed that then? Or believe it now? But it was a time in our history of great anxiety *and* idealism. The two impulses fed each other. And Shaw's passion, enthusiasm, and boyish idealism carried him through all his years. The impossible expectation he placed upon music was a tool. He used it to build his Cleveland and Atlanta choirs, and for transforming them from glorified community choruses to refined musical instruments. Blinding idealism is part of what gave the Collegiate Chorale the confidence to sing for Toscanini. It is part of what made Atlanta singers believe they could be world-class. Shaw believed music can and will exert its own moral power. For him, this was a self-fulfilling prophecy. As Sylvia McNair said, "He made you believe."

Shaw believed that singing together could heal wounds and change hearts, and though the hope might have come harder in later years, and he promised himself and his musicians somewhat less than the moon and the stars in those last years, he never changed his mind: Music could change people. Singing together could make wounded souls whole.

In the very early days of the Collegiate Chorale, Shaw and some of his close friends and associates—Thomas Pyle was certainly one of them and Florence Kopleff was another—drafted what they unselfconsciously called a "Creed" for the Collegiate Chorale. It was a list of precepts that began with "We believe." Of course, Shaw was the primary author.

And what did they say they believed in this credo?

- That music is a community enterprise;
- That music is "one art, choral-orchestral, solo, ensemble"—one craft;
- That music is a doer's art;
- That the performer's craft is to "reveal, not to interpret";
- That "the choral instrument should assume a position of respect and musical responsibility commensurate ... to that of the major professional orchestra";
- That the choral art stands in a unique position to be of service to man and music.[25]

Musicians who worked with Shaw in later years would recognize all those tenets. His conviction only deepened.

The creed also had a preamble, which contained the first and founding principle: "We believe that in a world of political, economic, and personal

25 Shaw papers.

disintegration music is not a luxury but a necessity—not simply because it is therapeutic, nor because it is the universal language, but because it is the persistent focus of man's intelligence, aspiration, and goodwill."[26]

Music is the master art—the one that combines mind, soul, and brotherhood. It is not merely nice or lovely, but vital.

Once written, Shaw stuck to his creed. This was very early Shaw. Yet, he didn't stray much from it. He built on it, but did not throw any of it away. Coincidentally (but maybe not), there are six elements in it, as there are in the Christian Nicene Creed.

Here is a part of one of the first of Shaw's hundreds of letters to choruses—this to the fledgling Collegiate Chorale, written February 8, 1943. It is emblematic and foundational:

> *What they don't see—and what I'm afraid you don't see—and what you must see, is that the Collegiate Chorale is not a glee club or a stock company. You don't join the Collegiate Chorale. You believe it. It's very damn near a religion. It's a way of life. Either you feel the fellow next to you is an important human being and you like him and you try desperately to understand how he feels about what he sings about, and pool your creative passions to make something a damn sight bigger than either of you could make alone—or this isn't your kind of choir. Either the music you sing is torn out of you—or you ought not to be singing.*[27]

The language is the passionate language of a young man, and though Shaw never wrote anything so lacking in nuance, or in irony, in his later years, fundamentally, this is still how Shaw saw music at the end of his life.

26 Shaw papers.
27 Ibid.

Certainly he was less naïve as time marched on, but in some ways he became more idealistic and uncompromising in old age. Speaking to a Carnegie Hall chorus roughly 50 years later, Shaw said of the Hindemith *Lilacs*, "Singing a piece like this changes lives . . . Goddamn it, it changes lives . . . You're not the same. You don't think in the same way, you don't grieve in the same way; you don't love in the same way."[28]

But at the time Shaw wrote to the Collegiate Chorale in 1943, his personal transformation was still in progress. He was a man in a hurry then, albeit riddled with self-doubt. Occasionally he would collapse, the victim of a combination of exhaustion and that doubt. He would recover quickly, however—drawn back by the music and all he wanted to do. And he would resolve to better educate himself and improve his skills.

In 1949, frustrated by his slowness at score study, lack of ease and fluidity with the orchestra, and even lack of time for listening to music (three frustrations that plagued him for virtually his entire career), Shaw made a plan of retreat and self-education—to study and "catch up" once and for all. He obtained leaves from Juilliard, Tanglewood, and the Collegiate Chorale and decided to go to Europe and study with Nadia Boulanger. Then he would return to the United States, tour a bit, and go to San Francisco to study with Pierre Monteux. The plan didn't quite work out, and various, similar plans made later in his life, to pull back, to retreat into study and writing, didn't work out either. For five decades he kept trying to get himself to sit down and write a book on choral techniques, and in late life he wanted to write a second book of musical commentary on the masterworks of oratorio literature, which he would have been singularly qualified to pen. To a degree, he did write both books, in piecemeal and epistolary form. They may be found, co-mingled and somewhat obscured by Shaw's own excess and extranea, in *The Robert Shaw Reader*. Thanks to this collection assembled by Robert Blocker, the thoughts on music that Robert Shaw committed to print exist between two covers. But the primary reason that Shaw's plans of retreat and study never came to fruition is that Shaw was a

28 *Robert Shaw: Preparing a Masterpiece,* Vol. V.

performer. He was monkish, but not a scholar. Music was only alive to him when performed. He would retreat to learn a work of music. But eventually, he always wanted to hear the scores "sound," as Toscanini put it. Shaw was no more an intellectual than Toscanini. To him, music was meant to be heard. Shaw was incredibly intelligent, and his emotional intelligence perhaps outran even his intellect. But he was not a man of abstraction. His self-discipline was great, but it depended on the next performance. As much as he hated the spotlight in some ways, Shaw *was* a performer. Music was for playing, not philosophizing. Granted, Shaw loved to philosophize about music, but on the way to the performance. It meant nothing to love a score if you could not awaken it. Loving Mozart or Brahms was not abstract either. It had to do with the nuts and bolts—understanding a composer's language and doing right by his piece.

Since Shaw was a natural teacher, he had various opportunities at various points in his life to enter the academic world on a full- or part-time basis.[29] He always declined. He knew himself in this regard. When he was on campus he always taught toward a specific performance.

Shaw did go to Europe in 1949, armed with letters of introduction from his friend Wilder to the likes of Gertrude Stein. Wilder also provided reading material for the trip—his own small anthology of various writers and some of his own musings, including a critique of Shaw's bearing and posture in concerts. Wilder thought Shaw slouched and feigned humility, which he found vain. But Shaw was intimidated and ill at ease in Paris and mostly got drunk with an American pal. His only serious and lasting contact in Europe was with the composer Francis Poulenc, with whom he would correspond for some years, and whose work he would champion and record for several

29 According to Shaw, the founder of Westminster Choir College, John Finley Williamson, offered him the presidency of Westminster. After he retired as music director of the Atlanta Symphony, John Silber, President of Boston University, offered him a chance to head, and to augment, the choral music program. Shaw could have had almost any title or salary he requested, had he accepted. Later, after his protégé Ann Howard Jones went to BU on his recommendation, Shaw began to go there twice a year to study and prepare a work. Again, Shaw was offered an academic title, again he declined. He insisted that he was not an academic, but a craftsman. In the one instance in which he did accept an academic title—Robert B. Woodruff Professor of Music and Fine Arts at Emory University, after his retirement from the Atlanta Symphony Orchestra—Shaw (and his wife) felt badly treated.

decades. (Poulenc wrote effusively and Shaw responded perfunctorily. Shaw corresponded little in his life, except for his one-way letters to his choruses.) Soon Shaw had returned from his European retreat and was back in New York studying with Julius Herford and planning new programs.

Shaw's concept of the choir as one spiritual family, with a somehow "unanimous sound," was in his head very early in the game. And at that time, the 1940s, he relied heavily on his tutor: Julius Herford.

As part of the writ Shaw issued him to "teach me everything," Herford grounded Shaw in the great German composers and taught him the methods of structural analysis and historical research that Shaw would employ in preparing music for the next 50 years. That method focused on discovering the individualized musical syntax of each particular composer. And it focused on history—the composer's history and the context of his time. This was 35 or 40 years before the great movement toward historical authenticity in musical performance came into vogue.

Herford shared Shaw's lofty goals. Shaw's idea was to marry amateur purity, spiritual authenticity, and technical dexterity in choral music. That was a grand ambition in 1946, 1947, and 1948. At that time the two men enjoyed an almost complete unanimity of vision—as to musical worth, tastes, values, scholarship, and preparation.

In the end, Shaw used most of his "leave of absence" not to study with a big name conductor or to absorb Europe, but to study scores and counterpoint back home at the piano with Herford. Two things happened: Shaw and Herford were soon working 10-hour days and they were working on the music Shaw was either engaged to perform or hoped to perform in the upcoming season, either with the Collegiate Chorale or the Robert Shaw Chorale, or some other entity. For Shaw, music could not exist in a vacuum. Study always related to performance.

As for Pierre Monteux, there was an exchange of letters and a visit arranged. Beginning in January of 1950, Shaw cleared almost three months for study and time with the great man and his assistant, Artur Rodzinski, in San Francisco. Shaw did go to San Francisco. Furthermore, Monteux and Shaw apparently liked each other very much. Monteux was sympathetic to Shaw's feelings of inadequacy and his desire to more completely educate himself as a conductor. Shaw explained that his keyboard skills were so minimal that he was, substantially, learning each part of each score by singing it to himself. There wasn't enough time in any day to prepare that way. And since Shaw didn't feel the natural ease with the orchestra that he felt with the choir, he wanted more time to prepare orchestral scores, and the orchestral sections of choral-orchestral pieces. Monteux assured Shaw that he understood the problem, but there was no real cure but time and experience. Again, to one degree or another, these were the problems Shaw would forever face. Monteux and Shaw did not actually spend much time together in the end. They met a few times. They talked music and looked at some scores. But it could not truly be said that Shaw "studied" with him, not in the way he had worked with Herford. Perhaps there was a misunderstanding about schedules and time. Perhaps the understanding had been too vague, and Shaw never tied the arrangement down. Perhaps, like Shaw, Monteux was a performer, not a scholar or teacher. In any case, he had a full schedule and little time for Shaw. Perhaps, also, he didn't see Shaw as so desperately incompetent as Shaw sometimes imagined himself. Again, a retreat and study plan failed. Shaw wandered around California a bit and saw friends and relatives, and drank. Then he went home to New York to get back to work—with Julius Herford. Their partnership was comfortable and pragmatic. Once home, Shaw focused again on learning by doing—diving into projects that were difficult for him. He was back to being "over his head," where he was strangely, painfully comfortable with being uncomfortable. He learned and got better, not from step-by-step instruction from a mentor-coach, but by continually throwing himself into increasingly turbulent waters. It was a somewhat masochistic approach, but it was Shaw's way. When he leapt into the waters of the Cleveland Orchestra, a few years later, it was the most masochistic of all his jumps. Sharks were in those depths.

He also learned by appropriating teachers and mentors, soaking up all he could, rather quickly, and moving on to the next guru. By the mid-1950s, Shaw was using Herford less and consulting him less. Julius Herford was an academic. That was a fault line. But the ultimate fault line was in Shaw's psyche. The restless student had moved on (just as he would rather quickly tire of George Szell years later).

It was in this era, the 1950s, that Shaw really began to change the ways Americans regarded choral music. Choral music may seem the easiest music to make on a simple level, but it is perhaps the hardest music to make on a complex, musically ambitious, and artistically demanding level. It may be true that anyone who can speak can sing. And an average voice doing simple music can make an emotional statement worthy of attention, memory, and admiration—consider pop ballads or country music. But singing complicated and demanding music, set to a profound text, within a group is, inherently, very, very difficult. Prior to Shaw, the assumption was that choral music simply could not be done with the precision of a great symphonic or chamber music performance—that it wasn't very serious music making because it *could* not be. It was still singing, and thus inherently imprecise and unrefined. Shaw demonstrated that choral singing could be precise and refined. Singers could be instrumentalists. Groups of singers could perform in harness. It had always been his goal to show that choral music could meet instrumental standards of precision and sonority. And in the mid-1950s—the heyday of the Robert Shaw Chorale—people began to believe that this might be so. Perhaps the voice is not only the Alpha of music, but also the Omega? When asked late in life whether he minded being remembered as a "choral master" instead of, simply, a musical master, Shaw would say "no" (20 years before, it would have been "yes"). Shaw said that the composer Paul Hindemith had told him that one day people would see that choral music was the highest and purest form of music, hence choral conducting must be the highest form of conducting. Shaw probably laughed when he heard this, and he may also have been editing what Hindemith said, but this is what Shaw himself had come to believe.

As for Herford, he and Shaw reconciled in later life. This was a matter of time and age. Partly it was also Bach. Shaw returned to Bach, and his love and understanding seemed to deepen in a way that is only possible with age. "I'm a Bach," Herford had answered when asked his religious affiliation. Shaw came to something like the same position (for him, it was more of a definition than a conclusion). At the end of his days, Shaw found that getting inside the music of Bach was the closest he could come to God.

Shaw didn't really found the Robert Shaw Chorale. It evolved. It grew out of the need to occasionally produce a smaller choir, or a smaller sound for a given occasion or a given piece of music. This smaller choir was extracted from the Collegiate Chorale. In the beginning it was known as "the small choir" or the "chapel choir." It was a group of 25 "pro" singers known also by its momentary affiliation: the "CBS Chorale" if it was performing a work for CBS radio or the "NBC Chorale" if the engagement was with NBC. Shaw's first two important recordings for RCA—the Bach *Mass in B Minor* and the Brahms *German Requiem* were both attributed to the "RCA Victor Chorale."

The group existed in its early form in 1947; it did not become the Robert Shaw Chorale until 1948, when it went on the road and began to tour under this name. Obviously it could not be the "CBS Chorale" and, alternately, the "RCA Victor Chorale" on the road. Thus, the road gave birth to the Robert Shaw Chorale. And since Shaw was famous by then, more people would come to see the "Robert Shaw Chorale" than something called the "Chapel Choir." The Robert Shaw Chorale became the nation's, and then the world's, best-known and most-respected professional touring vocal ensemble. But that's a misleading statement in itself because there was no true competition in professional touring choirs, other than Roger Wagner. Just as there had never been a group quite like the Collegiate Chorale, there had never been one like the Robert Shaw Chorale: a professional, touring, classical choir. It was as unique an idea then as it is today. Many choirs tour occasionally, but they are not touring choirs. They are not paid professionals. They are typically associated with colleges or universities—Westminster, St. Olaf, or various choirs out of Oxford and Cambridge. Some smaller choral ensembles, like the King's Singers, are on constant tour today, but they are small chamber groups, not choirs.

The original Chapel Choir grew to between 36 and 40 so that the choir could cut through the instruments, especially in public school auditoriums and gymnasiums—a frequent venue. Within a very few years, the Robert Shaw Chorale with orchestra began to tour America, doing not just glee club programs, but major works. Eventually the chorale toured Mozart's *Requiem*, Handel's *Messiah*, Bach's *Mass in B Minor* and *St. John Passion*. It also sang Stephen Foster songs, Appalachian folk songs, spirituals, art songs, and some Broadway and standard glee club material. The Robert Shaw Chorale's programs were astonishingly long, ambitious, and varied musically. Shaw would commonly deliver, in one concert, the equivalent of three programs—an oratorio or Mass, some art songs and chamber works, and some folk and pop. So the Chorale was not just a choir, but it also had to function as a symphonic chorus and an oversized chamber group. That sort of flexibility and expanse of repertoire might be a good working definition of a "Chorale." The Robert Shaw Chorale made 100 records (mostly LPs) for the RCA label, including the first Red Seal recording to sell in excess of a million copies (this was a Christmas record made in 1952: *Christmas Hymns and Carols, Vol. II)*.

The Robert Shaw Chorale was also, very quickly, immensely successful—one of the few groups of classical musicians in America to reach something like popular or mainstream status in its day. The Chorale performed on radio and appeared on TV regularly, and of course, its Christmas albums were a staple in thousands upon thousands of American homes.

The size and composition of the Robert Shaw Chorale is important. It was typically a group of 30 to 40 people. Again, that size made the group flexible. This meant that Americans were able to hear important Baroque musical works in live performance, sung by professional musicians, on something approaching a Baroque scale—a revelation for many people at the time. Not everyone was receptive. Americans like big choirs. Indeed, Shaw liked big choirs. But, ever the amateur musicologist, he knew what the music called for and wanted listeners to actually hear it performed on the scale intended by the composer.

The Chorale was known for its sound. It was powerful. Critics remarked on its crispness, clarity, and energy. But the greater accomplishment was the range of music performed, and the variety and length of the programs. Because the singers hired by Shaw for the Robert Shaw Chorale were so strong vocally, and so capable, they could do all sorts of music—from Byrd and Purcell, to the Mozart *Requiem*, to spirituals. And they could do it night after night.

Yet, because Shaw was always attentive to vocal balance and health, his singers did not wear out their instruments. Shaw would say the composers cultured and conserved the voices, but in truth, the youth and joy of the singers—along with Shaw's preference for balancing sound by redeploying singers rather than simply cranking up the volume—may have had more to do with the Chorale's endurance.

The Robert Shaw Chorale was also, in a sense, a pickup group. The membership was not constant. Its composition changed for virtually every tour. Most singers hired stayed a year or two. They could not and did not wish to live on the road. A core of Shaw friends and collaborators did. But each tour was its own entity and its own choir, for the Chorale was constantly being reconfigured and restocked.

Yet, the constant coming and going of singers didn't seem to change the sound of the Robert Shaw Chorale. Though each season the Chorale was a nearly new choir, it sounded essentially the same and in each incarnation many people assumed the membership of the choir was static. How was this possible? Well, it was Shaw. The choir sounded the way Shaw wanted it to sound. It was tuned to his ear. He did not build the Robert Shaw Chorale around particular voices but on a sound he heard in his own head. Later, in the Cleveland and Atlanta days, he built his choirs on the disciplines he had evolved to achieve unified rhythm and clear intonation. And the sound was a bit different. The Robert Shaw Chorale was perhaps more of a top-down rather than a bottom-up sound. It was based more on a sound rather than ensemble disciplines. But even in these early days, certain Shaw practices were in place. He tinkered and adjusted for balance, and he always balanced his choirs by moving voices from part to part, measure to measure, or even note to note. The Robert Shaw Chorale was, finally, more an aggregate of fine solo voices, whereas the later Shaw choirs were choirs of lesser voices unified by technique. In those later days, everything was designed to get the whole team breathing as one—in mental and musical sync. In the Chorale, one hears individual voices.

The quality of those individual voices was extraordinary. The sonority of the group was stunning. The sound was unapologetically robust and masculine.

At its peak, the Robert Shaw Chorale recorded two to four records for the RCA label each year. It visited hundreds of American towns and cities, and toured Europe, South America, and the Soviet Union. As noted, it toured the Bach *B Minor Mass* and *St. John Passion*, as well as Handel's *Messiah*, and the Mozart *Requiem*, with full orchestras—astonishing accomplishments physically and logistically, to say nothing of musically.

There is no doubt that, for Shaw, personally, the peak of the Robert Shaw Chorale's existence was the choir's tour of Russia. Shaw said so many times.

The group had already toured in Europe (in 1956), but this was different. For one thing, this was 1962, the time of the Cuban Missile Crisis and the high point of U.S.–Soviet tensions. For another, neither the Russians nor the U.S. State Department had much initial enthusiasm for a touring choir.

Not much was expected of a Robert Shaw Chorale tour of Russia. Shaw was told this.

Nevertheless, the Chorale was booked for Russia: 11 cities and 30 concerts in six weeks. The group also did four concerts in Yugoslavia and six in West Berlin on the way.

There were three basic Robert Shaw Chorale programs for the Russia tour. But the group adapted to different venues and mixed and matched various parts of programs for concerts that might include everything from sixteenth-century madrigals to the American spiritual, "Dry Bones," which brought down the house in Moscow. (Supposedly, Shaw was handed a note before another concert some days later, which read, "Dear Mr. Shou. Very ask you perform Negro sperichuelle 'Decay bone.' Very ask you please").[30] In any case, the first basic program was a traditional classical concert—a Schubert Mass, some Renaissance material, hymns, and spirituals at the end. The second was a program of mostly modern composers, with spirituals as encores, which later formed the core of one of the Chorale's best LPs: *The Robert Shaw Chorale on Tour*—with selections from Debussy, Ravel, Ives, and the Schoenberg *Friede auf Erden*. But it was the third concert program that caused the most reaction: the Bach *Mass in B Minor*, which Shaw had been advised was not the wisest choice for audiences in the U.S.S.R. That advice, indeed all of the conventional wisdom surrounding the tour, turned out to be wrong. Though the Chorale was dubbed "a sleeper act" by the Department of State, the Chorale's tour of Russia was a sensation. The sleeper awoke. And the "hit" was Bach's Mass. Audiences would remain in the halls after the concerts, often for up to an hour, and often on their feet. Soviet Radio broadcast this American touring choir and orchestra's performance of Bach's lifework—a "reactionary" piece of Western religious music, according to Soviet orthodoxy—not only in its entirety, but including 10 minutes of applause at the end. Shaw recalled leaving the stage in Moscow after many, many encores, then dressing and returning to look out on the house one last time. To his amazement, most of the audience was still in

30 Mussulman, p. 154.

the theater, some 30 minutes after the conclusion of the concert. They were standing in silence. In Leningrad, several hundred people stood in line all night to get coupons from a government bureau that would entitle them to *again* stand in line the following day to try to get actual tickets. The tickets were for standing room only. According to Shaw (in one of his letters to one of his choruses), the Leningrad audience's reaction "easily surpassed the Moscow demonstration of our opening week." Also, according to Shaw, the Leningrad concert coincided with President Kennedy's decision to blockade Cuba. Shaw was advised that there could be anti-American demonstrations that night. Not only did that not happen, but the Chorale was showered with affection.

The audience reaction to the Chorale was like this everywhere the group went in Russia and, more important from Shaw's point of view, the reaction to the Mass, which they performed 10 times while in the country, was sometimes near pandemonium. In the city of Lvov, a riot broke out when several hundred people, unable to get tickets, knocked down the door and pushed their way in to an already full concert hall to hear the Mass.

Shaw liked to tell a story of a conversation he had with the group's tour guide, tutor, and guardian angel, an old man named Petrov. According to Shaw, in his last conversation with Petrov on the way to the Moscow airport, Shaw asked why the response of the Russians had been so tumultuous. The old man's first response was that the American visitors may have underestimated their audience. But then he went on to say, in words that sound awfully like Shaw himself talking: "I was with you in every audience, you know. And it never failed; within three minutes after you had begun to sing, people forgot that you were Americans or performers, and that they were in a concert hall. They were simply hearing, *Kyrie eleison,* 'Lord our God have mercy,' or *Dona nobis pacem*, 'Give us peace.' It was like one heart talking to another heart—or more like Bach's heart talking to all of us."[31]

Shaw also said that, for many years, Russian musicians would come up to him after this or that concert in the United States and say that the Chorale

31 Mussulman, p. 155.

had struck a blow for artistic freedom in the former U.S.S.R. One musician told Shaw, "You have no idea how those concerts changed the musical life of our country."

It all sounds a bit fantastic, and no doubt Shaw engaged in some hyperbole and self-mythologizing as the years piled up. But there is also no doubt that the "sleeper act" rocked Russia. The Robert Shaw Chorale tour made international news. *The New York Times* ran a page-one story about the Chorale's first triumphant concert in Moscow and the *New York Herald Tribune* ran an editorial. *Newsweek* weighed in with a report. The *Tribune* headline was, "The Night Moscow Listened." It is evident that Shaw had gotten away with doing something that would have normally been ideologically unacceptable. Not only did the choir perform Bach's Mass, and *Friede auf Erden* by a decadent composer, but most of the music, being choral music, was sacred music—the Schubert Mass, parts of the Mozart *Vespers* and, of course, the spirituals, in an ostensibly godless regime. Moreover, aside from the Mass, the spirituals were the biggest crowd pleasers. The *New York World Telegram* wrote: "The tour was a musical, diplomatic, and spiritual triumph almost without parallel in our time."[32]

Shaw could probably not have pulled all this off if his intent had been to advertise America, or to promote Christianity. He cared only about bringing the music to the Russian people. Certainly he could not have pulled it off had he not possessed his naïve but unshakable belief in music's power.

There had never been such a musical group as the Robert Shaw Chorale, and there is no such group today. There has never been a group that attempted such programs, such tours, or perhaps achieved as much popular success with music of such seriousness and high purpose. When Shaw shut down the Chorale, the general sense among those involved was that it was

32 Shaw papers.

too soon. But in reality, it is amazing that Shaw sustained it for so long with so much touring and recording. Choirs today, professional as well as amateur and scholastic, do brief tours. Choirs from Oxford and Cambridge, the Yale Glee Club, and many American university choirs, may tour for one week a year. Philippe Herreweghe, Helmuth Rilling, and John Eliot Gardiner, three European conductors of great eminence, all record often. Herreweghe and Rilling tour extensively—but not constantly. The Shaw Chorale was an aberration. It is almost impossible to imagine a commercially popular American conductor of today taking a professional choir on a tour of America with the *Mass in B Minor.*

The Robert Shaw Chorale, at its peak, was a "crossover" musical commodity in the best sense. It enjoyed popularity akin, perhaps, to James Galway, or the Three Tenors, or the Eroica Trio today. Shaw was a recording "star." The Chorale was a household name, and was even featured in a "Peanuts" comic strip.

The Collegiate Chorale had a slogan, printed on posters and press releases: "This shall be for music . . . these songs for love of singing." Shaw took it absolutely seriously. The music, and only the music, mattered. He claimed that his Russian friend, Petrov, told another Russian, after watching Shaw and his choir set up a hall for a concert, "If this man cares as much about the music as he does the risers, this concert will be different."

But for all the popularity of the Chorale, Shaw would not dumb down or pander. And though he sold many records for RCA, he would not sell himself. Moreover, if anything, Shaw became more uncompromising as he aged. Indeed the process of aging for Shaw, musically and personally, was one of progressive clarification and refinement. He was a guileless human being in many ways, one who was almost compelled to act on his beliefs and say only what he really thought. He took the Creeds of Christian churches at face value, for example, and he therefore found he could not say them. Shaw wanted music to be pure—the incarnation of the creators, and perhaps also the creator's spirit—not a product to be consumed.

By the mid to late 1960s, Shaw's longstanding distaste for anything "popular" had only grown more acute. And this meant he was losing interest in his most famous creation—the Robert Shaw Chorale. It was complicated. As a melodist, he actually loved Kern, Gershwin, even Rogers and Hammerstein. But he loathed the commercialization and trivialization of music. And he'd come to agree with Charles Ives—that, in music, familiarity breeds complacency and even contempt. Hence, he began to be repelled by some of the music RCA and the public expected of him—the Glee Club and folk material. And his interest in sacred music and contemporary composition was deepening and becoming less compromising. The spiritual, on the other hand, remained close to his heart, always, and he never stopped performing spirituals. Black music was born of suffering, after all, and this aspect of art spoke to him, be it in Beethoven or the music of slaves. Shaw *always* intuitively connected suffering with art. Now he was outgrowing the audience he had built: a sort of middlebrow audience. He was all for the middlebrow, if it meant a larger audience for good music, but his own core interests were always in sacred music and music that seemed to him sacred. He now found he had no tolerance for show tunes or "Polly-Wolly-Doodle." And he felt more at home in long musical forms and with the orchestra. So rather than be trapped by his own success, he disbanded the Chorale. He walked away. Partly, it had to do with his audience and his recording career. If he could have recorded only the Bach Passions and cantatas and the modern works of Stravinsky and Poulenc, Shaw might well have kept the group together in some form. But he knew the public and the record company wanted a certain amount of pop from the Chorale, and Shaw had always given it. The only way out was to disband. Alas, the Chorale had become a kind of musical prison cell to him. And he wanted release. Ironically, Shaw recorded far more Bach with the Chorale and RCA than he did in his second recording career with Telarc. With Telarc he recorded only the *Mass in B Minor*—his third recording of that work—and the *Magnificat*.

By 1965 and 1966, Shaw's interest in his own creation was waning. And partly it had to do with Shaw, the man. He was not, by nature, middlebrow himself. He was the highest of highbrows, and the lowest of lowbrows. But he was not a "Time/Life" sort of fellow. Shaw might quote the King James Bible or something he read on a bathroom wall. He was unlikely to quote Rev. Peale or Dale Carnegie.

Finally, by this time Shaw had also developed a parallel career as a symphonic conductor, and this was where his focus was now aimed. He had been conducting orchestras for 20 years by then and he had been with the Cleveland Orchestra since 1957. He had moved into orchestral work as his primary path of musical exploration.

The last Robert Shaw Chorale recording was of Irish folk songs, issued in 1967, and Shaw pretty much turned the whole project over to Alice Parker, his long-time co-arranger. One story has it that on one particular day, he simply handed Parker the baton and walked out of the recording session, never to return. (Parker does not remember it that way. Rather, she recalls a lessening of overall interest and increasing reliance upon her.) But Shaw had definitely "moved on" mentally. By that time Shaw had landed the Atlanta job and was thinking about what he would do with the Atlanta Symphony Orchestra. There is no reason the Chorale could not have existed alongside the ASO, as it had alongside the Cleveland job. But he was going to give Atlanta what he'd not given Cleveland—full service of his time and self.

Shaw conducted the Collegiate Chorale from 1941 until 1954.

He conducted the Robert Shaw Chorale from 1947/48 to 1968.

He now embarked on his third major pastorate.

Economics was also a factor in the demise of the Robert Shaw Chorale. One might think constant touring and recording had made Shaw a rich man. Not so. He was in the habit of subsidizing his dreams with his own earnings. Shaw would use his profits to hire more musicians for a given performance or tour, to send a musician with whom he was associated to Marlboro or

Tanglewood on "scholarship," or to commission a new work. There was never, in the life of the Chorale, a time when such needs did not exist. This was how Shaw always operated, before and after the Robert Shaw Chorale. "Look, this is the only way I know to make the kind of music I believe in with the kind of people I believe in for the kind of audience I believe in," he said.[33] In 1952, for example, Shaw canceled part of a choral masterworks series he had set up in New York because he had already lost $40,000 of his own funds on the venture. His manager and his wife both raised their voices. In 1956, he added a workshop to the San Diego Symphony summer series. He financed it himself. In fact, by the time he had drawn up all his plans and negotiated a budget with the symphony and San Diego State University, it was clear that his San Diego job was actually going to cost him money that year. He went ahead with his plans anyway. When, in the 1990s, he lost funding for the choral music festival he had established in France, he and his wife Caroline paid for the whole thing—room board and musical support for 40 singers—themselves. (This terrified the second Mrs. Shaw. She wondered if they would be on the hook every year.) Shaw never thought twice about such things. He was happy to pay for the music he wanted to make. He felt art *ought* to cost, in all senses of the word. And Shaw always wanted better singers, better instruments, better players. But this approach partly explains why the highly successful Robert Shaw Chorale, recording phenomenon and a household name, was never truly a profitable venture. By the late 1960s, their tours were no longer viable in economic terms. It had become too expensive to move that many musicians around that constantly—as it would be today.

Shaw did not publicize his generosity; indeed, he went out of his way to hide it. And in a real sense, it was not altruism. When he wanted to do something, or re-do something, and there was no other money, he did not want to delay or dither, so he paid to get what he wanted. When he wished to replace a singer or cancel a recording for which singers had already been engaged, which he rarely but occasionally did, he willingly paid from his

33 Mussulman, p. 105.

own pocket. Make lots of money, the better to live well, he felt. But more important, make lots of money in order to do the music that you want to do. In his later life, perhaps nothing gave him as much satisfaction as his annual week-long workshops at Carnegie Hall. Once as they were preparing to go to New York for one of these workshops, he asked Nola Frink, "Do I get paid for this?" "Yes," she replied, "and very handsomely, too." Shaw was amazed, and shook his head in a sort of "I'll be darned" way.

Shaw always used his capital—moral, musical, and financial—to get the music he sought and the instruments he needed: the choir being his most important instrument. At any given point in his life, Shaw usually had at least two choirs to direct, one large and one small. But by the end of the 1960s, the Robert Shaw Chorale was too expensive an instrument and he craved another anyway.

But none of it had to do with making a living, or a fortune, or for that matter becoming established as a legend. It had to do with growth and passion. Shaw's musical life was marked and divided by a series of mentors—Toscanini, George Szell, and Julius Herford—and by a series of growth spurts, often caused by self-administered blunt-force trauma.

All of the musicians Shaw respected most did the same thing he did: they suffered, or so Shaw believed. Hindemith, Pablo Casals, and Rudolf Serkin had all taken risks in order to grow—they left the safe and known material that they had conquered behind and moved into uncharted waters. That is what Shaw wanted to do by 1967 and 1968. He didn't want another gold record with the Chorale, or another successful tour and another collection of rave reviews. He wanted to be music director of a major American orchestra. That was the only way to deepen his musicianship. He knew that to become a truly great musician, he had to move beyond the choral corner, even if it would forever remain his home base. He had to learn and conduct all the Beethoven and Brahms symphonies, and all of Hindemith's eccentric concertos, and not only the song forms of Ned Rorem or Poulenc, but also their larger works. He had to do this to achieve fluency in the language of the composers he loved. He knew it would be difficult, and that he would often be miserable. One of the lines he often repeated in those speeches he gave about music, art, meaning, and worship was this one: "Mystery and sensitivity to pain are irreducible conditions of worship." Worship? When Shaw spoke of music, he inevitably spoke of worship.

CHAPTER 14

RCA—The First Recording Career

Shaw began to record with RCA in 1944—as chorusmaster for the recording of Broadway's *Carmen Jones*. In 1945, he made his first recording as leader—*Six Chansons*, by Paul Hindemith. His choir was then called the "Victor Chorale." Shaw made a recording, as narrator, of A. A. Milne's *In Which a House Is Built at Pooh Corner* that same year, and he made his first Christmas album that year. According to Shaw, his mother sang on that album.[34] By 1946, he was recording the Bach *Magnificat* and the *Christ lag in Todesbanden*, as well as an album of Bach arias with Marian Anderson. By 1947, he was making his first recording of the Bach *Mass in B Minor* and the Brahms *Ein Deutsches Requiem*—a landmark recording because no professional conductor had yet recorded the work in the United States.

Commercially speaking, the Chorale's tours supported the records and the records promoted the tours. Shaw's artistic ambition then was large, as it always was, but also naïve. He later said that had he fully understood how much he did not know at that stage of his life, he would never have undertaken to record some of the works he recorded. He recorded Bach *Cantatas No. 4* and *No. 140* in 1946, for example, when he was still relatively

34 At least one of his sisters, possibly both, may have also sung on the first Christmas record. Memories differ on this. Florence Kopleff believed no family members were on that recording.

new to Bach. He made early recordings of the Bach *Aus der Tiefe* and *Jesu Meine Freude* (in 1949)—two works he held in such awe that he dares not to record them in later years. And there was the first (of three) Shaw recording of the mighty Bach Mass. Shaw did not look back on this period with any particular pride. "Oh Lord, I was dumb . . . My God, I was green." When someone raised the matter of his 1950 recording of the *St. John Passion*, and the possibility of reissuing it, he was dismissive, saying, "I was a *child*." He said he doubted the recording would be of any value to contemporary students of music. But Shaw wasn't "a child" in 1950. He was 34 when he made the *St. John* recording. What he was really saying, perhaps, was that his understanding of music, choral techniques, Bach, or all of the above, was childish at that point in his life. And compared to his later life, and his later performances of these pieces, of course, it was. When he made his early Bach recordings, Shaw had barely begun to develop, with Herford, his ideas about Bach phrasing. The only really worthy early Shaw Bach recordings, Shaw felt, were the ones he made with the baritone Mack Harrell. Bach *Cantatas No. 56* and *No. 82* were issued by RCA in 1958. This was the same year he issued new recordings of *Jesu, Meine Freude* and *Christ lag in Todesbanden.* (These 1958 Bach recordings might well be greeted by choral CD-buyers with enthusiasm today.) Shaw was recording a great deal in the very early days, and no one stopped him from recording Bach. But certainly these early recordings show that he did not "discover" the monumental classical works, or even orchestral conducting, in mid-career. It was actually his pop career that was brief, except that he continued to record Broadway and other accessible material for RCA Victor into the 1960s. His performances were overwhelmingly of classical material. In the very early days of his career, Shaw made his living and his name in radio, just as he would later make his living as an orchestral conductor, but his deepest affections were remarkably consistent. They were for the sacred choral works.

There wasn't much tension as to musical taste or interest within Shaw. He never much liked the lighter fare and eventually refused to do it at all. But there was *always* a tension with Victor. The record company tended to want at least a somewhat commercial product and Shaw tended to want art. They began with opposite sensibilities, and both sides continued to move apart from the other—to opposite polarities. But it took years for the hardening of positions to occur. Shaw was willing to accommodate and so was the company for most of the years they were together, and they forged an agreeable and remarkably productive partnership of almost 25 years, making multiple recordings most of those years. Shaw and Victor came to an understanding: For every one record they made together that Shaw wanted, he would record two or three commercial LPs (more or less) that Victor wanted. Toward the end of the relationship, RCA management wanted more pop and Shaw had less and less patience for anything that smacked of pop, or Broadway, or what he thought was in bad taste. But for more than two decades, they co-existed happily.

Shaw did not deny that the record company's position was reasonable. To record a Bach *St. John Passion* was expensive and such a record was considered unlikely to sell in large commercial quantities. The Chorale brought RCA surefire dollars when it did a recording of Broadway hits or Christmas carols. Once, in later years, while having a drink with a friend in his study, Shaw pulled out five or six of his albums from the 1950s. "This, this, and this, and this," he said, "they were all so I could do this," and he pulled out the record jacket of the Bach *Mass in B Minor* (1960 version).

The year he recorded the *B Minor*, for example, Shaw also made a popular record of sea shanties and an LP of songs from Victor Herbert operettas.

Shaw was not exactly ashamed of records like *The Many Moods of Christmas* or *This Is My Country* or *Yours Is My Heart Alone*, and he prepared for these records as thoroughly as he prepared for a recording of Brahms or Schubert. He was the same musical perfectionist he rehearsed the national anthem as when he rehearsed a Bach cantata. But he regarded his commercial records as ways to pay his freight, and he simply became less and less patient with spending his time on that sort of music and less and less willing to expend his energy on it. Still, these recordings did make it possible for him to record Bach's *Aus der Tiefe* or the *St. John Passion* or Stravinsky's

Symphony of Psalms. Ironically, listening in later years, Shaw felt that the Robert Shaw Chorale often sounded better on the lighter albums.

Sometimes Shaw improved upon his high-art to folk-pop ratio. In 1958, he made the two Bach recordings previously noted. He also made *The Stephen Foster Song Book* and *On Stage with Robert Shaw* that year—fine records. But, increasingly, not the kind of recording Shaw wanted to do.

The management of RCA and Shaw were on two planets at times, with Shaw casting himself in the role of purist and his nemesis (or nemeses) as philistines. (A similar dynamic occurred with Shaw and various Atlanta Symphony boards and board members years later.) The tension increased as the years passed, and Shaw grew ever more severe musically. But as Shaw saw it, it was RCA that was changing—becoming more commercially minded. Consider the following exchange of letters.

In late September of 1958, Richard Mohr, musical director of Red Seal Recording at RCA, wrote to Shaw with a request Shaw found both bizarre and infuriating:

> *Dear Bob,*
>
> *Would you be interested in recording an album for release in 1961 tentatively titled* The War Between the States? *I understand from Alan this would be a choral treatment of Union as well as Confederate war songs, and songs typical of the period, and that the 1961 release would commemorate the 1861 firing on Fort Sumter.*[35]

Mohr reviewed other possible Shaw/RCA recordings then on the front or back burner. These were a mix: the Bach *Christmas Oratorio*, which did not happen; a recording of songs from *The Music Man* and *My Fair Lady*, which did not happen (though in 1958 Shaw did make *On Stage with Robert Shaw*, which included Gershwin, Rogers, Porter, and Kern, and in 1965 he made *The Robert Shaw Chorale on Broadway*); a recording of operatic choruses, which was made in 1959; the Brahms *Liebeslieder Waltzes*, which eventually

35 Shaw papers.

did happen, but later, in 1965. Most tantalizing was a final paragraph in which Mohr said that RCA was querying the Boston Symphony Orchestra about a recording of the Stravinsky *Symphony of Psalms*, to be paired with either the Haydn *Symphony No. 104* or the Hindemith *Mathis der Mahler*. That recording, very sadly, was never made. Shaw never recorded the Hindemith piece, which he conducted a number of times, and which he loved. One wonders what killed this project. This letter was roughly a year after Shaw went to the Cleveland Orchestra. Did he have a crisis of confidence and decide he was not ready? Did George Szell somehow discourage the project? (*He* perhaps did not think Shaw was ready to make that recording in 1958.) Did RCA manipulate Shaw, or the situation? For the material the company wanted to record generally got done eventually, and in some form. Shaw had many more ideas for classical recordings than were realized. And Shaw would be recording glee club and folk and pop choral material for another 10 years, whereas he would make only a few more recordings of serious classical choral works with large instrumental forces in the remaining years of his career at RCA. He did make his great 1960 recording of the *Mass in B Minor* (perhaps his finest recording), and the *Symphony of Psalms* paired with the Poulenc *Gloria* with the Victor orchestra (1964), as well as a Vivaldi album—*Chamber Mass* and *Gloria* (1965). And he did record Handel's *Messiah* with RCA (1966). The Bach, Stravinsky, and Handel records all won Grammies. But RCA, mostly, was pushing Shaw toward more accessible works and he made many more of those records. The ratio was now more like four to one. Two "pops" recordings that Shaw thought corny but most musicians nevertheless thought very well done were *The Many Moods of Christmas*, orchestrated by Robert Russell Bennett, and *This Is My Country* (1962)—patriotic songs, service songs and, yes, some songs of the Confederacy and Union. These are big albums, with big forces. They are fun and still sound splendid. But both are a long way from *Mathis der Mahler.*

Here is Shaw's response to Mohr's original idea for a recording celebrating the war of the states:

Dear Richard,

Your projected album, The War Between the States, *must be equally as couth as a belch during communion. I understand the necessity of keeping up with the Columbias, and I have nothing against the repertoire, but there certainly must be a less grotesque way to market such a commodity. One might, for instance, call it "Our own 100 years war."*

As noted, Shaw did some of the repertoire on *This Is My Country*, but it was released as a celebration of patriotism, rather than civil war. And even then Shaw was doubtless unhappy. At the end of his letter, Shaw wrote something fascinating to his RCA colleagues: "If I am able to make a pleasant severance here (Cleveland), you very likely will have me on your hands year round beginning August or September, 1959." Of course, there was no such severance. Shaw stayed in Cleveland another nine years. But this is perhaps an early hint at how severe the strains were between Shaw and George Szell. Would he have made more of his kind of recordings if he'd had more time to devote to recording? Perhaps.

Three years later, Shaw would send out an even more adamant howl. To D. D. Slick of RCA he wrote:

Dear Danny,

I have your letter of March 24 together with your corporate recommendations for recording this summer. I use 'corporate' because I am sure neither of us some years back would consider making an album called I Believe, *which has in it the musical and religious shit which was the original presentation. It is an incredibly pompous title, and, when coupled with music of this stature, it belittles the whole inhuman race.*

The album Glee Club Favorites *is not a bad idea, though it occurs to me that a better repertoire could be built by consulting 25 years of Yale Glee Club programs or the programs of the University Glee Club of New York—the adult post-college singing and drinking society, which certainly must have had in its repertoire in the last 20 years everything nostalgic.*

My 'Encore' album would have in it the Gale Kubik things, two or three Liebeslieder Waltzes, *the* Echo Song *of de Lassus,* Fa Una Canzona *of Vecchi, some Negro spirituals, perhaps even one of the Debussy or Ravel chansons, or the Hindemith* Since All Is Passing. *I am sure Alice Parker would have some good suggestions as to what are, or could be considered, encores of the Robert Shaw Chorale. In this regard it is interesting to read the last paragraph of the Frankenstein review of our concert in San Francisco: 'A program as beautifully chosen as this is seldom to be found on the circuit of commercial concert giving. The payoff came with the encores, a considerable number of them Negro spirituals and other folk songs, sung in arrangements of unrelieved vulgarity. They drew lots of applause mingled with the soft splash of the cognoscenti being quietly sick in their hats.'*

As to Songs America Loves Best *would you consider the title* Once in the Dear Dead Days? *I have nothing in principle against 75 percent of the repertoire except the ungodly presumption of the title. This is material which in sensitive, isolated instances could be beautifully effective—in, for instance the encore situation—but to make a meal out of it is certainly indigestible.*

I assume you will be counting on recording at least a few minutes of my repertoire this summer. I am counting on the Singet dem Herrn *and the Carissimi* Jephthah.

I hope you get a chance to lay out this repertoire which you sent me on your desk all in one lump. What you are proposing in the name of Victor is a sort of musical-o-moral suicide.

I was pretty serious in my language to Alan the other day about the promotion which I feel that Wagner was receiving for his records as against that which I was receiving from Victor. If this is Victor's answer, fuck it.

Bob[36]

Quite a letter.

And the reference to "my repertoire" is interesting.

The *Singet* and the *Jephthah* were *not* recorded.

Shaw's disgust at being pigeonholed, contained, and marketed as a Robert Shaw he does not wish to be—lightweight—is palpable. His revulsion at musical bad taste and, further, the demeaning of his art is manifest. Shaw even tells his record company to consult his associate, Alice Parker, about what an album of Robert Shaw encores might contain. When presented with an approach to and understanding of choral music that seemed to him cheap and banal, his rage is barely contained. He then invokes a critic who calls such an approach nauseating. He calls RCA's proposed repertoire musical and moral suicide. And he reminds Mr. Slick not only that they made better records in the past, but of Robert Shaw's *actual* repertoire at that point in his life.

And what was his actual repertoire at this time? Shaw was doing *Jephthah* on tour at that point and sometimes *Singet*. Both went in and out of various programs. Shaw wanted to record them. He wasn't doing much pop or folk or glee club material on the road, except in the infamous encores. And he never made this recording—*Jephthah* and *Singet dem Herrn*—for Telarc in his later years either. It is a pity. For only a year prior he had made his vivid and majestic recording of the Bach *Mass in B Minor*. Shaw's understanding

36 Shaw papers.

of Bach was mature by this time. The 1960 recording is so clear, precise, and passionate that one longs to hear his mature *Singet*. Alas, it was not to be.

The paths of Shaw and his record company were diverging. RCA was moving in a more commercial direction. The Robert Shaw Chorale was doing the most high-minded and exquisite of programs in its history, but only on the road. It was doing middlebrow and glee club material on records. Arguably, the record-buying public never heard the best of the mature Robert Shaw Chorale. For Shaw, all this was terribly painful. RCA was winning more of the battles now: patriotic tunes, yes; but *Singet dem Herrn*, no.

Shaw would record Handel's *Messiah* in 1966. It was to be the last victory of his RCA years. He would make his renouncement of both the Chorale and RCA a year later. It is hard to recall, now, how clean, lean, robust, and startling this recording was at the time. In its way, it seems as new today as the *B Minor* recording. It was a *radical* recording—opening minds and stunning many a listener and musician. For American choral conductors of a certain generation, this recording was, perhaps, the one that, more than any other, gave them a whole new concept of choral singing and, for that matter, Handel. People had simply not heard an athletic and airborne Handel, especially in this piece.

Three other serious recordings of this final Shaw period with RCA are also very fine: the Vivaldi *Gloria* and *Chamber Mass*, 1965; the Britten *Ceremony of Carols* and *Rejoice in the Lamb*, 1963; and, at long last, after many years of lobbying and venting, in 1964, the Stravinsky *Symphony of Psalms*.

Though many of the later Robert Shaw Chorale pop or semi-pop records between 1958 and 1967 were splendid—*Sea Shanties* comes to mind—they did not fully engage Shaw's imagination.

When he disbanded the Chorale, Shaw was frustrated with George Szell, frustrated with RCA, and frustrated with himself—with what he felt was a lack of growth and a continual lack of mastery of the orchestra. Shaw now wanted to begin anew; turn the page. He wanted to work on big canvases, but somewhat out of the limelight. That is precisely the opportunity that his move to Atlanta in 1967 afforded.

After ending things with RCA, Shaw would not make a recording for eight years. This was a Christmas recording. He would not make a recording purely for orchestra, with the ASO, until the Stravinsky *Firebird Suite* in 1977. That was his debut with Telarc records.

The conflict between lighter and heavier fare dogged Shaw through much of his career. It existed, to a lesser extent, on tour. Shaw wanted to do passions and oratorios, Renaissance and Baroque *a cappella* material, as well as the art songs and other compositions of modern composers. Agents and promoters and bookers tended to want glee club and folk programs. Shaw claimed that when he first proposed an American tour of the Bach *Mass in B Minor,* the reaction was laughter.

But in the case of the tour-booking agents, more often than not, Shaw prevailed. He generally won fights over programming with bookers, agents and, later, the Atlanta Symphony board and management. But with record companies he could not always prevail. Even in his later collaboration with Telarc, he did not always get what he wanted.

Still, the RCA legacy is impressive. And it is interesting that he did so much Bach while at RCA. The great scholar and conductor Alfred Mann believed Shaw's second *Mass in B Minor* recording to be Shaw's single most important achievement. Bringing the work to a wide public, with a truly Bachian sound, Mann thought, was a noble, almost miraculous, thing that only Robert Shaw could have done.[37] But the recording is an accomplishment in a purely performance sense as well. Shaw and his forces seem to defy gravity. The sound is luminous.

With RCA, Shaw did what no one had thought of doing. He made those very early recordings of the Mozart *Requiem* (1950), Bach cantatas (1946), the Brahms *German Requiem* (1947), and the aforementioned Bach *Passion According to St. John* (1950). He introduced American record-buying audiences to Britten, Poulenc, and Bartók. It took nerve, fervor, and perhaps a certain naïveté.

And, for the first twelve years or so, the Shaw-RCA Victor partnership worked handsomely. It was later that things changed. For the last eight years, the marriage was strained. There probably was no single moment when Shaw's relationship with RCA finally broke down. But when a relationship became painful, or broken in Shaw's mind, he tended to close the door and move on. This happened in his emotional life—with his mother, with his sister Holly, and with his first wife Maxine. And it happened later in his professional life with George Szell. But if there was a season when Shaw began to close the door on RCA, it might have been 1966/67. Shaw wanted to record the Haydn *Creation* with RCA that year. RCA said it would be too costly. The company wanted an album of Irish songs. They got it, but it was the *last* recording RCA got from Shaw.

RCA deserves enormous credit, nonetheless, for allowing Shaw to record the *St. John*, and the Brahms, and the Bach Mass (twice)—and this in the era of Eisenhower, Joe McCarthy, and the *Man in the Gray Flannel Suit*. The first great burst of intellectual growth in Robert Shaw's life, which occurred from roughly 1948 to 1956 (more or less the Herford period), surely did not coincide with an intellectual and artistic blooming in America. Fred Waring was probably closer to the artistic mainstream of the day. Shaw always pushed the boundaries, and he was ahead of his public, and his own abilities, in the RCA years. But for a time, RCA let him have the reins, and some amazing things resulted.

37 Burris-Mann interviews.

If the Chorale and RCA had Shaw in one kind of box, the critics had him in another. The success of the Chorale, and its success with popular material, identified Shaw, until rather late in his life, as "middlebrow" and, thus, not on a level with conductors like Eugene Ormandy or even, say, George Solti, who was of Shaw's own generation. Smoke from radio's "Chesterfield Hour" seemed to hang over him no matter how difficult or noble his musical endeavors. This showed a lack of knowledge of Shaw's work, of course, to say nothing of his approach to music, but reputations are just that—inflated hearsay and gossip. The middlebrow view of Shaw was never accurate. He knew how to do Glee Club and Broadway music, and do it well. But it was never, even early in his career, all of what he did or what he cared most about. To be sure, Shaw did far more of the lighter material with RCA than he wanted to do. Much more. But at the same time he did as much challenging and difficult material, modern and classical, as anyone working in music. He had to do both to satisfy his public and pay the bills on the one hand and satisfy his own soul on the other. His solution was simply to double his output.

His RCA career—though it included a recording of the Handel *Messiah* that knocked American musicians on their ears, and though it included one of the great Bach recordings of all time, both of which were giant steps toward proper historical understanding and performance—was still somehow thought of by many as predominantly pop-ish, Glee Club-ish, and thus lighter fare.

Few critics or orchestra managers seemed to notice that Shaw had, for example, been one of the first American conductors to champion Béla Bartók. Shaw worked on his own translation of the *Cantata Profana*, with the help of knowledgeable scholars, for the first U.S. performance. And his head was often buried in Bach scholarship or his latest Passion translation.[38]

Shaw was a bit stigmatized by his early work with Waring and then some of the RCA recordings. The middlebrow aura dogged Shaw a bit, as it did Arthur Fiedler, and as with Fiedler, quite unfairly. Shaw did not package himself as such, but the core and focus of his work was as highbrow as it gets. Certainly his repertoire, from season to season, was as difficult as any in music. (Not for nothing did the Robert Shaw Chorale patrons include Ives and Toscanini). So Shaw waited a long time to be elevated to icon status. But this was perfectly fine with Shaw, mired as he was in the bog of his own sense of inadequacy. In fact, it gave him a degree of effacement from the cold light of fame.

Certainly, there were things Shaw did less well than others, as is true of any conductor, and as he was the first to point out. But even allowing that Shaw was something of a specialist, as is also true of any conductor, and even allowing that he was tentative with some works and some orchestras, it seems bizarre, given the range of his work, that he was for so long, and to some extent still is, ghettoized as "the choral guy," the old "radio guy," the "Christmas guy," or a "middlebrow musician."

Interestingly, Shaw was quite indifferent to his reputation. He didn't think of himself as being on a par with Ormandy, never mind Szell, and if "middlebrow" meant "accessible," that was fine. "I am a *part* of the great unwashed," he said. And even though he spent so much of his career trying to get out of the choral conductor ghetto, and trying to master the orchestra, his late-life one-liner was that he'd been dropped into a pigeonhole "big enough to get lost in."

38 Yet, to this day, a music fan goes into a large record store in New York (if one can still be found) and sees a section marked "Conductors," and does not see Shaw's name among them. One finds his recorded work in the "Choral" section, or by composer. Indeed, orchestral management in America did not begin to think of Shaw as a "first-tier" orchestral conductor until very late in his life (though he'd run his own orchestra for 22 years and had been George Szell's deputy in Cleveland for 11 years before that). Shaw didn't get credit for the depth of his musical seriousness until his later years, and perhaps not enough then, but it mattered little to him. If he seemed more the musical everyman than, say, a Solti, that made it easier to bring an uninitiated music lover to Johann Sebastian Bach.

Something else was at work in Shaw's management of his career and his fame. To say Shaw was ambivalent about the "maestro" title is to engage in massive understatement. He generally scoffed at "maestro" status for himself, and for a long time forbade anyone to call him that to his face. He thought of himself as a *maestro-not*—more often a craftsman than a true artist. Shaw was profoundly uncomfortable with pretension and airs of any kind. Moreover, he simply felt unworthy. He did not believe he was good enough for the music he was performing. He doubted anyone was. But he believed he was less up to it than most, at least in his formative years, which, in a sense, ran into his sixties. He could not relax and enjoy praise or fame until the end of his life. Mostly, he tried to push it away. He hated criticism, but he hated praise even more. Only in his eighth decade did he sometimes allow himself to think he wasn't so bad.

Indeed, being "Robert Shaw" often embarrassed him, though he enjoyed the possibilities afforded by fame.

He did like speaking and preaching. This came easier to him than music. And this actually contributed to the middlebrow image. "Maestros" who cultivate an air of mystery and distance do not give speeches to Rotary clubs.

Yet, his temperament and yearning were profound and deeply artistic. He was both an aristocrat (of taste, talent, and dedication) and a radical democrat. He wanted to bring the Mozart *Requiem* and the Bach *B Minor Mass* to the "unwashed," *and* he wanted to bring them first-rate, stately performances, not dumbed-down or "good enough" versions.

For years he declined many, if not most, press interviews and profiles, and grumbled about the ones he granted. (He usually enjoyed them once he did them. It was a chance to preach and teach.) Generally, he professed the wish to be left alone in some little corner of the world, or his study at home, to do his work—to analyze and mark scores, the better to prepare his forces in rehearsal, and finally release the work in performance. In Shaw's mind, a true incarnation of a piece of music allowed him, as the conductor, to become transparent. Many famous people want more fame. They cannot get enough. Part of Shaw hated fame, especially in his youth. As he aged, he found that he liked parts of it, mostly for the perks—money to use for more music and good hotel rooms, restaurants, and airplane seats. But he had no ambition to be on the cover of *Time* or be thought Number One.

Still, his artistic *ambitions* were always immense. In the Robert Shaw Chorale heyday, if he was not touring a Bach *Passion*, the *Messiah*, or the Mozart *Requiem*, the program was, as Shaw said, typically a Haydn or Mozart Mass; some Renaissance and/or Baroque music; four or five pieces by moderns like Hindemith, Britten, and Ives; and *then* spirituals. They were incredibly long programs. And they were incredibly demanding—for everyone: musicians *and* audience.

What Shaw expected of the Robert Shaw Chorale and its audience was often thought, at first blush, rather daft back then. Today such ambitions for a touring choir would be laughed at and dismissed. There were three tours of the Bach *Mass in B Minor* (in the United States, the U.S.S.R., and Latin America); three tours of the Mozart *Requiem;* a tour of the Handel *Messiah;* and a tour of the Bach *St. John Passion*—all with full orchestras, and most in mid-sized cities where they were performed in school auditoriums and gyms. These were often three-hour programs, with music spanning the sixteenth to twentieth centuries. Who else would have attempted such things? On the podium, according to critic Michael Steinberg, the Shaw of the early years was a performer—and a charismatic one. "He was a showman." In the early days, Shaw himself might sing "If I Got My Ticket"—the showstopper. "But," said Steinberg, "the late Shaw—the one I saw 40 years later—wanted to *disappear* on the podium. He wanted to be invisible, irrelevant to the audience—inside the music."[39]

Again, Shaw's desire was not so much to interpret as to re-create the composition and call forth the composer. Shaw eventually became a "learned

39 Burris-Steinberg interview.

musician," in the sense that Bach's biographer, Christoph Wolff, applies the term. Though a performer by choice and a craftsman by necessity, Shaw was essentially scholarly and reverential. Music, he felt, should point to that other invisible life—sacred, mystical, eternal.

Shaw had rejected the religion of his father and mother. But he still needed a faith of his own. Each time he performed a great work, he approached the task with awe and devotion. As the years accumulated, his awe and devotion deepened.

Music was, for Shaw, holiness, wholeness, his Christian, and humanist, and pantheist, and universal church. The arts were his theology. Choral musicians were his denomination. (He was, as we shall see, enormously pastoral when he felt he needed to be, or when someone was sick, broke, or troubled enough to get his attention.) Great works were his holy texts. The podium was his pulpit. The stage was his altar, which is why he arranged it and rearranged it so carefully for every performance.

Each performance was sacrament.

Broadway material "did not feed him," as he said so often. He doubted it could feed anyone. He doubted it could point to that other life. That is why Shaw became so angry with RCA when they wanted him to do pap, or to saccharinize simple, honest music.

None of this theologizing of music, or little of it, was done consciously. It was simply Shaw's nature and upbringing reapplied. And it didn't keep him from being enormously bawdy and, in younger years, self-indulgent and self-destructive.

Shaw knew how to entertain. He came from church music and popular music, and the necessity of both to persuade. He understood the showbiz aspects of music very well. He could "sell it." He was also a superb musical dramatist and was keenly aware of how to accentuate the emotional and the dramatic contours of the music of Brahms, or Verdi, for example. But as he aged, he grew more and more impatient with the entertainment aspects of music. He wanted the music to sell itself—for the listener to meet the composer face to face. He hated the notion of music as background or muscle-relaxer or romantic mood-enhancer. (He was forever amused by a letter writer who informed him that he had tried to use the Robert Shaw Chorale's most romantic Broadway LP as a mild aphrodisiac, but the mood was shattered by the choir bursting into "Wintergreen for President.") Mind you, the mature Shaw was a very pragmatic musician, well aware of what halls and orchestras cost, how singers scrap for a living, and what audiences might or might not respond to. But he always wanted to *teach* the audience, challenge it, and lift it, as he had lifted himself, to music of great imagination and moral seriousness. To do that he had to set his vanity, and to the extent possible his ego, aside so the music could come through unscathed and uninterpreted. He wanted to be part of the greening of great music in America, and the enlightenment and ennoblement of musicians and listeners. And it happened. One reason Shaw was so wary of the entertainment impulse is that he was a natural entertainer. It came easily to him. Art came hard. Michael Steinberg was right. Shaw *willed* Shaw the showman to disappear, and indeed, even the famous conductor to disappear. He wished the *composer* to descend like the Holy Spirit. If Robert Shaw could just get out of the way and "be a clear glass," this Eucharistic reappearance might be possible.

CHAPTER 15

"32 Tempestuous Years"

"You will be forced to share a room with me."

Those are the words Maxine Shaw wrote to her husband Robert as she briefed him, by letter, on the arrangements she had made for their daughter's marriage.

Robert and Maxine Shaw's marriage was never right. They fell into it because they were each other's "firsts," and desire made them blind to their differences. Perhaps people thought less about marital compatibility in 1939. Certainly people were less inclined to seek escape in the case of gross incompatibility. Divorce was a sign of failure. It was letting down the kids. Robert and Maxine stayed together, more or less (mostly less), as man and wife for three decades. If they began as two planets spinning in different orbits, they only spun further apart, out of each other's pull. Certainly they always loved each other on some level, but they could barely function together, never mind live together, and in spite of intermittent efforts to revive or improve the marriage, they only grew more miserable as a couple.

Shaw effectively opted out of his marriage fairly early on—becoming a husband in name only. He was an unfaithful husband and absentee father. He was seldom at home and he made little room in his life for his family, no matter where he was. Later he got a second chance—a second marriage that was an opportunity to redeem himself and a chance to succeed as a father. But he failed his first family miserably. And he knew it.

Children in a failed marriage suffer in all sorts of ways, of course, but one way they suffer is that their loss is final. They may find love as adults, but they will never have another opportunity to be loved by a mother or a father. Dad can try being a dad again—with new progeny. No one gets to try being a son or daughter again. No child in a broken family will be awarded a second, intact, family. Shaw never quite forgave himself for the failure of his first marriage. Nor did his first children forgive him. In time, he moved on and found peace and happiness. He may have granted himself a larger measure of forgiveness than his first three children felt he deserved.

But Shaw changed. His heart changed. His behavior changed. His second marriage succeeded, in some measure, because Shaw so desperately wanted it to succeed and was so determined, this time, to get it right. His second family was a success for other reasons as well: the marriage to Caroline Hitz was such a natural and seemingly destined partnership. He and Caroline were in sync from the start. And she was willing to be subsumed into his life and career. He and Maxine had always been in conflict. Shaw was repulsed by conflict and retreated from it. His first marriage failed, in part, because he could not bear constant battle. At some point, he closed the door. Even when he was present with the family, which was seldom, he wasn't there.

Shaw did not become a saint, or someone other than himself, when he remarried. He was still impatient, grouchy, nonverbal at the dinner table when the day's work had not gone well. But he was a virtual teddy bear compared to the first Shaw as husband and father.

One major change, with his second family, was that he was "there"—physically—for Thomas Shaw, Alex Hitz, and their mother, Caroline Shaw. Shaw was busy, but mostly around—in town. His work was not on the road but in Atlanta where he lived. Shaw traveled some and went on mini or regional tours with the Atlanta Symphony Orchestra. But he was not gone for extended periods. He was not out late at night or all night. His office was at home. When he was married to Maxine, "work" was often on a bus, or on a stage, or in a coffee shop, or at a bar. His family home, in Scarsdale, might as well have been a million miles away.

The second time around, Shaw was a resident father and husband, and he worked at it. Indeed, he enjoyed it. He cared enough to enjoy it. He once, famously, held up an ASO board meeting while he finished building a go-cart with his son Thomas.

Nothing like this happened the first time around.

In the first Shaw household, the children were to be seen and not heard. Occasionally, when home, Shaw would remember them and commandeer one of the boys to chop wood with him, or he would enlist their assistance in making the one dish he could cook—a kind of American chop suey. But mostly he was in Manhattan or on the road. And when he was at home, he worked, and was "not to be disturbed." He worked in the dining room of the house—on a card table—and the children were not to make noise if they were in the house. Later he built an office on the side porch and worked there. But it was clear to the children that the best thing they could do when father was working was to vacate the premises.

Shaw was faithful to his second wife. He had not been faithful to Maxine, and worse, he made no great effort to camouflage his dalliances. Women threw themselves at the young Shaw, particularly singers. And Shaw liked it. He took full advantage. He was a preacher's kid and he had married the first woman with whom he had a serious and intimate relationship. It was *fun* being a bad boy. Meanwhile, while he was on the road, Maxine would hold down the fort and write him frequent letters about his children and his home.

Robert would, in late years, ascribe the failure of his marriage to Maxine Farley to his own lack of maturity and stability—100 percent. That was not wrong. It is not the whole story either. In the early years of the marriage, when it first went awry, Shaw was not mature or stable. He was peripatetic. He was working at night. He was thinking only of the music he wanted to make. He was not a pipe-and-slippers type and could not have been building his career as he was if he had been. But he also did not want to be home—

any time. He liked the nightlife and travel, and he did not want to be in Scarsdale with Maxine, for there would be a fight. And Shaw tried to avoid fights, perhaps because he knew his own temper to be fierce, and he feared it.

He left all the arrangements of home and children to Maxine, and showed little interest in her updates of family progress and problems. From his mid-20s to his mid-30s, Shaw lived for his work, himself, and his pleasure. Although he had a wife, he lived as a single man, with a virtually unlimited capacity for drink and extramarital affairs. He was involved with a succession of women, including Maureen O'Sullivan, the first Jane in the "Tarzan" movies, and the first woman to appear naked—very briefly and furtively—in American movies. O'Sullivan later became known as the mother of Mia Farrow and as a prominent and devout Roman Catholic. Shaw carried on with a succession of women. Generally (as a somewhat sheepish defender said), he was a "one woman" man—that is to say, one "other" woman at a time. Maxine knew of the affairs, indeed she knew many of the women, including a close friend. Shaw's behavior was abominable. His excuse, and the excuse made for him by friends, was that many of these women were the aggressors, which was a convenient and complimentary excuse, and had the virtue of being true. Shaw had a kind of rock star persona in those days. But the serial and flagrant nature of his adultery was shockingly indifferent and brutal. He didn't seem much troubled that he had humiliated his wife—until later years added perspective. The strange thing—the contradiction that he did not see in himself, or perhaps simply could not help—was that he didn't mind moralizing about music, "humanism," and music's power to unite and heal, while he was simultaneously breaking his marriage vows and his wife's heart.

There were, perhaps, two important women in Shaw's life B.C. (before Caroline Hitz Shaw). One was a singer named Gretchen. Caroline was *the* love of Robert Shaw's life. But before her, Gretchen was certainly an important love/romance. Theirs was an intense, passionate, and somewhat sophomoric affair. But, for whatever reason, Shaw was unwilling to end his unhappy marriage for her. (He apparently told her that if he ever *did* end his marriage to Maxine, he would marry her. At least that is how she remembered things.)

The second woman was Edna Lea Burrus, who was Shaw's assistant at the Cleveland Orchestra, and would follow Shaw to Atlanta. Theirs was not a passionate affair. She was more in the mold of worshiper, enabler, and servant. She was, in some ways, what Shaw felt a wife should be. Eddie cared for Shaw's every need and was on call 24 hours a day, 7 days a week. When Shaw finally did divorce Maxine and married Caroline, Eddie was banished—to retirement and another state.

Part of the problem with Maxine was that she was not worshipful. Not at all. She was competent (she managed one of the Robert Shaw Chorale tours when the road manager quit suddenly) and independent and, Shaw told his son Thomas and friends in later years, *cold*. That was Robert's rap on Maxine: she was cold. Indeed, even her defenders and admirers tend to describe her as "austere," "arch," and "sardonic."

The pose Maxine tended to strike was one of detached, if not cynical, sophistication. She wished to be droll, but some thought she could not quite carry it off. Perhaps the pose was defensive. She often had a brittleness that Robert could not bear—what seemed to him a core of hardness. She would sometimes make her husband return expensive gifts he had purchased for her, saying they could not afford them. (He was big on fur coats.) Maxine also had a limited enthusiasm for bearing children, and in one instance when she thought she might be pregnant a fourth time, suggested the possibility of abortion, which shocked Robert. To him, a softness, a warmth that Maxine could not manufacture, was the essence of femininity. To him, motherhood was the essence of womanhood (a degree of servitude was, as well). Still, *he* wasn't going to spend any significant time raising his children.

On one occasion, Shaw was preparing for an evening concert at Carnegie Hall and was about to dispatch a factotum to the lobby with tickets for

Maxine. The messenger did not know Mrs. Shaw and asked her husband how he might recognize her. Shaw's reply was, "Look for a handsome woman, exceedingly well-dressed, and standing in two buckets of ice."

This was Shaw's devastatingly frank, and final, assessment of his wife, delivered, on this occasion, to a stranger.

Maxine possessed a sort of small-town haughtiness. She had, some who knew her thought, an exaggerated sense of her own importance and cleverness. She was an attractive woman and she did know how to dress and present herself. She was not intimidated by Paul Hindemith or George Szell or Thornton Wilder. And perhaps Shaw thought she should be. (*He* was.) She had opinions on topics ranging from the politics of the day, to the theater, to music, and she had no particular expertise in any of those things. Some of Shaw's friends, Thornton Wilder for one, liked her very much. Wilder saw strength and native savvy and cunning. He thought her plucky. But some of Shaw's family saw Maxine as rather small.

Maxine was working in a department store in New York when she and Shaw met. Perhaps the archness was a matter of self-protection and preservation. Perhaps it grew out of a certain naïveté. (After all, if one is not intimidated by someone like George Szell, one may not have a sufficient understanding of one's own limitations.) She was an innocent, and haughty, too. Maybe that's another reason Wilder liked her. Maxine was a modestly wealthy Midwestern girl. Her father was a politically connected car dealer from Indiana. She was an elegant retail clerk—the sort of character one might find in a Claire Booth Luce play. Maxine had a Barbara Stanwick demeanor, which masked her lack of in-depth knowledge about much of anything. She was smart and classy, but actually knew little about music or poetry—her husband's two favorite subjects. Harrison (Buzz) Price—Anne's husband, Shaw's half-Jewish brother-in-law—detected a not-so-mild anti-Semitism in Maxine. She occasionally would make remarks like, "Don't you think so-and-so is too *obviously* Jewish?" Her stance, Price said, was, "It's not a problem for me, but it is a problem for others." On the other hand, she detested the racism she believed she perceived in Atlanta in her short residency there.

Interestingly, Shaw's other sister, Holly, was a great friend to Maxine. The two were close. But then Holly was a great friend to virtually every living being she encountered, the more so if the other living being needed help.

Maxine needed a lot of help. She was a proud and pathetic cucquean—in over her head with most of her husband's friends, and pitied by the friends who were close. She was raising three children, essentially on her own. She and her husband had loved each other once. And they stayed together more than thirty years. So some of that love must have remained. But they fought, and there was a dreadful, omnipresent tension when they were together, followed by Robert's retreat into solitude and de facto bachelorhood. Maxine didn't, and couldn't, get much help from Robert. At times she was forced to enlist the aid of Eddie Burrus, the woman Maxine knew was her husband's mistress, just to reach him.

For months at a time Maxine's only contact with her husband was receiving his dirty shirts in the mail, taking them to the local Chinese laundry to be done, and mailing them back. She wrote to him with each package, usually with businesslike reports about the children, the house, and their summer home in Nantucket—"Sevendoors"—a place they both loved. (It was one of the few things they agreed upon.) Occasionally, the letters contained plaintive and pitiful pleas for some kind of fresh start and relief from the alienation and hostility that plagued them. Shaw didn't know how to respond. Bach's Passions could make him weep. Lincoln's *Second Inaugural Address* could, too. A direct emotional appeal from his estranged wife sent him into further retreat.

Maxine was bright enough to know that Robert thought she was an over-reacher. What must it have been like to live with that awareness? And to live with Robert's blatant (even for the time) male chauvinism—his needs, his demands, his ups and downs—to top off his physical and emotional absence?

Even after he reined in his late-night drinking and carousing, Shaw did not come home to Maxine. He went to Cleveland to work in 1957. He adopted a much quieter lifestyle. Initially, Maxine stayed in New York. When she moved to Cleveland with the children, things of course got worse. She moved away again. She began to spend more time in Nantucket.

When Shaw was first appointed music director of the Atlanta Symphony Orchestra, Maxine moved to Atlanta. She was a good sport and willing to try again. She was still Mrs. Robert Shaw. But she loathed Atlanta and looked down upon it even when she was trying to do the right thing and play her part. She urged the ASO Women's Guild to integrate racially, and Robert was proud of that. But there were more and more conversationless dinners in which intermediaries were told to arrange the next day with the spouse at the end of the table. Not long after the move to Atlanta, Maxine repaired to Nantucket a final time, never to return. The two were divorced a few years later, just weeks before Robert remarried.

The scars remained.

Shaw told this story, which, in his mind, epitomized Maxine's persona: Following his first purely symphonic concert with the Cleveland Orchestra, which had been a source of enormous anxiety for Shaw (and which was, the next day, positively reviewed in the Cleveland papers), Shaw returned home. Maxine, though still living in New York, was in Cleveland for the concert. "Well," she said, "You're certainly no George Szell."

He told that story many years after it happened.

He sometimes prefaced it with, "My wife of 32 tempestuous years said to me." And he laughed his trademark cackle. He had absorbed Maxine's comment into his repertoire of self-deprecation. But the line was stored on the dark side of his emotional hard drive, along with "It should have been you."

On at least one occasion, he prefaced this story with a story of George Szell saying to him, "Bob, you had no right to that fine performance after the *miserable* rehearsals you conducted all week." One of the last times he told the Maxine story, he told his chorus how much his second wife Caroline had enjoyed the previous day's dress rehearsal. "Caroline," he said, "always says the right thing."

Truth to tell, Maxine did not know music well enough to compare Shaw's conducting with Szell's. (Perhaps 3 percent of concertgoers would.) Since her review obviously wasn't part of a constructive conversation about music, it must have been intended, on some level, as a hit. Was the remark only a passing moment of malice? Or did it manifest Maxine's long-simmering anger at being left out of her husband's world?

Shaw knew full well that Maxine was no great critic of music. (For that matter, Caroline wasn't, either.) He might have shaken it off on that basis. He didn't. Shaw needed a certain response from the women in his life. And when he got otherwise, it was hard to forget.

Sometimes Shaw called the entire first family "cold"—his wife *and* children, as opposed to only Maxine. This shocks. Shaw apparently held his children to a higher standard than he held himself to at that time.

Why on earth did Robert and Maxine remain married for so long, when both were in such pain?

Maybe it was simply what you did then.

Maybe they did it "for sake of the children."

Maybe they loved each other—still, even amid constant fights and disappointments and misunderstandings.

Maxine was there with Robert in the early years—doing office work for the Collegiate Chorale and the Robert Shaw Chorale. But after the children started to come, she stayed with them. She lost touch with him—with what was then the only part of his life that was real to him: music. But the problem was more than that, deeper than that. Something also went terribly wrong *between* these two people. And whatever went wrong was exacerbated by words and events like the Szell remark, or a returned gift, or Maxine's lack of enthusiasm for child bearing. At some point, Shaw closed the door on Maxine. He wrote her off. Her archness only increased the expanse between them. His cheating surely increased her pain and tendency to lash out. There was no way for the two of them to recover their innocent beginnings or to get to higher ground.

Shaw would eventually find a measure of personal happiness and stability in his life, and in the institution of marriage, but not until his second time around.

Meanwhile, Maxine Shaw—very much alone—had raised the Shaw's three children: Thad, Peter, and Johanna.

What about those children? How did they feel about a man whose unique position in American music was partly defined by a sort of call to virtue and who was seen by many who worked with him as a deeply sensitive, deeply good man?

They saw him differently, to be sure. They saw him as a father who'd abandoned them. They found the canonization of their father by much of the outside world tough to take. And when he succeeded at marriage and fatherhood on his second try, and this fact was widely celebrated by Shaw and his friends, it nauseated them.

Thad was the youngest. In his late adolescence, Shaw brought him to live in Atlanta for awhile. Justifying the move, Shaw told a friend, "He is much man and I love him very much." Shaw wasn't playing the father when he wrote those words. He didn't do that sort of thing. He did love and admire Thad. But it was too late to truly be a dad, and tragically, one of the things the father taught the son was how to drink hard liquor. Shaw was deeply ashamed of this.

The wounds Shaw perpetrated on his first three children by his absenteeism and distance never healed. The combination of this distance from his children, his neglect and mistreatment of their mother, and his public image as classical music's premier humanist were too much to bear in youth and too much to fully forgive in adulthood.

For his part, Shaw never sought pardon, only a measure of forgiveness. Late in life he began to truly comprehend what he had done. It brought him enormous grief. He knew his alienation from his children could not be "fixed." But he hoped for a modicum of reconciliation. He did try to reach out at times. He sent his children greetings and money and good wishes. He tried to see them when he was performing in or near cities where they lived. But it never quite jelled. It was too late.

With Peter, Robert achieved a measure of peace. They had it out one night in a California restaurant—when Peter was a middle-aged man. They made a scene—cleared the place. But they found their way to some sort of honest regret and détente. Robert also greatly admired Peter, as he actually admired all three children when they were grown. Peter had been a soldier. He had gone to war—a stupid and brutal war (Vietnam). He was an individualist who did his own thinking. He didn't try to sugarcoat their common history. His father respected that.

Perhaps Shaw found reconciliation with Johanna, as well, for she was at his side when Shaw died in New Haven in 1999.

But the agonies of the failed first family were never overcome. And it is hard to see how they could have been. Certainly, Shaw's almost total lack of discretion about his womanizing must have manifested itself at some terrible moment for all three children, and that would be a moment hard to forgive and forget.

One is amazed and disturbed at Shaw's cognitive dissonance during his first marriage. He was a moralist and a preacher by nature. How did he reconcile this with his treatment of his wife and of his children? Politics and the church are, of course, full of moralists who make generous exceptions for themselves. But Shaw was, generally, ruthlessly honest, including with and about himself.

Two other factors certainly added to the hurt of the first Shaw children. One is that Caroline Shaw, once she created a new home and a new private life for Robert, did not want him to have much to do with his old life. The first children didn't have a place in the new portrait. Neither did certain old friends. This did not apply to professional colleagues and associations of a certain stature. Caroline wanted Robert to stay in contact with old New York pals like William Schuman and Rudolf Serkin. But the personal circle, small as it was, was broken up and replaced with her alone. Eddie Burrus was exiled to Florida retirement. Florence Kopleff was marginalized—not invited to parties or dinners at the Shaw home. (This was a person whose association with Robert as singer, soloist, soul mate, personal assistant, and friend predated Caroline by roughly 30 years.) Caroline was also this way about the Shaw children. She didn't insult or attack them; she didn't overtly deny their existence. But they could not belong in Shaw's new life unless either Caroline or Shaw himself made a place for them. And realistically, only Caroline could have done that. Shaw was a man who, when working, sometimes had to be reminded that he had children. In his second new family, he was reminded daily of Caroline's son, his stepson, Alex, and of their own son, Thomas. Johanna, Peter, and Thad? Not so much. And they got the message. They felt they were second-class citizens when their father was married to their mother. They felt they were non-persons after he remarried—forgotten details. Shaw had *not* forgotten them. But he never had much time for any family member because he worked constantly, and there was not much occasion to see people other than at a dinner or a reception after a concert. And by then, Shaw was spent. Shaw's really close associations were not only through music, but *in* music—in the making of it. Caroline, very wisely (though she, like Maxine, could not read music), sang in Shaw's choruses. She knew that was where Shaw truly lived and it was the place to be with him.

In a way, Shaw's domestic success in his later life was seen as a second rejection by the first Shaw children. If someone has failed to behave as if he loved you, but displays great love for someone who takes your place, that's a bitter blow.

Shaw said that his failure as a father to Johanna, Peter, and Thad Shaw was *the* great tragedy of his life. Nola Frink once asked him, "Why *did* you drink so much in the old days?" "Because," he said, "I was a failure." And he explained that he meant, primarily, as a husband and father. But the failure was deeper than a role. He had failed as a human being. Shaw's sense of what it meant to be a man and to be a musician were always connected. Until he could be a better musician, *and* a better man, he would be a failure in his own eyes.

The young, philandering, and heavy-drinking Shaw, who was also hyperactive professionally, was certainly running away from himself. That was not Maxine's responsibility, whatever her faults. But the middle-aged Shaw was not at peace with himself, either. He knew his marriage had failed, but he hadn't the will to end it. He was still on the run. He was trying to hold down his Cleveland duties, keep the Robert Shaw Chorale on the road, and keep recording. And he was not particularly happy with the result in any sphere. If only he could study more, he said again and again. Amid Shaw's artistic ambition, insecurity, and motion, the lives of his children were obscured.

The tragedy was that it was evident to anyone to whom he spoke about them that Robert did love Johanna, Thad, and Peter. Like a lot of men of his generation, his pride was clearly displayed for everyone but those who should have seen it. He could tell others. He could not tell the three, directly.

Robert and Maxine were not meant to be coupled. They cared for each other. They created a family and shared its history and memory, but they could not connect. Or be at peace with each other.

Maxine Shaw, in Florence Kopleff's apt and stately phrase, "made an estate" for Robert Shaw. She managed his finances, his schedule, his laundry, his home. She raised his first three children. She gave him structure and support, though not, sadly, the emotional support he craved. His early career would not have been possible without her. And his children Johanna, Peter, and Thad would not have existed without her.

Shaw did receive a measure of forgiveness from Maxine. On his 80th birthday, she wrote to him. It was short, simple, heartfelt, and restrained. She congratulated him on his life and work, and wished him well. It was a remarkable gesture of grace and abiding affection. For the children, forgiveness was tougher. He agreed with them.

CHAPTER 16

Demons

Throughout his life, Shaw had bouts of acute stage fright, though he was usually fine once on the podium. This abated in his later years. But he never overcame the feeling of being ill prepared for his chosen work—the feeling that he was, in his oft-repeated phrase, "playing catch up." This was more than insecurity. This was a feeling of insufficiency. He never got over feeling badly about his remedial keyboard skills. They improved because he practiced. But he said his poor keyboard skills were his biggest deficiency and he insisted that one of the best preparations for conducting was mastery of the piano—the conductor can hear the whole piece, all of the notes written by the composer, he said. Shaw had to sing through each part or rely on an accompanist to play the score for him. The slowness of his study process maddened him.

Shaw was intimidated by orchestras for roughly the first twenty years he conducted orchestras. Gradually, that intimidation subsided somewhat but he experienced some degree of trepidation until the end of his days. Shaw believed he knew the voice, it felt like home to him. He knew, even before he really understood the structure of music, how to shape the voice. But who was he to tell fine instrumentalists how to play? He felt particularly unsteadied and cornered by big and famous orchestras. But he forced himself to do what he saw as his job. He would insist upon using *his* edits of the score. (But if he particularly liked and trusted the concertmaster, he would invite collaboration, editorial changes, even a small degree of improvisation.) He would call attention to "undisciplined playing." By undisciplined playing he meant many things—poor intonation, lack of rhythmic precision and unification, lack of attention to edits. His directions were made in a gentlemanly, even courtly fashion, but firmly. The mature Shaw often felt he detected deep flaws among American orchestras when he guest conducted: lack of commitment and passion, lack of close listening, and lack of musical close-knittedness. But he chose not to be vocal or outspoken about this. While he found technical deficiency in some singers, he found the problem among many players to be an absence of sufficient affection—a loss of their original ardor for music. Thus a player could become, Shaw felt, more enamored of his own cleverness or proficiency than awed by a composer's work. That hardening of the heart, he believed, led to indifferent preparation and listless execution.

The big change in Shaw's confidence level with the orchestra came from working with and shaping the Atlanta Symphony Orchestra. He learned a lot of music in his years with George Szell and the Cleveland Orchestra. But he did not find grace in conducting until he'd led his own forces in Atlanta for several years. He may have actually *lost* confidence in Cleveland. Atlanta was the church *he* built. And the players were his flock—indeed, his extended family. The Atlanta choristers were another story. They were flock, but not family. He was more involved on a micro level musically with chorus members, but was not generally involved personally.

Shaw never fully overcame his abiding sense of insufficiency with the orchestra. He seldom "let go" in a purely symphonic piece. He felt he could do adequately, and sometimes even well, with an orchestra, but he could not mold and refine the sound as he could with the chorus, which was once his stated goal in music. But it is also true that when he had the *two*, orchestra and chorus together, he *could almost* meet his own standard. When he conducted the orchestra in a choral/symphonic work, the fear drained off rapidly and Shaw's innate, natural musicality took over. The presence of the chorus rooted him. His instrument was on the stage. Indeed, it is in this corner of music—orchestra and chorus together—that Shaw is perhaps without peer. For while there were others who could do much with a small choir or a large chorus, and many who could do more with the orchestra alone, Shaw achieved a unique mastery in the combination of the orchestra and chorus. One watches him on film, conducting the orchestra in the Handel *Messiah* or the Beethoven *Symphony No. 9*, and there is no evidence of nerves or insecurity. He conducts every note for every player and directs the symphony with great fluency. Indeed, according to former Atlanta and Cleveland concertmaster William Preucil, for a certain kind of instrumentalist—perhaps he or she is less jaded, or less technical, and more poetical in nature—Shaw was actually a *preferred* conductor.[40] Instead of terror or intimidation, he offered inspiration and liberation. With the Orchestra of St. Luke's in New York City, a young orchestra with roots in Baroque music, there was the feeling of collaboration and deep respect. Shaw led them with devotion. With the New York Philharmonic, Shaw felt two things: first, many of the players did not wish to listen to him, or *any* conductor; and second, the orchestra was undisciplined. But with St. Luke's, Shaw was like a grandfather at a great holiday feast—instantly in his element, respected, and beloved. Shaw and St. Luke's formed a unique and sustained partnership in the last decade of his life. The Cleveland Orchestra was something of an exception as well because there was so much history between Shaw and the orchestra and so much mutual respect. He could be relaxed and confident with the players when he returned to that orchestra in the 1990s. Even during his tenure there, some Cleveland players, far from seeing his humility as a weakness, loved Shaw for it. Still others preferred playing for Shaw to playing for Szell because, knowing they would never be good enough for Szell, they could relax into the music a bit with Shaw. When Shaw returned to conduct in Cleveland in the 1990s after so many years, the musicians who'd been present in the Shaw-Szell years were amazed at

40 Burris-Preucil interview.

his calm and confidence. "Big-time conductors are supposed to be like lion tamers," said Cleveland Orchestra English horn player Felix Kraus. "Shaw was not like that. He was a colleague, entirely devoted to the music, and asking for our help to serve it."[41]

Insecurity was the father of all of Shaw's demons. It drove his alcoholism and his philandering. He lived with a constant, nagging fear that not only was he inadequate but that he always would be. He might not only fail, but fail to learn. What if he diminished the piece? Or perverted it? Or made it dull? He lived with the fear that he was, at bottom, a fraud no matter how good the reviews were or how hard he tried. He lived with the fear that he would never be fully capable of the work he had chosen.

The life he had been given wasn't handed to him, after all. He sought it and made it. Yes, his life did involve some luck, as he often said. Being brought to New York by Waring was luck. But mostly he made his own luck. Much of his life was a matter of sweat—striving, digging deeper, and creating a distinctive persona for himself. Yet he always felt that it would never be enough. "*Every* performance is a failure," he said.

The secondary looming demon was the bottle. At one or two points in Shaw's life, his drinking problem approached a life-threatening level. There was little doubt that during much of the 1950s and 1960s he was a "functional" alcoholic. He seldom missed a rehearsal, and he could carry on through hangovers: he was incredibly strong, both physically and mentally. Shaw had an enormous physical capacity for alcohol, just as he loved food and was a natural and fierce athlete and lover. But he also drank self-destructively. Lore has it that he drank twelve martinis at an embassy party in Moscow during the Russia tour. (That's very hard to believe, even if it occurred over the course of many hours and the glasses were small.) But as the story goes, Shaw was only somewhat the worse for the wear. (Also hard to believe. This sounds like one of those Shaw stories rooted somewhat loosely in reality.) At any rate, lore from one period in his life tells us about Shaw's reputation in that period. He did drink copiously and maniacally. If

41 Burris–Kraus interview.

he was "with" Dylan Thomas the night the poet drank himself to death, it is an indication of the seriousness of Shaw's own habit. The 1950s pride in alcohol abuse is only slightly less embarrassing than the prevailing attitude toward male sexual conquest in that period. Shaw "got" that as he grew older and was sincerely mortified at his past excesses. He also sometimes said that he never really began to make good music until he'd settled his own psyche and found a way to contain, if not quite manage, his addictions. One reason he pooh-poohed much of his 1950s work is that those were his "drinking days." They were a bit of a blur and there was much pain in those years that he preferred to consign to lost memory. Certainly his own tales of his heavy drinking portrayed Shaw more as a fool than a macho prince. In those wild days, he was seldom, if ever, a falling down drunk, but he was adamant that he would make no decision at night. He knew what his condition and state of mind would be. Nothing of consequence could be decided after supper—a rule he kept throughout his life.

Shaw also smoked through middle age. One day he simply quit. Cold turkey.

Shaw never quit booze entirely, only boozing as an active hobby and off-duty way of life. He limited his intake without becoming a teetotaler. He was quite open and frank about all this, though his honesty sometimes put off some die-hard fans and embarrassed family and protectors.

In later life, he mostly drank beer, perhaps a good wine with dinner, and occasionally after a quite successful concert, some vodka. But sometimes during the Christmas season, he got drunk, and was not pleasant. He cursed the holiday and all its pretense of "good will toward men." Astonishingly, Robert Shaw did not much like Christmas. He loved his concerts, and the theology he had contrived for the Christmas concerts (protesting all the way that this Jesus stuff was not his bag). And he loved the *idea* of Christmas, as both a Christian and a humanist holiday. But he hated Christmas as he found it—the hype and commercialism. A shopping mall nativity, like televangelism or any sort of pious pageantry, got under Shaw's skin.

In the hard drinking days, Shaw drank every night, he drank everything he could get his hands on, and he sometimes drank until he was obliterated. The next day, he worked—sweating it out.

Shaw's fear that he was a failure, both as man and musician, and that he was a fraud who might be found out were palpable then. He drank when his marriage was crumbling. He drank when reunited with his wife. He drank after the marriage had finally come apart. He drank heavily in his early career—when the career seemed to him so far ahead of his aptitude and knowledge. He drank on the road. He drank heavily in the early days in Atlanta. He was lonely then, certainly. He was also a frustrated artist. He was not getting anything like the sound he wanted out of the orchestra *or* the chorus. So he was failing at the thing that defined him. And he was failing now that the big chance had come. Not at fame. He'd had fame for years and retreated from it. The big chance was to make his own instrument—to get the musical product he wanted, on his own, his way. In the early days in Atlanta it seemed to be slipping away. In sum, he drank at all the big moments: good *and* bad.

What makes a man so doubt his own destiny and yet drive himself to fulfill it?

How did Shaw get off that fast track to self-destruction?

The first question is unanswerable. It is the mystery and nobility of Shaw. The second question has an answer: Caroline Sauls Hitz. She believed in him. She was all he wanted a woman to be—all graciousness and warmth. She was all he thought a wife should be—she lived for him and did everything for him. But unlike some of the women he'd more or less appropriated to serve him through the years, Caroline was, as he saw it, his equal intellectually. Indeed, she knew *more* about literature and poetry than he did. She knew infinitely more about the visual arts. She knew about Europe—a place that frightened him in his youth. She could stand up to him, and she did. She married him on the condition that he stop the heavy drinking. He didn't stop drinking entirely; he did stop being a drunk.

But Caroline comes later in the story. She does not appear until 1972. In fact, Shaw actually made much fine music in his wild and dark days. And surely he knew that. But he was not centered, not grounded, as a man; and for Shaw, it was not possible to be a great musician and an indifferent man. He was still far from the human being he wanted to be.

CHAPTER 17

American as Corn

"American as corn." The phrase fit. There was an "aw shucks" quality about Robert Shaw that he never lost. That's something you would not say about other homegrown musical geniuses of America. Bernstein and Aaron Copland were somehow European, almost from the start. Lenny was Byronic—anything but "aw shucks." Shaw was Jimmy Stewart. There was a raw and innocent aspect to him. He never lost his small-town California awe, the demeanor of modesty, his Red Bluffness. It transmogrified from boyish awkwardness (at 30, even 40) to idiosyncratic, stammering wisdom (at 60), to bluntness, clarity, and even (occasionally) confidence (at 80). He mellowed—a little. But he did not soften. His impatience never flagged. There was a reason he was impatient: he was playing "catch up" and could not win. A few of Shaw's friends understood his plight and didn't lie or condescend to him. When William Schuman met him in 1942, Shaw was rehearsing the Collegiate Chorale in a Brahms motet. Schuman had never heard anything quite like that *sound* before. But it was also clear that Shaw had no understanding of counterpoint in Brahms. One of Shaw's favorite quotes about himself came from what Schuman said when reminiscing about those early days: "My God, Bob, you were dumb."

Shaw's compensatory study was endless and neurotic, but essentially self-directed. His auto-didacticism is part of his American-ness. He became something of a self-made musical scholar. Shaw's letters to his choruses are at least 35 percent Music Theory 101 and 102. They were written lectures, designed not only to pass on what he had learned in years of independent study and practice, but also to work through what he knew—for himself, first of all.

"American as corn." Yes: The idealism. The radical democratic sense that art is for all. The all-American mania to build, improve, and perfect. Consuming passion. The love of beautiful objects and people. And justice (or fair play). The obsession with race. Optimism. Drive. Personal wreckage and tragedy—all quintessentially American.

Shaw's inherent and self-imposed modesty also figured in his American-ness. He never quite believed his luck. The "aw shucks" maestro not only put on few airs, he cast them off. He liked the role of *craftsman*, a sort of American "working man" in music. Lenny could pull off wearing a cape. Shaw was most comfortable in his rehearsal blues—blue shirt and matching blue slacks—a working man's clothing. ("At least Caroline got him out of polyester," mused Sylvia McNair.)

But modesty is not the same as simplicity. And modest manners and claims are not the same as modest artistic ambitions. Shaw's intellectual, musical, and spiritual aspirations (as opposed to personal ambitions) were as grand as any dreaming American's. He was classically American in that way, too. What is art, or the artist, without vision? There is nothing modest about the Beethoven *Missa Solemnis*, or the Britten *War Requiem*, or the Bach *Mass in B Minor*, to name three technically, textually, and *theologically* difficult compositions that Shaw championed and devoted himself to mastering. He did not wish the vision to be personalized in his own image, quite the contrary. But the attempt to realize the vision of a Beethoven or a Bach, at the peak of *his* powers, was a reason to get out of bed every day. And it was not a modest ambition.

Shaw's story is an American story, but not a simple American story: more F. Scott Fitzgerald than Horatio Alger. It is appropriate that Shaw's first true nemesis was Norman Vincent Peale—high priest of positive thinking. For Shaw, positive thinking was a contradiction in terms—a way to turn Bach or Brahms into, well, Broadway or the "Hour of Charm."

But like almost every other seemingly apt generalization about Robert Shaw, this one—"American as corn"—is spectacularly true and spectacularly inadequate. To see Shaw as a Huck Finn—homespun and folksy, a native talent who sprang forth from the California soil (Rousseau's American if he had created one)—is to understand a central truth about the man. He did sometimes behave like he'd just gotten off the raft. That was who he was, and who he wanted to be: part of the great unwashed; part of Sandburg's *The People, Yes*. But it is also important to see the work, and the discipline it required to become Robert Shaw, and the growth it entailed. Shaw *also* wanted to be a part of great art and to delve ever deeper into its mystery and its cost.

Somehow, Shaw retained his enthusiasm, his earnestness, his boyishness. But to see him *only* as a simple, humble, self-made, and self-effacing soul would be like seeing the characters in Mark Twain's fiction as Walt Disney people.

Shaw never stopped being a "son of a preacher," an evangelical, a westerner. Had he not been who he was, he could not have reached people as he did. *But* he could not have done what he did had he not outgrown the man he thought he was supposed to be when he went to Pomona College, as well the partying rebel who hated being the son of a preacher.

So, *how* did he grow? Who were his great teachers?

In one sense the answer is perfectly clear: Arturo Toscanini, George Szell, and Julius Herford were the chief ones. Paul Hindemith, Pablo Casals, and

Rudolf Serkin were collaborators who exerted a huge influence and served as mentors and models.

But, in a true sense, Shaw was his own teacher. He was a craftsman who learned by doing. He venerated scholarship, but he grew from the making and remaking.

Eventually, the great composers themselves became his guiding stars. He outgrew or outlived everyone else. Eventually, the works he performed and studied over and over again fed him—as scripture and as sacrament. They formed his values. They informed his heart. These works were not bound to a time, place, or culture, like Shaw's actual teachers. The masterworks at the core of Shaw's career were, to him, endlessly exploitable spiritual resources.

Great music is not limited by the musician's own experience, or even the composer's. A work like Paul Hindemith's *When lilacs last in the dooryard bloom'd* is not a work of personal expression, but an impersonal reflection on the mess of history and the sorrows of human hearts caught up in history. That work is, unexpectedly, an *American* musical classic—a tribute to Franklin Roosevelt and Abraham Lincoln, based on the words of Walt Whitman—and composed by a German neoclassicist. Shaw was its greatest champion. Similarly, Shaw, ever the "golly-gee" kid from San Diego, all but worshiped Bach, Beethoven, and Brahms. The California preacher's son produced landmark recordings of the Verdi *Requiem*, the Bach *Mass in B Minor*, and the Duruflé *Requiem*—works born of traditions utterly foreign to his own and far more ancient and knotted than what he called his "Welch's Grape Juice" Protestant youth.

No artist was more American than Shaw, none was less parochial.

PART TWO

FORMATION

Mystery and sensitivity to pain are the
irreducible conditions for worship.

—Robert Shaw

CHAPTER 18

TOSCANINI: *THE* MAESTRO

Simultaneous with the prime of the Robert Shaw Chorale was the most important collaboration of Shaw's life—with Arturo Toscanini: Shaw was his fair-haired boy. He was not Toscanini's only protégé, but Shaw worked with Toscanini repeatedly, over a long period of time. And his endorsement of the young man was almost unconditional. Shaw said that Toscanini "pulled me up out of popular music and brought me into the classical world." That's not quite true, as we have seen. Almost from the moment he arrived in New York, Shaw knew he wanted more than pop music could offer and he had begun to look for it on his own by the time he commenced working with "*the* maestro" (Shaw's term). But Toscanini did inspire Shaw in a way that no one else ever did. The maestro possessed a combination of high dignity and carnality that seemed to Shaw to embody art. Still, Shaw had only *begun* to imagine music making as art. Toscanini showed it to him as a practical reality.

Shaw began to record with Toscanini in 1948. He had already made his recordings of the Brahms *German Requiem* and the Bach *Mass in B Minor* in 1947. And he had recorded the Beethoven *Ninth Symphony* as chorusmaster for Serge Koussevitzky in 1947. Shaw would not record that piece with Toscanini until 1952. But that recording changed Shaw's life—his musical life and his inner life—and it cemented his bond with the grand old man. In Shaw's mind, he was not truly a serious musician until he worked with Toscanini, perhaps not even until that 1952 *Ninth*. The first time they worked on the piece together was for a live performance; they met to discuss problems and adjustments and *Toscanini* addressed *Shaw* as "Maestro," which made Shaw blush, even decades later.

What did Toscanini impart to Shaw? The first lesson was musical intensity and concentration; the second, Shaw termed "forward motion." He said that Toscanini infused every performance with a forward motion that could not be denied. For Shaw it was a vital principle that music must never be static. Toscanini conducted this way. He created a motion, which became a wave, and stopped only on the final note or chord.

Toscanini also taught Shaw about Verdi and about opera, neither of which Shaw had taken to initially. A romantic by nature, Shaw instead embraced the Baroque and Classical. He distrusted himself. He trusted form. He initially found Verdi, he said, a bit too "show biz" and a bit too inclined to display emotion. Toscanini forced Shaw to look deeper. Shaw came to see the craft in Verdi's music, and also to appreciate the well of emotion. Somehow Verdian melodies, Shaw came to feel, pierced straight to the heart—accessing emotions directly—because of the music's simple honesty and beauty. (Shaw felt the same way about Handel.) Shaw also discovered, to his delight, that Verdi was an anti-clerical, populist democrat.

Toscanini *taught* Shaw, but he did not *instruct* him in didactic fashion. George Szell would do that. Szell would hold forth. And Shaw, who himself loved to teach, was somewhat resistant to Szell. According to Shaw, Toscanini discussed "music" as an abstraction, very little. Almost never. And absolutely never on a grand or philosophic level. His teaching was in the work—the music making itself. Their discussions were pragmatic, having to do with editing, forces, and balance—never vision or theory. When he and Shaw met to consider possible difficulties in the score or upcoming performance, the conference was a brief and to-the-point exercise in problem solving.

Shaw made eleven landmark recordings with Toscanini in the maestro's last active years:

1. Brahms *Gesang der Parzen*
2. Verdi *Aida*
3. Cherubini *Requiem Mass in C Minor*
4. Verdi *Falstaff*
5. Verdi *Manzoni Requiem*
6. Beethoven *Ninth Symphony*
7. Gluck *Orfeo ed Euridice*
8. Beethoven *Missa Solemnis*
9. Verdi *Un Ballo in Maschera*
10. Boito *Mefistofele (Prologue)*
11. Verdi *Te Deum*

All with the NBC orchestra. All with Toscanini conducting.

Shaw also assisted on *Rigoletto* and *Il Trovatore* with conductor Renato Cellini and *Carmen* and *Die Fledermaus* with Fritz Reiner in that time period—1947 to 1955. Shaw provided and prepared the chorus for a lot of opera in those days, with a variety of conductors and soloists. He was himself recording all manner of music in that period, ranging in genre—from an album called *Music of the Sixteenth Century* in 1949, to a folk record called *Sweet and Low* (which also included Schubert songs), to a recording with his Chorale and Margaret Truman, to a *Porgy and Bess* record with Robert Russell Bennett. He did that all in 1950 alone. This was the same year he made his recording of Bach's *Passion According to St. John.* In that year RCA marketed an astounding 15 recordings featuring Robert Shaw, either as principal conductor or as chorusmaster. Shaw was in overdrive. But the opera recordings are fascinating because Shaw was thought in later life to hate opera, or worse, to know nothing about it. Certainly the second contention is untrue. And he didn't dislike opera exactly. He just didn't like it much. Yet, Shaw's collaboration with Toscanini on these operas surely enhanced Shaw's sense of musical drama, and while he never cared much for musical acting, he did have a keen sense of musical drama.

This body of work—eleven recordings, plus the famous live Beethoven *Ninth* performance under Toscanini's tutelage—constituted one of Shaw's sub- or mini-careers. Primarily, he was working with his own chorus for his own concerts and recordings. And he was already hiring and conducting orchestras. But he fit in the Toscanini (and Reiner and Cellini) collaborations as part of his "post-graduate" education. Shaw recognized his luck and treasured, and archived in his memory, every moment with the master. The maestro's influence is directly manifested in Shaw's own recording of the Verdi *Manzoni Requiem* in 1988. This recording is generally thought to be one of Shaw's finest. Indeed it is widely thought to be one of the outstanding recordings of the work.[42]

In the Shaw recording of Verdi's *Requiem*, Shaw's mastery of quiet, slow choral music and his feeling for musical drama came together. And Shaw's ability to command and organize large forces paid off. One member of the Cleveland Orchestra recalled that a Shaw rehearsal for a benefit performance of the Verdi *Requiem*, in 1990, was the most moving experience in his musical life. How so? The player gave an interesting answer: Efficiency. He was astounded by Shaw's command of the material and his mastery of forces in limited rehearsal time. Behaving as a pragmatic craftsman, as Toscanini had taught him, Shaw quickly and unemotionally pulled the many complex strands together. He took hold of the piece, rather than being overwhelmed by it, and thus allowed the piece itself to exert its own natural force. The

42 Listeners overwhelmed by Shaw in concert sometimes felt disappointed by the recorded Shaw. This has generated much debate and discussion among colleagues and fans. Some blame digital sound, others the acoustics at Atlanta's Symphony Hall, which seemed to muffle sound. Some people have criticized Telarc records, Shaw's second recording home, and believe the company produced a distant sound. (But Telarc and Shaw made many fine, unmuffled and immediate-sounding, recordings.) To some degree, according to Robert Woods of Telarc, the quality of a recording is a matter of chance. As with a film that has all the right ingredients—script, actors, directors—yet does not gel. One mitigating factor was Shaw's extreme tidiness and obsession with technical perfection, which recordings sometimes exaggerated. His Telarc Brahms *Requiem* recording with the ASO with particularly fine soloists, Arleen Auger and Richard Stilwell, is an example. Many conductors swear it is "best overall" and in keeping with Brahms's own restraint. But it lets down some listeners. Shaw's perfectionism could create a chilling effect in recording sessions. Some singers swear there were instances when performance grew worse each time he fiddled and tightened and became more evidently unhappy. The opposite occurred on his final recording—the Dvorák *Stabat Mater*. Shaw's delight in discovering the piece, in his singers, in the quality of the orchestra's playing, and in the recording process itself, allowed him to loosen the bolts rather than continually and maniacally tighten them.

Cleveland performance was a fundraiser for an organization seeking nuclear disarmament, and only three hours were available for rehearsal. The Cleveland player said he had never seen such unification of a conductor and a composition. Shaw knew exactly what he wanted and needed to do. (This was the mature Shaw.) He proceeded in "hurry-up offense" mode and whipped together an explosive performance. Yet somehow it was the assured putting-it-together aspect of the entire project that impressed the Cleveland player.[43]

Shaw's approach—detailed attention to organization and extreme attention to musical architecture until, in theory anyway, the composer's language begins to sink in to the musicians' bones—was not so much derived from Toscanini. It was a bit of George Szell, and a bit of Julius Herford, and a lot of Shaw. But love for Verdi and the *Manzoni Requiem* came from Toscanini, undoubtedly inspired, in turn, by direct acquaintance with and access to the composer. Shaw liked to think of himself as once removed from Verdi, via Toscanini, though in *no way* Toscanini's equal as a purveyor of the work. (Suggestions along those lines would likely be met by violent denunciation or laughter.) But Shaw felt comfortable and confident with the piece. He learned it from one who had Verdi in his blood.

Toscanini recorded the *Requiem* for RCA in 1951, with Shaw as his chorusmaster—39 years prior to Shaw's appearance at the benefit performance in Cleveland, and 36 years prior to Shaw's own recording. Toscanini's RCA rendition of the work was one of the handful of recordings Shaw listened to more than once, for reasons other than checking tempo indications.

What Shaw *may* also have inherited from Toscanini, in terms of approach, was a sense of the grandeur of the Verdi *Requiem* and an ability to build the grandeur cumulatively by keeping the composition moving forward in performance.

43 Though Shaw was an accomplished and prolific recording artist, his sense of music, and its execution, was inextricably linked to live performance, just as Glenn Gould, for example, found the recording studio a natural habitat. Shaw could be visceral and "in the moment" in concert. This was not often possible for him when recording. To him, music essentially happened in a time and place, and that moment defies capture. Moreover, a recording is "for the ages," a huge responsibility, especially for a musician like Shaw. The Verdi *Requiem* and the Dvorák recordings are exceptions. They are wonderful because they are more like a Shaw live performance.

According to Robert Woods of Telarc International, Shaw's own recording of the piece at last granted him international stature as a symphonic maestro and helped put Telarc records on the map. And for once, Shaw agreed that his recording was "good." But he felt that accomplishment owed everything to *the* maestro. Shaw often said that as an evangelical Protestant he had simply not understood Verdi's dramatic language or intent until Toscanini opened the door for him. Some listeners and at least one critic—Ted Libbey—feel Shaw was too modest. They have said his Verdi recording is not good, but great, and in some ways even better than Toscanini's.

This is how the Toscanini-Shaw relationship began: In 1945, Shaw was hired to prepare the Collegiate Chorale to sing the final movement of the Beethoven *Symphony No. 9* for a performance with Toscanini. Every performer, including Shaw, was nervous, for they had heard the stories about the great man's rages. But when Toscanini came to hear the choir rehearse a few days before the performance, the maestro had nothing but praise. He listened for a brief time, with Shaw conducting, and then embraced the younger man, telling him, "It's the first time I hear it sung!" Two years later, Shaw began to record with him. Later, Toscanini would say, famously, "In Robert Shaw I have found the conductor I have been looking for." Now what did he mean by that? In biographies and critical works on Toscanini, Shaw is invariably credited with being the maestro's favorite choral man. But Toscanini did not say he had found "the *choral* conductor, or *chorusmaster* I have been looking for." Could Toscanini have meant that he had found the young conductor of the future? Well, he didn't say that either. And we cannot know. But it seems possible, if not probable, that he saw in Shaw more than a choral assistant—that he saw what collaborators of later years saw: an outstanding musician, period. In any event, Toscanini did not dole out praise lightly.

Shaw adopted Toscanini as his role model. Not that he tried to ape or imitate him. Not at all. And not that he tried to duplicate his repertoire. But Shaw did try to learn from and emulate the maestro's concentration, stillness, and intensity on the podium in performance. (The very young Shaw, in contrast to Toscanini and to the mature Shaw, was rather hyper when conducting.) Shaw was moved also by the dignity of Toscanini, who was hardly calm or still in rehearsal. Finally, Shaw admired the conducting economy of Toscanini. He similarly admired this quality in Igor Stravinsky, for whom Shaw prepared the *Symphony of Psalms* for performance—no extra gestures and no excessive ones.

Like almost all of Toscanini's fans at the time, Shaw was taken with the man's zeal and passion. But Shaw felt that Toscanini's contained fervor never led him to self-importance, or self-advertisement, or self-gratification but instead made it possible for him to appeal to a wide audience, transcending class. Toscanini was a communicator; he could transmit the work to an audience.

Perhaps most of all, Shaw was touched by Toscanini's humility before the music. When the two met to go over the score for Beethoven's *Ninth* for the first time, Toscanini told him he had never conducted what he thought to be a successful performance of the work. "Sometimes," he said, "the orchestra is bad. Sometimes the soloists are bad. Often *I* am terrible."

Their backgrounds could not have been more different. But something in Toscanini spoke deeply and directly to Robert Shaw.

One year, on Christmas Eve, Shaw brought members of the Robert Shaw Chorale to Toscanini. Shaw and his forces had just completed a radio broadcast of Christmas music with Guido Cantelli. Shaw arranged with Toscanini's son to have the group stop by the maestro's estate, "Wave Hill," after the show. The maestro had recently ceased to conduct. When the choir arrived, the old man was in his bathrobe watching wrestling on TV. Shaw lined up the singers on a staircase outside Toscanini's den. The song commenced, and when Toscanini emerged, he was in tears. According to

Shaw, the group stayed until 4:00 a.m. and Toscanini spent time with every member of the choir, assuring the singers that he didn't sleep much anyway. (Since Shaw was with Toscanini into the early hours of Christmas morning, Christmas preparations for his own children must have fallen entirely on Maxine.)

Shaw never bragged about the experience or exploited it, but perhaps his closeness to Toscanini has never been fully known. For example, Toscanini brought Shaw and Maxine to his home in Italy one summer. And Shaw told a typical, perfectly formed, and slightly fantastic story about that visit. According to Shaw, Toscanini had his own small island called, of course, Isle Toscanini. His was the only home there—a sort of castle. And an amazing thing happened one night on Isle Toscanini: Shaw and Maxine and Toscanini's daughter and granddaughter took a small rowboat to another island to have a glass of wine. The maestro, who had his evening bowl of soup at 4:30, stayed home. When the rowing party landed at the other island, they were advised that a storm was coming in and they should return immediately. They set out, but were caught in the storm and ran aground on yet a third island. "Then," Shaw recounted, "we made a common decision to try to get home," for Toscanini might "die of worry." It was evidently a terrifying voyage, with night blindness, struggle against the wind and rain, and undisguised fear. As Shaw wrestled with the storm, the Italian women prayed—aloud. Eventually they made it back but only because, Shaw said, Toscanini lit and placed a candle in every window of the villa—hoping to make it visible from the sea and bring the travelers safely home. Shaw recalled that the next morning the maestro consented to be photographed with the Shaws before they departed, something he did not usually allow.

The force and luminosity that Toscanini brought to the podium never left Shaw. He respected George Szell. He loved Toscanini.

In a 1964 *New York Review of Books* essay on the book *This Was Toscanini* by Samuel Antek, B. H. Haggin wrote: ". . . outsiders . . . who reported accurately what they had heard in performances or observed at working rehearsals could not report the experience of sitting in an orchestra and rehearsing or performing under Toscanini." Haggin described Antek as an insider who made "vividly real for us the extraordinary powers with which Toscanini operated; the complete, selfless, and intense dedication to the artistic task he made into a moral quest for truth."

A rehearsal as a moral quest for truth? This is not a usual concept in professional, classical music. And, in a way, it seems a vain absurdity. But it was Toscanini's quest, and it became Shaw's.

Antek speaks of how Toscanini got performances out of musicians that exceeded what they knew to be their capacities. He quotes a wind player who upon hearing himself in recording said, "I don't play that good."

Antek also wrote:

> *When you played with him you felt you were once more an individual, an artist, not a nonentity. This made you bring, to everything you did, everything you played, the same intensity and expressiveness you sought when playing alone. You were once more stimulated, challenged to give your best . . . we played to please the old man, but . . . we were inspired to play and satisfy our highest standards and instincts, in pursuit of our common goal. The terrors and abuses Toscanini hurled at us were accepted and tolerated because they sprang from his own humility, sincerity, and love for the music . . . the performances were ours, not only Toscanini's, for he was but the voice of our own musical consciences. Few musicians ever gave such complete, unswerving dedication to high ideals, and few imbued music-making with such deep emotion, stature, and nobility.*

These words are uncanny, for they apply as precisely to Shaw as to his mentor. Indeed, virtually identical words have been spoken by musicians as diverse as Peter Serkin, Sylvia McNair, Dawn Upshaw, William Preucil, and Jeffrey Kahane, to say nothing of countless players and singers in Cleveland and Atlanta.

Antek's account of Toscanini's accomplishments described Shaw's goal: to allow the musician to be, once more, an individual and an artist, not a cog in a machine. Further, it was Shaw's hope that as a conductor he could be not so much "the leader" as the voice of a collective musical conscience.

Toscanini's gift was not technical, or perhaps even tangible. What made him great was devotion to the music and ability to inspire. The same could be, and often was, said of Shaw—though he obsessed over technical matters.

Players, soloists, and choristers all felt that with Shaw they were at once empowered and swallowed up in something large. Almost all of them say they played, or sang, above their game because Shaw opened the music before them and then stepped aside.

Shaw believed that when Toscanini told him that he had never gotten Beethoven's *Ninth Symphony* absolutely right, the maestro meant it literally. Toscanini was not posturing or speaking hyperbolically. He really meant—*I have never* fully realized this piece. And he surely felt, or so Shaw believed, *no one* could fully realize it.

Fred Scott, a former Atlanta Symphony Orchestra Associate Conductor and later the musical director of Atlanta's resident opera company, said that when Shaw would tell him, as he often did, "I've never done the *St. Matthew Passion* to my own satisfaction," Scott would roll his eyes and think to himself: "Give it up. Learn a new piece." "But eventually," admitted Scott, "it became clear to me that Shaw was being perfectly serious and literal. Shaw truly felt he had never really gotten the piece right, and therefore he had to keep trying."

"*All* performances are failures," quoth Shaw to Peter Serkin.

That doesn't mean that most performances cannot go well technically, do not do credit to the composer, or do not add beauty to the world. It does mean that they never fully realize the piece's own ideal, or even the full human potential of the musicians. Shaw was a perfectionist who scoffed at the notion that any performance could be "too perfect," as some critics said, or even too tidy and clean. But Shaw didn't believe artistic perfection existed (technical perfection, maybe on good days).

Antek revealed that Toscanini would sometimes freeze up in performance. He would lose confidence and drop the reins. Shaw, too, could be thrown off by an error and then bury himself in the score, scarcely looking up. (Some thought this was punishment. He said it was fright—holding on for dear life.)

Toscanini's gestures would become smaller and smaller, less emotive as he aged. But according to many accounts, in rehearsal he could be almost wild. Antek wrote that "the performance was what mattered to the audience," but "Toscanini's greatness for the players was what they felt in him—the unimpeachable honesty and integrity, the warm humanity in his working process, and the tremendous power and incandescence he inspired in them." The *working process* is where the real artist, and the real man, shone through—for Toscanini and for Shaw.

What moved musicians about Toscanini was how hard he worked in rehearsal. So, too, Shaw. What moved musicians about Toscanini was what he did *for the work itself*, not for the audience. The same was true of Shaw.

This was the essence of Shaw's aesthetic: The composer and the composition come first. The performer and the audience second.

Did Shaw learn this from Toscanini? Or was it already in him and thus he was drawn to Toscanini, who affirmed his instinct?

Probably both. This instinct—to place the composer first—was natural to Shaw and the master fed and reinforced it. Certainly, neither man was *indifferent* to the performance or the audience. But the audience and the performance represent the dividend, not the product.

The pianist Peter Serkin, a true artist like his father, loved Shaw. When asked the most revealing thing he knew about Shaw, he answered: "Twelve hours of rehearsal for the Schoenberg piano concerto!"

Most symphony orchestras and symphony music directors would schedule one, maybe two rehearsals perhaps for an hour-and-a-half to two hours for such a work with a visiting soloist. Shaw scheduled five rehearsals. Serkin said Shaw threw himself into this difficult work. When Serkin discovered that Shaw had scheduled so much preparation, he was both stunned and elated and when the work—rehearsal and performance—was over, Shaw, who was thirty-odd years Serkin's senior, said to him, "Peter, I would like to study with you." Serkin was speechless. Shaw as *his* student? He'd been trying to think of a way to ask if he could study with Shaw.[44]

This is the strange, opaque, and deeply felt way that profound musicians connect: They find truth in the seeking of musical fidelity. They find a freedom and timelessness and escape from the ego. They see each other without masks—face to face. They hear the creator's voice. They are within the music together.

Perhaps Shaw could not mold particular orchestral sound the way George Szell or Eugene Ormandy could. Neither could he mold orchestral sound in the same way that he could naturally mold choral sound. (Nor could any orchestral conductor mold choral sound the way Shaw could.) But he could listen and collaborate—a great gift. Shaw's chief talent on the technical end of conducting was perhaps in seeking and achieving balance. As an orchestral leader, it was in editing parts carefully—which he'd partly learned from Szell, though Shaw took it further—and in meshing the orchestral sound with choral and vocal sounds. His ear was so fine that he could continually edit and adjust to achieve his purpose; he took into account the piece, the forces, the hall—not as a dictator from the podium but by calibrating and balancing all musical elements.

But Shaw also had a nontechnical ability akin to his mentor's: the capacity to liberate and inspire musicians—to make them love the music as they did when they first came to music. This rediscovery process could only come from the rehearsal process. Krista Feeney, concertmaster for the Orchestra of St. Luke's, said that Shaw's devotion and enthusiasm were irresistible.

44 Peter Serkin and Shaw had a personal connection going back many years. Serkin remembered traveling to San Diego with his father, Rudolf, when the elder pianist played with Shaw. He claimed Shaw took him to Disneyland, although as Anne Price remembered it, she took the boy there. Peter Serkin recorded both Brahms piano concertos with Shaw, certainly the conductor's finest non-choral work on record.

Musicians could not help but get caught up in it, and pulled up by it. She felt the same sort of unimpeachable integrity and warmth coming from Shaw that musicians felt from Toscanini.

It is usually said that Toscanini designated no musical heirs, except perhaps for Guido Cantelli, who died young in an airplane crash. But Toscanini had *two* protégés. The other was Shaw. Though Shaw never sought to be Toscanini's heir, his ability to inspire musicians to think and feel as individuals and as artists was like Toscanini's.

With a choir, Shaw was the *über* didact. With an orchestra—like his mentor—he led by the force and purity of his love for the music.

An interesting parenthetical: It was commonly noted that as an old man, Toscanini's tempos got faster and faster. Shaw's tempos, as an old man of 79, 80, 81, got slower and slower. "I hate to see the music slip by," Shaw said of the Brahms *Requiem* when he was preparing a round of performances two years before his death.

If Toscanini "lifted" Shaw to a higher level of musicianship, as Shaw claimed, Shaw believed it was his own responsibility to continually educate and challenge himself. He did this in two ways.

First was his repertoire. His repertoire on the road tours with the Robert Shaw Chorale was, as noted, incredibly varied, ambitious, and challenging. For example, he prepared three alternative programs for a tour of South America in 1964. One was the Bach *B Minor Mass*. Another featured pieces by Tomás Luis de Victoria, Heinrich Schütz, Orlando di Lasso, the Schubert *Mass in G*, and ended with Charles Ives. The third included Mozart, Schoenberg, Barber, Copland, Gershwin, and Villa-Lobos.

Why did he take on *so much* and expect *so much* of his musicians and his audience? First, for the same reason that a gourmand, or glutton cannot stop: sheer appetite. Second, for the reason that a teacher tries to cover too much material: the desire to inform and excite, as well as the desire to rediscover and dig deeper. Finally, for the same reason Sartre or Whitman sometimes wrote too many words: urgency. It was a quality he shared with Toscanini. At times, Shaw overdid it. This much music in one night, of such seriousness and variety, was like a feast, followed by dinner, followed by dessert, then a light supper. A human being can only ingest and process so much.

Shaw always did programs of this length, variety, and ambition in the Robert Shaw Chorale years, and his programs with the Atlanta Symphony Orchestra, while not as lengthy and meandering, were no less artistically ambitious.

The second way Shaw pulled himself into the classical world was by beginning to conduct symphony orchestras. At first they were the orchestras he formed for the purpose of accompanying his choirs and doing particular pieces. But in the 1950s he accepted the post of music director in San Diego, and began to guest conduct widely. And of course, in 1957 he accepted the Cleveland post. Why? Why Cleveland? Why then? Well, as Florence Kopleff put it rather economically, "Where else did he have to go?" Especially, once Toscanini had left the scene, it was the only way to grow."

Actually, Shaw had *two* options. He could have chosen opera. After all, he had done extensive opera choral work during the years of his association with Toscanini. He might have gone full-tilt into opera as, for example, James Levine did years later. Or, he could become a conductor of symphony orchestras. Those were the two possibilities if Shaw was to spread his wings and break free of the "choral conductor" cage. Shaw chose the orchestra. It was an interesting, and in some respects, curious choice. Opera would be the more logical leap since it would retain the emphasis on voice and words. And Shaw was obsessed, on every level, by the human voice. He was nearly as transfixed by words. Yet he chose the symphony, he who played no instrument. Indeed, in the early days of his orchestral work, Shaw wrote words into his score to help him visualize the music he needed to hear. There is no certain answer. But perhaps he chose the orchestra, in part, because the orchestral route was harder—the greater challenge. Second, Shaw saw opera as play-acting and symphonic music as closer to poetry. Opera made him uncomfortable. Opera *people* made him uncomfortable. Shaw felt opera was showy, self-regarding, and less intellectually serious than symphonic music. He was suspicious of acting. He loved that in the Bach Passions a singer had to reach into himself to convey words and notes as Truth, whereas in opera, a singer "plays" someone else. Shaw never felt a singer should "play" Jesus in the Passions, he believed the singer should instead "represent" Jesus simply by conveying the Gospel texts, as if "reading the lesson" in church. That is exactly what baritone Mack Harrell did under Shaw's tutoring. Harrell said he tried to sing as if he were opening and reading the Book for the faithful on Sunday, never as if he were Jesus. And Harrell was Shaw's idea of a great singer. Yes, but surely what Harrell did was a form of acting—it was theatrical communication as all fine singing is. Ah, but it was not *play*-acting.

In symphonic music Shaw found a high level of intellectual discipline and moral seriousness that spoke to him and spoke to him in a way he felt opera never could. Shaw also had a practical motive, rooted in craft, for learning to conduct the symphony and acquiring a symphonic repertoire: the invented, internal language of particular composers was of specific interest. He had fallen in love with Beethoven because of the *Ninth* and the *Missa*. He wanted, therefore, to know everything about Beethoven's world. Shaw felt that if he knew the symphonies intimately he could better conduct the *Missa*. The same held true for Brahms. If he wanted to truly master the *German Requiem* he needed to master the part songs, the four symphonies, and the concertos.

It is hard to imagine Shaw happily at work in the world of opera. For one thing, he would have had to fit in. That was not necessary in the choral world because he was able to mold it in his own image. Very soon in his career the choral world became *his* world. The world of opera could not be so easily remade, even if that had been Shaw's intent. But perhaps more to the point, it is a world of both musical and personal flamboyance of a kind that Shaw abhorred. Shaw made one full-blown, late-life attempt at conducting opera. In 1978, he conducted *The Damnation of Faust* in Boston, for a production supervised by Sarah Caldwell. He enjoyed nothing about the experience but the city of Boston. Mainly he thought a great deal of his time was wasted, and he was always jealous of his time. Shaw liked and respected Caldwell, but he quickly concluded that the engagement was a mistake he would not make again. Still, his experience preparing the choruses for various operatic recordings in the 1950s (again, roughly a dozen) was invaluable. He learned about musical narrative, pace, and drama, just as he learned to master time from his radio work. And he could not have disliked the material too much (the music, as opposed to the culture of opera), for he made two recordings of operatic choruses under his own baton. Shaw did present a concert version of Beethoven's *Fidelio* in Atlanta and became, for a time, fascinated by that work. And he also performed an unstaged version of *Porgy and Bess*. Finally, he premiered Scott Joplin's *Treemonisha* in Atlanta, an event we shall consider more fully in later pages. But Shaw's choice to perform the latter had little to do with an interest in opera, and not all that much to do with a deep interest in Joplin or ragtime. It was his interest in race, racial injustice in America, and racial outreach in Atlanta, and the fact that Joplin had never been able to hear his own master effort performed. Joplin had never been taken seriously as a composer—Shaw felt an injustice had been done.

Thus, particular operas by particular composers held an interest. And, again, he felt that if he were to realize the Verdi *Requiem*, he had to know something about Verdi's operas, too. But opera, generally? No. Too much flash; too much show biz. Symphonic music had solemnity and dignity, and all that quiet space for us to inhale and exhale and escape our present and ourselves. When we really listen to music that is truly great, we are nowhere.

Toscanini was, without question, the mentor Shaw *treasured* most. In fact, Shaw wrote a letter to his Atlanta choruses after viewing a video of Toscanini he'd spotted in a Paris record store. Shaw's summary of the video and of Toscanini's conducting style could, uncannily, serve as a description of the late-life Shaw on the podium. He wrote:

First, I had either forgotten—or never had seen—so severe and unconditional a concentration. His face might have been a sleepwalker's masque of outward blindness and inward sight.

And second, I had forgotten the astonishing economy of his gesture. An absolute minimum of "cueing"—almost never—if the section or player could be counted upon to enter without it. A clear beating of time and tempo with a beat that referred to the conventional patterns but was free, fluent, and personal enough to encourage hard corners and rough edges or smooth contours and warm moistness.

In the above first instance not only was music never to be used for personal "exhibitionism," but with Toscanini it was so chaste that one doubted that music could be or should be used for personal enjoyment. Certainly no "audience" was even consciously in his choreography.

And in the second instance, watching again the rapture and energy with which players like cellist Frank Miller and violinist Josef Gingold responded to Toscanini's simple, persuasive gesture, I was conscious, for the first time, I think, of how much personal involvement and individual creativity he not only allowed—but inspired . . .

The book which came out in these days was entitled Dictators of the Baton. *And Toscanini, of course, was Exhibit A. Such was the folklore and the fable, encouraged by publicists and other merchants. Some of the stories did have a basis in fact. The "Maestro" was capable of anger. But none of us, I think, ever saw him "sorry for himself"; rather it was the composer who had been betrayed, not the conductor; and, like the tantrum of a "terrible-*

> *two," it was soon over. The point is that his conducting invited exceptional and enthusiastic personal involvement. The finer the player and the finer the artist—the greater could be his or her participation. Dictatorship? Phooey! Nonsense! Artists played with Toscanini, not for him. And more often more than not they played the very same piece he was conducting that day.* (See Appendix VI for complete letter.)

To some degree Shaw created his own Toscanini myth to combat the prevailing one. For example, Shaw recounted how Toscanini would growl to the orchestra, "play, pigs"; but in Shaw's mind this was not derisive, it was plaintive. Shaw claimed that Toscanini would mutter "porco miseria" if displeased with his musicians, and "porco dio" if pleased. What Shaw is describing in his letter, however, is not only the Toscanini he knew and wished to remember, but the conductor Robert Shaw wished to be. He is describing the self he sought on the podium: economy of gesture, concentration, a certain indifference to the audience, "cueing" as the least important work of a conductor, and the ability to invite collaboration and inspiration. Shaw's remark that Toscanini's artistic purity cast doubt on the notion of music as a commodity for personal enjoyment is also self-revelatory. Again, in no way is Shaw suggesting, nor did he ever suggest, that he was an equal to Toscanini. But Shaw *is* saying: *This is what every serious conductor should seek to be.* Even if Shaw's Toscanini is as reified as the mythical Toscanini he attacks, the ideal reveals Shaw's ambition. The ideal is un-showy and unobtrusive conducting that shines the light on the composer, and impassions the players. The ideal is a conductor who is as self-*less* as possible and as clear a glass as possible.

Shaw was a lifelong student, enthusiast, and (his favorite word) "amateur" in the sense of one who is always new to his art—enthralled, humbled, and seduced by it. He never took it for granted. And he was moved by artists who had this same sense of awe, discovery, and personal insignificance. Pablo

Casals, Rudolf Serkin, and Mack Harrell were in this pantheon. Isaac Stern was on or near Shaw's pedestal. Claudio Arrau, with whom Shaw worked only once, might well have been had Shaw known him better. These artists didn't necessarily approach music in the same way Shaw did on a working practical level, but they were similarly humbled by and devoted to music, if not always personally humble. It is surely not coincidental that Shaw was simpatico with extraordinary soloists, particularly pianists. He was a kind of soloist himself. Toscanini surely was.

Toscanini remained at the top of Shaw's mythic musical mountain. The Maestro's purity—his lack of personal vanity and distraction, or what Shaw called his "artistic chastity"—set him utterly apart. His child-like shudder at the sheer grandeur of music, a thrill like the experience of seeing the Grand Canyon or the Manhattan skyline for the first time, only multiplied and was never lost. At least as Shaw saw Toscanini. For *Shaw* never lost it, hence his desire to be a musical soldier or monk—to work, indeed live, for the music alone. Shaw never failed to be bowled over or emotionally overwhelmed by the music of Beethoven, for example. He was forever awestruck. The same was true of Toscanini, and that was what touched Shaw most in the great man. Toscanini was a servant of the composer and his music.

Indeed, musical piety, or what Shaw thought of as the amateur spirit, was the quality that attracted him to all the musicians he loved and admired. It may have been what helped him endure George Szell. Shaw did not love Szell the way he loved Toscanini; he often found Szell rather unlikable. But he respected Szell, not only for his knowledge and craft, but for *his* piety. For Szell, who (rightly in Shaw's view) saw himself as superior to most musicians, trembled at the prospect of performing Beethoven.

If Toscanini influenced Shaw most deeply, it was Szell, so often his nemesis, who influenced Shaw most completely. Szell, too, would "lift" Robert Shaw.

CHAPTER 19

Mr. Szell and Cleveland—A Splendid Misery

From 1953 to 1957, Shaw conducted the San Diego Symphony, his first such post. It was a very happy experience. He was home in California. (One of his father's churches had been in San Diego.) Shaw brought with him some of his closest associates from New York—like Julius Herford, his teacher and co-programmer, and Alice Parker, his partner in arranging folk material and spirituals, her husband Tom Pyle, and singer-conductor Clayton Krehbiel. Shaw engaged noted musicians he knew and admired from New York, such as Rudolf Serkin, Isaac Stern, and Lukas Foss. California singers, some of whom also had Hollywood affiliations, including John Raitt and Harve Presnell, sang with him in San Diego. A few non-singing actors and actresses came to serve as narrators in various projects. The Los Angeles connection added a degree of Hollywood glamour and panache to Shaw's San Diego years. Shaw expanded the symphony's number of appearances—doing indoor evening concerts at Hoover High School as well as outdoor concerts in Balboa Park's Ford Bowl. He developed a chamber music series, and, with Herford's help, a choral workshop at San Diego State University. Shaw conducted several choral-orchestral masterworks in San Diego, like the *Missa Solemnis*, in which his sister Anne performed, and the Berlioz *Requiem*. And he got significant symphonic experience. San Diego was still, essentially, a summer orchestra, but it was *his*. Shaw conducted a few lighter classical works, some Beethoven, some Brahms, and some pops material. The first year, a few of the players gave Shaw a hard time, but with his discipline and study, and improvement in technique, he brought most of them around the second season. And instead of allowing himself to be hectored, he had the players submit questions to him through the concertmaster. Shaw told a reporter at the time, "My fingers taste the sound. My ears taste the sound. I can't explain it . . . I am just closer."

Since the symphony's programs were done over a period of weeks in the summer, its concert schedule could be designed to fit around Shaw's touring and recording with the Robert Shaw Chorale.

But in 1956, Shaw became Associate Conductor of the Cleveland Orchestra, then under the direction of George Szell. Shaw held this post from 1956 to the beginning of 1967. His job was to direct the choruses *and* to be Szell's assistant—responsible for most of the programs Szell did not do. That meant several subscription concerts; several out-of-town concerts; and all of the children's concerts, which were many in Cleveland at that time. Shaw was to carry the ball on the choral repertoire *and* be the Cleveland Orchestra's number two symphonic man. Moreover, he would be responsible for Szell's programs if Szell became ill or incapacitated. It was a big job. And Shaw did not intend to give up touring with the Robert Shaw Chorale or recording with RCA. The plan was to now do *that* in the summer. He would, with a year's notice, relinquish the San Diego position.

San Diego was Shaw's first symphonic sandbox. And he was creating the place, or recreating it, virtually in his own image. Seldom did anyone in San Diego say no to anything he suggested, and the audiences were enormously responsive. Shaw was having fun. But the resources and possibilities were, finally, too narrow. Money was often a problem. The season was short. The capabilities of a part-time orchestra were limited. While there was no one to deny him programming, there was little structure to support or feed him artistically.

So he took the Szellian plunge.

Cleveland was, of course, a quantum leap from the San Diego Symphony—in range, depth, history, and virtuosity. And Shaw was becoming an employee. For the first time since Waring, he would not be the boss. The transition (from the Robert Shaw Chorale and San Diego) was comparable, perhaps, to an actor moving from his own repertory company of friends doing plays in church basements in Greenwich Village, to appearing with Lawrence Olivier in *King Lear* at the National Theater.

Shaw was playing in the Big Leagues now. The players in Cleveland were known to be "little Szells"—brilliant technicians, well educated, rather ruthless, and a little cold, both musically and humanly. Shaw wanted to learn a lot fast, swim with the big fish, and maybe punish himself a bit along the way. (There was a masochistic element to Shaw's dues paying.) Indeed, Shaw was somewhat suspicious of any pleasure in music making. Joy, or satisfaction, might be a by-product, but sweat and suffering were the ground of art. Shaw's hair-shirt approach often got him into impossible positions. Partly, or mostly, in order to learn. But it may be that it was part emotional self-flagellation as well. Working for someone as gifted, erudite, and unforgiving as Szell would surely be an education. But it was also likely to be grueling. On the other hand, Shaw was eager to work with some of the other fine musicians in Cleveland, like violinist Rafael Druian. Ironically, there was less harassment of Shaw by players in Cleveland than there had been in the beginning by San Diego players.

But something was also lost. Not until the last ten or twelve years of his life would Shaw again experience the joy of the early Collegiate Chorale years, the Toscanini collaboration, and the San Diego years. Joy was replaced with an interminable feeling of playing catch-up; always slogging away, always behind the eight ball. This began in the Cleveland years. In this period Shaw would often tell anyone who would listen that he was a failure. Certainly there were moments of great joy in rehearsal and in performance. But in 1956, Shaw entered what he once called a "period of penance"—a period of struggle and constant misery at the feet of George Szell.

Shaw resigned or threatened to resign from the Cleveland job several times, but in the end he stayed until he went to Atlanta.

It was the only way he knew how to grow. After all, the Cleveland years were rich musically. But because of his habit of throwing himself into ever deeper and more turbulent seas to test his swimming ability, the anxiety and distress in Shaw's life from 1956 to 1967 was considerable. Shaw felt Szell continually condescended to him. He feared the players were privately laughing at him. And the more he learned about repertoire, about conducting, about instruments and instrumentalists, the more inadequate he felt.

Moreover, Shaw's personal relationship with Szell was as troubled and tense as his relationship with Toscanini had been easy and harmonious. One might think that a man with an inferiority complex and a man with a superiority complex would get on famously. But that is not the way it was. Both men were high strung and used to control. Szell had superior knowledge and power—and he wielded neither asset with subtlety. Shaw wanted Szell's wisdom but rebelled at his overbearing nature. Further, in time Shaw came to feel that Szell was less than fully honest with him.

Szell did not think Shaw his musical equal. That's what Shaw thought too. He was "no George Szell." But Toscanini *treated* Shaw as a young colleague. Szell treated him as a junior apprentice. Szell, for his part, felt Shaw did not put Szell and Cleveland first. And there was one more layer to Shaw's misery: Shaw's marriage to Maxine had come completely undone by the time he arrived in Cleveland. On at least one occasion, Shaw's health collapsed. What his physicians found bespeaks the anguish of those years: "back pain, stomach pain, chronic sick headaches, and stomach disorders." It was a confluence of miseries—it is possible that the condition of his private life made Cleveland and Szell seem even worse than they were.

Yet Shaw got what he wanted: a crash course in orchestral conducting and repertoire. Whereas Toscanini, an intuitive genius, had responded to Shaw's native talent, Szell, an analytic genius, saw Shaw's lack of instrumental knowledge and orchestral comfort and responded to *that*. Szell was particularly perplexed by Shaw's habit of spreading himself so thin. It displeased him and he said so. Shaw, in turn, found the severity of Szell's judgments a heavy weight to bear. As Shaw put it, "We became antagonistic early on." Shaw spent his whole life detailing his deficiencies, but that was *his* job, not Szell's. He had always attached himself to extraordinary mentors. But *he* liked to pick them. Szell anointed himself as Shaw's teacher and chose the lessons. Finally, most of his mentors were boosters. Szell was a booster, too, but he coached in the persona of scold and nemesis.

Shaw was a self-directed man and mostly had been his own master. True, he and Waring had clashed, on occasion. But that had to do with their egos, temperament, and taste. Waring, mostly, left Shaw alone to do the job he was hired to do. He left Shaw to teach himself. Waring was a mentor as sponsor. Toscanini was a mentor as model. Herford was a mentor as employee. But Szell was a boss. He was hands-on. And always there. The orchestra was *his* baby. Not just a place that gave him a title and a "base." Szell was not a traveling conductor. He lived in Cleveland. He attended many of Shaw's rehearsals—both for orchestra and for chorus, but especially for orchestra. For that was when "Bob," as Szell called him (his *friends* called him "Robert") needed, Szell felt, Szell's help the most. "Mr. Szell" (as Shaw called him) was a micro-musician and a micro-manager whose job it was, in this instance, to manage his protegé.

Shaw had come to Cleveland, as he said to Szell and said in public often, "to learn." But Szell gave him more than he bargained for. And Shaw endured it. Shaw also attended Szell's rehearsals, for he was Szell's backup. It was part of what he had wanted, if not to this degree. Recall that Shaw was in his forties at this time, and famous and successful in his own right. He'd done all those RCA records, all those radio broadcasts, and was hailed by the critics. He was fifty when he finally left Cleveland. He wanted to learn, and learn from a master, but being infantilized by Szell was harsh medicine.

The problem was not merely Szell's personality. It was style—he and Shaw had two different ways of leading, learning, making music. Shaw was not a didactic learner. He learned by doing, not by listening to a guru or by having someone watch, criticize, and correct him. Szell was the *über* didact, and that continually complicated the relationship between the two men. With Szell, Shaw found himself back in a familiar position—the position he'd been in with his father, his mother, and his wife: approval was often withheld.

So why did Shaw go to Cleveland and why did he stay?

First, because Szell was still Szell—one of the finest musicians in the world. And the Cleveland Orchestra was still Cleveland—one of the three or four finest orchestras in the world. Szell was already a legendary figure when he hired Shaw to come to the Cleveland Orchestra. He said he wanted a chorusmaster to bring the chorus up to the level of his orchestra players. Also, Szell wanted the orchestra to be able to perform the major oratorios and the grand choral literature. Cleveland had done some of this music, of course, but not in a quantity or quality to satisfy Szell. And he wanted a choral man to do it. Humble is not a word that springs to mind when one thinks of Mr. Szell, but he was a big enough and wise enough man to know that the choral literature was not his forte and he needed someone else to do it. For several years he'd had one, and only one, candidate in mind: Robert Shaw.

It took some time to make it happen. Shaw was reluctant. As would be his pattern—he did it with Waring and later the Atlanta Symphony too—he initially said no. Eventually, Szell convinced him, or Shaw became convinced that he and Szell needed each other. They knew each other only slightly. Years before he had gone to Cleveland; Shaw had arranged, through William Schuman, to hire Szell as his tutor. Szell was teaching at the Mannes School at the time and had been engaged to conduct at the Metropolitan Opera. Schuman, the composer and head of Juilliard who would appoint Shaw to run the choral program there, was one of Shaw's greatest friends and backers in the early years. Schuman knew how raw Shaw was and told him so, in no uncertain terms. He told Shaw that he had tremendous talent but needed to educate himself. Shaw agreed and asked Schuman to take him on. Schuman could not, but sent him to Szell. That arrangement lasted four sessions. And of course, it was Herford who eventually took that job and taught Shaw what and as he liked. But Shaw and Herford focused on Shaw's already existing choirs by working toward and through actual programs. It was a performance-oriented education. It was practical. And Shaw was in control. It was his sandbox.

By the time the Cleveland offer came, Shaw needed something more, just as Szell did. The eventual bargain was: *You will create a first-rate chorus for the Cleveland Orchestra and in return I will give you a chance to master the orchestra—with the finest symphony orchestra in the land.*

The attraction, the challenge, and the burden was that Shaw would not just be master of the chorus, but Szell's orchestral deputy. That was the bargain. Shaw would either overcome his insecurities about conducting orchestras or lose his mind trying.

What kept the Shaw-Szell marriage together, rocky as it was from the start, was music. Szell seemed to Shaw, at times, to simply know everything about music, and he was a gifted pianist. Shaw felt Szell was the most broadly talented musician he'd ever known. Szell was a font of knowledge and he poured forth. Sometimes to excess, or into arcana. Szell loved cars, for example (as did Shaw). But he didn't just tell you about his newest car and his enthusiasm for it; he told you at length why it was the best car. He told you how it was engineered, where it was made, and how much horsepower it had. Szell was like this about everything, said Shaw. He was an ultra-perfectionist, a born teacher, a gifted virtuoso. He was arrogant, autocratic, brilliant, brutal, enormously demanding, elegant and, in his music making, clear, clean, and unsentimental.

It was very hard for *anyone* to meet Szell's standards, including George Szell. He could also be generous financially, though he wanted no one to know it. He was, in ways that mattered most to Shaw, usually quite generous professionally. For example: for the most part Szell did not have Shaw prepare the chorus and turn it over to him for performance of choral-orchestral works. Shaw mostly prepared the choral masterpieces for *his own* final performances. He reaped the rewards of his own choral preparation.

Szell didn't usurp it. Szell was not a selfish boss, just a tough one. The first choral piece Shaw worked on in Cleveland was Beethoven's *Missa Solemnis.* He, not Szell, conducted the performances. This was indicative of Szell's generosity to Shaw, and of his confidence in Shaw in all matters choral. For all his criticism and second-guessing, Szell deferred to and trusted Shaw in Shaw's realm.

Szell had been a child prodigy. Some said that Szell's conducting was more fluid when he led the orchestra from the piano. It has also been said, by some who played for him, that his best performances were in rehearsals.

Shaw said that Szell "could easily have been a Class B composer. Instead, he chose to be a Class A conductor." Szell was a cosmopolitan European—a Hungarian of German sensibilities. When he conducted *La Mer* by Debussy, the joke in Cleveland was that it became *Das Mer.* His music making emphasized precision, clarity, preparation, and ensemble playing. Some people found his music, as well as the man, cold.

Szell scared people. No one dared call *him* middlebrow. It seemed, sometimes, as if he wanted to intimidate audiences into art. He once left the stage and interrupted a performance because there was, he felt, excessive coughing in the audience during a *pianissimo* passage. "I give you five minutes to clear your throats," he announced. When he returned to the stage to resume the concert, precisely five minutes later, Szell said: "Ladies and gentleman, we here on stage are only trying to do our best. Would you please do the same?" That was quintessential Szell.

According to Shaw, Szell regularly told his orchestra (and it was *his*), "Gentlemen, we begin our rehearsals where other orchestras begin their performance."

He was an odd match for Shaw, as their early association should have warned them both. One was a sophisticate, the other was not; one was a piano prodigy, the other had to struggle to reach remedial skill levels on the keyboard; one was cool and one was warm. Both were maniacal perfectionists who paid obsessive attention to detail. But Shaw, by nature and in later life by intent, could let go in performance: One prepared and prepared so that it was *possible* to let go in the performance. Certainly Szell was as devoted as Shaw to the composer and just as much in awe of musical greatness. But Szell really could not remove himself and trust the musicians—even if they were little Szells. The mature Shaw wanted to "get out of the way."

Arguably, Shaw's initial response to Szell—to turn down the Cleveland offer—may have been the right one. Shaw had a full career in progress in New York. He still felt insecure with an orchestra. But he might have overcome this in his own time and fashion. Cleveland was the most demanding orchestra in the United States. Its music director was the most formidable in the land. Why do it? Why trade success for agony? Of course this is the reason Shaw *did* do it.

Also, as Florence Kopleff said, Toscanini was gone. *The* maestro retired in 1954. He and Shaw made their last recordings together that year: Verdi's *Un ballo in Maschera* and *Te Deum* and the Prologue from Boito's *Mefistofele*. (Shaw would record the latter two himself a quarter century later.) The year before, they had recorded Toscanini's version of the *Missa Solemnis*. Toscanini died in 1957.

Moreover, Szell was persistent. He kept after Shaw with the Cleveland offer. There was no urgency, no deadline, because no "opening" existed. Szell planned to create one once Shaw said "yes."

In the end, Shaw decided that going to Cleveland was now the best way to challenge himself as a musician—to identify deficiencies in knowledge of the orchestra and to conquer his fears and doubts about that complex instrument. With Toscanini's departure from the scene, Szell and Cleveland represented the next step.

Finally, the Cleveland move was a renunciation of sorts, an act of self-denial and mortification.

After discussing it with his friend, the great pianist Rudolf Serkin, Shaw finally accepted Szell's offer. Serkin told Shaw that Szell, with whom Serkin had often collaborated, would be a difficult but brilliant teacher.

To friends and colleagues in New York, Shaw's going to Cleveland was a bizarre decision—strange personally and almost inexplicable professionally.

In truth, it was totally explicable in Shaw's terms: He was making himself less visible professionally, and less happy, in order to "get closer."

After he went to Cleveland, Shaw's personal behavior began to change. He became a far more studious and reclusive man. He often ended conversations with friends and colleagues abruptly in those years, pleading, "I have to study." He studied scores perpetually when not rehearsing or performing—sometimes sleeping three or four hours a night. This was not the Shaw of New York City.

When Szell announced the appointment, Shaw made his oft-quoted public statement that he "expected to learn a lot," which caused some huffing and puffing in the city of Cleveland: Shouldn't a conductor have learned *before* he decided to come to work at the Cleveland Orchestra? Further, a popular associate conductor was being displaced to make way for the choral guru. Rudolph Ringwall, Ph.D., was the current associate conductor and had to be forced out to accommodate Shaw. Feathers were ruffled. And Shaw put a bull's eye on his own back by speaking honestly.

How *much* did he still not know when he went to Cleveland? A lot. Shaw was speaking frankly, not hyperbolically. He knew his musical Achilles' heel was, chiefly, his lack of breadth and experience with a broad range of orchestral repertoire. It is not so amazing that he wanted to correct this, but that he wanted to correct it on such a conspicuous stage. He knew his second weakness was that, because of poor keyboard skills, he was a slow study—it took him considerable time to learn new scores. Yet as associate conductor, he was constantly learning works he'd never conducted and, in some cases, never heard.

His agreement with Szell was also that Shaw would be able to continue with the Chorale and other activities like summer choral workshops, though he would give up the music directorship of the San Diego Symphony. But this agreement, to give Shaw freedom to keep doing other things, was an ongoing source of tension and perhaps *the* major source of tension between the two men. Shaw had once again put himself in an impossible position. Szell did not understand that this was how Shaw needed to do things. Nor did Szell understand that Shaw needed choral music making like breath, and needed the Chorale because it was *his*. His view was: Cleveland is where you will learn the most.

The two were hopelessly at odds, partly because of ego, but mostly because their mental and emotional processes were so different.

During Shaw's eleven years in Cleveland, he continued guest conducting, recording and touring with the Chorale, and participating in festivals. (The historic Robert Shaw Chorale tour of the U.S.S.R. was during his Cleveland years.) Shaw was peripatetic in those days. He always had several balls in the air at once. If he freed himself of one commitment, he would pick up a new one.

Szell wanted him to *settle*—to limit and focus his activity chiefly to Cleveland. Szell wanted this for his own and the orchestra's sakes, but also to benefit Shaw's musicianship. Shaw couldn't do it, not then. Would he have given Toscanini 100 percent of his time and devotion? Toscanini would not have asked it.

Yet Shaw did apprentice himself to Szell, and did humble himself. He felt he was "rounding the learning curve" in the early days with the Cleveland Orchestra, though doing so slowly. Despite the tensions between Shaw and Szell, and despite the frequent threats of resignation (and sometimes he did tell Szell he quit), the pain was worth it to Shaw. He *was* learning, though, again mostly by doing. He never hid what he did not know or understand. Some Cleveland orchestra players felt sorry for him, for he was obviously, they thought, having such a difficult time of it, especially in the first four or five Cleveland years. Conductors are not supposed to visibly struggle. But none of the Cleveland players tried to sabotage Shaw's efforts. (According to lore, while guest conducting another orchestra, the brass section intentionally played wrong notes to see if "the choral guy" would notice. He did.) Shaw could not or would not make it easier on himself. He would not study less, conduct less, or do more music he already knew. In fact he continually made life harder for himself. That was the idea behind his coming to Cleveland, and he made it harder still by continually increasing his non-Cleveland commitments. It was as if he intended to wring all crassness (musical and personal) out of himself and lift himself to art by force of will and might of labor.

Overall, the trial by fire worked. Shaw had to learn and learn fast—both new music and how to become more comfortable with the orchestra—because he had so many programs to conduct. He averaged more than a concert a week in Cleveland during the season. And Shaw never approached any musical commitment, even in these years, without extensive preparation.

His Cleveland work ethic suited his personal needs at that time. In some sense, he was on the run—from his failed marriage and wrecked family. The family he wrecked.

Years later, Shaw said he regretted not attending more closely to Szell and spending more time with him, as Louis Lane had done in Cleveland.[45] Eventually, Shaw *did* finally settle, pick one path, one place, and one job—Atlanta. There he would have his own orchestra and learn even more.

Musicians in the Cleveland orchestra were actually astounded at the things Shaw had never even heard—even a warhorse like the Mendelssohn *Violin Concerto*. (Then again, most of them probably did not know Mendelssohn's Psalms or American Negro spirituals.) Like many musicians, the music Shaw knew was the music he'd played. He often lamented that he never had time for simply listening to music. He was usually preparing for the next concert—"playing catch up." Granted, Shaw was not schooled in

45 Louis Lane was, in succession, rehearsal pianist, assistant conductor, and associate conductor in Cleveland. It was at Shaw's request that Lane be elevated to equal status with Shaw in Cleveland. Shaw simply felt there were many things Lane could do better than he could. Later, at Shaw's invitation, Lane became "co-conductor" in Atlanta. An incredibly versatile and gifted musician, Lane was a Shaw colleague and confidante for almost thirty years. Lane was a perfect deputy for Shaw as music director in Atlanta. He had all the orchestral prowess and keyboard facility Shaw lacked. He did not suffer the same anxieties or deficiencies. It is said by some that he also seldom ignited a performance as Shaw did. He was a cool-headed conductor. But he had enormous fluency and Shaw admired him greatly and relied upon his talent, taste, and experience heavily. The building of the Atlanta Symphony was mostly a matter of Shaw's will, determination, and push. But he needed Lane's knowledge, advice, and complementary abilities to make it happen. After Lane, a young man named James Levine became the rehearsal pianist in Cleveland. No wonder the Szell era was, and is still, regarded by many musicians in Cleveland as the Golden Age.

symphonic literature. This was a "big deal" to him. However, Shaw had not been schooled in choral music either—not really. He simply did it, lived it. Orchestral work could not be approached the same way. Conductor Vance George has written, astutely, that the lines between Shaw and his early New York circle (Herford, Parker, Pyle, Hillis) blurred distinctions between teacher and student. Shaw thought of them as equals, certainly. He could not operate as a fellow musician as a conductor of the Cleveland Orchestra.

Because Shaw was responsible for so many programs in Cleveland—the youth concerts, a number of "run-outs" (regional out-of-town concerts), several subscription concerts that were non-choral, and all the choral-orchestral concerts—he did learn a great deal of new repertoire. In this period he grew very fond of the concerto form. He felt comfortable as an accompanist. After Shaw persuaded Szell to elevate Louis Lane from Assistant Conductor to a fellow Associate Conductor, the two deputies split these many responsibilities, which reduced Shaw's workload. Lane took over a number of the youth concerts and understudied Szell. Lane's abilities were something Shaw and Szell could agree on.

Shaw did roughly sixty concerts in Cleveland in his first year there. As the ultimate conductor for virtually all choral-orchestral masterworks in Cleveland, Shaw was able to test and stretch himself. But Shaw was sometimes quite literally overwhelmed with his Cleveland and Robert Shaw Chorale duties and with studying scores. That was when the medical maladies kicked in.

Szell did reserve the Beethoven *Symphony No. 9* for himself. Moreover, some years following his arrival in Cleveland, Shaw asked Szell to conduct the *Missa*, convinced that Szell would bring something special to it. (After Szell did, Shaw was less sure about that.) But Szell turned Shaw loose on all the rest of the latter's core repertoire: all the oratorios and requiems and cantatas and Masses. The extent of Shaw's responsibilities and freedom under Szell, and Szell's generosity and ultimate trust, may be unique in the history of American symphony orchestras.

When Shaw told Szell he wanted his *very* first concert in Cleveland to be the *Missa Solemnis*, Szell's initial reaction to that choice was: "Are you sure?" But after the concert, he embraced Shaw and told him: "I should never have doubted you." (This didn't stop Szell from questioning Shaw's future choices, both professional and musical.) "I don't feel as comfortable with the orchestra as the chorus, and I want to find out why," Shaw said when he took the Cleveland job.[46] It's not clear that he found out, though the answer seems clear from a distance—the chorus was his instrument.

Shaw was no longer the *wunderkind* when he went to Cleveland in 1956. Nor was he new to the orchestra. He had been conducting large professional orchestras on a regular basis for ten years: his purely orchestral conducting debut was with the Naumburg Orchestra (a summer festival ensemble) in New York in May of 1946, and, as noted, he first conducted the NBC Symphony in purely symphonic works in August of 1946. Moreover, 11 months before that, in 1945, he had conducted the premiere of Hindemith *Lilacs* with the CBS Orchestra on radio. Prior even to this, he'd conducted a pickup orchestra for an RCA recording with Marian Anderson. At about that same time, he'd conducted a full orchestra for an outdoor concert with Paul Robeson in Philadelphia. And, of course, he had begun making his own recordings of masterworks, as well as more popular music, in 1946 and 1947 (most notably, the *Mass in B Minor* and *Ein Deutsches Requiem* recordings, both in 1947). Prior to going to Cleveland, he had guest conducted throughout the country, including a series of concerts with the Boston Symphony. Thus, when he went to Cleveland, Shaw actually had a fair amount of experience conducting orchestras. What he did not have, in his own mind, was mastery. He lacked confidence. He wanted Cleveland to be a shock to his system, and it was. He did learn—he had to. He gained in knowledge of musical literature and conducting technique. He gained a more intimate understanding of the orchestra. But his confidence was, in fact, further eroded, not built. In San Diego he felt he was "getting closer." In Cleveland, he sometimes felt, in the lyrics of "Wondrous Love," that he was "sinking down, sinking down."

46 Shaw papers.

Shaw often said the players of the Cleveland Orchestra were his teachers. This sounds characteristically self-deprecating. But it is also true. Some of the Cleveland players did pull him through some tight spots; others, like Druian, befriended him. All who were willing taught him. He was quite willing to admit he needed help.

Shaw never did come to feel as comfortable with orchestras as with choirs. He knew he *knew* the voice. He knew, somehow, even before he was musically educated. He knew intuitively. Although he tried to learn the rudiments of every orchestral instrument (when he was at Juilliard as head of choral music, in his spare time), and although he constantly peppered musicians with questions, and although he was forever trying to improve his keyboard skills, and though no one ever knew a score like Shaw, and he could tinker with balances in an orchestra like few in the business, he did not know any instruments the way he knew the voice, nor any collection of instruments the way he knew how to mold a collection of voices.

It is said that Duke Ellington's true instrument was his orchestra, though he was a fine pianist. Shaw's instrument was the *choir.*

Of course, most conductors know only one instrument as a player. A conductor may have been a violinist, a cellist, a reed player, or a pianist. Instrumentalists may and often do say of a conductor, "What does he know about strings, he's a reed man." Or "what does he know about reeds, he's a pianist." Unless you play everything, and know everything, you are vulnerable to second-guessing and criticism by players. Szell "knew everything" and even he was criticized. Because Shaw so acutely lacked confidence, he was always highly vulnerable. Music is so vast that all conductors have pockets of ignorance. (Sir Georg Solti was preparing the *St. John Passion* for the first time when he died.) But Shaw felt all his ignorance and all he lacked acutely.

Robert Shaw's first professional job in choral work was on national radio; so, too, his first all-orchestral program. His classroom was a natural audience. He didn't have the luxury of learning on college orchestras (except for Juilliard); he learned on the high wire. He put himself in very difficult situations. Cleveland was another sort of high wire—an agony, but for him a necessary agony.

Years after he left Cleveland, Shaw told friends that he was grateful for the opportunity but he didn't miss it when he was gone. When Shaw told Szell he felt unprepared and unworthy of his profession, Szell *agreed.* Constantly telling an insecure man, in small ways and large, that indeed he doesn't measure up may seem rather sadistic. But in a sense, this was the European tradition of musical pedagogy—allegedly tracing back to Mozart's father. Szell adopted the father-teacher role toward Shaw, which at times included behaving like a bastard well and true. But if Szell was something of a sadist, Shaw was a masochist.

Shaw, in later years, would say, "I didn't use Szell nearly enough . . . we became antagonistic relatively early and I didn't take full advantage of him." But he also said, "Everything I know, sort of, I learned from him."[47] Cleveland marked the third of five crucial events in Shaw's career—five points at which, like a child on a trampoline, he bounced to a new and higher level. The first was coming to New York to work for Fred Waring. The second was Shaw's association with Toscanini. The third was the move to Cleveland. The fourth was building a world-class orchestra and chorus in Atlanta. And the fifth was recording his own favored and most often repeated repertoire—the great symphonic-choral masterworks and a number of smaller, *a cappella* choral works by composers closest to his heart—some for RCA, but mostly for Telarc in the later portion of his life.

George Szell may not have imagined that Shaw would, or should, ever graduate from his tutelage. Indeed, Szell advised Shaw not to go to Atlanta. He told him he wouldn't have access to the talent he needed to do what he wanted to do. And that was true. In a sense, Szell always sought what was

47 *Preparing a Masterpiece,* unused footage.

best for Shaw, *and* tried to keep him down on the farm. Szell felt that all he did for, and to, "Bob" was "for his own good."

By the time the Atlanta call came, Shaw had grown tired and somewhat wary of Szell. As with other mentors, chiefly Herford, Shaw had absorbed what he could and had begun his real learning on his own after only three or four years. He relied on score study, performance experience, and a few trusted friends who were Cleveland players, like Rafael Druian, the concertmaster. But George Szell had handed him a "Stradivarius" on which to learn. And when he looked back, despite the tension that grew between them, Shaw felt he really did owe Szell a huge debt.

Did Shaw become a great orchestral conductor thanks to Szell?

That sounds like a simple question. It's not. He became more competent and literate thanks to the Cleveland experience. He gained some of the tools he needed for the Atlanta job. Eventually he would become familiar and comfortable with a handful of orchestral pieces, like the Brahms symphonies. He also did all the Beethoven symphonies, several of them many times over, and by all accounts, he did them well. But these experiences came in Atlanta. Most musicians who worked with him say his greatest fluency and mastery came when he conducted both—the orchestra *with* the chorus. When he was doing his highly specialized repertoire with the combination of forces, his musicianship soared. In that instance, commanding that combination of vocal and instrumental musicians, and balancing those forces both in temper and in tone, he was at his best and he was unique—peerless. Is this too narrow a range for "greatness"? Some would argue so. The more common idea of a great conductor is one who can "do anything," can do it fast, and can do it with drama. Shaw was not a fast study. He would often recommend that someone else conduct a work ("he could do this better"), and he had no desire to be dramatic. The great conductor is supposed to be able to do Broadway, *and* John Cage. And actually, Shaw did. Literally. But the pieces he returned to again and again were choral-orchestral—the little pigeonhole in which he said he could get lost. Yet that core repertoire was, perhaps, forty works. And the range of Shaw's tastes was perhaps wider than that of most conductors. Still, a violinist does not play a horn concerto. He plays works written for his instrument. All musicianship is built upon some kind of initial talent and core intuition. If greatness is measured by depth of understanding, communicativeness, and spirit (however we might understand all of these terms), Shaw was great. If it is measured by flash, dexterity, speed, and versatility, he was not. What makes Shaw's life as a conductor interesting is that he turns the conventional idea of a conductor on its head. He could not "do anything," do it fast, and do it with flash. He didn't want to. Perhaps that is one reason why most musicians, when asked, "Was Robert Shaw a great conductor?" reply, "Robert Shaw was a great musician."

How much of his growth was Shaw himself and how much was Szell? Shaw certainly became *the* master of choral-symphonic literature, whether it was Verdi's *Requiem* or Britten's *War Requiem*, and this mastery deepened in Cleveland. But its completion was in Atlanta. Shaw's true coming of age with the orchestra would also have to wait for his own podium. Szell simply cast too long a shadow.

Shaw never treated an orchestra the way he treated a chorus. With a chorus he was the father, the Dutch uncle, the coach. With an orchestra he worked quickly, professionally, but also with more suggestion than overt command. With the orchestra he was a colleague. The reasons were partly philosophical and partly biographical. He felt the players were professionals, that they knew their instruments better than he did, and that they should not be micro-managed. (Atlanta Symphony Orchestra players who felt they did not get enough direction from Shaw when he was principal conductor and music director found they loved him when he came back as the conductor laureate. His successor *was* a micro-manager.) If a player with the Cleveland

Orchestra rejected his help, Shaw not only backed off but could become wobbly and unsure of himself. And even with the ASO, he did not press many players—only ones whose work ethic he doubted. If he respected an instrumentalist, he tended to give that player a lot of room. Not so singers. The more he loved the singer (we are speaking of soloists), the more hands-on he was. A singer who ignored or opposed Shaw did so at his or her peril. On the other hand, with a fine instrumentalist who shared Shaw's vision and temperament and related to him personally, like violinist and ASO concertmaster William Preucil (later concertmaster of the Cleveland Orchestra), Shaw could be an inspired collaborator. The same was true for Rudolf or Peter Serkin. As Preucil put it, one isn't looking to be walked though a piece step by step by the conductor, but to be ignited by something, perhaps something like the composer's original spark. Shaw, according to Preucil, had the ability to rediscover the work, find the creator's voice, and bring the player along—if the player wished to make the journey. Preucil believed Shaw's vulnerability, his knowledge, but most of all his devotion, set him apart.[48]

Shaw did not try to hide his flaws. To the contrary. He freely admitted to anyone that he did not quickly learn scores, and did not memorize them at all, and he was the first to say that he sometimes missed cutoffs and cues in the heat of performance. He told players, "I know I will make some stupid mistake." He tried to compensate by knowing the piece he was working on absolutely thoroughly. And, indeed, composer Ned Rorem attested that when Shaw conducted Rorem's *String Symphony*, Shaw knew the piece better than the composer.[49] Often this worked handsomely. When players responded to Shaw's work ethic, his preparation and organization, his love of music and devotion to the work at hand, he could lead them. If the game was, "Either intimidate us or be intimidated," the result might not be so good.

Cleveland players and audiences were astonished at the growth of Shaw's technical dexterity and confidence when he returned to conduct a series of

48 Burris–Preucil interview.
49 Burris–Rorem interview.

concerts in the 1990s. Atlanta had changed him. But Shaw had to endure the years of the Cleveland experience—his Purgatory—to reach his place of promise. Atlanta was that place. And it was perhaps in Cleveland that he became almost uniquely adept at managing large forces—large chorus or double chorus and a full orchestra. The Berlioz *Requiem* and the Beethoven *Missa Solemnis*, said Ann Howard Jones, "drive many conductors to drink." They were red meat to Shaw. Cleveland provided Shaw a vast canvas—program after program. And he came to feel quite comfortable with a canvas that size.

Different orchestras elicited the best in Shaw in a variety of ways. With openhearted young musicians, like the Orchestra of St. Luke's in New York, with whom Shaw worked in later life, he settled into an unspoiled and noncynical element. They saw Shaw as a poetic father figure, and he saw them as innocent and new. He could relax. When Shaw worked with people he saw as pure musicians, it was a love fest. The Orchestra of St. Luke's officially bestowed upon Shaw its "Gift of Music" award in 1998. But long before that, it had given him its heart. But Shaw's conducting trips back to Cleveland in the mid and late 1990s were also warm, deeply respectful, and loving.

Shaw's success with an orchestra depended partly on where he was in his journey, and partly on the specific orchestra. The St. Luke's experience happened roughly 45 years after he arrived in Cleveland and 35 years after he had departed. He'd grown. In some ways, he'd grown up. But also, they were his kind of musicians—in it for love.

Only at the end of his life could Shaw let down and let go in a way he never could in the early Cleveland days. (Szell never let down either. *No one* in Cleveland ever did in those days. To use Shaw's own terminology, this made it hard for the orchestra "to sing.") To watch Shaw in his later years conduct the Beethoven *Ninth,* which is, of course, not primarily choral, was to see a conductor totally involved with the orchestra, quite free of the score, and in a place of total comfort, fluidity, and command. Atlanta singer and choral educator Pam Elrod has said, "His pacing of that work was mind blowing." But this level of confidence, comfort, and command had been hard earned. Though he already knew the piece well by then, Shaw could not have conducted it with such grace during his Cleveland tenure.

Shaw was a *figure* in the Cleveland community. When he died, the local obituaries treated him with reverence, more so in some ways than the coverage given in Atlanta. Partly it was nostalgia—Shaw was a last living element of the Szell legacy in Cleveland. But it also had to do with the role Shaw played in Cleveland's cultural life. In New York in the early on-fire days, he'd been a celebrity. But in Cleveland, as he would later be in Atlanta, Shaw was a good citizen, a local teacher, an accessible guru.

Shaw's obsession with preparation began in Cleveland. Szell required Orchestra members to walk into rehearsal prepared to play a performance. Shaw fell in love with the idea, and with Szell's phrase—"We begin where others end." Why, thought Shaw, should it not be so for the chorus as well? Why not edit scores so singers could come prepared to sing a performance? Shaw developed his "disciplines" and work ethic over the years, but they began to compound in Cleveland. Further, the Cleveland Orchestra was the model for what he tried to do in Atlanta with both orchestra and chorus. (Musicians joked that the ASO was "Cleveland South." Szell's head was once imposed on a picture of Shaw on an ASO bulletin board.)

The ideal sound for the Cleveland Orchestra was clear, clean, and *in harness*—like a string quartet. At least that was how Shaw saw it, and it became a choral ideal for him as well as the standard he applied to the orchestra in Atlanta. The Cleveland approach, as perceived by Shaw and then applied by him, posited that music making, at its highest level, is built on listening. Not by "blending" but by leaning in, tuning toward, and playing *with* fellow musicians.

When Shaw gave choral-orchestral concerts in Cleveland, they were "events"—"happenings" for almost everyone who participated. When Shaw did the *Messiah* in Cleveland, it was a hot ticket indeed. Those who were amazed and moved by these concerts, though they had not expected to be, included grizzled veterans of the orchestra who, when Shaw did purely orchestral pieces, were sometimes most impressed with how difficult it was for him. But Shaw had also begun to play the role of missionary. He viewed conducting the youth concerts in Cleveland not as grim duty, but as unique teaching opportunities—for himself as well as the audience. He presented the *Messiah*, in its entirety, on local television. Stravinsky's *Histoire du Soldat* was also televised locally, with Shaw conducting and making his "acting debut" as narrator. Shaw also began to do something he did a lot more of in Atlanta—public speaking before schools and civic groups. Shaw was scheduled to conduct the *Missa Solemnis* (a second time) in Cleveland after the death of John F. Kennedy. Before his downbeat, he delivered a short meditation on JFK's life and his devotion to the arts. Shaw was also a fixture at Cleveland/Akron area colleges and universities, especially Kent State, where he conducted a memorial concert days after the 1970 shootings. So a second kind of maturity came to him in Cleveland: He found a public persona. And because he was "warm," especially next to the aristocratic Szell, Shaw was much loved by the Cleveland music-going public.

Shaw was far more visible, and more revered, than most associate conductors of most symphonies in most cities, then and now. Furthermore, he was more universally and unequivocally beloved and honored in Cleveland than he would be for many years in Atlanta.

But Shaw did not truly begin to "feel the music in his fingers" with the orchestra until he left Cleveland for Atlanta. When he arrived in Atlanta, Shaw was still unhappy with his skill level with the orchestra. So, if Shaw was having trouble communicating what he wanted, or felt in some way inadequate, he simply said so. To some players this meant he was weak. He could not tame them. He was not their ruler. But others were moved by Shaw's selflessness and his humility before the music. Said ASO cellist Christopher Rex: "There was nothing he would not do, or ask a musician to do, in service to the music. And there was nothing he asked in service to himself."[50]

Don't most conductors feel reverence for the music and insignificant in the shadow of the composer? The question seems simple, but is not. All conductors have respect, but it is a matter of degree. Toscanini was utterly humbled before the music. So was Casals. And Szell. One musician recalls that Szell literally shook with fear when he came to record the Beethoven *Eroica*, which he had known most of his life and been preparing for recording for two years. A contemporary conductor and teacher of conducting, when asked " Don't *most* conductors feel awe and reverence?" responded with a laugh and these words: "Hell no." Most conductors, he said, are worried about the impact of their performance—and how the performance will be received by the audience and reviewed by the critics. Some worry a lot about how they look. Shaw was of an alternative polarity. He was constantly trying to reduce his own centrality, which for many conductors is the antithesis of being a conductor. When it came to curtain calls, for example, Shaw stood to the side and pointed to others. He usually took one bow at the end.[51]

Musicians like William Preucil or Krista Feeney, of the Orchestra of St. Luke's, as well as pianists like Peter Serkin and Jeffrey Kahane, said that Shaw's gift was not "stick work" but love. He wanted to "get out of the way," let the piece "sound," and let the composer be heard. In practical terms, Shaw's devotion led to detailed preparation, which meant he knew the music and had a plan—a detailed plan of battle—heading into rehearsal. He had read the scholarship on the work. He had analyzed the score structurally, melodically, and harmonically. He had set up a rhythm, a pulse, which he might slightly adapt, but which would stay pretty constant. He knew where

50 Burris–Rex interview.
51 Burris interview with Peter Sacco of the University of Connecticut.

all the joints, intersections, and transitions were, *and* at that moment, he loved *that piece* he was preparing and rehearsing more than anything in music. At that moment, he loved preparing that piece more than anything else in life.

That's not to say that Shaw's gifts were chiefly verbal and pedagogical (a criticism made in his younger days). But perhaps this was the *core* of his gifts. Maybe this was the springboard to voice and chorus—words and ideas—the need to communicate and the power of words in that quest. But Shaw's musicianship was not limited to choral music or vocalists. His time before the orchestras in Cleveland and Atlanta was not a fluke, or résumé building. It was learning the orchestra so he could combine it properly and most effectively with chorus. It was learning the language of composers he loved. It was learning another instrument so he could hear his first instrument more clearly, as it was for Glenn Gould to play harpsichord or organ. It was, finally, making music with instrumentalists he loved and looked to for musical insight.

Shaw was both thinker and mystic—rare qualities in any profession. He brought these attributes to the podium. Most conductors are technicians, though they often approach a work with less technical precision than Shaw did. And many conductors, *according* to conductors, simply do not want to work as hard as Shaw did on any given piece. They may feel, for example, that they don't have time. In his later years, Shaw accepted fewer and fewer engagements so that he *could* devote more time to each piece he was doing that particular season. Few conductors have that luxury, and for most conductors, the more engagements the better. Again, Shaw was a kind of anti-maestro.

In Cleveland, Shaw did a good deal of contemporary music for orchestra and was, by all accounts, quite good at it. This may be because he was acting out of conviction: a mission always energized Shaw and diminished his insecurities. The conviction was that modern men and women should hear the "music of their time" and support the artists of their time. He did this in the early days in New York—commissioning one new piece of music annually, if possible. He championed the contemporary composer when he went to Atlanta as well. Shaw did not always love this music. But he was committed to new composers, to challenging concertgoers with unfamiliar sounds, and to the proposition that music is not a dead language but a living one. If nothing worth hearing has been written since Mozart, Mozart will never be heard as new. Soon after Shaw left Cleveland, Szell would expressly recruit Pierre Boulez to conduct modern works in Cleveland, just as he had recruited Shaw for choral work.

Once Shaw got his own orchestra, he began to conduct works that he would not have dreamed of conducting during his association with Szell—the Brahms symphonies, piano concertos, and Hungarian dances, for example. Almost everyone who heard him do the Brahms symphonies in Atlanta, especially in later years, talks about what a wonderful Brahms conductor Shaw was. Shaw's recordings of the Brahms piano concertos with Peter Serkin affirm this. Initially, the concerto form was a gentle way into the orchestra and it came to be a form Shaw loved, for its collaborative nature de-emphasized *his* prominence.

To hear the Serkin recordings, or see and hear Shaw conduct, for example, the third movement of the Beethoven *Symphony No. 9* during his lifetime was to witness what he ultimately brought to the orchestra—how he could make it sing. He worked by metaphor. He looked for "the long line." With the choir, and with solo singers, he sought, always, more Szell-like definition and particularity: "For a chorus needs to learn how to play." But to find his own way with the orchestra, to become the best he could be with the orchestra, to teach it to sing, he had to be Shaw—the lover, worshipper, of music.

Shaw always held the Cleveland Orchestra in ultimate esteem. Szell's idea of the orchestra as a highly disciplined and closely-knit chamber group, grown large, became Shaw's. Szell's preference for elegance and clarity over romantic lush sonorities is what Shaw wanted for the Atlanta Symphony

Orchestra. So Shaw established a relationship between Cleveland and the ASO—with a fluid movement of players and administrators back and forth—that continues today.

Shaw's difficulties in Cleveland were, perhaps, one part Szell and two parts Shaw—his lack of self-confidence. But there was no dramatic and embarrassing incident. There was no disastrous performance. The crisis was ongoing and internal.

Shaw would return to Cleveland triumphantly for a number of notable performances, and as a guest conductor after he had retired as music director in Atlanta. In the mid- and late-1990s, he conducted the Beethoven *Symphony No. 9*, the Brahms *German Requiem*, the Mahler *Symphony No. 8*, among others. He repeated the Mahler with Cleveland forces at a famous performance at Carnegie Hall, in which Shaw filled the first level of the hall with singers.

Shaw's years in Cleveland took more than a pound of flesh from him. Some of the players worried about him. There was anxiety, sickness, loneliness and, in his mind, abject artistic failure—not in performance, but in understanding, mastery, and depth.

And yet, it was what he had to experience. Decades after he left Cleveland, concertgoers still talked about Shaw's Handel and Bach concerts, and *The Soldier's Tale*. And stories flowed: Remember the time Shaw locked latecomers out of a chorus rehearsal and refused to unbar the door? Remember the time he put his head down in a *St. Matthew Passion* rehearsal and we thought he was ill, but he was weeping?

Cleveland was purgatorial for Shaw, but in many ways a splendid misery. He made some great music there and edged closer to what he wanted to be. The penance was paid. By the time he conducted the Cleveland Orchestra in the Mahler almost thirty years after leaving his Szell apprenticeship, there was no doubt in anyone's mind that Shaw belonged on that podium.

CHAPTER 20

A Polyphony of Three Men

From Toscanini, Shaw learned concentration, economy of gesture, and severity on the podium. He reinforced his own instinct to build and sustain musical momentum. Toscanini, said Shaw, could imagine and realize the entire piece, not just aspects of it—swallow it whole, in a way. Shaw said, "Toscanini saw farther into the distance than Mr. Szell ever wanted to see."

From Szell, Shaw learned to be dispassionate and clear. For Szell, the composer, not the devil, was in the details. Shaw said that Szell "developed the whole out of the microcosm."

Shaw was, by will and likely by disposition as well, more Szellian. He worked from the small cell up. If things did not go well, he might never look into the distance. He could not. But if they did, he was capable of wrapping his arms around the entire *Missa Solemnis* or *Mass in B Minor*. He could ride the wave and see into the far horizon, like *the* maestro.

One mentor was intellect and the other inspiration. From Szell, Shaw adopted the idea of extensive pre-rehearsal preparation so that players could truly listen to each other and play as chamber musicians. In Toscanini, Shaw witnessed lift-off—a jet defying gravity. Shaw said that "the chief thing that

Toscanini communicated was a vitality of forward motion . . . if it's a little rough here, you continue to fly."[52]

From Toscanini, Shaw took the big picture, the long line, and the ability to conceive the composer's entire vision. This fit with the Herford-Shaw notion of absorbing each composer's own particular musical language. Shaw also embraced the maestro's emphasis on constant musical locomotion. Here again, Shaw was drawn toward a characteristic that was already his own.

Cleveland Orchestra musicians were supposed to be able to turn in a performance at the first rehearsal. Once Shaw adopted that standard, he had to decide how he would accomplish it. He settled upon the idea of a map. He would give the musicians—chorus and singing soloists as well as players—a road map at the start of their musical journey together: microscopically detailed edits on each player's part. That was Shaw's own extension of Szell. Shaw began the practice with chorus and extended it to orchestra, thus increasing his own preparation time. Szell did not do this, to that extent at least. Toscanini certainly did not do it. Indeed, no one has identified a conductor who did it so extensively. Szell made extensive adjustments and edits in rehearsal. Shaw knew he would not and could not do that. Shaw's editing was a vital organizational device that also became, for him, a vital form of study and even a kind of spiritual exercise.

Shaw's editing involved some direction for virtually every note, in every musician's part—instrumentalists, chorus, and vocal soloists. He would play through every part on the piano, or sing it through, or in his very last years, occasionally have it played through for him by his accompanist and choral deputy in Atlanta, Norman Mackenzie (Shaw singing along). Shaw would also play, for example, a violin part on the piano, while singing a vocal part against it to test proportion and balance. In preparation for conducting the Bach *Mass in B Minor* at the University of Kansas in 1990, Shaw sent the UK chorusmaster *three* piano-vocal scores he had edited. The first "clarified choral and concertist roles." The second dealt with "approximate tempi" and

52 Shaw papers.

prescribed "structural and expressive dynamics and occasional articulation," and a third dealt with phrasing.[53]

Shaw discovered that editing could be an enormously practical tool for the conductor: It saved time. The conductor could prepare for the first rehearsal and create a game plan that everyone could see and begin to understand even before the first meeting.

When preparing, Shaw would also re-orchestrate. This might seem to contradict his "original intent" doctrine. But in Shaw's mind there was no contradiction. His view was that Beethoven had bigger things to do than worry about the nitty-gritty of realizing his creation. ("He should be writing his 10th symphony," Shaw said.) So if Shaw thought a certain passage needed more woodwinds or fewer strings to bring out what he thought the composer was trying to say melodically at that point, or if he felt an important theme might not be well heard, he would adjust the number of harmonizing instruments accordingly.

He did make adjustments during rehearsals to compensate, he said, "for my own stupidity." But even so, the changes were sent to the library, penciled into the parts, and then distributed to all forces. The goal was unanimity of sound and psyche. And there were the inevitable practical considerations, like adjusting to the hall or the strengths and weaknesses of principals or soloists. But Shaw felt it was irresponsible to wait for rehearsals to begin working on these matters of clarification and balance. Usually Shaw's changes were small—adding some slight amplification or punctuation where nothing was indicated or, quite often, lowering one section a dynamic level so another could be heard. Thus his design was not to "improve" or dramatize, and certainly not to place *his* stamp on a piece. Shaw's aim was transparency for the music.

In his attention to the small cell, Shaw was out-Szelling Szell. Except that the contrasting emotional make-ups of these two apostles of microcosm produced two very different results. With Shaw, detailed preparation could lead to a final release of energy. For Shaw could not help being a romantic and emotional person.

53 Shaw's letter on preparations for this performance, Shaw papers.

Shaw regarded his editing not as interpreting but rather, in a sense, as gardening—bringing out the melodies that were obscured by weeds. He was trying to reveal the composer's structure and language, not put his own spin on a piece. His goal was to serve a rediscovered intention, not to recast or re-imagine.

Shaw's two mentors, Toscanini and Szell, shared humility before the composer. Both men affirmed the notion of fidelity to the composer's intent. Szell and Toscanini, as different as they were, both disliked laying the conductor's persona upon a composer's work. The two were, one might say, strict musical constructionists. So, once more, Shaw responded to what he already felt intuitively. Shaw would, for all his days as an orchestral conductor, emphasize the notion of trying to hear a piece of music "as the composer heard it"; being present "when the composer took pen to paper." It was, now and forever, Beethoven's piece, not Toscanini's; Haydn's piece, not Szell's; Brahms's piece, not Shaw's.

Shaw's goals as a conductor—(1) editing to bring out all the sounds in the composer's arsenal and (2) "to be a clear glass . . . or as clear as possible," to let Beethoven or Brahms shine through—exist in tension. But they are not contradictory in practice. The former is the instinct to weed and garden, the latter the instinct to step aside and let the music exert "its own grace" (Shaw's phrase). But for Shaw, both goals were to serve the composer. He knew, he said, that to be a "clear glass" was, strictly speaking, impossible. But he felt this should be the conductor's intent. He understood his small adjustments would inescapably leave his footprints. But he hoped they were footprints in the snow.

Though the methods and personas of Shaw's two great mentors were drastically unalike, their musical value systems were very much in sync. At his best, in his later years, Shaw combined the finest qualities of his two great teachers. He became a master of musical microcosm *and* inspiration, of clinical analysis *and* forward motion. One could hear this in Shaw's performance of a piece like the Beethoven *Missa Solemnis,* which requires both the engineer and the visionary, the organizer and the poet.

Richard Dyer, then a music critic for the *Boston Globe*, attempted to examine why and how Shaw did what he did in an August 26, 1997 review of a Shaw performance of Beethoven's *Ninth Symphony* with the Boston Symphony Orchestra at Tanglewood. Dyer wrote:

> *Shaw prepared choruses for the now legendary performances of the Beethoven* Ninth *by Arturo Toscanini and George Szell. His own performance Sunday afternoon may become legendary too. It had the clarity of vision of his two great mentors, but it also boasted Shaw's own mellower human qualities. Shaw's approach was leisurely and spacious. Intensity came not from speed, volume, and whiplash attack but instead from the accumulation of proportionate detail. Nearly everything about the performance was memorable, but the Adagio seemed particularly profound in the way the utmost simplicity can be—the simplicity that can be arrived at only by the very wise and the very experienced. The tempo relationships in the last movement were superbly judged because they were stages in an emotional progression too.*

Dyer concluded his thoughtful review: "You could hear every note in this performance, but what made the experience of Shaw's performance so profoundly moving—and so appropriate—was that you could also hear the function of every note and its meaning."

This was high praise certainly, but particularly because it mirrors so closely what Shaw was trying to achieve. This is where respect for the composer and editorial markings unite—the *function of every note* is manifest and the cumulative revelation of emotion and spirit are revealed in the "accumulation of proportionate detail."

Shaw synthesized Szell's particularity and Toscanini's passion, along with his own nature—his sense of warming the note and his rhythmic intuition. Shaw built like Szell and flew like the maestro, *if* all went well, and it didn't always. The synthesis was not only the Shaw musical result (the Shaw sound) but the Shaw *experience* of music; the Shaw idea of music.

There is no question which man Shaw loved: Toscanini. But Szell was a profound influence on Shaw's craft—the breaking down and preparation process that Shaw was forever perfecting. Shaw already had passion. Szell taught him how to inform his passion. He showed him a way to work from the small cell up, which was the way Shaw tended to work. And Szell taught Shaw how to make reverence for music real, not just pious. Reverence, piety is a good place to start. But, according to the Gospel of Shaw, without comprehension and preparation musical piety can become a mere posture, or worse, a pose. Szell, as an old man, was as much in awe of Beethoven as Shaw had been as a young man. But it was a pragmatic awe. Szell knew something of what it had cost Beethoven to be Beethoven.

Shaw didn't much *like* George Szell personally. His days in Cleveland were, in many ways, hell. Moreover, there was a breach. Shaw felt Szell lied to him. Szell told Shaw he could not go with the orchestra on a tour of Russia because the State Department didn't want Shaw to go. Shaw discovered this was not the case. The government was glad to have Shaw, for this would have been a return Shaw appearance, after the Robert Shaw Chorale's triumphant tour. Evidently, *Szell* did not want Shaw on the trip. After that, Shaw wrote Szell off personally as he tended to write off those he felt had let him down, though he stayed with the orchestra several more years. The Shaw-Szell personal relationship was troubled. And by Shaw's own testimony, it was that way, virtually, from the start. But Shaw's own words that he "taught me practically all I know of music," also ring true. Fairly or unfairly, Shaw felt he was something of a musical adolescent until he went to Cleveland. Szell threw him into cold water and made him swim.

Julius Herford's dictum, refined by Shaw, was that out of structure musical spirit would flow. Szell went Herford one better. He was even more structural, cool, and analytical, and he was a virtuoso, as opposed to an academic. Shaw felt that, though it was harsh medicine, what Szell prescribed was what he needed. Shaw tried to know himself. He knew he was a romantic. He felt he should tether himself to structure and musical coolness to temper his own ardor. Szell wanted the music as clean and technically perfect as it could be. Shaw agreed. Moreover, Shaw felt there should be no easy road to beauty, to faith—whatever the faith—indeed, to Bach. This precise, mathematical approach was, for him, the narrow road. Certainly, Shaw felt, the listener should ultimately respond to the Bach Passions, for example, emotionally. But he believed that a conductor had no right to such a response without first delving into these works with intensive study and preparation. And yes, ultimately, suffering the piece. A musician must *earn* the right to an emotional response to great music, Shaw believed, by mastering matters of craft and by many hours of toil. Szell made him suffer.

Thus, out of structure, true freedom. And out of transparency, beauty. The influence of Shaw's study of the Baroque is as important as the influence of Herford and Szell in forming his aesthetic. Shaw knew the emotion would come on its own, in the end. He knew *he* would respond emotionally. The emotional content was, in a sense, the easy part. The greater challenge was to become absorbed in the composer's world, learn his language; then the composer's message would come—not the performer's message laid over the composition, like icing on a cake, but the composer's own message.

Perhaps for Szell, as some players held, the emotion was the hard part. But Szell had a great mind. And Shaw respected intellect above all else. When asked by Martin Goldsmith on National Public Radio if a Christmas carol sung by a rag-tag door-to-door group was not as profound an artistic and human achievement in its way as a Haydn symphony, Shaw, who was being interviewed about Christmas music at the time, responded swiftly, "No, I don't think so." The massive intelligence it takes to construct a symphony *has* to count for more, he said. And weeks of rehearsal are more likely to lead to human nobility than spur-of-the-moment good intentions. Shaw would often tell choruses, "the audience is welcome, but they cannot possibly understand the piece the way we do" after living with it and struggling with it.

Shaw was committed to the intellect, just as he was committed to musical analysis. But his nature was emotive, just as Szell's was cool. Even to analysis and rehearsal, Shaw brought emotion. After all, the original musical influences on Shaw were Protestant hymnody, folk music and spirituals. Later, under Herford's tutelage, Baroque music became the dominant influence. Shaw did most of his musical analysis as Herford had taught him to analyze Bach: Structure revels spirit. But Shaw's personality was not Baroque. It was more nearly Byronic. Shaw knew this, thought it a weakness, and tried to compensate. Actually, it was not a weakness. It was his power. It was the essence of his ability to connect and communicate.

Robert Shaw came from the warmth of Southern California and held memories of that place and its climate dear. He lived a good part of his life in Atlanta. He liked the sun, the earth, wine, food, and beautiful women. He was not *by nature* a watchmaker. He was a watchmaker by vow. He was by nature a Romantic poet who forced himself to focus on the microcosm—to work cell by cell. His practices were Szellian, but his heart would always be closer to *the* maestro. When Shaw finally recorded the Verdi *Requiem*, which he said he loved partly because he loved Verdi's democratic and anticlerical beliefs, he claimed it put him in touch again somehow with Toscanini and working with the master on his recording of the work. Toscanini is indeed present in Shaw's towering recording. So is Verdi. That recording was Shaw's homage to his spiritual and musical godfather.

Shaw would hold back his choirs and never release their full might until the performance. That restraint—never letting his forces release with full, open throttle until the very end—was a potent tool. It allowed him to dam emotion and reserve it for performance, hence to bring some spontaneity to his highly structural approach. "Prepare as dryly and in as detached a fashion as possible," he said, "and then 'let it rip' in performance."[54]

Shaw imposed his "disciplines" upon himself as well as others. Indeed, he disciplined himself most of all, for he distrusted his own emotion so: *First, get the music in order, construct and deconstruct. Emotion must not come cheaply, or too soon. And it must never be about you, Shaw.*

He had been a flamboyant conductor when young but then, inspired by Toscanini and Stravinsky on the podium, he'd consciously changed his style. His gestures became contained. Emotion was discernible only in his eyes and the movement of his right hand or forefinger. There was no waving or gyration, no thrusting up of the torso toward the players in mock religio-sexual ecstasy. From behind, the audience saw very little. Shaw admired the restraint of Toscanini, Szell, and Fritz Reiner, above the grandiosity of others. Yet Shaw did *not* resemble them in performance. He was more likely to be swept up, in spite of all the disciplines. Late in life, in one of the Carnegie Hall videos, he said, "I know that 25 percent of the disciplines will wear off in performance (especially in a temporary or young choir) and I *enjoy* it when it wears off—as long as it is blood and visceral and enthusiasm and passion." Shaw might not have said such a thing 20 or even 10 years earlier. As a mature artist, he reconciled his trinity of impulses—Toscaninian passion, Szellian precision, Shavian savoring. He gave everything when he was conducting. His eyes and hands were incredibly expressive—powerful, and pleading. Once inside the music, he held nothing back. And maybe, sometimes, he also managed to disappear, as he wished, into the music.

"You're no George Szell," Maxine Shaw had said so devastatingly. Eventually, Shaw discovered that he did not need to be. Critic James Oestreich wrote, after Shaw's last performance of the Brahms *Requiem* in Carnegie Hall in 1997: "There are times when it is simply a privilege to be in the hall . . . at last Brahms has his requiem."

54 Shaw speaking to the ASO chorus.

In Cleveland, as noted, Shaw began to do what he'd only touched upon in New York and would do a great deal of in Atlanta: public speaking—semi-preaching. This was one way he broke out of his loneliness. Some of these were remarkable addresses. And they were a lifelong habit with Shaw. He liked to speak and to preach. He wrote and rewrote almost every speech, no matter the audience. Be it a men's service club or a graduate symposium, he wrote, and spoke, at length—trying to make his meaning plainer, his message more urgent. He had no "mainstream" speech. He didn't pitch at one level to civic leaders and at another to music teachers. Everyone got Bach, Buber, Beethoven, and Lincoln. Everyone got a sermon on the gospel of music, according to Shaw's Christian humanism, via the sainted composers. He loved these occasions and spent a lot of time on them, which mystified colleagues like Szell and friends like Lane and Herford. Why take time from music—time that Shaw always guarded as so dear? Why take time—when he could spare little of it for his friends or family—to write a speech for a Rotary club?

Yet these speeches—secular sermons and meditations, really—served as therapy for Shaw. They replaced some of his New York party life with study and cogitation, yet still allowed him to let off steam. For he was preaching, first of all, to himself. And he got a chance to be an evangelist again. Besides, as hard as he worked on his speeches, they were not nearly as physically and psychologically demanding as music.

But there must have been some good town fathers of Cleveland, as there later were in Atlanta, who thought to themselves, "Say what?" when they heard some of these talks. A Shaw speech might be 5,000 or 6,000 words—an *address* in other words—with 1,000 words on Charles Ives alone.

To the Cleveland Rotary Club Shaw threw out this little ditty on "the meaning of a circle," apparently a work of his own devising. (Shaw took credit for it when someone wrote to him and asked, and it would not have been his way to do so had it not been his work; but it has the feel of something, or some version of something that may have been circulating at the time—in the 1965 approximation of the Internet.) On the other hand, it sounds very much like Shaw. Some might think it a bit sophomoric. It is naïve and primitive, but it is very much Shaw:

A Circle means
an infinite number of points
absolutely the same distance
from a certain point.

The first thing you face
is the idea of infinity
It's a big idea—
People haven't always had it.

Then there's the idea of
—a Point.
That's a big idea—
it's the idea of one,
the Indivisible—
that's monotheism.

A Circle also means
no beginning
and no end.
That's forever –
Eternality —
Everlasting.

Now one more thing—
Set that Infinite Indivisible Eternal Circle in Motion,
—a wheel, no less,
Let it move—
Point after infinite circumference point.

How long then,
Before this infinite number of points
Will begin to repeat themselves?
—and if they do—
if the wheel really goes once around —
can the points really be Infinite?
Can Infinity repeat itself
on into Infinity?

Or what about the axis point?
Does it turn 'round too?
—Because if it does—
then part of it's up
while the other part's down
or part of it's facing East
while the rest
faces West.
—And anything that can face two ways
at once
has two or more sides—and is no Point.

The axis, then,
cannot really be said
to move at all.

And at the center of Infinite Motion
—we have Infinite stillness.
And the radii of Infinity
Revolve with what friction
Around the Immovable?

If it sounds silly—
Take that circle.

CHAPTER 21

Church Musician—A Happy Parenthetical

Shaw made a lot of great music in Cleveland. But, for him, there was not much happiness—with one exception. In 1960, Shaw took over the music program at a Unitarian church. This was not something Shaw did primarily as a matter of civic or professional duty, though it was to some degree perceived that way at the time. He did it to feed his soul.

It happened this way:

First, Shaw, at this point in his life, desperately needed a friend—a real confidante with whom he could talk—in Cleveland. He found such a friend in Robert Killam, minister of the First Unitarian Church of that city. Second, Killam was Shaw's kind of minister. He was deeply pastoral; he was a social and political liberal; and he was an intellectual. More, he was at least as many parts secular humanist and Christian philosopher as he was Christian evangelist. Killam's field of scholarship was not the Old Testament or the Psalms, but Shakespeare. Shaw found in Killam a man who shared his own idea of what the Christian Church ought to be—essentially humanist and mystic. Killam gave Shaw a bridge between his interest in religious faith and his distaste for organized religion, between his spiritual attraction to sacred music and his desire to reject "that old-time religion," between his past and his present, between his parents and himself.

As Shaw saw it, Jesus was not an organization man and would not have been seen in a cathedral or a church on 5th Avenue in New York. "Jesus," said Shaw, "had trouble with a temple made of mud." Further, Jesus wanted to change minds and souls, and bring charity and non-violence to the world. Man's interpretation of concepts like divinity and eternity, superimposed on Jesus of Nazareth, were, for Shaw, distracting and perhaps even idolatrous. Shaw found in Unitarianism a way to reconcile his own skepticism and his longing for faith. In Killam, he found a kindred spirit; a fellow pilgrim. He found, perhaps, the man his father might have become in another time and place, given more time to live and more exposure to different ideas. He found the man Robert Shaw might have become had he stayed in the preaching business. Killam encouraged Shaw to continue his reading in the Eastern religions—an interest sparked during Shaw's studies with Dr. Alexander at Pomona College. It may well have been Killam who introduced Shaw to the Jewish theologian and mystic Martin Buber, whom Shaw discovered in middle age, read closely for the rest of his life, and came to love.

Shaw said, years later, that he found Unitarianism "quite supportable." In the Unitarian Church he discovered a denomination and doctrine (or anti-doctrine) that did not require him "to check one's mind at the door." It was gratifying to be, briefly, not at odds with something so deeply imbedded in his psyche.

What really made Shaw happy was what grew out of the Shaw-Killam friendship. Killam persuaded Shaw to become the church's part-time minister of music (of course the old one had to be dispatched). Shaw had long been fascinated by the idea of developing purely musical liturgies, and he returned to that idea in his old age. Eventually, he began to think of his concerts as quasi-liturgical. (Not all the time, and not all concerts.) But at First Unitarian he could try out his idea. And he did. Shaw took the job as minister of music at Killam's church on the condition that he would be allowed to create his own sacred services. There might be a brief meditation or two—but the music would *be* the worship. Shaw would conceive and execute such services several times a year. And he would assume responsibility for music for all other Sundays as well. He would also hire an organist/assistant music minister to handle routine Sunday chores. The church, Shaw stipulated, would pay him no salary, but would hire a string quartet and soloists of his choosing. It would also purchase a harpsichord, a grand piano, and commission and pay for a Baroque organ. Killam agreed to the conductor's conditions and found donors to pay. Shaw had complete artistic freedom. And during his tenure, he gave two, and possibly three, sermons. Of course, once word got out that Shaw was the music minister at the First Unitarian Church of Cleveland, the church needed to double the number of Sunday services.

Killam was not trying to "land" Shaw or to put his church on the map. Shaw stimulated his mind as much as he stimulated Shaw's. Just as Killam introduced Shaw to the Bard, Shaw introduced Killam to Bach. Just as Killam considered the plays of Shakespeare to be, in some sense, sacred texts, Shaw found great music to be a sacred language. Both men were excited by the notion of redefining church and faith and by exploring the diversity of religious experience by a less-traveled secular route. Killam loved Shaw's idea that if there is a Creator responsible for the world, he must still be creating somewhere, by some means.

Shaw's part-time job as music director of a small church was an oasis during the busy Cleveland years, and Shaw had, along with close friends and colleagues he brought from the orchestra, a glorious time. He became, for the first time since his youth and the last time in his life, a church musician. Cleveland Orchestra players earned supplementary incomes doing music not often available to them, and in the warm, familial setting of the church. (Shaw saw that they were paid handsomely, dipping into his own pocket when necessary and seeing that those who needed transportation on Sunday were driven to the church, in his Bentley.) Shaw's select ensemble of musicians played the music of Bach, Handel, Vivaldi, Schubert, and more, Sunday after Sunday. Shaw loved working on this intimate, chamber music scale. He was contributing as a *fellow* chamber musician, with friends, out of the limelight, and only for the glory of the music, which was his way of glorifying the Great Spirit at the source of this music. ("God" was seldom mentioned in sermons by Killam or Shaw.) The harpsichord and organ were customized to meet Shaw's specifications. And soon the First Unitarian Church was fending off converts on "Shaw Sundays." For these unique events, performed by the city's finest musicians, were free. Interestingly, Shaw formed no permanent personnel at the church. The musical ingredients—string quartet, harpsichord, and baroque organ, plus voices—were the set items. Actual players varied. The musicians came from the Cleveland Orchestra and Chorus on a pickup basis, as with the Robert Shaw Chorale.

Shaw hardly needed another job, for he also had the Chorale's touring and recording schedule, guest conducting engagements, and workshops on his plate, in addition to his Cleveland Orchestra responsibilities. But his post at First Unitarian was Shaw's happy parenthetical in Ohio. It had no commercial element. Shaw was making music with friends whom he respected and loved. He was making music for the purpose of divine praise and contemplation, just as Bach had done, albeit in a modern, more secular context. But it was not for RCA, George Szell, or tour audiences. If not for God, expressly, it *was* for worship—some sort of embrace of the spirit and the divine. In this intimate musical and human context, Shaw could be free and happy. The extra job he didn't "need" was the one he needed for his sanity.

In Killam, Shaw also found someone who could hold his own intellectually—one of the few in Shaw's lifetime. Killam was a man whose mind and character Shaw admired and whose company he enjoyed enormously. He was Shaw's kind of Christian and Shaw's kind of pastor. He loved the man.

The First Unitarian gig lasted roughly four years. Shaw's schedule grew overwhelmingly busy. Then Killam fell ill and eventually died. Shaw lost interest in the church and church participation after that; though half a lifetime later, he did sometimes attend his wife Caroline's church, Trinity Presbyterian in Atlanta, and he took a great liking to its minister, Allison Williams. He even appeared in a series of concerts and gave a series of lectures there.[55] But Shaw was never much for sitting in a pew. And never again

55 Burris-Williams interview.

would he be a church musician. Indeed, never again would Shaw make a church *his* home. Caroline's church was her church. The Unitarian interlude in Cleveland was a blessed time in a chapter of little peace.

Shaw's act of renouncement—his self-exile from Manhattan and his rigorous, often punishing, residence in Cleveland—helped him to become the learned musician he wanted to be. If he did not entirely achieve the mastery of the orchestra that he sought, he grew enormously—intellectually and artistically. All of his Cleveland experiences made him a better musician: the church work; the youth concerts and TV appearances; the collaboration with fine players; and, obviously, the primary work with Szell. Shaw stuck it out because he felt Szell really *was* a know-it-all where the orchestra was concerned. And he felt Szell was even harder on himself than others. Shaw told Louis Lane, "We must suffer if we want to make great music."

In the Cleveland years, it was often only the choral-orchestral works that took flight when Shaw held the baton. The rest was schooling, and penance for being a dumb undereducated kid from a hick town in California. He still did not entirely trust himself with the orchestra. But at least he knew his way around it now. When he arrived in Atlanta, he felt he was no longer ignorant or lacking in musical insight.

Cleveland also complicated Shaw's already difficult marriage. Robert and Maxine had grown increasingly unhappy with each other. She moved from Scarsdale to Cleveland and back again. In Cleveland, Shaw sometimes lived in a hotel. His philandering was less generalized, but also less hidden. He spent his time with his assistant Edna Lea Burrus. That was convenient for Robert but excruciating for Maxine since the nature of "Eddie's" relationship to Robert was well known. Eddie had also been a sort of ex-officio family member. Shaw's treatment of his wife was beyond shabby and the way he sometimes used other women throughout his life was just that—*use*.

Some were only too happy to be used. Edna Lea Burrus enslaved herself willingly. But Shaw's treatment of Maxine, and of women in general, was shockingly out of sync with his own values and capacity for empathy and friendship. Even in the context of the period (the 1930s and 1940s and 1950s), his behavior toward Maxine, and toward women generally, is inexplicable and inexcusable. It is a dark side of Shaw and one that later caused him shame. Shaw was in a great deal of pain in the Cleveland years. He caused much pain as well. He believed artists should suffer. Maxine Shaw was not trying to be an artist.

The Cleveland years were, in many ways, what Shaw anticipated—learning and struggling, and an apprenticeship to a brilliant and difficult man. But there was perhaps more misery than he expected. Shaw *did* call Szell "Mr. Szell" until Shaw's own final days. ("George" in person, but "Mr. Szell" when referring to him. This was Shaw's choice. Szell did not require it. Shaw called Toscanini by his surname when telling stories about him and called him "Maestro" when addressing him directly.)

Shaw transformed musically in Cleveland. He learned a great deal of music that he had not known previously, as he did in Atlanta as well. He became more careful, more scholarly, a better listener, and also more tentative. Musical tightness and cohesion became increasingly important. But he emerged from his purgatorial post-graduate education with even less self-confidence. He felt his own inadequacies before going to work for Szell. Now, knowing more, he understood his limitations in agonizing detail. In his very late years, Shaw became more Toscanini-like—with emphasis on locomotion and exaltation. It was not until then, and a return to New York City, that the joy of his early professional years returned.

CHAPTER 22

Fathers and Sons

Robert Shaw's life was all about his own fatherhood and son-hood. The two mentors of Shaw's college years—"Prof." (Ralph) Lyman and Hartley Burr Alexander—were saintly men, "Mr. Chips" sort of figures on the leafy Pomona College campus. Lyman gave "Bob" Shaw responsibility. He saw such talent in the young man—then very raw—that he turned his choir over to him. Surely more experienced hands were available. But Lyman was dazzled by the young man's innate ability to create a rich choral sound. Indeed, he may have realized young Shaw possessed a talent he himself did not have. (Interestingly, Shaw in his eighties, sat with Nola Frink and listened to two recordings of the Pomona Glee Clubs, one under the direction of Lyman and one dating from the year he replaced the ailing teacher. Though sheepishly, Shaw had to admit that the chorus on the second recording had a fuller, richer sonority.)

Alexander, the professor of comparative religion, gave Shaw something his parents could not—permission, and then encouragement, to question in matters of the spirit. Without Alexander, it would have been, perhaps, harder for Shaw to throw off his bonds to the Christian church and fashion his own faith. Not unlike Shaw's biological father, Alexander embraced the ethic of Jesus. But unlike Rev. Shaw, Alexander emphasized the humanity of Christ.

Robert Shaw turned the dial one notch higher. For him, the personhood of Christ was preferable to God-hood. Humanity trumped divinity. Shaw eventually embraced other religions, along with secular humanism, as part of his own eclectic mosaic of belief. Eventually, music became not an augmentation of worship but rather, to him, a purer form of worship than a Christian prayer service. Art was not an intimation of the divine, or even an expression of it, but a concrete manifestation of the divine, or in Shaw's words: "flesh becomes word." Hartley Burr Alexander opened this door for Shaw. It was he who introduced Shaw to comparative religion and to mysticism.

Fred Waring, the third father-figure to enter Shaw's formative years, was a sort of upside down Shirley Shaw—selfish, profane, vain, ambitious, worldly, and somewhat avaricious. No one would mistake him for Mr. Chips. But Waring was the great liberator: the man who took Bob Shaw away from the local church and college choir to New York and opened that door—a door that opened to show girls and saloons, too. Shaw liked Waring's world, if not Waring himself.

Julius Herford came next. He was Shaw's first *true* teacher. Shaw sought him out and asked him to teach him "everything." Together they read and analyzed the choral masterworks of Haydn, Mozart, Brahms and, of course, Bach. They worked hardest and by far the longest hours on Bach. Herford was primarily a choral scholar and undoubtedly the key influence on Shaw in preparation of music, beginning with score analysis. Herford was the man who introduced Shaw to much of the literature that would become his own repertoire. And Herford taught him how to study and prepare. He not only taught him Bach, but how to be a "Bachian." But Shaw outgrew Herford as he would outgrow the previous and the subsequent father figures. Herford scarcely influenced Shaw after those early years together. They saw each other infrequently. First, because Shaw left New York, and second, because their needs and interests diverged. Herford was essentially an academic and Shaw a performer. When Herford prepared a work, his goal was to gain understanding—scholarly insight. When Shaw studied and prepared a work, even in an academic setting, it was with an eye toward realizing and performing the creator's conception.

When Shaw began to conduct the San Diego Symphony in 1953, he brought Herford on board—running workshops on musical analysis for the musicians. Herford was doing the same sort of teaching he had done in New York for Shaw's Collegiate Chorale. But by then, though Herford was offering the conductor interpretive advice, Shaw didn't want it. The next phase of their relationship was detachment and alienation. The final phase was reconciliation.

But in their early days together, Herford submerged Shaw in the music of Bach. This was enormously important, for it influenced Shaw's approach to music. Bach's abiding musical pulse spoke to Shaw's sense of *rhythm as essence* in music. Shaw applied his approach to "Bach phrasing," which he worked out with Herford and wrote about in letters to his choruses, to most oratorio works. For example, Shaw believed musical phrases trumped linguistic phrases in most works and that musical clauses within phrases were also entitled to their own time and space. Musical sense and syntax had to take precedence over linguistic sense and syntax. Musical clarity was more important than textual message, despite the significance of the text. A pop singer could bend the musical line to accommodate text. Not so, a chorus. This may seem like another contradiction for a word man who began in music with the song. But for Shaw, pulse came even before song, and musical language actually *was* language—language of a higher order.

Bach's profound spirituality obviously also moved Shaw deeply (though Bach's piety and religious steadfastness also scared and perplexed him). Bach's extraordinary sense of structure and musical architecture fascinated and absorbed Shaw, as it does so many musicians. Ultimately, Shaw found the Bach Passions to be the greatest dramas ever written. To him, the Passions were unique meditation on both divine and human nature. And what appealed to Shaw particularly was getting there via artifice and intellect, not sweep of emotion. Indeed, for better *and* worse Shaw approached preparation of even the music of Verdi and Mahler in this essentially Bachian, structural way. Shaw tackled scores the way Herford taught him—analyze texturally (critics would say mechanistically), presuming that taking apart the watch and putting it back together will reveal the spirit, the temperament, of the composer. Out of musical structure, Holy Spirit. Shaw's roots in Bach, which were thanks principally to Herford, sustained him all of his musical life.

Obviously, the fifth and sixth father figures were Toscanini and Szell. But with a caveat. Toscanini was more of a grandfather, or perhaps godfather—the greatest overall influence on Shaw and the only one Shaw did not tire of or outgrow. But Toscanini was an influence and an inspiration, not a tutor, like Herford or Szell.

There are three other men who also figure prominently in Shaw's pantheon, and who were father figures, though far less involved in Shaw's life than were Herford, Szell, or Toscanini. These were idealized father figures. One might compare them to a boy's favorite uncle, or a coach, or a scoutmaster. Shaw revered Pablo Casals, Paul Hindemith, and Rudolf Serkin.

Shaw worked with Casals for two summers at the Casals Festival in Puerto Rico. Though Shaw conducted the Casals Festival orchestra and the choirs he had imported from Cleveland, he also prepared the chorus for Casals to conduct the Bach *St. John Passion.* He stepped back into the chorus-master role for Casals. There was perhaps no one else he would have done that for at that stage of his career. On one occasion they also collaborated on a single performance in New York—bringing the festival forces and program to Carnegie Hall. No evidence exists to show that the two corresponded or otherwise became close. Casals was in his last years when he and Shaw worked together. But Shaw and Casals hit it off. Shaw looked upon Casals as had Toscanini. He saw him as a great humanitarian as well as a master musician. Shaw spent a good deal of time *watching* Casals conduct. He also talked to Casals about the cello at some length. He didn't much like to watch or study Szell. He loved to observe Casals.

Though Casals offered some of the warmth Szell lacked, he c(equally dogmatic. What Shaw loved was not Casals's dogmatism, innocence—his *devotion* to music and his ability to be freshly awed by it. Shaw called him a consummate artist with an amateur's heart. He told of Casals setting down his baton in rehearsal and saying, "Gentlemen, we're the luckiest people alive." For Shaw, Pablo Casals was a sort of saint of music.

Similar attributes could be applied to Rudolf Serkin, with whom Shaw *was* close personally and with whom Shaw collaborated quite often—engagements in Atlanta, San Diego, Cleveland, at the Curtis Institute, and at the Marlboro Festival, spanning three decades. To Shaw, Serkin was a pure man, and a pure musician—unsullied by vanity or commercialism, and focused entirely on the selfless pursuit of music. Shaw truly loved him. Perhaps even more than Casals, Serkin had the amateur spirit, or what might be called innocence—he was constantly surprised, exalted, and humbled by his art. He and Shaw kept in touch and confided in each other.

Shaw also loved all that the Marlboro Festival stood for. He conducted there in August 1961 (the Beethoven *Choral Fantasy*, which traditionally closes the Marlboro season) and again in 1962 (the *Choral Fantasy* once more and the Schubert *Mass in G)* and visited there briefly several other summers. Shaw always wanted to study and observe great instrumentalists and he liked to hear and see chamber disciplines. His choral institute in France, founded in the 1990s, was in a sense "Shaw's Marlboro"—not in a literal sense, since Marlboro's program is chamber music made by mentors and students working together. But Shaw imagined his festival in France to be born of the same spirit (similar to his church work in Cleveland). The Shaw Festival was supposed to be amateur in tenor—done for love. It was planned as a communion of artists, living in community and existing only for music. Much of their work was done on a chamber scale—even a "small" *Mass in B Minor*. And though the singers, even the young ones, were mostly pros, there were indeed some student-teacher relationships. The festival had only one real mentor though—Shaw.

Robert Shaw was an ambitious musician. But his ambition was not to be on the cover of *Time* magazine. It was to become like Casals and Serkin—to exude and inspire a certain love or innocence that placed ego in a hip pocket. The critic Edward Said called Shaw's appearance on the podium "saintly," which caused Shaw's intimates to smile, as he too may have done. His manner was most unsaintly in everyday life. But he *did* convey grace and reverence on the podium in later years, much like those two heroes from his past.

Shaw wanted to be like the teachers and elders he admired. It meant making war on his own ego and regarding most of life, other than music, as a distraction. And he did become like them. As with Casals and Serkin, the music listening public could sense something special—quiet, lonely, and yes, in a way, holy—in a Shaw performance.

Many successful human beings are helped along by mentors—teachers who may also be substitute father or mother figures. But Shaw, the Bob Shaw who became Robert Shaw, was in many ways formed by his father figures. And yet, Shaw chose *them* as much as they chose him. And he seemed to choose them based upon a truth, an instinct, or a direction he had already intuited.

Further, in forming each mentor-disciple partnership, Shaw seemed to seek out teachers who were, each in his own and different way, the antithesis of his father. Alexander emphasized Christ's humanity over his divinity. Waring was profane. Toscanini, Casals, and Serkin were open hearted and passionate. Herford's church was Bach.

It was as if Shaw was pulled by some inward light toward the man he wanted to be. The campus liberal in Pomona could not have imagined the work he would do in choral music or in Atlanta. He could not have imagined himself as the force in music that he became, or the type of conductor he became. But he knew, almost from the moment he arrived in New York, that he wanted to be a part of serious music and he knew that his life in music would not be, principally, about fame or entertainment. So, as in Plato's cave, Shaw was guided by an ideal, a form, a partial vision, however obscured it may have been at times.

Shaw chose mentors who would help him to form a church outside of, and larger than, the Christian church—a church of music. Each teacher struck a chord in Shaw that already existed. And each one helped him place a stone in his personal cathedral.

But none of his teachers, including Fred Waring and Toscanini, took him in hand and said, "Look here, Robert, that's the wrong path for you, go this way instead." Shaw was already on a path—always. His path. Only Szell tried to redirect him from the outside. And Shaw resisted him. The father figure he heeded was more like a Spencer Tracy or Robert Young character—strong, compassionate, wise, inspiring, but detached. An example, not a nanny.[56]

Thornton Wilder and William Schuman were also strong influences for a while—tutors mostly in the ways of the world. Both shared Shaw's inherent and, later, well-developed interest in new artistic forms—in the theater and music of his time.

Shaw took what he could use from each of his teachers, and once he found the thing the teacher had to give, he soaked up every drop he could. Then he moved on.

Shaw was not unlike Szell in that he was himself a natural teacher. The difference between them was that Shaw was also a preacher, or an enthusiast (in his friend Wilder's word). He was giving workshops on choral music and holding forth on the art in the early 1940s. But in truth, Shaw began to teach before he knew all that much about music—he knew only his passion, his credo, and his instinct for choral sound.

56 It was during the Szell period of his life, and after Toscanini's passing, that Shaw worked with Casals at the festival in Puerto Rico. Their instant closeness, much like what occurred with Toscanini, reflected the tension in the Shaw–Szell relationship. Szell was not nourishing Shaw emotionally or spiritually. Shaw was a man with a chronic case of the Protestant work ethic. He always wanted the best. But he was also one who generated, and required, warmth. He could not live with Szell's harshness any more than he could live with Maxine's. In Casals, he found a child-like sunnyness.

As he matured into "generativity" and middle age, Shaw began to be a mentor/father figure himself. By then he knew musical structure, most choral and much symphonic literature, and the management of large ensembles, and he had begun the slow, painful process of coming to himself and relaxing into some degree of self-knowledge. He had always been expository by nature, but now, he could truly teach. He knew his craft. And of course, by his seventies and eighties he had become a very great teacher indeed, for he had honed his aphorisms, his technical tricks and his shortcuts.

It was necessary for Shaw to love, or at least respect, his artistic mentors and to look up to them as human beings. If he could not love them, or lost respect for them, he stopped listening. There was a period of time when he turned away from Julius Herford and stopped listening. The same thing happened with Szell. Possibly Thornton Wilder fell from grace similarly. No information exists to explain why the friendship seemed to stop abruptly. Wilder was very fond of Maxine Shaw, so that may have been a factor.

Eventually, in Atlanta, there were no more mentors. Shaw stood alone. Some might argue that it was high time, for Shaw was then in his early fifties. Nonetheless, in Atlanta from 1967 to the end of his life, he finally acquired assurance and fluidity before the orchestra. Experience became his penultimate teacher and, in due course, the composers became the final teachers—teachers he could not outgrow.

Eventually, son-ship gave way to fatherhood.

Shaw had numerous surrogate sons. This was another injury to his real sons from his first marriage. He didn't spend much time with Peter or Thad. But he did take time to mentor, and even "father" to a point, various young musicians. Here, too, musical and personal admiration necessarily overlapped.

Mack Harrell, a great American baritone and father of cellist Lynn Harrell, was Shaw's dear friend. Mack Harrell was a sort of brother to

Shaw. He was the kind of man Shaw liked and admired—humble but not affected; artistic yet robust, even profane; naturally physical and athletic. Shaw not only loved Mack Harrell the musician, he loved the man. Harrell died young and Lynn Harrell, who was Shaw's godson, became a surrogate Shaw son. Shaw looked in on him and interceded for him in various ways for many years, culminating in securing an audition for Harrell with Szell and the Cleveland Orchestra. Harrell was hired, though not because Shaw pulled strings. Szell did not operate that way. Shaw's influence got Harrell the audition. Harrell's talent got him the job. Young Harrell and Shaw then became colleagues and confidantes in Cleveland and Harrell later played with Shaw as a soloist in Atlanta and New York. Shaw truly loved him like a son and Harrell knew it well. Unlike Shaw's own sons, Shaw could communicate with Harrell through music.

And there were other protégés, much beloved by Shaw. Bill Preucil, concertmaster in Atlanta and then Cleveland, could do no wrong in Shaw's mind. First as musician and then as a man. Preucil felt that way about Shaw, too. Christopher Rex, first cellist in Atlanta, whom Shaw hired from the Philadelphia Orchestra, was another surrogate son. And later, two choral musicians, Craig Jessop and Norman Mackenzie, became surrogate sons. Again, the avenue of fraternity, the language of understanding and affection, was music. Jessop sang with Shaw in France. He was a conductor of U.S. Armed Forces bands. He became, for several years, the principal conductor of the Mormon Tabernacle Choir. Mackenzie was Shaw's faithful and flawless accompanist and assistant choral conductor in Atlanta. He eventually was able to anticipate Shaw's dictates, and know what Shaw was thinking almost before he articulated it. After Shaw's death, Mackenzie became director of choruses for the Atlanta Symphony Orchestra.

There were brother figures too. As well as Mack Harrell, there was Clayton Krehbiel—the same sort of man. Krehbiel was a big strapping fellow from Kansas, a sort of all-American outdoorsman who happened to have an incredible natural tenor voice—a classic American folk voice that seemed to come out of the land and express nature itself. He sang in the Robert Shaw

Chorale and for many years was part of the inner circle—the phalanx of aides, allies, and enablers; the Shaw entourage. Krehbiel succeeded Shaw briefly in the chorusmaster's role in Cleveland and finished out his career teaching choral music at Florida State. He was close to Shaw for the rest of his life. They collaborated occasionally. Krehbiel provided student voices for a Shaw performance of the Mahler *Eighth Symphony* in 1978. Many years after their old road days, Krehbiel would show up unannounced at Shaw ASO concerts, which absolutely made Shaw's day. Clayton Krehbiel came, as Shaw put it, "from Mennonite stock" (one of the few religious sects Shaw respected). He seemed to Shaw one of those rare people who had internalized a bit of Christian charity and serenity. Or maybe he was just naturally decent and kind. Shaw was perhaps closer to Krehbiel and Harrell, emotionally, than anyone in his life, though it is doubtful that they ever discussed their "feelings." They talked music. Or talked not much at all.

There were other brothers as well. John Wustman, the prototype for the sort of accompanist Shaw was lucky to find several times in his career. Wustman had exquisite taste and the ability to almost read Shaw's mind. Not many fine pianists grasp the choral animal. Wustman, who went on to a distinguished teaching career at Illinois, and accompanied Luciano Pavarotti, shared Shaw's perfectionism and big heartedness. Maurice Casey, a longtime Shaw choral colleague and deputy, who taught at Ohio State and often pushed Shaw toward new repertoire, was another brother. Walter Gould, Shaw's agent, surely was beloved kin. And, in later life, David Lowance, Shaw's physician, became his Atlanta pal—his fellow punster and bad boy. Like Caroline Shaw, Lowance was "old Atlanta." Like Robert, he liked to puncture pretension.

Robert Porco, long of Indiana University, and later the Cleveland Orchestra, fell somewhere between a son and brother. A choral conductor and educator a generation younger than Shaw, he was held in much esteem, partly because Shaw saw in Porco a musician who cared as much as he did. The first time Shaw heard a choir Porco directed, he said, "I want to meet that man."

In the Atlanta years there was also Harry Keuper, one of Shaw's singers who became the transcriber and keeper of Shaw's edits. Keuper made the original Shaw markings neat and readable—"pretty," Shaw said—and kept them all in order. He wasn't quite son or brother, but more a faithful aide, a Sancho Panza, invaluable to and beloved by Shaw.

Christ supposedly told his disciples, "I have called you friends not slaves." Shaw sometimes forgot there was a difference. But his inner circle, his aides and assistants, were devoted friends to him. He was blessed by their competence and affection, and he knew it. He was blessed by their devotion and intimacy derived from making music.

Shaw liked people less complicated than himself. He liked people who were unspoiled and direct, and a little rough around the edges. It is profoundly ironic that for many years some music critics thought of him as middlebrow, for Shaw was either very high brow (always in the arts and philosophy) or rather low (habits, tastes, and language used in private). The same man who studied, yes studied, the works of Martin Buber told the randiest of randy jokes and, in his seventies, bragged to anyone who happened to be in the room about his sex life, if that subject came to mind. ("Sex on the kitchen floor is pretty good, even at my age.")[57]

Shaw's world was predominantly male. Certainly he desired, and sometimes adored, and more than occasionally exploited women. But seldom were they confidantes; seldom were females admitted to the inner sanctum. That was for fathers and sons and brothers. At least this was so until Shaw's very late years, when he'd begun to change. He always tried to transcend his upbringing and his nature. But even so, Shaw's idea of the world was of a man's world. No woman received the buddy treatment from "R.S." that, say, Mack or Lynn Harrell did. Shaw was a product of his own generation. He often called his long-time colleague and assistant, Nola Frink, "Dear."

Ann Howard Jones was a late-life exception, to a degree. She was a much-trusted assistant in Atlanta. Shaw even called her "Jones"—a sign of comfort and trust. And perhaps of all American choral conductors who knew

57 Burris interview with ASO chorus members.

or studied with Shaw, she is the one who today best incorporates Shaw's spirit and techniques, without trying to mimic him. When Jones was gravely ill, Shaw telephoned her virtually every day. She belonged to his group of "beloveds." Yet one day, impressed by the way she had prepared the ASO chorus in one section of a work, he said, "It's just too bad you're a woman." (Jones became the director of the choral music program at Boston University.)

Only two women were ever really treated as absolute equals by Shaw, and that was late in life: Caroline Sauls Hitz Shaw (the second Mrs. Robert Shaw) and Judith Arron, head of Carnegie Hall and the person most responsible for much of the esteem that befell Shaw late in life.

There was one surrogate daughter, and that was soprano Sylvia McNair. Possessed of the angelic voice Shaw felt his sister had—always light, and never dragging—as well as of Holly's radiant disposition. McNair was informally adopted by Shaw, both personally and professionally. Shaw gave McNair a European debut, her New York debut, and her recording debut. Sylvia became close to Caroline Shaw. Her relationship to Caroline was part sister and part daughter, and she remained close in Caroline's final illness. When McNair made her debut at the Metropolitan Opera, Robert and Caroline flew to New York to support her. McNair sang at the funerals of both Robert and Caroline, as well as at the wedding of their son, Thomas. Shaw adored her and could let down his guard around her, though if she had not been an extraordinary talent, Shaw might never have opened the door to her in the first place. It was a matter of warmth responding to warmth and musicality responding to musicality. Again, a relationship not possible with Shaw's real daughter was possible within music.

In his old age, Shaw did begin to figure out how to better relate to women through this father-daughter dynamic, rather than as servants or sexual conquests. Christine Goerke was another young musician Shaw treated almost as a daughter or granddaughter. He plucked her from the chorus and made her a soloist, and she became an opera star. The personal relationships always grew out of musical collaboration. He was also very fond of Atlanta singer-musician Pam Elrod, another music educator. Shaw loved her for her voice, musicality, intelligence, and warmth. But Shaw, being Shaw (then nearly eighty), also said she had "great legs."

Shaw mentored so many, while failing woefully to parent his own first children—Johanna, Peter, and Thad. But the only way he could find his full humanity was within the music. Here he found a safe place for his religious explorations *and* for fatherhood, brotherhood, and sonhood. Everyday life was not so readily navigable.

Key "familial" relationships in Robert Shaw's life

FATHERS		SONS/BROTHERS	
SIGNIFICANT	IMPORTANT	SON (DAUGHTER)	BROTHER (SISTER)
Prof. Alexander (comparative religion)	Prof. Lyman (chorus)		Clayton Krehbiel (singer, choral educator)
	Howard Swan (choral educator)	Seth McCoy (singer)	Mack Harrell (singer)
Fred Waring (band leader)		Daniel Lewis (conductor, music educator)	
Julius Herford (music educator and scholar)		Lynn Harrell (cellist)	Maurice Casey (choral educator)
ArturoToscanini (conductor)			John Wustman (pianist, accompanist, educator)
George Szell (conductor)		Peter Serkin (pianist)	Walter Gould (agent, business associate)
	William Schuman (composer, Juilliard President)	Robert Porco (choral educator, conductor)	
Pablo Casals (cellist, conductor)		Bill Preucil (violinist, concertmaster)	
	ThorntonWilder (playwright)		
Paul Hindemith (composer)		Craig Jessop (conductor, Shaw singer, protégé)	
Rudolf Serkin (pianist)		Norman Mackenzie (accompanist, rehearsal pianist, choral conductor)	
		Ann Howard Jones (Shaw conducting assistant, choral educator, conductor)	
		Sylvia McNair (epitomized Shaw soprano sound)	
		Jeffrey Kahane (pianist)	
		Garrick Olsson (pianist)	

PART THREE

MISSION

"How can I reach all those people?"

—Robert Shaw

CHAPTER 23

ATLANTA

W*hy* Atlanta?

Why did Shaw leave Cleveland for what then seemed a cultural backwater, at least to many of his fans and friends? A decade before, when he decided to leave New York City, though his career was in high gear there, it was to become a better musician. The Cleveland Orchestra was a great orchestra. But why did he go to the Atlanta Symphony Orchestra in 1967?

The short answers: (1) He was ready to move on after eleven years with Szell and (2) Atlanta came after him. There were not then, just as there are not now, frequent leadership openings among the symphony orchestras of the nation. Besides, no one else had made an offer. There had been an earlier flirtation with Portland, but when Shaw discovered that Cleveland players were being not-so-discreetly polled by Portland Symphony representatives, he became enraged and called it off.

Still, Atlanta was a curious move. Atlanta at that time was a part-time, regional orchestra in a city without an established fine arts culture. It was in a part of the world that many of Shaw's contemporaries and intimates, not least among them his then-wife Maxine, regarded as primitive. Indeed, Shaw himself knew little of the South. He was a West Coast man whose career had been based in New York and Cleveland. When the Robert Shaw Chorale toured the South with African-American soloist Seth McCoy, it encountered difficulty booking halls and hotel accommodations. Further, Shaw had been warned there could be "trouble" when he insisted on a wide-open ticket policy and an integrated audience. There was no trouble, but there was tension, and McCoy had to pretty much keep to his hotel room and take his meals there, often joined by Shaw and other Chorale colleagues.

If his intent was merely to escape Szell, Shaw might have simply gone back to New York, revived and augmented his Manhattan presence, and established the Chorale as a resident, as well as touring, choir. He could have assembled his own orchestras as he'd done in New York in the early 1950s and for recordings all along. A masterworks series could have been mounted, like the ones he'd done with the Collegiate Chorale, pre-Szell. It would have been easier to market than it was in the early 1950s. If he'd simply gone back to New York, Shaw would have had more time to record and tour. There was always pressure on him to do just that, and each time he almost quit in Cleveland, he told RCA that he intended to follow such a course. This was welcome news to RCA and Shaw's management, both of which could more easily promote a full-time choral Shaw than a part-time one. The touring Robert Shaw Chorale and its records remained in demand. As things stood, Shaw had only part of his summers to give to the Chorale. And touring was increasingly less profitable, for Shaw insisted on engaging large forces and paying his musicians well. Furthermore, other touring costs, like transportation and insurance, had increased. But reviews for the Chorale, both on record and on tour, were usually rapturous. Moreover, Shaw's reputation in music had only grown since leaving New York. With a restored New York base and eleven years in Cleveland under his belt, Shaw could certainly have taken guest-conducting dates as well. He surely would have had plenty, for even in those days he turned down many more than he accepted. He might have done very handsomely back in New York as the nation's premier choral and choral-symphonic conductor. He could have written his own ticket. It would have been a lucrative and prestigious career, unburdened by the politics and responsibilities of leading an orchestra, especially an undistinguished orchestra in a "backwater." Yes, it was time to leave Cleveland. But why Atlanta? Once again, Shaw was taking the hard way.

Moreover, George Szell did not want Shaw to leave, and told him so. After Shaw informed Szell of his decision to accept the music directorship in Atlanta, Szell tried to change Shaw's mind. Shaw had told Szell he was quitting before. Several times. But he told Szell that this time his mind was made up. Szell then urged Shaw to keep an ongoing and official relationship with the Cleveland Orchestra. Shaw declined. Though he did agree to make his transition out of Cleveland on a gradual, two-year schedule. This meant that in his first full year in Atlanta, he would still have several concerts to do in Cleveland.[58]

As it happened, Szell lived only another five years. What if Shaw *had* stayed? Might he have become Szell's successor? Shaw was a much-respected figure in Cleveland, and rooted in the community—a community with a fine music conservatory, several colleges and universities, a world-class art museum, and an ample supply of singers for his symphony chorus—all things he would lack in Atlanta.

It seems unlikely. Shaw was in awe of many of the Cleveland players and could not relax before them.

It is possible that had he stayed and become, along with Lane, an interim director after Szell's death, Shaw might have been propelled to a more visible podium where there was less building to do than in Atlanta. But Shaw didn't want a podium that was as visible as New York or Cleveland. He *wanted* a backwater. For in that environment, he could grow in the way he now needed to. He could build his own instrument and build his confidence and skill with it. Shaw knew what he was doing when he told the Atlantans "Yes." A continuing renouncement—of the fast track and the white spotlight—was

58 Szell thought Atlanta unworthy of his deputy. He still saw Shaw as without equal in choral-orchestral work. From Szell's point of view, there was no one who could replace Shaw in Cleveland. Szell may have been unaware of the extent of Shaw's disillusionment. He may not have seen how Shaw was beginning to chafe and feel oppressed by Szell. Or he may have been inattentive because such a sentiment would matter little to him.

necessary. A new challenge was necessary. He needed to find out if he could handle an orchestra on his own. Could he be a good music director? Could he settle in one place? Could he build an orchestra from the bottom up? Shaw was not sure. But he thought it possible that he knew enough now. He wanted to try.

The Atlanta Symphony needed strengthening and rebuilding in almost every area. Its funding base was rickety, at best. Most of the players had day jobs. Its choruses needed formation, or re-formation. (Shaw would have *both* jobs, choral and orchestral.) Nor did the Atlanta Symphony have stores of human capital to draw upon. There were not enough devoted patrons, not a deep enough well of local musicians, not even a reserve of fine singers. Atlanta had a lot of church singers, good ones. But Cleveland had scores of trained musicians, some of whom were amateur vocalists. The Cleveland Orchestra was a glittering jewel. Shaw believed it to be the finest orchestra in the world. Atlanta was, at best, a diamond in the rough. Shaw was leaving the Ritz to do missionary work in Appalachia. And that's one of the reasons he took the job. Shaw was a man who liked big jobs and long odds. Moreover, in Atlanta he would be the master teacher, the needed leader, and maybe a kind of savior. In Atlanta, he would be called upon to do the impossible and to do it quickly. And finally, in Atlanta he would, he believed, be a part of the civil rights revolution in the United States. This was a major factor for Shaw. He and the Atlanta Symphony would take part in history. So was his hope.

But Shaw *always* made strange career choices. He chose music over the ministry; he chose sacred music over popular music; he chose Atlanta over remaining in Cleveland or going back to New York. He tended to pick the unknown and rocky over the safe path. As Shaw's son Thomas said, "He loved to sweat." Suffering teaches.

As noted, to go to Atlanta and give himself fully to the job, Shaw felt it necessary to shut down the Robert Shaw Chorale. He was ready to close that door and move on. This shocked, angered, and hurt old associates like Alice Parker and Thomas Pyle. Shaw could do whatever works he wanted on the road with the Chorale, with virtually whatever singers and players he wanted. And he did not necessarily need to stay with RCA. They pleaded with him to keep the Chorale afloat. But Shaw's mind was made up. It seemed crazy to many of Shaw's old friends. He'd spent almost 20 years building both a musical instrument and a musical franchise. Now he would scrap it for Atlanta—a vehicle of dubious promise. It seemed to them also thoughtless, for it deprived loyal old friends, like Parker and Pyle, of their livelihoods. But Shaw wanted to write a new chapter on a fresh slate.

Shaw kept to his pattern of saying "no" the first time he was asked to come to Atlanta, just as he had initially turned down Fred Waring and Szell. He had deliberated and hesitated with Juilliard too. After a prolonged and amorous courtship, Shaw told the Atlanta Symphony Orchestra search committee (he was dealing chiefly with Charles Yates, President of the Board of Sponsors) that it should widen the search. He said there was no honor in being first on a list of one. He told them there were more ideal conductors for the job. Most obvious, in Shaw's mind, was his Cleveland colleague, Louis Lane. Lane was better with the orchestra than he was, said Shaw. Much better. On Shaw's recommendation, the search committee brought Lane to Atlanta and interviewed him. But Lane didn't have the name, charisma, or warmth they found in Shaw. The Atlantans didn't want a better orchestral technician than Shaw. They wanted a leader. And a star. They wanted Shaw. Yates went back to Shaw and told him he was still the man Atlanta needed. Shaw accepted.

Shaw's family took the back seat again. Shaw's daughter Johanna was grown and living on her own by then, but his sons Peter and Thad had already been bounced back and forth between Cleveland and New York. As for Maxine, her feeling for the South was somewhere between dislike and loathing. In any case, the family members had no vote. This may well have made the already bad situation worse. But Shaw didn't know how to make things better at home and he felt "called" to Atlanta.

In due course, Atlanta's city fathers of the day convinced Shaw that, along with a performing arts center, they intended to create a rich cultural life in Atlanta, and the orchestra, under Shaw, would be the driving engine of it all. Amazingly, though there were disappointments along the way, that is pretty much what happened.

The arts center was to be the Atlanta Memorial Arts Center. (It eventually became the Woodruff Arts Center, named after Robert W. Woodruff, past president of The Coca-Cola Company, who was its major benefactor.) The "memorial" honored 106 members of the Atlanta Art Association who were killed in an airline crash at Orly Field in Paris in 1962. These Atlantans—the core of the arts community in the city and all that it hoped to become—had been on their way home from a tour of European museums. Their deaths dealt a psychic and spiritual blow to the city that would echo for decades. And their memorial was to be not just the building, the Woodruff Arts Center, but the cultural life that Shaw, Woodruff, and others would establish and nurture. Those others included Atlanta mayor Ivan Allen, Andrew Young, Roberto Goizueta (a later chairman of the board of Coca-Cola), Wych Fowler (who became a U.S. senator), and Robert Edge, a prominent Atlanta lawyer and music lover who sometimes acted as Shaw's defender, confidante, and Dutch Uncle. Shaw had a small band of intensely loyal friends and allies in Atlanta. They not only shared his vision of a New South and a progressive Atlanta, but they informed it, for they were natives and had the vision and fought for it long before Shaw came to town.

When Shaw came to Atlanta, it was as a missionary. And his behavior, if not his cause, mirrored his father's. Shirley Shaw had essentially built several of his churches: not the buildings literally, but the human and spiritual infrastructure. Now Shaw, working with his new instrument, would build his musical parish. The ASO would not be Henry Sopkin's orchestra (the man who had paved the way for Shaw). It would not be Szell's. It would not be a pickup group, as were all those that had accompanied the Robert Shaw Chorale on record or tour. But the orchestra would be Atlanta's own. And it would be "for keeps."

Shaw, too, would be Atlanta's. Atlanta's alone. He would give himself to this city as Szell had given himself to Cleveland—totally. That was how Shaw envisioned things, and that was how things went. Atlanta became Robert Shaw's permanent home.

The ASO had no reputation beyond being a noble regional outpost of musical good intention. Most members of the orchestra earned only a portion of their living playing for it. None were full-time players. They were schoolteachers, insurance agents, and the like. One of Shaw's first acts was to ask the players to choose: Do you want to be a full-time musician or stick with your day job? The opportunity was thrilling for some players and terrifying for others. To choose music did not guarantee success in music, and there was no guarantee that Shaw would succeed in upgrading the orchestra, financing that upgrade, or even that he would stay in Atlanta. Yet many players opted to forsake financial stability for a leap of faith. (The weekly wage for the players was $135 a week and the principals earned less than $7000 a year.) Szell had warned him, "Bob, you are going backward."

In a way, he was. And he knew it: The ASO was *not* one of the top 10, or 20, or even 30 in America. It was a far cry, not only from Cleveland and New York, but from Boston, Chicago, Philadelphia, and Cincinnati—all places conductors sought to conduct, all places where Shaw had conducted. The ASO was not so very different from the summer orchestra Shaw had run in San Diego in the early 1950s. And this was the late 1960s, and Shaw himself was in his fifties. On the other hand, Shaw saw in Atlanta a chance to mold a group that was relatively uncorrupted by the cynicism of the big cities and orchestras. Shaw found many symphony orchestra organizations bureaucratic and brittle, and many players hardened. Here was a chance to upgrade and remake a musical institution, Shaw said, based on love of music. Here was also a chance, because of relative obscurity and insulation from the national arts press, to grow an orchestra and chorus together. Atlanta would be a laboratory. At last he could do it his way, and teach both his players and his audience how to love the compositions and composers he loved. But first he had to make the ASO into a full-time orchestra and hire some good players to reinforce the ranks. This he did quickly—moving to a full-time orchestra in the first year and hiring players during the first two and three. He was his whirlwind self in these years, dazzling and frightening the trustees and prominent locals.

While he consciously took himself to the margins of the nation's classical music scene, Shaw's choice allowed him to let his guard down with a stable group of musicians, all of whom were there because he wanted them there—Shaw had hired them or asked them to stay. He was father, pastor, leader—he could try new things and dare to fail. Shaw had such a reservoir of goodwill when he first came to Atlanta that he had little fear of his bosses, the press, or the local gentry.

When a "name" conductor becomes music director or principal conductor in a place like Cleveland (after Szell), or San Francisco, Pittsburgh, or Chicago, he builds on a reputation already long established, something that may be quite fine. He hopes to leave a distinctive mark, of course. But it is unlikely that he will be the defining influence. The orchestra is already too well established. Its performance standards, its professional reputation, its listening audience (locally and on recordings, radio, and TV) are all pretty well set. The conductor is adding to a tradition—not creating it. Shaw had no such luxury. The ASO needed to be re-founded in all three areas: performance standards, reputation, and audience. Shaw was *establishing* the tradition. Shaw saw this as an opportunity.

Henry Sopkin was the original Founder of the ASO; Shaw the second Founder. But rather like the men at the Constitutional Convention who re-founded the government, Shaw had to make something different. The nation existed as a confederation; the revolution had been won and a second founding was necessary to assure consolidation, survival, and growth. The ASO was a fine regional, part-time orchestra. Sopkin had literally made something out of nothing. He had taken a youth orchestra and made something greater. Now Shaw had to take a local orchestra and transform it into a professional and, hopefully, *national* orchestra.

Thus, Shaw was not just the new conductor in town, but the man who had come to fundamentally change the ASO. And he did. Shaw effected change in practical ways: by hiring fine players, often from established orchestras; by extending the concert season; by constantly agitating for an increase in the budget to do these things (he generally prevailed); by hiring Louis Lane to be his deputy and to help instill Szellian discipline; by bringing outstanding guest artists; by developing ambitious programs; by sending musicians to festivals and workshops (sometimes at his own expense); and by constantly harassing his board of trustees and beseeching his audience to care. Perhaps most of all, Shaw raised the performance level of the orchestra through his own example: his enthusiasm, hours of study, rehearsal hours, programming, and high standards. A player who came unprepared or played indifferently was likely to be called to Shaw's dressing room for a talking to. It was not pleasant. No player who had heard about such an audience wanted to get called in. No player who experienced it would let it happen again.

The ASO became Shaw's orchestra, as Cleveland had been Szell's—cast in his image. That meant that it became a precise and rhythmic group, but with a warm sound—an "orchestra that could sing," in Shaw's parlance. It also meant that the ASO performed a lot of new music—commissioned fare. It was an orchestra with a social conscience—traveling, for example, to all-black schools to perform for the students. Shaw also commissioned works by African-American composers like T. J. Anderson. And, of course, the ASO performed many choral compositions, eventually had two choruses attached to it, and recorded myriad choral and choral-orchestral works.

Not long after arriving in Atlanta, Shaw founded an ASO chamber chorus (1967), and later the Atlanta Symphony Orchestra Chorus (1970). So actually, his attentions were somewhat divided, if locally concentrated. He had two jobs again. And for most of his time as music director in Atlanta—1967 to 1989—he was his own chorusmaster. The ASOC eventually became, in the eyes and ears of many, the finest amateur orchestral chorus in the nation, perhaps the world. And admittedly it was not the vastly and quickly improved orchestra that got the attention of the region, critics, and the two young men who were beginning a record company called Telarc, in Cleveland. Rather, it was the fact that Shaw was forming new choruses that could produce Shavian sounds with an orchestra modeled on the Cleveland Orchestra. It was the choral-orchestral pairing that put the ASO and ASOC on the map.

Ironically, Shaw's success in Atlanta eventually changed that city, so it was no longer the quiet place where Shaw could work quasi-anonymously. By putting the ASO on the map, Shaw drew attention to himself. Most who have considered the matter, or were participants during those times, have said that in his 22 years there Shaw catapulted the Atlanta Symphony into the top 10 of American orchestras. Certainly he, and Telarc International, made the ASO one of the best-known and best-selling *recording* orchestras.

Yet, in his first years in Atlanta, Shaw declined offers to record. The Robert Shaw Chorale was no more and he felt the ASO was not ready. When he did record again, he found the audience was still there. In fact, it was wider and even more respectful. His Telarc recordings and the Grammy Awards he won during his music directorship in Atlanta made him a household name once again. And the recordings made the ASO into a household name as well. Indeed, the ASO's grip was so firm on a sector of the classical music audience in America that its recordings enjoyed robust sales in the 1990s and 2000s. Meanwhile, other orchestras of equal and greater prestige had no recording contracts or had to record and sell independently of any established label. The ASO's success was built on the foundation Shaw had laid. People bought the Shaw Telarc recordings, and National Public Radio aired them, because of Shaw's reputation for careful and soulful music making.

Nick Jones, an Atlantan and distinguished program annotator, was long the ASO's primary in-house critic and scholar; he was also for many years a member of Robert Shaw's choruses. As author of the ASO's program notes during Shaw's tenure, he helped Shaw educate the Atlanta audience. He is probably *the* expert on Shaw's music directorship in Atlanta. In 1999, after Shaw's death, Jones wrote of the "whirlwind" that was Shaw's music directorship. Quoted here at length, Jones's essay gives an insider's view of those furious two decades (the ASO continues to post the complete version on its Web site):

> *He came in like a whirlwind, presenting ambitious concerts of difficult music, speaking about Atlanta's need for a conservatory of music, looking for black musicians to play in the all-white orchestra, successfully lobbying to have black members added to the ASO's Board, and introducing the city to more contemporary music than it had ever heard before. Hard though he may have driven his players and singers, he pushed himself harder. His attention to detail and his capacity for endless hours of score study and preparation were phenomenal. Unlike most high-profile conductors, he had no other orchestra half a globe away, and he accepted few dates to conduct elsewhere. Shaw had come to Atlanta to be Music Director, and he considered it a full-time commitment. Shaw immediately began his efforts at expansion and outreach. In addition to continuing the main subscription series and the Suburban Series at Westminster School, he inaugurated a Chamber Series to present works for smaller ensembles, a Connoisseur Series at Emory University, and a Promenade Series of lighter fare. He took the Orchestra for a week-long Festival of Contemporary Music, much of it by black composers, at Spelman College. He also began the ASO Chamber Chorus in order to enhance the choral offerings of the Orchestra. He turned Chamber Chorus rehearsals into seminars on vocal technique and choral conducting methods, with academic credit available through Georgia State University . . . .*

Shaw's opening season brought a raise in pay for musicians, expansion of the subscription series from 14 to 18 concerts and lengthening of the playing season from 26 to 30 weeks. The following season, further expansion and increased salaries made it possible for the first time to institute daytime rehearsals and to regard playing in the ASO as full-time employment. The ensuing years saw the ASO become a year-round orchestra, its schedule based upon a Master Season of 24 subscription-concert weekends. Musicians' pay continued to increase, enhancing the Orchestra's ability to attract and retain notable players. The roster was increased by several positions. The organization heeded Shaw's early pleas for better instruments by purchasing some of them directly and setting up loan funds to help players obtain others.

During his first season, Shaw spearheaded the drive to raise one million dollars in order to qualify for a matching Ford Foundation grant of 1.75 million dollars. A portion of that began the ASO's endowment fund, which continues to grow as the foundation of the Orchestra's financial security. The initial season set the tone for the Robert Shaw era to follow. Its emphases persisted and widened. The Chamber Series evolved to the point of sending ASO performing groups into Atlanta schools . . . Shaw and his conducting staff regularly led the Orchestra in locations throughout Georgia and the Southeastern region, supported by grants from the National Endowment for the Arts. National touring began in 1970, and subsequent years drew Shaw and the ASO to Western states, to Chicago and the Midwest, and repeatedly to the Northeast and New York City. In 1980 he took the ASO to Mexico for a four-concert residency at the National University. Crowning his period of leadership was the ASO's first concert tour of Europe, preceded by concerts in New York's Carnegie Hall and Avery Fisher Hall. The ASO and Chorus became the largest performing arts group ever to travel from the USA to Europe. Greeted with tears and standing ovations, concerts were given in East Berlin, Zürich, Ludwigsburg, Paris and the Bath Music Festival, climaxing with Beethoven's Ninth Symphony at London's Royal Festival Hall.

Regarding programming, Jones wrote:

. . . His programs returned constantly to the works of the Classical era of Haydn and Mozart, both for their musical value and because they are great trainers of instrumental and ensemble skills within the orchestra. He was generous with selections from the Romantic era, the monumental and much-loved works from Beethoven through Brahms and beyond to Sibelius and Rachmaninoff. He was also unflinching in presenting the music of our own time, not just the now-familiar sounds of Mahler and Prokofiev, but representatives of the latest trends and experiments. In his first speech to the ASO Board of Sponsors, he affirmed his intention to commit a portion of his programming to "that sound of this moment upon which one has no right or means of exercising a judgment: the absolutely absurd, experimental, unconventional, uncensored, inconceivable, unbearable anti-music."

His first seasons included Theater Set by Ulysses Kay, which he had commissioned with funds from the Junior League of Atlanta, as well as works by Penderecki, Schoenberg, Webern, Lutosławski, Ligeti and Gunther Schuller, among other contemporary composers . . .

The years that followed brought . . . works by Alberto Ginastera, and a spring festival of concerts devoted to Bartók and Beethoven (1981). Under the American Music Project, Shaw commissioned a total of 15 new works from American composers, including Bernstein, Schuman, and Menotti, with premieres extending from 1984 through 1992. Every season brought first ASO performances of anywhere from 15 to 30 musical works.

Regarding the African-American community:

> *Throughout his career, Shaw was known for his commitment to racial equality and to broadening opportunities for minority musicians in the classical field. Under his leadership, the ASO actively sought black and other minority instrumentalists for vacancies in the Orchestra. During the 1980s the Atlanta Symphony participated in the Music Assistance Fund's "Orchestra Fellows Program," designed to help rising black string players gain the experience for successful symphonic careers. At the front of the stage, many black soloists, both instrumental and vocal, performed with the ASO. His commitment was further reflected in his full staging in 1972 of the world premiere of Scott Joplin's opera* Treemonisha, *in his frequent work with glee clubs from Morehouse and Spelman Colleges, in his leading the ASO at the inaugural ceremony for Maynard Jackson, Atlanta's first black mayor, and in his commissioning of new music by composers such as Frederick Tillis, Billy Taylor, John Lewis, T. J. Anderson and Alvin Singleton. Anderson and Singleton were also chosen by Shaw to be Composers in Residence with the ASO.*

Finally:

> *. . . To the Chamber Chorus he added the larger ASO Chorus in 1970, supervising the recruitment, auditioning and training of more than 200 volunteer singers and conducting their debut in Beethoven's* Ninth Symphony *. . . Highlights of the collaboration of the Chorus and Chamber Chorus with the ASO under Shaw included a Carnegie Hall debut in 1976, featured status in the inaugural Concert for President Jimmy Carter in 1977, hosting additional guest choruses for mammoth performances of Mahler's* Symphony of a Thousand *in 1978 and 1991, returning to Carnegie*

> *Hall for a series of three great Requiems during Easter weekend in 1980, and participation in most of the ASO's award-winning recordings. The Chorus also performed in Carnegie Hall with other orchestras under Shaw's baton for Mahler's* Eighth Symphony *in 1995 and the Brahms* German Requiem *in 1997.*

It is an astonishing record of action and accomplishment. As one long-time Shaw-ASO backer said: "He just wore us out."

Shaw went to Atlanta to build a musical instrument that would mature as he did and become, in some sense, his own instrument—not Szell's or Toscanini's—his own family, his own parish, at last. He went to bring culture to people he felt deserved more than they had. And he went to be part of the new South. This was the chief non-artistic reason for coming to Atlanta. But it was as important as the musical challenge and the psychological attraction of building his own musical organization. Civil rights mattered to Shaw. He wanted his musicians and musical programs to not just acknowledge social action in America and the American South, but to also comment on it and to take part in it. And he, personally, wanted to be a witness to change.

It was G. K. Chesterton who described the United States as a nation with the soul of a church. That's certainly how Shaw saw America. And he saw civil rights as the essential secular drama of American redemption—the essence of the struggle to realize its own creed. Atlanta was the capitol of the South. Not only was Martin Luther King, Jr. in Atlanta, but so was the crusading newspaper editor, Ralph McGill. Both men were Shaw's heroes. Shaw had followed McGill's career closely (McGill was a nationally syndicated columnist). Unfortunately, the two men never had the opportunity to become friends, as McGill died in February of 1969, when Shaw was still new to the city. Wendell Whalum was also in Atlanta, at Morehouse College. Shaw regarded him as a venerable guardian of black music and as *the* premier black music educator in the country. These two men would become close friends and collaborators. Andrew Young became a dear friend also, as did a moderate progressive candidate for governor of Georgia seeking to succeed the segregationist Lester Maddox—James Earl "Jimmy" Carter, Jr.

Atlanta's evolution as a city played a key role in the great American drama of race and the quest for social justice in the south. This was widely understood, even at the time. Because of the residence of Dr. King, Atlanta was the de facto capital of the Civil Rights Movement. Shaw desperately wanted to be a part of this movement. He wanted music to be a part of the realization of the true American dream—racial justice and social equality. But Shaw was not certain how this could happen. How could he bring music to the struggle for equality? He was personally committed to civil rights and excited about Atlanta's centrality in the drama. He was convinced the arts should play a role. But how?

Atlanta was poised to become a cosmopolitan city, one rooted in racial diversity and tolerance. Perhaps it could also be the city in which classical music became "the people's" music: the music of all peoples—united. Perhaps it could be the first major American city in which 50 percent of the symphony's musicians were people of color. Perhaps the ASO could be a symphony orchestra with as many black listeners and ticket buyers and patrons as white.

Alas, all this was not to be.

Shaw succeeded only very modestly in bringing classical music to black Atlanta. Or in integrating the city through music. Or even in integrating the orchestra. Shaw dreamed lofty dreams but he collided with reality. There were only so many black cellists available for hire in the county, for example. And symphony goers remained upper middle-class whites. Things changed a little. But not nearly as much as Shaw had hoped. Shaw did, certainly, have an impact on music education in Atlanta area schools. And the ASO became an important part of Atlanta's life. Under Shaw's directorship, a youth orchestra, which he did not train but did lead in final concerts, was established. The ensemble reached out to black students. And Shaw developed his partnership with Morehouse College, as Nick Jones noted. But Shaw was not truly able to use his musicianship to contribute to civil rights directly. The tragedies and triumphs of the movement mostly happened around him.

But, Shaw's long friendship with Wendell Whalum, and his frequent collaborations with him when both men were at the zeniths of their careers, did establish a bridge between Morehouse College and the ASO, and between Atlanta's black community and the white concert-going community that stands today. Shaw used Whalum's forces whenever he could, including in many Christmas programs, and he conducted on the campus, not only his own forces, but Whalum's.

Moreover, Shaw made a huge splash when the world heard, for the first time with full symphonic forces and orchestration, an opera by Scott Joplin, as Jones also notes. Joplin had written a serious, large-scale piece about a black heroine's triumph over racism and social injustice by dint of literacy and self-education. Joplin called the work *Treemonisha*—referring to the "tree of knowledge." The work was published in Joplin's lifetime—1911—and performed once with piano accompaniment. (Joplin died in 1917.) But it was never performed on a full musical or dramatic scale. Clearly the composer regarded it as "the best of me," as Elgar wrote of his most ambitious piece. Joplin wanted to be a serious composer, not merely an entertainer. This was his magnum opus. Shaw was moved by Joplin's dedication to a dream deferred.

Shaw, who perhaps personally identified with Joplin's reach for something he could never quite attain (as he was moved by Francis Poulenc's ambition to be a "true" composer), was determined that the piece be heard—heard by the public and heard as the composer (more or less) imagined it. The idea also fit Shaw's dream of what Atlanta might be as a cultural center—a place where experiment, rediscovery, and artistic embrace of social justice might all simultaneously occur. And it would be an act of outreach to black Atlanta and to black America.

Treemonisha was performed in January of 1972, with Shaw conducting a black cast, and with orchestration by resident ASO composer T. J. Anderson. It was accompanied by student choruses from Morehouse and Spelman Colleges, as well as an interpretive dance troop from the Southern Illinois University. Anderson and Whalum supervised the production, which Shaw financed with a $25,000 grant from the Rockefeller Foundation. Joplin's opera, at last, was realized.

Treemonisha was broadcast live on National Public Radio, with an accompanying interview with Shaw, in which he dodged the question of the work's inherent and long-term artistic value and focused instead on its emotional qualities and social vision. The work was recorded by the Houston Grand Opera under the baton of Gunther Schuller in 1975. (While several critics erroneously reported that Schuller's was the first full orchestral performance, it was the first fully staged one. The ASO version, while dramatized, was not fully staged.)[59]

So was Shaw softening toward opera?

Not really. Shaw's commitment to *Treemonisha* had to do with, first, fulfilling Joplin's vision and, second, with Shaw's desire to bridge the racial gap with music.

His reaction to *most* opera remained impatience. Shaw understood musical drama very well, both intuitively and from his years with Toscanini. He knew a story could move people—and he knew how to "milk" emotion, whether he was conducting *The Creation* or *Elijah*, or had a soloist singing "All the Things You Are." But he knew qualities of musical form and structure moved *him* even more. Still, especially in the early years in Atlanta, Shaw would do semi-staged versions of several operas. He loved

59 According to Nick Jones, the one performance in Joplin's lifetime may have been overseen by the composer and may have even been semi-staged. Gunther Schuller, an eminent jazz scholar as well as classical conductor and composer, has championed the piece, conducting it again in subsequent decades.

doing *Porgy and Bess* and once imported Cab Calloway to Atlanta to play "Sportin' Life." He conducted the *Marriage of Figaro* semi-staged, and he became quite enamored of Beethoven's *Fidelio* when he semi-staged it in Atlanta. *Fidelio* was a minor obsession for a year or more. And, of course, there was the Joplin. Shaw also conducted the Handel *Semele* in Cleveland with Beverly Sills. He did it only the one time, there were two performances, and both were in concert format.

Shaw also semi-staged the Bernstein Mass in Atlanta, a somewhat daring thing to do at the time because the piece was controversial, and the composer was enduring much criticism for the work. Conductors were not rushing to champion and perform the Mass. But Shaw was always pushing the envelope in Atlanta and people came to expect this from him. This performance received much local media attention as did *Treemonisha.*

Still, these outings were, in a sense, the exceptions that proved the rule about Shaw and opera. His basic view was that it was contrived drama and not the most interesting music (only *Fidelio* qualified as great music in his mind). Shaw found greater drama in the Bach Passions than in any opera. For him, the deep drama in music was beyond the narrative just as it was beyond the words. The life-changing drama in music was in the music itself—structure and melody and overtones.

One could nonetheless argue that Shaw "opera"-tized, or brought out the dramatic elements in, for example, the Mendelssohn *Elijah,* not to mention the Verdi *Requiem.* He knew well that some works were "performance" pieces and had to be treated as such. He deplored the chorus singer's loss of innocence—"the discovery that he is, in a certain sense, in show biz" (Shaw). But he knew it to be sometimes true. For Shaw, it was almost as if acting and staging demeaned music and trivialized its inner force. And this is surely one reason why he also hated flashy conducting.

The New York years had been hungry, fast, and fertile—the star years. The Cleveland years had been the learning years. The Atlanta years were the years of building—artistic maturation and acquisition of command—years in which Shaw began to formulate his ideas with some assurance and in some detail. Here is Shaw speaking to his forces, at the peak of his Atlanta idealism:

Let's realize first that the arts are not an ivory tower of retreat. They are a doing.

They are a making. In their Sanskrit etymology "art" and "arm" have the same word-root: something made "by hand."

They are sweat, strain, cramps, blisters, tears, blood, profanity, and mocking laughter.

This is what Shaw was offering Atlanta: hard work, strain, blisters, and profanity. He was true to his word. But Atlanta was not always overwhelmed with joy. Sometimes the city rather hoped for comfort and consolation instead—less art, more entertainment.

Shaw also wrote:

Music is the organization of tone and timbre in time. Its concern is to organize Time, to give it beauty and meaning.

Shaw was obsessed with all matters of time—the allocation of time in rehearsal, beginning and ending on time, people keeping personal appointments to the second, his tempo watch, the comparative times it took various conductors to perform a piece. All matters of time.

It was in Atlanta that Shaw's focus on rhythm flourished and he began to feel confident enough to develop ways to enhance rhythmic values in rehearsals through his counting technique. Counting in time—"keeping" time—was, to Shaw, of central musical importance.

Maestro Louis Lane worked with Shaw in Cleveland and in Atlanta—first as an accompanist and assistant conductor, then as a fellow associate conductor under George Szell, and later as Shaw's co-conductor and principal guest conductor at the Atlanta Symphony Orchestra. Lane said: "I thought I had learned a lot from George Szell, and I had. But Robert came with a different way of making music based on the melody and how its inflections could be used to interpret and perform music more successfully. This was an eye opener . . . I also thought George Szell had taught me all I could learn about rhythm, but I was wrong."[60]

Melody and rhythm were Shaw's natural strengths and his dual Holy Grail. Shaw was a self-described "nut" about rhythm and tempo which, he told his choruses, "together form pulse." He used his tempo watch the way a track coach uses a stopwatch—as a measure of success and accuracy. Many conductors use it only as a point of reference or information. For Shaw, it was like a second heart. He could drive singers to distraction with the little device. But this continuous emphasis on musical force and motion could be heard in a Shaw performance, and can still be heard in many Shaw recordings. In a piece like the Vivaldi *Gloria,* the pulse is never lost and this helps hold the work together as a whole. It is never lost in the Handel *Messiah,* a piece that can be deadly in performance when the drive and motion wane, as they so often do. *Messiah*, Shaw used to say, "Must 'snap, crackle and pop.'" The performances most of us have heard drag, dawdle, and plod.

Atlantans also discovered that Shaw had learned a thing or two from his Waring days, and the many folk and quasi-Broadway records: Shaw knew melody. Among Shaw's most popular concerts in the early days were his "pops" offerings, mostly in the summers at Chastaine Park. They were concerts Shaw did not actually like doing very much. But he brought the same ear for melody to the lighter classical pieces he programmed—much Mozart, Schubert, Strauss, and Gershwin, among others, and a surprising

60 Burris-Lane interview.

amount of Tchaikovsky—as he had to Broadway, folk and ballads for radio. To some musicians, this sense of lilt, or dance, is the essence of musicality.

Alice Parker has said that when they did arrangements of folk tunes and spirituals together, Shaw "based everything on melody": the original choice of the tunes, where to place each voice, how to write lines for each part, what the audience would accept or not accept. "His first rule in arranging was not to stray too far from the melody, and his second was to continually re-use and recycle the melody."[61]

In Atlanta, Shaw rediscovered the sense of mission he'd had in the Collegiate Chorale days. He was building and preaching again. He'd always had the leadership gene, even when his friend Schuman had deplored his ignorance. But now, at last, unlike the Collegiate Chorale days, Shaw was beginning to feel he also knew *music,* just a little. The natural force of his personality began to be less manic and he settled into a degree of comfort with his own judgments. He was very comfortable in the role of ultimate authority regarding things musical at the ASO.

But it was not until he got to Atlanta that Shaw's highly individualized musicality could fully flourish and be recognized, including by himself. Lane again: "Robert was a genius . . . How so? Three things: superior musical sense (and here he cited Shaw's feeling for pulse and melody), charisma, and a mission."

Shaw was a tireless civic booster in Atlanta. He spoke and wrote about the symphony season constantly, not only to subscribers, but also to men's clubs, women's groups, and schools. He did special concerts for civic events and conventions. He brought symphony players and/or choirs to the celebrations and funerals of local eminences. He even toyed, on one occasion, urged on by some of his Atlanta civic pals, with the idea of running for mayor. (What

61 Burris–Parker interview.

a misappropriation of talent that would have been.) In terms of his musical life and, without question, in terms of his national reputation as a musician, Shaw spent way too much time and energy on Atlanta civic involvements. But his view was that he and the orchestra were *of Atlanta*, and they would grow in virtue and excellence together, or not at all.

"Let's get down to the nitty gritty," Shaw told a local Rotary Club in a 1967 speech:

> *What if it were really true that we of the white pigmentation are the "deprived" and "underdeveloped" people of our time?*
>
> *What if it were really true that the arts might bring a sanity and a logic and a hope into our too-little and too-late and too-shaky attempts to staunch the flow of wounds too deep and too old?*
>
> *What if an Arts Alliance [of Atlanta] were really an alliance of, by, and for the people—all the people?*
>
> *I wish I could describe to you the strange shame of playing a children's concert in Midgeville, Georgia, for twice three thousand beautiful little children hearing a symphony orchestra for the first time. And not a single white face in the audience—and not a single black face in the orchestra.*
>
> *In Atlanta, "the arts" have a chance to become what the history of man has shown that they should be—the guide and impetus to human understanding, individual integrity, and the common good.*
>
> *They are not an opiate, an avoidance, or a barrier, but a unifying spirit and labor.*

This was vintage Shaw. And it did not always go over well in Atlanta, especially in the early days of his tenure. Sometimes the reaction was bewilderment, sometimes outrage. He seemed at times as much preacher, reformer, and visionary as musician. And yet he was not. He was a musician first and last—"obsessed with music," as Virgil Thomson had said. His missionary qualities sometimes obscured his musicianship.

Robert Shaw's energies were focused on one place and one job from 1967 to 1989, and really for the first time. The man who so loved touring decided that the only culture that mattered was the kind grown locally. He sometimes exhausted his fellow laborers in the vineyard. For just as with the Collegiate Chorale and the Robert Shaw Chorale, the ASO and ASO chorus were his life, and he expected that this would be true for all who joined the cause. One former staff member says that when Shaw entered Symphony Hall, electricity and tension snaked quickly through the building. He said it was a feeling, every day, of both excitement and foreboding. Shaw was demanding, exacting, exhausting. He had, he said, "a job to do," and it was urgent.

A slightly different form of electricity and tension were present when Shaw was in a room with the Atlanta Symphony board of trustees. He would get angry, sometimes spontaneously and sometimes after pre-meditation. And just as with a chorus, he would tell the board members that they just didn't care, or didn't care enough, and that they were letting down the community and music. Shaw regularly told his board it was failing to live up to its responsibilities. Often, they didn't much like it.

In 1972, Shaw was fired.

It happened this way: Shaw loved the work of Charles Ives. In the 1971–72 season, he decided to focus on two composers and do all the major works of those two composers—Brahms and Ives. It was the latter's centenary. But Ives is a tough sell anywhere and Atlanta was no exception. Attendance plummeted. There had been grumblings about Shaw's programming throughout the five years he had been there. It was, his critics said, too weighted toward the heavy and intellectual, toward requiems, and toward modern compositions. All this was true. Shaw did not deny it. But this was the music he was passionate about, felt people should hear, and felt he could do well. In truth, it is unlikely that Shaw himself loved Ives the way he loved Brahms. Shaw was a melodist and *by nature* actually a musical conservative—one who paid homage to the masters, who venerated musical tradition, and who wanted, always, to return to musical roots and "get back to Handel's line," or Bach's, or Haydn's. But that is not the same as a musical reactionary or a closed mind. *By conviction*, Shaw was a modernist. And he loved Ives as much for his intellect and moral courage as for his music.

Shaw did not pretend that the music of his time was equal to the music of Bach. But he felt the music of his time was important and that classical concertgoers should support living music, lest the music of the past become dead music. To close one's mind and ears to the music of one's own time would be to despair of that time, and to make of the great music of the past a mere relic.

What Shaw also loved about Ives was the nobility, daring, and Americanness of the composer's musical mind. He loved that Ives was attempting the new, while in line with tradition. He loved that Ives was attempting to connect high and low culture in America, and that he was attempting to weave our history and music together. And he admired Ives's invention, self-invention, and orneriness. Ives didn't pander. Ives didn't care if his music was easily accessible. Indeed, though he would have thought it presumptuous to think so consciously, Shaw must have subconsciously aligned himself with Ives. They were both American auto-didactics and both rebels. (And Ives had been one of the early patrons of the Collegiate Chorale in New York. Shaw was programming Ives even then, though the composer was by that time too ill to work with the Chorale.)

Robert Shaw had championed Charles Ives's music since the late 1940s. *Damn it*, Shaw felt, Atlanta *needs* to hear Ives.

Shaw was committed to the notion that audiences and orchestras should support this great American original, as well as other new voices in music. So, this year—the 1971–72 season—was to be the year of Ives at the ASO.

In other times and seasons it was the year of Britten, Hindemith, Rorem, Tippett, Glass, Harbison (find a pattern if you can). Shaw felt a responsibility to support contemporary composers and to introduce them to the American audience. And he did this as much, or more, than any conductor of his generation.

But audiences and boards in Atlanta grumbled. Ives was challenging. Ives *is* challenging. And when audiences grumbled, Shaw grumbled right back. And kept on doing what he thought he should be doing. He was a populist and a democrat. But he believed the people needed leadership—teaching.

Shaw's "this-will-be-good-for-you" attitude, however, and insistence on shoving Ives, in particular, down the throats of his board and public alienated many people in Atlanta. Did Shaw think he knew better what was good for Atlanta than Atlanta? Why yes, he did. He didn't mind telling people they needed to dig a little deeper and force themselves to grow up artistically. Shaw was not a compromising or conciliating fellow in these matters.

That same year Shaw programmed a series of five concerts of "romantic favorites." He wrote to subscribers: "The rationale of this series derives directly from the imbalanced statements of symphony orchestras in general and the response of the ASO's trustees in particular, and it is simply stated: People like best what they know best and will pay good hard cash to hear it again." And he added: "Every sunrise and sunset, face in the direction of the Memorial Arts Center, bow low to the ground and repeat after me, Familiarity breeds—box office."

Trustees, long-term patrons, and bluebloods of Atlanta were not amused.

Shaw didn't care. He was a realist. He didn't like to kid himself. But that didn't mean he had to like or endorse reality. He was determined not to spoon-feed or pander; he was going to challenge and lift up, at least beyond a certain point; and he wasn't going to apologize for art. He believed Atlantans could learn to love Charles Ives and other new sounds and voices. And he intended to keep trying to prove his point until he was proven right.

It all came to a head.

The year of Ives, and Shaw's obvious contempt for what was familiar, popular, or desired by his board, had made him enemies and worn out some of his allies. In February of 1972, the executive committee of the symphony board requested, and received, Shaw's resignation. But when word got out (actually when word spread that it was not Shaw's idea to go, for many Atlantans had assumed it was Shaw's decision to move on), there was a huge public outcry. A spontaneous but well-organized public campaign was ignited. Its scores of volunteers felt they were involved in something akin to an idealistic political campaign, or the peace movement in its heyday. The campaign's goal was first to persuade Shaw to stay, for he had not intended to fight the board's decision or even to make public that he was being fired. The campaign would then persuade the full board to withdraw the request for Shaw's resignation. In short, the goal was to reverse the will of the powers that were, and to keep Shaw in Atlanta.

Shaw had concluded that maybe Atlanta was just too tough a nut to crack; or maybe he and the board were simply too far apart. (It is interesting that his initial reaction was one of equanimity.) He knew he was pushing the board and indeed the friends and patrons of the symphony. He knew the risk of his behavior. He thought it necessary. He was often self-righteous, even ill tempered when dealing with board members. But when he was fired, he was the soul of calm. He remarked, philosophically, that when visions are vastly at odds, communication inevitably breaks down, and with it trust. It wasn't quite, "Maybe it's for the best," but more like, "I gave it my best shot." Shaw was not surprised or devastated. And, of course, he was not without options. He could have returned to New York, and full-time freelancing, touring and recording with the Chorale, and lived an easier life.

In any case, the campaign grew—in size, intensity, and momentum. And the full board, in time, retracted the decision. The public was told Shaw would be asked to stay, and had agreed to stay—*if* the 1972–73 subscription series sold out.

It did.

Subscribers were instructed by the "Keep Shaw" brigades to make out their subscription checks *to Robert Shaw*. Many—3,500—did just that, which put the board on the spot. The board spun the whole thing as a great victory for all, as if keeping Shaw was really what most board members wanted all along. Shaw said, chuckling but also proud, that it was "the first time in history that a community had hired the music director."

One person active in the campaign was Caroline Sauls Hitz, who was to become the second Mrs. Robert Shaw.

After Shaw's departure was reversed, he threw himself into his work with new vigor. He remained demanding, challenging, artistically ambitious, combative, and irascible for the next 17 years. He still cited what other symphonies were doing and asked why the ASO was not doing as much. He still threatened to quit on occasion. He was very often, in the words of one ex-ASO staffer, "a pain in the ass."

The ASO board fired Shaw after five years. He stayed 22. Tensions rose and fell several more times and so did box office proceeds. But no one ever said Shaw's agitations were about his needs, wants, or ego. It is amazing that his music directorship lasted so long. It should also be said that in the Shaw era, the ASO staff mostly all felt it had a mission and was unified in this mission—great music for all people. Pettiness had no place at Shaw's ASO.

In the end—1987 and 1988—Shaw *was* pushed out, though it was done with care, indeed with reverence, and presented as a retirement that was Shaw's idea. He was of age, and almost no one in Atlanta knew it was, again, not his idea.

There was, by 1987 and 1988, a sense on the ASO board that it was time for Shaw to step aside and let in new life and new approaches. While Shaw didn't disagree, he did not see that this goal required him to retire. He still felt strong and full of new ideas. But the board felt that the orchestra needed an instrumentalist to "polish up the sound"—though few, if any, could say what that meant. Some players were saying such things out loud. Shaw was over 70 by then, and had been there for two decades. The quiet, internal line was that the ASO had gone as far as it could under Robert Shaw and that it needed something else now as well as, perhaps, a slightly new direction in programming—less choral music. ("Enough God damn requiems!" in the infamous words of one board member.)

Shaw was to be ushered out with the greatest delicacy, with all honor and gratitude, and if he was willing, there was to be an ongoing and lucrative contract to maintain an ASO affiliation. After all, by this time Robert Shaw's name was synonymous with the ASO. He would be retained as "conductor laureate," doing several programs each year, including his popular Christmas programs. He would continue to direct the choruses and, importantly, record with the ASO and ASOC. This was prudential, after all. When NPR played the Shaw Telarc recordings all across the nation, the announcer did not tend to say, "the Atlanta Symphony Orchestra, Robert Shaw conducting," but "Robert Shaw, conducting the Atlanta Symphony Orchestra."

All went more or less according to plan, but the ASO board did have to push Shaw a bit to become emeritus anything. He was not ready to go into that good night. He certainly was not ready to retire from conducting. He would be a mere 72 years of age at the appointed time of transition. He'd made Atlanta and the ASO his home. He'd married Caroline Sauls Hitz and she'd made him an Atlantan. He had no desire to live elsewhere, nor did she. He felt he was, in a sense, just beginning as a musician. And at first, the board's will came as a shock to him. But in a short while, Shaw adjusted remarkably. He began to see the musical merits of a new music director for the ASO, and he felt the board's decision a defensible one. He had little bitterness or anger, and at first helped the board in its search for his successor. Caroline Shaw was not so sanguine. She felt deeply hurt for Robert and felt the board was profoundly ungrateful, a point impossible to dispute.

Interestingly, Shaw did not assume he would be in demand elsewhere once freed of his duties as a music director. He was genuinely concerned about how he would make a living once he left the ASO. As it turned out, he was eventually paid as much to be a music director emeritus and conductor laureate as he had been to be full-time resident conductor and programmer. Shaw had been the lowest paid music director in the nation throughout most of his tenure in Atlanta, largely by his own choice. He generally used his bargaining power at contract time to get another player, or a better player, for the orchestra. He felt he was paid enough and that the orchestra's funds were better spent on an infusion of musicianship or on publicity campaigns, education and outreach, or resident composers. And Shaw had other income, from royalties and the like. But once he was convinced the orchestra would be fine, maybe even better off, he was genuinely concerned with what he would do next.

For all his agitating, most members of most of the ASO boards were genuinely fond of "Robert," and they knew they were in his debt. In fact, when he did retire, the ASO board gave him a Picasso. Moreover, in the last ten years of his life, as he became quite famous again, the ASO board saw him in a light that demanded ever more handsome remuneration. So while he was not particularly well paid as music director, he was extremely well paid as the former music director.

Shaw soon discovered how seriously he had underestimated the extent to which he would be in demand as a guest conductor around the nation, once freed from Atlanta. He'd anticipated working on four or five choral-orchestral and Christmas programs in Atlanta, which he had agreed to do in his emeritus status; forming a small group of chamber singers to perform in and around Atlanta; and teaching at Emory University, which had agreed to sponsor a to-be-formed Robert Shaw choral institute (this became his summer festival in France). Shaw also planned to continue to record with Telarc, both with the ASO and ASOC, and his chamber singers in Atlanta and France. All of this he did do, although the Emory arrangement did not last, due primarily to academic jealousy and Shaw's usual lack of willingness to play the game. But thanks in large measure to Judith Arron—executive and artistic director of Carnegie Hall, who became a great advocate for Shaw late in both of their lives—Shaw re-emerged as an American musical elder. Arron put Shaw back on the map in New York City and he was then in enormous demand nationally. Virtually every orchestra and university music program of note in the nation asked him to conduct. Shaw enjoyed a sort of third career in his last decade of life. He had much more guest conducting offered to him than he could or would accept. His career reached its height, in terms of both artistic merit *and* public prestige, in his very last years. Many conductors, many artists, are still going long after, in John Cheever's wonderful phrase, "Their leaves have fallen." They work, but their powers are diminished. Not Shaw. He was lucky. He did some of his best work in his last years, and at the end of his life he was at, or near, the peak of his powers. Shaw had fretted that, after the ASO, no one would want him and that he would not be able to support his family. (They lived well.) He accepted the appointment at Emory partly for health insurance. But he was to have no such worries. He was, actually, as his last decade progressed, exponentially more in-demand and better remunerated than he had been in his life. He had no worries about work or income. And, more important, he was, often, able to do music on the high plane he had sought all his life. He had to think only about music now and, at that, only the music that he wanted to do. The ASO board, by putting him out to pasture, had done Shaw, musicians, and music listeners generally, a great service. Robert Shaw had been given back to the nation.

Perhaps not surprisingly, upon retirement Shaw also became, almost instantly, the beloved old man in Atlanta. When the "emeritus" returned, as he did each year for twelve to eighteen concerts at Symphony Hall, orchestra members (some of whom had been critics) were amazed anew at his ability to get them to "sing." You don't know what you've got 'til it's gone. And you don't know the perils of the new until you get it. Most of Shaw's returns to the ASO between 1989 and 1999—for concert series several times a year, and for recording sessions once, twice, or even three times a year—were love-ins.

Shaw's tenure as music director in Atlanta is now almost universally recalled as uniquely productive, co-operative, and free of small-mindedness—a time of great music making because the focus was *on* the music, not personalities. And it *was* all that, if also exhausting. As one member of the orchestra said:

> *Many conductors demand your personal loyalty. Robert never did that. He never asked me to, in any way, "be loyal" to him. He only asked that I feel responsibility to the composer. As a result, I felt tremendously loyal to Robert Shaw.*

ASO musicians Martin Chalifour, who became concertmaster with the Los Angeles Philharmonic, and William Preucil, who became concertmaster in Cleveland, occupied, respectively, the second and first violin chairs in Atlanta under Shaw. They have, together, now played with countless numbers of the top musicians in the world. Preucil remembers their time with Shaw in Atlanta as the best music making of their lives.

But hindsight can paint a rosy picture. Shaw got plenty of criticism in Atlanta toward the end of his tenure as music director. It was said that he was too apt to repeat his favorite pieces and composers, which is ironic since the complaint in the early Atlanta years was that there was too much unknown, unfamiliar, "modern stuff." But Shaw did have a core of works he returned to again and again. (Brahms and Beethoven symphonies, and piano concerti by both, for example.) Shaw also presented a fair amount of Bartók, and always lots of Bach, Mozart, Mendelssohn, and Haydn. And there were the moderns he loved: Hindemith, Britten, Stravinsky and, surprisingly, Prokofiev. Finally, of course, there was Charles Ives. Far from steering clear of Ives after his "firing," Shaw returned every few years to his Ives campaign. This might seem masochistic, or just stubborn. It was more than that. To be fired over Charles Ives! For Shaw this was a badge of artistic merit. Then to be re-hired by the people! That was worth a belly laugh.

In fact, the year following his firing Shaw was perhaps even less cautious. He programmed Luciano Berio, Eliot Carter, and Anton Webern.

By 1975 there were again many empty seats at ASO concerts, though many had been paid for. It was a constant tug of war. Shaw was always under pressure to dumb it down or lighten it up. He was always pushing to expand local tastes and his own and his musicians' boundaries. He tried, not always successfully, to remain aware that he had to stop that push just before he lost his audience, his allies in Atlanta, or his board.

Shaw came to love Atlanta and consider it his hometown. But in his years as music director Atlanta also frustrated Shaw enormously. He had a love/hate relationship with the city. He never felt he had the support for the orchestra and chorus that he thought he should have. (In fairness, this might not have been possible.) He never had the sort of financial resources available to him that, say, the Cleveland Orchestra, with its decades-old endowment, made available to its music director. He never had the cultural richness or resources to draw upon that Cleveland offered, or San Francisco, or even Cincinnati. There is a down side to missionary work: building from scratch is wearing.

Cleveland had, along with universities, a distinguished music conservatory. Atlanta had nothing like this. ASO cellist Christopher Rex says, surely rightly, that the best memorial to Robert Shaw would be a conservatory in Atlanta.

Shaw himself dreamed of what he called a "musical performance society"—a faculty of roughly 150 musicians who would play all sorts of music and mount a wide variety of musical performances, as well as teach.

Shaw succeeded in leading the ASO into its period of excellence and national prominence (the task for which he was hired). He professionalized the orchestra, hired great musicians (not just out of the best music schools but from other orchestras), imposed Szellian standards of preparation and performance, and continually challenged his musicians to dig deeper, better themselves, and rediscover their love of music. This he did by personally challenging people in private conversations ("read more poetry dear," he told one musician, who was hurt and offended) and with fervor—the fervor with which he approached almost every piece he rehearsed and performed. In the Atlanta years Shaw really did stay home. He focused on the orchestra and the chorus and the audience in Atlanta. He had decided that "the arts are not transportable." A community needs its own great music, he said.

It cannot wait for fine musical artists to come to town, and it cannot be sustained by art that merely visits.

Pushing Shaw into "retirement" in 1989 *may* have been incredibly ungrateful, for the ASO under Shaw had now won a slew of Grammies, and played Carnegie Hall regularly, and accompanied a presidential inauguration (that Carter fella). But ultimately Shaw's retirement freed him for ten amazingly fertile years. Energy that might have gone into administration went to projects like rethinking his approach to Mahler's *Symphony No. 8* (the so-called symphony of a thousand), and presenting it in Carnegie Hall with a hall (audience) full of choristers. Or it went to doing favorite pieces, like the Beethoven *Missa Solemni*s, with new orchestras and choruses.

Shaw came to accept Atlanta in a "lover's quarrel with the world" sort of way, and Atlanta forgot, in Shaw's old age—when he was so honored throughout the world—what a demanding and difficult rabble-rouser he had been. Shaw chose to continue living in Atlanta after he retired as music director, though there were other possibilities, especially after Caroline Shaw's death in 1995. John Silber wanted him to come to Boston University to head and remake the choral music program there. Judith Arron wanted him to live in New York at least part-time and become, essentially, the house conductor at Carnegie Hall. She argued that this was not a matter of friendship or altruism, since Shaw's concerts got the best reviews of Carnegie's season, and often the best attendance. (But Arron was also looking out for her friend Robert and trying to help him to create a new and full life after his wife's death.) Shaw did not want to live in New York or Boston. He could have returned to the West Coast, too—his true love was not France, which his wife taught him to love, but the Pacific. He did become principal guest conductor of the San Diego Symphony Orchestra, but that was a quite limited and sentimental commitment. That orchestra was struggling, in any event. No, Atlanta had become his home. (When guest-conducting in Minnesota, he once told a chorister whom he'd discovered was from below the Mason Dixon line, "Talk Southern to me, boy.") For all his quarrels with Atlanta, he felt grateful. He'd found professional fulfillment there. He'd done his best work there. He *was* part of the civil rights struggle, albeit as a musical footnote. Most of all he'd found personal happiness for the first time in his life in Atlanta. There he'd met Caroline, who changed him.

Further, in his second recording career, which was based on his Atlanta tenure—with Telarc—he finally escaped the *a cappella*, glee club, and folk repertoires and was able to put most of his classical repertoire of choral-orchestral masterworks, plus much more, on disc (some 60 recordings). Without Atlanta and the ASO, Shaw might have remained "the choral guy." Yes, he was grateful. He felt loyal. In the last year of Shaw's life, the government of France was to award him an honorary knighthood, and make the presentation in Washington, where he was guest conducting the National Symphony. Shaw said, "No." Let them make the presentation in Atlanta, he said. It had been his home, professionally and personally for 30-odd years. It was only due to Atlanta, he said, that he had become whatever he had become.

Shaw was proud of building a symphony and molding its basic personality in what New Yorkers might think of as a provincial spot. It was part of his contrariness—part of going against the grain. His theory was that a really great symphony *needed* to be built and sustained outside of New York, Boston, Chicago, or Philadelphia. What challenge would it be to put one's stamp on the already great orchestras in those cities? Great music is not just for the few; it is not just for those who feel they know it, but for those who might discover it. He also wanted to make Atlanta a regional Mecca. For Mecca is a long way for most people. As Shaw put it: "There should be one place where *all* the notes are sung, and it might as well be Atlanta."

Years after his retirement, Shaw was flying back to Atlanta after an out-of-town engagement with his faithful aide, Nola Frink, at his side. Shaw loved to fly and was looking out the window, analyzing the pilot's approach. He said to Frink: "I used to fly home and look out over the city and wonder, 'How can I reach all those people?'"

Once, near the end of his tenure as music director, Shaw was asked what the most memorable moment had been. He skirted the question, for he didn't much care for it. But then he began talk about an Atlanta performance of the Brahms *Ein Deutsches Requiem* in which, during the baritone solo in movement three, singer Tom Krause was delivering the words from Psalm 39—"Lord make me to know there must be an end of me and my life has a term"—and huge tears began to roll down his cheeks. Like the Mozart moment in Boston, so many years before, everyone in the hall was caught up in the depth of Brahms's text, music, and emotion. It was a moment of utter, raw truth, and for Shaw truth was beauty.

Shaw's early years in Atlanta were miserable in many ways. He was building all right, but meeting much resistance. He had nothing like the talent pool he'd had in Cleveland from which to choose singers, and many of his early Atlanta singers put church choir first. He was also living, again, as a solitary. The first Mrs. Shaw did not last long in Atlanta and retreated to the family home in Nantucket early on. These were the days when Shaw would drink with almost anyone in a local hotel bar—"Black Jack and Coke," with a beer chaser—one set after another. It was not the dignified behavior expected from the august leader of a symphony orchestra. And it was not the life he wanted. But private life, ordinary living outside music, was always a bit of a mystery to him. He never quite knew what to do with himself. Until an Atlanta woman changed that.

And eventually, the choirs got better, the players got better, Shaw got better. Things started to click in Atlanta. "It begins to be music," he said, in the middle 1970s.

The audience? That never quite clicked in the same way. The cycle of action and reaction in Atlanta was something like this: The box office went up and down as Shaw attempted to educate the public in choral literature and the sounds (and composers) "of our time." The public resisted, and the board asked for programs that would sell. Shaw relented, for a time. But then he became angry and, retreated from relenting, indeed came back with even more challenging programs and an even more determined and defiant attitude. Shaw's greatest popularity in Atlanta came after he retired and was rediscovered by the rest of the world. The prophet was not without honor in his homeland, but he was often seen as a wearing pain in the neck until he began to wander in the higher regions and gather praise and disciples there.

Shaw celebrated the end of his tenure in Atlanta by taking the ASO and ASOC on a tour of Europe, with a stop first in New York. They did 8 concerts in 12 days. His forces—340 people, at that time the largest American arts contingent ever to tour Europe, as Nick Jones noted—were acclaimed, especially for performances of the Beethoven *Ninth Symphony* in East Berlin and London. The tour, said Shaw, would be a test of the ASO's growth and skill. The climax of the tour was the performance in East Berlin—it concluded with eight curtain calls and applause that continued for 12 minutes after Shaw led the concertmaster, followed by the orchestra, from the stage. Shaw was mobbed by an enthusiastic throng when he finally left the dressing room for his car. It was a moment reminiscent of the Moscow performance with the Robert Shaw Chorale 27 years earlier. Prior to the London concert, one player was warned that English audiences simply do not "do" curtain calls or standing ovations, an odd remark in any case, but one proven untrue that night. The attitude seemed to be: What can an orchestra from the American provinces teach *us* about this piece? But the response was rapturous. And on this occasion Shaw, conducting the ASO in the *Ninth Symphony* for the last time, put down his baton and conducted the finale with his fists.

During his tenure, Shaw took the Atlanta Symphony Orchestra and chorus to Carnegie Hall 12 times. The reviews were almost always positive and respectful, but never worshipful, as they became after Shaw began to do the Carnegie Hall workshops in the 1990s. One might say the public was ahead of the critics in its appreciation of Shaw, for during all the Atlanta years, when he was recording his oeuvre with Telarc, the public was buying Shaw, radio stations were playing him, and Grammies were accumulating.

Shaw made his life and career in Atlanta, as Szell had done in Cleveland. When asked why he did not guest conduct more, he would respond, "Why go out for a hamburger when you have a steak at home?"

Sometimes he would say he'd learned that you grow the best vegetables in your own back yard. Now headed for what would be the last chapter of his life, the final ten years, he was about to experience an artistic re-birth.

CHAPTER 24

From Choral Master to Complete Musician

Many people assume Shaw began to conduct orchestras after he came to Atlanta. As we have seen, this is very far from true. By the early 1950s, Shaw was routinely conducting choral-orchestral works and orchestras on his own. Even during Shaw's Toscanini period—from 1949 to 1954—indeed, even prior to his work with Toscanini, Shaw mostly prepared choruses for *his own* performances with his own pickup or touring orchestras. Shaw was also, of course, already making his own records of classical choral and oratorio literature by the time he began to work with Toscanini.

The centerpiece of Shaw's orchestral debut with the Naumburg Symphony was Beethoven's *Symphony No. 1*. That was 1945. He first led the NBC Symphony in a purely orchestral program in August of 1946—conducting Beethoven's *Symphony No. 2*, among other works. He had begun to work his way through Beethoven. He believed that if he could handle Beethoven, he'd truly be a conductor. Maybe that's one reason he loved the *Ninth* so much—it represented graduation.

But even from the formative days of the Collegiate Chorale, and the occasional small chamber choirs he plucked out of it, Shaw *never* confined himself to *a cappella* work, and as the years progressed, he spent only a small amount of time on strictly choral material. He loved *a cappella* literature, built much of the Robert Shaw Chorale's following on it, and regretted that he had little time for it in the 1960s, 1970s, and 1980s when his main jobs were with symphony orchestras. (He returned to recording such works in the 1990s after retiring from the Atlanta Symphony Orchestra.) But from the beginning, he was drawn to large-scale works involving orchestra and chorus, and from the very early stages of his career he wanted all the available colors of the musical palette at his beckon.

Ironically, when he went to the Cleveland Orchestra, Shaw became *primarily* an orchestra conductor. His basic job description and his time commitment were primarily orchestral. He was spending 65 to 75 percent of the time he gave to Cleveland on purely orchestral works. And yet he was hired because he was a choral wizard. In Atlanta, 80 to 85 percent of his time was to be devoted to the orchestra and orchestral matters. Shaw's task, in Shaw's mind, was to go from choral wizard to total musician. This was his task when he went to Cleveland. But it remained his task when he went to Atlanta. He felt he'd never entirely "licked it" in Cleveland, in part because of his own insecurities, in part because of the long shadow of Szell and all the "little Szells," and in part because of his many other commitments.

It was only after he got to Atlanta, and then only after many years—having hired orchestra members, disciplined some players, been tested by others, and learned and repeated many orchestra pieces—that Shaw began to be comfortable with the orchestra. Once again, he was learning by doing; and once again he was, musically anyway, his own boss. But even this newfound degree of comfort he'd found could become shaky with a different orchestra (like the New York Philharmonic, which he nonetheless felt was "undisciplined"). In Atlanta, there was no steely glare upon him, except from within. And he could focus as Szell had wanted him to because he'd given up his other jobs—the Robert Shaw Chorale, most touring, and (in the early Atlanta years) making records. He had only one sideline in Atlanta—Atlanta's choruses.

Shaw had to treat the chorus as an extra job—after already putting in fifty or sixty hours a week on the orchestra. This makes what he eventually accomplished with the chorus all the more astounding. Mind you, Shaw needed and used help—most notably his assistant Nola Frink, herself a well-trained choral musician. And in later years, he used assistant conductors Norman Mackenzie and Ann Jones. On a couple of occasions he spoke of hiring a chorusmaster other than himself, and at one point, in a two-decade-plus rule as music director, he actually did hire a choral conductor to handle the choir. (He was angry at the choir.) But it didn't last. The chorus was his own personal, hand-built go-cart. Though his first responsibility was to the orchestra—building it, programming for it, studying scores—the chorus was his first love.

The sheer workload of doing both jobs in Atlanta sometimes pushed him to the brink of breakdown, but it was his choice and nobody was going to talk him into a different way. He had to do *both* to be a total and complete musician.

His orchestral work changed the way Shaw thought about the chorus.

He had always been rhythmically driven. But now he became rhythm obsessive. He decided that what the chorus needed was orchestral clarity and particularity.

Szell was a master of the small cell of music—a detail and small-picture man. The essence of good playing to him was not emotion but clarity and cleanness. Why, Shaw wondered, could this standard not apply to the choir?

He concluded that the choral art needed "instrumental disciplines."

And he felt that if a great orchestra, like Cleveland, could play with the attentiveness and synchronization of a string quartet, a small choir could do the same. (And the large choir could imitate the small choir.) He admitted that the larger the choir, the harder this task was to accomplish. Yet Shaw usually had large choirs—another story.

It is possible that Shaw's greatest contribution to the choral art may be this idea of instrumental particularity. Shaw showed that the goo and gauze in the choral sound *could* be removed. He learned instrumental disciplines by working with instrumentalists. He studied the technique of Serkin, Casals, Stern, and others. *His* instrument was the voice—or voices—he knew that. But what could he glean from the instrumentalists? Cleanliness of sound and clarity of line.

He had taken at least a few lessons in most of the instruments in the orchestra, beginning at Juilliard, as well as during the Cleveland years. He had taught himself the guitar. And there was the ongoing attempt to improve his keyboard skills. Shaw liked singers who were trained on an instrument. He always told young conductors: "The better your keyboard skills, the better a conductor you will be." Shaw said the piano, unlike the other instruments, granted access to the whole work. He knew he would never be an instrumentalist, but he could make his choirs instruments, and teach them precision. Shaw's aphorism that an orchestra needs to be taught to sing while a chorus must be taught to play was not a clever phrase to him, but one of his sincere quasi-theological tenets.

Trying to instruct both—the orchestra to sing and the choir to play—taught Shaw a great deal about one very practical matter: balance. It made him attentive to balancing the sound of the orchestra with the chorus in a concrete way that few orchestra conductors are concerned with at all. He also sought to balance the sound *within* the chorus and *within* the orchestra—problems many conductors never truly face. Because of his unique background—and temperament—Shaw was almost uniquely attentive to choral–instrumental conversation and complement. This matters enormously. For what often happens is that chorus and orchestra rehearse separately, at different dynamic levels and variations, and then are put together—for perhaps two rehearsals—like a cake and gravy. Often, no one is even looking for the balance problems. The conductor is simply trying to cram all that sound together and shut the door. The hopeful working assumption is that problems of balance will work themselves out in the moment of performance. But Shaw, having walked both sides of the street, would have been thinking about balance problems all along and marked virtually every note in the score, for every player and choral section, for dynamics. All this was done to balance the sound. Then, in rehearsal he would test and listen for balance problems and adjust his edits. He would also adjust for the hall—adjusting sound and, in a sense, tuning for the hall. Thus, with the Shaw method, in the final coming together of players and singers, there is a chance that the musicians can hear each other and actually play *together.* Instead of trying to adjust a train wreck, the conductor can refine and calibrate a conversation.

Shaw was, all his life, obsessed with rhythm, with tempo, and with metric precision. This is unusual for someone coming out of choral work. But thanks to his orchestral submersion, his near-obsession with metrics actually sharpened his sense of musical energy and calibration.

Shaw's symphonic and orchestral background made a difference in what he brought to the American public. He was not just bringing "a sound," but great choral literature, in well-considered sound proportions.

Shaw adopted Szell's meticulous attention to detail and Toscanini's feel for the long line. Once he was free to really be himself (in Atlanta), he added, as critic Richard Dyer noted, his own unique qualities—his rhythmic sense, his ability to instrumentalize choral music and choralize instrumental music—his warmth.

Shaw actually worked on music more the way Szell did—the slow, methodical, microcosmic, inch-by-inch march through the composer's blueprints; taking the watch apart and putting it back together. But he did not want it delivered that way. He wanted each work he performed to be whole and well proportioned.

It was from Szell that Shaw took the idea of an orchestra as essentially a large chamber group. But Shaw went Szell one better. Shaw believed that the orchestra could be so tightly knit by score study, by solid and well-organized rehearsals, and by the musicians listening to each other that the conductor could be, and should be, virtually irrelevant by performance time. Shaw said that if he did his job properly, the conductor ought to be able to step out of the way in the moment of performance and let Beethoven (or any other composer) and Saint Cecilia take over. Certainly, Shaw felt that when ideal music making occurs, the conductor should not be needed for cueing and other traffic cop duties.

In a sense, Shaw attempted to lay Toscanini's style over Szell's: The conductor on the podium in performance should be there not so much to beat time and direct traffic as to establish a shared internal clock, a musical groove, and hold the ensemble together and invite individual inspiration within a common spirit, gestalt, or trance. In Shaw's mind, and eventually in his practice, the conductor's coaching should be a subtle gesture of motion, just a tilt of the hand or leaning in. The conductor should never upstage the composer and his music. (In this sense, Shaw on the podium was the antithesis of Bernstein, who so many conductors now mindlessly ape.) Nor should the conductor upstage the musicians. He should allow the music to unfold and to be newly made.

Szell, said Shaw, developed the whole out of the small cell. Toscanini did the opposite, working backward, or downward from the mountaintop, and perhaps never reaching the ground. But both men spoke to Shaw. And he carried both to his own orchestra in Atlanta. Both men, giants though they were, *enfants terribles* though they were, conceived of the conductor's role as limited. For Szell, at least as Shaw saw Szell, the ensemble—the listening, playing ensemble—was king. For Toscanini, the composer, and the score, ruled.

Shaw was sometimes criticized for his lack of dynamism on the podium, for burying his head in the text, even for missing cues. And it is true that he was not a method actor of the podium. Nor was he a nanny. He did not pantomime angst or begin to weep at tragic passages. But musicians in Atlanta saw the light in his eyes and sensed, said one player, that "he could hear with his fingertips."

Shaw felt that good music making needed *less* conducting in performance, not more, though preparation required the conductor's maximum attention as editor, gardener, and coach in the rehearsal phase. Many conductors, consciously or unconsciously, believe the opposite is true—"this is my performance; the audience expects me to be in charge and will hold me responsible for boredom, failure, or fiasco." Yet they rush through their preparations. Shaw believed his real work was in rehearsal.

In later life Shaw's conducting was particularly spare but powerful in its inwardness and control. He could enrich the sound by rubbing his forefinger against his thumb. He could sweeten a violin solo by beckoning with the same finger. He could deepen the sound with an open hand or call out a choral sonic boom by raising his left hand in a fist and miming the words "come on."

One musician, an oboist, said, "Shaw would turn to you and just hand it to you . . . it made you feel very responsible and very powerful."

Shaw was more specific and hands-on with singers. He felt they *needed* micro-management to become more instrumental. Again, we are speaking of rehearsal and preparation. In order to "play," singers needed to tighten up, and down; to get in harness with the composer and in sync with each other. In order to "sing," players needed to be set free. More, Shaw believed vocal musicians need patient coaching and psychological manipulation, while instrumental musicians chiefly need instruction as to degree and shading. It's simply easier, Shaw said, to make an instrument do what you want it to do than to get ready and quick compliance from a voice. With the voice there are infinitely more possibilities and potential problems. He said it's harder to tune a voice, for example, than it is to tune almost any other instrument, though eventual pitches can be more centered than most instruments. The instrumentalist usually knows how to get the exact sound he or the conductor wants; the singer may not know how to get it. And the problems people have singing *together*, said Shaw, are profound. For each human voice is a distinctive instrument. We can all hear that. Almost any pair of ears can hear that the voices of Pavarotti and Domingo sound different. So is each piano distinctive, Glenn Gould might say. True enough, but not to the same degree. Not as dramatically. (And one seldom has the problem of a hundred pianos playing together.) So singers must be approached with a long-range battle plan and much patience, while players need great economy and efficiency in rehearsal and must be addressed in a kind of shorthand. Finally, said Shaw, singers need many hours of rehearsal to be knit together, while instrumentalists generally rehearse together for a few hours and achieve all they will achieve.

For both, Shaw prepared endlessly. Every minute of every rehearsal was mapped out. He allowed himself to be tyrannized by the tempo watch *and* the watch, for he was always determined to stick to his rehearsal plan. Of course, he did not always stick to the *musical* plan. He revised his edits endlessly. If he had four and a half days of rehearsal, as he did for the Carnegie Hall workshops in the 1990s, for example, he edited his editing each night in his hotel room. Working with a fresh score for each performance or performance series, he often, inevitably, returned to old musical ideas and habits. But he changed his mind too—deciding an edited passage had to be altered because he'd missed something, or had simply been wrong. The last time he performed the work, he decided he had been "*all* wrong" about the Mahler's *Symphony Number 8*, though no one quite had the courage to ask how so. (One associate speculated that Shaw may have decided his previous performances presented too unified a sound, and not an emotionally-wrought enough sound. A unified sound was a hallmark of later Shaw choirs. But was it what Mahler wanted? Shaw decided perhaps it was not. If the sound was wrong for Mahler, it would have to change.) Similarly, the last time he performed the Rachmaninoff *Vespers,* Shaw re-thought it. He decided to make the sound darker, more masculine, and more raw than his Telarc recording. Many people consider Shaw's recording of that piece to be as near to definitive as a recording can be. Shaw liked it, but decided it was not Russian enough. And certainly in the case of the Bach *Mass in B Minor* he was constantly rethinking. Shaw moved more and more toward breaking it down into a series of solos and quartets and away from not only a big choral sound but also, fascinatingly, choral dominance of the work. For him, that piece became essentially instrumental.

Of course all conductors, through the years, try new things. But Shaw wasn't actually much interested in the new, per se. And certainly he was not interested in a daring new take on this piece or that. For him it was: Is it right? Is it in the composer's language, vision, and intent? Is it musical truth? He was not after novelty, but the Holy Grail.

Shaw's insistence on the fresh score and on rethinking works he had prepared and performed many times, note by note, was typically Shaw and typically extreme. He put himself through re-marking a new score, in detail, whether the score was choral, orchestral, or choral-orchestral. He felt the exercise was *especially* necessary if he had done the piece many times. His idea was to be not so much interpretive as resurrective. To make the score "sound" (the phrase Toscanini used and Shaw liked) meant, to Shaw, clarity and sonority. But also, somehow, it meant mystic re-creation.

Shaw's rehearsal techniques were based on drills and repetition. These, he hoped, would lead to a shared consciousness. Everyone would be in sync so that Shaw's smallest movements in performance triggered a known response by the musicians. Cueing and stick work were really not the point. Robert Woods of Telarc said: "RS could conduct a concert with his eyes."[62]

When Shaw went to Cleveland it was to master the orchestra (or, negatively, to master his fear of it). After a decade or so, he simply wanted to

62 Burris-Woods Interview.

be a fine musician—a complete musician. Did Shaw attain his goal? Did he accomplish the complete or learned musicianship he sought?

Certainly *he* was never entirely satisfied. And there were, of course, flawed and failed and just plain unlucky performances in Atlanta. Perceptive critics could find weaknesses in some literature or in some technique, and they did. So, too, with Szell, Toscanini, and every other big name conductor. The giants create an expectation they cannot always meet. And music is too vast for any one musician to master every musical challenge. For Shaw, the ambition was in tackling the music, not in what he achieved personally.

Shaw would seem a paradox: The great choral guru who was not, strictly or simply speaking, a choral conductor; an orchestral conductor who never was as comfortable with the orchestra as with the chorus; the man who remade choral music, but ran a symphony orchestra.

But perhaps he was not a paradox if you consider what he was trying to do and the way he approached music. For growth was his be-all and end-all. And how could he grow if he could not sometimes fail? His goals in Atlanta were to perfect his own musicianship, build the orchestra, and expand the audience for great music in the city, state, and region. And perhaps along the way, via music, strike a blow for human rights and dignity.

As the years passed, Shaw cared less and less about how others regarded him or categorized him. It was the piece before him—the work at hand—and trying to realize it that mattered. He cared very little about his standing or his reputation but very much about his own continuing musical education.

Shaw never did fully escape the prison of categorization—the ghettoization of "the choral guru," or even the erroneous "chorusmaster"—though he came close in his final years. And, admittedly, he specialized. Most conductors specialize, to one degree or another. Shaw specialized in the choral repertoire, just as some conductors specialize in Mahler or the

Baroque. Virgil Thomson suggested that Toscanini was most "spiritually enlightening" when he did Italian music and not all that compelling when he did other material. Again, critics can find the chink in the armor—not surprising considering the virtual impossibility of some musical tasks. But most of us would wish to hear Toscanini conduct anything, including traffic. One would perhaps *most* want to hear him conduct Verdi. Yet one would not call Toscanini a conductor of Italian music.

In his early and middle years, Shaw wanted to escape the "pigeonhole." In his late years, as we have noted, he said that the pigeonhole had been, for him, "a space big enough to get lost in." On another occasion Shaw quoted Paul Hindemith in a private conservation. The composer said two things to Shaw: first, that the greatest music ever written was choral music, and second, that J. S. Bach was, after all, a choir conductor and choral educator.

In any case, Shaw again changed his mind, and himself. He ceased to seek mastery, or even assurance. Now he was seeking musical wisdom and depth. He wasn't after control any more. That seemed an illusion. He was seeking a profound participation in the music.

In Europe in the decade after Shaw's death, John Eliot Gardiner and Philippe Herreweghe perhaps approximated Shaw's overall importance and visibility in the United States in his time. And of course, Eric Ericson was the European Shaw of his day. Yet it would not be quite right to call *them* "choral conductors" either. The scope of their work is too broad. They are conductors, period. Musicians period.

In order to become a complete musician, Shaw had to overcome his insecurity with the orchestra. Second, he had to polish his specialty—large works that called for large forces. The Verdi and Berlioz Requiems are two obvious examples. For these, he had to learn to listen for orchestral textures and balances. And he had to learn the orchestral language of the great choral composers. Take Brahms, for example. Shaw took advantage of many chances to conduct the four Brahms symphonies and the two piano concertos while in Atlanta. Becoming an able Brahms conductor made him a more knowing conductor of Brahms's choral music. And it gave him dimension when conducting a choral-orchestral work like the *German Requiem*—a dimension that many conductors lack. Brahms, Shaw held, was an expert writer of songs. The *German Requiem* was a collection of song forms. Few *symphonic* conductors get an opportunity to work with song forms, just as few *choral* conductors ever get a chance to conduct a Brahms symphony. Again, the goal was a profound participation in the music of Brahms.

It does seem plausible that once a musician reaches a certain level, the music of a great composer becomes indivisible. This was Shaw's notion. It is sensible to think that Shaw was able to deliver near-definitive performances of the Brahms *Requiem* because he not only knew the choir, he knew Brahms. Leonard Slatkin once said that Shaw's Beethoven *Ninth Symphony* was fresh because Shaw always approached the piece as if he were conducting it for first time. This is true. But Shaw's sense of awe was also fed by his broad knowledge of the composer's total body of work. Shaw had conducted all of Beethoven's other symphonies and had a fifty-year relationship with this particular composer as well as this particular work—going back to Shaw's days with Toscanini. The significance of making the leap to the orchestra for Shaw was not so much personal and careerist as musical. It meant total immersion in the work of each composer when his composition was at hand. When Shaw conducted the *Missa,* for example, he studied Beethoven's late string quartets.

Every conductor has to *come* from somewhere: the woodwinds, the strings, the keyboard. Shaw's instrument was the voice, especially voices in common. He tuned the choir before performances the way Segovia tuned his guitar. But when he conducted Beethoven or Brahms, he conducted every note for every instrument.

Despite deep, and what turned out to be abiding, insecurities about his sufficiency, almost from the beginning Shaw wanted to stand before the players as well as the singers as a complete musician. It wasn't about power, but music. It wasn't about ego, but study, understanding, and insight. Never did he simply conduct the chorus and let the orchestra guide itself. He didn't think that way.

Bobby Shaw with his parents and siblings. He is front right.

A very young Shaw in rehearsal with the collegiate chorale -- more force and enthusiasm than musical knowledge.

Shaw was athletic, musically and personally. He said a yawn and a stretch "Don't hurt anything."

Shaw with his mother and brother John, circa 1945.

Two early publicity shots of Shaw. A colleague said, "There was a faint whiff of Hollywood about him in those days."

Shaw did what was necessary for the work. If he needed to stand on a table or chair to be seen, he did not hesitate.

Shaw with Koussevitzky at Tanglewood, summer of 1947.

Shaw enjoying rare down time with his first wife Maxine and his children, Peter and Johanna.

Shaw with Paul Hindemith

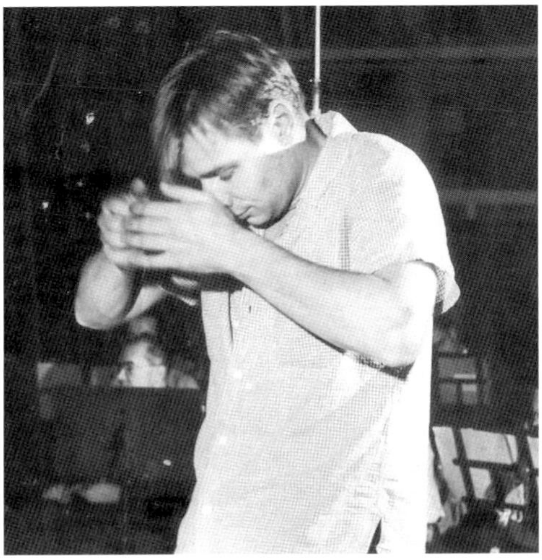

Listening.

Shaw with Julius Herford.

An early Robert Shaw Chorale program.

A poster for the Robert Shaw Chorale, containing a line of its Credo.

The Chorale on its way to Europe and the Middle East, 1956.

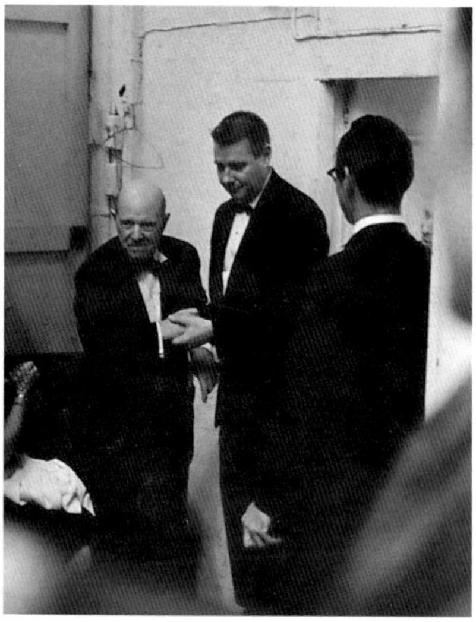

Shaw with Pablo Casals.

Shaw with his step-son Alex and President and Mrs. Carter, at the White House. Shaw liked and admired Carter and even campaigned for him.

Shaw in St. Moritz with members of the Atlanta Symphony Chorus, after a brief summer tour in 1982. Caroline Shaw stands before him and Thomas Shaw is to his right.

Shaw conducting the ASO and Chorus, and keeping both in time.

Shaw backstage in Paris with fellow conductors Christoph von Dohnányi and Pierre Boulez, 1990.

Conducting in one of his favorite halls, 1995.

Shaw conducting in Salt Lake in 1981. His intensity became more concentrated with age.

Shaw with his second family -- Alex, Thomas, and Caroline, in Atlanta.

Shaw with his stepson Alex. He was determined to get fatherhood right the second time around.

A poetic shot of sweat and toil.

Still listening.

He studied, researched, analyzed, and prepared the entire piece. Success as a conductor, for him, meant uncovering and rediscovering the composer in his entirety—with his fellow musicians. It would be no good to find the Holy Grail alone.

CHAPTER 25

Understanding the Words

Shaw's insistence on verbal clarity in singing, whether by a choir, a quartet, or an individual singer, certainly came initially from his own love of words. And Fred Waring reinforced it. Waring may have leaned toward the corny, but much of what he tried to do with pop music, Shaw appropriated for classical and sacred music: Articulate and communicate "*every sound of every syllable.*" Every sound within every word—every diphthong and tripthong—mattered. Perhaps not many students at Curtis or the Yale School of Music looked upon Fred Waring as a master craftsman, but in Shaw's view that was too bad. Shaw felt that many an august musician was strangely indifferent to the communication of text. Shaw felt these musicians could learn a thing or two from a Waring—or a Frank Sinatra. Shaw was quite an admirer of Sinatra. For one thing, he felt that Sinatra (like Waring) always knew exactly what he was doing musically. He would not bend a musical line because that is where his voice went at that moment but, very consciously, to emphasize a part of a text. Moreover, Sinatra, Shaw felt, always had complete control of his vibrato, and used it for musical purposes. That Robert Shaw could wax eloquent on Frank Sinatra often shocked musicians Shaw was instructing. But Sinatra, whose diction was so precise, so flawless, understood words and their importance.

The mature Shaw's concern with balance and with musical clarity, and what he called a "clean" quality, was a sort of extension of his early-life emphasis on text and communicating text. Shaw saw it as the duty of the musician to communicate the individual composer's *musical* language. This could only be done with particularity. Shaw hated what he called a musical "smear"—a blur of sound that wiped out musical tapestry. And without clarity and balance, a smear was inevitable. A composer by definition, he said, creates his own language—a language in music that is meant to communicate *beyond* words and is completely the composer's own. This must be as clear as an actor reciting Emily Dickinson. Words were Shaw's youthful preoccupation and a lifelong love. But musical languages beyond words, and communicating those languages, these were his later, mature obsessions.

Shaw's insistence that the audience understand the words in choral music was the basis of much of his early success. People had generally accepted that many of the words in a choral concert would be heard, if at all, as if through gauze—understood only if a text were provided. Shaw made the words matter in classical choral music because he made sure they were heard and understood. The later Shaw wanted, just as urgently, for the score to sound and for its internal grammar and poetry to be heard and taken in.

Shaw would devote himself to fully realizing all of the words of a *Missa Solemnis*. (This was not totally and absolutely possible, but Shaw's performance of the piece did tend to be much more articulate than renditions by other famous conductors.) So, too, did he demand articulation in the last movement of Beethoven's *Ninth Symphony*. Great and good conductors have long assumed that in some spots, in some choral-orchestral pieces, it is virtually impossible to get clear words across to an audience. Shaw would never make that concession. He never quit working on trying to get the words clean and clear, and then even more clean and clear—*every sound* within every word, in order to get every word. But so, too, the notes. Shaw's obsession with clarity, which began with words, extended to sound—and not only the big notes. Little notes, he said, have the same rights as big notes.

Each must be given, he said, its "itness." And the more subdivision within a note, the more clarity, and the more "itness."

Shaw was a word child who concluded that words (with the occasional exception of the popular song) must be subservient to musical values—musical language, cadence, and tone. If the words had been enough, if they conveyed all that could be conveyed, there would be no need to set them to music.

Shaw as a young man was schooled in literature, particularly American literature and religious literature. Literature, comparative religion, and philosophy would not seem to be great preparations for music. But for Shaw, they were. Shaw always heard the music in words and the language and syntax of music.

Because of his background in words, Shaw brought a quest for meaning—which, after all, is a part of the composer's quest, particularly in something like a requiem—to music. He was also born and bred to evangelical preaching, where there is always a message, and the message always derives from a text. He poured this fervor into music—his own true faith. He wrote or remarked to his Atlanta forces more than once that, though we recite, "God is love," we seldom seem to consider that it might be *literally* the case. "What if," Shaw asked, "God *is* love?" "Not," as Shaw put it, "God loves, or God is to be loved, or God commands us to love, but God IS love." G=L. "And what if," Shaw then wondered, "we discovered and agreed that singing together is a profound expression of charity or fraternity, or Augustinian love: '*Music* is love.'" "Hence," Shaw concluded, "G=L=M." This is the Shavian theology in fortune cookie form.

If music is meaning, indeed divine meaning, it must be done with the utmost care. And there must be a communion—of music maker and taker.

Shaw's roots in evangelical Protestantism and American folk music made him pragmatic: We are not here to express the arts for our personal pleasure, but to communicate a message. Why? In order to bring to life the artist's conception of the absolute. Thus the source of love (whoever and whatever Divinity might be) provides the means to love—making music together.

Music was Shaw's political philosophy as well as his cosmology. His concepts of community and of personal responsibility were bound up in his ideas of how to make music: find the message; communicate the message.

If nothing else, Shaw, given his background, which he saw as such a disadvantage, brought something unique to music making. And, as violinist William Preucil said, most fine musicians are not looking for a time beater to conduct them. They are looking for something extra. If they wish to be conducted at all, they seek inspiration—someone who somehow makes you see, feel, and give more. Shaw inspired his players and singers, said Preucil, to give more than they had a right to expect or get from themselves.[63] In part, this was because of his facility with, love of, and loyalty to language. Words carry messages. He had learned, in the church of his childhood, about "the message in song." But song carries messages, too, and takes you beyond the textual message to something deeper. To Shaw, that was the promise of music.

When he went to Atlanta, Shaw was responding to what his father, the pastor, would have dubbed "a call." When his time in Atlanta ended, especially after Caroline's death, the mission changed again. It was no longer Atlanta or the South, or even choral music, per se, but great music—music of transcendence and nobility—to which he was obliged. The mission now became, again, bringing great music to the American public—those who, like himself, were a part of the great unwashed. He would again ride the circuit and preach the word. The word, for Shaw, was not just text, but the mind of the great composer, as revealed in his compositions. His musical grammar.

It is one thing to view a music performance as a technical problem to be solved, or a job to be done. It is quite another to believe that "G=L=M." But Shaw bet his life on this equation.

63 Burris–Preucil interview.

Shaw used to talk to Nola Frink about the "nameless artisans" who built the great cathedrals of Europe. Tellingly, when he was asked by a participant in one of the Carnegie Hall workshops if he "considered himself a teacher," Shaw answered: "If I'm lucky, I don't consider myself."

Shaw acquired, in time, a sort of Benedictine self-denial. It had to do not just with gestures or sentiments of humility, but with his profound desire to be a medium for the music, rather than an interpreter or performer: to unleash the music and then vanish. Perhaps this harkened back to his father's "message in song" each Sunday. What matters is the message, not the messenger.

Shaw's view of himself as a musician was of a man with a handicap. But Sylvia McNair has said that the conservatory or more conventional music school education, which Shaw so lamented lacking, might have produced a lesser Shaw.[64] A number of observers, ranging from critic Tim Page to conductor (and one-time Shaw colleague) Alice Parker, have remarked that perhaps no other conductor has so penetrated the spiritual mysteries of the canonical choral-orchestral masterworks—such as the *Missa Solemnis* or the Bach *Mass in B Minor*. Would this have been possible if Shaw had been more a technician than a mystic? His grounding in text, and in structure, his focus on message, source and reception, were what made him a unique musician. Shaw saw the Beethoven *Missa* as the composer's personal meditation on suffering, immortality, and divinity. He saw the rage and the prayer of a composer at once at the height of his powers and aware of losing them; a composer at once affirming life and drowning in fear and despair. In short, Shaw understood the piece, and in an utterly personal way. No one else could have prepared and conducted it the way he did.

64 Burris–McNair interview.

CHAPTER 26

Disciplines and Necessities

Perhaps it had to do with his psychic architecture, his Protestant hyper-work ethic, or the guilt his parents bred in him, but Shaw did things the hard way. Music did not generally come easy to him. And if something did come easily, he made it hard. After he got to Atlanta, he would tell Fred Scott, one of his assistant conductors there, what he had told Louis Lane in Cleveland: "Suffering is good for musicians." Art, like grace, should not be cheap. Shaw made artistic straight jackets for himself as a way of earning artistic grace. At any given time, two goals were always in tension: technical perfection and spiritual enlightenment; dryness and emotion; skepticism and faith. He decided the tension was not contradiction but dialectic. Shaw was always working against himself. But this was his formula for art—or rather, the possibility of it—creative tension.

As people age they become more extreme versions of themselves, and Shaw was no exception. He became, in old age, at once more spiritual, more yogi-like, *and* more obsessive about vocal tidiness and choral "disciplines."

Asked about his approach to choral technique, or the vocal tricks of the trade he had developed, Shaw would give a consistent answer: musical technique should be practical problem solving. It is not a matter of this school or that, or of one form of musical correctness or another. That's why there was no Shaw "school" of choral methods and why he didn't want little blue-shirted Shavians running around the country leading choirs in count singing simply for the sake of count singing. For Shaw, technique in music, in all art, is problem solving. Not formulaic and not imitative, no matter how flattering.

Certainly Shaw had *principles*. One was that rhythm is the foundation of music. Another was that singers are responsible for identifying and being able to achieve pitches as of the first rehearsal—that is, they must have learned notes on their own. (Shaw was very fast at teaching notes but hated to "waste time" doing so and felt the individual singer should be accountable.) But once notes are learned, rhythm should come first. It is the first layer. One might call learning the notes the timber. Rhythm is the foundation.

Rhythmic unification of a choir is difficult to achieve, Shaw said, but ultimately helps with unification of pitch. Pitch refinement must come later. "Count singing" was Shaw's primary means of achieving rhythmic unification.

What is "count singing?" It's not rocket science. Shaw would have the choir sing "one and two and *tee* and four and" rather than text on the notes. ("Tee" was used instead of three because "three" takes too long to sing.) The point is to get singers thinking and making music like instrumentalists. You sing a note in time rather than attempt to sing a word fragment on a note. The idea is to get pitches and rhythms perfectly in alignment.

Again, the essence of what Shaw did as a conductor was in rehearsal, not performance. In a Shaw rehearsal, metrics came first. Lyrics came last. After he felt he had all the musical elements in place, textual drills were run on a single chord or whole-tone cluster of Shaw's devising. But even then, Shaw might return a choir to "numbers"(count singing) to reinforce rhythmic alignment. Only after dealing with metrics, pitch problems, tone quality, choral unification, and synchronization would Shaw move on to matters of dynamics and "color." Interpretation and emotional qualities were not even allowed to knock on the door until almost the end of the process.

It's not that Shaw believed that music should be unemotional. Quite the contrary. But Shaw generally touched on the meaning of text only tangentially as he built the piece musically, except for the Britten *War Requiem*—in that case he treated the text independently. When he did get to the text, Shaw did not interpret it any more than he sought to interpret the music before him. He treated it as truth. At that moment, the composer's truth was Shaw's truth and the truth of his forces. And, as Sylvia McNair said, "You had to believe it." Whatever the words were, you had to believe them.

Shaw believed that musical deconstruction and reconstruction, and the preparation of a performance should be as unemotional and clinical as humanly possible. "At first, don't be artists," he said in rehearsal, "be slaves." "Don't try to satisfy science and art. Just worry about the science." The science will unleash the art. A clinical performance of a Brahms *Requiem* or Bach *St. John Passion,* which some conductors have perhaps sought, would seem a very strange thing to Shaw—a clever conceit just clever enough to guarantee destruction of the heart of the piece. But clinical preparation? Absolutely. Shaw believed musicians were not entitled to *feel* the music until they had done everything they could to *understand* the music and prepare it. Then, perhaps in the moment of performance, "the piece will make itself known."

Shaw would return the choir to counting so he and the musicians did not get ahead of themselves. He sometimes did this even at the dress rehearsal. Again, he was holding back emotion and reinforcing musical parsimony and precision. In the words of one singer, "Shaw never wanted to release the dove until the last possible instant."

Shaw always insisted that those who came to his workshops should use what they could use of his methods, but incorporate them into their own styles and their own needs. He firmly believed in count singing as a method of locking in metrics and lining up metrical values with text. But he thought people ought to know why they were count singing and understand its value for them, not simply ape him because he was Robert Shaw. He felt younger conductors should simply discard any technique, including any one of his own, that did not work for them.

Filmmaker Nick Doob said that the most interesting thing he observed while filming several Carnegie Hall workshops was that Shaw was always adapting his own lessons and notions to the reality he found that particular year with that particular piece and that particular choir. If count singing wasn't working, Shaw would have a choir make percussive sounds instead, for example. If he was not achieving a feeling of locomotion, he would have the choir march. He was "going for what's necessary at that moment," Shaw said. If that meant clapping, singing in circles, or swaying back and forth, he did it. And he didn't fall in love with his own brainstorms. If something did not work, he dropped it. Some people think that, since Shaw sometimes broke the choir into quartets, this was an article of doctrine. But Shaw had no doctrine. He would organize a small choir in quartets in polyphonic music, but not in symphonic music. It was a practical matter. All techniques depended on the particular need. In some instances, for example, placing singers near the instruments that doubled their parts was effective, and in others it was not so effective. He did what he thought the situation called for.

Shaw geared his rehearsals to the needs of each composition, choir, hall, and performance. He was not only a pragmatist, but he was a man who might change his mind, and change it again—not based on whim but on the desire to more perfectly realize the piece in question. Shaw was known as the great advocate of using English translations for performances of the Bach Passions, for instance, and he certainly was. He felt the Passions, performed live, should be heard in the language of the listeners. But he also once wrote to an acquaintance that if he ever *did* record the *St. Matthew*, he would record it in German. The point of English was to create a living scripture for a living, and participating, American audience. It should be, "interactive," as it were. Hence, Shaw usually had the audience sing the Passion chorales. A person listening to a recording is participating in the piece in a different way—he is a listener, not an active partaker. What is more, he may be listening in any time or place. His listening is not bound to a specific time or place, for a recording is an artifact, part of the historical record. It is not of the moment.

But Shaw might have changed his mind about this had he made a recording of the *St. Matthew*. As Shaw himself said, "The scholarship changes almost by the day." Some scholars now say, for instance, that the congregations did not sing chorales in Bach's time.

Shaw recorded Haydn's *Die Schöpfung (The Creation)* in English for Telarc, but performed it in German the last time he conducted it at Carnegie Hall, saying, "Let's hear it the way Haydn heard it." (This would seem to flip Shaw's Bach Passion thinking on its head.) The point is, Shaw's wisdom, "tricks," and techniques were situational. He was not ideological, rigid or doctrinaire. Musical craft, for him, had to be a matter of pragmatic adaptation to circumstance.

He also felt that what he called "the disciplines" should serve musical needs. They were not ends in themselves.

What did he mean by "the disciplines"? He meant the tried and true lessons he'd gleaned over the years. The lessons he'd learned about centering and sustaining pitch quality; achieving a unified rhythmic pulse; and accomplishing clear diction. But truth to tell, sometimes the most effective Shaw "disciplines" were just him: Shaw going over and over a spot of music in his way and trying one trick (marching, clapping, singing in a circle) after another, one metaphor after another, one bit of coaxing or another—improvising, adapting, and overcoming—until the whole choir heard the ebbs and flows as he wanted them to be heard. Some musicians will say that they found Shaw's techniques and methods less persuasive than Shaw himself—the sheer force of the man's personality. It's fair to ask: To what extent were Shaw's methods responsible for the Shaw sound and to what extent were Shavian sonorities produced by him—his taste, his ear, his instincts, his experience and adaptations? It's an open question.

It is possible that Shaw's methods worked completely only for him. Count singing, for example, might be useful for any conductor, but perhaps only yielded great results for Shaw because he was Shaw. Many have tried Shaw techniques, but no one else gets his sound. One thing is sure, simply aping Shaw's count singing will not change the sound at all. The key Shaw concept—principle really—is to build the sound layer by layer, with rhythm as the foundation. Each layer, and the musical problem attendant to it, must be dealt with individually.

The important thing about count singing for Shaw was not count singing per se, but metric precision—if a conductor has another way to get there, fine. But Shaw believed that no good conductor could fail to deal with metrics and rhythm.

Shaw did devise dicta—precepts and practices that are now widely known and shared by choral conductors. They may not turn every conductor into a Robert Shaw, but they do help to break the music down and guide musicians in the practical matters of preparing a work for performance.

Here is my own brief summary of Shaw's "rules" of choral discipline, which might almost be "rules for choral conductors." Certainly others might amend or improve upon my list.

1) ***All of music's disciplines cannot be satisfied at once.***

Rhythm and tempo, notes, color, and dynamics must each be isolated and dealt with one at a time. And *this is the most important rule*—the lynchpin.

2) ***Never waste vocal gold.***

The voice is a finite resource. Always save the voice when possible. (Don't talk incessantly on concert day.)

Remember that amateur singers are not professional singers; they have less vocal capital to spend. Logically, the amateur voice needs more care, not less, than the professional's voice.

Therefore, sing *quietly* for as long as you may in the rehearsal process; and sing intelligently. Don't "just sing." Think. Don't "sing out." Listen. In theory, Shaw said, one could just think the notes in early rehearsals.

3) Loudness is the enemy of musicality.

Loudness positively wrecks and destroys, especially if there is too much volume *before* collective pitch centeredness and rhythmic solidity are achieved. The conductor must unify the choir before he lets singers pull out even one stop.

Loud singing early in the rehearsal process makes it very difficult to build choral unanimity because people begin by not listening to each other and never *start* listening to each other. Everyone just keeps cranking up the volume.

4) Don't rehearse the mistakes.

Isolate trouble areas and fix them right away. Don't sing over them, or sing through or past them, or simply repeat and repeat, hoping they will fix themselves, or until everyone is too tired to learn or correct.

"Try it again" for trouble spots in a piece of music will not do. A conductor must diagnose the mistake, prescribe, and treat. He must not warm up the singers' voices (they should do that themselves prior to rehearsal) so much as warm up their minds—increasing their awareness of pitch precision. There is a natural, physical limit to how many times a singer can subdivide a single note, for example, or how many times he can sharpen up or flatten down. But by making singers do these things a ridiculous number of times, Shaw sharpened pitch awareness and warmed up the musical mind.

5) Text matters.

Every word of every line must be pronounced so that it can be understood. Every *sound within each word* must be articulated and communicated. The deepest meaning will come out of constituent sounds, for the meaning transcends the words.

6) Every note (and every subdivision within every note) should have dynamic value.

You have to do something—a mini crescendo or diminuendo—with every musical particle. "Every note," said Shaw again and again, "deserves its 'it-ness,'" which he defined as a chance to "blossom, decay, and die," even if within a prescribed narrow range. (This was one of the reasons for his "hyper-editing" of the score.)

7) ***Don't "flash" or call attention to yourself.***

One is not a member of a chorus for star turns. Even among soloists—stars by definition—Shaw disliked conspicuous shows of vanity. We are not speaking only of gesture or demeanor here, but musical qualities. He insisted, for example, on very little vibrato. He felt it could be hammy and distracting and he felt it could pervert the pitch. He wanted the voice to have a straight, narrow, and natural sound. He disliked many opera singers, but had near reverence for Mack Harrell, who sang with such an unaffected tone. Ultimately, to Shaw, this was a matter of respect for the composer. Shaw would say: "Why not sing what he wrote?"

8) ***Listen, listen, listen.***

Listen for textures, for balance, for pitch-centeredness.

Listen to each other to help gain a unified sound. The reason Shaw often rehearsed in circles was so that singers could really hear each other. "If you look into the eyes of another singer," says one conductor who worked with Shaw, "it's harder to have your own private moment."

9) ***Make sure all musicians have the conductor's editing of the music in detail before rehearsals, so they can begin to grapple with it.***

They must all have the same "road map." This saves time and confusion in rehearsal, even if you have to make changes later.

10) ***Shift voices to get vocal balance in certain passages.***

Don't ask singers to simply sing louder to achieve balance. "The singer," said Shaw, "will simply strip his gears." Achieve balance by constant adjustment of forces rather than turning volume up and down. Send a soprano down or a baritone up on a few notes, rather than increasing loudness by all.

11) ***The conductor must do his homework.***

He must search for the piece itself, and the composer's intent, as if searching for food, water, or love. Remember, it is about the composer's music, not what the conductor does with his music. Therefore, read the scholarship and do intensive score study and structural analysis, and encourage musicians to do the same.

12) The primary job of a musician is not self-expression or self-gratification but communication of a given composer's creation.

One thinks of the watch metaphor again: taking the music apart and putting it back together. Shaw made his musical disability—the inability to simply play a piece through and swallow it whole—a virtue. He had to learn a piece of music element by element, note by note, cell by cell, part by part, and he deconstructed and reconstructed a piece of music for performance the same way. No doctrine; only "disciplines" and "necessities."

Sad to say, as great as Shaw's impact was, many choral directors still don't fully fathom, or internalize, his most fundamental conviction about preparing music—that music must be broken down, its elements handled one by one. This principle is more important than any particular technique. Many conductors, maybe even most choral conductors, still attempt pitches, rhythms, good diction, balance, dynamics, and emotional contours with choirs all at once—sometimes on the first read-through. The result is usually that singers wind up not doing any of these things well—no element is mastered. Making choral music Shaw's way swiftly teaches how sound and well-considered Shaw's basic approach was. It shows how many elements there are to be considered, and thus, acknowledges how difficult it really is to make music.

Shaw would not allow even professional soloists to attempt "artistic" singing from the get go. All musicians were expected to master each structural element of a piece of music. Unlike many orchestral conductors, and many operatic conductors who are accustomed to big, strong voices, Shaw had an acute sense of the expendability of the voice at his disposal. "Saving vocal gold" was not a truism to him but a critical operational guideline. What were the singers "saving the voice" for? The performance.

Shaw did not approach the orchestra in precisely this layered, building-blocks way. He edited and marked all parts based upon this same structural approach. For instance, he did his analysis of harmonic structure separately from his rhythmic analysis and determinations as to tempo. But partly because choral texture is a different animal, and partly because no conductor, not even Shaw, ever has the sort of time with an orchestra that Shaw had with the chorus, Shaw's approach to the orchestra was somewhat different. Here he relied on his editing, believing that he had given the "road map" to seasoned travelers. Like Szell, he expected quality at the first rehearsal. (And he was shocked when players of the New York Philharmonic or Boston Symphony would not, or could not, do as they were asked, or seemed indifferent to the rehearsal or the markings. "No discipline," he would mutter.) He did not expect the same immediate results from choruses because he knew that he was frequently not dealing with the same skill level and because the voice is, as he put it, "infinitely harder to manipulate than a string or a reed."

Shaw's editing for orchestra had much to do with balance—not only section to section, but within sections and, if a chorus or singers were involved, players against voices. Here is another instance in which Shaw turned a shortcoming into a virtue. Perhaps because of his vocal background, Shaw was obsessive about balance, and his ear was incredibly sensitive to it. He gave the problem huge attention and it paid off. Surprisingly, many orchestra conductors pay little attention to balance and, particularly when they try to conduct large choruses with orchestras, they can utterly lose control of the sound. In such a circumstance, a Berlioz *Requiem* might wind up sounding like the mass slaughtering of goats.

After rehearsing the chorus and the orchestra individually, Shaw rebalanced again at the first rehearsal of the two together. He also—always—tuned for and recalibrated balance again for the hall.

Shaw was loathe to correct players in the same way he corrected singers; though he was less hesitant in later years. But he may have had something to teach orchestral conductors in a mundane but all-important area: management of time in rehearsal. Many conductors never get through all the material they want to cover in rehearsal. Because of his detailed battle plans and his meticulous editing, Shaw generally got his work done in the time allotted, and he and the orchestra were usually well prepared and in sync, which of course does not prevent errors or problems in performance, or guarantee a good performance, but it makes it easier to recover from errors and problems and makes a good performance possible.

Anyone who has done it both ways—all musical elements at once, or one element at a time—knows that Shaw's way gets far better results, even among highly trained musicians. And anyone who has played for, sung for, or merely observed a conductor who wastes time in rehearsal knows that lack of focus tends to deflate and de-energize musicians and ultimately degrade performance. And yet the temptation seems always strong to go for instant and inspired music, rather than work at Shaw's slowly earned beauty.

Mind you, Shaw could wear out his charges and himself in a maniacal pursuit of musical order and cleanliness. If he got manic and convinced things were not working, he could drive the emotional content of the music out. He could even do this with the music he loved most deeply—that of Brahms, Bach, and Beethoven. He knew it. But he sometimes could not help himself, just as the disorganized conductor can sometimes not help himself.

The "disciplines"—that word Shaw used constantly—*could* sometimes be a cage from which there was no escape and for which no entry was possible by the dove. Shaw could occasionally get so bogged down in seeking clarity and order that the spirit he was really after would be snuffed out rather than invited.

Yet, when a critic accused him of seeking "too much perfection," he replied (in a private conversation with friends, never to the critic), "bushwa." "How can you have too much perfection?" he huffed. Point taken. But if Shaw had a major musical weakness it was in not recognizing that some music requires rawness, or a degree of spontaneity and surprise. Shaw both admired and was appalled by the fact that Leonard Bernstein never conducted a piece of music the same way twice, even in a single series of performances. Some of the musicians who loved him most nonetheless say Shaw sometimes should have trusted in the moment, and himself, more. Some of his relative failures—a Beethoven symphony in the early days in San Diego, a Verdi *Requiem* in the very late years in New York, any number of performances in Atlanta, several of the recordings (arguably the Mozart and Brahms Requiems)—were the result of his obsessive ordering, organizing, editing, and worrying a piece to death.

Shaw truly believed an imperfection in a critical place could ruin a very good performance of a work like the *St. Matthew Passion.* In the building years, of his own musicianship and in the Atlanta organization, mistakes haunted him after performances—particularly if they were his. It was hard for Shaw to shake off defeat. One performer who shared a dressing room on the road with Shaw said that if a performance went off the rail, Shaw grabbed his clothes and vacated the building swiftly after leaving the stage. He might walk the streets of New York, or a strange city the Chorale was visiting, for hours after a bad performance. So long as Shaw remained there on such a night, the dressing room was no place to be. Sometimes furniture got broken. More than once a fist collided with a wall.

But this was mostly early years, and in his first years in Atlanta. Once after a disastrous performance in Atlanta, Shaw walked home in his sweaty tux, muttering and cursing all the way. When the evening's offending soprano stopped and offered him a lift, he turned scarlet. Sometimes, when a performance went wrong, seriously wrong, and he could not recover, Shaw looked down at his score and never looked back up. Florence Kopleff called this a punishment—a cruel one—though Shaw denied that was his intent.

But in later years, such self-destructive behavior was increasingly rare.

Maybe he was "growing up," as he said. Maybe there were more satisfying performances. Maybe he had begun to believe, as Kopleff told him, that Bach and Brahms have big shoulders and cannot be ruined by one mistake.

In the last decade of his life, when his techniques melded into his persona and became a part of his second nature, Shaw began to feel something like the musician he had long been trying to become. What he attempted to do at that point was to prepare so thoroughly that the craft aspect of the music was internalized and became incarnated *within* each person and the assembly of musicians at the same time. He tried to set a collective clock that would tick to the same time in every musician assembled. His voice would be the ticking of the clock, but the rhythm would be inside each one of them.

When Shaw picked the right moment to switch from drillmaster to poet—moving from prosaic rehearsal technician to Yeatsian performance artist—the result could cause the scales to fall from the eyes of a cynic (frequently a player in the orchestra he was conducting for the first time).

But the creation of the musical community, and its collective heartbeat, was a precious and private thing to him, and Shaw viewed intrusions into the rehearsal process with alarm—sometimes violent alarm. Rehearsals were to Shaw the intimate conversations of family members, and those who wished to listen in were "intruders," "peeping Toms"—violating a sacred privacy. The delicate flower he was trying to nurture—a musical composition reborn; a choir born—needed the hothouse and the gardeners. Outside forces could kill the flower.

His final speech to the chorus before performance—a sort of "mystic huddle"—was especially intimate and fragile, and intruders were most unwelcome. When someone once tried to take a photograph of him during one of these private, pre-concert benedictions, Shaw exploded. He raged that such a person would no doubt be pleased to come into his bedroom with a camera as well.

The performance, after all the study and preparation, was also a sacred event to him, but no longer familial and private. Now it was public ceremony. That is why Shaw personally prepared every stage he performed on—"dressing the altar." That is why he drew endless, detailed diagrams of where instruments, chorus, and soloists would be placed on stage for each concert. That is why he tested every new hall acoustically with his own personal repertoire of shouts and claps and *humms* and *omms*. That is why he personally placed every chair for the chorus members and lined them up within fractions of inches for both purposes of auditory balance and sight lines (his and the singers'). He did it himself for every stage and every performance for 60 years, in hundreds of halls.

No concert is "just a concert," he told Martin Goldsmith. To Shaw, a concert was a contract with the dead. It was really for the composer. "Disciplines" make it possible to meet this heavy obligation. "The flesh becomes word," he said.

CHAPTER 27

Musical Cathedrals and Monsters

Shaw was an outspoken champion of modern classical music—a commissioner, performer, popularizer and, again, proselytizer of such work. He won praise, loyalty, and admiration for his commitment to the music of his own time and land, from Samuel Barber to John Adams. Several of Shaw's last recordings for Telarc included twentieth-century works, and he won Grammy Awards for some of them. He was devoted to the work of Charles Ives, of course, and having lost and regained his job in Atlanta over that composer did nothing to dim Shaw's enthusiasm—quite the opposite. Shaw also knew Ives, Hindemith, Poulenc, Barber, and other modern composers personally—some of them well.

And yet, when one thinks of the composers Shaw most deeply loved, and the pieces with which he was most at home, one thinks of the eighteenth- and nineteenth-century greats and the grand oratorios of the masters of those years. For though Shaw knew well and appreciated the pre-Baroque and the pre-Classical—madrigals, Renaissance motets, and plainsong—just as he knew modern compositions, he was most in his element in the massive sacred, liturgical or Biblical settings that, one might say, begin with Bach and end with Berlioz. These are the masterpieces of the Classical era and, not incidentally, of the Protestant reformation. As Louis Lane put it, "Robert Shaw just needed big works." By "big" one means big musically, numerically, theologically, and intellectually.

So one thinks of Shaw and thinks first, and perhaps last, of the Beethoven *Missa Solemnis,* the Requiems of Mozart and Brahms and Verdi, the Haydn *Creation*, Mendelssohn's two great oratorios, the mighty Bach *Mass in B Minor* and the Passions, the Handel *Messiah*, and so on. Shaw went beyond Berlioz to include in this canon, his canon, two twentieth-century works that are, in a sense, throwbacks to the nineteenth century but, to Shaw anyway, were also twenty-first century works in terms of poetic and philosophic power: the *War Requiem* by Benjamin Britten and *When lilacs last in the dooryard bloom'd* by Paul Hindemith. Shaw "believed" (his term) in these works whole-heartedly. That is to say, he was convinced of their urgency both as musical art and as messages for humankind.

One other grand work, essentially non-choral until the climax in the final movement, came to be closely associated with Robert Shaw—the Beethoven *Symphony No. 9*. But this work is in its own category, both as a work and as part of Shaw's repertoire.

These compositions are the great cathedrals and green-eyed monsters of classical music. These are works that almost all conductors hope to conduct—but rarely get to conduct. For many conductors, to do a Bach Passion once in a career would be a blessing sufficient enough. That is because, although such works are thrilling, there is a degree of impossibility associated with them: such is their scope and size, such are the balancing problems between chorus and orchestra, such is the talent required, such are the organizational and preparatory demands. Bernstein, for example, did the *Missa* only a few times, and according to one conductor who sang it with him in New York: "It was great fun to be with him, but it was a shouting match." Shaw specialized in and repeated what others could or would do rarely. While there are pieces and composers in the purely orchestral realm that Shaw did once, or seldom, his frequent repetition of these enormously complex choral-orchestral works, which many conductors know only fleetingly, is utterly singular. (Again, music is so vast that even the greatest musicians have gaps of knowledge and experience.)

Because Shaw so loved the oratorio, the sacred Mass, the requiem, and all nearly impossible combinations of choral and orchestral forces (Britten's *War Requiem*, like Beethoven's *Missa* is almost *conceived* as an impossibility), and because he so concentrated on these works—and knew them backward and forward and did them over and over again, restudying and re-editing each time he did them—he really made them, by the end of his life, a part of himself. (See Appendix II for Shaw's "core" and Appendix IV for some of his key recordings.) His relationship to some of these pieces, simply by virtue of years of familiarity and repetition, is unique in the history of music.

Dr. Ann Howard Jones, Director of Choral Activities at Boston University (and one of Shaw's most beloved pupils and associates), has suggested, for example, that Shaw may well have conducted the Mozart *Requiem* more times than any conductor in musical history. From the records that exist, which are incomplete, Shaw seems to have conducted the work approximately 150 times. Florence Kopleff, who made her own count, agreed with this number, more or less. First, Shaw performed it over many years—as early as 1944 and perhaps before that. Second, he took it on tour with the Robert Shaw Chorale in 1951. Consider this arc: That Chorale tour ended at Symphony Hall, Boston. This was the performance in which the instrumentalists were weeping at the end, and it was this performance that proved to Shaw that in music, familiarity (if it is really with the piece itself) breeds love rather than contempt. Cut to the end of the story—Shaw was slated to lead a mostly student performance at Boston University in January of 1999. The performance instead became a memorial to him. (It was conducted by Jones.) Thus, almost half century of close relationship with one remarkable composition.

It is also probable that Shaw performed the Brahms *German Requiem* and the Bach *Mass in B Minor* more than any other modern conductor, and possible that he conducted these two works more than any conductor in history. He toured the *Mass in B Minor* both in the United States and abroad, and he recorded it three times. The first recording was in 1947, and the last performance in 1998. Again, it was a lifetime of familiarity, of study, courtship, and performance. And it is no exaggeration or hyperbole to speak of Shaw's *relationship* with these works and their creators. His final performances of these two works, in particular, in the last months of his life were, everyone knew, a culmination and a crowning. Touted by musicians and critics for their sense of familial intimacy and naturalness, these performances were Robert Shaw's last will and testament. One critic said privately that Shaw did things that seemed dubious to him musically—odd or old-fashioned: the heavy reliance on ripienists in Bach, the homemade Shaw English translations that were part King James and part Hemingway, the slow tempi, the big choirs. And yet Shaw did them with such care, consideration, and homage and with such exemplary results, that one had to assent, at least in this case, time, and place. It seemed right.

After his last time at bat with the Brahms—after hundreds of performances—Shaw told several friends and colleagues: "I think I am finally beginning to understand this piece." That's not hyperbole, either. Shaw's willingness to put his performance of Bach on record when he was 31, and his reluctance to do so at 81 after 50 years of seeking to realize Bach's music, summarizes the change in the man and the musician over that five-decade expanse.

Throughout most of his career, Shaw dodged such questions as "What is your favorite piece?" or even "What is the most fun, the most delightful, to conduct?" Though his fondness for the Beethoven *Symphony No. 9* was pretty clear, since he ended most seasons in Atlanta with it and began and ended his musical directorship at the ASO with it. He also took every opportunity he could to perform the Beethoven *Missa*. It is certainly the piece that challenged him the most. It, along with the Britten *War Requiem*, piece that he wrote the most about.[65] On the other hand, the Bach *Mass in B Minor* is the piece he devoted the most time to over the years, and the Bach *St. Matthew Passion* is without question the piece that moved him most, especially in his mature years. Shaw's pat answer was that his favorite piece was the one he was working on at that moment. And this was honest. It was the way he kept himself totally, obsessively, focused on the job at hand. But in later years he strayed a bit from his own non-commitment. He called the Bach *St. Matthew Passion*, "my current obsession." He went back to it in the 1990s, even when he was not editing and preparing it for performance. He also, on several occasions, again late in life, called the work the most noble expression of art and "human aspiration" that he knew. This makes Shaw's profound reservations about recording the work all the more poignant.

Shaw actually did answer a written query about his "favorite requiems," perhaps an odd question to address to an octogenarian conductor. His answer is surprising. Shaw said he had four favorites: Britten, Verdi, Brahms, and Duruflé.

Brahms is not surprising, for by the end of Shaw's life, he and the piece almost melded together as a great actor and a favorite role become one. Brahms made his own liturgical text rather than follow the Mass (though he was not the first to do so and Heinrich Schütz's earlier weaving together of Biblical texts of his own choosing is thought to have influenced Brahms). Few have dared to do it since. (Though Britten did.) But this boldness, this taking prayer into one's own hands, spoke to Shaw. One almost feels it is something Shaw would have done had he the talent and temperament to compose. All the scriptural texts used by Brahms were ones Shaw knew well. Thus, the piece resonated with Shaw's pre-musical life. Musically, its structure is Baroque and its sound Romantic—this was Shaw's own nature. The song form in the composition was a natural habitat for Shaw. And though it might be too simple to say that almost all the passages chosen by Brahms emphasized the humanism of Jesus—the humanity that so fascinated Shaw and his father—that was certainly the emphasis. The directness, warmth, and

65 See *The Robert Shaw Reader.*

practicality of a requiem written to console the living, spoke to Shaw, heart to heart. Once he became a serious conductor, this piece and Shaw were bound for a shared destiny.

Many people who knew Shaw well thought of the Brahms *Requiem* as his signature piece. Certainly he was closely associated with it in the later years of his life. *The New York Times* critic James Oestrich has written these striking words of Shaw's last Carnegie Hall performance, "At last Brahms has his requiem."

Shaw loved the Duruflé piece for some of the same reasons—its consolation, humanity, and compassion. Shaw also mentioned his and Mrs. Shaw's friendship with Mme. Duruflé—a most un-Shaw-like reason for musical loyalty, but Shaw had been converted by the second Mrs. Shaw to Francophilia.

Shaw listed the Verdi *Requiem* for interesting reasons—the musical drama of the piece, but also its "musical health and vigor." Again, he mentions a non-musical reason: Verdi's "republicanism." Verdi was a populist and anti-cleric, both qualities that appealed to Shaw.

Britten's "anti-" *War Requiem* contains many of Shaw's own values—pacifism, distain for religious consolation in the face of slaughter, and disdain for religious rigidity in the face of great suffering. And these ideas are expressed not only in Britten's text, but in his bold and, to Shaw, shocking imposition of his own requiem text into the Catholic rite. Like Brahms, he re-made the requiem in man's image. But Britten, instead of replacing the liturgical structure of the Mass with biblical text, re-fashions the liturgy. This appealed deeply to Shaw. Shaw's enthusiasm for the work had as much to do with Britten's daring, his theology, his use of poetry, and his anti-war message as with his music.

So, two of Shaw's "favorite" requiems bend the form.

But the Verdi, the most traditional, might be Shaw's most important recording.

Shaw's recording of the Verdi *Requiem* in 1987 is considered definitive by some (Shaw was not among them). One of the many things Shaw valued about Toscanini was his direct link to the composer. Via *the* Maestro, Shaw could connect with Verdi. Again, Shaw conducted the piece innumerable times, almost certainly more times than Toscanini. When Toscanini made his historic recording of the Verdi in 1951, his chorusmaster was, of course, Robert Shaw. Ironically, and peculiarly, Shaw perhaps never gave a live performance of the Verdi *Requiem* as stirring as his recording. (It usually worked the other way.) Certainly his Carnegie Hall workshop performance in the last decade of his life was not as stirring as his recording. Many who heard it thought it was too tidy and almost un-Verdi-an.

In 1984, Shaw drew up a fascinating graph that dealt with some of these musical monsters—the three mega-requiems:

October 3, 1984

Dear Group:

Got groupier last Monday, didn't it?

How would you like to ponder an adjectival graph? No full-fleshed argument, and certainly not above rebuttal, but perhaps enough truth to titillate:

	Brahms *Requiem*	Berlioz *Requiem*	Verdi *Requiem*
Musical Language	Traditional; cumulative; crowning	Individual; exploratory; unfinished	Traditional; cumulative; crowning
Intent	Rumanative; introspective; philosophic; comforting	Fantastic; exhibitionistic; psychopathic; provocative; prophetic	Dramatic; ordered; extroverted; well scripted; clear minded
Treatment of Text	Seminal; the word as a spur to musical meditation and exegesis	Vehicular; scalpel for exploratory psychic surgery	Illustrative; text as actor in a musical drama

At the end of the graph/letter, Shaw wrote: "'Tain't 100 percent true, but 'tain't no lie, neither.—R."

Maybe it's not 100 percent, no. But Shaw's chart is fascinating and insightful. And it's hard to think of another conductor who would come up with such a thing.

The great and grandiose choral-orchestral works, be they oratorio or requiem, provided Shaw an opportunity to manage it all: words and music; singers and players; musical microcosm and musical tidal wave. It was at this juncture of the musical arts, and the amalgamation of them, that Shaw found his true home.

Shaw was also drawn to the gargantuan and improbable musical creation. Two perfect examples are the Beethoven *Missa* and the Mahler *Symphony of a Thousand*. He was drawn to musical mass, force, and power. He was drawn to the nearly impossible musical task of realizing such creations. It was not so much that Shaw loved big choirs. Shaw loved big dreams and big musical-theological statements. He liked a puzzle and a challenge, too.

Between 1967 and 1988 in Atlanta, Shaw was necessarily spending much of his time on study of orchestral pieces, but his interests, such as his interest in the smaller choral scale in the early music movement, were always expanding. His repertoire in later life was also growing in ways unusual for an octogenarian conductor, such as learning, performing and recording the Dvorák *Stabat Mater* and considering doing the same for the Elgar *Dream of Gerontius*. Still, the real core of Shaw's repertoire was a few key choral-orchestral masterworks he'd been doing for years. The combination of experience and familiarity, along with constant rethinking, gave Shaw's last performances of some of these works—the Brahms *Requiem* is perhaps the best example—a musical and emotional depth that will not soon be equaled.

Shaw *hoped* his last Brahms *Requiem* or Bach *Mass in B Minor* would be the best he had ever done—the accumulation of all his acquired knowledge and affection. It's fair to say he got his wish.

As Shaw saw it, if he was in competition with anyone, he was in competition with himself. He never sought to match Toscanini. (Shaw would have regarded such an ambition for himself as preposterous.) But he could improve his 1998 performance over what it had been in 1988, or '78, or '68.

The good news is that Shaw's performances of these gargantuan choral/symphonic masterpieces—his core—are almost all preserved and on record or disk. Of course, as some rock-and-roll fans say, "Live music is better." Shaw agreed. And the axiom generally proves true in his case (the Verdi exception having been noted). Many of the recordings of Shaw's signature work pale in comparison to his in-the-moment performance. Still, a testament exists.

Ironically, for one who did so much recording, Shaw was profoundly ambivalent about the whole concept of records. He wondered whether music could ever be carved in time—kept. The greater the music, the more he doubted his own, or anyone's, ability to capture it. He was not entirely happy with many of his recordings and saw good qualities in relatively few of them. He mostly stopped listening to playbacks in his Telarc period and decided to trust the final versions of many of his recordings to the producer and engineer. He may never have listened to some of his recordings. Still, most of us are happy to have replicas of some of Shaw's signature performances. Some of them, like his Robert Shaw Chorale recordings of the Bach *St. John Passion* or *Christ Lag in Todesbanden,* for example, will surely be reissued from the old RCA vaults and will be of interest to music lovers and scholars for years to come. More, they help those who heard the live performances to remember magical and transcendent moments. It is Telarc that gave us the heritage of most of the Shaw core repertoire on disc. Only a Shaw recording of the *St. Matthew Passion* is conspicuously missing. And this was corrected, in a sense, by the Cleveland Orchestra's issuance of a radio recording of a live

Shaw performance of the work. (One doubts Shaw would have approved its release. But one is grateful for it nonetheless.)

In his last NPR interview, again with Martin Goldsmith, essentially admitting that a Robert Shaw recording of the *St. Matthew* would never happen, Shaw wondered if that particular piece, which he loved so deeply, was simply not meant to be recorded. Maybe, he said, a performance of this work is always so rough an approximation of Bach's imagination, and necessarily such a living thing, that a recording is just wrong. Maybe, he said, it is a sort of "sin" (Shaw's word) to make a "grooven image" (his words again) of the Bach *St. Matthew Passion*. Was this musing? Or was it a rationalization, given that he knew his recording would not happen? It is hard to believe that Shaw would not have liked to *work on* a recording of the piece. But release it? He so revered the composition that he may not have ever been satisfied with a recording. Shaw certainly could have tried harder to make the recording than he did. He might have insisted. But Shaw had mixed feelings about recording *anything*, and this was sometimes manifest in his rather tight-fisted results. (In contrast, his greatest recordings, like those of the Verdi and Berlioz Requiems and the Rachmaninoff *Vespers*, convey the feeling of Shaw trusting in the performance and performers enough to let go.) But he was especially wary of and humbled by Bach, particularly Bach's Passions. The absence of the *St. Matthew* recording is testament to his inherent doubts about recording, about realizing this work by Bach, and about himself. He may well have truly believed, by the end of his life, that the piece he saw as the "most noble expression of human aspiration" could never be captured in recorded sound.

CHAPTER 28

Demons Again

Most creative artists have their demons, and Shaw was frank about his. All his life, he was stalked by insecurity—by the feeling that he was just not good enough: not at music and not at being human. Feeling that he had failed at marriage, Shaw made his marriage worse by running away from his wife and children, isolating himself, and engaging in blatant and repeated infidelities. He also wrestled with the bottle for many years, never entirely giving it up, though he was able to stop getting habitually drunk. When, late in his life, Nola Frink asked him why he drank so much in earlier years, he said, "Because I was a failure."

There were times when Shaw felt overwhelmed with a general sense of inadequacy and doom, not just for himself but the whole human race. All human beings who are awake at all, have felt such despair. When this feeling cannot be overcome, lived through, or deconstructed, we call it depression. And it is certainly true that sometimes Shaw had trouble climbing out of the pit, though he was never disabled for any extended period or hospitalized. It's just that the highs were rather high and the lows rather low. And in the heavy drinking years of his late youth, a lot of energy must have been lost to hangovers. Shaw did love to drink in those days, in part to come down from some of the highs and in part to enhance the melodrama of the lows.

There were occasions, though few in later years, when rehearsals were cancelled because Shaw was "down," or "recovering." We have noted the myriad illnesses of the Cleveland years, and his cancellation of a Chicago Symphony conducting date because of a sort of panic attack—"I cannot do this, I am not up to this." Again, most good musicians have felt this at least once. Great ones may feel it constantly. Even George Szell sometimes felt that a work or a performance was simply beyond him. Only the grossest of mediocrities have never felt thus. With Shaw, there were also the post-partum crashes after particularly dramatic, important, or stressful concerts, though this was rather less typical in later years. Shaw would stay in bed for two or three days. Partly, he was physically exhausted.

So Shaw had some tendency toward manic depression. His father, also, tended toward polarities of exultation and exhaustion. Mostly, Shaw pushed through it, with sheer will power and by the guiding light of the next project. He had an overdrive gear—a generalized energy level that carried him through and past the mood swings.

More, when Shaw got into one of his low moods, it sometimes really *was* about the state of the world or the human race. Man's inhumanity to man and the march of human folly were impossible for the old campus liberal to deny, and hard to shake off. Shaw had tremendous faith in the redemptive power of the human race, so he took reports of criminal cruelty, war, racial bigotry, and assassination very much to heart. The deaths of John Kennedy, Martin Luther King, Jr., and four students at Kent State University in 1970, in particular, shook him deeply. In the case of Kennedy, Shaw threw himself into an already scheduled performance of the *Missa Solemnis* as personal requiem and therapy. As we have noted, he spoke, briefly, before the performance, which he seldom did. In the Kent case, he went to Kent after the shootings to conduct a memorial concert—the Cherubini *Requiem.*

Some of the demons that haunted Shaw in New York and Cleveland returned in the early days of struggle in Atlanta—including high indulgence in alcohol. It wasn't just the ASO board, or mixed public reaction to some of his programming. Shaw was frustrated with what he was able to do with the ASO and ASO chorus musically. He was often unhappy with the quality of talent available to him. He was trying to fashion a choral sound, and he felt he lacked the ingredients. He was also trying to build the orchestra as well as his own orchestral chops. And nothing seemed to be going terribly well. Shaw was frustrated with himself. He once said that in the first five or so years in Atlanta, he sometimes felt as if he were trying to swim through cement.

Those were years of great stress and frustration. The nemesis was no longer Szell, but Shaw himself. And Shaw was alone. Maxine had departed permanently for Nantucket (not that her presence would have made things better). And so he drank, becoming a sort of barfly at a local downtown hotel, among other places, and further mortifying and alienating some prominent Atlantans.

Shaw was not generally a boorish drunk. He usually kept control and usually met all of his professional obligations. But this was a period of heavy drinking. He needed release from the frustration and anger he felt at "being Robert Shaw" and not getting it right. In that time, between wives, he brought soloists and instrumentalists home more to unwind than to entertain; more to drink with than to share a fine meal and wine. He also drank alone, at the end of the day—a housekeeper, friend, or assistant who drank nothing, or far less, might help him get upstairs to bed. He occasionally availed himself of good old boys at a bar so he did not have to talk music. He didn't like to talk about anything serious (music) after the sun went down. Better to talk politics, sports, and nonsense.

There is some considerable disagreement about how much Shaw drank in the dark and solitary periods of his life. (Not about constancy of alcoholic intake, but volume.) Some say they *never* saw him falling down drunk. Some say they did. He'd become a living legend for them, so mythology and gossip grew freely. This much does seem clear: Shaw's drinking in the early Atlanta years was less the wild party mode of New York—the running away—and more the self-medicating of a middle-aged man disappointed in himself.

In the Robert Shaw Chorale days, he was a whisky drinker and, off and on, a martini man. But in the Atlanta days, it was Jack Daniels or (occasionally) vodka with beer chasers. Though some old Shaw associates, like Kopleff, think the assessment overly dramatic (and they have a point because Shaw always pulled himself back from despondency and despair), Shaw himself said often that he might have destroyed his career or drunk himself to death had it not been for what he saw as an almost divine intervention that came in the person of a comely Southern woman.

By his own declaration—for it was more than an admission, it was self-analysis and testimony—Shaw's emotional maturation did not catch up to his intellectual and artistic maturity for many years. (And in some respects, it never did fully catch up. If he became angry with you, even the mature Shaw might simply not speak to you for days—perhaps for weeks—until *you* apologized to *him*. And this could be over arriving 10 minutes late for lunch.)

But a calm descended on his spirit after his marriage to Caroline Hitz. And for Shaw a normal home and family life provided the order and solace that allowed him to move to the highest level artistically. Having a home and a family life grounded and sustained him. He felt infinitely more prepared, confident, calm and ready to perform a given piece in the 1980s or 1990s than he had in the 1950s or 1960s. Of course, part of this was simply time and experience. But it was also the result of order in his life. "Music," Shaw wrote, "is order." He probably didn't mean that in a limited way. For Shaw also believed that music was spirit—partaking of Godliness. Preparing the way for music, either as composer or performer, was a matter of order. As he quipped once, "Sometimes cleanliness [a euphemism for order in his mind] is so close to Godliness, that Godliness just slides over." He felt that order in his own life not only saved his health but extended his life in music.

Perhaps this wasn't as true as it felt to Shaw. Sometimes agony *is* good for art. And Shaw did some of his most successful tours and recordings when his personal life was chaos and misery. But *he* believed that he did not achieve sustained focus on his music, or worthiness of great music, until Caroline brought order to his life. So Shaw's gratitude to Caroline was not just for health and longevity, but for the calm that made him a better musician. He felt he owed the last third of his life and career to her. "Isn't marriage great?" Shaw asked a recently married visiting soprano one day in the early 1990s. He wasn't kidding. The singer was actually having a hard time of it at that particular juncture in her own marriage. She also knew something of Shaw's personal history. "Yeah, right," she said. But Shaw possessed the zealotry of the convert where marriage was concerned. He was convinced that his second marriage rescued him from despair and dissolution.

Shaw never beat the insecurity demon. But he transformed it within himself. The insecurity became less egocentric, less about how he felt and more about the relative insignificance of the performer in the light of a great piece, or a great composer. His humility became less a matter of posture and less an assumed role than something deeply felt—something from within.

Was Shaw a manic depressive? Probably. If so, he was a functional one, just as he was a so-called functional alcoholic. He certainly worked his way up to full ecstasy when preparing and finally performing a piece like the *Missa Solemnis*. After performing the *St. Matthew Passion*, he was often unable to speak. It was not that he didn't feel much like socializing. He could not summon speech. He was spent, numb. This may be depressive behavior. Surely it is also the only sane response to the work.

Some years after their marriage, Mr. and Mrs. Robert Shaw had dinner with Mr. and Mrs. Walter Gould. Near the end of the evening a drunk made a scene and disrupted the entire restaurant. Caroline departed for the restroom when the unpleasantness reached a crest. As the drunk was being escorted out of the building and Caroline was making her way back to the table, Robert, nodding his head at the man, said, "That is who I would be today if it were not for the woman walking toward our table."

CHAPTER 29

Caroline

She had auburn hair, a lovely figure, and one of those honeyed Southern voices, both flirtatious and assured. She moved with grace and confidence. Her perfume, hair, and attire were always flawless but never overbearing. Like her husband, she could be ferocious. But the first line of attack was charm.

He met her, she met him, in the great "campaign" of 1972—to "Save Our Symphony," and to "Keep Robert Shaw." She was one of the volunteers—a lifelong Atlantan and a devoted backer of the ASO and its new conductor. She was a lover of the arts, indeed one of the leading cultural denizens of the city. She had studied in France as a girl and those who knew her thought her to be as competent as she was gracious and refined. She was deeply involved in Atlanta civic work and charities, perhaps most notably the Atlanta Historical Society. Many looked upon her as a kind of executive of local volunteerism. She adored music, but knew little about it.

She was an accomplished decorator. In this, she was as particular and demanding as her future husband was in musical rehearsal. Their eventual homes in Atlanta and France were works of art. She was always certain about what she wanted.

Caroline Sauls Hitz was a Southern belle with a clear mind, great intellectual curiosity, and an abiding love of all things bright and beautiful. She also could be very strong, almost ruthless.

When they were married, the justice of the peace asked Robert how long he'd been divorced. Shaw had not bothered to formally end his first marriage until he'd fallen in love with his next wife, though the first Mrs. Shaw had long ago absented herself. "About two weeks," replied the groom.

Caroline said that when he proposed, "it was like me Tarzan, you Jane." She drew and drawled out the line. They were middle aged. He was 57. But that's how they saw each other. And he was pleased to tell anyone who could not cover his ears fast enough that they enjoyed an athletic sex life. "Even at my age, sex on the kitchen floor is pretty good," he told a horrified colleague. He was 70ish then.

She was from Atlanta's "upper crust." After their marriage, Caroline guided Shaw through Atlanta's social terrain. She had deep roots in Atlanta and she led her husband through symphony, local, and corporate politics, none of which he ever understood (or wished to understand). She made an enormous difference to Shaw in his adopted city. It is possible that without Caroline he would have been fired again, but with a more permanent result. She made a difference, also, in how he viewed Atlanta and the South. He came to see Atlanta through a native's eyes rather than those of a Westerner or Northerner. He saw without condescension, and with affection. After 30 years there, Shaw would describe the South and Atlanta as a place of warm-hearted people.

Caroline changed Shaw's tastes and habits. She got him to reduce his drinking to (mostly) an occasional beer or two and/or wine with supper. She also introduced him to good wine. She got him out of polyester. She brought him to the visual arts—painting, sculpture, and design. Most important, she showed him he could succeed as head of a family, albeit on his own terms. (She did the day-to-day parenting.)

Caroline Hitz would seem an odd match for Robert Shaw. She was cultured in a broad and finished way. He was not. She knew little about music's language and structure. Robert thought about its nuts and bolts during virtually every waking hour. Truly, he was cultured *only* in music, and though his sensitivity and understanding in this one area was profound, he understood the arts mostly through music. And he was anything but refined in his own tastes and habits. He knew virtually nothing about other cultures or languages, and his knowledge of American literature was pretty much confined to nineteenth-century American poetry and the speeches of Lincoln. He knew a lot about religion, or felt he did, but not about the Presbyterian Church, to which Caroline belonged.

Caroline was a *grande dame* who came from, and was comfortable around, money and power. Robert was suspicious of money and power—he felt pretense and abuse came of both. He was rather proud he'd grown up a boy of modest circumstance. "I'm the only member of my family," he told an Atlanta friend, "who has ever done manual labor."

Caroline was enamored of all things European, especially anything French. Robert's idea of continental food was French fries.

She had spent her life in Atlanta; he had been a nomad. She was a sort of Dixie aristocrat. He was a populist, a mystic, a Californian proud of the sand in his toes, though he had not lived there since college.

Moreover, Caroline might be described as feathers on the outside and granite inside. Robert, beneath his gruffness and roughness, and occasional ill temper, was a pussycat—a romantic, a sentimentalist, an easy mark, a bleeding heart.

Yet Caroline and Robert, in some way, to those who knew them as a couple and saw how they entwined, seemed almost predestined for each other.

Their marriage was probably not constant bliss; no marriage is. But they seemed, to themselves as much as to others, that rare Platonic match—two people who were only completely fulfilled when in each other's company.

They both came from unhappy first marriages. When they began to see each other, they were both wary. Some of their early dates, at her insistence, were walks outdoors. They both came to the marriage seeing the other's flaws. He saw that she was somewhat spoiled and was used to deference. She saw that he was "high maintenance" and a man of lofty ideals and occasional low moods. He disliked the "society" that was her natural habitat. He hated that she smoked. She hated his drinking. It scared her. Her mother had been a drinker.

It was agreed, before marriage, that he quit hard liquor and she quit smoking. Neither was *entirely* true to his pledge. But he quit being a drunk because he wanted to marry Caroline. And he continued to not be a drunk because he had married Caroline.

Perhaps only she could have tamed him. Certainly she was one of very few who could hold her own with him. She devoted the last 22 years of her life to him, attending to his every need and bringing not only order to his life, but her total focus. She gave up most of her personal and social life, confining both in large measure to the telephone. (He found her phone use excessive and bizarre.) All Robert had to worry about was the music because Caroline took care of everything else—from packing for him to making all household decisions. (After her death someone discovered that he did not know how to write a check.)

She kept her hand in Atlanta charities and boards, but to a great extent, she felt she needed to be home. For when Robert came out of his study at the end of the day, he wanted her there, and he did not want to go anywhere except to the TV set to watch the *MacNeil-Lehrer News Hour,* and then to the dinner table. She knew him to be a great artist and a great man, and she was willing to subordinate herself, willing to hold his coat and calm his nerves, and towel him down and rub his shoulders and feet during intermissions of performances. Caroline Shaw made her own considerable renouncement.

Shaw said he "never knew a marriage like it, other than my parents"—a very interesting comparison for him to make. He didn't always like his mother and father, but he aspired to a marriage like theirs—one of total devotion, to each other and to a higher cause. Again—as he did by making music his faith, and the chorus his church, and conducting his pastorate—Shaw seemed to have adopted and adapted his parents' ideals to the life he made.

Where others saw Caroline as the ultimate "iron lady," Robert saw her as feminine, stoic, and delicate. She shared fully with her irreverent and slightly wicked sense of humor. She read constantly and was ever deepening her love of the French, whose language she deformed uniquely with her own cadences and pronunciations.

He saw her as exotic and nurturing. She saw him as primal and prophetic.

Cynics said the devotion was rather one-sided. And, to be sure, Caroline gave the greater part. But, if anything, Robert was the more starry-eyed of the two—more oblivious to her faults. He saw them. He knew they existed. He knew, for example, that his wife tended to treat colleagues, and even friends, like servants at times, and to sometimes treat servants quite coldly. He knew she loved fine things, like caviar and furs, perhaps a bit too much. He knew she still snuck a cigarette here and there. He knew, but he chose not to see. Or, if he saw, he chose not to dwell upon the knowledge. She was all sunlight around him, and this is what he saw and responded to—the warmth, the strength, the devotion, and the light.

But he worried aloud that in extending his life, she had perhaps shortened her own.

There is no doubt that Shaw was totally in love with Caroline. And when she preceded him in death, which, of course, no one had imagined because she was 20 years younger than him, Shaw was disconsolate. He lived for work then, and froze his personal life in grief. He had no intention of replacing her. He never wanted to get over Caroline's death.

He was "very sure," he told friends, that he would not have had the most productive years of his musical life had it not been for her and her unconditional love and admiration. He didn't need it from an audience, but he did need it from a wife.

In 1995, Caroline succumbed to her long battle with cancer, four years almost to the day before Shaw's own death. Just days before, she had accompanied him to New York for a workshop performance of Hindemith's *Lilacs*. She had insisted that he not cancel. But she became so ill in New York that she had to be flown home and hospitalized. Also on that Carnegie program was Caroline's favorite piece—Brahms's *Nänie,* lyrically built around the strophe that "even beauty must die." Caroline was able to hear it one last time at dress rehearsal.

Robert stayed with Caroline in the last days, living at the hospital. Neither of them permitted the other to give up hope, or even to speak of the possibility that the end was near. Shaw would later lament that he had "not had the opportunity to say goodbye."

He went back to work as soon after Caroline's death as he was able. He said it would be weeks. But it was days. After Caroline, he spent less and less time in Atlanta.

Shaw's emotional landscape changed when he met and married Caroline Hitz. He no longer had to be at war with the world and himself, at least not constantly. Moreover, if there was a battle, she would be at his side. They would curse the barbarians together.

She was a nearly perfect mother—in the eyes of Shaw and her sons—as perfect as a mother could be. She organized the boys' lives, set high standards, and made sure the father made his cameo appearances. And while her Southern charm and erudition always dazzled Shaw, her son (his stepson), and their own natural son, it was her maternal warmth that sustained them all.

Shaw's mother had wounded him. His first wife, Maxine, became his nemesis. Caroline healed him.

A comment like "You're certainly no George Szell" was too cutting for a man like Shaw to take—too heartless, too icy. Robert and Maxine were two wounded birds who could only hurt each other more. Caroline and Robert were sun and storm meeting. "She always says the right thing," Shaw told the Carnegie chorus the day after they sang *Nänie* for her.

She always said the right thing—to him. To others she could be cutting, demanding, condescending. All for the sake of Robert. In a way, Caroline was the person Maxine wanted to be. She was from real money and status; she was deeply intelligent as well as educated and cultured; she was a force in her own right. She could be scary. Without doubt, she was the woman Robert wanted Maxine to be; the woman he needed his wife to be. Caroline granted Robert total support and limitless devotion and admiration.

Caroline was not a saint. But what she did for Shaw was saintly.

She gave him her life and gave him back his.

CHAPTER 30

Supporting Players

It wasn't easy being Robert Shaw. He needed help—help even beyond what Caroline could give. And he got it. Throughout his life he built a sort of surrogate family around him. The family's purpose was not to be family, however. Its purpose was to make music, just as the purpose of his father's family, and extended family (his congregations), was church, or Christian mission.

The function of Robert Shaw's extended family, cynics in Atlanta said, was to serve Shaw. Actually, it was to serve music making in the Robert Shaw vein. But that did entail serving the man, too. For good and ill, the two things were indivisible. The people in this extended family did make Shaw's work possible and, in a way, his *life* possible, just as Caroline did. For his life and his work were also indivisible. These were the people who were closest to Shaw, and who took the most abuse from him, and yet loved him most unreservedly.

Abuse?

Well, yes. Shaw was always demanding, and sometimes he went beyond that to a level of abuse. It was verbal. And it didn't happen often. But his wit could be stinging and his temper profoundly unsettling. Perhaps what jarred people is that the dark side of Shaw was so at odds, not only with his public image, but with what those who loved him thought of as the essential man—the man whose nature was revealed in acts of friendship, of pastoral concern and, of course, in music making.

These episodes, Shaw out of sorts, were mostly a result of his impatience and something going wrong. (Shaw was to impatience what Casals was to the cello.) He also built certain frustrations into his life: the high standards, the impossible tasks, and the never-ending problem of not having enough time to read, edit, prepare, and rehearse. All this caused him no end of grief. The supporting players were there all along the way—trying to fix things, trying to calm Shaw, absorbing the blows. We have met Edna "Eddie" Lea Burrus, his Girl Friday in the Cleveland years. Nola Frink was his Girl Friday in Atlanta (though Eddie had come to Atlanta initially, as noted). Nola's line was, "I prepare the water for Mr. Shaw to walk on." In the New York years, Florence Kopleff, one of Shaw's greatest vocalists and musical protégés, also served as his secretary and special assistant. She later moved to Atlanta to teach at Georgia State University and, of course, to sing with Shaw. One reason she moved there was to "care for Robert," after Maxine's departure. When he was music director in Atlanta, Bill Segal, who was the ASO general manager, was a trusted friend. And such persons as Gary Hanson, Jonathan Martin, and Nancy Chalifour, who held various administrative titles and who all started at fairly low levels but rose through the ranks, helped with Shaw support. The two gentlemen went on to run the Cleveland Orchestra, with Martin later becoming President and Executive Director of the Charlotte Symphony Orchestra and then President and CEO of the Dallas Symphony Orchestra. Chalifour became an important West Coast arts consultant. All formed their conceptions of arts management working for and with Shaw.

Certainly, after his "retirement" in Atlanta, and following Caroline's death, Frink became the primary caretaker. When he began to travel again, the Atlanta choruses needed a new assistant to help Frink because she was on the road attending to Shaw, and that was Jeff Baxter, a choral musician with a Ph.D. in music.

Through the later Atlanta years, Norman Mackenzie and Ann Jones served as Shaw's top musical assistants, as Louis Lane had been the key orchestral deputy.

At Carnegie Hall, Shaw's dear friend Judy Arron was his advocate, protector, and angel, but so were staffers who did the grunt work—like Nancy Dobbs and Kristian Kuhr. Of course, there were the agents: Walter Gould and, later, Martin Shaw (no relation). And back in the early days, there were the various assistant conductors and/or accompanists, like Daniel Lewis and John Wustman. All were "family" to Shaw.

There were others. Harry Keuper not only duplicated Shaw's score markings for him but also carried things and helped Shaw build things. In many ways, Keuper based his life around Shaw. Dr. Charles Hamilton was a "pal," a gifted member of the chorus, and sometimes expected to be the on-call travel doctor. Bob (Robert) O'Brien, the ASO librarian, was also on call on Christmas and New Year's Days for changes in score edits. After Shaw retired from the ASO, O'Brien was not obliged to provide that service. But he chose to. Shaw didn't ask for the devotion of these people, but he needed it in one way, and they, perhaps in another, needed to provide it. His affection for this extended family was real. They were his only social life. They aided the re-creation—that was their privilege. And if a problem came to his attention—an illness in the family, a need for money, in one case an intervention before alcohol took the person down, as it had almost taken Shaw down—he was there for them. It took something large to get Shaw's attention, however. In order to make the music, Shaw took far more than he gave, from many people. The giving back had to be, principally, in the music.

This long list no doubt leaves out several people—people at RCA and Telarc who at various points gave their lives over to this man, and began a regime of anti-acids. Certainly Robert Woods comes to mind. He and Shaw fought like brothers. Woods's standards were as high, and for soloists, perhaps higher. He was a trained and true musician, not just a technician. His ear was nearly as good as Shaw's and his will nearly as strong. He had his own ideas about making music. Woods took some major grief from Shaw and gave it as good as he got. Without him, there would be no Shaw recording legacy in many of the major works and no Shaw recording legacy from the later part of his life.

They—all these accomplices and enablers and supporting players—to one degree or another, all became family to Shaw. A handful of singers and players did, as well. More to the point, it *took* this many people to keep him going, protect his time, and protect him from daily cares so that he could think only about scores and performances and new ways to get a beautiful, natural, and true sound.

His last agent, Hugh Kaylor, was not a person Shaw knew well. Sometimes Shaw forgot who he was and he had to ask Frink for his name. But like most, even on the outer rims of the inner circle, he came to love Shaw. Kaylor was an agent for many musicians and conductors, yet he had only one picture on the wall in his office: Shaw. No family or friends' pictures, either. Just Shaw, whom he knew he did not know well. When asked "Why?" he answered, "I don't know, there was something very profound in him. Very beautiful. He went so deeply into the music."

And this list of supporting players would not be complete without acknowledging Shaw's two wives: the first who helped administer the choirs, maintain his home, run tours, and raise his children essentially alone; and the second who raised two sons, with more help from him, but still having essentially forsaken her former life and the outside world.

The extended family saw all the warts.

Shaw made it a point to be collegial and cordial. Indeed, he was sometimes overly deferential to orchestral players, especially when guest conducting, and this could lead to the mistaken impression that he felt he was not in charge or was unsure of what he wanted. This overly practiced civility caused problems of its own.

But Shaw's impatience and loss of temper, which, though only occasionally explosive were monumental, tended to be directed at his inner circle—his extended family of associates, assistants, friends, protégés, close musical collaborators, and occasional brown-nosers and flunkies.

Because he usually felt himself to be behind the curve, Shaw was generally in a hurry. He hated having even five minutes of his time wasted. That can make for some tension at the workplace—and in the home if it is a workplace. Also, as Sylvia McNair put it, "RS had a small mean streak . . . We all do." When under pressure, tired, or feeling out of time, he could be not only demanding but also sharp-tongued and cutting. Again, it was not the rule, and he usually tried to make it up to the victim. Moreover, his volcanic rages, especially when directed at a chorus, distressed and embarrassed him deeply. There were fewer as the years wound down, but they never entirely ceased.

Shaw didn't suffer fools. He was impatient in this sense as well—impatient with stupidity and incompetence as well as mental and physical slowness. Like Toscanini, he always wanted forward progress. He didn't suffer poor preparation or lack of commitment. He didn't accept answers he did not want to hear. Or other people's agendas. Or, really, anything distracting to his focus. In his desire and determination to stay on task, he was lucky, and well served, because most people close to him felt the focus was important.

Always, in the end, Shaw was grateful for the help he received. But he was not always grateful along the way—in the throes of preparation. Sometimes people who just happened to be in Shaw's path when that thing that was bound to go wrong went wrong got clobbered. And their only sin had been trying to help.

A prime function of the supporting players was to protect Shaw from small talk, socializing, and gossip—except when *he* decided to relax and waste his own time. In that case, the supporting player became a pal if Shaw was in a reflective mood.

Shaw took rare vacations. He read fewer and fewer serious books as he aged. He saw ever fewer people. Of course, time was the issue again. In his last years, he knew he was really running out of time, for all time, and he still had a lot he wanted to do. "Everything," said a chorister.

Shaw had a long-standing rule to not make decisions or discuss serious matters after supper. That was when he flipped the switch. In the early years, there was partying. In middle years, more solitary drinking. In his later years, those hours might well go to the evening news, a detective novel, sports on TV, or just a good meal. In those years, he wasn't *looking* for intellectual stimulation, though he might find it, and be grateful for it, at a place like Boston University, where he became a frequent visitor and fond of its president, John Silber. (Silber, like Judith Arron at Carnegie Hall, would have liked an even closer and more permanent association for his institution, but Shaw declined.) In the last years, Caroline's was the only company he truly sought. And sometimes his son Thomas. Or Walter Gould, his old business partner and agent. Or David Lowance, his physician. These two were the closest thing he had to brothers. After Caroline, he often preferred solitude. In the early years, he couldn't get enough of poets and dancers and actors and eggheads. The late Shaw often didn't want to talk music, or theology, or culture. Just sports, trash, or nothing.

Shaw's supporting players were always there, holding the score or the coat, or warming up the car. They were the truest of the true believers. And what Shaw gave them was the music. When they were with him in private, he was exhausted and there was little left to give. But when they made music together, he gave them everything he had and took them to the heavens.

When people are up close and personal with a "great" man, or woman, they come to loathe that person or love him all the more. Loathing occurs, perhaps, not because of combat duty, or even abuse, but because some falseness is detected at the core. But when the aide, or devotee, is up close and personal and discovers the hero is real—that his core is deep, or even more genuine, or more complex than first imagined—the love and devotion actually deepen. (The actress Dixie Carter once said of her husband Hal

Holbrook, "He's even finer than he appears.") The second phenomenon is what happened with Shaw. Some of the outward behaviors of both the false hero and the true one might be the same—childishness, bad temper, a certain selfishness, and abuse of privilege. Both persons are, as the phrase goes, "high maintenance." But when one says, "It is all about the music," he's only mouthing pieties. When the other says it, for all his faults and vanities, it's an actual expression of his ethic, his practice, his humility, and his psyche.

Still, when people consent to be used, and feel they are doing so for art or love, it does not always end well.

Shaw also tended to see women, in particular, as servants. He was a man of a certain generation, and the way he saw the role of assistant, or wife, was blurred. Eddie Burrus, in addition to being faithful servant, protector, and number one fan, was also his lover. And when the second Mrs. Shaw came along, Caroline quickly dispatched Eddie, froze out Florence Kopleff, and took the role of "chief cook and bottle washer." Fair enough. But Kopleff lost a part of her friendship with Robert. And Eddie Burrus lost her identity—a big part of her life. She was suddenly and coldly discarded, obviously, not just by Caroline, but by Robert. She was fit to be a servant, but not a wife.

Caroline tolerated Nola Frink, and eventually was something like a friend to her; but this is partly because she treated Frink as *her* servant as well. Frink gave much of her life to Shaw. She said she felt as many others did—he took her to artistic heights that she could never have achieved on her own.

The supporting players were exploited in some cases. But it was with their assent. Shaw could be a bear, but they knew his heart was large, his humility real, his art unique. Their common endeavor was noble. Maybe music was worship, after all.

PART FOUR

HERITAGE

I suppose the first scriptural enigma any of us memorize as a child is "God is love." In my case it was some years before I realized that there was a possibility that it said exactly what it meant and meant exactly what it said. Not "God is to be loved" or "God loves," but God IS Love. G = L. At least by analogy (I would say by absolute coincidence) music is love, and so is a chorus and so is singing together.

—Robert Shaw

CHAPTER 31

Telarc: Recording the Canon

It is almost true that no two musicians, indeed no two listeners, can agree on anything about a musical performance or a musical composition. But most Shaw accompanists and listeners seem to agree that Shaw's live performances were often superior to his recordings. This does not necessarily negate the accomplishments of his recording careers—the first with the Robert Shaw Chorale, and the second with the ASO and ASOC. The first is a legacy of sound. The Chorale was a new sound in music. The second—the Telarc legacy—was a legacy of choral literature. It was not only Shaw's core repertoire, and then some, but it was the core of the choral/symphonic repertoire. This was Shaw's testament. And he knew it.

But for Shaw the act of recording was somewhat stifling: how to justify a permanent record of any masterpiece?

Perhaps Shaw pulled back on some of his recordings; not wanting to utter his own last word on something as awesome as the Handel *Messiah* or the Brahms *German Requiem*. Certainly he believed there could be no definitive version, or last word on such works.

Or perhaps Shaw was so nervous about committing his performances of certain great works to history that he became overly organized, detail driven, controlling, tight, and thus he constrained or stifled the performance somewhat. All this is conjecture.

But Here is the paradox of Shaw's recording career: Some of the Shaw recordings in which one would have expected the most of him are the most disappointing—not because they are bad but because they seem prosaic, workmanlike, too controlled. And some of the recordings where little was expected of Shaw, or the piece, or both, are superb. An example of let-down, as previously noted, is his ASO-Telarc *Messiah*. Another, for some, is his ASO-Telarc Bach *Mass in B Minor.* His RCA recordings of both are quite electric and alive. Many listeners thought his ASO-Telarc recording of the Brahms *Requiem* properly somber but, for this piece and this conductor, rather staid. And yet his Verdi and Berlioz Requiems recordings were far greater than anyone expected—they blew away record buyers and critics. It's curious.

All generalizations are dangerous, of course, especially with Shaw. But it does also seem that if he was recording a work in which something less than the monumental might be expected of him, such as Schubert's songs for male chorus, or the Rachmaninoff *Vespers*, or the Duruflé *Requiem*, or the Beethoven *Mass in C*, he could relax into the music and do some of his best work. That is, while he shrank a bit from the monumental works, feeling himself unworthy, he infused his own sound and sensibility into works that were not closely identified with him or were considered "less great." And he did so without self-consciousness. The Rachmaninoff *Vespers* is widely considered one of Shaw's finest recordings, as is the Duruflé *Requiem.* Neither bore the weight of a Brahms *Requiem*. But the Schubert *Songs* and the Beethoven *Mass in C* are just as wonderful. Both achieve a sublime lightness, and a sonic beauty that is not a bit showy, but simply, exquisitely gentle.

Recording the Mozart *Requiem*, a piece that, as we have seen, Shaw performed scores of times, might have been reasonably expected to be a defining moment for Shaw. But Shaw seemed to recoil from such a presumption. His Telarc Mozart *Requiem* recording seems a bit generic—as if he most wanted to *avoid* putting a Shaw stamp on it. Yet, in the smaller or less-expected works, Shaw surprises the listener and seems to breathe life into and expand the work. Perhaps this has to do with this legacy matter, per se. A "maestro" must leave a legacy of major recordings or major works. But clearly, the whole notion of a legacy was problematic for the self-doubting Shaw. Aside from the Rachmaninoff *Vespers*, his Schubert Masses might be his most surprisingly sublime recording on CD. Hardly minor works, but not the great and grand ones with which he had such a close association.

There was a part of Shaw that functioned best when no one much was looking. He perhaps never conducted the New York Philharmonic as well as he conducted the ASO, and that was not just because the ASO was his baby; it was also because he could let down with his friends, colleagues, and protégés. Part of making the bulk of his career out of New York—on the road, in Cleveland, in Atlanta—was about his desire to work out of the limelight. His choral festival in France was practically a secret. He did not seek European critics, a large stage, a fancy venue, or even, particularly, an audience. The whole festival was really for the musicians themselves, and Shaw. One year in France, he did a "small version" of the Bach *Mass in B Minor*—perhaps the work into which Shaw had invested the most study, time, and love in his life. The choir, the orchestra, *and the audience* were "chamber" sized. It may have been his greatest performance of the piece. Everyone who was there rhapsodizes about it. But not many people were there. It was a hot night, in a very ancient church in a small village in France. No one recorded it clandestinely, not even on a hand-held tape recorder. For then it would have been a "grooven image" and not what Shaw really loved—the purest performance of the greatest of music—as free as possible of vanity and "impact." It was done for love, and recorded only by memory, the void, or God.

Shaw often used to joke, "It is a shame the audience has to come and spoil it." But, like many of his jokes, it was only a half-joke.

It was in 1978 that Robert Shaw entered into a relationship with Telarc Records—a Cleveland-based outfit that was so fledgling it scarcely yet existed. The partnership was to last until Shaw's death in 1999. Once again, Shaw took the obscure, less-traveled route. Once again, he helped to put something on the map that had not been there before. Once again, he seemed to place himself, if not in a backwater, in a back row.

Telarc's two founders, Jack Renner and Robert Woods, could hardly believe that Robert Shaw, who had been such a huge musical figure in their generation, especially in Cleveland where Telarc was to be based, was not recording. And it *is* amazing, in a way, that Telarc, so new and undercapitalized, snagged Shaw. After all, he'd been a recording "star" with RCA.

But that had been with the Robert Shaw Chorale, and Shaw had shut the group down. And that had been Robert Shaw doing choral music—a genre in which he was the acknowledged master without peer. But now Shaw had made another renouncement and gone to Atlanta so that he could grow musically. He didn't want to record choral music per se, especially lighter choral music, even (perhaps especially) if it sold well. He was a conductor of orchestras now. And as of the early 1970s, he still felt the Atlanta Symphony Orchestra was not ready to record. They were not yet good enough. He was not yet good enough.

Shaw did made a Christmas album with his Atlanta forces in 1975. It was called *Nativity: A Christmas Concert with Robert Shaw and the Atlanta Symphony Orchestra and Chorus*. The label was Vox. But that had to do with Robert Shaw and Christmas. His name will forever be linked with Christmas, and many people who know nothing of his Atlanta work, or Cleveland, or his New York careers, hear the name Robert Shaw and think, "*Christmas with*."

What made this record different from previous Shaw Christmas re was that it was done with amateur singers and with an orchestra thε truly Shaw's own—not a pickup orchestra. Also, it was the first time Shaw, in essence, recorded his annual Christmas Concert—a program he originated in New York, moved with him to Cleveland, and then took to Atlanta.

As with TV preachers, the "Hallmark format" of Christmas could get Shaw quite agitated. His own participation in such "commodification" of the birth of the Christ child, which was inevitable in the selling of many Christmas albums, and in the repeated yearly performance of a Christmas concert, caused him anger, listlessness, impatience, depression, and even shame. He was actually ashamed of *The Many Moods of Christmas*, though he made it twice and venerated Robert Russell Bennett. Some thought Shaw regarded the music as a schlock. He did, sometimes. It *is* much more akin to the music he did in his early career than in his mature days. But the music was honest and well crafted and did not pretend to be what it was not. Moreover, it cheered and touched many listeners. It was perhaps selling a Christmas product that disturbed Shaw. He actually enjoyed the repetition of his Christmas programs for the chance they offered to hone and perfect. But he hated being put in a box.

In his annual Christmas concert, Shaw arranged the music according to themes:

I. Advent and Human Yearning
II. Nativity and the Manger
III. Under the Christmas Tree (the secular celebration of the pagan feast)
IV. The Meaning of Christ's Life

Shaw tied together the music for this concert not only by theme and the linkage of specific texts, but by key relationships. He interspersed Biblical readings, often performing them himself. He tinkered with this program for almost 50 years. It became a narrative symphonic suite—his symphony and commentary on Christmas. His Christmas liturgy. And most years, he complained that he had to do it again.

Christmas was a time when Shaw became grumpy and self-righteous about greed and commercialism, and generally hard to deal with. He liked buying gifts, but not on cue. In his drinking days, he sometimes took more heavily to the bottle as the holidays approached. "Learned behavior," said one of his sons. From whom? Some friends speculate that Shaw's father had been difficult around the holidays.

The Shaw Christmas program was televised several times from Atlanta (the last time in the final year of Shaw's life for national distribution). It was televised at least once in Cleveland and was often on radio there. It was broadcast on radio in New York in its early days.

Some people think Shaw made *scores* of Christmas records. But actually, that's not so. He made the original one for RCA that made him famous—*Christmas Hymns and Carols*. And he made a follow-up—*Vol. II* in 1952. He re-made the first album in 1957, with new arrangements by himself and Alice Parker. And in 1962, he made the blockbuster, in every sense of the word—*The Many Moods of Christmas*. The album had 17 tunes arranged by the Broadway genius Robert Russell Bennett. It was a record with a big orchestra and a huge brass sound, and the record, which was enormously popular, was also much copied as to style (Doc Severinson said he shamelessly "stole" ideas from it for 40 years).[66] Often Shaw claimed to hate it. He once said it was an instance in which he had really "sold out" and cheapened his vocation. He only did it the first time, he said, to pay back RCA for the Bach recordings, and he did it the second time only to help Telarc and the ASO. Was this mythologizing? Perhaps. Shaw liked to depict and contrast the forces of light and the forces of darkness, but he didn't do much that he did not want to do. In any case, many people still love the album. Other than the re-make of *Moods*, Shaw made only two Christmas albums for Telarc, both superbly tasteful and justly beloved.

That's seven Christmas albums—three for RCA and three for Telarc, plus the one for Vox in the early Atlanta days. Only one of these presented

66 Burris-Severinson interview.

Christmas music in Shaw's own preferred framework—something like the way he presented music at the Unitarian Church in Cleveland and something like a worship service that was all musical in structure and content—and that was the album for Vox.

For almost a decade after accepting the Atlanta post, Shaw said the ASO was still building, and he was still learning.

In 1977, the ASO under Shaw's baton made its non-choral, non-Christmas recording debut. The record was made by Vox Cum Laude and the music was Bernstein's "Symphonic Dances" from *West Side Story*, a piece Shaw liked to conduct and did conduct often, including as a guest conductor, and Tchaikovsky's *Romeo and Juliet*. It was an interesting choice. It is not clear what happened next. Apparently there was very little critical or popular response. Perhaps Shaw was happy with the product, though it seems unlikely. But Shaw with the ASO was not snatched up by any major record label. The recording disappeared into the ether.

Meanwhile the fledgling Telarc had begun to court Shaw.

Record companies are often run by people who think in categories. They know that's how many critics and many of their customers are thinking. But Telarc's founders did not want Robert Shaw Chorale-type recordings of glee club favorites. They knew that Shaw had been performing major choral-orchestral works for 25 years, many of which he had not recorded. They knew that Shaw's name was as strong as ever. They knew that he had only grown in scope and depth in his years away from the recording business. They also had a hunch that the public would buy a Shaw recording no matter what orchestra he was conducting—so long as the quality was high and it was not purely orchestral.

For their first record together, Shaw and Telarc decided to do Stravinsky's *Firebird Suite*. It was a gutsy choice. As a backup, they added the *Overture* and Polovetsian Dances from Borodin's *Prince Igor*—big, lush Romantic sound with chorus. The record was a mild commercial and critical success, and both Shaw and Woods were proud of it. They were off.

In Robert Woods, who would become Shaw's executive producer, and more often than not his producer on the Telarc records, Shaw met his equal in perfectionism and desire for control. As with most of his contract-oriented relationships, Shaw thought, and spoke, of quitting more than once. Shaw found Woods too opinionated and too prone to interrupting the recording sessions for critiques that Shaw sometimes found arbitrary and vague. Certainly, once Shaw's recording career with the ASO and ASOC had been established, it would not have been hard to find another label. Yet Shaw stuck with Telarc. He felt grateful and he was loyal. And, in the end, he loved and respected Woods. He was a musician, and a driven one. Occasionally Shaw also felt a bit too categorized and hemmed in, as he had at RCA.

Shaw did make three recordings of the works of contemporary composers with other labels—works by Alvin Singleton with Nonesuch, sharing conducting duties with Louis Lane; the (Stephen) Paulus *Violin Concerto* with soloist William Preucil, for New World Records; and a splendid recording of two major works by Philip Glass for Sony Classical—*Itaipú* and *The Canyon*. In the last case, it was because the composer was contractually bound to Sony. Shaw's original contract agreement with Telarc was a handshake. So he was bound only by sentiment. The whole of the partnership was amazingly prolific. In that same year as the Glass recording—1990—Shaw brought out three major recordings for Telarc, including a third recording of the Bach *Mass in B Minor*.

Shaw's Telarc recordings are among the best-selling and the most-played (particulary on public radio) classical recordings. Shaw didn't, in the end, make many purely orchestral recordings. Telarc stuck with Shaw's core repertoire and with the choral-orchestral formula shifting, in Shaw's later years, to recordings by his small chamber choirs, mostly recorded in France.

For whatever reasons, Shaw and Telarc never recorded the Beethoven *Ninth Symphony*, though they talked about it more than once and began planning such a recording on at least one occasion. Shaw did record it for a label called Intersound Pro Arte in 1985.

Could Shaw really build a first-class musical instrument in Atlanta? It turned out he could, and did. And it turned out that Telarc could sell recordings by an orchestra not thought of as one of the Big Five or Big Ten—if they were fine, and led by Robert Shaw. Indeed, the Atlanta Symphony Orchestra kept recording with Telarc—and selling recordings—long after the blight on orchestral recording contracts hit the major orchestras in New York, Boston, Chicago, and Cleveland.

Shaw put Telarc on the map and Telarc put the ASO on the map. Telarc allowed Shaw to record his core repertoire and leave a recorded legacy. It was symbiotic.

Was there a tipping point? A point at which it became clear that this partnership was going to work? Were there several?

Well, the ASO's 1980 recording of *Carmina Burana* did get people's attention and was widely played. It is still considered one of the best recordings of the piece. Indeed, many years after making the recording, Shaw got a royalty check that was inexplicable to him. It turned out the ASO's version of the piece had been used in Oliver Stone's film *The Doors*. "The who?" asked Shaw. "In the what?" And he went back to work.

This recording may have gotten more attention than anything he had done up until that time with the ASO because the chorus had such power and yet was so nuanced. People had not heard *Carmina* that way. Shaw liked the recording, as much as he liked any of his recordings, but ultimately decided he disliked the piece. It was one of the very few pieces he performed and recorded but disliked. His thinking on *Carmina* apparently evolved. He eventually decided it was unworthy, "trashy." Shaw told people that he was offered the American premiere of the piece and turned it down. This implied that he had *always* disliked it. What seems more likely is that Shaw's distaste grew through the years. The composer was "a Nazi prototype," Shaw told one friend. "R.S. wasn't bothered by Wagner," quipped another associate, "but then *he* was a greater composer." Still, for some years *Carmina Burana* was a piece in Shaw's repertoire, so he must have seen some merit in it at one point. As for recording it, Shaw was undoubtedly trying to balance the commercial needs of Telarc, which he thought reasonable, with his own artistic ambition. Indeed, the LP version of this recording contains a second piece—Hindemith's *Symphonic Metamorphosis on Themes of Carl Maria von Weber*. Shaw *kept* that piece in his repertoire. He thought it noble. He loved and respected Hindemith. Shaw was forever balancing his own taste with commercial reality; his need to learn and teach with his pragmatic obligations to his orchestra and his record company. The Orff recording does have Haken Hagegard as the baritone and the CD still sells.

Shaw and the ASO did not record again until 1982, and then it was only one recording—works by Poulenc, a composer Shaw had championed since 1947.

In 1983, the Telarc–Shaw relationship was in full blossom. That year, Telarc issued an astonishing four full-length Shaw recordings: the Berlioz *Les Nuits d'été* with Elly Ameling paired with the Fauré *Pelléas et Mélisande*; a re-make of *The Many Moods of Christmas*, this time with the ASO; the Stravinsky *Symphony of Psalms* paired with the Poulenc *Gloria* (two pieces Shaw dearly loved, repeated often, and recorded with aplomb and confidence); and two records that were expected to be Shaw triumphs—yet somehow were not—the Handel *Messiah* and the Brahms *Ein Deutsches Requiem*. Maybe it was a matter of too much recording in a short span of time. Shaw recorded the Brahms on November 5, 6, and 7 of 1983, and he recorded the Handel on December 18, 19, and 20 in that same year. This would be a lot for anyone, but given Shaw's demanding schedule at the time, and given his nervousness about recording and about recording seminal works, it may have simply been too much.

Shaw's relationship to Handel's *Messiah* is long, close, and confounding. It is a work Shaw conducted scores of times, and virtually every year of his professional career at Christmas or Easter. The Christmas portion of

Messiah, along with the Bach *Magnificat,* is the last thing Shaw conducted in his life—roughly a month before his death. The ASO recording was his second recording of the full work, and while very fine, and loved by many as a standard recording with modern instruments, to the ears of some musicians and more than a few listeners, it was not nearly so good as the earlier RCA recording. This *Messiah* is not as lean and light as his 1966 recording with the Robert Shaw Chorale. Robert Woods recalled that the recording process for this Telarc version of *Messiah* was not pleasant. Shaw was feeling insecure, and as if he should perhaps try for an early musical sound. But he was not in a position to do so. (The movement was in its infancy and Shaw was conversant. Indeed, he presaged it in some ways with his own earlier work. But he was not a true believer, and never would be.) He was also unhappy with his chorus that year, which was often the case. But when he was unhappy on the eve of a recording, it was not a good sign. Woods recalls that Shaw warned him that this 1987 recording would not be "new" or, in the musicological sense, old. It would be old-fashioned, and more Victorian than Baroque, Shaw said. He rather doubted he had anything new to say.

This is strange. For it was, after all, Shaw who first brought what was then thought to be an almost shockingly "small" sound to this piece in American performances in the 1950s and 1960s. He was thought revolutionary by some and arrogant by others for performing the piece as a chamber work rather than a heroic message from a small army of jubilant Christians. Shaw was one of the earliest American champions of "getting us back to Handel's line." His 1966 recording *was* new; indeed, was seminal. Conductor Richard Coffey said, "It changed the way everyone in American music thought of the piece." Shaw's performances of the work in the 1950s and 1960s were "small," especially for their day. He used 35 to 40 singers. And yet in the 1980s, he chose to do it on a large scale with large forces.

Shaw's 1983 *Messiah* does have something of the Shaw wonder and sound. In No. 21 of the score, "His yoke is easy," the final phrase, "and his burden is light," becomes a moment of pathos one will not hear on any other recording, including Shaw's own first one. But, generally, the Telarc recording does not sound like the culmination of Shaw's years with this work and this composer. Again, it is as if he somehow shrinks from the responsibility of recording for all time so timeless and monumental a work.

Shaw said once, during a break in rehearsals of *Messiah* for a TV recording (and to no one in particular): "He's always surprising you, isn't he? Always surprising you." His RCA *Messiah* has that sense of surprise—of snap, crackle, and pop. As for the large forces for the ASO recording, Shaw knew better, but as with the Bach Passions, he sometimes opted for greater congregational participation over musical correctness. The pastor trumped the conductor.

The Telarc Brahms *Requiem* recording is an even greater puzzlement. It, along with the Beethoven *Missa* and the great Bach Mass and Passions, was perhaps the work Shaw loved most. It was one of the pieces closest to his talents and temperament. It virtually became a Shaw signature piece. Shaw made the first American recording of the work in 1947, and it was new to many people. That seems amazing now, since performances of the work seem almost ubiquitous around the world and there are now many, many recordings of it. Again, the Brahms was somehow a piece Shaw himself might have written had he been placed in Brahms's time and endowed with Brahms's talents. The work is an ingenious composite. It is Baroque in structure and Romantic in temper; at once melodic, old-fashioned, daring, and totally unique. And it encompasses, almost eerily, Shaw's own theology—the theology of the individual not the institution, of the suffering mourner, and of the *humanist* Christian.

Yet the dove did not descend in the ASO–Telarc recording in 1983.

Mind you, it is a perfectly decent and respectable recording. But it simply hasn't the feeling or the depth that Shaw usually brought to his performances, particularly in later-life performances.

Perhaps he'd not yet lived some of the life wisdom and agony that he eventually brought to this piece. Or, he was not yet willing, subconsciously, to deliver his last word on it.

Shaw spent much of his time in the last months of his life on his own translation of the Brahms *Requiem* into English, and he was to have recorded the piece one more time, using his own new translation, with the Mormon Tabernacle Choir. He missed the date by only a few weeks. He might have made something very special. As with the *St. Matthew*, there is a later, live version of the Brahms *Requiem*, again issued by the Cleveland Orchestra after Shaw's death, and hence unsanctioned by him. This recording has more of Shaw's passion and less of the perfectionism of the Telarc recording. The chorus is not nearly so good in the Cleveland recording as in the ASO recording, but the feelings for life and death, fragility, gratitude, and last things is tangible. There is no woodenness.[67] It can't be accidental that this was a live performance—*not* for the ages, so Shaw was not constricted by his doubts about recording, or himself.

As previously noted, the breakthroughs for Shaw and Telarc were the recordings of the Verdi *Requiem* and the Berlioz *Requiem*.

The Berlioz, released in 1984, startled nearly everyone in the music world.

That included Shaw's Telarc Boswell, Bob Woods.

The work is grand and grandiose. It is almost ungainly. It is romantic, lush, at times meditative and at times hysterical. For many people it is over the top, musically. The piece was not one of Shaw's favorites, particularly. Not then. Nothing in his training with Herford and Szell would have led one to believe it particularly congenial for him. It is not tightly or predictably structured. *But* Shaw was a romantic at heart, and brought much of himself

67 As with most things Shavian, there is no consensus. Some musicians feel his late performances of the Brahms were too slow—painfully slow. And Shaw himself said, "I know these tempi are slow." "And," he agreed, "a bit hard to justify musically." He said he was going for a meditative quality. On another occasion, speaking of the work, he said, "I hate to see the music slip by." Critic Tim Page, on the other hand, hailed the Cleveland Orchestra's live recording of the Brahms *Requiem* as something of a treasure. The Cleveland recording is, in a sense, compromised by not having been offered to the listening public by Shaw himself. But given Shaw's tendency to control some of his recordings a bit too much, perhaps Cleveland has done Shaw, and his listeners, a service.

to the over-the-top-ness of the composition—and not just his own large heart, but also his sense of restraint and taste. Berlioz needs this, perhaps.

The piece requires, as well, great organization and balancing technique by a conductor because the forces are not only large, but competitive. (The sound seems at times to be coming from all points—north, south, east, and west. Berlioz tosses in brass from the heavens at one point.) This sort of musical problem *was* right up Shaw's alley.

But something else, something seldom noticed or commented upon—the mystic, repetitive, almost Eastern feeling of the piece in places, which some cynics and critics call its non-musical spots—was also something Shaw could bring out. The piece needs order, and reining in, and Shaw was an obvious choice in conductors for that. But it also has a spiritual quality that was accessible for Shaw intuitively.

The reaction of some critics, according to Woods, was that they didn't know Shaw was capable of work of such richness and depth.

Shaw knew the recording was good, but did not see it as a musical breakthrough—just another difficult job. But it was a critical breakthrough, an opening of the door for Shaw and the ASO.

The Verdi *Requiem* in 1987 was, Woods believed, "the tipping point" for Shaw, for the ASO, and for Telarc.

This piece was, by then, a Shaw favorite. He loved it because he'd done it with Toscanini. But he'd changed his mind about it as a composition. Structurally, Shaw loved that "all the joints fit together," and he could tell where. It called for great passion and clarity—all that Shaw could illuminate, muster, and inspire. It called for a very high-quality chorus, not only knit together well, but vocally beautiful. Shaw felt his chorus had improved from the previous year. He felt that doing the *Missa Solemnis* earlier the same season had paved the way. It made the Verdi "duck soup," he said. "This choir grew up this season." That became Shaw's line. Recall Woods's rule of thumb: "If Shaw is happy with his chorus, you will get a good recording." He was happy with the chorus when he made his great Verdi recording.

Finally, the Verdi called for great soloists. And on this occasion, Shaw had them. They were neither of the Shaw extended family or of the inner circle, nor were they "names" as Woods wanted. They were simply splendid. They were: Susan Dunn, soprano; Diane Curry, mezzo-soprano; Jerry Hadley, tenor; and Paul Plishka, bass. Only Hadley had been something of a Shaw protégé.

Shaw attributed some of the artistic success, as well as critical success, of the recording to sheer dumb luck: It came together in a lucky way and was released and heard at the right time. But *heard* it was.

One perhaps overwrought British critic called it "the greatest Verdi recording ever."

In any case, the recording changed everything for Shaw and for Telarc as his label. The critics, including European critics, who had never taken the ASO, Shaw, or Telarc seriously, now did.

The record won a Grammy and began a steady stream of Grammies to Shaw and his forces. (Shaw won 17, ultimately.)

Interestingly, Shaw's luck with the Verdi *Requiem* was not always consistent, as we have seen.

Atlanta audiences saw mixed results.

There was the riveting version in Cleveland a few years after the recording to aid the cause of disarmament.

On the other hand, his performance for the Carnegie Hall workshop series, in the last decade of his life, some felt went off the rails. On the occasion of that performance, Shaw decided the piece was sacred music and not opera—in line with something Verdi had written his publisher, which Shaw had read. Shaw went back and forth on this issue, sometimes deciding the *Requiem* was Verdi's ultimate opera, sometimes deciding it should be "anything but opera," as Verdi had written.

At the time he made his still-shattering recording, Shaw thought the Verdi *Requiem* was opera, sacred opera, a Robert Shaw sort of opera, but opera. On this recording, the conductor successfully "got out of the way."

The Verdi may be Shaw's finest work for Telarc. Arguably, it was his most important.

But others, less expectable, stand out—such as his Rachmaninoff *Vespers*—a recording quite un-Shaw-like because the forces are not large and it is anything but the sort of rhythmic, propulsive work in which he excelled. Several of his France recordings for Telarc are also remarkable—notably *Evocation of the Spirit* and the posthumously assembled *Magnum Mysterium.* And virtually every singer loves Shaw's collection *of American Spirituals*, mostly using Shaw-Parker arrangements. (This, too, was recorded in France.) The Schubert *Songs for Male Chorus* and the Beethoven *Mass in C* recording—two instances of another kind of Shaw "best"—have been previously noted. When he was not on the high wire, Shaw could simply make music. In these instances, Shaw's love of choral beauty and his instinctive feel for it overrode his nervousness, his examinations of the scholarship, and his structural fixations. This happened in the Schubert songs recording—quiet, gentle music—and in the Beethoven—often (ludicrously) categorized as "minor" Beethoven.

One constant source of tension between Shaw and Woods in the Telarc years was Shaw's frequent use of rather ordinary soloists (at least Woods thought them ordinary) when Woods felt exceptional, star soloists would have better served the recording, and such soloists could have been secured.

The best explanation may be Shaw's pastoral side.

Shaw always felt bound to his extended family—his "parish" of musicians, if you will. And even though he was neurotically perfectionist, he was willing to endure imperfection in order to keep the family together. The use of large forces in recording of the Telarc Handel *Messiah* and Bach *B Minor Mass* when he himself had pioneered the use of chamber-sized forces is another example. He may have also felt that hiring perfection was cheating—it had to be earned, earned by suffering and hard work or not achieved at all. Also, he knew full well that a dry or clinical professional could ruin music and that he himself tended that way. So, sometimes he intentionally threw a wrench into his own well-oiled machine. He knew it would be harder to get the sound he wanted with a large chorus, but what a challenge! And meanwhile, more singers could partake of Handel or Bach. "When volunteer singers sing for love" he said, "it is hard to exclude them from the greatest works that can be sung."

The later Shaw method was this: Prepare as dryly and professionally as you can, and *then* open the floodgates. Or, turn the dryness on its head. Thus, after carefully preparing the Britten *War Requiem* for one of his workshops at Carnegie Hall and putting every detail in place, Shaw revealed to the chorus that one of the soloists was now essentially deaf. But the baritone, Benjamin Luxon, had actually sung the piece with the composer and knew it as well as Shaw did. And, Shaw explained, "Ben brings something very special to this piece." Shaw was not trying to do Luxon a favor. But he *was* trying to bring an extra-musical value to bear. Neurotic perfectionist though he was, Shaw knew that a truly great and living performance needed some additional X-factor—Passion? Grief? Ecstasy? Uncertainty? All of the above? But this factor could only come, for Shaw, *after* mechanical approximations of certitude were achieved. Otherwise, the love and passion are only cheap grace. Just as Shaw would sometimes, in the rehearsal process, artificially create chaos and crisis so that he could lead his forces into the promised land, he would sometimes wreck his own sandcastle so that he could rebuild it. This was partially premeditated and partially intuitive. But it was always necessary to Shaw's music making. For Shaw, art required order. But also struggle. There can be no art without cost.

CHAPTER 32

FRANCE

Robert Shaw loved the Pacific Ocean. Periodically, during his years as music director of the Atlantic Symphony, he and his wife Caroline contemplated a summer home somewhere near Big Sur or in the Pacific Northwest. Robert, at least, contemplated it seriously. A part of his spirit remained always on the West Coast and the great Pacific Ocean (which he considered "far nobler" than the Atlantic). Shaw also considered, less seriously, spending his semi-retirement, after leaving the music directorship of the ASO, there. He was popular with the orchestras in Los Angeles and San Francisco, and had turned down more guest conducting offers than he could accept from either. Moreover, after his retirement from the ASO, he agreed to be the principle guest conductor for his first orchestra in San Diego, which was regrettably and perpetually broke. So a return to the West Coast in his golden years, or a partial return, keeping one foot there and one in Atlanta, was possible. It was at least worth Shaw's consideration and contemplation because he so loved the Pacific.

The Shaws took one trip out West to look at properties and concluded that California was too expensive and too far from Atlanta. They would have to content themselves with vacations to Florida.

But Caroline Shaw had a place she loved as much as Robert loved the Pacific—France. And she made a convert of her husband.

Caroline Shaw was a devout Francophile. She had been briefly in school there, spoke the language—albeit with a Georgia peach accent—and loved all things French: the music, literature, food, fashions, geography, and people of France. For a long time, his wife's passion did not quite register with Shaw. Robert liked to eat and drink, but he could not have cared less about fine vintages. Matters of taste, in general, were not of much interest to him. He was intensely interested in where to place and how to configure singers on a stage. But interior design went right by him. Caroline had taught Robert to enjoy a glass of wine rather than simply blasting away at his brain cells with various and sundry combinations of hard liquor after a tough concert. But Shaw was no more interested in a wine *discussion* or critique than he was in the professional standards of certified public accountants. Caroline also taught Robert a bit about painting and sculpture. He'd never much noticed either. Most of all, she taught him about the joys of southwestern France.

Caroline began to arrange family vacations there, and then a summer rental. And, finally, she found a home. The Shaws purchased a property in the Dordogne Valley, partly because it was not a high tourist area—in the little village of Couzou. Fewer than 50 people live there.

Caroline totally rehabilitated, actually rebuilt, their home in Couzou. It was to be very elegant *and* very French. And it was, when completed. It took months and Caroline was, in effect, the general contractor. She had the chicken coop on the property converted into a combination guesthouse and study for Robert. She had now prepared a place for retreat for their family.

Robert had other ideas, or rather, other impulses.

Caroline's notion of the house in France was that it would be an oasis, a hideaway—a place for Robert to rest, study, and recharge his batteries. And it would be a place for the family to have time together. She knew there could be no Robert without music. But if she got him to France, without ASO duties, she reckoned there would be more of him for the family to share with the music. All he would be able to do there would be to study. When they re-built the house, Caroline won a sort of victory: Robert was beginning to like France, and once he retired from the ASO, she hoped they could spend more than a couple of weeks there together.

But Shaw recharged himself the same way he exhausted himself—by working, by preparing a musical performance. Why not, he said, hold a summer workshop of his own for choral music? He had done it for decades for various schools. Why not have his *own* summer festival in the spirit of the Marlboro Festival at Marlboro College in Vermont? Shaw thought that festival, founded by his friend Rudolf Serkin, was much the best of all summer music events because it mixed teaching with playing and the new, young players with old veterans. Why not such a festival for choral music—with choral educators making up the bulk of the choir? And why not do it in France?

Poor Caroline.

Once Shaw did retire as music director of the ASO and began to consider things he wanted to do, he began to think about small choirs and repertoire for a small choir. But this time, the small choir would not be professional singers or the best of his volunteer chorus, but mostly music educators who had professional-caliber musical knowledge and, often, voices. Shaw was more and more an educator as he aged, and he greatly admired music educators. Besides, who better to spread the gospel?

The Shaw "sound" with the Robert Shaw Chorale is not the sound he got out of the ASO chorus. His France choirs would change the sound again. Shaw was not so much *aiming* for a different sound. Rather, he was once again adapting to circumstance—primarily the voices he had, as well as the old French churches in which he and his singers would make music in France. This was a choir whose chief attribute was not sonority or enthusiasm, but intelligence and informed sensitivity. Shaw was not seeking a richer sound now, so much as compositional transparency. Waring had taught him that every sound of every word counted. But Shaw wanted every note, and every subdivision within every note, to count. That way, every musical idea of the composer would count. Shaw felt a choir of music educators could think this way. The sound of the Robert Shaw Festival Singers was softer, more rounded, and obviously lighter, owing to the smaller forces. Shaw was not looking for protégés or seeking to build a cult or a movement. He wasn't trying to pass along his techniques in one, and only one, form either. Rather, Shaw was following a natural instinct to teach, which he'd always had, and an increasingly strong desire to be among other learned musicians.

After his pending retirement from the ASO was made public, Shaw's appointment as professor at Emory University was announced with pride, fanfare, and a gala dinner and inaugural address by Shaw. What Shaw thought was the university's commitment to help him found an "institute" of music seemed to him the perfect platform for his return to the small choir—one that would be devoted to teaching and learning rather than touring and recording. He assumed that his new vocation would split him between Atlanta (where the institute would be based at Emory) and France (where Shaw would hold, and Emory would sponsor, a summer choral festival and workshop).

But the Emory arrangement began to unravel almost as soon as it was put in place. There were key flaws in the appointment: Shaw's duties had not really been defined. There was no clear budget or income stream for the Robert Shaw Institute, which Shaw assumed the university would fund. Indeed, Shaw assumed the university would be supporting his activities, somewhat unquestioningly. University officials assumed Shaw's operation would be self-supporting and would lend prestige to the university. Myriad problems of direction and perception developed on both sides. Neither side had thought things through.

Shaw had begun to dream again, as in the old Collegiate Chorale days. He hoped a full-fledged institute of sacred music would develop and perhaps, eventually, so would his "musical performance society"—Shaw's conception of a modern conservatory/association of players. But how was that supposed to happen? Shaw had always been free to conceptualize and focus on music. There was always a Thomas Pyle, an Alice Parker, a Nola Frink, a Bill Segel, or more likely a team of such people, around to operationalize the vision and take care of details. There was no such person at Emory. Ann Jones, who might have been that person, was on the faculty but left for a position at the University of Illinois. Charles Schissler was brought from Westminster, then at Princeton, to head the Institute in Atlanta, but by then the problems had begun to develop, and Schissler did not have years of intimate experience at reading Shaw and anticipating his moods and thoughts.

The main problem was lack of institutional support. Emory's then-president and his top deputies had, evidently, not fully considered the nature or extent of their commitment to Shaw. And Shaw had not considered that he would be an employee. He did not think of himself that way. He had never thought of himself that way. He had been an employee of the orchestras in Cleveland and Atlanta, but he'd never been treated as a hired hand. Shaw was also not an academic. He didn't have a slow speed, and he lacked the intrigue gene. He was no politician and no diplomat. When it was expected that he genuflect, or when he was the victim of professional jealously, Shaw simply didn't engage. As when he was "fired" by the ASO, Shaw didn't really fight back when the long knives came out. He might have politicked a bit and mended fences at Emory, and made it work. But that was not Shaw. He didn't have time for such "nonsense." His response to dysfunctional organizations and organization, throughout his life, was not-so-benign neglect. His attitude was: People do what they do. My work is there for anyone to evaluate if they wish. He'd come to Emory with skeptics, perhaps even enemies, just as he had come with them at the Cleveland Orchestra and the Atlanta Symphony. But in the case of Emory, the music and the Shaw charisma did not carry the day.

Within two years, the Shaw-Emory partnership had collapsed. And ironically, the University profited handsomely from its brief association with Shaw because it was entitled to royalties from the recording made during the first France institute in the summer of 1989—the Rachmaninoff *Vespers*.[68]

But Shaw was not giving up on the France festival. So he had to scramble to find funding for his yearly choral boot camp. For a time Shaw himself, and Caroline, carried the cost of it. The expense frightened Mrs. Shaw, and appalled her. She had gone to France for peace, not penury (which was not a real danger). In the end, two temporary partners were secured—Ohio State University, because longtime Shaw associate Maurice Casey taught there, and Los Angeles State University, where old Shaw pal and associate Don Neuen was on the faculty. Finally, Boston University, and its president John Silber, came on board with a true and deep commitment to Shaw and what he was trying to do. Alas, by that time, Shaw was running out of steam—he had only a few more years to live.

Robert Shaw always had his "baby"; his big dream; the sailboat he was building in the garage. His first was the Collegiate Chorale. The last was the choral festival and institute. The dream of the moment might be one of his early masterworks series in New York. Or it might be commissioning and performing Hindemith's *Lilacs*. Or, his "current obsession" might be translating the *Cantata Profana* of Bartók. But there was always a passion and burning vision. The Robert Shaw Choral Festival in Southern France and the Robert Shaw Festival Singers were his last big, innovative "projects." But, really, the dream was always the same: rediscovering and re-creating great music out of a process of rigorous study, rehearsal, and collaboration, at least once removed from commercial considerations. Every great Shaw project contained the same elements—daring and ambition, a family or community of musicians, scholarship and vocational devotion.

68 Shaw himself thought this CD "not bad" and "the best I have been able to accomplish." Incredibly, Shaw tried to call off this recording at the last minute, telling Bob Woods, whom he reached at La Guardia Airport with his recording crew, that the choir was not ready.

Two other positive things happened in Shaw's "retirement" that no one expected, least of all Shaw. The first was his new celebrity-hood in New York. The second was the overall rediscovery of Robert Shaw: in his eighth and ninth decades, Shaw was in great demand. He had not assumed this would be the case after the ASO. In fact, he rather assumed it would *not* be the case. Ultimately, this meant that Shaw didn't have the time to develop new forms of chorally based worship or to write the book he wanted to write. He was still a performer. Moreover, Bob Woods was tremendously interested in the sounds Shaw was getting from his new small choirs—the Robert Shaw Festival Singers and the Robert Shaw Chamber Singers—and Woods wanted to record what they were able to do, particularly in the ancient churches of France. (Woods, like Shaw, was excited by the availability of acoustical spaces not previously available to Shaw and his choirs. Heretofore, they had been recording in Atlanta.) So, in spite of Emory, Shaw had work. Plenty of it. And his small choirs had a reason for being. Despite being in the autumn of his life, he remained a working musician. His joy was study and rehearsal, but performance concentrated the mind.

Shaw's summers rehearsing, performing, and recording with his own hand-picked choirs in France became the happiest interludes in later life.

Shaw rented a lycée, empty in the summer. He engaged a local cooking school, up the hill and to the west, for lunches and dinners. The number of participants varied, but hovered around 60, give or take. The festival lasted two weeks and there were two major concerts. On two occasions the second was with orchestra. Shaw worked the singers hard by day. There was very good food and much wine in the evenings. Shaw put the orchestras together from around Europe, often using members of the U.S. Army Band of Europe, with the assistance of Craig Jessop. The "school," part of his Festival, consisted of score study, rehearsal techniques, more rehearsal, and, finally, performance. Many of the singers were people Shaw had used often and knew well—again, his parish or extended family. Many had PhDs or DMEs were established regional conductors, or well-known academicians and graduate educators. The core group of singers were repeat scholars, people who were favorites of Shaw's and had been in other Shaw choirs.

Several of the best of these summer festival sessions were not recorded. An all-American program, the centerpiece of which was Gershwin's *Porgy and Bess,* surprised some singers. Shaw seemed very happily at home in this music. (Of course, he had done it in New York, Cleveland, and Atlanta, many times, and it combined his classical, pop, and folk instincts.) Many thought it was one of the best performances in France. The small-scale *B Minor Mass*, as well as a program of Bach cantatas and motets, was *the* crowning Shaw concert for several of the singers and maybe for Shaw, too. He was working on more of a chamber scale again, and in intimate relation with his musicians, just as in the old Robert Shaw Chorale days. But, no recording was made. (Some who participated feel this is almost tragic.) Everyone felt "RS" worked hardest of all, of course. And when evening came, he paid for most of the wine. The singers also noticed how happy and relaxed the often-irascible teacher was these days. Shaw was doing music in the purist way he could, with people he most loved and respected. The format was similar to the workshop he had done at the Westminster Choir College in Princeton for a decade. But Shaw had ended that when it began to feel cult-like to him. This was different. These musicians were peers. Again, Shaw had found a quiet, almost invisible place to work. He and his troops were, substantially, making music only for each other. Both recording and performing were afterthoughts as far as Shaw was concerned, although, after the Rachmaninoff *Vespers* recording, Woods rather counted on a good record from France each summer. Typically, Shaw was not satisfied even with this recording, fine as it is (and now thought of as almost a classic recording). The next time he performed it in Atlanta, he told several of the singers, "We're going to put the balls back in it." He felt the recording, though the best he'd done sonically, had too little bass, for which he blamed himself, and Woods, and too little soulfulness and grit. It was too precious. It was not Russian enough. Nothing can be "too perfect." Any performance can be improved.

The summer institute/festival actually led to Shaw's yearly workshop at Carnegie Hall. Judith Arron, an old acquaintance from their collaboration at the Cincinnati May Festival, had just assumed leadership at Carnegie Hall. She came to France to see what Shaw was doing, was fascinated, transfixed, and seduced. It was then that she decided Shaw had to be shared with New York, America, and the world.[69]

Shaw and his choir were in seventh heaven in France. They were working only for each other and the composer. And they were reveling in the ancient churches of the area. Shaw performed with the choir in Gramat, Rocamadour, Toulouse, and Souillac, where the choir lived. He and Woods recorded in Gramat, in the Church of St. Pierre. Shaw particularly loved hearing the Baroque and chamber echoes in those spaces.

Though the Robert Shaw Institute never became a full-fledged institute and the Festival was really just Shaw and his forces performing two programs in two or three churches, usually for very tiny audiences (most of France never knew Shaw and his merry band were there), the musicians who came to France were changed by it. Four superb records were done for Telarc. And great music was made—for its own sake.

Alas, there were only four of those glorious France summers. Caroline Shaw's battle with cancer forced the cancellation of one, and after her death, though Shaw wanted to continue the Festival, he did not wish to do so in France. Shaw decided to take the festival to Park City, Utah. This, too, was cancelled due to Shaw's own health problems (exacerbated by altitude). The last Festival was at Furman University, in South Carolina, in the last summer of Shaw's life.

Shaw also started a similar group—the Robert Shaw Chamber Singers—to use as his choral laboratory in Atlanta (with some overlapping

69 Arron was then relatively new as head of Carnegie Hall. Shaw's partnership with Arron was to be one of the most important of his life. Although they had known each other through the Cincinnati Music Festival (Shaw had conducted there often and Arron had been director of the Festival), after she saw Shaw work in France, Arron became fully enamored of Shaw and convinced of his historic importance to American music.

membership), often paying their expenses out of his own pocket. These were his "beloveds"—not so much his disciples as his children.

Shaw still talked, sometimes, of his "musical performance society" that would have 150 to 200 musicians, a staff of 3 to 6 conductors, and would "engage in all conceivable types of musical performance, education, and outreach." That—Shaw's dream of a kind of floating conservatory—did not happen. But something wonderful did. The Robert Shaw Institute morphed into the Robert Shaw Festival and the Robert Shaw Festival Singers, who also participated in Shaw's Carnegie Hall workshops. (Indeed, they formed the core of the workshop choir.) He'd long had an ASO chamber group, of course. But this was an intimate group, and he could lead smaller, elegant, and quiet works. The ultimate "big choir guy" was a small choir man again.

CHAPTER 33

Return to the Small Choir

When in the summer of 1998 the Robert Shaw Chorale Institute and Summer Festival moved to Furman University in Greenville, South Carolina, Shaw and some of his close associates, like Bill Thomas of the Furman faculty, saw it as a jump start for the festival—a new beginning. In fact, this was to be the last year, for Shaw died the following January. But he would have a last chance to work with his "beloveds"—the singers he'd trained and knew best—in a small choir setting.

Shaw had become, over many years, master of the large chorus and the Leviathan works for chorus and orchestra—whether tragic as with the Britten *War Requiem*, or merry as with the Haydn *Creation*. But now in the last years of his life, post-ASO, he wanted to work again with more intimate groups of musicians and with more intimate musical works. Now, in his last months of life, he would gather his small group of colleagues and friends, not in France, but near to home.

Throughout his career, Shaw almost always kept a large choir and a small choir at hand: a large and a small canvas. In the early days, for example, the Collegiate Chorale tackled the *Missa Solemnis*, and a sub-group, for a long time simply called "the small choir," which became the basis of the Robert Shaw Chorale, took on Bach.

In Atlanta, Shaw actually formed the Atlanta Symphony Orchestra Chamber Chorus first (1967), and later (1970) the ASO Chorus. Now, his "festival" singers and the Robert Shaw Chamber Singers would be his small canvases.

It is easy to underestimate Shaw's small group work. He spent so much time on the large works that they are rather naturally associated with him. The choruses of symphony orchestras are typically 150 people and up, and Shaw worked with such groups in Cleveland and Atlanta from 1957 to 1989. Also, Shaw did innumerable workshops with large choirs through the years. Here, again, pastoral considerations often trumped musical ones. His Westminster choral workshops, in Princeton, were huge musical and cultural events. Shaw did many of the major choral-orchestral works—every summer was some monumental work—and the whole thing usually culminated in an acclaimed New York performance, or two, sometimes with the Mostly Mozart Festival, and always with the finest New York orchestral players. For singers, it was like crossing the Red Sea. So many people wanted to get into that workshop, and Shaw, the preacher and pastor, wanted to accommodate the maximum. This was also true with ongoing festivals in Atlanta, Michigan, and San Diego in the years he did festivals in those places. Many of his singers, along with Louis Lane, believe Shaw was intuitively drawn toward big works, big forces, and big musical ideas.

But like all Shaw truisms, this is only a part of the truth. Shaw loved small choirs, too. He liked horsepower. But agility mattered to him as well. Shaw did not like to be boxed in musically and always wanted to test new and deeper waters. Again, it was Shaw who brought Baroque performance practices to the performance of Bach's choral music in America in late 1940s and 1950s. Virgil Thomson praised Shaw's use of 60 singers and 35 instruments for the *Mass in B Minor* (by today's standards, not so small) as the "returning of Bach to Bach." Thomson said Shaw allowed the proportions of the work to take on full majesty without any heaviness. In the 1990s, and his own 70s, freed of his ASO teaching and pastoral responsibilities as he saw them, Shaw began to think again of what small choirs could do and to again consider proportion in choral music.

Ironically, in his early days, Shaw was primarily associated with a small professional choir. In his guru years, he was thought the quintessential big choir guy. But now, with the Carnegie, France, and small Atlanta choirs, he was willing to limit size to sculpt the music back to its essentials. "Let's see the girders," he said.

His grounding in Bach gave Shaw a sense of skeleton, musculature, and proportion. And it's not coincidental that he returned to Bach when he returned to the small choir. Bach's impact on Shaw—on his sense of construction, and of choral phrasing, and most of all balance, was profound.

Just as he could make large choirs sound lean and precise (to a point), the characteristic warmth of the Shaw sound came through in his performances with small choirs. There is nothing tinny, dry, or "early" there. Indeed, this is a sound that some of today's purists might regard as too rich for the Baroque. Yet the sheer beauty and the driving pulse of Shaw's second recording of the *Mass in B Minor* or his first *Messiah* (both for RCA Victor) may outlast passing fashions. And the same thing might be said of his late life (1992) small choir performance of Schubert's songs for male chorus.

The ASO chorus really became the Collegiate Chorale of Shaw's later life—1967 to 1999. For it is fair to say that Shaw demanded religious commitment from these amateur singers. Like the Collegiate Chorale so many years before, and the Cleveland Orchestra Chorus later, a chorister had to "believe"—in the music, his vocational call to perform it to the best of his ability, the choir itself, and the sacredness of the whole endeavor. The small France and Atlanta groups of the late part of Shaw's life were the mature versions of the Robert Shaw Chorale.

Rather like a man who keeps a two-seater Porsche in his garage as well as a long Cadillac sedan, Shaw liked to have both instruments—the large choir and the small—available.

The small choir work that Shaw did with Telarc in his final decade was less commercial than much of his RCA output. In fact, much of his post-retirement programming and recording was of unabashedly and unapologetically "serious" music by composers like Bartók and John Adams.

It was very far from the commercial appeal of *Yours Is My Heart Alone* or the Robert Shaw Chorale men singing Mallotte's "The Lord's Prayer" with Perry Como. (Perhaps as a hedge, Telarc tended to market some of the recordings with titles that contained the word "spirit.") One producer said that Shaw was making records that no other American conductor, of any age, would dare to place before the public. But Shaw had at last, and very certainly, escaped glee club fare. No longer did anyone go to a Shaw concert expecting to hear *Shenandoah*. No one blanched at being asked to listen to the *Cantata Profana* when they went to a Shaw concert. The Telarc-Shaw legacy is one of great intellectual integrity.

The further greatness of Telarc was that it not only encouraged Shaw to put his core repertoire on disk for posterity, but it also encouraged him to experiment with modern composers and to expand his personal repertoire, as he did in his very last recording—the Dvorák *Stabat Mater.* Shaw brought to it the poignancy of last gestures and accumulated wisdom. (Shaw had been studying various Stabat Maters for several years, at that point. He had been pouring over ancient texts and works on Marianology—an eye opener to a skeptical protestant humanist.) Shaw was moved by, and drawn to, the suffering in Dvorák's life, his yearning for consolation, and his drift toward mysticism. What others found to be excess in Dvorák's *Stabat Mater,* Shaw found to be reflective and meditative. "His wanderings are precious," said Shaw, as if to insist that a dark night of the soul cannot be rushed. Conducting the piece in his own twilight yet with renewed zest, Shaw seemed, said Bob Woods, to be unspooling the music, as if from Dvorák's suffering psyche. In the recording sessions, Shaw seemed passionately engaged and more physically energetic than in years. He also seemed to some to be letting go. Shaw's own frame of mind and soul when he made this record, and his fresh look at the work, evoke a sound never quite heard before in this piece—a palpable grief and prayer for light.

This final recording was also a big, ungainly piece, with a huge choir and a massive score that Shaw said employed and evoked many musical folk, as well as sacred, idioms.

As we have said, Robert Shaw could be seen as a folk musician working in the classical vein. For all his intellectualism about music, for all his hard-won technique, for all his assertions that the disciplines of music must be satisfied if there is to be any art, at bottom, a certain visceral and intuitive response was always at work in him. For Shaw, music came out of life and was about life and was essential to life—like greenery coming from the earth. Music was not abstraction, but toil and love. Just as he grew deep intellectual roots in Bach, Shaw had deep personal roots in American folk music: black music, American Protestant hymnody, and what he called Appalachian folk tunes.

His arrangements of American folk songs, done with Alice Parker in the 1950s and performed throughout the world by the Robert Shaw Chorale, made this noble music widely known and sung. With Parker, Shaw celebrated, elevated, and propagated the American folk legacy. The Shaw-Parker songbook became a core part of the choral music curriculum in elementary and high schools. This is one of the ways Shaw "taught America to sing." His first small choir spawned these arrangements and was fed by them. His late-life celebration of this folk legacy is *Amazing Grace*, released by Telarc in 1993. Thus, Shaw's last small choir returned to these songs. He did not actually change the old Shaw-Parker arrangements much, but he did seem to simplify them—to make them less adorned and showy than in the Chorale days. He also respected the distance between black music and white singers, as perhaps he had not fully done 40 years before. And he always tried to give Parker the bulk of the credit for the arrangements.

Shaw *was* a teacher, preacher, and pastor. He was instructing and giving workshops in choral methods long before he had mastered conducting, and in years when he was still doing his own self-designed graduate course in music. That's not because he was arrogant. It is because he could not help himself. It is one of the reasons he stayed on the road with the Chorale for so many years—the desire to teach. In a sense, his recording legacy is best seen as part of Shaw's teaching and preaching call. After all, Shaw had doubts about the ability of recordings to capture music. He had very deep reservations about the commercial aspects of making and selling records. And, finally, he doubted his own right to set down "groovin images" of masterpieces. Still, records *were* a way to "reach all those people."

CHAPTER 34

By His Work Shall We Know Him

In 1996, a critic for *The Wall Street Journal* wrote of Robert Shaw: "Only a handful of musicians in any era can really be claimed as the greatest in their field. Indeed, greatness as a concept has become so stale from overuse that it has become obsolete. Yet, who would deny that Shaw, now 80 years old, is the greatest chorusmaster of our time?"

But as we have seen, Shaw was actually *not* exactly a chorusmaster for most of his career. A chorusmaster prepares the chorus for others. Shaw did this in his very early years—for Fred Waring on radio and for Broadway shows. And in what one might call his later early years (after World War II), Shaw acted as chorusmaster for Toscanini and, occasionally, for a series of other great conductors of a magnitude equal or similar to that of Toscanini: Fritz Reiner, Renato Cellini, Leopold Stokowski, Charles Munch (once), Thomas Beecham (once), as well as, on one occasion, Igor Stravinsky, conducting his own work. Those occasions were by arrangement, and Shaw took these assignments very consciously, to learn at the feet of masters. This was his graduate education. But, as we have seen, even during Shaw's Toscanini period—from 1949 to 1954—indeed, even prior to his work with Toscanini, Shaw mostly prepared choruses for his own performances with his own orchestras. As we have also noted, Shaw was already making his own records of classical choral literature and oratorio by the time he began to work with Toscanini. He had recorded the Bach *Mass in B Minor* and the Brahms *German Requiem* in 1947. And in 1949, the year he acted as chorusmaster for Toscanini's recording of *Aida*, he made seven other recordings on his own for RCA, including the Poulenc *Mass in G* and the Bach *Jesu, Meine Freude*.

Later, he was a chorusmaster who worked as an orchestral conductor. After 1956, when he went to the Cleveland Orchestra, his job description and his time commitment were primarily orchestral.

So what was the art, or area, in which he was great? One might say, at being Robert Shaw—a thing he'd invented and a thing he found it difficult to be.

His specialty, as it were, was in the strange in-between of chorus and orchestra. The large-scale works for both (and soloists) were his meat. Whereas choral conductors often only prepare for the orchestral leader and seldom get to lead an orchestra, and orchestral conductors sometimes wander into the no-man's land of choral music accidentally and continue aimlessly, Shaw's true home was the meeting of the two forms. His last recording, for example, of the Dvorák is a tour de force in management of large choral and orchestral forces that seem, in the score, at times almost at war with each other.

Even from the formative days of the Collegiate Chorale, and the small chamber choirs he occasional plucked out of it, Shaw never confined himself to *a cappella* work. Indeed, as the years progressed, he spent only a small amount of time on strictly choral material. He loved the *a cappella* choral literature, built much of the early following of the Robert Shaw Chorale on it, and regretted that he had little time for it in the 1960s, 1970s, and 1980s when his main jobs were with symphony orchestras. But from the beginning, he was drawn to large-scale works involving instrumental *and* vocal forces. He wanted to do monumental works that said something and stood as literature as well as music.

Shaw was attracted to large statements—musical and poetical. And whether it was Verdi, Bach, Britten, or Dvorák, these required large forces, and the clashing and balancing of those forces. Managing both forces, together, was his special call. In Cleveland, he began to learn how chorus and orchestra could be "knit together" in his phrase. In Atlanta, he learned more.

Those who preceded him and succeeded him in Cleveland as director of choruses (Clayton Krehbiel, Margaret Hillis, and Robert Page) *were*, primarily, preparers and chorusmasters, getting an occasional chance to conduct the orchestra and chorus, but not many or regular chances. And none of the chorusmasters conducted purely orchestral programs on a regular basis. Shaw was lucky. He got an opportunity few choral conductors get. And he became more than a choral conductor because of the opportunity.

So if Shaw was not the "greatest chorusmaster" of our time, or any time, or indeed, primarily a chorusmaster, what was he?

Shaw would perhaps insist that, for his kind of music making—music which is both sung and played; music which is also literature—greatness has no more meaning than eye color. For him, the things that make it possible for music to happen (for "the dove to descend") are discipline and devotion: Work very hard at understanding and preparing the composition, and then "get out of the way"—let the musicians play and the music bloom.

And this brings us to a very Shavian issue: What are we trying to do, exactly, when we make music? Are we trying to play notes? Make "magic"? Entertain?

Shaw was different. He was not trying to perform or entertain. In his early days, he *was* trying for magic—a home run. But the mature Shaw was trying to initiate a sacrament—to invoke the creator and his creation, and by so doing perhaps also *the* Creator. It is possible that this is Shaw's lasting contribution—not choral techniques, or a choral sound, but a way to understand music. For Shaw, music is sacramental. A sacrament is defined as a rite "that confers sanctifying grace."

One may understand music as essentially a performance art. And Shaw spent his life as a performer. He knew the requirements. But Shaw imagined music as a calling down of the Divine. A rough analogy may be the difference between a Protestant minister and a Catholic priest. The minister preaches the word. He never ceases to be a fellow sinner or worshiper. Catholics believe that the priest, acting in his sacramental role, mediates between the worshipers and the worshiped—he has the duty to call God forth. His is not a personal power, but a sacramental one. So, too, the conductor. For Shaw, collaborative music making—not of one musician, but music making on its highest level and with pure intent—was grace: divinity working within and around us. It therefore required a solemnity about the musician's duty and a seriousness about musical story and practice that one finds, for example, in the life of Bach or Beethoven, but seldom—in sustained form—in modern professional musicians.

Perhaps more fitting than being the "greatest" anything, and more in keeping with Shaw's lifelong intention to be a complete man and artist, was what the pianist Lee Luvisi muttered almost to himself as he watched Shaw working with the National Symphony Orchestra in 1998, just a few weeks before Shaw's death: "What a *musician* that man is."

Almost to a person, other fine American musicians tend to use this word about Shaw—from Jeffrey Kahane, to Dawn Upshaw, to Ned Rorem. They speak of Shaw not as a chorusmaster or choral conductor; but as a great American musician. Period.[70]

And what do they mean by this, exactly? Partly they are speaking of instinct—for rhythm and for melody and for balance. But what fellow musicians saw and described in Shaw was also the totality of his giving. He gave his all to the music—everything he had and everything he was, holding nothing in reserve.

For Shaw, music was a life in vows. Shaw's searching, study, mania for excellence, his drive to improve what he'd done before, and his willingness to

70 Burris interviews.

do what he had never done before, all of his striving and suffering, suggest the idea of musicianship as a vocation. A musician has a solemn and sacred duty. It is a duty he must approach with great care, reverence, and humility. Shaw's faith was almost childlike, and utterly unlike the way most professionals approach music. That is part of what made his music making so powerful.

Consider a short Shaw catechism:

- Music must be broken down to its basic elements.
- Music must be studied and prepared before it is performed, that is, mastered technically before it can be thought of as music.
- No one is *entitled* to attempt to make music until technical competence and understanding are achieved.
- Music is built on small units and on even smaller details within those units.
- Music is punctuated by a series of metaphors, which attempt to divide time and fill space.
- Music can be taught, but cannot be led.
- Music is corrupted if it is done for anything but love. Money, ego, fame, even personal pleasure, can destroy music.
- Music is somehow a holy endeavor.
- Musicianship is a calling.

Some of these precepts are so simplistic as to be almost elementary school truisms. They are also *elemental*, fundamental, and almost impossible to achieve, which is why almost no one really attempts to make music according to these dictates, and why the attempt to make music by these dictates is unsettling and challenging and singular.

Many musicians will say that some of Shaw's vocational values are their own. But they do not actually attempt to live those values, as Shaw did.

Why should it matter? Why should music *not* be another business, another career—show biz, after all?

Can't the cool and clinical craftsman sufficiently avoid sloppy emotionalism, which ruins music? Why ask more? Why ask for an intellectual and spiritual ambition that can become vain or delusional? These are fair questions.

Shaw saw music the way a great poet sees poetry. It is first a craft, but ultimately, eventually, a way of hearing and being. All of Shaw's edicts and all of his metaphors lead to his ultimate formula:

G = L = M.

God is love. He is not *like* love. He *is* love. And music isn't like love. It *is* love.

So if G = L = M, then M = L = G.

CHAPTER 35

Enigma Variations

"Maestro"—the term embarrassed Robert Shaw. For much of his life, he asked that he not be addressed that way. He claimed the first person who did call him maestro, in direct conversation, was Toscanini—the only man Shaw thought truly worthy of the title.

Think of Casals, Rudolf Serkin, or Toscanini. Shaw's own idols had priestly qualities (when making music). True "mastery" in a musician is a mixture of technical mastery, a physical presence that attracts and commands, and inspiration—inspiration as to the composer, the composition, and the moment of performance. There are different mixtures of these qualities, in different percentages and manifestations, but these are the obvious qualities of mastery in musical art. It is almost impossible to explain or dissect them. But it is not hard to see them.

When Shaw met his first great mentor, Julius Herford, in 1944, he said, "I want to begin at the beginning and learn everything." He never lost that drive, inquisitiveness, or sense of his own ignorance and insignificance. He always saw himself as a student. He always felt keenly his own lack. Thirty years after meeting Herford, Shaw asked pianist Peter Serkin, the son of his old friend and colleague Rudolf Serkin, and a man roughly the age of Shaw's older sons, if he (Shaw) could study with *him*. Shaw was always playing "catch-up." "I'll never be worthy," might be neurosis. It might, simultaneously, be wisdom.

Shaw's aura of command, by the end of his career, issued in part from his technical innovations, in part from sheer time spent with various pieces, and in part from performing experience. Moreover, he had the bearing of a leader, even in youth. But in his case, orchestral musicians (who are famously jaded and often looking for reasons to be dismissive of a conductor) listened. They listened because they were moved by his desire to serve the music and by his obviously genuine conviction that it was so much bigger than he was. To them, some of them anyway, this was the essence of a maestro.

Not all masters of music, or any other art, are great human beings or great humanists. One thinks of Picasso, Sinatra, and Karajan: great artists all but not great human beings. For Shaw, however, art had to be a form of humanism, just as religion and spirituality had to be a form of humanism. He really did not believe that a bad man could make good Mozart. That is one reason he worked so hard to become a better man.

He also believed that great art could not fail to change receptive human hearts.

Is this true? It is what Shaw bet his life on.

Shaw's father told Buzz Price, "You have to want to join." Robert Shaw was absolutely certain that if a human heart was open, a Mozart or a Bach could bring a person to higher ground.

And because he staked his life on this proposition, Shaw dignified the music he played. He never trivialized it. He brought profound respect to masterworks such as the Haydn *Die Schöpfung*, and curiosity and affection to lesser works, like the Dvorák *Stabat Mater.* His commitment was the essence of Shaw's ability to fire the imaginations of musicians and audiences. To get singers to perform above their game, to get professional musicians to play like eager children, to get audiences to listen intently, to help everyone find "it" in performance, Shaw had to elicit participation in his own fundamental seriousness about music—his piety about musical creation and re-creation.

Like other remarkable American musicians—"Lenny," Paul Robeson, and Marian Anderson come to mind—Shaw had an innate ability to communicate the music—to connect. And he wanted others to experience music as he had—as food for the soul.

Shaw believed it was his responsibility to help Every Man and Every Woman discover his church of music—if they were willing. (And never by dumbing down; if anything, he taught up.) Second, he believed it was up to him to challenge the professional to rediscover his love of music. The message was: Bach is here (or Mozart or Stravinsky), let's listen. And if we are not hearing it for the first time, what will it take to hear it *as if* for the first time?

Shaw drew musicians and audiences to himself precisely because music making wasn't for him—for his glorification, or even his delight. Being led by the mature Shaw was like being led through Greek or Roman ruins by a wise old guide. He was showing you what was really there, something you might not otherwise see. One player in the Orchestra of St. Luke's in New York City said, "Every time he conducted us . . . was as if he was unraveling the music before us."[71]

Shaw, writing about George Szell, said, "He was an enigma. Even to himself."

Shaw was an enigma to others.

He was an irreducible and irresolvable mix of soft and rough; confident and self-doubting; driving and humble; monk and icon.

But he was none of this to himself. To himself he was a craftsman, maybe just a workman, a handyman, and a rather inadequate one. Shaw did not much share the twentieth-century fascination with the self. And unlike many a musician, probably Szell included, Shaw did not find himself particularly interesting.

What Shaw found interesting was distinctive musical language and structure, rhythm, melody, theology, the religions of the East, some great leaders of history and their oratory (Jesus and Lincoln), sports and, once he discovered fatherhood with his second family, his family. Those things were interesting. The self was not.

71 It is astonishing how often this description, or something very much like it, is used by disparate musicians to describe Shaw's conducting.

Shaw was raised by people who believed in something, and because of that belief, they had a mission—something to say, work to do. What Shaw believed was different from what his parents believed. But belief is what drove and sustained him, just as it had driven and sustained them.

Music was not Shaw's profession, but his calling. More, it was not just a religion substitute, psychologically—something to throw himself into and fill himself up with. For Shaw, music *was* faith. He felt divine presence at the moment he stepped aside in a performance and the music exerted "its own grace."

Thus, the enigma that interested Shaw was not himself but the finally inexplicable mystery of great art and how to make it.

Music was his temple. The great compositions, the scores, his scripture. The musicians his parishioners. And all listeners were potential converts. Fame was merely a pulpit.

Performances were sacraments; holy reenactments—like the Mass. One sees this in film of him conducting the Beethoven *Ninth Symphony*—not only a mastery of the orchestra (which he had striven so long to achieve) and not only mastery of the score (to which physical reality he is not, at last, tethered), but his intensity, visceral strength, and sheer childlike joy in the music. There he is, unfolding the music again, seemingly not conducting it, but discovering it—as if all his editing and rigorous rehearsal procedures were only preparations for opening the great book of life for the first time.

Shaw made music with religious devotion, with self-sacrificing, self-critical, and sometimes self-immolating passion, with propulsive drive, and with the unwavering conviction that great music changes souls.

But is it true?

Does great music change souls?

There is, of course, the classic rebuttal: Hitler loved Wagner. And Beethoven and Mozart allegedly brought Eichmann and other Nazis to tears. The pianist Jeffrey Kahane, speaking of Shaw, said that he believed Shaw's answer would be, "So what?" Obviously, the music did not change them because their hearts were not open and receptive. They consumed; they did not believe and partake. They did not wish to join. Though they'd heard Mozart, they'd never really heard Mozart's music.

It's not that music always *does* change the human heart, but that it *can.* Music has the power to change us, if properly communicated and if properly received, and if we desire to be transformed.[72]

Again, this is rather like standard Christian dogma. We are saved by Grace, freely offered, if we accept it. For Shaw, music offers its power to change, and one may accept or reject it.

Shaw's wager is a wager. One may doubt that art can "save" a culture, or even a single human soul, and still admire the belief, and the believer.

But there is *no question* that music changed Shaw. He was his own controlled experiment. In many years of living, he found further evidence that music could heal and save.

Coming out of a Shaw performance of the Verdi *Requiem*, one young woman said to her companion, "I just want to say, '*Help us*,'" and she began to weep. Shaw would have been moved by this. He would have felt he communicated Verdi's piece to that person—not an audience member, or a consumer of live music but, for Shaw, another yearning soul he urgently needed to reach.

A critic, in the 1950s, once complained that Shaw had made the Bach *St. John Passion* both "American" and "evangelical." Shaw wore that review (though he claimed to never read reviews) like a badge of honor. Bach had intended universality, Shaw said, and he had intended to evangelize.

Shaw despised any attempt to appropriate a composer on behalf of a message, a fad, an era, or a denomination. He warned that any attempt "to impose one's own religiosity on Bach would blind one to *Bach's* religiosity." But he did want to convey Bach's message, if he could. Shaw had no doubt that the composers he loved intended to change, and in some way save,

72 Burris-Kahane interview.

souls—not necessarily in the way that Jerry Falwell, or even Shaw's father, or the Pope does. But in the sense that the composer's music puts the individual in touch with the ground of his own being.

Shaw liked to tell singers playing the Evangelist in the Bach *St. Matthew Passion* about Mack Harrell. Harrell, Shaw said, never tried to play a part or to be an actor. Sing it, Shaw would say, as if you are reading the lesson in church on Sunday. That's what Mack Harrell did. But to one prospective singer, Shaw went even further. It should be sung, he said, as if everyone in the audience knows this piece of scripture and we are all singing it together, "but silently."

Shaw saw his own work as custodial. Clean up the score. Get the musicians ready. Maybe the dove will descend. Yet soprano Sylvia McNair once said: "Mr. Shaw is far and away the most spiritual conductor I've ever worked with. His spirituality is cosmic. It is enormous. You have to believe the words."

Shaw was never far, for all his rebellion and occasional disgust, from that "long line of preachers," and he drew the line himself, innumerable times, from their faith to his own. He said he found faith in established Christian religions unsustainable—"You have to check your mind at the door." He said he thought the Christian church had been corrupted. He thought even less of politics. But there was a faith he could sustain. For him, the arts were the last sacred thing; and to him, music was the most sacred, most mystical, and most communicative art form. And choral music was the most purely communal form of music other than, perhaps, the string quartet.

Shaw knew that he'd plugged music into the place in his heart where his parents kept Jesus. It was no revelation to him that he approached music with the same fervor that his father and maternal grandfather brought to the Christian church. It is no news to those who knew him that Shaw found in music not only mystic sustenance but also a means of conversion.

Shaw's inherited evangelical religiosity gave him fervor—the fervor he brought to the music and the fervor that produced almost every other quality he brought to the music—ardor, urgency, and transparency.

What did he say about the popular music he forsook? "It didn't feed you back." Great music fed him, and he wanted others to be fed by it.

A major epiphany for Shaw was the concluding concert of the Mozart *Requiem* tour with the Robert Shaw Chorale at Symphony Hall in Boston, in 1950. We have already noted its effect on the other musicians. But what about Shaw? When, at the 63rd performance, he found that he was still learning from the piece, still discovering it, and that it was more deeply informing his heart, Shaw felt that, yes, this was the music he'd been seeking for so long.

PART FIVE

TOWARD PURITY

These hands make no sounds.

—Robert Shaw

CHAPTER 36

SAGE

Judith Arron was one of those amazing artistic collaborators who blessed Shaw's life. It was she who brought Shaw back to New York and made Carnegie Hall his platform, via his Carnegie Hall workshops and concerts, and the "Preparing a Masterpiece" films that she commissioned to be made of the workshops. It was she who was constantly pushing Shaw to program more concerts in New York.

Thanks to Arron, Shaw became a New York icon in the last decade of his life. He caught the attention of the New York concert-going public and the press, as there was no dominant maestro, Leonard Bernstein having passed in 1990. New York needed a musical guru, and Shaw filled the need. It was Arron who made it possible for Robert Shaw to do the programs he really wanted to do and in the way he wanted to do them. Above all, she wanted him to pass on his not-so-secret secrets in a venue where he would be seen and heard. Arron believed Shaw was such a unique and important artist that once New Yorkers saw what he did, they would become ardent fans. She was right, as it happened.

Shaw might have shunned this kind of attention a few years earlier. Indeed, he had received it once and renounced it. He'd left New York and mostly avoided the big stage and the mainstream when he could. He preferred to work away from the brightest lights, whether in Atlanta or France. Only in his last decade did he find those lights tolerable, and even, at times, agreeable. This may have been because this late-life fame allowed him certain artistic possibilities. It was a matter of relaxing into himself and his art after so many years of struggle. But certainly, it was also a matter of his trust in Arron.

Judith Arron was a perfectionist like him; an idealist like him; a workaholic like him; a person who loved music and the arts more than her own success or reputation, or even health. She was not in arts management for the cocktail parties, but because she cared about music. She was also gentle and compassionate—the kind of woman who could give Shaw the comfort and support he needed. She felt her friend Robert was a restless but big-hearted soul who would give all he had to the project at hand. Shaw felt the same way about her.

Arron seemed to understand what Shaw was seeking at this stage of his life. He had attained a degree of mastery in music, a degree still insufficient by his lights, but even Shaw had to acknowledge that he wasn't bumping into the furniture on stage and that his hands did not shake when conducting anymore. He'd found some peace and order in his life. He'd been famous, a recording star, a failure in his own mind, a re-maker of a discipline, a builder of an orchestra. Now he was being offered Carnegie Hall as a national classroom. He could impart what he had learned about music on a national stage. Why not? He had nothing to lose and nothing to prove.

But he was still looking for something. What? Shaw felt an increasing devotion to the composers. He felt a greater need than ever to study. He felt a greater desire than ever to get certain pieces right, or as right as he could get them, at last. He also wanted to do pieces he'd not done. He felt a greater indifference than ever to the audience. In that last decade or so of his life, he was looking for a kind of purity.

After watching him work in France, Arron became convinced that Shaw was one of the world's pre-eminent musicians—a one-of-a-kind original—

and she was determined to share that knowledge with the world. She wanted very much to preserve and pass along Shaw's methods, but also to preserve something of his persona and spirit. So she insisted that each year of the Carnegie workshop be filmed and that the documentaries of Shaw's preparation be sold and widely distributed. Sadly, none of the films contain a full and final concert performance.

The France and Carnegie projects, and the choirs Shaw created for both, were the capstone of Shaw's career. Not only did they bring him great visibility and honor, and allow him to teach at the highest level, but they also made it possible for Shaw to do his very best work at the end of his life.

This is what Bernard Holland wrote in *The New York Times* on November 20, 1990—the beginning, really, of Shaw's Carnegie Hall years with the choral workshops, the Orchestra of St. Luke's, and Judy Arron:

> *Seldom does Carnegie Hall offer a musical event in the form of a final exam, but Sunday afternoon's performance of* A German Requiem *by Brahms was roughly that: the proof of what a gathering of choral directors, orchestra conductors, music administrators, and singers had learned under Robert Shaw during five days of seminars and rehearsals.*
>
> *The afternoon was much more; indeed, one of the more powerful communications between musician and listener that this reviewer has experienced in the past 10 years. That Sunday's audience stood for over five minutes at the end, that the Orchestra of St. Luke's applauded Mr. Shaw's efforts for the same amount of time, went beyond concert decorum. It was a special few hours.*
>
> *Choral conducting, of course, is at the center of Mr. Shaw's career, although he retired only recently as music director of the Atlanta Symphony. This presumably has given him more time for the choral institute he runs in southwestern France. Forty-eight of Sunday's 150 singers were from this Robert Shaw Institute of Music.*

One could infer some of the things that had passed between him and his students at Carnegie Hall last week. Among them, assuredly, was this: that the sincerest Passions don't do much good without the thoughtful application of detail.

First impressions were of deep, round choral tone, in which, however, the listener heard everything.

Gradually one heard why: precise placement of accents; smaller swells of loud and soft within bigger ones. Mr. Shaw's singers were obviously hungry for this music. He made sure, however, that each flavor was tasted. Fascination for detail includes the deep danger of getting lost in it. Mr. Shaw doesn't.

We know that sometimes Shaw *did* get lost in the detail. So why didn't he at this stage of his life? When he did succeed, how did he find the balance between what he called "art" and "science"?

Shaw had his bag of "tricks" (his word) from count singing, to circles, to quartets, to marching, to clapping, to singing text on four monotones—all dependent on the music, choir, space, and performance or performer problems at hand. Quiet singing seems like very simple notion, but it is not often employed. Shaw began rehearsals with very quiet singing and often kept it quiet for a long, seemingly abnormal time. Part of the idea was to "save vocal gold," or as he put it, negatively, to not "strip vocal gears." But it was also to facilitate the choir in really listening to the piece, not just the notes for each singer on each part, but the architecture of the piece.

Shaw tended to think of the count singing as the most important trick of his trade because there was no instance in which it did not helpsynchronicity, and to clean and clarify. Count singing helped with more than one problem—time, rhythm, intonation, and full values for all of the notes.

But his best and biggest trick may have been something that was no trick at all, and that was the way Shaw held his singers back—seldom letting them sing in full voice until the performance, or very near it. This created a tremendous buildup, anticipation and, eventually, release. Shaw did not really allow the choir, or himself, to let go until the moment of performance. No spontaneity, or loss of discipline, until then. Then the dam could break.

If Shaw had adequate rehearsal time—he didn't always if he was guest conducting—the musicians (particularly choristers) had all been through a layered process of gradually mastering each element of the music. The singers had also been returned to basic disciplines, like count singing, in final rehearsals to create, and lock in, a common pulse. This created a sort of mantra effect, which was calming and confidence boosting. With each musical layer, Shaw would add just a little more Shavian philosophy or confession. But each layer was added only after the previous one was mastered. Again, this instilled calm and assurance and "unanimity of psyche" (his phrase).

An analogy for Shaw's pedagogy—coaching, really—might be a track coach who re-teaches a runner how to walk, stretch, and sprint before every race. And, indeed, many great coaches, from John Wooden to Bill Belichick, do engage in this sort of breaking down of the basic elements of play and review of fundamentals. (Wooden famously would spend the first practice on how to properly put on a sock and tie a shoe.) But Shaw, in his mature years, was aware that he could go too deeply into rote detail and kill emotion with technique. He knew there was risk in his method. So he tried with each choir and performance to calibrate. It was important, he said, to keep the game interesting and not schoolmasterish. But this "holding back" of full musical force and emotion was less a trick than intuition behind the tricks—as if to say, we don't get the pot of gold until we have made the whole journey.

An example: Shaw loved Stravinsky's *Symphony of Psalms*. He knew it very well, having prepared it many times and once prepared the chorus for a performance by the composer himself. He considered it the greatest of all twentieth-century choral symphonic works. He recorded it twice. Yet when he prepared, he did so very dryly, technically, and attending to the most basic elemental matters. It was as if he were preparing a high school orchestra and chorus, said one disgusted player. Shaw would spend much of his preparation time focusing on rhythmic qualities—and therefore on counting. His approach would be highly mechanistic, and he would address the humanity and poetry of the piece only near the end of preparation, and only briefly and obliquely.

Get all the pieces in place and the emotion will take care of itself—that was the theory. The music will emerge from structure.

The theory works better, perhaps, with Stravinsky than Berlioz. Shaw thought so, too. That is why he reserved the right to adjust even his own methods to circumstance. Whereas he feared excessive emotionalism might destroy some pieces and generally thought music benefited from a cool, analytical foundation, he felt the Hindemith *Lilacs* was so intellectual, and so intentionally wary of cheap emotionality, that it needed a more passionate approach. And so, in rehearsing this piece, Shaw was more the poet and preacher from day one. Ditto, the Britten *War Requiem*. He would read and discuss the poetry of the text from the first day of rehearsals. In both pieces the texts are paramount, and highly emotional, but lest the composer's artifice obscure them, Shaw adopted a warming approach. Of course, Shaw himself was highly emotional about these two works. But he loved the *Symphony of Psalms* no less.

There is no doubt that, as Robert Woods said, a conductor gets better at his craft after doing it for decades. He develops a second sight. Taste and a sense of direction in music come from experience, not genes. In time, Shaw learned, as he put it, "what is necessary at that moment."

One choral conductor who sang with Shaw tells of a rehearsal that was growing tense because Shaw was not getting what he wanted. Many feared a rage was forthcoming. Before beginning a passage for the umpteenth time, Shaw closed his eyes and clenched his teeth: "Now . . . don't take off like a scalded dog," which the chorister thought was one of the funniest things he'd ever heard, at least in a Classical music setting. The tension was defused and the rehearsal came back together. At that point in his life, Shaw knew that humor and not anger would soothe raw nerves.

Another chorister tells of Shaw at work on the Stravinsky piece. It had been a day of many starts and stops, and many four-letter words. Everyone was tired, hot, and drained, including the conductor, and the task before the group was that final, slow movement of the *Symphony of Psalms*. Shaw stopped the rehearsal at this near breaking point, only briefly, and said, with eyes shut and sweat pouring down his forehead, "People, this is a glimpse of immortality." And then a pause of four to six beats. And then the punch line: "Let's see if we can sing it."

Under such circumstances, musicians, like players on a battered high school football team intensely loyal to their harsh but beloved coach, were willing to reach deeper and go the extra mile for Shaw.

One singer put it his way: "He just manipulated the hell out of you. But since he was right there with you, and since he demanded more of himself than anyone, and since he was hypnotizing himself, too, you let him hypnotize you."

In this last decade of his life, three things were happening, and they were converging. First, Shaw was finding that he was surprisingly free of insecurities and worries; second, he was mellowing (thanks to Caroline); and third, musicians, the music business, and the music press had come to recognize him as a sage. To his further astonishment, he liked the role. He told one interviewer that he had surprised himself with his lack of nerves and stage fright on some recent occasions. "If we lick the fundamentals," he said, "we can relax."

CHAPTER 37

Channeling the Masters

In this last decade of life—his 70s and the nation's 90s—Shaw began to delve more deeply into the composers he most loved. His days as missionary and administrator in Atlanta were behind him. He was, more than ever, the musical scholar and monk of his own design. This tendency became acute after the death of Caroline Shaw. Basically, after Mrs. Shaw's death, Robert wanted to be in his den studying if he was not rehearsing or performing. He came out to watch "The News Hour" on PBS, the ritual by which he ended the day when he was at home. And on weekends he emerged to watch sports and curse the televangelists. But he'd become hermit-like.

What was he *doing* down there in his study all day? There weren't many new scores to learn by that time in his life and even he could only come up with so many new edits for pieces he'd done multiple times.

For the first time in his life, Shaw was not playing so much "catch-up," he was not behind the curve. He was sometimes now studying works he was *not* preparing for performance—like the Bach Passions.

Or he was working on his English translation of the Brahms *Requiem.*

Shaw was entering into his own personal, autumnal dialogue with the masters.

As we have seen, several important composers were, more or less, contemporaries and friends. Shaw met Ives and knew Hindemith, Poulenc, and Rorem well. He was a close friend and, in the early days, a protégé of William Schuman. Lukas Foss was a good close friend and collaborator in the early years. Shaw was among the first to champion composers such as Stephen Paulus and Alvin Singleton. The prelude to John Harbison's opera, *The Great Gatsby*, was a piece commissioned by Shaw for the Atlanta Symphony: *Remembering Gatsby*.

We know he loved Ives's work and was a tireless advocate for it. He was a great booster of Poulenc, as well. Shaw was fascinated, some have said beyond musical justice, by Poulenc's mystical experience: his desire to transform himself from entertainer to mystic and his re-conversion to Catholicism. Perhaps more than any other musician, Shaw was responsible for bringing Poulenc's music to America. Shaw also admired Bartók greatly. He introduced Bartók's *Cantata Profana* to the United States, and some Bartók scholars say Shaw's recording of the piece, late in Shaw's life, and roughly four decades after premiering it, is an important musical milestone. Of course, Hindemith and Stravinsky formed a part of Shaw's musical pantheon. Shaw believed the *Symphony of Psalms* to be the greatest of all modern compositions. And he often said that Paul Hindemith was the greatest overall musical mind of his time.

Shaw was devoted to the work of these men. He would seem, in some ways, a quintessential modernist. Certainly, Hindemith's whole conception of music was very close to Shaw's own.

Yet, as we have noted, Shaw's deepest affections, sympathies, and abiding devotions were for the monumental eighteenth- and nineteenth-century masterworks for symphony and chorus: the Beethoven *Missa Solemnis*, the Mozart *Requiem*, the Brahms *A German Requiem*, the Verdi *Requiem*, the Berlioz *Requiem*, Haydn's *The Creation*, the Mendelssohn *Elijah*, and their Baroque precursors—the mighty Bach *B Minor Mass*, the Bach Passions, and Handel's *Messiah*. The other two works at the center of Shaw's canon hearken back to the eighteenth and nineteenth centuries: the *War Requiem* by Benjamin Britten, which borrows from the Verdi and Berlioz Requiems, and *When lilacs last in the dooryard bloom'd*, by Hindemith, which Shaw commissioned. The latter work might have been constructed by Brahms had he lived in the twentieth century (or so Shaw believed), though perhaps with more choral beauty. But this is the point: This work, like the *War Requiem*, is a throwback to the humanistic reinvention of the oratorio—the grand Classical and Enlightenment statements about life, brotherhood, God, and war. In the theology of nineteenth-century music, as Shaw liked to say, God was recreated in man's image. Britten was not the first to redefine sacred music. He was a throwback to Beethoven and Brahms. Shaw was a throwback, too, not a modern man at all really. He lived, theologically, and idealistically, very much in a world somewhere between Beethoven and Brahms. God is not dead in this world. Nor is God sleeping. But the seekers are attempting to write a new language for their prayers.

Shaw was a true friend of modern music. But his heart was with the masters 200 years dead. His roots were in Haydn and Mozart and Bach, from his early study with Julius Herford. The musical language and ideas of the nineteenth century and the oratorio formed his intellectual imagination. The creators of this epoch spoke to him and would likely have drawn him in, even if he had never met Herford.

So Shaw stood upon a platform—his core repertoire—while, in the course of his career, simultaneously performing hundreds of purely orchestral programs and scores of modern works, as well as Christmas programs and recordings, folk material, and spirituals, and even, in the early days in New York and the early days in Atlanta, pops and Broadway material.

But he returned to these core works again and again, hoping to perfect them. They were pieces people wanted to hear Shaw perform. And they were works that he had a unique opportunity to hone. Because Shaw lived so long, specialized even while doing orchestral programs, and toured most of these major choral-orchestral works, he had an opportunity, which no other conductor has ever really had.

Recall Ann Howard Jones's suggestion that Shaw may have conducted the Mozart *Requiem* more times than any conductor in musical history. He performed it in Boston with the Robert Shaw Chorale in 1951, for example (the performance at the end of the RSC tour during which the musicians wept at the conclusion of the piece), and he was slated to do so at Boston University in the winter of 1999. (Shaw died a week before the performance.) Shaw took the Mozart *Requiem* on tour with the Robert Shaw Chorale and Orchestra three times, conducting it 63, 65, and 27 times, on those tours—hence, 155 performances with the Chorale. He conducted it another 30 times with Cleveland, the ASO, and other professional, academic, and workshop orchestras. He conducted the piece in its entirety with the Springfield Symphony in 1945, which may have been the first time he did it professionally. Shaw knew this piece as an extension of himself—like a lifelong Henry James scholar would know James; or a preacher would know the letters of St. Paul. He knew the piece as only one who has lived with, struggled to realize, and pondered such a work for half a century could.

Consider Hindemith's *Lilacs*. Shaw did it more than any conductor had the desire or chance to do it. He probably did most of the piece's major performances in the United States in his lifetime. As we have noted, this is probably true of the Bach *B Minor Mass* and the Bach Passions as well. Shaw gave 37 performances of the *B Minor Mass* on tour in the states and approximately the same number on the two overseas tours. Again, no one else in music has ever had the opportunity to do the work as often. Shaw's mastery of this piece, according to the eminent conductor and musicologist Alfred Mann, and his bringing of it to America on a Bachian scale, via tours and at least two of his three recordings, was perhaps Robert Shaw's greatest accomplishment. Shaw's 1960 recording of the piece, with the Robert Shaw Chorale, has been re-issued and re-discovered. It is amazingly attuned to contemporary conceptions of the vocal scale of the Mass. In Mann's view, the sheer beauty of the recording has yet to be surpassed.[73]

---

73 Burris-Mann interview.

Dr. John Silber, of Boston University, told of the excitement on college campuses when Shaw released his first recording of the Mass—how students would gather around and play it for hours upon hours in near silence.[74] William F. Buckley said he was eternally grateful to Shaw for that recording. At the time it was released, said Buckley, "I was transfixed."[75] Critic Michael Steinberg said that he "had never really heard Bach" as a young man until Shaw's performances of the Mass in the 1950s. "We only knew the freight train Bach—heavy, slow, weighed down by large, gelatinous choirs."[76]

Anticipating the early music movement by two generations, Shaw performed the Mass with Baroque lightness, grace, and motion. He used four to eight voices on a part, depending on the size of the hall, and he used concertists (one voice or a small group of voices on a part) when Shaw felt Bach's score called for instrumental vocal precision. This was revolutionary at the time.

Shaw gave the same treatment—de-Victorianizing and re-Baroque-ifying with smaller, lighter choirs and leaner, quicker orchestras—to Handel. He wasn't being particularly scholarly, or even a purist. He wasn't trying for something "new" (albeit "old"). He simply wanted people to *hear* Handel. Getting back to Handel's line and scale was the best way to do this. Again, Shaw was not interested in musical ideology so much as pragmatics. Handel's *Messiah* is another piece Shaw toured *and* performed virtually every year for 45 years. So again, Shaw had a singular opportunity to do the piece scores of times (over 80 by this author's count). Some years ago, in a *New York Times* report, Shaw's *Messiah* recording was listed as No. 1 for overall impact and influence on later performances and recordings.

Shaw's recordings of Baroque music, and there were not enough of them, are now considered "old-fashioned." His approach—stripping away the glue and varnish, yet still cultivating beauty—produced recordings still valid and unique. Shaw's 1988 recording of the Vivaldi *Gloria* and the Bach *Magnificat* is not "new" or "modern" in the sense of "period" approach,

74 Burris-Silber interview.
75 Burris-Buckley correspondence.
76 Burris-Steinberg interview.

nor is it "ancient." However, it is a pulsating, crackling recording and true to the two composers. Certainly, the period influence has been so profound that much of what has been recorded in the many years since Shaw made this recording is lighter, faster, and done with smaller forces. But might there be a difference between honoring a period and honoring compositional spirit and intent? There is something to be said for beauty. Shaw's 1960 recording of the Bach Mass, for example, is not "period," but it is surely "Baroque" and a recording of great beauty. It is both light and sacred—surely Bach's hope.[77]

Shaw obviously also returned to the Brahms *German Requiem* many times over many years. He made the first American recording in 1947, as noted, and recorded it again in 1983. He staged historic performances in Carnegie Hall in 1991 and 1997. I have mentioned the Atlanta and Cleveland performances, which resulted in live recordings of his later-life takes on the piece. Here we get not so much the propulsive Shaw but the very reflective Shaw—he tended to slow down the piece more and more. Shaw did not see this piece as propulsive and light, but very grave, very solemn, and in some spots very grand indeed—engulfing the grief-stricken with compassion. How much could he slow it, he wondered, and keep it musical?

Shaw's final performances of the Brahms *German Requiem*, the Bach *Mass in B Minor*, the Beethoven *Symphony No. 9*, and the *Messiah* (Part 1) in the last months of his life were really a unique culmination of six decades of study, struggle, searching, and repetition.

There can be no doubt that the two pieces Shaw studied and contemplated the most in the later part of his life were the Bach *Mass in B Minor* and the

77 According to conductor Vance George, longtime chorusmaster for the San Francisco Symphony Orchestra, Shaw was driven to distraction by the orchestra's inability to make the sounds of Bach. Shaw enjoyed a long and fruitful relationship with that orchestra and had conducted a shattering and much-praised Brahms *Requiem* there in 1983. But when, in 1992, he conducted a *B Minor Mass* in San Francisco, he was beside himself with his own, and the players', inability to transform the orchestra into something resembling a Baroque instrument.

St. Matthew Passion. In some way, these stood outside of the rest of music for him. Near the end of his life, he called the Mass the ultimate metaphor of the human struggle. He called the *Passion* "my current obsession," and on several occasions, "the greatest work of art and worship in Western civilization."

As we know, Shaw's own true musical education, not in conducting, but in musical construction and composition—in the late 1940s and early 1950s—was based upon study, rehearsal, and performance of Bach. His cell-by-cell and layer-by-layer approach to both music scholarship and performance preparation was deeply influenced by his early Bach study with Julius Herford.

Just as he returned to the small chorus in his last years, he returned to the study of Bach in those years. In the last months of his life, Shaw was again conducting "the three Bs" in their great signature choral works—the Beethoven *Missa* and *Ninth*; the Brahms *German Requiem,* which Shaw was lovingly translating into English; and the Bach *Mass in B Minor* and *Magnificat.* He was thinking a great deal about each composer, delving into his life and works. He spent a great deal of time on the Brahms project—mostly trying to get syllabic compatibility with Brahms's notation and finding it frustrating. Shaw's study process was always analytical, but now it was, increasingly, ruminative. When preparing a performance, he lived with the composer and little else. He thought about little else. He wished to talk about little else. Sometimes he came to dinner and barely spoke. He might read some scholarship or a new biography of the composer. He would eventually listen to some recordings. But mostly he kept taking the piece apart—layer by layer, phrase by phrase, cell by cell—at his desk or piano in his downstairs study, armed with only colored pencils, experience, and new hunger. Shaw pursued the composer whose work he was studying like an obsessed lover. And in the case of these particular composers and these particular works, he had engaged in this pursuit many times over many years.

Shaw knew, as Brahms did, the Biblical passages that formed the text of *A German Requiem* by heart. He had learned them in his childhood. He loved Brahms's application and editing of those texts. And by now he knew the language, the colors, of Brahms intimately. We have previously noted that Shaw frequently conducted the Brahms symphonies and the piano concertos, the latter having been his finest non-choral recordings. These engagements deepened Shaw's understanding of the consistent textures in Brahms's music, and the context and foundation of his choral/symphonic masterpiece, just as Shaw hoped they would. To many musicians, Shaw was a born Brahmsian. There was some sort of primordial connection between this composer and this conductor. The rich, romantic, golden tones of Brahms were just up Shaw's alley. Brahms's romanticism layered upon Baroque structures made intuitive sense to Shaw and fit like a glove his own inclinations. Shaw was a kind of "romantic rationalist," to use Iris Murdoch's label for Sartre. Perhaps Brahms was a rational romantic. (So, too, Hindemith, who spoke to Shaw in a similar way.) The Brahmsian sense of grandeur, mixed with a certain earthiness and a somehow unexpected sense of delicacy and intimacy, spoke to Shaw—heart to heart. (The *First* and *Fourth Symphonies* are grandeur manifest.) And what Shaw called Brahms's "depressive" choral works—*Nänie*, *Gesang der Parzen*, and the *Alto Rhapsody*—were perfectly formed miniature Brahmsian dramas. Brahms's sighing melancholy in the face of human loss, longing, and aging were "hard to beat," Shaw said, as poetry for the seasoned soul. Indeed, these pieces seem almost written for Shaw to conduct, just as he seemed to have lived his entire life so that he could conduct the *German Requiem* for the last time, in the last year of his life, in Atlanta and New York. Shaw brought and gave all of himself to those performances. It seems fitting that his work on an English version of the Brahms *Requiem* was the last active musical effort of his life—his open score and worksheets for the translation were found in his study after his death.

The Brahms temper and the Shavian one seemed almost uniquely matched. The Brahms sound, which Shaw once described as chocolate syrup coming from a soda fountain until it covers the floor (Shaw had briefly been a soda jerk in California), and which Grieg described as "a landscape torn by mists and clouds," was one Shaw could taste with his fingers.

But some who made music with him will tell you that it was Beethoven who was closest to Shaw's nature. Shaw loved the protean and heroic qualities of the composer. He loved Beethoven shaking his fist at his fellow men, at religion, and indeed, at times, at God himself. Here, again, there was a long and rich relationship. Shaw's orchestral debut, without chorus, was Beethoven's *First Symphony.* And Shaw's NBC symphony debut was Beethoven's *Second Symphony.* Of all the pieces he conducted, the one he wrote the most words about was the *Missa Solemnis.* Shaw was drawn to the monumental intellectual and spiritual ambition, and struggle, in Beethoven's work. Some Atlantans remember particularly memorable performances of the odd-numbered Beethoven symphonies. One singer even accused Shaw of "Beethoven-izing" Haydn's *Creation.*

The Beethoven *Missa Solemnis* was constantly on Shaw's mind, of course. And again, he performed it probably more than any conductor of his, or any other, age. He did it in New York and San Diego in the early days. He did it twice in Cleveland, when he was with that orchestra, and every third or fourth year during his tenure in Atlanta. And there were multiple performances most of the times he did it. He performed the work several times in his later years when he returned to the guest conductor circuit. He did it whenever he could at festivals, music schools, and universities. So, Shaw probably performed the piece 50 to 60 times. Most conductors get a chance to do it once, maybe twice, in a lifetime. Shaw was fond of saying, "the un-performable nature of the work is what it's about."

The *Ninth Symphony* was Shaw's first concert as music director with the ASO and his last. He ended almost every season with it. Late in his life, he performed it with the Cleveland Orchestra at the Blossom Music Center and with the Boston Symphony Orchestra at Tanglewood. Just months before he died, he did the *Missa*, the *Choral Fantasy*, and the *Ninth* with the National Symphony in Washington (at a two-week-long Beethoven festival), and just days after that, he opened the Boston Symphony's season with the *Ninth* when its music director, Seiji Ozawa, took ill. This was Shaw's last out-of-town concert.

As with Brahms, Shaw's many years of work on the Beethoven symphonies were in their way preparations for the *Missa* and the *Symphony No. 9*. The latter became a set piece, some said a "party piece," for him. But when Maestro Leonard Slatkin heard Shaw do it in Washington, he found it electrifying and new. He asked Shaw if it ever seemed old hat to him. Shaw said, "Oh, no. No, no." He told Slatkin that every single performance of the *Symphony No. 9* was different, challenging, and scary. This is essentially what Toscanini had told Shaw 50 years earlier.

In the case of the Bach Passions, Shaw not only had more opportunities to do them than most conductors (George Solti was studying the *St. John* at the end of his life and had never done it), but Shaw (with help) translated them into English for performance. Moreover, he had done his close study and spent his "monastic" time with both of them year after year. The translation experience gave him a hands-on intimacy that few find the time to develop or are privileged to experience. And each time he performed the Passions, Shaw tinkered with his translations. The *St. John Passion* was another piece he toured. So, here too, we are talking about a unique opportunity to conduct this piece 50 times or more, rather than 1, or 3, or 5 times. And unlike the *St. Matthew*, Shaw recorded the *St. John* in his own translation—the first of many translations, done with Julius Herford. Naturally, Shaw didn't like the recording, and even called it a "youthful indiscretion." It was released in 1950, so he would have been 33 when he made it—not that youthful. He did like Mack Harrell's singing on the recording, however.

As music director at the ASO, Shaw had to learn hundreds of pieces new to him (he had never done, for example, Robert Schumann's symphonies before he went to Atlanta). And he was, we know, a slow study. He once said he needed 20 hours of preparation for every hour of rehearsal. But he kept exploring anyway. At the end of his life, he was still doing pieces that were new to him—like the Dvorák *Stabat Mater*. He'd hoped to tackle the Elgar *Dream of Gerontius*, too. In a way, it is amazing that Shaw had never done either piece. But music is so vast it humbles even a Solti or Shaw.[78]

78 Maestro Andre Previn has made the point about the humbling effect of music's vastness—with reference to jazz. Previn once said he was amused and disturbed by a classical singer who told him she might record a jazz record but confessed she knew nothing about jazz. Previn said he didn't see how music could make its way into such a recording. (Burris-McNair interview)

Still, he returned again and again to his core repertoire—his other "beloveds." Some would hold that this is not what "great" conductors are supposed to do. But Shaw didn't care. He kept going back to Bach, Beethoven, or Mozart to dig a little deeper, to plumb the depths, to get to the heart of the composer and his work. This instinct is comparable, perhaps, to a scripture scholar who, in preparation to teach a seminar on the gospel of Matthew, digs in anew, though he has already written three books on the subject. Sylvia McNair once wrote to Shaw after a performance: "Mr. Shaw, you *own* the *Missa Solemnis*." No response was made. But if he had responded, Shaw might well have said something like, "That's not possible, dear."

Author, music critic, and annotator Michael Steinberg said that each late-life Shaw performance of one of the masterworks so closely identified with him, and by now so deeply internalized in him, seemed simply to be more profound than what other conductors could achieve, and indeed, deeper than what Shaw himself had previously achieved. Each exploration of a familiar and deeply loved piece, such as the Bach *St. Matthew*, or Beethoven *Missa*, especially in the last years, was more meditative and probing and personal, without being personalized. "The late Shaw," said Steinberg so memorably "wanted to 'disappear' on the podium—vanish into the music."[79]

Shaw would always say that a composer had to have great faith and hope: faith that his composition would last and would speak to future generations, hope that future musicians would be able to communicate it.

"He was sure depending on somebody," Shaw said. "There is something holy about that."

So how can we summarize Shaw's relationship to the dead composers whose work he most treasured? Let us take one last look at Robert Shaw and his three Bs:

79 Burris–Steinberg interview.

Bach

Shaw admired the rock-like faith of Bach, and perhaps even envied it a bit, but felt Bach's sort of religiosity was out of the reach of an intellectually honest modern man. He also felt that Bach's choral music could only be properly understood as worship. This created a problem for Shaw personally. How to reconcile the intellectual honesty of a modern man with the Bachian inspiration of Christian belief?

Bach, Shaw said, did not write music for a music hall or songs for consumption. Bach wrote praises to be sung, not concert music for an audience to watch. Handel was an entertainer, not a liturgist. But Bach's music was part of a liturgy and of congregational prayer. For Shaw, who always sought to honor the composer's intent, one of the profound problems for the modern musician was that Bach's audience knew Bach's music, sometimes sang it, *and* believed it. Fellow believers did not observe and critique, they participated. That unity of psyche, faith, art, and community was part of the music. It was deeply attractive to Shaw, and not just because he loved Bach, but because, fundamentally, he believed in the idea of music as prayer. So one of the problems with Bach's Passions is that the modern performer must find some way to *believe* them, on some level, while preparing and performing them. Shaw respected, and ruefully savored and pondered, the Lutheran lady who told him, "You have no right to this music if you do not believe it."

From the beginning of his career in music to the end of his life, Shaw talked about wanting to develop a new liturgical form that would be all musical. He didn't see how the old forms and the old prayers could work. And he was horrified at much of the "praise music" in vogue in Christian churches at the end of his life. He saw it simply as bad music—cheap. And to Shaw, praise and thanksgiving in the form of cheap unmusical music was a cruel joke. It mocked God.

Like his book on choral methods, Shaw never got around to his new liturgy. And yet, like the book, in a way he did. He simply did it in installments. (The letters in *The Robert Shaw Reader* really deliver that book on choral methods, and much more.) He did do all the musical liturgy in Cleveland. No text except the text in the choral work. No sermon. No announcements. No communion. No "fellowship" except in what was created by the learning, preparing, and approximate realization of the music. As Shaw imagined it, the themes of each "service" could be developed by several musical pieces arranged together according to related ideas, musical forms, and keys—rather like his Christmas programs. In Cleveland, in his Unitarian phase, Shaw created several such programs or liturgies. To Shaw, this was emulating Bach in the twentieth century. But, more to the point, Shaw created a sort of liturgy in much of his programming, and in many of his performances, in his later years, particularly in sacred pieces like the Bach Passions. If he could not believe what Bach believed, Shaw could believe in Bach's music, and what it could do to and for people. No one who was present would dispute that Shaw's final performances of the *St. Matthew Passion*—in Atlanta and New York, in 1996—were sacred meditations.

So, too, his Christmas programs. They were Shaw musical suites, but also Shaw worship services. To many audiences, and perhaps to the management of the ASO, the Christmas programs were shows, pageants. But to Shaw, they were gospel, worship, prayer. Ann Jones said: "Shaw would not allow applause to enter the hall," and thus trivialize his Christmas liturgy, "until the end, and then you should have heard the eruption."

To some in the audience at Tanglewood two summers before Shaw died, a program of the *Symphony of Psalms* and the Mozart *Requiem* was music to drink white wine by. For Shaw, it was liturgy—the only real liturgy available in our time

Julius Herford, asked his religion, said, "I'm a Bach." And so was Shaw—especially in his later years. Shaw did not think of himself as a Christian. He doubted the divinity of Christ. He doubted the meaning of the term. A Christian humanist, maybe. But then, he often said, why not just humanist? But a Bach? Yes, he could join that church.

Is it possible for a modern "congregation" to feel directly connected, as one body, to a divine Creator, as in Bach's day? Shaw doubted it. Not in the shadow of World War I and World War II, to name two obvious examples of modern barbarism ever present in Shaw's consciousness. But a *choral congregation* might connect as one to Bach. And Bach might be as close as mortals can get to God. In short, some form of connection to the Divine and to grace might still be achievable through music.

When conducting Bach, Shaw insisted on the clarity and motion of contrapuntal lines, while also conveying the swell of congregational aspiration—especially in the chorales. This warming, or Shaw-ifying, of Bach may not be, strictly speaking, thought musicologically correct today, but it represents the convergence of pastor and musician in Shaw, and there is surely something deeply Bachian in that.

All his life, Shaw was trying to get back to what he called the amateur spirit, epitomized, for him, by Hindemith's, Serkin's, and Casals's musicianship. But he was also trying to get back to *Bach's* musicianship: To play and to sing for love, and gratitude, is to approach, however unsteadily, worship in music.

Beethoven

He was more than a hero to Shaw, as Lincoln was, and Hindemith and Toscanini were. Beethoven was an *idol.* First, because Beethoven struggled and suffered so much with life and for music. Second, because as Shaw put it, "Beethoven tried to reinvent Christianity." Did he exactly? This is what Shaw believed the *Missa Solemnis* was all about. Beethoven, to Shaw, was a figure who stripped both Christianity and music back to their root elements and then re-created both. To Shaw, Beethoven was rebel, creator, mystic. Beethoven's take-no-prisoners approach to the nature and meaning of life, music, and God, and the psychological cost of that stance (Shaw insisted that the *Missa* ended with the muffled pessimism of distant war drums), inspired Shaw.

Shaw liked to collect and write down things that Beethoven had written to himself. There is one paragraph that Shaw particularly admired and quoted to more than one choir: "Every real creation of art is independent, more powerful than the artist himself, and returns to the Divine through its manifestations. It is one with man only in this, that it bears testimony to the mediation of the Divine in him." This is what Shaw believed about art and artists.

Brahms

He, too, sought to take the traditions of the Christian faith and classical music and both preserve and renew them. Less a rebel or revolutionary than a renewer and re-inventor of tradition, Brahms was a "conservative" artist in the best sense, by Shaw's lights. As noted, Brahms spoke very personally to Shaw's earthy qualities. Even his by-turns sentimental and gruff nature is echoed in Shaw's own, as was Brahms's love of good, simple things: good food and drink, meaningful conversation and companionship, habitual routines and time to hear oneself think. Both men knew loneliness, self-doubt, and grief. One sees other similarities: a certain bawdiness, a certain humility and peasant quality, acute intelligence, independence, underlying shyness, and some emotional retardation. Brahms had an ear for the lullaby and the folk tune, and so did Shaw. Brahms was a master of melody. So was Shaw. (Shaw told Alice Parker that the way to ruin a hymn or folk tune was to write an arrangement that strays too far from the melody.) Robert Shaw was born for the music of Brahms. But his long experience with the music of Brahms is what made him a unique Brahms conductor. His Brahms recordings showcase the melodic sensitivity of both men—the ability to keep the emotional contours without violating them. One especially heard this, perhaps, in Shaw's recording of the *Alto Rhapsody*, with Marilyn Horne; *Gesang der Parzen*; and *Nänie;* as well as his many performances of those pieces with various soloists.

Nänie was certainly a particular Shaw favorite. He performed it scores of times—whenever he could. He felt it was a perfect Brahms miniature. The work was his wife Caroline's favorite piece of music. Shaw did it last in New York in 1995. Caroline was ill with cancer but had insisted he not cancel his engagement. She heard the dress rehearsal performance of *Nänie* and thought it the most beautiful she had ever heard, but then she had to fly back to Atlanta and be hospitalized. She died days later.

And then there was the *Requiem*. Shaw truly internalized the piece. He didn't have to apply Shaw-reiteration. It became a part of him, and Shaw seemed, in concert, to step off the podium to make way for Brahms.

As John Silber noted, the *Requiem* makes Christian consolation available to agnostics. "One need not believe in resurrection, only hope," he said.

Most conductors do not prepare music as Robert Shaw did. They are pressed for time and in a hurry even when not pressed for time. Shaw took the time to immerse himself in the piece before him—the one he was next to conduct. Shaw insisted on the luxury of turning down work to make time, and was blessed with the ability to do so. He was blessed also, perhaps, with the curse of being a slow study, for that forced him to learn a piece of music note by note, inch by inch, from the inside out. Many conductors would much rather go to the dinners and receptions that Shaw loathed than sit alone in a hotel or dressing room studying a score for the umpteenth time. Shaw preferred the company of the composers.

Not all conductors *try* to get penetrate the music, seek to be inhabited by it, or fret about how and why it *must* be communicated. They may say they do. But they don't. That may seem strange. But it is true. Many conductors simply learn the piece well enough to perform it and then try to perform it with a bit of dash. (If they can learn it quickly or can memorize it and conduct without a score, they are considered proficient, maybe brilliant.) Shaw loved being alone with the composer, agonizing over the music, emptying himself into the score and the score into himself. He loved this part the most. He knew he was smaller than the composer and the composition, and he wanted to stay that way.

Many conductors are in show biz. Shaw was not in show business. He spent much of his life trying to get out of it. Of course, some would assume entertainment was precisely Shaw's field of endeavor. It's certainly how he started, just as he started out as a kind of junior minister. But he came to despise the show-biz aspects of his profession and his life, almost as much as he loathed the institutional church. The shallowness of both the church and the music business brought his blood to an instant boil.

Shaw also disliked a purely scholarly approach to music. Music, he felt, must be a living thing, not a relic. It must not only be "ancient" or "period" in the sense that the composer's line is honored, but it must be heard and felt anew. Music is written to be heard and it should be "made" to be communicated. Rhythm and melody save us from schoolmasterish pseudo-music.

Shaw understood that music does not end with the musician's pursuit of the composer. Granted, that's where *Shaw* liked to dwell. Music only begins there. Shaw's obligation as a musician was to connect the composer to the listener. Toscanini's question to the young Shaw was: "Will it make the score sound?" If the listener happened to be part of the "great unwashed," all the better.

Shaw was neither a pure performer nor a pure scholar, but a sort of hybrid of his own making—part surgeon or mechanic working to get the machine started, part itinerant preacher, part troubadour with a classic repertoire, part secret monk who'd taken his own private vow of fidelity to music itself.

He was not in the music business: he had answered a call to music.

Shaw made his life complicated in ways that don't occur or appeal to others in the conducting fraternity. And they are right, in a sense—symphony audiences and boards don't care about a conductor's scholarship or musical piety. They just want a good show, a not-too-intolerably-long show and, as Charles Ives said, sounds that are reasonably familiar and comforting to their ears.

Shaw had his own ideas of what a conductor should be—a teacher, a homilist, a Mr. Fixit, but perhaps most importantly, a medium and communicator. The musician's job is to go to the source of the music (the composer) and then take the music to the intended (the listener whose life might be changed).

It took Shaw a lifetime to figure out the first part of the assignment. The second part was in him from the start—his preacher DNA. Dr. David Lowance, Shaw's longtime friend and physician, said this: "Robert communicated music so urgently because he *could* communicate. And he could communicate because to him the message was urgent. He understood everyone in the audience: the poor man because he'd been poor, the rich man because he'd been rich, the artist because he *was* an artist, the bubba because he *was* a bubba. There was no one he could not reach, because he was so fucking human."

CHAPTER 38

Three Lesser Greats: Britten, Poulenc, and Hindemith

Shaw had great affection for Benjamin Britten's work, and in the case of the *War Requiem*, there was as much theological and poetical basis for that affection as musical basis. This was unusual. Shaw had spent his adult life transforming himself from a wordsmith to a molder of musical sentences. The musical line almost always came first.

Moreover, Shaw was generally not a great fan, or student, of English music. But he loved Britten. He performed Britten's *Ceremony of Carols* many times and also recorded it. He also loved *Rejoice in the Lamb*, but here, too, he tended to talk about the poetry in it, not the notes. He rediscovered Britten at the end of his life and put together two more or less identical programs of Britten's shorter works (which Shaw was supposed to record, though he changed his mind). But all this may have been another case of Shaw wanting to do as many works as possible by the composer because he truly loved one piece by the composer. That piece was, of course, the *War Requiem.*

In terms of a work that Shaw spent his own study and words on, only the *Missa Solemnis* and *Mass in B Minor* got more attention. Through the years, Shaw amassed scores of pages of analytical notes and observations on Britten's *War Requiem*, many of which he shared with choruses and workshops. But these notes, as with most of his writing, were not intended for publication and were written as much for himself as for any audience. What was it about this work that moved him so? Shaw himself said that Britten's musical language and structure in this piece borrowed heavily from Verdi and Berlioz. So it wasn't structure or melody that attracted Shaw. Indeed, some critics and students of music find the work admirable but pedantic and unlovely. So what was it that so fascinated him? Well, Shaw was explicit. It was Britten's message. It was his message of pacifism and, on a deeper level, Britten's outrage at innocence violated and young life discarded. It was Britten's humanistic theology, and his profound disgust at false patriotism and false religion. The work was *supposed* to be unlovely.

Here was another composer doing as Beethoven and Brahms had done—creating a requiem of his own devising—and more: a form of sacred worship and a sense of religiosity of his own devising. For Britten inserted his outrage *into* the Mass—an act Shaw found bold and thrilling.

By embedding his protest into the Roman Catholic liturgy, Britten had, Shaw felt, made the requiem prayer an impious and primal cry for help. Standing alone, that cry would be mere politics. Everyday politics did not engage Shaw deeply. But the fundamental political questions of war and justice did.

How, Shaw wondered, could any religious man, any just man, any sane man, consider the slaughter and absurdity of war and *not* plea to the Almighty: *Why?* This was Britten's question in his requiem. It had been Shaw's question ever since Jim Shaw died.

Shaw wanted every person in the world to hear the question. He felt no one asked it more eloquently than Britten. And each time Shaw conducted the work, he was more energized by it.

But Shaw conducted this work differently than most pieces. First, in rehearsals he gave the text precedence. He did not delay textual considerations to the end. He was less hesitant to discuss meaning or to editorialize on what he perceived to be the meaning of the poetry that made the libretto. (He took musical rehearsal time to read some of the Wilfred Owen poems, upon which the work is based. The only other time he did such a thing was with the Hindemith *Lilacs.*) Second, he treated it more as a work of drama than a work of music (proving again that he was not lacking in an operatic sense but only, by choice, operatic repertoire). And third, since meaning was more important than musical beauty in this instance—in the piece beauty is a foil—Shaw could conduct it more viscerally. And that he did. Shaw, if you will, conducted ugly. He was still Shaw, but there was far less tidiness.

The *War Requiem* can be ponderous. Some musicians find it almost unmusical. At times its message is like a 2 x 4 to the side of the head. For Shaw, the challenge was to avoid ponderousness and to convey the tragic sense and emptiness that comes from facing a horrible truth: war is simply the butchering of the young. An entire generation becomes Isaac. Except that governments, in the role of Abraham, do not pull the knife back. They slaughter.

Shaw's performance of the *War Requiem*—and Telarc did capture Shaw's musical energy on this monumental recording—is raw and angry and heart breaking. It is a Beethovian shaking of the fist and a pleading—both with God and man. The piece is disturbing. It is unsettling. Britten wanted it to be. And so did Shaw. Shaw's live performances were even more emotional, especially his final performance with the Minnesota Orchestra in the last months of his life. It was one of those Shaw concerts that left many in the audience stunned, shaken, and silent. By this time, Shaw felt more strongly than ever about the *War Requiem*, about young life (he knew his own life was drawing to a close), about war, and about the need for *new* requiems—new modes of spirituality and worship. His final performance of the piece was raw and blistering.

Robert Shaw also championed the work of Francis Poulenc for over 40 years. Shaw recorded Poulenc's *Mass in G* in 1949. He re-recorded it four decades later, along with the *Gloria*, with Sylvia McNair, in 1982. With his festival chorus in France, he also recorded Poulenc's *Tenebrae Responses* and *Prayers of St. Francis*. Shaw often programmed Poulenc's work in concerts through the years, and the *Gloria* became a popular choice for him when guest conducting.

Poulenc, of course, said that Shaw understood him better than he understood himself. And the two men, while Poulenc was living, were cordial. Yet the relationship does not quite compute. Poulenc's sensibilities were, in many ways, inherently pop, tinged with jazz. Poulenc was a swell who wanted to be a monk, a sort of French Gershwin "lite" who wanted to be a sacred composer. Given Shaw's aversion to entertainment music, what was the attraction?

Partly, Shaw may have loved what was so different from his own experience—the lightness, French-ness, non-Germanic quality, and the Catholicity. Further, Poulenc was a "fallen" Catholic who, in mid-life, had a reconversion, a mystical experience. (It happened at the Shrine of Our Lady in Rocamadour near the place Caroline and Robert would settle in France.) Mystics and mysticism always spoke to Shaw. The Catholic embrace of what Martin Buber called "I and thou"-ness was totally foreign to Shaw's own Protestantism, which made him fascinated.

But mostly, Shaw admired Poulenc for what Poulenc desperately wanted to be—*not* a showman but a serious, and indeed, devout musician. For that was what Robert Shaw wanted to be. When Poulenc, in tears, told Shaw that thanks to him, the world would see him as he really was, it surely made an impression.[80]

Once Caroline Shaw got Robert interested in France, Shaw's affection for Poulenc fed into that, and he even re-traced some of Poulenc's steps along the latter's journey to Catholic rediscovery.

Shaw's feeling for Poulenc's music, so foreign to his own musical roots and usual tastes, is interesting for two things it suggests about Shaw.

First, although Shaw wished to approach music analytically and clinically, he responded emotionally. He always responded, for example, to a fine African-

80 Shaw papers.

American voice, trained or untrained. The first time he heard the great tenor Seth McCoy, Shaw wept. McCoy was essentially untrained at the time Shaw helped McCoy change that. But Shaw heard in the African-American voice (and in McCoy's voice in particular) suffering and resilience. His own response to music was, for all his successful effort to educate and discipline himself, essentially visceral. Second, Shaw did not really detest show tunes any more than folk tunes or gospel tunes. For many of the best ones touched him. What he detested was the *use* of music as a soporific, or as wallpaper.

Shaw had a natural feeling for the music of Jerome Kern and Richard Rogers, as much as he harassed his sister Holly for her commitment to Broadway. This is, after all, just another form of folk music. Shaw admired all music that was honest and came from somewhere—a tradition or a lone voice. He appreciated the music the folk keep around for longer than a week or two. He hated manufactured music that had been given the Hollywood treatment, whether hymns or ballads. In later years, he returned to the old Robert Shaw Chorale practice of ending concerts with spirituals and what he called "Appalachian folk hymns." The melodist in Shaw precedes, and succeeds, the musical engineer. One hears this again in Shaw's very last recording—the Dvorák *Stabat Mater.* Shaw made that piece new, in part by bringing out the folk qualities in it. His recordings of Schubert's songs for male chorus shows the same inherent feeling for the folk idiom. It is a recording that is breathtakingly beautiful because it succeeds in unfolding the quiet, modest beauty of Schubert's songs.

Poulenc was French Broadway. He was a melodist. Shaw could get an extraordinarily light sound out of Poulenc's work—a light and a tender sound not easily accessible to many American musicians. He could also raise it to the holy level where Poulenc wanted it to be.m That was how Poulenc heard his music. Few others did. But Shaw heard Poulenc's true voice.

Shaw's life may be read as a kind of Protestant parallel to Poulenc's wayward Catholic one. Poulenc sought, almost desperately, two things that Shaw also yearned for: musical seriousness and the mystic religious experience. They were two essentially secular, worldly, and physical men, both with powerful hedonistic streaks, obsessed with the idea of holiness. Each, in his own way, was trying to find his path to some sort of sanctity. Here was Poulenc, who began as a salon jazz artist in café society, seeking to be a sacred composer. Here was Shaw, a glee club director who went to radio and Broadway, trying to discern the meaning and realize the sounds of the *Missa Solemnis*. Shaw understood what Poulenc was striving to become and what he was striving to escape—a suspicion of his own shallowness.

Shaw's most abiding musical affections were for the greatest of great composers, and the deepest of deep composers. And despite Poulenc's best efforts, his Cabaret-Broadway slip is always showing. But listening to Shaw's rendition of the Poulenc *Tenebrae Responses*, one feels they *do* achieve a sort of Gregorian stateliness. Shaw and Poulenc realize musical seriousness together. Maybe it takes the spiritual seeking of one entertainer to understand the spiritual seeking of another.

The relationship of Robert Shaw to Paul Hindemith was a unique one for a composer and conductor. They were not buddies, as Shaw and Samuel Barber were. And Hindemith was neither a father figure nor a grandfather figure (as Toscanini was). Nor was he a mentor, as Szell and Herford were. They did not spend that kind of time together. Yet Hindemith exerted a deep intellectual and spiritual influence on Shaw. And one reason is that, as with so many of the people and forces that shaped Shaw's life, Hindemith, as musician, man, and musical philosopher, spoke to Shaw—to something that was already in Shaw. Intuitively and philosophically, they began on the same page. Hindemith articulated values and perceptions Shaw felt.

Hindemith wanted serious music to be *made*, not just heard. He disliked recordings. He disliked, in fact despised, music as a consumer good. He composed music for amateurs to sing and play. Indeed, Lukas Foss noted that much of Hindemith's music has been forgotten because the people he wrote it for no longer make music, but "listen to hi-fis." The musical amateur of old is now the audiophile.

Shaw, too, put his faith in the amateur musician and in the humanizing force of human beings making music together. Both men saw listening as an inherent part of good music making. But simply listening to music, with no thought of making it, was quite foreign to both Shaw and Hindemith—indeed, almost a perversion. Observing music, or talking music, without making music was as strange to Shaw, and Hindemith, as talking love, or observing love, without ever loving.

Both men were musical moralists. They believed music—properly understood, heard, and played—could change humanity, soul by soul. Of course, both would insist that the necessary conditions for conversion are almost never met. Music is almost never properly understood, heard, or played. But this is the *potential* of music, in the views of both Shaw and Hindemith: it *can* transform us.

Here are some powerful and poetic words of Hindemith's, as quoted by Shaw in one of his letters to the ASOC. They speak to the essentially common vision of the two men. First:

> *Life in and with music, being essentially a victory over external forces and a final allegiance to spiritual sovereignty, can only be a life of humility, of giving one's best to one's fellow men. This gift will not be like the alms passed on to the beggar; it will be the sharing of man's every possession with a friend.*

Next:

> *A life in, for, and with music is a "victory" over "external forces"—over the material world, and it requires total death of the ego.*

And finally:

> *The ultimate reason for this humility will be the musician's conviction that beyond all the rational knowledge he has amassed and all his dexterity as a craftsman there is a region of visionary irrationality in which the veiled secrets of art dwell, sensed but not understood, implored but not commanded, imparting but not yielding. He cannot enter this region, he can only pray to be elected one of its messengers. If his prayers are granted and he, armed with wisdom and gifted with reverence for the unknowable, is the man whom heaven has blessed with this genius of creation, we may see in him the donor of the precious present we all long for: the great music of our time.*

This is the Shaw-Hindemith ethic and aesthetic in brief. The true musician serves music—in humility. His "disciplines" guarantee only transportation to the door of art. Entry is not ensured. He can never, on his own power, possess the secrets of art. But he can be its messenger.

Hindemith also said, "Music has to be converted into moral power." It is an audacious, and debatable, statement. But it could have been Shaw's short creed, his mantra, his epitaph.

We don't really know what Hindemith thought of Shaw. When they first knew each other and worked together on *When lilacs last in the dooryard bloom'd: A Requiem "For those we love,"* in 1946, Shaw was a young man and Hindemith an old man. And soon Hindemith would go back to Europe. Shaw himself hinted that Hindemith thought him green and a bit unmoored. (This may be Shaw's view of himself at that time.) But Hindemith was religiously serious about music. Shaw claimed that when Koussevitsky conducted *Mathis der Mahler* at Tanglewood, Hindemith walked to the stage during an orchestra break, picked up the score, closed it, and walked away with it, saying, "You don't know it." It is another Shaw story that seems a bit too perfect and too fantastic. But it certainly conveys Hindemith as Shaw saw him. And it is certainly possible that, as Shaw claimed, Hindemith turned his back on Shaw at a New York luncheon in honor of both men when the conductor told the composer he was working on a "theatrical" production of the *St. Matthew Passion,* with Lillian Gish as the Virgin Mary and a yellow spotlight as Jesus. (The ringmaster of this circus was Leopold Stokowski.) It is also possible that this is simply one of Shaw's slightly exaggerated old reliable tales—one that never failed to amuse him.

Shaw commissioned *Lilacs* for the Collegiate Chorale in 1945. By 1945, the Collegiate Chorale was an established and respected group. But it was young in every sense. And its leader was 29 and still very much "playing catch up" musically. According to Shaw, Hindemith was considered one of the big four living composers—Bartók, Stravinsky, and Schoenberg were the other three. Shaw was to conduct the American premiere of the *Cantata Profana* and to prepare a chorus for a rendering of the *Symphony of Psalms* under the baton of the composer. His contact with musical giants is perhaps a testament to both luck and longevity. But it was surely a reach at this stage of the Chorale's and Shaw's professional life to ask a composer of Hindemith's stature to compose an original piece for a large amateur chorus. Yet, if one assumes that Hindemith had internalized his own value system, that he was sincere in his beliefs, it makes complete sense. The Collegiate Chorale was supposed to be a "melting pot that sings." It was devoted to the amateur art (though many of its singers were actually pros) and the amateur spirit. Hindemith believed that instrumentalists should sing in choirs, and the smaller the choir, the better. The Collegiate Chorale was devoted both to great historical music and to the most noble of modern compositions. It was supposed to change hearts and minds through music. Again, Shaw was already singing Hindemith's tune.

Further, a year before, the Collegiate Chorale had already commissioned and performed *The Prairie* by Lukas Foss, who was one of Hindemith's students. So Hindemith might have known something of Shaw's work.

And we do know that, in preparing the work for performance, Hindemith gave Shaw his time unstintingly. They went over the score together, in more than one session. And Hindemith came to at least one rehearsal. Shaw had many questions. Hindemith, the ultimate teacher, engaged them all.

Shaw would conduct many Hindemith pieces in his later role as an orchestral conductor, most notably *Mathis der Mahler* (symphonic version) and *Symphonic Variations on a Theme by Carl Maria von Weber*. But he did not know or perform much of Hindemith's work before Hindemith left the country and returned home to Germany. Hindemith never knew the calmer, accomplished Shaw of the Cleveland and Atlanta years—only the young, green, nervous, and enthusiastic Shaw of the 1940s. But Shaw knew the mature and assured Hindemith, and worked with him on a composition dear to Hindemith's heart. The composer made a deep impression, and his book, *A Composer's World*, became a kind of Talmud for Shaw.

Shaw premiered another Hindemith choral work, though it was on a very different scale, in fact, rather intimate—*Apparebit Repentina Dies,* for a symposium on modern music at Harvard. Shaw returned to this grave and stately piece several times, though he was never able to record it.

Finally, astonishingly, on at least one occasion, Shaw and Hindemith played Bach together: Hindemith played the viola da gamba in a performance of the *St. John Passion* with the Juilliard Orchestra and chorus with Shaw conducting. (This would seem to indicate that Hindemith, however undemonstrative, or even gruff, thought rather highly of the young man.) Shaw claimed that when Hindemith was not playing his own part, he quietly sang all the chorales from his seat in the orchestra—from memory.

Lilacs bound these two men. They came together for and in the work. *Lilacs* is usually said to be Hindemith's tribute to the recently dead Franklin Roosevelt and the American war dead of World War II, though the vehicle is the words of Walt Whitman in praise of Lincoln and the Civil War dead. It is an artistic bridge between the two epochs, tragedies, and two great men. But perhaps it is more. Some have compared *Lilacs*, at least in the scope of Hindemith's intentions, to Brahms's *German Requiem*. And *Lilacs* does seem to be about more than the Civil War and dead presidents. Even to call it Hindemith's anti-war hymn seems too limiting. Like Brahms's masterpiece, *Lilacs* is a *human* requiem—it is about loss and sorrow. And it is for the living. But there is precious little consolation other than truth. As Shaw himself wrote: "It has nothing to do with proclamations of national mourning, the public beating of breasts, but with private quiet grief and a lonely broken heart." The subtitle, "requiem for those we love," points us in that direction—the spiritual rather than the political. It is Hindemith's hymn to human pity. Like Brahms, Hindemith wrote a requiem of compassion for those left to mourn. It is all the more tender for not being sentimental. All of this Shaw understood intuitively. He understood the humanity of Lincoln (Shaw's personal hero)—a humanity that transcended politics. He understood the humanity of Whitman—the one-time cheerleader for war who became an orderly in a hospital and a chronicler of the costs of war. He understood Hindemith's combination of severity and magnanimity, of idealism and sorrow.

Lilacs united the American ideal with Bachian counterpoint; a noble American text and a modern, neo-classical German composer; an American idealist and a German one. This work, like *Mathis der Mahler*, perhaps Hindemith's other really great work, expressed the composer's longing for and belief in human nobility. "He hated anything even a little Hollywood," Shaw said of Hindemith. Such hatred came naturally to the composer. It came later to Shaw. Shaw changed, and became the man and musician he wanted to become, but he had a lot of Hollywood in him when he met and worked with Hindemith, and he knew it.

Shaw, as we have noted, conducted *Lilacs* more than any conductor in the world. After Hindemith went back to Europe in 1953, Shaw became the work's leading advocate in America. Each time he performed the work, he proselytized for it. "Vote yes for *Lilacs*," he told the Atlanta Symphony Chorus in 1974. "Vote hundreds of times each day."

In 1996, Shaw went to Yale, Hindemith's American home where he had made such a lasting impact as a teacher, to conduct *Lilacs* one last time on the 100th centenary of Hindemith's birth. There, Shaw conducted Yale students and faculty in a performance of the requiem infused with a half century of knowledge and love. Shaw also made the case for the importance of Hindemith as a composer in a public talk and an interview with a local reporter. Hindemith, Shaw insisted, was a genius of the nineteenth century confined to the twentieth, and would yet be rediscovered.

It is sometimes said now that Hindemith is not held in such high regard as Bartók and Stravinsky, and that no one has stepped forward as Hindemith's great advocate in the way Robert Craft did for Stravinsky. But Shaw did try to advocate in the same way for Hindemith. It's just that Shaw was doing many other things, and from 1957 to 1990, he was seldom center stage in New York.

But Shaw did everything he could for *Lilacs*. He conducted it at Carnegie Hall in 1995 as part of his Carnegie Hall masterwork-workshop series, putting it on a par with the Verdi and Brahms Requiems. And that, too, was a performance that rattled people. Somehow, in *Lilacs*, as with the Britten *War Requiem*, Shaw could let go. He'd been conducting the piece since its birth, after all. (It bothered him that the Collegiate Chorale's commission was not noted on the score.) His Telarc recording is still regarded by many as definitive.

Shaw marveled at Hindemith's skill with setting text (almost to the detriment of the music, some say). Hindemith "never wanted it to be too pretty," Shaw said. He wanted it to be thoughtful and, like Ives, not comfortable. Shaw quoted Hindemith, "I write so much music because so much of it is bad." Which was true, said Shaw. "But he put it out there and up against the *St. Matthew Passion* and the *B Minor Mass*." And Shaw added, "it *is* bad next to the *B Minor Mass*. So is the rest of humanity."[81]

81 Video of Carnegie Hall Choral Workshop on *Lilacs*.

In a Q&A session with singers during the Carnegie Hall workshop preparation that year, Shaw allowed himself to muse and look backward, which he seldom did. He talked about how much Caroline had enjoyed the rehearsals, and he even talked about his first wife and their tempestuous years together. He spoke of Hindemith telling him that in one place in the score, "I put all the wrong notes I could in so it would sound swirlier." Shaw said that, above all, Hindemith "despised music not made for love." And Shaw talked about what *Lilacs* meant to him. "Singing a piece like this changes lives. God damn it, it changes lives. You don't think the same way. You don't cry over the same things. You don't love the same way . . . You're different . . . and its just too damn bad humanity isn't ready for it."

The other work on the Carnegie program in 1995 was the Brahms *Nänie,* which Caroline would hear that last time. Later Shaw told the chorus, "We'll say goodbye during the performance, and remember that goodbye means we'll meet again." His beloved wife was dying. "Caroline sends her love." Shaw told the chorus. "She thinks this is the best chorus (Carnegie Hall Workshop Chorus) we've had."

Some musicologists do not agree with Shaw that *When lilacs last in the dooryard bloom'd* is a seminal or lasting work. They see it, as Hindemith himself said, as "gray/brown," and as Shaw said, "knotted" and "difficult." But hearing Shaw speak of the piece, and hearing the piece as he and his forces rendered it, particularly with the great Jan DeGaetani on the recording (a spirit as noble as Shaw), it is impossible to believe they are right and Shaw was wrong. *Lilacs* is "gray/brown" and not easily accessible, just as Hindemith wished it to be. But its heart is large.

The Collegiate Chorale paid Paul Hindemith a $1000 commission for *Lilacs* in 1945. Shaw found this paltry sum absurd and embarrassing. But the great man had accepted it. No one knew it at the time, or wondered about its source, but the money came out of Robert Shaw's own checking account.

CHAPTER 39

Clarity, Energy, and Devotion

It was perhaps during the Robert Shaw Chorale period that the term "the Shaw sound" was coined. Shaw hated the term and he hated the notion. He wanted Bach's sound, or Brahms's sound, or Handel's sound.

But there *was* a distinctive Shaw sound. One hears it quintessentially on his RCA *Mass in B Minor*, his Telarc recordings of Schubert's Mass and *Songs for Male Chorus*, and in several other Telarc recordings—the Rachmaninoff *Vespers*; the Christmas recordings; and his final recording, the Dvorák *Stabat Mater.* Most musicians would say that they can tell a Shaw recording in the first minute or two of hearing it, unidentified, on the radio. Critic Richard Dyer of the *Boston Globe* noted that, amazingly, Shaw could get "the sound" from a workshop choir, or a choir he was guest conducting, and he could get it very fast. Shaw would probably insist "only to a point." But whether the choir was big or small, amateur or professional, his own choir or one he was guest conducting, it acquired the Shaw sound if Shaw rehearsed and conducted it. Dyer compared the phenomenon to Eugene Ormandy, who, he said, made every orchestra he conducted sound rather like the Philadelphia Orchestra.

So what is this "Shaw sound"? Veteran Shaw singers and listeners tend to list four things. First, it is healthy, robust. It is *not* the sound of English schoolboys. There is nothing precious in it. Men sound manly and women sound womanly. Moreover, part of its robustness is that it is an *American* sound. The Robert Shaw Chorale sounded more full and more uniform than the softer sound of the Atlanta Symphony Chorus and Chamber Chorus. The Chorale was, of course, not only a small professional chorus, but the product of a younger, more aggressive man. Second, the Shaw sound builds on a strong bass line. The basses are not an undertow or an undercurrent, but a floor upon which to stand. The other voices stand upon bass shoulders. Third, and related intrinsically to the bass foundation, the Shaw sound is warm and rounded, never tin-like or brittle, even in Baroque music. Fourth, there is unanimity of sound almost certainly derived from Shaw's unique rehearsal methods and obsession with rhythm—the internal synchronization, the collective clock he sought between musicians. Again, this fourth characteristic is more the case in his later choirs.

No two Shaw choirs sounded exactly alike. But every Shaw choir had "the Shaw sound."

The Cleveland Orchestra's chorus under Shaw sounded more virile, if you will, than the Atlanta Symphony Chorus, where Shaw adopted a softer, more rounded sound. His Atlanta singers, in the early years, did not have the collective vocal muscle of the Cleveland singers, and they certainly did not have the heft of the Collegiate Chorale or Robert Shaw Chorale. A choir "has to be built up," Shaw said, through rehearsal discipline over weeks, months, and years. He said that his Atlantans eventually surpassed all his other choirs in quality of intonation and enunciation. As always, Shaw made a virtue (and a slightly different sound) out of necessity.

The Robert Shaw Chorale had a more pointed and hungry sound than the Atlanta Symphony Chamber Chorus or the Robert Shaw Festival Singers of his late years. Shaw himself said there had never been, and never was again, such a collection of vocal gold as the Robert Shaw Chorale. Because times always seemed to be lean for singers in New York, and because they were especially lean in the years immediately after the war, Shaw was able to pick and choose from the very best: he had enormous vocal talent and power at his disposal. His later choirs were either symphonic choruses, in which Shaw sought unifying sectional sounds so that he could make 160 people sound like 40, or handpicked small choirs. Ironically, he loved amateur singers—in a poetic sense, as he defined the term—though his own choirs were mostly not composed of singers who were *literally* amateur. Mostly, his singers were well educated in music. Quite often, especially in the case of the later choirs, they were music educators. As Shaw himself put it: "Most of us do not make our livings singing, but are related to music and singing circumferentially." It is interesting that he used the word "us." The Atlanta choirs, especially in the early years of his music directorship, were less knowledgeable and talented than the Cleveland choirs. But that changed as Shaw built the Atlanta choirs and the musical culture of the region. And, in terms of musical knowledge and understanding, the France and Carnegie Hall choirs were the best he had ever had to work with. Sometimes there were a tiny few literal musical amateurs—people who could barely read music—in Shaw's choirs. They tended to be family and friends. Caroline Shaw certainly could never have passed an audition for a Shaw choir. On the other hand, Shaw was rather hard on his niece, who was a very fine singer/musician. Her name? Holly.

Shaw's later choirs were older than the Robert Shaw Chorale singers had been and less naturally gifted, but, Shaw claimed, they were generally more sensitive and more attuned to musical subtlety. He claimed that, in Atlanta, he achieved not only better intonation and better enunciation but, finally, the "unanimity of psyche" he'd always sought. He was also proud of his Atlanta and France choirs for the obstacles they had overcome with text in various modern compositions—from Adams to Bartók (or in the case of the France choirs, Rachmaninoff).

In both large and small choirs in his later years, Shaw seemed to sometimes choose nuance and articulation over sonic power. But not always. In his final recording—the Dvorák *Stabat Mater*—there is sonic power to spare.

What is true is that in the latter half of his career, Shaw worked with choristers who had other jobs and made music not for a paycheck, but for love. For this, he loved them. And it made him feel true to his amateur ethic.

But Shaw had also, essentially, founded the touring professional choir. And all his life he worked with professional soloists. Everyone who worked with him had to be gifted, educated, and devoted, or they worked with him only once.

Shaw's approach to some singing soloists was specific and detailed. It depended on how well he knew the person. Richard Clement and Christine Goerke were two successful soloists who had come out of Shaw's choruses. He took a particular interest in them and set a particularly high bar for them, just as he did for his own chorus. With soloists and choirs he did not know well, he was more solicitous and flattering. But, generally, Shaw did not hand to a star a star turn to do as he or she liked with the music. He drew a map and expected soloists to follow. If they followed well, he then allowed for some individuality, especially instrumental soloists. But creativity had to be within the lines. Shaw felt that real creativity came out of discipline. Once the music was ready, he could step back.

The chorus was Shaw's instrument, just as a band, not a piano, was Duke Ellington's first instrument. Shaw could tune it as a great violinist tunes his fiddle. And indeed, his "warmups" were not literally designed to clear or warm the voice, which he assumed individual singers did on their own. They were tuning exercises—singers listening and tuning to each other. Shaw could manipulate a choral sonority the way a cellist tinkers with bowings. He moved voices around the way a clarinetist might change reeds. And this ability to shape a choral sound, though he refined it, seems to have been innate—he had it as a college student. Shaw simply had a built-in sense of the choral textures he wanted—like Hemingway's sense of the shape and resonance of a sentence. Shaw also never lost the pulse. He preached rhythm, and he felt pulse.

In the obvious and traditional sense, Shaw was anything but a musical prodigy. He was a fumble fingers at the piano and all of his life was painfully aware of his limits at the keyboard, though he got much better. (The early Cleveland years heavily featured the personal penitential rite of practicing scales. This, at a time when he was conducting the *Missa Solemnis.*) But Shaw *was* a choral prodigy. He somehow knew, instinctively, with virtually no training, what to do with a choir. His mentor at Pomona College, Ralph Lyman, may have taught him the elementals (his mother had taught him before Lyman). But Shaw's instincts guided him, and his feeling for choral sound was there from the start.

The critic, Edward Rothstein once said Shaw's musicality could be summarized in three words: "Clarity, energy, and devotion." Let us consider those three instincts, all of which Shaw refined, but all of which are instincts.

- *Clarity.* Shaw deeply distrusted emotionality in music, partly because he distrusted his own emotions and, to a degree, until his very late years, his own taste. He loathed, and sought to avoid, sentimentality. As different as he and George Szell were as human beings, Shaw responded to the Szell approach to music: make it clean, precise, and elegant—the neo-classic instead of the neo-romantic. Szell may not have consciously thought of himself as the anti-Bernstein, but Shaw believed Szell positioned himself that way. (It bothered Szell, said Shaw, that Bernstein's records outsold Szell's.) Shaw saw the Szell approach as anti-excess, and that seemed right to him. It was Shaw's conviction that if you got music "clean" enough, clear enough, orderly enough, lined up (rhythmically), and in tune enough, then, and perhaps only then, the most genuine and deepest of emotions could be released. The emotion could be, in a sense, true, or fresh, and not hackneyed or reflexive. Having gone through the discipline, cheap emotion would be impossible. And having imposed so much discipline, cheap emotion would be checked.

- *Energy.* Shaw hated flaccidness in music. He *held the pulse.* His *Messiah* was a wonder to many in the early years because he did it stripped of not only its Victorian plumage and layers of propriety, but also its lugubriousness. He made it dance. His leaner, meaner Handel was a revelation to many (a disappointment to others who wanted to hear it the grand old way). When Shaw toured *Messiah* in the United States, he educated Americans in this athletic Handelian sound.

There is a mythic tale that Shaw took a small choir of the usual 35 to 40 singers on the road for what was then thought to be a big choir job because no one could afford to tour *Messiah* with a large choir; and it was then that he "discovered" a lighter, cleaner, rhythmic Handel—by accident, as it were. This is nonsense. Dr. Alfred Mann, the eminent American musicologist and conductor, and the critic Michael Steinberg, as well as those who performed with Shaw then, like Florence Kopleff, had no doubt that Shaw toured with a small group of singers because he had studied the music and read the Handel scholarship and felt that *Messiah* should, at last, be communicated in a light, aerobic way—by a small choir.

Even in later years, with larger symphonic choirs, a Shaw performance of *Messiah* crackled with energy. Shaw described the piece as "one hit after another; a miracle of virtuosity and invention . . . melodically just fabulous." He called the piece "acrobatic." But in the 1950s, and even early1960s, the notion that *Messiah* should, above all else, dance was still new and strange to many. Indeed, though lip service is paid to the notion today, one could make a case that this understanding of Handelian performance has still not been fully absorbed in the United States.

For Shaw, music must have motion. In fact, it *is* motion—motion and energy—in sound.

Shaw wanted *Messiah* not only lighter and leaner, but also filled with life force so it could *fly*. The piece never became academic, studied, or gluey if he could help it. This was partly because of the emotion Shaw brought to any final performance and partly because of his concern to express a text he knew well and loved dearly. But it was also because of his insistent rhythmic discipline and sense of pulse. To be music, he said, notes must be moving toward, going away, or arriving at. Ann Jones said: "There was never an unintentional pause in the energy, even from movement to movement," in a Shaw *Messiah* performance.[82]

- *Devotion.* This, in so many ways, was at the core of Robert Shaw, as man, musician, and displaced pastor, theologian, and teacher. First, he felt that one does not become a musician to make a living but to answer a call. Music is not a job but a vocation. Second, all re-creations of great musical compositions are sacramental. A sacrament is, by definition, a sign of divine grace. For Shaw, great music—which is great because of the quality of its construction, the depth of the composer's imagination, and because it exists for all time and for all human beings—partakes directly of the Divine. It does not allude, it partakes. Therefore, a classical musician is not an entertainer but a caretaker of something precious and timeless.

This matter of devotion relates directly to Bach and to Shaw's devotion to Bach. In the early years of Shaw's music making, he was, of his nature, attracted to the qualities of clarity, energy, and devotion. But he did not know how to achieve them. Yet he saw all three virtues, *par excellence*, in the music of Bach. And that is why he attached himself to Bachian scholars like Julius Herford, Alfred Mann and, some years later, Gerhard Hertz.

Shaw's study of the Bach Passions and the *B Minor Mass* began when he met Herford and, actually, never did end. Still the pupil, Shaw was studying the *St. Matthew* when he died, though now, 50-odd years later, he was his own Herford. Or rather, Bach was his teacher. Each time Shaw performed the Passions, he refined his English translations of them. This was part of his ritual of devotion. But ritual must not be understood in the colloquial sense here. Shaw developed his own rituals, and they were not simply matters of habit. They were disciplines of reverence.

82 Burris–Jones interview.

The Bachian sense of sacredness in musical form and craft suffused Shaw's work patterns and work ethic. For Bach, music was worship—in a practical, literal sense. For Shaw, in his own idiosyncratic and modern (or post-modern) sense, music was worship, for it was the only viable replacement for traditional worship. It was the one form of fellowship that seemed honorable, sustainable, and true. It was the only offering that could stand as prayer.

Shaw's clarity, energy, and devotion formed the core of a homemade, working musical aesthetic, indeed, a musical ethic—a contrary and alternative approach to the musical arts for our time. It is a vocational concept of music making. It owes much to Hindemith, but it comes from the viewpoint of a performer, not a theorist: a builder, not an architect.

To clarity, energy, and devotion, one would have to add, again, a word we have already encountered: "warmth." In truth, this word is not adequate, but it is perhaps the best available word for conveying the deep texture and embracing quality of the Shaw sound and persona.

Shaw's stepson, Alex Hitz, when a boy, nicknamed Robert "Warm." To a boy this might be a matter of body heat, or visible perspiration. Shaw generated plenty of both. But children have a way of getting at the essence of things. And warmth was a part of Shaw as surely as it was characteristic of his musical tone. (Florence Kopleff said the German word *innigkeit* is a better, less vague word than warm. She understood it to mean: soul, ardor, fervor, intimacy, sincerity.)

Robert Shaw liked warm, sunny places. His speaking voice was a familiar, folksy, warming voice. His public persona and stage presence were warm and familial. His preaching and orating voice was fervent and pleading. He was not of Marshall McLuhan's "cool" age. His manner of communication was direct and engaged, not ironic, detached, or effaced. And he did have a *preaching* voice. When he gave his set speech about worship and the arts, and when he quoted the old hymns of his youth, he would pound out the cadence of the hymn on the podium with his fist as he spoke: "There is power, power, wonder, working *POWER in the BLOOD of the Lamb.*"

Shaw liked to cradle and warm words as he did musical phrases. He read scriptural passages during his Christmas programs (even though he was a doubting Christian) in part because he loved the words. He loved public speech. He did not play recordings for his son Thomas, but he would show him great speeches and poetry, and sometimes read passages aloud. He handed over his baton and read Lincoln's words in Copland's *A Lincoln Portrait* himself, both with the ASO and the Orchestra of St. Luke's, not because he was a ham, but because he so loved Lincoln and his words. (He also edited Copland's text a bit, taking out all the "this is what Abraham Lincoln said" prefaces so that there would be no dilution of Lincoln's words.)

No, there was nothing "cool," in any sense of the word, about Shaw's personality.

Shaw had a way of talking to musicians, especially singers, as if each one were the most important person in the world—maybe the only person in the world. And as if what they were about to do (perform music) was the most important activity in the world. His "warmup" for singers included, at the very end, prior to performance, his "mystic huddle." He would tell the choir how special they were, how important the days of rehearsal had been to him, what an awesome performance was about to take place, and how honored they all were to be doing this particular piece. Shaw always reminded them as well that, at this moment, the composer was depending on them.

Warmth could also turn to heat. Shaw's temper could come quickly if someone rubbed him the wrong way, something he cared about went wrong, or he felt the pressure of time against his own high standards.

In the Robert Shaw Chorale days, Shaw was often agitated and angry. The rehearsal time never seemed adequate. The hall was often bad. Maybe the hotel was bad, too. Maybe he was hung over. The instrumentalists never seemed to be well enough prepared, committed enough. And he was never good enough.

Some say that, sometimes in his middle years, Shaw would use his temper intentionally, as a tool to make a point, to get the attention of musicians. Allegedly, these tantrums were more or less staged.

But in later years, a show of temper embarrassed him greatly. He concluded that they were demeaning and (always an important consideration for Shaw) counterproductive. Also, Shaw simply mellowed. One conductor recalls seeing him conduct at Yale in the 1990s. Two timpanists missed their entrances. Shaw stopped and simply said, "Come on, guys." "In another time," said the observer, "they would have left the hall eunuchs."[83]

Shaw had an edge. He always had nervous energy (drumming with fingers and crumpling papers). He was often anxious. He always wanted to get to it. Or, if he'd just finished something, go on to the next thing.

Shaw's impatience was tempered over time but never flagged. Jonathan Martin, once of the ASO, later the Cleveland Orchestra, and the Charlotte (NC) Symphony, said Shaw was perhaps the most impatient man he ever met. Shaw, said Martin, always seemed to be saying (internally): "GET OUT OF MY WAY. I've got things to do."[84] Sometimes he said as much, expressly. Shaw always felt time was precious and should not be wasted. He was always very jealous of his time because there never, ever seemed to be enough. But as he aged, he learned to better control his anger and impatience. Not always. Not perfectly. But he was better. And Caroline and the supporting players could soothe him. But Shaw's occasional loss of control mortified him. As with his drinking, he wanted to tame his demons, or at least outlast them.

Here is what Shaw wrote to his chorus about the subject.[85] They were working at the time on Mendelssohn's *Elijah:*

---

83 Burris interview with choral conductor Henley Denmead.
84 Burris-Martin interview.
85 Shaw papers.

October 16, 1974

Friends,

It's a terribly shaming thing to get mad at rehearsals. Anyone with an ounce of sense or honesty knows that music and anger don't really mix. For two very good reasons.

First, nothing technically sick, broken, or out-of-sync is cured. On some occasions (I can think of none) when skills and schooling are perfect, everyone may have to guard against indifference or lassitude, but for the most part conductors of choruses get mad when they don't know how to fix the fool thing—so they kick its tires.

And, of course, in the second place, anger is completely alien to the whole purpose of music—or of a chorus, for that matter.

The purpose of these is communication (it does seem to me that "communion" is a more suitable word except for its religious connotations) and anger is a barrier, an isolation. The dilemma of this particular conductor is that though the teaching (and for him, the learning) of "fundamentals" is an extraordinarily pleasurable experience—except when it gets racked up by the pressure of schedules and performances—there's really not a great deal of stimulus or "point" to learning (or teaching) a performing art unless somebody performs.

Since my failure of Monday night I've spent some hours outlining and starting to assemble a handbook, tentatively titled Fundamentals of Choral Musicianship, *a syllabus of drills and exercises for the choral rehearsal.*

For years I've written (letters and articles) and lectured on the "principles and rules of choral technique" and tried, so long as I could stand the sound of my own tape, to apply them to the repertoire at hand. But "principles" and "rules" somehow are convincing principally, and as a rule mostly, to those who "invent" or "discover" them. And to become effective, efficient, and dependable, they need to be isolated from other technical complexities and psychological urgencies, and repeatedly drilled, and comprehended in the "doing."

So—as your one-time choral-scout bows his way out of the door with rue on wry for his inability to lead you sweetly, bloodlessly, and dryly across Kishon's brook—lift them eyes—oh lift them eyes unto the mountains of exercises that even now begin to take shape hill by drill and from whence if any help cometh at all who can afford to say it neigh?

Au reve—

R

CHAPTER 40

Repetition, Epistles, and Melody

Toscanini said: "Make the score sound."

Shaw spoke of "the necessity" of making the music new, rediscovering it.

To Shaw, this was not an existential question but an organizational one, not a matter of inspiration but fundamentals: Get the rhythmic structure; adhere to tempo; learn the composer's language; communicate the text. "If we can lick the fundamentals, we'll be fine," he said. In short, clarity, energy, and devotion.

Shaw repeatedly used three devices to attack the fundamentals: repetition, teaching letters, and fidelity to the melodic line and sense.

Shaw loved repetition. He liked to repeat stories, concerts, rehearsal axioms, even speeches. He used repetition to perfect and invoke, but also to reveal. The best illustration of what Shaw felt repetition could do for musical understanding, and perhaps what he thought it did for him, was his oft-retold story of the Robert Shaw Chorale tour of the Mozart *Requiem*: We have already told it in these pages. At the end of the final performance of the six-week tour, the musicians wept. (A cynic said they wept out of relief.) But Shaw drew what was, for him, the obvious conclusion: The piece had broken down their sense of separation and detachment. It had exerted its own grace.

The Robert Shaw Chorale and Orchestra had performed it enough times to begin to really fathom it. The piece needed that many repetitions.

Shaw believed that it often took scores, if not hundreds, of tries to master a great piece of music technically. Second, to unlock the spirit of a great work of art, you had to live with it and meditate upon it. Again, the obvious analogies are scholarship and art. A scholar who has written a long book on Renoir's *Liseuse Blanche* has probably spent as many hours staring at the painting as he has producing pages of type on it. An actor who finds a great part might play it hundreds of times. (Henry Fonda played "Mr. Roberts" more than 1,000 times.)

Repetition was key to Shaw's sacramental approach to music. Repeat the piece. Repeat the recording. Repeat the one-liner or punch line. Repeat the lesson. Practice scales. Repeat the notes, now the measure, now the phrase, now the line. Again, with words. Again, with numbers (count singing). Again, with nonsense sounds.

Again.

Repeat.

Repeat the speech.

Start over. From the beginning. A new score (if time allowed). Remember what you do not know and all that you do not understand and that every performance, on some level, is a failure.

Shaw gave the same two speeches—about "The Conservative Arts" and "Worship and the Arts"—over and over again for 40 years. And just as if he were conducting *A German Requiem* again, he started with a fresh sheet of paper.

When Shaw repeated a story, he didn't make it more fantastic, as most good Irish Americans do. He didn't embellish. He tried to elaborate and perfect.

A mantra, after all, is a prayer. And it is not about zoning out. It is about zoning in. A mantra is an act of focusing and concentration, of homage and devotion, and of summoning—of calling forth.

Almost every week for most of his life as a conductor, Shaw wrote letters to his choruses. This was one more of his repetitive rituals. But it was more. Via his letters, Shaw could think through a piece of music with his chorus. In the case of the Beethoven *Missa Solemnis* and Britten's *War Requiem,* Shaw wrote his choruses 50-page letters of compositional and performance analysis. Each time he did these works, he thought them through again and added length to the previous letter on the subject.

For Shaw, writing had to do with the urgency he always felt to communicate and convert: "How can I reach all those people?" Shaw told a chorus, during a rehearsal, only a few months before his death: "We are here such a short time . . . It's necessary to talk."

Of course, Shaw, a word man all his life—a romancer of words and jouster with words—was convinced that words fail to communicate the deepest emotion and the deepest truths. For that, you need art. "One of the proofs," he said a few weeks before he died, "that music is necessary and important is that you can't explain it."

So, it is also necessary to *listen* for the communication that transcends words.

Consider the following letter, a mix of Shavian wisdom and wit:

> *Someone asked this week why I had occasionally advised a phrasing (or an implied phrasing) in the middle of a syllable—"Does this not interrupt the meaning of the words?" There are two answers to this question, and many of you have heard them before.*
>
> *The first is practical: Most frequently this advice has been given with reference to subsidiary or accompanying materials. The composer, of course, begins with his text, and his principal concern is to create a musical statement which will fit and enhance*

the given elements of speech, and which will, in addition, enrich and deepen the meaning of the text. If he is a composer of song-forms (as is Brahms), then his principal melody will bear close relationship to the line of text. But as he creates other voice lines, which accompany and comment, his text is liable to be fragmented, extended, or turned around to make it more usable. In these instances one frequently recommends phrasings, which go with the music rather than with text—for the composer's attention here would seem to have been primarily musical rather than textual.

The second answer is a bit more in the field of general ideas and purposes. The truth is that only the most primitive sort of song has a kind of "one-to-one" relationship between tune and text ("all alone by the telephone"). All great melody, however, assumes a great deal more independence for itself. For instance, all of us can think of melodies where we may have as many as 5 to 20 notes to sing on a single vowel. ("Ich hoffe," p. 37, Requiem.*) While great melody does manage to "fit" (in varying degrees) the mechanics of speech, the thing that really makes it great is its ability to illuminate the spirit of the text—even occasionally by employing little inner musical groupings which imply textual interpretations. This is not to say that music is independent of the text or that the composer is not "inspired" by it. Rather, it is to say that music is also a language: It has its own laws and methods of structure and expressivity. The great composer does not merely "highlight" or "underline" text; he creates a musical fabric in tone and time, which matches or transcends or illumines the text, but is also law unto itself and its own reason for being.*

As artists—and as human beings—our concern is not with how we feel about death or the textual imagery of the German Requiem *but how Brahms felt about these things. And the way we learn about his feelings is by learning to "speak" his language—as perfectly and as trustingly as we can.*

We have to believe that Brahms has something to say: We have to recognize that for the next few weeks and in this place we are his voice. We have to realize that he speaks in terms of intonation and tone "colors" and rhythms, and that we are privileged to be truly the sound of his mind.

When one obeys traffic laws he may reasonably expect fewer traffic tickets and an increased chance of survival—not much, but something. But when one lovingly and earnestly obeys the laws of great music, there is always the chance that the flesh will be made word and dwell among us.[86]

This is vintage Shaw. This is Shaw at his most clear-eyed *and* most lyrical. 1) The composer creates a musical fabric that may transcend the text. 2) Melody is the major strand in that fabric. 3) We, the performers, must learn to speak the language of Brahms, or whoever the composer is at hand.

This was Shaw communicating through words the limits of words. This was Shaw pouring out himself—an act that came so naturally to him on a podium or from behind a lectern and with such difficulty in personal relationships. He opened himself via musical dissertations, in his hundreds of letters to his choruses. He could not do so in a sphere other than music making.

According to Alice Parker, "employing little musical groupings" and creating "a musical fabric in tone and time" is exactly how Shaw worked when creating arrangements of folk tunes. Recall Shaw's warning rule to Parker: Don't stray too far from the melody. Great melody will "illuminate the spirit of the text." Shaw stuck to that rule, as did Parker, which is one reason their arrangements have endured.

86 Shaw papers. My italics.

The Shaw theorem on melody is as follows: "Think of melody as musical energy . . . *melody is a note looking for a place to sit down* . . . the quality of tension or relaxation passed by each note to its successor . . . until the moment of rest occurs."[87] There is grist enough in these few lines for a master class or a graduate seminar.

Not everyone thought every Shaw-Parker arrangement (or Parker-Shaw, as he preferred to say) flawless. Recall also Roger Wagner, Shaw's rival in the Chorale days, remarking that a Shaw arrangement of *Shenandoah* "sounded like *The Art of the Fugue*." But Shaw had both a practical and a temperamental reason for keeping the melody always in clear sight. Practically, he didn't want the tune cluttered, obscured, or slowed. The folkiness, or singability, might be lost. It would lose its genuineness and honesty. Temperamentally, he wanted to stay close to the composer so that he could hear the composer's voice. Where did the creator want the notes to move or rest?

Music, Shaw said again, again, and again, was 90 percent discipline, toil, and suffering. The other 10 percent of music—the earned 10 percent bonus—is inspiration, luck, letting the "disciplines" that brought you to this point go. The magic of creation that might come in the moment of completion of craft—performance. The mystic level above that of technical mastery might arrive as a gift, or it might not. But it certainly would and could not come without dues paying, without toil. The poetry is dependent on the prose.

"Come Holy Spirit," runs the ancient poem, "fill the hearts of your faithful and kindle in them the fire of your love." Shaw's much-repeated prayer was: "If you clean the cage, the dove may come."

87 Ibid.

CHAPTER 41

Icons Are Meant to Be Broken

Virtually everyone who knew him and worked closely with him has spoken about Robert Shaw's "humanity." But what do they mean? Passion, obviously, perhaps also temper, talent, drive, and compassion. But Shaw also had an infectious laugh and a highly individuated sense of humor.

Shaw could be droll, puckish, downright outrageous—such as when he told the ASOC bass section that the sounds they were making sounded like they were coming out of the wrong orifice of their bodies.

Shaw wrote this poem to his chorus in preparation for a "festival of requiems"—his astonishing staging of three requiems in three nights—in New York City in 1980. It's an example of his wit, which was never far from his obsession with music, or his pedagogy:

Introit:
Berlioz, Verdi, and Brahms
Was a trio of singers of Psalms.
What Berlioz wanted he never quite got,
And Verdi went "oom-pah" as often as not,
While, as for Brahms's love-life, it wasn't so hot.
But nothing impaired the musical charms

Of Berlioz, Verdi —
Of Berlioz, Verdi—
Of Berlioz, Verdi, and Brahms!

Ballade:
Hector's love for his music
—And make no mistakes here—Was short of his passion
For W. Shakespeare.
He offered to France Benvenuto Cellini,
But all Paris wanted
Was works by Rossini.

Held by those in his time
Less sublime than deplorable,
The balance still wavers:
Banal to adorable.

Like the ghost in Macbeth—A sorrowing spectre—He hovers and haunts
The theatrical sector.
He challenged the heavens;—And half his frustration
Is being renowned
For his "fine orchestration."

Cabalette:
Verdi kept by his desk
A composing machine. (The recent invention
of mean-well Joe Green.)

As quick as a flash
Or ahbrahcahdahbrah!

He put in a mass—
And out popped an opera!

Calzona:

His operatic plots, it's clear, Were frequently intended
As parables of social wrongs And how to get them mended.

If he were writing wrongs today we'd call him humanistic.
He'd not a womanizer be,
—But might be womanistic.

Liebeslied:

Brahms's morning star was slow to rise—Vienna had its slights:
His little wick of flame was dimmed by Wagner's acolytes.

He won his first esteem as a Piano virtuoso;
But soon his songs—as well as hands—Were known, and as maybe more so.

Some say he had affairs of heart—If not, he'd not be human.
(One hopes he helped to dry the tears of Mrs. Robert Schumann.)

He must have viewed his times askew:
Among his legacies
Are triplets over bars in two and duplets over threes.
Forever probing after Form, By nature and upbringing
His large designs all sheltered first the song and then the singing.

And so Vienna grew to love His walks and habitats;
And even folk across the street would nod and tip their hats.
And we who love his Requiem confess it and concede here:
The final Brahmsian pilgrimage still takes us to his Lieder.

See you Monday,
R
April 22, 1980[88]

88 Shaw papers.

Several of the singers who worked with Shaw in France say their favorite image of him is of a recording session at the tiny church in Gramat, the church of St. Pierre, where the Telarc Shaw small-choir recordings were made.

On this occasion, the pews had been removed from the church and Shaw was in his stocking feet. He had arranged the choir in circles and was moving, somewhat maniacally, as he sometimes did in rehearsal, from circle to circle conducting them. He was shoeless because the acoustics in the church were such that the conductor's shoes were potentially too distracting and could interfere with the recording. But the singers were now distracted by the fear that the maestro would step on the floor spikes that had formerly held the pews. The producers and engineers from Telarc were distracted by something else: Shaw was grunting under his breath as he conducted, as he always did. But in this medieval acoustic the sound was coming through. The technicians feared it would not be possible to clean up the recording. So Shaw had to be told about the problem, and no one wanted to be the bearer of that news. Everyone knew Shaw grunted when conducting (as several of the great pianists have), but Shaw didn't seem to know it.

No one quite remembers who had to do it. The consensus is that it was Bob Woods. Shaw was eventually told something like: Mr. Shaw, your grunting is disrupting the session. It is coming through on the recording.

There commenced much muttering, sputtering, cursing, and grinding of teeth. "I've been recording for 50 years," he said, "and in all that time nobody *ever* said I grunted." (There may have been an adjective or two in front of years.)

Then Shaw walked out of the session. As he passed Ann Jones in the circle of singers, he said, "You finish it. They don't want me." She went after him. After tempers had cooled a bit, Shaw went to work on solving the problem. He asked for tape and had it placed over his mouth.

Thus the indelible image, as one singer recalled, was of one of the world's greatest musicians, in his golden years, running around a tiny, musty old French church in his socks—red faced and gagged. "He looked like a crazed elf," she said.

The singers watched Shaw's mischievous eyes even more closely that day.

The concerts in France were under- or un-publicized and sparsely attended. Shaw did not mind. In fact, he seemed to like it that way. Indeed, his favorite concert was said to be the one that no one attended—there was, literally, no audience. (No publicity had been done, or signs hung, because of a misunderstanding on the part of the person charged with publicity.) The concert took place in Toulouse, in the cloister of the Cathedral. "We sang," said one participant, "only for each other." There was no vestige of entertainment here. There were none of his dreaded "deception" receptions. There was nothing but the music, the fellowship, and good food and wine after the music making. And there was the background of the Dordogne Valley and its small villages and ancient spires. For Shaw, it was a grand night.

Some singers noticed for the first time that night that Shaw was not a large or tall man. They noticed his great shyness. And there were times that they suddenly realized he was old. But not when they were making music together. In those moments, he seemed to be getting younger.

Making music in France was not possible for him after Caroline's death. "The problem," he said of his post-Caroline life, "is simply loneliness." But the problem was more severe than simple. His stepson Alex Hitz said, "He would not be consoled." Indeed, Shaw kept a quote from Dietrich Bonhoeffer in his desk, and often sent a copy to friends who had lost a loved one. This was his standard sympathy message when he needed to be Shaw the pastor. The passage reads:

> *. . . nothing can make up for the absence of someone whom we love, and it would be wrong to try to find a substitute; we must simply hold out and see it through.*

That sounds very hard at first, but at the same time it is a great consolation, for the gap, as long as it remains unfilled, preserves the bond between us.

It is nonsense to say that God fills the gap; he doesn't fill it, but on the contrary, he keeps it empty and so helps us to keep alive our former communion with each other, even at the cost of pain.[89]

Shaw the pastor and empathetic friend was the Shaw who showed up unannounced on his friend Walter Gould's front step after Gould's wife died. Gould lived in Manhasset, Long Island and Shaw was, of course, in Atlanta. But Shaw had an out-of-town conducting engagement and decided to fly to New York on the way. With no warning, Shaw showed up on Gould's doorstep early in the morning. He stayed only a few minutes. He did not come inside. He mumbled a few words of consolation and left. This was the same Shaw who said to Gould, after Gould's brother Morton died, "I'll be your brother now."

Shaw's compassion was not the compassion of a pose struck or the copious tears of a busybody. Rather, he had a great capacity for empathy and a deep and abiding pity for broken souls. It did not quickly kick in. He could be slow to notice, hard to reach. But when it did, his sympathy was visceral and his follow-up was low-key and practical—a gift or a loan for someone who had fallen on hard times; his personal check for services rendered for a singer who hadn't worked out; inking in a different note when a singer could not hit the high or right one; a bit of his humorous doggerel to someone getting a divorce; daily phone calls to a friend, player, or chorister fighting some merciless disease.

The same Shaw who would summarily fire an unprepared singer, or order one of his assistants to do so, would take extra time to work with one who was sincerely trying, but failing—even to the technical detriment

89 *Bonhoeffer Letters and Papers from Prison,* Macmillan, 1972, p. 176.

of the performance. The same Shaw who could be mercilessly cutting to a promoter, board member, or orchestra administrator he thought a fraud would come to the defense of a wounded soul. (As, for instance, his saying to his Alaska deputy Daniel Lewis of their petrified organist, "Couldn't you smell the *fear* on that man?")

After France and after Caroline, Shaw was more than ever Father Music, the grand old man. Mellowed, but not done. And he was, more than he had ever been in his life, alone. It would be just four years from Caroline's death until his own. He enjoyed being celebrated and treated as a guru and a national treasure. But it didn't fill the gap. He did not want to fill that gap. And he didn't quite believe all the accolades anyway. When Walter Gould, in Shaw's presence, read a rave *New York Times* review of a Shaw performance, he exclaimed, "Robert, you're an icon," Shaw reply? "Icons are made to be broken."[90]

90 Burris–Gould interview.

PART SIX

M=L=G

There are two things that raise a man
above earthly things—simplicity and purity.

—Thomas à Kempis

CHAPTER 42

Last Days

By December of 1998, Shaw was failing physically. He knew it, and those close to him knew it. But what bothered him most was a lack of stamina: he was unable to work. Indeed, he was forced to cancel all but one of his December engagements with the ASO, and that one he conducted sitting down. Through the years, through a series of mini strokes—and one major one when he was still music director of the ASO—he had always been able to recover, come back, push through. Not this time. In hypertension and heart disease he again mirrored his father. But his father was progressively disabled by his hypertension, whereas Shaw, because of advances in medical science, was lucky enough to work—indeed to conduct—until almost the end of his life. Indeed, Shaw was able to work at his craft until the month before his death, albeit with considerable discomfort.

But now there was no techno-medical fix available. Shaw had long-standing problems with the electrical conduction system of his heart. (One name for this is cardiac skeletal sclerosis. Another is Brady-tachycardia syndrome.) In practical terms, it means the heart can beat both too rapidly and too slowly. Shaw had a pacemaker (he liked to say it could keep tempo in rehearsal if he was having an off day). He took blood thinners to prevent clots as well. But blood thinners can cause bleeds, and Shaw had developed a spontaneous bleed in his brain. This necessitated ending the use of blood thinners. Shaw was stabilized, but in a no-man's land medically—between the possibility of a blood clot that would kill him and a bleed that would kill him. He knew all this.

The patient was also suffering, that last Christmas, from a pinched nerve.

He was weak, in pain, unable to do much sustained work in his study. He was unable to do much of anything. He was miserable, and miserable to be around.

Shaw was forced to cancel his Carnegie Hall workshop for 1999, which was to have been a program of Stabat Maters. (Typically, he dove deeply into his research, and was becoming an amateur expert on the history of this ancient and noble prayer, which amused some of his cohorts. Robert Shaw, enemy of organized religion, was exploring Roman Catholic theology and symbol.)

Yet, sick as he was, at the end of January, Shaw decided to travel to New Haven to see his son Thomas, a senior drama major at Yale, in a play. The decision stunned some of his friends. They had some notion of how sick Shaw was and they saw how suddenly enfeebled he had become.

But Shaw understood his situation clearly and made a decision in light of that understanding. He knew that "something could happen" on the trip, but something could happen at home, too.

At about this time, Shaw told one or two orchestra pals that the doctors had assured him he could live another 10 years. This was perhaps a kind-hearted fiction invented by Shaw for worried friends. In reality, he had been told that there was little that could be done, and that he could die at any moment. Shaw had always had an acute sense of time, and he'd made clear to intimates that he knew his time was running out. He concluded there was no particular advantage in dying at home. If he stayed home, he could be monitored closely by doctors and friends who knew his situation. On the other hand, if he was not stricken and he was sitting at home in his room, and the play came and went, he would be sorry. Shaw decided that if the end was to be soon, it might as well be in New Haven as in Atlanta. He would be with Thomas. He would keep his promise.

Thomas had only one parent now. Caroline Shaw had been gone for four years. Shaw knew that, best-case scenario, he would not be around for many more plays. He had spent much of his life as a no-show father, too busy with the higher things to be there for his children. This might be his last chance to be a good dad.

So Shaw flew into Hartford with Nola Frink and they took a limo to New Haven, and ensconced themselves in a hotel there to prepare for the play—*Endgame* by Thomas Becket.

On the night of the performance, Shaw spoke to his son by phone. "I've finally read the play," he said. "It's about death, isn't it?"

Later, during supper, Shaw remarked quietly, and almost to himself: "I think it would be very difficult for me to ever conduct again."

That night, during the play—in the tiniest theater in New Haven—Shaw began to snore, and then snore a very deep and audible snore. Nola nudged him, and then shook him. To no avail. Shaw would not awaken. He had suffered a massive stroke.

Thomas and the other actors in the play, sensing trouble, went speeding through their lines. The play came crashing to an end. An ambulance and paramedics were summoned. The lights came up and the medics descended. The small audience, all aware of what had happened, and to whom it had happened, departed in silence.

For the next 24 hours, Shaw lingered in the hospital but never regained consciousness. Nola Frink sat beside him, held his hand, and sang to him. She sang every aria, every soprano part of every oratorio libretto, and every hymn that came to her mind. Occasionally, he would seem to squeeze her hand a bit, attempting to signal, Frink surmised, that she was slightly below the pitch.

Shaw had suffered severe brain damage. And everyone knew what he wanted in such a circumstance. He'd told his friend and physician David

Lowance many times that he wished to live a high-quality life as long as possible, but that he did not wish to have a poor quality of life, or worse, mere existence, prolonged. His wishes were respected. He died on January 25, 1999, at Yale-New Haven Hospital. Shaw's sons Thomas and Alex, Shaw's daughter Johanna, and his niece Laura Wallace were present.

Thomas Shaw was now an orphan. He had lost his mother in his senior year of high school and his father in his senior year of college. Now he would have to invent his own life—a new life—as Robert Shaw had done.

Only weeks before, Shaw's stepson Alex Hitz had remarked to a friend, "When that man cannot make music any more, he will simply die. He will just will himself to die."

CHAPTER 43

Last Music

Shaw's final performance just a month before he died was, fittingly, with the Atlanta Symphony and Chorus. It was the Christmas portion of the Handel *Messiah* and the Bach *Magnificat*—two propulsive, life-affirming, and life-giving musical essays. Although he was sitting—and no one could remember *that* happening before—it was an appropriate and noble last stand.

Indeed, Shaw's last year, musically, was blessed, and in the light of a backward glance, has a valedictory shape and tone.

In the last summer of his life, Shaw directed a final Robert Shaw Festival, with the Robert Shaw Festival Singers—his last handpicked small choir, his protégés, his friends and extended family: his flock. Shaw had moved the festival to Furman University, in Greenville, South Carolina, partly because it was close to Atlanta, partly because he liked the people there, and partly because it was not France. Shaw was in good musical form and his artistic appetites were as voracious as ever. He scheduled two major and distinct programs for the festival. As had been his practice, one was a program of larger works, in this case, Haydn and Mozart—with orchestra. The other program was composed of shorter works, purely choral, which ranged from some favorite Britten pieces to spirituals. Both were nearly as long as the old

Robert Shaw Chorale programs on the road. Shaw had grown mellow in recent years. But now he was in a hurry again—trying to "do it all" before he died.

The music making in Greenville that summer was on a high level, and Shaw was happy with the result as well as with being back with his "family." The Britten material was to have been a Telarc recording, but Shaw was displeased with the Furman acoustic and later decided that, as good as this choir was, it did not have something "new" to say about Britten's music in an era in which English choirs were generally superb. Shaw was also tired. And that was the other thing that was going on. Time was closing in. He lacked his old stamina and he wore himself out at Furman that summer. He was forced to cancel subsequent major engagements with the Boston Symphony at Tanglewood and the Cleveland Orchestra at the Blossom Festival. Nola Frink asked him if it was really necessary to conduct *all* the festival programs or, indeed, hold the festival at all. "These are the same people you have worked with again and again," she said. "They know your methods and ideas." Of course it was necessary, Shaw said. It was only at Nola's insistence that he cancelled Tanglewood, but even if she had not insisted, Shaw might not have made it onto the airplane.[91] He was that depleted. Perhaps the gathering of the flock and the repetitions of the familiar rehearsal rituals at Furman gave him a sense of comfort. He was gathering his clan. For Shaw knew, even then, that he was running out of days. It was about this time that

91 This writer witnessed 20 or so Shaw performances and rehearsals in the last few years of Shaw's life. One incident in particular stands out. It happened at Tanglewood: The writer, there with his family, was walking the grounds perhaps 40 minutes before a Sunday afternoon performance. One of this writer's children was holding his hand and another was riding on his shoulders. We heard singing in one of the sheds and moved slowly toward it. We weren't looking for anything, or expecting anything. Simply responding to warm sounds on a warm day. When we arrived at the shed, a crowd was already gathered around the door and open windows. Robert Shaw was warming up a chorus. The writer's daughter whispered, "It's Mr. Shaw." Shaw was telling a story about his old Tanglewood days. It was hard to hear, but it involved "Dr." Koussevitzky. The crowd had begun to swell, but Shaw had not noticed, so silent were the onlookers and so involved was he. Then Shaw looked up and saw the throng, perhaps 200 people now—the outsiders. His countenance changed, and he began to mutter and tap his baton against his leg. Then, "Let's go." He charged out through the chorus and past the crowd toward a waiting golf cart and driver. It was now 25 minutes or so before the performance and he was still in his rehearsal blues. Before Shaw reached the cart, a small boy, perhaps 8 or 9, approached him with a score, and asked him to sign it. Shaw drew back a bit. "We've *got* a *job* to do," he said. The boy's shoulders fell and Shaw quickly reversed, saying, "Alright, alright." He signed the score with the Sharpie in his pocket and said: "There you go, boy." Then he got into the golf cart and told the driver to "move." As one musician said, "You'd seen him naked."

Nola remarked to Shaw that his skin color seemed to be changing. He said, yes, he'd noticed, too, and added, "I'm just dying, you know."

Given his summer exhaustion and cancellations, many doubted Shaw would be able to conduct a two-week Beethoven festival with the National Symphony in Washington, DC. He was scheduled to conduct *Symphony No. 9*, the *Choral Fantasy*, and the *Missa Solemnis*, and that meant two weeks of arduous rehearsals and six performances. As Shaw himself liked to point out, Beethoven is "protean as hell," and the *Missa* an Everest. No, that would not be happening.

But it *did* happen. He did it.

Shaw loved nothing in music more than these pieces, especially the *Missa*, and if he were at all able, he *would* conduct them one last time. He also loved the National Symphony, Washington and, at this stage of his life, being visible and in the thick of things. Gone was any feeling that he wanted to work at his craft in the shadows. He had been given the Kennedy Center Honors a few years before and was happy to conduct in this hall. He also greatly respected Leonard Slatkin and felt Slatkin had improved the orchestra. (Slatkin, in turn, revered Shaw as a patriarch of American classical music and eagerly listened to Shaw talk of Toscanini and other legendary figures Shaw had known.)

For the *Choral Fantasy*, Shaw chose the pianist Lee Luvisi—a musician few at the Symphony knew. He was not a big-name recording artist of the kind that conductors and orchestras like to hire for such a performance series. Luvisi was a music scholar, an academic, a chamber musician. He was just the sort of musician Shaw liked most to work with—the sort who shared his devotion. They had worked together in Atlanta, and interestingly, like other pianists, Luvisi and Shaw had formed a bond based upon humility, study, and devotion to craft. This was a man who knew the score and tried to make *it* the star, just as Shaw did. Luvisi was stunned to get the high-profile assignment and pleased and surprised to hear from Shaw after many years.

Shaw did miss one rehearsal with the chorus. (He offered to send his pacemaker along.) But the performances were triumphs. Audiences quite literally leapt to their feet at the conclusion of the music. Shaw was particularly amused by what he called "a standing ovulation" for the *Choral Fantasy*. As they stood to receive the applause, an obviously pleased Shaw asked Luvisi if he could believe it. Many in Washington remarked on Shaw's sensitive pacing of the *Ninth*, which, after all, he knew by now like the back of his hand. Yet, Shaw told Slatkin, it always seemed to him an awesome responsibility to conduct the piece. The piece was never "old hat" to him, but was always intimidating. Musicians present remarked, as they often did after hearing this piece conducted by Shaw, that the unexpected pleasure was what he did with the third movement. As for the *Missa*, the headline on *Washington Post* critic Tim Page's review was: "A *Missa* for the ages."

This was not Shaw's only out-of-town triumph in that last year. Nor was it the last.

Just days after the Washington concerts, he was called by the Boston Symphony Orchestra at the last minute. Seiji Ozawa was ill. He would be unable to conduct the gala opening of the season. The program was Beethoven's *Ninth Symphony*. Would Mr. Shaw stand in? Shaw felt he owed the Boston Symphony one, for he had cancelled Tanglewood that summer. And even he would admit that he could conduct this piece without re-editing the score or any last-minute cramming.

With Kennedy Center Beethoven performances fresh in everyone's mind, including Shaw's, he accepted the challenge. Indeed, in Boston, there would be no time for *any* rehearsal. Luckily, Shaw knew all the soloists. And he knew the orchestra, having begun to conduct at Tanglewood again after 40-odd years' absence and having closed the previous Tanglewood season with just this piece. Due to airplanes and traffic snags, Shaw had only a little time to meet with the principals before the performance, and that was it. Of course, the audience and critics delighted in the old pro pulling it off as, in truth, did the old pro. "Did you hear what we did?" he asked his sister Anne.

In that last year of his life, Shaw also gave an amazing final performance of the Bach *Mass in B Minor* at Carnegie Hall with the Orchestra of St.

Luke's and the ASO Chamber Chorus. It was at Easter time and it was Shaw's last performance on that beloved stage, where he had done upward of 50 concerts over the years.

There were two occasions, both in Shaw's later years, in which he felt he was getting close to realizing Bach's intentions in his Mass. The first was in France, which some of the participants called the "small" *B Minor* performance. It was performed in a tiny, ancient church, the choir was small—chamber sized—and lithe, and the instrumentalists were also of chamber quality and scale. Even the audience was small. Shaw was playing with his friends again. All the musicians were singing and playing, for each other, and for Bach. The second time was Shaw's final performance at Carnegie Hall. He was able to scale it down and make the piece very intimate, as he'd long wanted. Shaw seemed barely to "conduct" that night. Certainly, he scarcely looked at the score. The music appeared to inhabit him. And he seemed to embody it. The bent old man at the podium grew younger and stronger with each note. He had finally "disappeared" into the music.

It was fitting that Shaw, who spent so much time on this piece, should have crowned his own performing life with it. And he seemed aware that both a summarizing and a summoning were taking place. "Remember," he told his forces, "someone in the audience is hearing this piece for the first time, and someone is hearing it for the last time."

He also told one interviewer that "if there is a heaven—and a God—the *Mass in B Minor* would surely be God's favorite music."

But Shaw's *very* last out-of-town performance was a very different sort of triumph. It was a kind of glorified sing-along, and its purpose was to raise money for something he believed in.

Shaw's old friend Elvera Voth, with whom he had worked in the Anchorage Music Festivals many years before, had founded an "Arts in Prison" program in Kansas. Its nucleus was music. Voth began with a men's choir. Would Shaw come to Newton College in Bethel, Kansas, and lead a benefit concert to raise seed money for the program?

Would he?

This was just up Shaw's alley and he was enormously excited by it.

Shaw also loved and admired Elvera Voth.

So, at a time in his life when he was trying to save some energy, and cancelling rather august engagements, Shaw traveled to a little Mennonite town in Kansas—at his own expense—to raise $25,000 by leading those who plunked down their money in a sing-along of some familiar choruses.

That initial funding *did* launch the "Arts in Prison" program in Kansas, which became quite successful and eventually expanded beyond choral music. Shaw made a Mennonite full circle—the help he extended to Voth might also be seen as a tip of the hat to his old friend Clayton Krehbiel, also a Mennonite.

Voth was a true Shavian. She did serious and difficult music with the prisoners, and insisted that the hard and damaged men she worked with meet exacting musical standards. She, too, insisted that music can change hearts and minds.

Shaw's spirits were high on that trip, and he talked at some length to the local newspaper and a small group of fans who had gathered around him, of that "long line of preachers" from whence he had come, adding that before long he would be joining them in the place to which they had gone, concluding with his trademark cackle, "It can't be long now."

It would be 71 days.[92]

The music continued after Shaw's death. In lieu of a church funeral (which no one who knew his thoughts on organized religion would have suggested), there was a memorial "celebration" of his life at the Woodruff Arts Center, where he had rehearsed, performed, and recorded for so many

92 For a fine account of this episode, see "Mother Teresa, How Can I Help You? The Story of Elvera Voth, Robert Shaw, and the Bethel College Benefit Sing-Along for Arts in Prison, Inc.," by Mary L. Cohen (*International Journal of Research in Choral Singing*, Vol. 3).

years. The Atlanta Symphony Orchestra, which he'd led and built, played the "Adagio" movement of Beethoven's *Symphony No. 9*. Various Shaw singers and choirs sang, ending the service with the "Hallelujah Chorus" from Handel's *Messiah*. And a memorial booklet, made up largely of Robert Shaw aphorisms and covered in his favorite color of midnight blue (the color of a seemingly endless supply of Shaw rehearsal work shirts), was distributed.

Symphony Hall was full that day. Hundreds of people came from all over the world to pay tribute. Some were managers of other symphony orchestras, some were executives with Coca-Cola, some were music students who traveled by night from their colleges and conservatories in beat-up old cars, and some were "amateurs" who had simply been touched by Shaw's music making. Hundreds more people posted memories and benedictions on an *Atlanta Constitution* Web site created expressly for the purpose of tributes to Shaw.

As the weeks and months drew on, the tributes kept coming. Professional musicians were, perhaps, uncommonly generous. Kurt Masur, then music director of the New York Philharmonic, described Shaw as a "musical priest" for singers, and dedicated a performance of the Beethoven *Missa Solemnis* at the Cathedral of Saint John the Divine to Shaw's memory. The Boston and Chicago Symphonies dedicated performances of the Brahms *German Requiem* to Shaw. The Cincinnati May Festival did an entire program of Shaw arrangements of folk songs, spirituals, and other short pieces associated with him, in memoriam. Yale, where Shaw died while visiting Thomas Shaw, held its own memorial service. Scores of local choirs did tribute concerts or tribute pieces within concerts. And almost three months after his death, *The New York Times* dedicated most of an entire page to a story about the sense of loss that now seemed to hang, as a cloud, over American singers and choruses. Conductor James Conlon said, "He was a gigantic figure, and it feels like a different world without him."

It still does.

For 60 years, Robert Shaw had been a founding father of American classical music. He seemed to be everywhere and always in motion. And he did seem to speed up in the last 10 years, and yet again in the last 5 years, of his life. Was there anything he felt he left undone?

Not much, but a little.

There was the undone *St. Matthew Passion* recording that he felt so ambivalent about.

He talked at the last Carnegie Workshop in 1998, at which he did the Haydn *Seasons* and *Creation* in one week, about a "Passion Week" at Carnegie in which orchestra and chorus would do the Bach *St. John* and *St. Matthew* and the Penderecki *St. Luke Passion.*

He spoke of learning and performing the Elgar *Dream of Gerontius,* which he'd never done.

These are tantalizing might-have-beens.

John Henry Newman said, "Growth is the only evidence of life." At the end of his life, Robert Shaw was still growing—still learning and recording new music, as the Dvorák *Stabat Mater* performances and recordings proved. It was just that his body had tired.

Bob Woods felt that some good Shaw Bach recordings "got away." Certainly a disc of Bach cantatas with the Shaw imprimatur would have sold, and perhaps revealed that Shaw had something new and fresh to say about Bach. But somehow the stars were never in alignment. Moreover, Shaw felt bound to use full ASO forces in his recordings as long as he was music director there.

Most fascinating, perhaps, is that Shaw once expressed to Sylvia McNair the desire to record the four Brahms symphonies. But he added: "That ain't gonna happen." He never pushed for it, thinking that there would be no market. He felt no one wanted to hear him conducting Brahms without voices. Simply as an economic matter, but also as an artistic one, he was wrong about that. At the end of his life, the record-buying public would very probably have bought a re-made or re-mastered *Winnie the Pooh* recording by Shaw. The Brahms symphonies might have been revelatory recordings.

Of course, a life like Shaw's is never finished. But it ended as it was lived—in labor and with music.

Shaw was working on his English translation of the Brahms *Requiem* when he left Atlanta for New Haven. He was to record it with the Utah Symphony and the Mormon Tabernacle Choir in the winter of 1999. Despite his remark in New Haven, that he did not see how he could conduct again, Shaw was scheduled to conduct again. Indeed, he was scheduled into the next year and the year beyond that. He knew otherwise. (Telarc did make the Brahms record with the Mormon Tabernacle Choir as a memorial to Shaw, under the direction of Shaw's friend and protégé Craig Jessop, with Bob Woods at the helm.)

Leaving aside the handful of things Shaw left undone, we have bushels of things Shaw wanted to do that he did do. Not only did he conduct dozens of major symphonic and choral-orchestral works by virtually every major composer, but he was able to record most of the great oratorio and choral-orchestral works, and make fresh statements about many of them—statements he hoped echoed the composer's vision and musical language. There are other small gems one treasures as much, like some of the *a cappella* recordings he made in France, and his recording of the Rachmaninoff *Vespers* and the Schubert songs for male chorus. There is his amazing final recording—the Dvorák *Stabat Mater* made on October 31 and November 1, 1998, less than three months before his death. Shaw was growing fragile by then and would take short naps at Symphony Hall, but he seemed to everyone 20 years younger and stronger on the podium. It was an extraordinarily happy recording session of a deeply sorrowful piece of music, which Shaw somehow infused with new life. And there are, for so many, the memories of countless live performances—timeless, transcendent, still intact. There is his life as a tireless musical road warrior—16 trips to the Crane School of Music over the course of 33 years, for example. Why? Crane is well off the beaten path. Another chance to conduct the Beethoven *Missa* (thrice). A chance to conduct the Bach *Mass in B Minor* (twice).

CHAPTEI

MENSCH

Robert Shaw's life and work may be the greatest love story in the history of American music.

As Romeo pursued Juliet, Shaw pursued music. As Abelard longed for Heloise, so Shaw sought a sound clear, warm, and true enough.

Shaw believed that music could change hearts and he began with himself: *his* heart, *his* psyche, *his* life. He was always a man of energy and passion. But he became a man of conscience and of reflection—in critic Richard Dyer's words, "a mensch."

One thinks of him saying to Nola Frink on the way to a Carnegie workshop, "Do I get paid for this?" Or of him saying to Walter Gould, "I'll be your brother now."

Did music really change Shaw? Or did Shaw change Shaw? We know what Shaw's answer would be. Perhaps no practical distinction can be made. The man and his musical education and vocation are inseparable.

Beethoven really was alive to him—his idol, mentor, inspiration, and friend.

And what about two of his favorite stories? The Robert Shaw Chorale and Orchestra musicians weeping the last time they did the Mozart *Requiem* at the end of the first tour. Or the mother who had just buried her child in

Alaska, who thanked him for bringing Mozart's grief, and life, to hers. In Shaw's words on Hindemith's *Requiem:* "It changes you . . . you're not the same."

One thinks of the St. Luke's musicians repeating the Shaw aphorism, "Music is always waxing and waning. Coming, going, or arriving."

Music is the life impulse and the soul impulse.

One thinks of Shaw telling musicians, the last time he did the Bach *Mass in B Minor*, to be aware of the responsibility of playing it for someone who is hearing it for the first time, and someone who is hearing it for the last.

Music is the right of many.

One thinks of an audience member at Carnegie Hall, at that last *Mass in B Minor* saying, "We don't know how long we'll have this man with us."

In the end, it wasn't so much Shaw's talent, his experience, or his discipline that mattered most. What was most distinctive was the way Shaw looked at his craft—his way of thinking about and making music.

Like Brahms, Shaw loved beauty, and had a vulnerable open heart, but, like Brahms, he kept an edge to protect himself and to avoid sentimentality.

Like Lincoln, his non-musical hero, Shaw was a self-made original.

Like both Brahms and Lincoln, Shaw was a large soul—always evolving, refining, rising—in the tradition of the American transcendentalists whose writings he loved.

He possessed the wonder of a child and the ferocity and focus of a warrior.

He changed American music by focusing on improving it and himself. That was his essential American-ness again: improve yourself, keep working, make it better.

Shaw saw music as something holy. Maybe the last thing that could be holy. So the problem became *how to make the making of music holy.*

CHAPTER 45

Music Alone

When you enter the Trappist monastery in Bardstown, Kentucky, called Gethsemane, the words above the gate are: "God alone."

Music became Shaw's church. He wanted to become a kind of contemplative within it—living a simple, focused life, devoted to the musical composition at hand. He'd started as an evangelist. He was ending as a monk. He desired only the music. Just as a monk tries to live for "God alone," and tries for what the Trappists call "conversion of life," Shaw wanted to convert his own heart. If he could live for music alone, this might happen, however haltingly.

A "saint," Fr. James Martin, SJ, tells us, "may be a patron whom one asks to intercede for him to the Divinity." That is the traditional understanding. But a saint may also be, says Martin, "a companion and example—someone who teaches the way." For Shaw, Beethoven was this kind of saint.

The composers became his companions.

For Shaw, the implied notion of "conversion of life" extended into his personal life. Not that Beethoven's notes would teach him to be a good father and husband, but he believed they did change his heart, and make it possible for him to, as he put it, "grow up."

Is this a kind of idolatry? Or a bizarre type of psychological displacement?

Was Shaw's spiritualization of music, even "churchification" of music, a matter of making "false gods"?

Perhaps it would seem so to some. One suspects it would seem so to his parents. But not to him. For Shaw music was another way; the only way. For Shaw the sanctity of music became obvious in the making of it. Once you delved into Mozart and began to understand the music, even a little, the Divine simply leapt out at you—Divine order, Divine beauty, Divine grace. That, Shaw said, will (can) seldom happen in a church. Outside of the arts, properly understood and embraced, what road to God is consistent, or possible at all?

One might well ask whether even Shaw had truly given up on the world's religions. What sort of self-professed agnostic is interested in new forms of worship, after all? Worship whom? What? To what end?

Thomas Lawson Shaw said, "I don't buy my father's alleged agnosticism, I think he protested too much."

But protest he did—routinely harassing Baptists and Methodists in his choir in a not-altogether-friendly fashion, and cursing away at the televangelists every Sunday morning. Maybe Shaw was impatient for those old, organized religions to finally fall and for a new day to come. Maybe he was not an agnostic at all, but a believer at heart—someone who had to believe in some unifying and eternal force for enlightenment and love and, equally, had to find his own way to it. But certainly he thought the "Crystal Christoramas" were holding back the church of music, which would open the way to a new enlightenment and a new humanism. This was the "agnostic" who loved his Unitarian church in Cleveland, and loved being a music minister there, and would say, even 40 years later, that this was a form of religion that he could support. Unitarianism is not exactly revolution, or nihilism. It wasn't that even in 1962. It is well north of agnosticism and well within the American tradition of religious freedom, at least in New England and the Midwest, if not in the Bible Belt.

Shaw was the "agnostic" who said a person "would have to be a damn fool" to listen to the Bach *Mass in B Minor* and not admit the possibility of Bach's kind of God—not a divine energy or influence but a divine being who somehow sustains both earthly and eternal goodness.

Shaw thought religious sensibility and exploration, like music, was too important to be left to the professionals. In some ways, Shaw took religion more seriously than modern religion takes itself. In one of the Carnegie Hall videos, Shaw wondered: "What would Jesus say about any church on Fifth Avenue in New York?" He answered his own question. Shaw said Jesus would be shocked and would ask, "*I* created this? This is what *I* made?" And Shaw added, "He had trouble with a temple made out of mud." Robert Shaw could take the evangelical church out of himself, but not the evangelist.

All his life Shaw was drawn to religious questions, religious metaphors, religious texts and mediations, and holy people. He was violently repulsed by every form of religious fundamentalism and almost as opposed to every form of religious institutionalization. (He did soften his feeling about churchgoing, slightly, just as he softened many feelings, after Caroline Shaw came into his life. He sometimes went, as we have noted, to Mrs. Shaw's church, Trinity Presbyterian, and he had deep respect for her minister there, the Rev. Allison Williams, who became a close friend. Shaw even conducted several chamber programs and gave his three Harvard lectures there—on the "conservative arts," worship and the arts, and conducting orchestra and chorus. But *he* did not join the church.) In later life, Shaw also formed a close association with the Mormon Tabernacle Choir, a group he had once regarded dismissively. One of Shaw's closest protégés, Craig Jessop, became music director of that choir, and Shaw was actually invited to deliver "the spoken word" on a weekly telecast from The Tabernacle—the only non-Mormon to be so honored, at least up to that time. It was a unique and ironic honor for an inveterate church basher. But to Jessup and others who knew him well, Shaw's spirituality was obvious.

Shaw deeply believed something he often said: that religion and politics had failed modern man and that the arts could and would serve as society's only viable substitute for both the church and the public square. As he saw it, music, and choral singing in particular, was the one remaining natural habitat for community and for the life of the spirit.

Perhaps Robert Shaw didn't lose *his* Christian faith, though he did, certainly, lose most of his parents' faith. Shaw's Christianity was a highly personalized combination of Christian mysticism, Christian agnosticism, pacifism, Beethoven, Brahms, and Shaw. Shaw doubted that contemporary organized Christianity had been faithful to Jesus; and he doubted that eternity was a *place* so much as a *state of being*—best imagined in Bach's music, or Beethoven's, or Mozart's.

Shaw well understood that form of profound faith that does not provide immunity to doubt but is intertwined with doubt. He was, actually, engaged all his life with the primary religious questions: Who is God, and what does He want from me? What is the purpose of life? What is my mission on earth?

Shaw saw Jesus as the greatest of all teachers and humanists. He left whatever else Jesus was to Bach and other orthodox believers. Though he felt Bach's Passions and *Mass in B Minor* were the greatest achievements of art known to man, Shaw's own theology was closer to Kierkegaard, Martin Buber, and Miguel de Unamuno than to Bach or to Luther. Shaw didn't need Jesus to be God. "For me," he said, "it is enough that he was a man."

At the memorial "celebration" concert for Shaw held at the Woodruff Arts Center after his death, Rev. Williams gave a meditation that he felt epitomized Shaw and that Sylvia McNair thought summarized Shaw's personal theology. It was borrowed from Mother Teresa. When Mother Teresa was asked what she said when she prayed to God, she replied, "I do not speak to God; I listen." She was then asked what God said to her. And she replied, "God does not speak; He listens." The Rev. Williams then said: "Let us pray." And there was silence.

CHAPTER 46

DISAPPEARING

Robert Shaw's humility was both aesthetic and neurotic: both natural and practiced. He never thought that he, or any conductor, was worthy of a great composer's finest work, but he also felt that he was less worthy than most because he believed he was inadequately prepared for his profession. Yet his humility and his insecurity, which were indivisible, granted him a precious gift: He came to music as its servant. Ever the student and ever striving, he rehearsed and performed each piece of music as though it was the composer's last will and testament.

After being shown part of a film of Shaw conducting the Beethoven *Symphony No. 9*, Peter Sacco, a University of Connecticut professor and orchestra conductor who played under Shaw as an instrumentalist several times, said, "It breaks me up to see him...partly because he is gone. But also, just his total, unselfish commitment to the music. It makes discussions of tempo and interpretation seem so trite. He had this quality...I don't know what to call it...maybe what Aristotle calls 'virtue.'"

For Aristotle, virtue was not simply goodness, or sweetness, but "excellence of character," or "dispositions which we praise," writes philosopher Roger Scruton. Aristotelian virtue might be said to be a combination of heart, soul, and discipline.

Once Shaw was visiting with the journalist Paul Hume, then the premier music critic in Washington, DC. Hume asked Shaw what he had not accomplished that he would like to accomplish. Shaw said he would just like to feel he had "gotten close," just once, when rehearsing and conducting the Bach *St. Matthew Passion.* Fred Scott, Shaw's longtime assistant in Atlanta, was present, and said he thought to himself, "Oh, for Pete's sake." But Scott came to realize that Shaw was totally in earnest. He really felt he had merely skimmed the surface in scores of performances. And he really thought it would take many more performances to "get close" to what Bach intended. Recall Shaw to Peter Serkin: "Every performance is a failure." (Serkin recalled this, as another true artist would, "That's beautiful.")

Shaw suffered from stage fright his entire life. Often he broke into a cold sweat and shakes before he went on stage. And though he became more relaxed and confident in later years, he did worry he would forget something or lose his place in a performance. (He knew this had happened to Toscanini, and may have actually seen it.) It wasn't the audience he feared, or even the critics in a place like New York. He knew he'd prepared the musicians as best he could. He feared letting down the composer.

At his final Carnegie Hall workshop in 1998, the works were Haydn's *The Creation* and *The Seasons.* Both pieces would be rehearsed in a single week. The performances of each would be two days apart. It was inspiring, and a little scary, to many that an 80-year-old man was putting himself through double rehearsals and two different concert programs. Sometimes, as the poet Eugene McCarthy wrote, "The last shot from the brittle bow is truest."[93]

Though Shaw talked about doing *three* pieces for the workshop the year *after* next (three Passions), there was a summing up and farewell quality to the days of the Haydn preparation. Maestros James Levine (in rehearsal togs) and Kurt Masur dropped by the dress rehearsal, for example, to pay

93 From "Courage at Sixty" (*Selected Poems,* 1997).

their respects. And the press and the public seemed to feel this was the last, or close to the last, time Robert Shaw would conduct in New York. Judy Arron felt everyone could sense it. She certainly did. "I somehow feel Robert will not be back next year," she told a friend. (And then, Arron died. Neither she nor Robert returned for the 1999 workshop.) And when he did the *B Minor* a few months later, there was an almost palpable sense in the hall that Robert Shaw was saying goodbye. There was also a sense of a family gathering, a homecoming, to both the Haydn and the Bach rehearsals. There was inherent joy in the music itself. And there was the joy Shaw found in a last chance to "get close." Shaw seemed to be giving everything he had left. This was evident even to the audience in the Bach performance. These are joyful pieces, of course. But the joy in doing them *right*, and knowing that he knew how to do them well, mattered enormously to Shaw. By "well" one does not mean definitive: he was way beyond such an aim. One means "clarity, energy, and devotion."

There was also perhaps a joy in not doing requiems—these were pieces about life: celebrating life. Shaw had seen death. He'd watched Caroline die and now Judy was ill, and he knew that he, too, was not far from death. Better to celebrate with Haydn and Bach—to ride the big wave out of this world.

Speaking in the Haydn rehearsals about the sound he was trying to get in the initial choral entry in the *Creation*, portraying the Blakean first moment of light on earth, Shaw said: "We are talking about the edge of language—the edge of communication and of understanding....We must have that edge; that emotional necessity."

Later, speaking about that same passage, he said: "It must sound, not like great voices, but great drama—as though everybody was overcome by the mystery of the thing."

He even allowed himself a bit of nostalgia in the rehearsals for the last workshop, noting that he'd been conducting on the Carnegie stage for 50 years. "Different floor," he deadpanned. But the hall, he told his "beloveds," was a great and precious instrument in its own right.

Shaw's stage fright, which he never totally overcame, usually did not last once the music began. He knew what to do then, and the music itself took over. But he always felt, on some level: I am not up to this. I am not worthy of this. *No one is*, but me, least of all. He approached music as a beggar, a penitent, a slave.

This penitential quality was, paradoxically, part of Shaw's allure and his power. Many musicians found his humility so raw that his urgent pleas for help in uncovering the music were impossible to resist. Emotionally, he'd caught them, drawn them in, even if they found his microscopic editing of the score more hindrance than help.

Those who knew him say they have never known anyone remotely like Robert Shaw. One singer who worked with him extensively in the last 15 years of his life, Richard Clement, said that it is silly to talk about who will be the "next Shaw." There was no one like Shaw before he came along, said Clement, so why should we expect another Shaw after him? He was without precursor and without successor. This is partly a comment about Shaw's choral legacy, of course. But it is also about the Shavian idea of what music is: life force, motion, and grace.

CHAPTER 47

Credo

Christians, when they gather, say a "creed"—Apostle's Creed or Nicene Creed. Shaw said that he ceased to be a Christian when he found he could not go beyond the Creed's first line: "I believe in God." And he was not absolutely sure about that line. But Shaw had his own creed. He wrote it down and he preached it and distributed it in interviews and commencements and convocations. There was a long version and a longer version. It is contained in his "conservative arts" address and, to a lesser degree, in his "worship and the arts" speech. But the short version of it is as follows: "We believe that in a world of political, economic, and personal disintegration, music is not a luxury, but a necessity...because it is the persistent focus of man's intelligence, aspiration, and goodwill."

This is a theological oath. It begins with "believe," and not just "I believe," but "we believe," in the manner of a classic Christian credo. Music was not only Shaw's life, it was his faith—his road to the highest level of human awareness, to the eternal, to the Divine.

The formulation of the core Shaw equation bears repeating: It begins "God is love." Not "God is to be loved," or "God loves," but "God *is* love." G = L. And, by analogy, he continues: "Music is love, and so is a chorus, and so is singing together." So, G = L = M. Shaw based his life on this equation, or rather, the equation reversed: M = L = G.

The intensity of his belief in music was Bach-like; the fervor and idiosyncratic nature of it were Beethoven-like. This musical faith—a spiritual approach to music and an evangelist's belief in what music could do for humanity—was not just patter for universities or interviewers, it was the basis of Shaw's work, his days, his being. Music was his daily compass. And as he aged, his musical theology crystallized and his performances became richer, more intense, more relaxed, focused, and passionate.

Shaw kept adding to that big speech—"the conservative arts." He gave it two or three times a year, year after year. He would adapt and perfect, but mostly add on. Shaw liked to give speeches, but he loved to give *that* speech. He did not deliver it; he preached it. He was affirming, testifying, and bolstering himself. He was saying his prayers.

Like a fundamentalist minister who has one basic sermon, "Repent, the end is near," Robert Shaw had one basic sermon (unless he was delivering a speech for the symphony, to an Atlanta civic group, or for a eulogy). That one basic sermon, that one central message came in slight variations: Make music and find dignity and uplift; embrace the arts and heal the soul; sing the notes as Beethoven (or Brahms or Mozart) actually wrote them and they will make you a better person. Decode the language of the composer, enter into it, and your heart—and, hence, the consciousness of the whole human community—will be purified, if only a little. But the basic message was: M = L = G: Music equals Love equals participation in the Divine.

Belief defined Robert Shaw's life. Struggle punctuated and propelled it. One might even say he believed in struggle. One had to struggle to get the music ready. One had to struggle to understand it. One had to struggle to perform it, to believe it, and to live within it.

Shaw struggled, strove, and believed. Music was the element with which and in which he struggled—the end *and* the means.

And though he spent thousands of words and hundreds of hours re-writing his credo, it was also succinctly summarized by Hindemith: "Music must be transformed into moral power." That summarizes what Shaw saw as "the necessity" of his mission, of his vocation. *Of course,* people had to be converted to music, and music to moral power—for music is love and love Divine.

In the second of his great, rambling Victorian-style stump speeches, "Worship and the Arts," Robert Shaw *equated* the arts with worship; in fact, he said that great musical art is the most unequaled and unparalleled act of worship. Then Shaw added what is an important concept for him:

> *Mystery and sensitivity to pain are irreducible conditions for worship.*

He wrote:

> *The Arts provide for the exchange of ideas or values otherwise incommunicable by alphabets, numbers, equations or grunts. The reason that our reaction to a Beethoven quartet cannot be described is that the Arts are not superfluous. They exist to convey that which cannot otherwise be conveyed.*
>
> *Off stage in an Anchorage High School auditorium a well-weathered woman of uncertain years waits for the students' programs to be autographed. This is at a time when Alaska has more light airplanes than automobiles, and more miles of unpaved landing strips than of paved roads. She has just listened to the first Alaskan performance of Mozart's* Requiem. *"This is the only Mozart I've ever heard," she says, "and I don't speak no Latin . . . I had a child who died last winter. Thank you very much."*
>
> *The truth is that it does not require a graduate degree in musicology or art history to what they call "appreciate" great art.*

What it does require is equal parts of modesty and vulnerability—
and a preference for the small truth over the big lie.

Shaw began his career in show business and never lost his understanding of the realities of the performing arts in the modern consumer age. But he was not in show biz. He was in vows—locked in his vocation and its ever more rigorous demands. Shaw worked until his body would no longer allow him to work. He felt he was doing the Lord's work, just as his father had. And when he could no longer do that work, Robert Shaw died.

In the narrow definitional sense of religion, it might be said that Shaw began life as an evangelical Christian and ended life as a Christian humanist.

But this is far too simple. Shaw often noted the length and degree of audience silence at the end of a great work as a measure of the performers' success in transmitting the composer's creation. He said the only fitting response to Bach, if you really hear Bach, is silence: awe. Shaw's concept of prayer was Mother Teresa's silence.

Shaw did not deny the truth of orthodox religion so much as he doubted its exclusive hold on the truth. He left himself open to a full pastel of possibilities—from nothingness to resurrection. Shaw liked to say that after considering the resurrection portion of the "Credo" in Bach's *Mass in B Minor*, it would be hard to be an atheist. "Whether one comes back as a beetle or a stone," he once said, "one would be a damn fool to deny the possibility of resurrection." But for Shaw, that was not what mattered. Sensitivity to pain and to art was *enough*—enough responsibility, and the only achievable responsibility in this life.

Chorus member in a seminar: "Do you consider yourself a teacher?"
Shaw: "If I'm lucky, I don't consider myself."

Shaw sought to achieve, and to a great extent did achieve, a rare thing for an artist or a man of fame: indifference to his legacy, his reputation, his place in history. He used to talk about the "nameless artisans" who built the cathedrals of France. They, he said, were the *true* artists. They made art only for its own sake, giving all they had to it, and knowing that no one would ever recognize or remember them. Nameless artisans—the ultimate amateurs. The purity of their motive and their art moved him deeply.

Not many years before he died, the filmmaker Ingmar Berman said something remarkably similar, and it fits Shaw's pursuit of purity in his craft.

> *I want to be one of the artists of the cathedral that rises on the plain. I want to occupy myself by carving out of stone the head of a dragon, an angel, or a demon, or perhaps a saint: it doesn't matter; I will find the same joy in any case. Whether I am a believer or an unbeliever, Christian or pagan, I work with all the world to build a cathedral because I am an artist and an artisan, and because I have learned to draw faces, limbs, and bodies out of stone. I will never worry about the judgment of posterity or of my contemporaries; my name is carved nowhere and will disappear with me. But a little part of myself will survive in the anonymous and triumphant totality.*

In 1940, F. Scott Fitzgerald wrote in a letter to his daughter:

> *I am not a great man, but sometimes I think the impersonal and objective equality of my talent and the sacrifices of it, in pieces, to preserve its essential value has some sort of epic grandeur.*

Robert Shaw did not sacrifice pieces of his talent to preserve the whole, but he did sacrifice pieces of himself. And there was grandeur in all his sweat and toil, though he insisted that it was modest. Now he has, at last, disappeared into the triumphant totality of the music, which remains.

"We are trying to get back," Shaw said in a rehearsal, "to what he (the composer) was feeling when he put pen to paper. The composer dips his pen to write and we begin to sing."

AUTHOR'S NOTE:

Why Deep River?

Why *Deep River?*

Biography, like theology, is the search for the right metaphor. Depth seems the right metaphor for what Robert Shaw was seeking, both in his life and in his music. Shaw always wanted to be a better musician and a better man.

He was not seeking height, if height is understood as the metaphor for superior position, fame, or power. What drove him was the desire for understanding and the pursuit of artistic perfection. He knew perfection was unattainable, of course.

River suggests force and movement. A current can take you, against your will.

Shaw often depicted his life this way. He said that his life had been a series of unexpected events and that he had been pulled along on a ride he'd not imagined or devised. That's not quite so. Many of the "unexpected opportunities" that came his way were the result of his own dreams and hard work.

Shaw's early dreams were large. By 1946, he wanted, perhaps more than anything, to be a part of the establishment of a serious and particularly *American* form of classical music.

He wanted, specifically, to help remake American choral music.

The dreams of his middle and late years were just as big, maybe bigger.

He wanted to make the Atlanta Symphony Orchestra competitive with the top five to ten "name" orchestras in America.

He wanted the ASO Symphony Chorus to be the best—as good or better than any in the world.

He wanted to set up a network of choral music educators who could support each other and share ideas.

Shaw never wanted disciples, in the slavish or sycophantic sense of the word, or to establish "the Shaw school" or "the Shaw method"—one way of making music. He believed in his methods, but he did not believe in musical tyranny. His idea was to strengthen the musical community as a whole and to continue maturating and perfecting his own little corner of music.

Depth, for Shaw, was a discernible path—a practical series of habits and disciplines: studying, practicing, polishing, and honing. This was the way to get closer to the composer and the mystery of great music and great music making.

The river was his own story—his struggles, loves, demons, and breakthroughs.

Deep River also suggests Shaw's connection to the Negro spiritual and the American folk idiom. He *was* a folk musician, both in terms of early background and temperament, and in terms of his primary musical associations with voice and rhythm. He happened to fall in love with the most majestic and complex of musical forms and literature, and to master those forms. But he was rooted in the American song. Shaw was a classical musician by will but a folk musician by nature. Indeed, a large part of Shaw's early career was concerned with spirituals and folk music. Sometimes the music was from Stephen Foster's mythic world. Sometimes it was the product of anonymous craftsmen. (Some of Shaw's favorite Christmas carols were by unknown authors.) Sometimes the "folk" had been slaves and their music was the music of suffering and desperate hope. Robert Shaw brought a good deal of African-American music to mainstream America and never lost his interest in, or sense of identification with, music born of suffering. At the same time he knew that he was a tourist in the land of the spiritual. It was not the music of *his* experience, or of *his* ancestors. But he knew it was music he wanted the vast American public to hear. In the days of the Robert Shaw Chorale, Shaw ended most concerts with spirituals. And he returned to performing them throughout his career. The spiritual was both a respite and a base.

Moreover, the questions of race, racial tolerance, and justice for the African-American were centrally important in Shaw's life. Racial integration was a part of what Shaw sought in his Collegiate Chorale. An integrated chorus and black soloists were a part of a Robert Shaw Chorale tour of the South when "separate but equal" was still the rule. The Chorale faced harassment, discomfort, and physical threats when it toured the South, just as jazz ensembles at the time did, because the Chorale was "a melting pot that sings," in Shaw's words.

What made a white pseudo-liberal Baptist from Southern California feel he could empathize with black Americans and record and perform their music?

On one level it was his background in the American Biblical culture, so much a part of the African-American experience. White Baptist Appalachia and black America share that Biblical culture, and some of the music born of it. The gospel his father preached—the ethic of Jesus—made it impossible for Shaw to be anything other than sympathetic. But more than this, his own suffering and feeling of being an outsider created a sense of identification. (For some years in Atlanta, Shaw drove around the city in a BMW with the initials SLAVE on the license plate.)

The spiritual, done with integrity, presents the human voice, both raw and refined. It has the same internal sense of dance and heartbeat as does another old form Shaw loved—the carol. Shaw's interest in the spiritual had an intellectual as well as an emotional component, though. For there is no doubt that Shaw saw the fate of the black man and woman as the central theme in the unfolding of the American drama. He saw black history as the tragic and redemptive essence of his country's story. Poet Langston Hughes must have sensed that Shaw was a lover and not a plunderer of the black oral and musical tradition, for he agreed to write the liner notes for one of the Robert Shaw Chorale's recordings of spirituals and folk tunes. Though the songs were, decidedly, black music sung by white folks (and perhaps sound embarrassingly so today), Hughes saw Shaw's devotion to the music. He knew the white Protestant boy from California understood the beauty of deep sorrow. Shaw reached Mozart and Bach via the spiritual.

One of these spirituals was "Deep River," which Shaw recorded in 1957 with the Robert Shaw Chorale, and which was the title of the album on which it appeared.

The lyrics of "Deep River" speak repeatedly of crossing over, of wanting to "cross over into campground." Shaw was always trying to cross over, and not from classical music into pop, or even the reverse as the term "crossover" now implies, but from music playing to music making, from Protestant religiosity to spiritual resonance, from entertainment to art, from the superficial to that which has depth.

The key verse in "Deep River" is:

Oh, chillun
Oh, don't you want to go, to that gospel feast
That promised land, that land where all is peace?
Walk into heaven and take a seat and cast my crown at Jesus' feet.

Shaw was a believer in the connotation of lyrics—in the implied deeper meaning of sound with words, or what one might call linguistic overtones. When Brahms, in the third movement of his *German Requiem*, has the baritone soloist sing the words from Psalm 39: "Lord, teach me to know, know the measure of my days on earth . . . ," he is setting a meaningful and noble text. And he draws upon the words. But he is also drawing out what is *within* the words with his musical craft. He mines the words with particular melodies, modulations, or changes of rhythm or dynamics.

It is finally, and most vitally, the connotations of "Deep River" that connect us with Shaw. He was always yearning for something more; always trying to get *somewhere,* somewhere deeper, maybe the other side of everyday humdrum or of human conflict and pain. He was struggling to connect music making to things eternal. The crown he cast at the Lord's feet was the body of his life's work in music.

Biography is an act of faith, hope, and love. One must love the subject, hope one can tell his story justly, and believe that people will care. Shaw was, as one of Mozart's biographers said of him, "not made for a peaceful life." Contrary to the fatherly or grandfatherly image of later years, Shaw was not a calm and even man. He made his path through life and music the hard way. (And if the way was easy, he *made* it hard.) Life and music were a struggle for Shaw, a battle. Furthermore, he associated suffering with emotional depth and he associated emotional depth with artistic seriousness.

Deep River suggests the flow of a long life that was seldom still or silent, though occasionally it was surprisingly serene. *Deep River* suggests mystery, as well as force and movement.

Shaw was always in motion almost to the end. The current that carried him, and flowed as much from within as without, was sometimes fierce and there was occasional wreckage. Indeed, he liked to say that music *is* motion—that a musical line is always going toward, passing through, or coming away from its source. Like a river, or a life.

Acknowledgments

I am indebted, first and last, to Nola Frink, Robert Shaw's longtime assistant and friend. I thank her for every conceivable form of support—for providing me access to Robert Shaw's personal papers in Atlanta (with the consent of his sons), for helping me to work through the papers and to make copies of many documents, for putting me in touch with many of Shaw's friends and colleagues from the last thirty years of his life, for being a sounding board, and most of all, for telling me stories. Nola's stories about and memories of Shaw gave me some access to the private man, as well as insight into what it cost him to be the public man. Ms. Frink also sustained and inspired me with her abiding devotion to Shaw and his mission. When this book was delayed because of health issues and the necessity of earning a living, Frink told me that the world needed to understand Shaw's conception of music making now more than ever—a very Shavian thing to say. Without Nola Frink, there would be no book.

I am indebted also to three of Shaw's sons: Peter Shaw, Thomas Shaw, and Alexander Hitz. They were not only generous with their time, but honest, open, and unafraid.

I owe deep thanks to Shaw's sister, Anne Shaw Price, who was enormously generous and helpful to me, as was her husband Harrison Price. The Prices, too, were utterly frank, and helped me to see the home Anne and her brother Robert knew as children.

I am grateful to several of Mr. Shaw's close associates, particularly Alice Parker, Craig Jessop, Jeff Baxter, Walter Gould, Sylvia McNair, Florence Kopleff, Ann Howard Jones, and Pam Elrod. Kopleff's was a grand, unique voice in her generation, and her contribution to this book was also unique. Her corrections and suggestions were copious and invaluable. Kopleff was "present at the creation" and she was a firm but loving critic. I am greatly obliged to her. I thank Jones and Elrod, in particular, for agreeing to read the book in manuscript form, for their excellent suggestions, honest but unflagging support, and for their friendship. These two fine musicians made it possible for me to run the last mile. They are responsible for making the book better, once it existed. To the extent that it is a "good" book, I have them to thank.

So too, Nathan Zullinger. He came late to the project but was a godsend. He worked on two of the more complicated appendices, and was a most perceptive reader.

Early in the project, at the interviewing stage, several Atlanta musicians were generous with their time and reflections. These include Christopher Rex, Paul Brittan, Laura Ardan, Fred Scott, Norman Mackenzie, and Robert O'Brien, then the Atlanta Symphony Orchestra librarian. Nick Jones, longtime ASO annotator and chorus member was an unfailing source of information and wisdom on the Shaw tenure in Atlanta. He is also *the* expert on Shaw's Atlanta conducting record and Shaw's discography from the beginning of the Atlanta period to the end of Shaw's life. I quote his history of Shaw's ASO music directorship at length in the Atlanta chapter because it is definitive.

Several conductors in my home state of Connecticut happened to have Shaw connections of one kind or another and they served as a sort of college of confessors. They are musicians of Shaw-like skill and dedication with whom I could check my perceptions and test my questions. Three of them, Peter Bagley, Ehren Brown, and Mark Singleton also read parts of the manuscript and rendered moral support along the way. I cannot repay them except in friendship. Three other conductors—Richard Coffey, Henley Denmead, and Peter Sacco—instructed, remembered, and listened.

My thanks go to a particular subset of the many musicians I interviewed. They stand out because their insights into Shaw were remarkable and their affection was palpable. These include Peter Serkin, Lynn Harrell, Lee Luvisi, John Wustman, Daniel Lewis, Krista Feeney, Jeffrey Kahane, Garrick Ohlsson, Christine Brewer, Marietta Simpson, Christine Goerke, Felix Kraus, and William Preucil.

Of the many people I interviewed, the most devoted were long-time members of the Atlanta Symphony Chorus and Atlanta Symphony Chamber Chorus, several of whom befriended and supported me early in the project. I wish to thank five in particular—Ellen Dukes, Annette Burton, Carole Jacobsen, Kiki Wilson, and Charles Hamilton. Members of the chorus are the people who had to work hardest to keep up with Shaw and seemed to love him most unconditionally.

I thank another Atlanta chorister, John Cooledge, for his insight into Shaw's time in Atlanta and relationship with the Atlanta Symphony Orchestra as well as Shaw's work as a recording artist.

All of these people gave so much help, so unselfishly, because they were inspired by Robert Shaw and believed in the importance of his life.

Three critics—Pierre Ruhe, Donald Rosenberg, and Tim Page encouraged this book. I am particularly grateful to Page a true friend of music and ideas.

The scholar and program annotator, Michael Steinberg, provided my first and truest sense of the musical scope of Shaw's career and the ways in which Shaw grew and changed. Steinberg gave me one of the most important lines in the book. I hope just a little of Steinberg's elegance and discernment are present in these pages. To me his work is the gold standard for critical writing about music and musicians.

The conductor and eminent Bach scholar, Alfred Mann, was wonderfully patient and, ultimately, made clear to me, in a way that no one else had, Shaw's contribution in bringing the master choral works of Bach to America.

Nearly 200 people besides those mentioned above were interviewed for this book—conductors, players, singers, educators, and critics. Some are well known, some less so. Some knew Shaw for many years and others knew him for perhaps one rehearsal cycle and performance, yet were especially in tune with him. Virtually every conversation about Shaw, it seemed, rendered some conundrum or an affecting musical or personal vignette. It was not hard to get people to talk about the man. I thank all of the interviewees with all the sincerity I can summon. Not all of their names appear in the text, but many of their thoughts and all of their good spirits do. There may be a few "Shaw people" I did not talk to and I am sorry for that. But Shaw cut a path so wide and so deep that an attempt to speak with everyone he influenced would have made my task virtually unending. At some point, I had to write.

Anyone interested in Robert Shaw is indebted to *Dear People...Robert Shaw* by Joseph A. Mussulman. This fellow, or succeeding, biographer is particularly indebted.

I went through the Shaw papers a second time at Yale University, where they are now archived in the Gilmore Library of the School of Music. I am indebted to Richard Boursy of the library staff—the man charged with care of the Shaw materials. Boursy had come to know Shaw by cataloging the surviving documents of his life and hence was a kind of biographical colleague. He indulged me as I searched for I knew not what.

I wish to acknowledge, also, all the wonderful staff of the South Windsor public library in South Windsor, Connecticut, particularly Matthew Barone and the library director Mary Etter. The library provided a quiet place to work and was a sort of haven, a sanctuary.

I am grateful, finally, to the chairman of the board of the Coca-Cola Company for a grant of $12,000 to assist me in the research phase of this book and to Mr. John White for securing that grant. I am indebted to my friends Austin and Kathy Linsley, who, on several occasions, offered me a solitary place to work on this book. In the early, interviewing days, Anne and Josh Weiss gave me shelter in New York City. David Lowance, Shaw's dear friend and personal physician, was a great source for *Deep River*. I am deeply appreciative of his help. Lowance was also fun and inspiring to talk with about Shaw, and twice, on visits to Atlanta, where I was four times a temporary resident, he provided me with a place to live. Lowance is one of the few people who really knew Shaw but had virtually no connection with music. He simply loved the man. A privilege of association with Shaw is the nature of the people who were drawn to him.

I must acknowledge the unflagging support of my assistant Barbara King.

I thank my friend and ex-boss, at my former day job, Elizabeth Ellis, for her enthusiasm and encouragement.

I thank my former colleague Kathy Tofflemire who read the early book proposals.

I owe a debt to Robert Laux-Bachand for reading a later manuscript and calling attention to many of my stupidities. And to the eagle-eyed Natasha Garnett, who read an even later one.

I thank Vanessa Weeks Page who advised us in the early editing process.

Almost last, but assuredly not least, I must acknowledge my publisher, Alec Harris, and my editors Edith Bicknell and Linda Vickers for their superhuman patience and professionalism. They are my collaborators and coaches, and I am eternally grateful to them. Ms. Vickers, in particular, went above and beyond the call of duty, again and again.

I thank my three children, Alec, Sophie, and Will, for inspiration.

Finally, I must thank my wife Amy for heroic assistance typing handwritten changes into the penultimate draft. I thank her, even more, for her faith and patience through the years of this project. I know that both virtues were tested.

One of the troubling thoughts, as one begins a book, is the knowledge that one cannot get everything absolutely right. This thought is even more haunting at the end of the process, when one is all too painfully aware of the limits of the writer and the form. Every biographical subject deserves 100 percent accuracy, wisdom, and insight and none gets it. I deeply regret this. Obviously, any errors of interpretation or judgment are mine alone and are the results of my limitations, not the thoughts or memories of others.

APPENDICES

Appendix I

Shaw Timeline and Awards

A.B., Pomona College (California), 1938.

Married Maxine Farley, October 15, 1939; divorced, 1973. Children: Johanna, Peter Thain, and John Thaddeus.

Married Caroline Sauls Hitz, December 19, 1973; deceased, January 22, 1995. Son: Thomas Lawson. Stepson: Alexander Hitz.

Professional Background:

1938–1945	Director, Fred Waring Glee Clubs
1941–1954	Founder/Conductor, Collegiate Chorale, New York City
1942–1943	Choral Director, Aquacades
1943	Choral Director, Carmen Jones
1944	Choral Director, Seven Lively Arts
1944	Director, Choral Workshop, School of Music Northwestern University
1945–1948	Director of Choral Music, Juilliard School of Music; New York City Choral Director, Berkshire Music Center, Tanglewood, Massachusetts
1948–1967	Founder/Conductor, The Robert Shaw Chorale
1953–1957	Conductor, Music Director, San Diego Symphony
1956–1975	Music Director, Alaska Festival of Music, Anchorage
1956–1967	Associate Conductor and Director of Choruses, Cleveland Orchestra
1967	Appointed Music Director and Conductor, Atlanta Symphony Orchestra
1967	Founded ASO Chamber Chorus

1970	Founded ASO Chorus
1984–1991	Robert W. Woodruff Professor of Music and the Fine Arts, Emory University, Atlanta
1988–1999	Music Director Emeritus/Conductor Laureate, Atlanta Symphony Orchestra
1988–1999	Ongoing conducting relationships with Cleveland Orchestra, Minnesota Symphony, Florida Symphony, National Symphony, San Diego Symphony, Orchestra of St. Luke's (New York City), Boston University, Ohio State University
1988–1999	Artistic Director, The Robert Shaw Choral Institute at Carnegie Hall
1992–1998	Founder/Conductor, The Robert Shaw Chamber Singers

Major Awards (Selected):

1943	National Association of American Composers and Conductors Award for Outstanding American-born Conductor of the Year
1944	Guggenheim Fellowship (first awarded to a conductor)
1955	Alice M. Ditson Award for Service to American Music (Columbia University)
1973	Governor's Award in the Arts (Georgia)
1976	ASCAP Award for Service to Contemporary Music
1977	Harvard Glee Club Medal
1979–1984	Member, National Council on the Arts
1980	ASCAP Award for Adventuresome Programming
1981	Samuel Simons Sanford Medal (presented by Yale University School of Music for contributions to musical life in America)

1981	American Choral Directors Association Award
1981	Distinguished Service Award (University of Georgia Department of Music)
1982	Martin Luther King, Jr., Award for Artistic Achievement
1983	Visiting Fellow (Indiana University Institute for Advanced Study)
1985	Fulton County Arts Council Award
1986	Fauré: *Pélleas et Mélisande* (Best Orchestral Performance)
1986	Berlioz: *Requiem* (Best Choral Performance) (Best Classical Recording)
1987	Hindemith: *When lilacs last in the dooryard bloom'd* (Best Choral Performance)
1988	Retires as music director of ASO; named Music Director Emeritus and Conductor Laureate
1988	David Prescott Burrows Award (Pomona College, California)
1988	Marlene and Morton Meyerson Centennial Visiting Professor of Music, University of Texas, Austin
1988	Mumm Champagne Classical Music Award
1988	Gramophone Award, Choral Recording of the Year – Verdi: *Requiem*
1988	Georgia Music Hall of Fame
1988	Verdi: *Requiem* and Five Opera Choruses (Best Classical Recording) (Best Choral Performance)
1988	Rorem: *String Symphony, Eagles, Sunday Morning* (Best Orchestral Performance)
1990	Britten: *War Requiem* (Best Choral Performance)

1991	Bernstein: *Chichester Psalms/Missa Brevis* *Belshazzar's Feast* (Best Choral Performance)
1991	Kennedy Center Honors
1992	"Musician of the Year" (Musical America)
1992	National Medal of the Arts (White House)
1993	Conductor's Guild Theodore Thomas Award
1997	"Officier des Arts et Lettres" Medal (from the government of France, equivalent to honorary knighthood)
1998	Adams/Rachmaninoff: *Harmonium/The Bells* (Best Choral Performance)
1999	Barber: *Prayers of Kierkegaard* (posthumous) Bartók: *Cantata Profana* Vaughn Williams: *Dona nobis pacem*
1998	Inducted into American Classical Music Hall of Fame
1998	"Gift of Music" Award (presented by Orchestra of St. Luke's)

Grammy Awards for Recordings with the Robert Shaw Chorale and Orchestra:

1961	Bach: *Mass in B Minor*
1964	Britten: *Ceremony of Carols*
1965	Poulenc: *Gloria* Stravinsky: *Symphony of Psalms*
1966	Handel: *Messiah*

Gold Record:

Christmas Hymns and Carols, Volume II (first RCA Red Seal recording to sell more than a million copies)

Grammy Awards for Recordings with the Atlanta Symphony Orchestra and Chorus and Robert Shaw Festival Singers:

(Best Classical Recording)
(Best Choral Performance)

Appendix II

Shaw's Core Repertoire: Summary of Performance History

A

1. Brahms: *Requiem*
70 to 80 performances (Perhaps as many as 90)

2. Bach: *B Minor Mass*
80 to 85 performances

3. Bach: *St. John Passion*
49 performances on RSC tour;
approximately 15 to 20 more with orchestras, festivals, workshops

4. Bach: *St. Matthew Passion*
20 to 25 performances

5. Mozart: *Requiem*
80 to 90 performances;
65 performances on tour with RSC

6. Bach: Cantatas
Shaw performed 31 different cantatas; several were repeated one or more times

7. Bach: Concertos
Shaw conducted 17 of the concertos, repeating several of them many times

8. Beethoven: *Missa Solemnis*
70 to 80 performances

9. Beethoven: *Symphony No. 9*
approximately 70 performances

10. Handel: *Messiah*
6-week RSC tour, 36 performances;
approximately 70 to 75 performances in all

B

First U.S. recordings of:

Brahms: *Requiem*
Mozart: *Requiem*
Bach: *Mass in B Minor*
Bach: *St. John Passion*
Bach: Cantatas by professional singers

NOTE: Shaw wrote more about the *Missa Solemnis* than anything else. He wrote very little on the Bach *Mass in B Minor*, on which he perhaps spent the most musical time—in preparation and analysis.

Appendix III

Non-vocal, Oft-repeated Works Conducted by Robert Shaw

NOTE: Works listed were programmed in at least 7 concert series, mostly—but not exclusively—with the Atlanta Symphony Orchestra.

BACH	Concerto No. 1 for Keyboard & Orchestra, BWV 1052 Suite No. 3 in D Major, S. 1068 (many Bach works, but with fewer than 6 repeats)
BARBER	*Medea's Meditation and Dance of Vengeance*
BARTÓK	Concerto for Orchestra (many other Bartók works, but few repeats)
BERG	Violin Concerto (several repeats)
BEETHOVEN	Concerto No. 3 in C minor for Piano & Orchestra, Op. 37 Concerto No. 4 in G Major for Piano & Orchestra Concerto in D Major for Violin & Orchestra, Op. 61 Overture to *Egmont,* Op. 84 Overture to *Leonore,* Op. 72B Symphony No. 3 in E-flat Major, Op. 55 ("Eroica") Symphony No. 6 in F minor, Op. 68 ("Pastorale") Symphony No. 7 in A Major, Op. 92
BERLIOZ	Overture – *Roman Carnival* (many Berlioz works, but few repeats)
BERNSTEIN	Overture to *Candide* "Symphonic Dances" from *Westside Story*
BIZET	Suite No. 2 – *L'Arlésienne*
BORODIN	"Polovtsian Dances" from *Prince Igor* (usually orchestra only, no chorus)
BRAHMS/ LEINSDORF	*There is a rose in flower*

BRAHMS	Concerto No. 1 for Piano & Orchestra (several repeats) Concerto No. 2 for Piano & Orchestra (several repeats) Concerto for Violin and Orchestra (many *Hungarian Dances*, mostly No. 5) Symphony No. 1 Symphony No. 2 Symphony No. 3 Symphony No. 4 *Tragic* Overture *Variations on a Theme by Haydn*, Op. 56A (many repeats)
COPLAND	*A Lincoln Portrait* (sometimes as conductor, sometimes as narrator)
DEBUSSY	*La Mer*
DVORÁK	*Slavonic Dance No. 1*, Op. 46
GERSHWIN	*Porgy and Bess* *Rhapsody in Blue*
GINASTERA	*Estancia* (ballet suite in four movements)
GLINKA	Overture to *Russian and Ludmilla*
GRIFFES	"White Peacock" from *Roman Sketches*, Op. 7, No. 1
HANDEL	*Royal Fireworks Music*
HARBISON	*Remembering Gatsby*
HAYDN	Symphony No. 87 and Symphony No. 92 (often repeated) (many Haydn symphonies, but few repeats)
HINDEMITH	*Nobilissima Visione: Suite* *Mathis der Maler* *Symphonic Metamorphosis*
IVES	*From Hanover Square North...* Symphony No. 1 *The Unanswered Question* *Variations on "America"*

MENDELSSOHN	Concerto in E minor for Violin & Orchestra, Op. 64 Incidental Music from *A Midsummer Night's Dream*
MOUSSORGSKY	*Pictures at an Exhibition*
MOZART	Concerto No. 21 for Piano & Orch. in C Major, K. 467 Concerto No. 23 for Piano & Orch. in A Major, K. 488 Concerto No. 24 for Piano & Orch. in C minor, K. 491 Overture to *The Magic Flute* Symphony No. 40 in G minor, K. 550 (many other piano concertos, but fewer than 6 series of each)
POULENC	Concerto in G minor for Organ, Strings & Timpani
PROKOFIEV	Symphony No. 5 in B-flat Major, Op. 100
RACHMANINOFF	Concerto No. 2 in C minor for Piano & Orchestra, Op. 18 Symphonic Dances, Op. 45
ROREM	*Symphony for Strings*
ROSSINI	(many overtures, few repeats)
SCHUBERT	Symphony No. 8 in B minor, "Unfinished" Symphony No. 9 in C Major (many symphonies, few repeats)
SCHUMAN, Wm.	(lots of Schuman, few repeats)
SCHUMANN	(lots of Schumann, few repeats)
SIBELIUS	*Finlandia*
SOUSA	*Semper Fidelis* *The Stars and Stripes Forever*
STRAUSS, R.	*Don Juan*, Op. 20
STRAVINSKY	*Firebird Suite*

TCHAIKOVSKY	*Romeo and Juliet* Symphony No. 4 in F minor, Op. 36 Symphony No. 5 in E minor, Op. 64 Symphony No. 6 in B minor, Op. 74 ("Pathétique")
VIVALDI	*The Four Seasons*
WAGNER	Prelude to Act III from *Lohengrin* Overture to *Die Meistersinger* Overture to *Tannhäuser*

Appendix IV

Most Important Shaw Recordings

Bach: *B Minor Mass*, RCA (second of three recordings Shaw made of this work)
Verdi: *Requiem,* Telarc
Beethoven: *Missa Solemnis,* Telarc
Rachmaninoff: *Vespers,* Telarc
Berlioz: *Requiem,* Telarc
Britten: *War Requiem,* Telarc
Handel: *Messiah,* RCA
Walton: *Belshazzar's Feast*
Bernstein: *Chichester Psalms, Missa Brevis,* Telarc
Schubert: *Masses,* Telarc
Duruflé and Fauré: *Requiems,* Telarc
Dvorák: *Stabat Mater, Evocations of the Spirit,* Telarc

Honorable Mention

Hindemith: *Lilacs,* Telarc
Haydn: *Creation,* Telarc
Schubert: *Songs for Male Chorus,* Telarc; *Spirituals,* RCA and Telarc
Vivaldi and Bach: *Gloria* and *Magnificat,* Telarc
Any of the later Christmas albums, Telarc
Barber: *Vaughan Williams, Bartók,* Telarc
Mendelssohn: *Elijah,* Telarc

Worthy of Note:
Cleveland Orchestra Robert Shaw Collection
(issued posthumously)

Bach: *St. Matthew Passion*
A flawed and dated rendition, to be sure, with a few small sections missing (it was taken from a tape of a radio broadcast). Shaw would certainly have found it "too thick," and it was far larger and heavier than what he was doing in the last decade of his life with this work. Still, parts of this recording are deeply touching, partly because of the robust Shaw sound, partly because of the congregational qualities in the chorales, and partly because of Shaw's translation.

Beethoven: *Ninth Symphony*
Not the most tidy, nor the most virile version, but perhaps one of the most warm and human.

Handel: *Semele*
Just great fun, very Handelium sound in a time when it wasn't heard.

Brahms: *Requiem*
This is a good recording though the choir is, understandably, not as good as Shaw's Atlanta chorus. Neither this, nor the 1983 ASO recording of this work for Telarc, represent Shaw's best performance or last word on a composition so closely associated with him. The closest thing to that is a live performance recorded and broadcast by National Public Radio. It is from Shaw's last cycle of Brahms's *Requiem* performances. If this recording could be tweaked for sufficient sound quality and NPR is willing and able to release it, a significant Shaw recording might still be out there.

Finally, one hopes also that RCA will some day get around to re-releasing the best of Shaw's 1950s Bach work, with quality as fine as the RCA *B Minor Mass* and *Messiah* recordings.

NOTE: I arrived at this "best of" list with a sort of sense-of-the-meeting process. I looked at reviews, including fan and customer reviews at Amazon.com. I asked three critics for their lists. When I interviewed musicians, conductors, and music educators, I asked them for their favorites. There was virtual consensus as to what should be at the top of the list.

Appendix V

Shaw Recordings with Toscanini

Shaw made 10 recordings in 6 years. All with the NBC Symphony under Toscanini's direction and with the Robert Shaw Chorale. All with RCA.

1948 Brahms: *Gesang der Parzen*

1949 Verdi: *Aida*

1950 Cherubini: *Requiem Mass in C Minor*

1950 Verdi: *Falstaff*

1951 Verdi: *Manzoni Requiem*

1952 Beethoven: *Ninth Symphony*

1952 Gluck: *Orfeo ed Euridice*, Act II

1953 Beethoven: *Missa Solemnis*

1954 Verdi: *Un Ballo in Maschera*

1955 Boito: *Mefistofele*, Prologue
Verdi: *Quattro Pezzi Sacri*, No. 4, *Te Deum* – NBC Symphony Orchestra RSC, cond. Toscanini (LM 1849)

In this same time period:

Shaw made 2 recordings with Fritz Reiner, both with the RCA Victor Orchestra and the Robert Shaw Chorale.

1950 Strauss: *Die Fledermaus* (excerpts)

1951 Bizet: *Carmen*

He also made 4 recordings with Renato Cellini.

1950 Verdi: *Rigoletto*

1951 *Milanov Sings*

1952 Verdi: *Il Trovatore*

1953 Mascagni: *Cavalleria Rusticana* (excerpts)
Leoncavallo: *I Pagliacci* (excerpts)
Verdi: *La Forza del Destino* (excerpts)

Taken together, these represent a surprising amount of experience in opera.

APPENDIX VI

A Shaw Letter on Toscanini
(written from France to the Atlanta Symphony Chorus)

19 September 1991
Couzou, France

Friends – (those neither seen nor heard for, lo!, these many months, and those of you never before seen or heard, whose friendship is still to be betrayed)

Had an extraordinary experience a short while back. Was in Paris seeing son Thomas off to Atlanta to begin high school with his peer group of incipient Rhett Butlers. C., T. and me (to begin talkin' American again) was makin' a first visit to the age's chiefest miracle of musical merchandising: The FNAC chain of storehouses of audio-video records, discs, tapes, etc. Tens upon twenties of thousands of platters, cassettes, discs and tapes (mostly now, of course, discs) in whatever period or style of composition or performance you might desire. CDs re-mastered from broadcasts of the 1930s and 1940s of friends from B'way days. Bin after bin of Teddy Wilson, Art Tatum, Benny Goodman, Tommy and Jimmy Dorsey. Red Norvo, Cozy Cole, Lionel Hampton. Many of them "first takes" that never were pressed or sold. T.L.S. was in eighth (Jazz) heaven.

(On to the "extraordinary experience"!) Caroline called me from my Baroque binge and beckoned towards another area around an aisle or two. When I was within a few feet of her I heard strains of *Aida*. We opened a glass door into a little theatre—and there was Arturo Toscanini—and a cast of all but the livestock: the NBC Symphony, soloists and chorus in Studio 8H of Radio City, when it was in Rockefeller Plaza, New York City, early 1940s, conducting the last act of Verdi's championship slam-dunk. It must have been one of the very first of musical telecasts. I had forgotten we had ever done it. But there, also, was very nearly the first of the professional "chorales," well before there was a touring or recording Same-Name Chorale. Close-ups of people whose names and faces had to be recalled over nearly fifty years. (None of us had changed a bit!)

(Get to the really exciting part!) The really exciting part was Arturo Toscanini, for all of us then, and still, the only "Maestro."

A few years after this telecast, I think it is fair to say, he was enough bedeviled by physical ailments or occasional lapses of memory (*very* rare) that his sheer *technical* mastery was not at every moment always so transcendent. (For instance, in later years he would seem to be conducting a performance that was taking place principally *in his mind*—without hearing occasional distressful events that were happening on stage.)

But here he was at the height of his powers, and with a score he might have written. (I had the feeling in those and subsequent days that there must seldom have existed in the history of music so strong an "identification" of composer and performer. Without much effort of imagination or will I could, with eyes open or closed, behold Verdi conducting Toscanini's *Requiem.*)

Now, it also is true that in those days, having "come to music" not only very late but quite by accident, and, never dreaming for a moment that I would one day have to stand in front of the NBC—or any other—Symphony, I was not as alert to the study of his "technique" as I should have been. My nose was in the score and I was listening for flaws in the *choral* collaboration.

(Alright—here's the extraordinary and exciting thing!) Most of the time, of course, the camera was upon the "Maestro." Toscanini had an awesomely "beautiful" face, with amazing skin and flesh textures. One could see no trace of a beard. His skin looked as though he never had shaved. One might have said he had a baby's skin—except that its color was not baby's pink, his head and upper torso looking almost as though they had been sculpted in white wax. Occasionally his eyes would dart from left to right or down to up. (Frequently this was his only "cue.") But his face would remain impassive—not unlike the concentration of a sculptor, working in his studio in clay or stone, who has no audience to impress or collaborators to "inspire."

The impressions of that day in Paris were these:

First, I had either forgotten—or never had seen—so severe and unconditional a concentration. His face might have been a sleep-walker's masque of outward blindness and inward sight.

And second, I had forgotten the astonishing economy of his gesture. An absolute minimum of "cueing"—almost never—if the section or player could be counted upon to enter without it. A clear beating of time and tempo with a beat that referred to the conventional patterns but was free, fluent and personal enough to encourage hard corners and rough edges or smooth contours and warm moistness.

In the above first instance not only was music never to be used for "personal exhibitionism," but with Toscanini, it was so chaste that one doubted that music could be or should be used for personal *enjoyment.* Certainly no "audience" was even consciously in his choreography.

And in the second instance, watching again the rapture and energy with which players like cellist Frank Miller and violinist Josef Gingold responded to Toscanini's simple, persuasive gesture I was conscious, for the first time, I think, of how much personal involvement and individual creativity he not only allowed—but inspired.

The book which came out in those days was entitled "Dictators of the Baton." And Toscanini, of course, was Exhibit A. Such was the folk-lore and the fable, encouraged by publicists and other merchants. Some of the stories did have a basis in fact. The "Maestro" was capable of anger. But, none of us, I think, ever saw him "sorry for himself"; rather it was the composer who had been betrayed, not the conductor; and, like the tantrum of a "terrible-two," it was soon over. The point is that his conducting invited exceptional and enthusiastic personal involvement. The finer the player and the finer the artist—the greater could be his or her participation. Dictatorship? Phooey! Nonsense! Artists played *with* Toscanini, not *for* him. And more often than not they played the very same piece he was conducting that day.

So, there! I suppose it's one of the advantages of "Alzheimer's": one is never too old to learn—for the first time, or at least for the "time being."

Questions: Is Poulenc's Stabat Mater Poulankier, equally Poulanky or less Poulanky than his *Gloria?* I've been re-studying Debussy's *Nocturnes* the past few days; and it's fun to recognize some of Poulenc's immediate forebears: the succession of 9th and 11th chords (Debussy's mostly in root positions, but Poulenc's inverted for dissonance) and the use of echoing phrase structures and sequences.

Don't go away. See you sooner than you may desire.

Appendix VII

Two Sermons Given by Shaw
(when he was in college and substituting for his father in the pulpit)

THE TRAGEDY OF GROWTH

Scripture
Isaiah 53: 3–9

He was despised and rejected of men; a man of sorrows and acquainted with grief: and as one from whom men hide their face, He was despised; and we esteemed Him not.

Surely it was our griefs that He bore, and our sorrows that He carried; while we accounted Him stricken, afflicted and smitten by God!

But He was wounded through our transgressions; He was bruised by our iniquities; the chastisement of our peace was upon Him; and with His stripes we are healed.

All we like sheep have gone astray; we have turned every one to his own way; and upon Him was made to fall the iniquity of us all.

He was oppressed, yet when He was afflicted He opened not His mouth; as a lamb that before its shearers is dumb, so He opened not His mouth.

So they made His grave with the wicked, His death like that of an oppressor; although He had done no violence, neither was any deceit in His mouth.

The Crucifixion
Luke 23:33–38, 44, 46, 47

Invocation

O God, forgive that I have seen
The beauty only, have not been
Awake to sorrow such as this;

That I have drunk the cup of bliss
Remembring not that those there be
Who drink the gregs of misery.

THE TRAGEDY OF GROWTH

Sunday Evening, July 18, 1937

One of the most beautiful passages of the Old Testament is the description of Jehovah's good servant. Because it so perfectly characterized the life of Jesus of Nazareth it has been seized by dogmaticians who find in it both proof and prophecy; which, however, does not lessen its beauty. Indeed, when the person of Jesus is added to its own literary richness, it is doubly compelling.

> "He was despised and rejected of men; a man of sorrows and acquainted with grief.
>
> "So they made His grave with the wicked, His death like that of an oppressor, although He had done no violence; neither was any deceit in His mouth."

Oscar Wilde has written in one of his Poems in Prose, "The master" an imaginary sequel to the crucifixion of Jesus:

> And when darkness came over the earth, Joseph of Arimathea having lighted a torch of pine-wood, passed down from the hill into the valley. For he had business in his own home.
>
> And kneeling on the flint stones of the Valley of Desolation he saw a young man who was naked and weeping. His hair was the color of honey, and his body was as a white flower; but he had wounded his body with thorns, and on his hair he had set ashoe as a crown.
>
> And he who had great possessions said to the young man who was naked: "I do not wonder that your sorrow is so great, for surely He was a just man."

> And the young men answered: "It is not for Him that I am weeping, but for myself. I, too, have changed water into wine, and I have healed the leper and given sight to the blind. I have walked upon the waters, and from the dwellers in the tombs I have cast out devils. I have fed the hungry and in the desert where there was no food, and I have raised the dead from their narrow houses; and at my bidding, had before a great multitude of people, a barren fig tree withered away. All things that this man has done I have done also. And yet they have not crucified me."

Rarely is cynicism so beautiful and so keen. But beneath the cynical evaluation of martyrdom, and the subtle implication of the paramount interest of the young man—himself—(which, of course, was the difference between himself and Him on the Cross); quite aside from these subtle and delicate cynicisms is the undertone of the significance of tragedy. The capacity for suffering is the difference between personalities which live and personalities which do not live! The experience of great pain yields moral greatness! Spiritual growth exists in conflict! It is a process, the inescapable conditions of which are pain, suffering, tragedy! Death is the inescapable premise of New Life—The Tragedy of Growth.

There is a winsome legend of old China which tells the story of a great bell. The Celestially August, Yong-Lo had commanded the worthy official Kouan-Yu that he should have a bell made which in beauty and strength of tone would have no equal. Therefore the worthy Kouan-Yu assembled the master moulders and bell-smiths of the empire and they laboured exceedingly, like giants, neglecting rest and sleep and the comforts of life. But when the metal had been cast, it was discovered that despite their great labour and ceaseless care, the result was void of worth, for the metals of the alloy had rebelled one against the other. The Son of Heaven heard, and was angry but spoke nothing.

A second time the bell was cast, and the result was even worse; there was no uniformity, the sides of it were cracked and fissured, the lips were split asunder. And when the Son of Heaven heard these things, he was angrier than before; and sent his messenger to Kouan-Yu with a letter:

> "Twice thou hast betrayed the trust we have deigned to place in thee; if thou fail a third time in fulfilling our command, thy head shall be severed from thy neck. Tremble, and obey!"

Now Kouan-Yu had a daughter of dazzling loveliness, and whose heart was even more beautiful than her face. In great distress she sought "Him of Great Wisdom that she might find a way to avert the awful doom. And after a long silence he made answer to her, saying; "Gold and brass will never meet in wedlock, silver and iron never will embrace, until the virgin flesh of a maiden be melted in the crucible." So Ko-Ngai returned home sorrowful at heart; but she kept secret all that she had heard.

At last came the awful day when the last effort to cast the bell was to be made; and Ko-Ngai accompanied her father to the foundry, and they took their places upon a platform overlooking the lava of liquified metal. The blood-red lake slowly brightened into vermillion, and then to a radiant glow of gold, and then the gold whitened blindingly; and Kouan-Yu prepared to give the signal to cast.

But ere ever he had lifted his finger a cry sounded sharply above the thunder of the fires, "For thy sake, O my Father." And the white flood of metal reared to receive the body of Ko-Ngai. And her father, wild with his grief, would have leaped in after her, but that strong man held him until he was born as one dead to his home.

Yet the glow of the metal seemed purer and whiter then before; and lo, when the casting was made and the metal had become cool, the bell was beautiful to look upon and perfect in form, and wonderful in color above all other bells. And when they sounded the bell, its tones were found to be deeper and mellower and mightier than the tones of any other bell, like the pealing of summer thunder.

Fritz Kreisler played last night with the Berlin Symphony, that which is for me certainly one of the greatest pieces of music ever written: the D Major Concerto for Violin and Orchestra by Beethoven. There is spiritual intensity in that music. There is magnificent melody. It crushes—and it lifts!

It came to mind (after there was a mind once more), that Beethoven had written this concerto, as well as his great Seventh Symphony, in what is known as the third period of his life. The first was that of the young musician, schooled and skilled in the arts of harmony and orchestration; and though his themes were not the shallow romantically personal or "pathetic" they were indifferent and relatively inconsequential.

And then Beethoven went deaf. And the second period is filled with music of fierce passion and rebellion; not merely against his own suffering (he was too big for that) but against the seemingly needless and brutal anguish of all mankind. That music throbs with bitterness.

...is replaced by quiet assurance. As though in his deafness he had discovered the meaning of tragedy, the music becomes wondrously purifying and exalting. Men must ever stand in awe and reverence at its nobility.

It is as though Pain were the only guide to understanding; Sorrow the only gate to Happiness. Born out of anguish and tragedy, the capacity for utter selflessness has given unity and purpose and power to personality.

God could have made an automatically perfect world where there was no suffering. He could have made man a perfect automaton. But he "made him in his own image" and shared with him the power of will. Man could choose between the Evil and the Good. Did he so desire, man could break the laws of God. No, man could break himself upon those laws; or he could grow in their understanding. He was not to be a puppet in the hands of a whimsical Prussian Fate. He was to be a free personality, moving at will in a world of change; of change and of crisis, of peril and of tragedy because they were the only conditions of the growth of character. God must have wanted that kind of a man.

And so it was that slowly and painfully, rising out of the mire of strict biological response and reflex and instinct, willing his devotion to higher laws—he knew not what, his spirit came suddenly to a strange and wondrous realization! For he beheld that which could resolve out of Tragedy, Growth; out of death—life; and he shared with God in that moment, the power of Love.

But he did it with the tragic sense that every organization of his existence, his government, his home, his church, was an obstacle to the realization of further possibilities. After it had been achieved it must be gotten out of the way to clear the path for further values—values which he could not conceive in terms of the present, but in the future disclosure of which he maintained a joyful faith. . .

And that is the real meaning of the story of the Cross. That is the real significance of nails, and a crown of thorns and a wounded side and a bleeding heart. Make no mistake! It was real tragedy! The most beautiful and benevolent and compelling person the world has ever known was brutally and summarily removed from his generation. That is tragic!

But if it was tragedy, it was also the only real hope! For out of that lifeless body on the cross there grew an amazing force, a force which is the only spiritual "constant" mankind has ever known.

For wherever men have lived in allegiance to something that was better than the best they knew, that spirit has led them.

Wherever men have been able to say concerning that institution to which they have given the whole of their lives, "This too must fall," that spirit has led them.

Wherever men have been able to see rising out of the ashes of a holocaust of Hate, new Love—

Wherever they have seen great Tragedy become the condition of new Growth, and know that even this, too, must be tragically consumed and out of its smouldering embers still other Growth—that spirit has led them.

Wherever men have stood beside the silent lips of Death and said, "Here is Life Everlasting," they have been led by the spirit of a Christ upon a cross.

"O cross that liftest up my head
I dare not ask to fly from Thee
I lay in dust life's glory dead
And from the ground there blossoms red
Life that shall endless be."

HEARTS ON FIRE

Sunday Evening, July 11, 1937

I've been thinking that the term "meditation" is a very fortunate and happy one. If an "address" or a "message" or a "sermon" were to be announced we might rightfully expect some finished work; we demand that one of these reach—after rather tedious but necessary steps—certain definite conclusions. But no one expects anything from a meditation. It is supposed to get anywhere in general and nowhere in particular. It is a sort of rhetorical escape valve for excess sputterings which otherwise might stew internally with disastrous effect. To change the figure—it is a sort of "end-of-the-month sale" on miscellaneous goods which have been hard to move.

We would express, however, that which is in our hearts of appreciation and thanks to Mr. Warren for his splendid artistry. We like to believe—because we can see it no other way—that the song is but the expression—and a very beautiful one—of the soul. As a young violinist at the Men's Club Dinner the other night concluded the last beautiful strains of Schubert's "Ave Maria," the man on my right leaned over and whispered, "I'm not so sure but that the soul speaks more clearly through music than anything else."

And it is probably demonstrable that you can get no more coffee out of a thermos bottle than there is in the thermos jug, or cookies out of a cookie jar than there are in that cookie jar. So because our hearts have been reached by the artistry of the evening, we feel that there must have been some outpouring of "the heart" of the artist; and we voice our thanks.

I recall two rather significant stories; the first of them a delightful little fairy tale by Oscar Wilde, called "The Birthday of the Infanta."

Now although the Infanta was the heiress to the "magnificent-and-knew-it" throne of Spain she had only one birthday each year, just like poor little boys and girls; so it behooved all of Nature to furnish the most perfect conditions and entertainment. All the rest of the year she was allowed to play only with children of her own station—and so she played alone; but on this special occasion she could have as playmates whomever of the children of the court she desired. And it was a gala affair. Bright rich costumes and gay laughing voices played at mild forms of hide-and-seek in the luxuriant gardens. And the Infanta was the most charming and beautiful of them all.

There was a mock bull-fight; there were jugglers, and gypsy dancers, but funniest of all was the dancing of a little grotesque misshapen dwarf. The children screamed with delight as his huge head with its rolling eyes and little black beard jerked loosely on the crippled and hunched shoulders. Strangest of all, the little dwarf seemed to enjoy it as much as they; and when the Infanta, laughing hysterically, threw him a white rose in mock courtesy, his eyes lighted with a new love. And when she demanded that he perform again that night his joy was boundless.

So great was his delight that that afternoon he decided to invite the Infanta to come to the forest with him, where he could show her the wonders of the birds and the trees and the flowers which he knew so well and which loved him so dearly. He hurried into the palace to find her, but to no avail. As he was about to leave he thought he saw her in a doorway at the end of a long room. Running to catch her—he stopped in surprise; for what he had thought was the Infanta was a short ugly hunchbacked little figure. He laughed—and it laughed back. He made a mocking bow—and it did the same. He ran toward it. It came to him step for step. And then he gave a wild cry and fell sobbing to the floor. He was the monster! It was at him that the Infanta had been laughing!

At that moment she entered the room with her companions, and went off into shouts of happy laughter as the little dwarf wildly beat the ground with his little misshapen arms—the hot tears pouring down his cheeks. Suddenly he gave a convulsive sob, a curious gasp, clutched his side—and fell back, quite still.

"That was funny. Now you must dance!"

There was no answer.

"A whipping master should be sent for!"

But the chamberlain looked grave, went over and put his hand on the little heart, rose, and shrugged his shoulders.

"But why will he not dance again?" asked the Infanta, laughing.

"Because his heart is broken," answered the chamberlain.

And the Infanta frowned, and her dainty rose-leaf lips curled in pretty disdain. "For the future, let those who come to play with me have no hearts," she cried, and she ran out into the garden.

And just here is where the first scripture of the evening is most piercing. "Out of the abundance of the heart, the mouth speaketh." And here is the first picture: "Out of the abundance of her heart," the Infanta cried, "For the future, let those who come to play with me have no hearts." There on the floor in front of her—so near she could have touched, but wouldn't dare—was the mute witness as to the abundance of her own heart.

"The world stands out on either side
No wider than the heart is wide."

And at that moment the world was pressing in tightly and the heart of the Infanta was smothered.

The second story is shorter—which is not its only virtues—for it is just as powerfully, and more positively, packed. It was the story which we read earlier in the evening of Jesus' reappearance to the two disciples. Here are two men, trudging a hot dusty road, grief-stricken over the death and disappearance of one whom they had called Master—and who was for them the meaning of existence. They are joined by a third figure who questions them concerning their apparent sadness, and then by quiet conversation with them so revitalizes their faith and lifts their spirits that, reaching the end of their journey, they are hesitant to part from his company, and demand that he have dinner with them. And as the stranger breaks the bread and offers thanks in prayer—they recognize Jesus. (It is perhaps significant that it is not until Jesus prays that their eyes and minds respond with recognition.) And then the figure disappears.

The most important thing about his story, however, is not the mystery of just what really did take place on the hot and dusty road to Emmaeus that day some 1900 years ago. The miracle of Jesus' reappearance after his crucifixion—whatever the manner might have been—is a story so beautiful it would have to be true. The thing of vital significance is the expressed reaction of the disciples to the presence which some way they felt so powerfully. "Was not our heart burning within us while he spake to us in the way?"

Wherever Jesus went, wherever the power of his personality was felt, men's hearts were on fire!

He so completely appealed to that which was already in them of Divinity, their own capacities for spiritual insight, their souls, their hearts—that there was lighted an answering flame of devotion not only to himself, but to the Good and the True and the Beautiful wherever it could be found or produced! The personalities which Jesus touched glowed with the radiance of a contented and joyous spirit, with the brilliance of a soul engaged in a cause greater than itself, with a warmth of human sympathy and good-will.

And the most wonderful miracle of all is the effect upon the hearts of man that Jesus of Nazareth was wrought in the centuries since that day, and is still working today, and will work for centuries to come; that wherever men have grown or are growing in closer companionship with this living vital force—the person of Jesus—through prayer and through practice, their spirits are strangely and contagiously—luminous. Their souls burn within them! Their hearts are on fire.

Appendix VIII

Thumbnail Sketch of Shaw's History with the Music of Bach

First, we have the recordings:

1 Arias and Cantatas from the *St. Matthew Passion* and the *Christmas Oratorio* with Marian Anderson – 1946

2 *Christ lag in Todesbanden* – 1946

3 Cantata 140 – *Wachet auf, ruft uns die Stimme* – 1946

4 First of three recordings of the *B Minor Mass* – 1947 (the first professional American recording of the work)

5 *Aus der Tiefe* (Cantata 131) – 1949

6 *Jesu, Meine Freude* – 1949

7 *St. John Passion* (in RS English translation, with Mack Harrell) – 1950

8 *Komm, Jesu, Komm* – 1953

9 Cantatas 41 and 42 – 1954

10 Cantatas 56 and 82, with Mack Harrell – 1958

11 Second recordings of *Jesu, Meine Freude* and *Christ lag in Todesbanden* – 1958

12 Second, and greatest, of the three *Mass in B Minor* recordings – 1960

The early recordings on this list are in the days of Julius Herford's work as teacher and mentor to Shaw, and show Herford's influence.

Moving into the mid and later 1950s, Shaw is in close touch with the scholar and conductor Alfred Mann. Mann came to believe that Shaw's greatest contribution to music was his ongoing work on the *Mass in B Minor*. In his view, Shaw brought it to an American audience; stimulated American music schools to study and perform it; and illuminated it with performances both learned and lively.

A third Bach scholar who influenced Shaw greatly and with whom he was in touch for decades was the late Gerhard Herz, who taught for many years at the University of Louisville.

After 1960s, Shaw does not release a Bach recording again for 28 years. This would be the Bach *Magnificat,* paired with the Vivaldi *Gloria*—in 1988.

Why would he have substantially stopped recording Bach, especially when he did so little in his early career?

Possible answers:

One, he may have felt he had reached his pinnacle in Bach in 1960 and decided it was time to move on. Two, there were likely commercial pressures. RCA may have been pushing him to make more records that were lighter and easier to sell. Even Telarc, later on, may have felt Bach recordings were not commercial winners. Moreover, they would have been expensive to make. (The Bach explosion in recordings was in the 1990s.) Third, the later Shaw was more intimidated by Bach than the younger Shaw.

By this time Shaw was spending most of his time in orchestra work and perhaps felt he had little time for the cantatas.

However, Shaw never stopped performing Bach. He did one of the Passions or the *Mass in B Minor* virtually every year and he programmed smaller Bach choral works and Bach instrumental works in Cleveland and Atlanta regularly.

Shaw also toured the *St. John Passion* and the *B Minor Mass* with the Chorale.

In 1990, Shaw does his third recording of the Mass. He uses a large choir, seemingly for reasons theological and pastoral: Involvement of the entire "congregation," as it were.

His performances in Atlanta in the 1980s were large and participatory, with audiences invited to sing the chorales, as he had also done in Cleveland and New York.

His last performances, in Atlanta and New York, in the late 1990s, however, were smaller in scale and more lean, athletic, and strictly baroque, though they never became dry or abstract and never lacked for fervor.

He was unhappy with his final recording of the Mass, which he said was "too thick." Not everyone agreed. The solo and quartet singers are wonderful, as are the rhythmic qualities in the recording.

What does all of this show about Shaw and Bach?

- It shows his roots in Bach.
- It shows, perhaps, the arrogance of youth. In his youth Shaw plows right into recording Bach. No other American conductor was recording this material at the time. In maturity he was unsure of himself with Bach, as with much. In old age, he was wary of recording, saying "the scholarship changes every week."
- Third, not only did Shaw never leave Bach, he rediscovered him.

In the 1990s, free of the responsibilities of running an orchestra, he began to delve into Bach study again, and perform him more often. Shaw began listening to period instrument recordings at this time, praising Ton Koopman, in particular. And he began to study and meditate upon the *St. Matthew Passion,* in particular, even when not preparing a performance of it. This was as rare as Shaw listening to records for sheer pleasure. He even called the *St. Matthew* "my current obsession."

Shaw's abiding love for Bach deepened in his last years.

Appendix IX

Three Shaw Meditations on Bach

The first two are excerpts from two Shaw letters to the Cleveland Orchestra Chorus written in February and March of 1960. They concern the *St. Matthew Passion.*

The third is a complete text of spoken program notes Shaw delivered before a performance of the *St. John Passion* at the Alaska Festival of Music in 1957. The notes were written in Shaw's hand on yellow legal paper and deciphered with the assistance of Nola Frink.

I.

Most of us are aware, I suppose, of the Roman Catholic doctrine of *transubstantiation,* according to which at the consecration of the Eucharist the bread and wine become the actual body and blood of Christ. Well, that may or may not be your faith, but it seems to me that something very like transubstantiation is operative in such master-works as the *St. Matthew Passion.* In the presence of such a creation—whose spirit *must* be very near to that of Jesus himself, "Sense is transfigured quite." We are no longer "play-actors"—and the music itself, I believe, is a Eucharist in which are dissolved the mutually exclusive boundaries of spirit and substance, time and space, the mortal and the immortal.

"Come ye daughters, share my anguish" is not the *picturization* of the spirit of anguish, it *is* the spirit of anguish. We do not engage to portray a mother or a world of mothers crying over the slaughter of their innocent sons. Herein anguish cries only unto anguish—and we *are* anguish.

"Let him be crucified!" is not the simple picturization of the cry of another crowd on another day. By the temper and the stature of this music time is obliterated, and we share that crucifixion. We're participants. We *crucify.* I don't mean figuratively. I don't mean "so to speak." I mean crucify. The scape-goat and the sacrificial slaughter of the Aztec innocents and the crucifixion of Jesus are one and the same. They are the obedience of the human spirit to the knowledge of its own guilt and its own mortality. There was no time when Jesus was not crucified; and his blood assuredly is on us and on our children. I believe the music of Bach says that.

The thing I think I'm trying to say is that we are *not* engaged in the *dramatization* of the death—and triumph—of Jesus. But by the dignity and integrity of this great music, the spirit of which reaches out to touch that of Jesus himself, we are forced to acknowledge our participation in that death and triumph. The *Passion* music is not dramatic in the theatrical sense of acting a part. It is drama in the cosmic sense—of being a part. It is not a series of masques to be put on and manipulated to the maximum "effect." It is—if you are sufficiently mystic—a sort of Eucharist whose physical properties issue in something quite transcending time and place.

It seems to me, therefore, treacherous and abortive to superimpose the imagined excitements of a given crowd on a given day by the devices of accelerando, ritendando and dynamic effect. By the spiritual genius of Bach the greater drama is already built into the musical structure. It is wrong to play the pit; the people must be brought to the music.

I wouldn't say that there is any great danger that it will be otherwise in this instance. But it's nice to keep sights high and feet dry. Anyway, I know now what I meant when I said two weeks ago that rehearsal on the *Passion* should be very nearly a sacrament.

II.

Have you had occasion during the work on the *Passion* to note the extraordinary range, depth and complexity of roles the chorus plays in the work? There are three major ones. First there are the various groups of participants in the drama—the disciples, priests, crowds, etc., who sing the "action" choruses. Second is the congregation of believers before whom the drama is being played, who respond to the most sensitive moments with their impulsive common chorale. (The first group responds to the act, the second to the retelling of the act. Each of these groups, then, has a time and a place.)

The third role of the chorus is the most complex of all—for it has of itself neither time nor place. Its locale is the universe of ideas, of morality; its time is long before and long after, as well as the instant of the work's creation and the instant of its retelling. The chorus in this role stands apart from both actor and audience, and bears witness to the meaning of the play, its intent and progress.

What is almost beyond understanding is the manner in which these roles are fantastically—almost surrealistically—mixed. For instance, what is the time and place of the opening chorus? Is it an invitation to the play we are about to see? Or is it an invitation to the crucifixion itself? (Note that the congregation in the form of the chorale, which enters at letter A, is responding to the drama before the drama has begun.)

Mark the curious mixture of congregational and priestly functions in No. 26. The chorus this time is an abstract company, somehow a part of, and responding within, the soloist's mind.

What are we to say of the chorus in No. 33? "Loose him! Halt ye! Bind him not!" Who is now singing—the actors, the congregation, or you and I? Who sings, "Have lightning and thunder all vanished? Then open thy fiery abysses, O Hell!" – And what a mixture is No. 35! Congregational chorale—but so developed musically that it stands apart from both actor and audience.

Perhaps these are the moments in which you and I here and now are most deeply involved.

It is as though there were a theatre on the stage of which a play is being acted—and that is one drama. In the hall of the theatre there is an audience, and this audience interrupts the actors on stage—and that is the second drama. And somewhere above this theatre watching both these dramas stand you and I. And at incredible moments (Think what craftsmanship this represents on Bach's part)—at incredible moments the actors on the stage are suddenly frozen, their posture or gesture transfixed, the audience in an instant is turned to stone, time holds breath, and you and I become a part of the third great drama—that of the meanings of things and events, of love and hate, of to live and to kill—a drama before and beyond time, before even this particular *Passion,* yet known to us here and now.

There are layers upon layers of art and awareness in the *St. Matthew Passion.*

III.

Ladies and Gentlemen –

I am Robert Shaw. (This before the concert begins—perhaps even without any lighting other than audience lighting. How am I dressed? Is there a curtain: Is it up or down?)

What we are about to witness tonight is a lynching. It is a lynching in abstract—and depending upon whether you are a Christian—and what sort of a Christian? How traditional is your theology—or a Mohammedan or a Jew or a Hedonist or an Atheist—will not determine the specific extent of your involvement in this drama. (to be continued)

(Written in margin beside above: "not quite good sense yet")

This is a musical drama. Opera has certain specifications. It asks you to believe that the people on the other side of the proscenium—the footlights—exist; that they are those whom they represent—that their tragedies and triumphs are real and their art plausible.

The true musical drama—the drama of the symphony or the string quartet, the solo sonata—and more particularly the oratorio—says that those people on the stage do not exist, except that you make them exist—that you "breathe into them the breath of life." They are a part of your imagination—or they do not live.

For many of us this is the story of the imminent triumph of evil over good. That Jesus was a man, that he lived, that he was good, history affirms and no man denies. That he was a God—some may question. But none of us will question that goodness is of necessary value—that its struggle against evil is the greatest human drama that the mind can conceive.

It must be said that in the mind of the man who created this drama—Jesus was Divine—with the necessary capitals. And for those of us who are heirs of that strict theology this drama will have meanings which others of us will not share.

Therefore three things need to be said about this musical drama.

The first is that it was written explicitly as a part of and function of religious dogma. Johann Sebastian Bach believed that Jesus of Nazareth was the Son of God. He signed his manuscripts J. S. Bach—to the Glory of God.

His audience was an audience of believers—perhaps no more—but very probably more than any congregation in today's churches is an audience of believers.

The second thing which is unique about this drama is its scale of time. Our contemporary theatre is built upon the premise that what occurs upon the stage happens within our own SCALE of living-time—if it does not happen within our SPAN of living-time. That is to say—as Thornton Wilder told me once: In today's theatre, if a man shoots another man—on the stage—the victim on the stage is the only man who dies. The people in the audience do not die.

Bach's drama is quite differently conceived. This span is not of living Body-Time, but of equally Living-Time of the Mind. Thus Bach will feel quite free to abandon the temporal struggle of Jesus for his physical life to inquire into how you and I should feel about it.

The success of this drama depends not upon how real the characters emerge on the other side of the footlights—but upon how clearly they may be awakened in your own life. It is you who breathe the breath of life into Pilate, and Peter, and the soldiers and the Chief Priests.

And in a greater sense—for as in the case of no opera ever written—this drama involves you as you have come to the theatre this evening—from whatever custom of occupation or home—for you are not asked to be listeners only but also participants. There is no doubt of that.

The cast of characters is in this manner detailed. We have first of all the Narrator—the evangelist who reads with all the incredible musical poetry that Bach prescribed, the story with which all of us are familiar. There are second, the actors in that story: Jesus, Pilate, Peter—he who is unsure of himself and his Lord—the maid, the soldiers, the priests. There are third, those of philosophical utterance, who at moments very precious to Bach will interrupt the story to caution us; to invite us to ponder the meaning of the event in the quiet of our minds—undisturbed by the measure of minutes—counting only the time it takes us to savor and think on these things. The opening and closing choruses share this meaning.

And there is finally the congregation of participants. For at moments during the drama—in the vision of him who created the drama—no man could be silent. The form of this participation is the Chorale—and they are simple tunes—known to every church-goer in Bach's day—the knowledge of which in our time would bring not only dignity to our worship but stature to our living. Insofar as you are moved by the events depicted—or find a resonance in your own life, we invite your participation in their singing—humming or speaking—however you wish. To symbolize that participation, members of your community are joining us from the audience in this performance.

Appendix X

"Worship and the Arts" Combined with "Conservative Arts"

Robert Shaw gave three major speeches in his lifetime that were also lectures and in two cases personal credos.

These three were:

"The Conservative Arts"

"Worship and the Arts"

"Reflections and Excursions on Orchestra and Chorus"

None changed in essence. But Shaw re-wrote all of them many times over. "The Conservative Arts," in particular, was re-written, refined, and delivered innumerable times. All three were delivered in more or less final form at Memorial Church, Harvard University in 1981.

All may be found in *The Robert Shaw Reader,* edited by Robert Blocker.

I have included a combined version (by Shaw) of "arts" and "worship" here.

WORSHIP AND THE ARTS COMBINED WITH THE CONSERVATIVE ARTS

by Robert Shaw

Minneapolis, Minnesota
March 21, 1985

Doctor Meisel

Ladies and Gentlemen – Good afternoon.

Like musical institutions around the world, the Atlanta Symphony and its choruses have scheduled celebratory performances of J. S. Bach's major choral and instrumental works during this tri-centennial season and focusing on this very special week of his birth.

During the last few days, while I have been trying to bring some coherency to a few years' random musings bearing on "Worship and the Arts," we also have been attempting to "mount"—as the saying goes—a series of performances of Bach's *St. Matthew Passion.*

Now, the *St. Matthew Passion* is a logistical Mt. Everest rising high above the entrapments and jungles of symphonic contracts and schedules: Nearly three times the length of the normal symphony concert, and calling for two orchestras, three, four or more choruses, a dozen vocal soloists and nearly that many instrumental soloists, and even inviting audience participation—to exist at all (in living sound) it must be brought before its public fully and handsomely clothed in something under ten hours of orchestral rehearsal.

And no piece of music in the history of Western Civilization (unless it be the *Mass in B Minor*) is so worth it.

Running through my mind—as I have tried to hang my "Worship and the Arts" notebooks on today's anniversary pegs—have been four questions concerning the *St. Matthew Passion.*

1. Is it not possible that during the entire—nearly twenty-century—history of Christianity, the *St. Matthew Passion* must be accounted its single most sensitive, beautiful consummate and profound act of worship?

2. Given a world of varying and different religions, given the fact that among them Christianity has been the one most concerned with proselytization and missionizing, and not infrequently guilty of unfriendly if not inhuman zeal, how is it that a relatively obscure church musician committed so literally and serenely to the dogma of his day and place could seemingly seek to embrace all mankind—for centuries still to come—in his exploration of grief and heroism—both human and divine.

   How is it that a conservative theology which seemingly led one solo musician two and one half centuries ago to reach out to comfort, could motivate a body of men and women who consider themselves uniquely moral—as proved by their majority—in our time to reach out for control—even exploitation?

3. Is it not possible that the *St. Matthew Passion* is as extraordinary as a Work of Art as it is an Act of Worship? If it is—as it appears to us to be—an intellectual achievement, so masterful in structure and expressivity as to match any of the half-dozen towering accomplishments of human history—what does that tell us of Bach's congregation—or our own forms of worship?

4. If any of the above are true—why don't we just pass out the music, and rehearse for an hour—instead of talking about it?

So that you can appreciate how far back it is possible for one man to have slidden, you should know that for three or more generations the Shaws and Lawsons—both of whose names I bear—have been ministers, chaplains and missionaries in the service of a denomination removed from Westminster Presbyterianism chiefly by water rites and Welch's grape juice. From one end of California to the other, our church called itself—modestly—the "*First* Christian Church."

In the age-old confrontation between reason and the heart as the royal road to salvation, we'd have been numbered among the "deep-feelers." In our home, Latin was acceptable as an intellectual discipline five days a week, but along with golf and card-playing, it was forbidden on Sunday. (I was allowed as a child to sing "Gloria in Excelsis" only because it was actually Hebrew for "bringing in the sheaves.")

As to the aesthetics of church architecture, our principal influences in California were Forest Lawn Cemetery, Alcatraz, and Grauman's Chinese Theatre.

Grandpa, in addition to being a "Disciples" minister, was head of the Anti-Saloon League in California—representing a conviction he apparently had reached somewhat late in life.

As a youth he must also have experienced other secularities, because Mother reported once with a wry combination of embarrassment and pride, that on a church "retreat" in the High Sierras (which really was an excuse for a fishing trip) the men of the church had finally one evening conned their pastor into a game of poker.

They carefully explained the game to him, and when it became his turn to deal, and the betting had been sufficiently vigorous, Grandpa laid down 5 Aces—saying something like "Go your way, and sin no more."

From infancy, "church" in our family was no sometime thing, but a seven-day, twenty-four hour shift. And, for a season fifteen years ago, and another period thirty years prior to that, I frequently found myself in the very critical condition we face today—somebody out there and me up here.

This, of course, was when I was much younger—and infinitely wiser.

For, from a pulpit one may begin with the incidental, but must end with the *essential.* One rummages through life's attic of intendables, accidents and witless repetitions to see if there be anything other than failure worth, as they say, "sharing."

So while it may be a charitable and Christian act to set out in search of the sheep that is lost, it is quite another matter, having found him, to put him in the pulpit.

I take as my texts for this morning's homily four verses from the contemporary scripture according to Charles Ives, and five from the gospel according to St. John.

Charles Ives's sentences are to be found in a post-face to his privately published volume of *114 Songs*. In a pungent essay which he randomly entitles: " . . . The Truth about Something . . . (or) How to write Music While Shaving . . ." he asks these questions:

> Is not beauty in music too often confused with something which lets the ears lie back in an easy-chair? Many sounds that we are used to do not bother us, and for that reason are we not too easily inclined to call them beautiful? Possibly the fondness for personal expression—which self-indulgence miscalls 'freedom'—may throw out a skin-deep arrangement which is accepted at first as beautiful . . . But if a composer's conception of his art, its functions and ideals, even if sincere, coincides to such an extent with these . . . tried out progressions in expediency . . . has he or has he not been drugged with an overdose of habit-forming sounds? And as a result do not the muscles of his clientele become flabbier and flabbier, until they give way altogether and find refuge only in platitudes, the sensual outbursts of an emasculated rubber-stamp?

The familiar opening verses of the Gospel according to John seem to me even more provocative in the translation of the New English Bible:

> When all things began the Word already was. The Word dwelt with God; and what God was, the Word was. The Word, then, was with God at the beginning, and through him all things came to be; no single thing was created without him. All that came to be was alive with his life, and that life was the light of men. The light shines on in the dark, and the darkness has never quenched it.

Let me suggest to you the questions which this morning's title suggest to me. Be sure that I presume no ministerial certainty for my answers. I speak to you as a lay member of the larger religious community concerned, as surely all of us are, with man's nature and condition as a brother—or sister—of Man, and a son—or daughter—of the Infinite.

The questions are:

1. What is the Nature of Worship?
2. What is the Nature of Art? . . . and

3. What, then, are the responsibilities of the Arts to Worship (and coincidentally the Church); and what are the responsibilities of the Church to the Arts?

First – What is the nature of worship?

"Anglo-Saxon S-C-I-P-E-: a suffix embodying a condition or state,
Preceded by W-E-O-R-T-H: that quality of a thing rendering it
valuable or useful; excellence, eminence, virtue."
Therefore: worship—the state or quality of worth.
From that: the courtesy or reverence paid to that which is worthy.
From that: divine worship—honor to divine worth.

Under what conditions does worship occur? What are the attitudes and states of being which allow it to happen?

For me, its absolutely minimum conditions are a sense of mystery and an admission of pain.

What wondrous love is this
O my soul
O my soul . . .
What wondrous love is this
O my soul?
What wondrous love is this
That caused the Lord of Bliss
To bear the dreadful curse
For my soul
For my soul . . .
To bear the dreadful curse
For my soul.

Amazing grace . . .
How sweet the sound!
That saved a wretch like me.
I once was lost
But now am found,
Was blind, but now I see!

Through many dangers, toils and snares
I have already come;
'Tis grace has brought me safe thus far,
And grace will bring me home.

Sometimes I feel like a mournin' dove
Sometimes I feel like a moanin' dove
Sometimes I feel like a morning dove
A long ways from home.

Sometimes I feel like a motherless child
Sometimes I feel like a eagle in the air
Sometimes I feel like I'm almost gone,
A long ways from home.

These words are miracles to me—of ungraven images and boundless mystery; and their melodies, shaped and worn by life-times of tears, are as perfect as anything I know in music.

This is not nostalgia; their saintliness and humility is the acquaintance of my later years. In my youth I was accustomed to a shoutier, boastier fare:

Oh, there's power . . . power
Wonder-working power
In the blood
        (In the blood)
Of the Lamb
        (Of the Lamb)

Oh, there's power . . . power
Wonder-working power
In the precious blood
Of the Lamb.

I was sinking deep in sin
Far from the peaceful shore,
Very deeply stained within
Sinking to rise no more—
When the Master of the sea
Heard my despairing cry,
From the waters lifted me—
Now SAFE . . . AM . . . I.

Blessed assurance, Jesus is *mine*!

Strangely, even these—viewed through the blurring of time—seem somewhat superior in poetic plausibility and just common decency to the sancti-monstrosities which, by the miracle of electronics, begin early every Sunday morning to violate what is called the Lord's Day—from Gethsemene Gardens, Florida to Chrystal Christ-o-rama, California.

In the great folk hymns and spirituals of the eighteenth and nineteenth centuries, there is a directness and a fervor of utterance, and a humility, which invoke man's nobility, and to me, a spark of divinity.

His voice as the sound of the dulcimer sweet
    Is heard through the shadow of death.

Swing low, sweet chariot,
    Comin' for to carry me home.

When Jesus wept,
    a falling tear
    in mercy flowed
    beyond all bound.

There is a balm in Gilead
    to make the wounded whole.

Broad is the road that leads to death,
    and thousands walk together there.

Angel, oh angel,
I don't want to be buried
    in the storm.

O tell me where the dove has flown
    and where he builds his nest. . .

Ev'ry time I feel the spirit
    movin' in my heart,
I will pray.

My Lord, what a mornin'
    When the stars begin to shine.

This little light of mine,
    let it shine
    let it shine
    let it shine.

Occasionally, of course, mystery and pain will find a contemporary voice: Robert Frost, writing,

"Dear Lord, forgive the little jokes I've played on Thee,
And I'll forgive the great big one on me."

Dylan Thomas, in his *Child's Christmas in Wales,* writing of finding breast-up always on that icy morning "by the post-office or the swings . . . a dead bird . . . perhaps a robin, all but one of its fires out;" and of receiving books that "told me everything I needed to know about the wasp . . . except 'Why?'"

There must be little in our national life so frightening as the Sunday Spectaculars of bigotry and contempt for men's minds so proudly exhibited by televangelism: Christianity pre-packaged and pre-digested in a succession of monologues and commercials starring that lovable 33-year-old Trail Boss "everybody knows" and his Big Daddy in the skies. These have to be a flat-out burlesque of Christ's compassion for the suffering souls of men.

The witticism about the Unitarian praying "To whom it may concern" is really only half-a-laugher, but totally disturbing. Hartley Burr Alexander in *God and Man's Destiny* concludes: "This is faith's humility, and the fountain of its prayer, never more feelingly uttered, as in the name of the souls of men, than by an Indian of the North American prairies, 'A man from the earth am I . . . have compassion upon me, Whoever, from above, you the Supreme.'"

"Nobody knows the trouble I've seen."
"Who is that a-comin' yonder on a cloud?"

Mystery and a sensitivity to pain are irreducible conditions for worship.

A second thing can be said about worship: it is that, though all of us on occasion have experienced in solitude what we felt to be a sudden flash of divine goodness and beauty, in a very important sense worship is a communion and a fellowship.

The chief contemporary prophet of this understanding may well be Martin Buber, the German-Jewish philosopher and theologian whom Dag Hammarskjold, shortly before he died, recommended for a Nobel Prize.

If I understand him correctly, the argument of his books *Between Man and Man* and *I and Thou* is (1) that man finds his being and his relationship to "the Other"—that Outside Mystery which some call God—only when he is confronted with and responsive to another human being, a *Thou;* (2) that *I* and the *Thou* and the Mysterious Other are inextricably intertwined; (3) that this "revelation" happens not in isolated retreat from the world, but in day-to-day living—perhaps even in day-to-day singing; and (4) that it is this communion which identifies man's manhood, and is of god.

That is to say: the Lord our God is One, but it takes at least two to find Him.

"Man's threefold Living relation," he writes, "is, first, his relation to the *world* and to *things*; second, his relation to *man*; and third, his relation to the *mystery of being* (which the philosopher calls 'the absolute' and the believer calls 'God') and which cannot in fact be eliminated from the situation even by a man who rejects both designations.)"

"A God reached only by renunciation" (of one or two of these elements) "cannot be the God who has made and held together all that is. The way (to this God) can only be a 'communion.'"

And then he says a remarkable thing: "I have given up the 'religious,' which is *nothing but . . . ecstasy*; or it has given me up. I possess nothing but the everyday out of which I am never taken. The mystery . . . has made its dwelling here where everything happens as it happens. I know of no fullness but each mortal hour's fullness of claim and responsibility. Though far from being equal to it, yet I know that in the claim I am claimed . . . and I know who speaks and demands a response."

Worship is a "communion."

A third thing can be said about worship: this seeking and celebration is approachable also on a formal and ritualistic basis. It is a good thing for communicants with whom one does not have a daily contact to come together with dependable frequency, to consider divinity's wonders, and man's relation to them and his fellow man.

It will surprise no one to suggest that this coming together must provide a variety of elements of worth, harmonious and supportive of one another, and so fashioned, that they make possible a deeper understanding of the Great Who/am.

And this, of course, is where the Arts knock on the church door: outside, trying to get in; or inside, trying to get out.

Precisely because it is occasional and structured, "Worship" itself becomes Art, or a confluence of the Arts, in that it has a certain amount of Space and Time during which to proportion and contemplate Truth and Beauty.

Small wonder that formal worship invokes the sensations of sight and sound—as well as of reason—not only as stimulants to quicken the perception, or as a balm for life's abrasions, but as factors of worth themselves.

Which leads us to our second major question: What are the meanings of Art? What can the Arts tell us of Man? What is Man trying to tell us of himself? Or of his mystery?

May I suggest to you four answers. First: for me, the Arts are the Flesh become Word. That "the Word became Flesh" is familiar doctrine. But what about the reciprocal miracle? The daily possibility of Matter becoming Spirit? Paint onto canvas in one century turned into tears six centuries later? Words onto paper today flung into a theatre tomorrow to change a life the year after? Little spots of ink transfigured into a miracle of symphonic sound, joining thousands of listeners and performers in a rare community of Brotherhood? Art is the Flesh become Word.

Second, facing the bewildering profusions of matter and sensation, the Arts testify to man's ability to isolate and to identify, and finally to relate and to order. These few pitches, those precise colors out of countless and contrary, out of confusion and chaos, emerge in perfect symmetry and heart-breaking recognizability, a Vittoria "O vos omnes" and "Swing Low, Sweet Chariot," *King Lear* and *Our Town,* cathedrals at Chartres and Coventry, "Blessed are the dead" and "The Lord is my shepherd."

Third, the arts provide for the exchange of ideas and values otherwise incommunicable by languages of numbers, symbols, alphabets or grunts.

The great creative artist is characterized not only by his capacity to order his experience, but by his capacity to *have* his experience. And while he cannot relate his experience to us, he can communicate how he feels about it. We recognize his feelings. We can find them consonant with our own experience, though experienced in an intensity beyond our dimmer comprehensions.

A work of art may indeed be a "revelation." It exists to convey that which is otherwise incommunicable.

And fourth, across boundaries of time, space, chance and malice, the Arts are the open hand of man reaching for his brother. Separate from both Church and State, unstructured to the point of near anarchy, alone—of the great ethical-social-intellectual efforts—they have been free of the inhumanities and excesses which seem eventually to beset all human institutions.

To humanity's shame, even that Church named after the "Good Shepherd" and "Holy Comforter" has had a history of persecutions and crusades—in just one of which, in the year of our Lord 1212, and in a much smaller world, fifty thousand innocent children were "shepherded" to their deaths by the sword, starvation and pestilence, and the few fortunate survivors "comforted" by being sold into prostitution and slavery.

The arts may indeed be not the luxury of the few but the last best hope of humanity—to inhabit with joy this planet.

What is it in the nature of the Arts that allows them to offer these hopes of maturity and survival?

In the first place, it is clear that a commitment to the creative process starts the human animal on a thorny and lonesome road of self-discovery, away from the comforts and compromises of institutions. "Forty days and forty nights" is a Biblical metaphor for what is more nearly a lifetime of wilderness and solitude. But the more deeply man delves into himself, the more surely he understands—and the more knowingly and tenderly returns to—his fellow man.

In the second place, the Arts are concerned not with the consumption, sale or other exploitation of earth's material wonders—not even with their recycling—but with their reincarnation. They propose not a mounting monopoly of a medium of exchange, but the sweet, quiet exchange of truth and beauty themselves.

Within our lifetime the technological explosions in the *means* of communication have substantially obliterated its *essence*. "Image-Making," with its armament of commercial propagandas and public relations—is an out and out attempt on the part of some of us to control the behaviour of the rest of us. Its avowed intention is to force a predictable response. It is the absolute antithesis of communication—the meaning of which originally was a "coming together—the way of, the fortress for."

Left to themselves, the arts propose not control—but simple truth and beauty.

And in the third place, in a time and a society whose values are geared to the biggest, the fastest, and the mostest, whose gaze is fixed desperately upon the future—as far as least as the next election or life after death or prosperity, whichever should happen to come first—the Arts offer an historical perspective. For their concern is with originality—meaning that which has origins. Thus the arts lead man to consider and build upon his own beginnings—his essence and his potential.

The Arts, then, are not merely "handmaidens" of worship; but, given creativity on the order of a Brahms *Requiem* or a *St. Matthew Passion,* they are themselves unqualified and unparalleled acts of worship.

There was one other question—though a double one. The first part of it was, "What are the responsibilities of the Arts to Worship and the Church?"

First, it seems to me that we have to agree that only the best is good enough. One does not sharpen his sensibilities to divine excellence by stuffing his ears with mediocrity. One does not gain strength for the stresses of virtue by gorging his muscles on unctuous fraud. A God of Truth, Goodness and Mercy is not honored by laying Saturday night's Disco Derivatives on Sunday's altar. The Minister of Music may indeed laugh himself all the way to the top of the Pop Charts—but God is only mocked—He is not worshipped.

This raises a few questions: On what grounds, and upon whose authority, are we to decide what is worthy and what is worthless for worship? May not one man's "Passion Chorale" be another man's "Old Rugged Cross"?

I suggest to you that the dilemma is more apparent than real, and that it can be solved by common sense, every-day good manners and a healthy combination of humility and industry which, however, lays upon very few of us the obligation to matriculate at a School of the Arts.

Let me lay before you four criteria which may help this evaluation.

The first is that of *motivation.* Let's say right out that purity of purpose dignifies. Not every continent-straddling evangelist is an Elmer Gantry. Similarly, 10,000 "How great Thou artists" are not irretrievably doomed for chanting softly and tenderly in the Cotton Bowl.

I can recall returning to my father's little yellow brick church when San Diego was still half-Navy and half-wetback, after my second exposure to the Bach Passions and Cantatas, to hear my mother and grandmother sing together "There were ninety and nine that safely lay—in the shelter of the fold." And tears started.

But how much greater an experience it would have been had we all been able to study and rehearse and perform competently together—as a service of worship—Bach's *Passion According to St. Matthew.*

Purity of purpose dignifies . . . But not all tears attest to equally deep springs of sorrow.

And just try to escape that cancerous explosion whose purpose is not so pure! "Positive pop puts Christian radio in mainstream," was the headline in a recent *Atlanta Constitution Sunday* Arts section. "It reflects bigger budgets and a move to pop professionalism, which counters the sincere amateurism that marked the early years." And these lines that lay it somewhere between Madison Avenue and Lynchburg: "There would have been a market ten years ago if there'd been a product." "To cross over into the market-place, you've got to take the cross over."

Jesus looked around and said to his disciples, "How hard it will be for those who have riches to enter the Kingdom of God." (Mark 10:23)

"And making a whip of cords, he drove them all, with the sheep and oxen, out of the temple; and he poured out the coins of the money changers and overturned their tables. And he told those who sold the pigeons, 'You shall not make my Father's house a house of trade.'" (John 2:15–16)

A second criterion must be craftmanship. Music is a craft, and it has rules and standards—and within reasonable limits these are knowable. We do not ask that every hymn or anthem be an unassailable masterpiece; but it ought at least to have the mortar, brick and girders specified in the contract.

Great text and great music do not meet in Nashville or Studio City.

The 50-year plague of that most popular "Lord's Prayer" cannot for long obscure the fact that it is more appropriate to Las Vegas than to the Mount of Olives—to Broadway than to Bethlehem. It cannot be considered an act of worship simply because it has "a fantastic lyric."

Great text and great music meet on the planes of purpose and craft, where music's edifice on its own terms is as honest and serviceable and as beautifully proportioned as the text it seeks to illumine.

In the third place, art and music worthy of worship will have historical perspective. They will have *origins*—which may, in time, even lead to originality. This criterion is very close to what we mean by "style," and it adds to *motivation* and *craftsmanship* the incalculable increments of *heritage* and tradition.

Note that this does not preclude, but embraces the legacy of folk-hymns, carols and spirituals: those tunes and texts, lovingly turned and polished by generations of nameless amateurs who loved their God and sought to praise Him.

These, folk-hymns and spirituals—Passions and Cantatas of Bach, the late Haydn Masses, and Requiems by Brahms and Britten and, perhaps, even Charles Ives's Psalms are really the people's music. The people think so little of pop music that every 6 to 10 weeks they have to have a new tune to dance to, to trade small talk above, to go up an elevator with, to make what some call "love" by. The real people's music is passed from generation to generation. Music worthy of worship will have a heritage.

And then—once in a very great while—we may come across a sculpture, a building, or a piece of music which is indeed a "revelation," evidence not only of the creator's capacity to "order his experience" but, more importantly, to "have his experience."

And that is the fourth and final criterion—the creative miracle of "revelation": a cathedral at Chartres or Coventry or St. Mary's in San Francisco, Bach's *Mass in B Minor,* Stravinsky's *Symphony of Psalms.* For, of course, the revelations themselves set the standards. We do not set them. Exposure becomes acquaintance, and acquaintance becomes "communion"; and finally we begin to understand what an act of worship really is . . . and what it asks of us.

Jesus was asked, "Which of the commandments is the first of all?" And he answered, "The Lord our God, the Lord is one; and you shall love the lord your God with all your heart, and with all your soul, and with all your mind, and with all your strength."

He did not say, ". . . all your heart, most of your soul, and—let's see—about 'half' your mind."

The truth is that worship should be a heart-wrenching, soul-searing, mind-stretching and generally exhausting experience. One should not be asked to check his mind at the door, should someone get him to the church on time.

What, finally, shall we say is the Church's responsibility to the Arts?

At present this answer is little more than a hunch, and perhaps I overvalue it because it's a recent idea, and they don't come all that frequently.

It seems to me that any institution—and churches run the same risks as symphony orchestras, banks, universities, divinity schools and governments—any institution runs the risk of becoming "set in its ways," rigid in its policies and doctrine, hard in the arteries and soft in the head.

My hunch is this: that in a world growing denser in population and poorer in sources of energy, we inevitably will have stricter political and economic organization in order to provide sufficient food, housing and occasional comforts. In this sort of world (so it seems to me) the creative arts will loom as the finest flower of a maturing mankind.

But, even more importantly, for me at least, the arts may provide the day-by-day confirmation of a Creator's hand still at work in the lives and affairs of men.

If the Christian Church can accept the doctrine of "eternal life"—and most of it has high hopes—does it not follow that this life is somehow a part of that eternal one (eternity being indivisible and having no beginning and no end); and, therefore, LIFE in the universal, eternal sense—of which ours is only a very small part—must be a "becoming"?

I am not arguing Genesis vs. Evolution. (What's a few million years to the Infinite?) I am simply suggesting that if there is a Creator—a God of Life and Love—He/She/It somehow/somewhere/somewhen must be doing exactly that: Living and Loving.

However we may view Creation, it strikes me as contrary to both reason and faith to argue that it is concluded. If so, when? And, if so, is God not dead? Or no longer God?

Is it not somehow shortsighted to raise up an eternal omnipotent Creator—and not give him anything to do since Day Six? Should not an everlasting Creator be somewhere lasting and creating? And if, indeed, man was made "in that image, after that likeness . . . male and female" (not hetero-, homo-, bi-, but BOTH! Simultaneously! Talk about equal rights!) . . . if, indeed, man was made "in that image," given a Timeless, Boundless Creator, is there a better place to see the Creator at work than "in that likeness?"

To me it follows that the Church, if it wants to keep in touch with the Creator, must provide a home for all that is—and all who are—creative, lest the church itself wither and drift into irrelevance.

Surely, basic to the responsibilities of a Church in the Christian tradition are the presentation and interpretation of ancient evidences of God's creative presence.

But, is it not also equally important to recognize and identify—wherever they occur—the Creator's continuing manifestations and processes, and celebrate the fruits of a Holy Spirit still at work in today's fleeting fraction of Time's continuum?

To refer again to Charles Ives, and to substitute about a word and a half:

> Is not (worship) too often confused with something which lets the (mind) lie back in an easy chair? Many sounds (or ideas) that we are used to, do not bother us, and for that reason, are we not too easily inclined to call them "worshipful?" . . . But if worship, even if sincere, coincides to such an extent with these tried-out progressions in expediency, have we or have we not been drugged with an overdose of habit-forming ideas? And, as a result, do not our minds become flabbier and flabbier until they give way altogether and find refuge only in . . . platitudes . . . ?
>
> When all things began, the Word already was. The Word dwelt with God; and what God was, the Word was. The Word, then, was with God at the beginning, and through him all things came to be; no single thing was created without him. All that came to be was alive with his life, and that life was the light of men. The light shines on . . . and the darkness has never quenched it.

You all have your own conclusions concerning the historical currents, tides and shapes of Theology and Christology. But, does it appear to anyone else that Christianity may have become so pre-occupied with the door-prizes attendant upon the divinity of Christ—that it has not nearly fathomed Jesus' humanity?

What if the "Son of God" were in truth the "Son of Man"? What heresies or truths lie hidden within this scriptural identity? What does it mean that he who is hailed as "Redeemer/Intercessor/Messiah/The Way/The Truth/and The Life" was in the beginning seen as "Emmanuel/God in us?" Is there any possibility that the emphasis upon the God-hood of the Son of Man, to the exclusion of the Man-hood of the Son of God affords a blanket of endliss bliss in preference to a hair-shirt of responsibility? Knowing that the gospels do, in fact, attest to Jesus' awareness of his very special relationship to what he called "the Spirit" and "the Father," have we been slow to understand, or unwilling to credit, the language and the confidence with which he reached out to touch the souls of those around him—as, also the soul of Everyman through all time?

"Whoever receives this child in my name receives me; and whoever receives me receives the One who sent me." (Luke 9:48)

"My daughter, your faith has made you whole." (Mark 5:34}

"You are the salt to the world . . . You are the light for the world." (Matthew 5:14)

"'The seed sown on rock' stands for those who receive the word with joy when they hear, but have no root in themselves . . ." (Luke 8:13)

"Why do you call me good? No one is good but God alone." (Mark 10:18)

"In very truth I tell you, the Son can do nothing by himself . . . I cannot act by myself . . . my aim is not my own will, but the will of him who sent me." (John 5:30)

"You cannot tell by observation when the kingdom of God comes. There will be no saying, 'Look, here it is!' or 'There it is!' for in fact the Kingdom of God is (already?) within you." (John 5:19)

"I am not myself the source of the words I speak to you; it is the Father dwelling in me doing his work . . . In very truth I tell you, he who believes in me will do what I am doing; and he will do greater things still . . ." (John 14:10,12)

"When the time comes, the words will be given you: for it is not you who will be speaking: it will be the Spirit . . . speaking in you." (Matthew 10:20)

". . . The light shines on . . . and the darkness has never quenched it."

Appendix XI

Shaw on His Connection to African-Americans and Their Music

Martin Luther King Center
"An Evening of Tribute"
August 27, 1982
Remarks by Robert Shaw

Miss Dorsey, Mrs. Coretta Scott King, Yolanda King, Daddy King, Members of the Kings' Royal Family—and Fellow Peasants.

It is very gracious, indeed, for you to include the Conductor of the Atlanta Symphony Orchestra among this evening's honored guests.

But I really must use my few minutes on this occasion, to say a few words of thanks—for the social changes—mostly non-violent—and the inner changes—occasionally violent—which some of you, personally, and many of your friends and some of your forbearers have made in my life.

For most of the years since 1970 you have invited me to take part in the observance of Martin Luther King, Jr's. Birthday.

But you have substantially—and perhaps wisely—limited my participation to one word only: Hallelujah!

Tonight I would like to say "Thank you"—"Hallelujah."

My daddy was a preacher; my mother was a very special singer—I'm almost fourth-generation Californian. And my very earliest memories—as we traveled up and down that coast, from pastorate to convention to camp-meetings—were of my mother singing "Swing Low, Sweet Chariot" and "Deep River" unaccompanied or in arrangements by Harry T. Burleigh, the way she'd been taught to sing them by Roland Hayes, whom she adored. Isn't that some kind of heritage for a little bitty piece of White Trash?

1937 My very first paid conducting job was as the student conductor of the Pomona College Glee Club. The Faculty conductor fell ill, and I had to conduct at the Annual Intercollegiate Choral Competition. The piece was Nathaniel Dett's "Listen to the Lambs" and we lost to arch-rival Occidental who sang "Swing Low, Sweet Chariot."

1943 The first time I even worked for and with a symphony orchestra was when our inter-racial New York City Chorus—the Collegiate Chorale—appeared with the New York Philharmonic accompanying Paul Robeson in *The Ballad for Americans*—both the music and the man pioneers of Social Change.

1943 The first opera on which I worked was *Carmen Jones,* with Muriel Smith and Cozy Cole. Broadway shows in those days had six weeks of rehearsal. By the end of the first week, the chorus had memorized its music. So there was ample time for the stage director and choreographer to louse it up. When we got to Philadelphia for the tryouts, Billy Rose said, "Robert, what happened to the chorus?" Oscar Hammerstein stepped up, tapped him, "Billy, why don't you just line them up across the front of the stage and turn 'em loose!" Which was the way it went—and Broadway was never the same.

1946 The first record on which I conducted a chamber orchestra was a series of Bach arias including: "Sorrow, Sighing, Trouble, Crying" and "Have Mercy, Lord, On Me" with Marian Anderson.

1954 Among the very first tours of the Robert Shaw Chorale—even before Montgomery—Eugene Brice (brother of Carol) and Howard Roberts (wonderful and important musician) walked out on stage with us in Jackson, Mississippi, where whites and blacks never had appeared together. We had been told the audience would leave, only a few did. It was the same two men—the very same year—and the other three-score singers and musicians who first integrated in Atlanta, Georgia, the Georgian Terrace Hotel, because the hotel decided it preferred a total sleep-in to a total walk-out. We all ate nickel hamburgers brought in from outside to the conductor's room.

In 1962—and the first tour of the Soviet Union—the totally surprising triumph was performances of Bach's *B Minor Mass,* with Seth McCoy and Diane White as soloists. The only encores with sufficient musical and human integrity to follow such a masterpiece after a proper interval were "My God Is a Rock in a Weary Land" and "Sometimes I Feel Like a Motherless Child."

During the first United States tour of Handel's *Messiah* in 1966, on Easter Sunday afternoon in Birmingham, Alabama—It had been rumored in the press that the performers would leave the stage if the hall was not integrated. And when Seth McCoy stood to sing "Comfort Ye, My People," for the first ten rows he looked out on faces of his own color.

In the Second International Choral Festival in 1969 in Lincoln Center, the 6 to 800 students from 20 to 30 schools—from as many countries—and all the continents there were had met for the first time in a social evening in the arena-type basement of St. Peter's and Paul's Church. Twenty to thirty languages, but no communication. Wendell Whalum's *Men from Morehouse* began chanting "We Shall Overcome." Everybody there knew all the verses. For one solid hour, 800 voices in vocal improvisation serpenting and slow dancing: Never a night like it in choral musical history.

Three years later—the first fully staged opera I had ever conducted: T. J. Anderson's re-scoring and Wendell Whalum doing everything else of Scott Joplin's *Treemonisha.*

The same season, *The Men from Morehouse* saved the symphony's first staged oratorio, *Oedipus Rex.* At the end of the oratorio the lights are supposed to go out on Oedipus' face to signal his blindness. But the lights went out all over the house—no orchestra lights—no chorus lights—no conductor's light. And the Morehouse Men saved the Atlanta Symphony Orchestra and Atlanta Symphony Orchestra Chorus, singing the final two minutes from memory.

And in the past decade there have been the Birthday Celebrations.

And just this year, for the first time anywhere, T. J. Anderson's *Spirituals.*

For so many "firsts" and so many "social" and "inner" changes—Thank you.

Appendix XII

A Keith Burris Letter to Several Friends on Seeing/Hearing a Partially Staged Contemporary Performance of the *St. Matthew Passion*, in Shaw's English Translation

On Good Friday, I went to The Brooklyn Academy of music to hear/see the so-called Jonathan Miller "production" of Bach's *St. Matthew Passion.* The conductor was Paul Goodwin, an early music guy who had conducted in the previous two BAM *St. Matthews* in 1996 and 2001. He used Mr. Shaw's English translation.

The idea was simple: Do it as a semi-staged opera. Since it *is* a narrative, and it *is* a drama, treat it as such. The rationale was also simple: Make it new. Rather, let it be as alive as it truly is.

The two choirs were organized as two mobs/choruses on either side of the stage (right/left). The two orchestras were front and back. There was no children's choir. All the cast were informally dressed. There were three singers per part in each chorus. The singers/actors did some acting. I would call it semi-acting, just as this was semi-staged. The theater was small and many of the sold seats were on stage, including mine. There was no set to speak of, save a table with bread and wine, where the evangelist (Rick Clement the night I saw it) sat, at first. The proper term for what was done is probably semi-choreographed, not semi-staged. Singers moved around; came on and off stage; took center stage and left it; twice a violinist came forward to play outside the orchestra to the audience or a player. I must say, I found *movement* effective—taking the singers and players out of the line-up formation. Bach's music never *stops* moving.

Also (obviously, I guess), the singers were mixed together, not grouped by section.

Movement fits Bach. So does any attempt to free the drama. But you don't need to do that much to free it. And I thought *acting* per se did not. You don't need to *dramatize.* The greatest drama in human history, literature, or art is there before you. You need only to open it up. When the BAM production was *acted,* I found it often corny, contrived, and self-conscious. (At one point, Jesus sang to an apple.) When it was sung with passion, by fine (mostly) young singers in the chorus, and they let themselves be moved by the music, it was deeply affective.

I know I am influenced by RS's ideas here. I can say that his last *St. Matthew* at Carnegie was more dramatic, to me, than this dramatization because of his pacing and dynamics—acquired over so many years and so much study and living. He freed the drama with musical sense and values.

Still, I think Mr. Shaw would have been intrigued by this production. And also put off by any sign of *cleverness.* You can bring your own vanity to Berlioz or Verdi. It might even help. With Bach's *Passions,* you have to check it at the door. This is prayer, not entertainment. It is meditation, not only on the Christus, but on life, hate, love, death and suffering. This ain't show biz. (Is there anything in this world more absurd than a Standing O for a Bach Passion?) But this is how audience and performer are trained. We all pretend for two hours and the lights go up.

There were performance problems, of course—so what? The big problem, I think, was Miller's conception. It's *not* opera. It is drama. If cleverness or cuteness or stage business replace fervor, you've missed the train.

Recall the Lutheran lady in Minnesota saying to RS: "You're not entitled to this music if you do not believe," and he respected that. His answer: Believing *somehow*; believing in the music, if not all the theology behind it, believing at that moment.

This is the essential thing for me: To Shaw a performance of a Bach Passion was not playacting but re-enactment. "We are witnesses," Shaw writes. "It's happening again. Bach is here; to show us that and pull us up and out." It's not dramatization he's after. It's not like any play. Not even like *Hamlet.* It's transubstantiation: from life into art, and back into life.

Mack Harrell said he was not playing Jesus, but telling his story. R.S. was not "interpreting" Bach but enacting Bach's setting of the *St. Matthew Passion.* Much like a priest saying Mass, Shaw sought to recreate musical compositions rather ritualistically, but within the ritual and the rigor, Shaw hoped to find the essence of the music.

Musically, the problem of the Bach performance was that of so many "period" or early music performances, sometimes the worst of both worlds. Too fast to linger long enough for beauty, but not clear, not clean, not light, not precise enough. But Bach has broad shoulders. The chorus was magnificent. The translation heart-felt. Bach shone through.

This tells me that the Shaw approach *can* work: The music can be reborn and it can change us.

Post-script:

I attended Good Friday services at a Catholic Church near Grand Central. And what I saw surprised me: a full church; incredibly quiet; busy New Yorkers trying to pray, in true piety and humility. And I thought about that Minnesota lady, and Bach, and Shaw.

Bach didn't write music for dancing or elevators. And Shaw, certainly by the end of his life, had no interest in entertainment music.

The music, and music making, that moved him most was the music that was done for some kind of worship, praise, thanksgiving, supplication, and/or some kind of love. And it seems to me that what separates Shaw from the classical musical "business" is that this became virtually the only way he could approach music. And maybe this is the most important thing I can convey in the book.

I realize how privileged I was to hear Shaw doing it for his last time—because it was a culmination of all he'd sought, learned and felt about the work and this composer, and in some sense, a culmination of all is life.

APPENDIX XIII

Documentary Films of Robert Shaw Choral Workshops at Carnegie Hall

1. Preparing a Masterpiece, Vol. I
   Brahms: *German Requiem*
   Year of Performance: 1990

2. Preparing a Masterpiece, Vol. II
   Beethoven: *Missa Solemnis*
   Year of Performance: 1992

3. Preparing a Masterpiece, Vol. III
   Berlioz: *Requiem*
   Year of Performance: 1993

4. Preparing a Masterpiece, Vol. IV
   Britten: *War Requiem*
   Year of Performance: 1994

5. Preparing a Masterpiece, Vol. V
   Hindemith: *When When lilacs last in the dooryard bloom'd: A Requiem "For those we love"*
   Year of Performance: 1995

6. Preparing a Masterpiece, Vol. VI
   Verdi: *Requiem*
   Year of Performance: 1996

7. Preparing a Masterpiece, Vol. VII
   Mendelssohn: *Elijah*
   Year of Performance: 1997

8. Preparing a Masterpiece, Vol. VIII
   Haydn: *Creation* and *The Seasons*
   Year of Performance: 1998

Appendix XIV

Major Tours of the Robert Shaw Chorale (1948–1967)
(Compiled by Nathan Zullinger)

15 touring seasons

20 domestic tours to 46 states

(excluding Alaska, Hawaii, Nevada, North Dakota)

3 international tours to 30 foreign countries

DOMESTIC TOURS

TOUR #1: October 2 – November 13, 1948

Repertoire (PROGRAM A)

Bach: *Cantata 131, Aus der Tiefe*
Janequin: *Le Chant des Oiseaux*
Victoria: *O Vos Omnes*
Gibbons: *The Silver Swan*
Leisring: *Lift Up Your Heads*
Morley: *Agnus Dei*
Le Jeune: *Revecy Venir de Printemps*
Monteverdi: *Lacsiatemi Morire*
di Lasso: *Olá! O Che Bon Eccho! (Echo Song)*
Brahms: *Liebeslieder Walzer*, Opus 52 (Nos. 8–16)
Copland: *In the Beginning*
Hindemith: *Six Chansons*
Kubik: *American Folk-Song Sketches*
Dawson, arr.: *My Lord, What a Morning*
Kubik, arr.: *Soon One Morning*
Shaw, arr.: *If I Got My Ticket, Can I Ride?*
Brant, arr.: American Show Music (Rodgers, Porter, Gershwin, Kern)

Repertoire (PROGRAM B)

Bach: *Jesu, Meine Freude*

Brahms: Five Partsongs (Nachtwache I and II, Letztes Gluck, Verlorene Jugend, Im Herbst)

Janequin, Victoria, Gibbons, Leisring, Morley, Le Jeune, Monteverdi, di Lasso (from Program A)

Poulenc: *Mass in G Major*

Hindemith, Copland (from Program A)

Performance Locations

Cleveland, OH; Wheeling, WV; Athens, OH; Toledo, OH; Valparaiso, IN; Green Bay, WI; Cedar Falls, IA; Chicago, IL; Milwaukee, WI; Davenport, IA; Burlington, IA; Lincoln, NE; Kansas City, MO; Wichita, KS; Tulsa, OK; Stillwater, OK; Pittsburg, KS; Little Rock, AK; Ruston, LA; Galveston, TX; Houston, TX; Baton Rouge, LA; Pensacola, FL; Auburn, AL; Atlanta, GA; Greensboro, NC; Richmond, VA; Petersburg, VA; Birmingham, AL; Athens, GA; Clemson, SC; Rock Hill, SC; Fredericksburg, VA; Newburgh, NY; Hanover, NH; Saratoga, NY; Philadelphia, PA; Allentown, PA; Lewisburg, PA

TOUR #2: March 21 – April 10, 1949

Repertoire – See Tour #1

Performance Locations

Princeton, NJ; Ithaca, NY; Potsdam, NY; Canton, NY; Buffalo, NY; Fort Wayne, IN; Dubuque, IA; Mankato, MN; Minneapolis, MN; St. Cloud, MN; Moorhead, MN; Sioux Falls, SD; St. Louis, MO; Fort Wayne, IN; East Lansing, MI; Oberlin, OH; Syracuse, NY; Worcester, MA; Washington, DC; Hampton, VA

TOUR #3: October 2 – December 10, 1949

Repertoire

Handel: *Coronation Anthem No. 4, "Let Thy Hand Be Strengthened"*
Bach: *Cantata No. 4, "Christ Lag in Todesbanden"*
Schubert: *La Pastorella, An den Frühling, Ständchen, Widerspruch*
Gibbons: *This Is the Record of John*
Vecchi: *Fa una canzona*
Victoria: *O Magnum Mysterium*
Debussy: *Trois Chansons*
Poulenc: *Motets for a Time of Penitence*
Rameau: *Danse de Grand Clumet de la Paix (Les Indes Galantes)*
Mussorgsky: *The Death of Boris (Boris Godonov)*
Verdi: *Chorus of the Scotch Fugitives (Macbeth), Rataplan (La Forze del Destino)*
Kubik: *American Folk-Song Sketches*

Performance Locations

Syracuse, NY; Akron, OH; Toledo, OH, Bowling Green, OH; Lafayette, IN; Chicago, IL; South Bend, IN; Bloomington, IN; Terre Haute IN; Wheaton, IL; Cedar Falls, IA; Topeka, KS; Omaha, NE; St. Joseph, MO; Columbia, MO; Kansas City, MO; Beatrice, NE; Des Moines, IA; Lawrence, KS; Emporia, KS; Springfield, MO; Fayetteville, AK; Stillwater, OK; Amarillo, TX; Denton, TX; Fort Worth, TX; Dallas, TX; Abilene, TX; Austin, TX; Harlingen, TX; Laredo, TX; San Antonio, TX; College Station, TX; Beaumont, TX; Vicksburg, MS; Gadsden, AL; Anniston, AL; Pensacola, FL; Tallahassee, FL; Gainesville, FL; Orlando, FL; Miami, FL; Tampa, FL; Macon, GA; Opelika, AL; Savannah, GA; Augusta, GA; Montgomery, AL; Birmingham, AL; Atlanta, GA; Nashville, TN; Knoxville, TN; Asheville, NC; Lexington, KY, Huntington, WV; Charlottesville, VA; Philadelphia, PA; West Chester, PA; Port Jefferson, NY

TOUR #4: March 10 – March 31, 1950

Repertoire – See Tour #3

Performance Locations

Detroit, MI; Buffalo, NY; Detroit, MI; Harrisburg, PA; Lynchburg, VA; Charlotte, NC; Winston-Salem, NC; High Point, NC; Raleigh, NC; Greensboro, NC; Roanoke, VA; Staunton, VA; Washington, DC; Richmond, VA; Norfolk, VA; Amherst, MA; Montclair, NJ

TOUR #5: January 7 – March 18, 1951

Repertoire

Mozart: *Requiem*

Brahms: *Liebeslieder Walzer* (Nos. 8-16)

Ravel: *Trois Chansons*

Gershwin: "It Ain't Necessarily So" and "Gone, Gone, Gone" from *Porgy and Bess*

Performance Locations

Harrisonburg, VA; Chapel Hill, NC; Davidson, NC; Columbia, SC; Clemson, SC; Atlanta, GA; Knoxville, TN; Birmingham, AL; Tuscaloosa, AL; Montgomery, AL; Columbus, GA; Savannah, GA; St. Augustine, FL; Fort Pierce, FL; St. Petersburg, FL; Lakeland, FL; Jacksonville, FL; Athens, GA; Johnson City, TN; Bristol, VA; Cullowhee, NC; Nashville, TN; Oxford, MS; Monroe, LA; Jackson, MS; Mobile, AL; Baton Rouge, LA; Houston, TX; Corpus Christi, TX; Denton, TX; Lubbock, TX; Dallas, TX; Wichita Falls, KS; Chickasha, OK; Manhattan, KN; Kansas City, MO; Pittsburg, KS; Tulsa, OK; Springfield, MO; St. Louis, MO; Peoria, IL; Danville, IL; Normal, IL; Beloit, WI; Naperville, IL; Chicago, IL; East Lansing, MI; Oxford, OH; Wheaton, IL; Ashland, OH; Jamestown, NY; Mt. Lebanon, PA; Washington, DC; Reading, PA; Norfolk, VA; Durham, NC; Southern Pines, NC; Syracuse, NY; Ithaca, NY; Huntingdon, PA; New London, CT; Port Jefferson, NY; Boston, MA

TOUR #6: September 29 – December 16, 1951

Repertoire – See Tour #5

Performance Locations

Wausau, WI; Eau Claire, WI; Austin, MN; Minneapolis, MN; Rapid City, SD; Casper, WY; Laramie, WY; Denver, CO; Boulder, CO; Grand Junction, CO; Salt Lake City, UT; Ogden, UT; Pocatello, ID; Boise, ID; Lewiston, ID; Spokane WA; Missoula, MT; Helena, MT; Great Falls, MT; Billings, MT: Butte, MN; Walla Walla, WA; Yakima, WA; Wenatchee, WA; Tacoma, WA; Vancouver, BC; Seattle, WA; Longview, WA; Portland, OR; Salem, OR; Corvallis, OR; Eugene, OR; Klamath Falls, OR; Chico, CA; Sacramento, CA; San Francisco, CA; Berkeley, CA; Fresno, CA; San Jose, FA; Oakland, CA; Visalia, CA; Claremont, CA; Los Angeles, CA; Pasadena, CA; Bakersfield, CA; San Diego, CA; Yuma, AZ; Phoenix, AZ; Tucson, AZ; El Paso, TX; Roswell, NM; Los Alamos, NM; Albuquerque, NM; Wichita, KS; Lawrence, KS; Columbia, MS; Springfield, IL; Des Moines, IA; Waverly, IA; Rochester, MN; Kenosha, WI; Rockford, IL; Hillsdale, MI; Oberlin, OH; Pittsburgh, PA

TOUR #7: February 27 – March 28, 1952

Repertoire – See Tour #5

Performance Locations

Williamsport, PA; Wilkes-Barre, PA; Norristown, PA; Portland, ME; Orono, ME; Hanover, NH; Worcester, MA; Allentown, PA; Baltimore, MD; Lynchburg, VA; Lexington, KY; Louisville, KY; Dayton, OH; Mount Vernon, OH; Wauseon, OH; Fort Wayne, IN; Chicago, IL; Flint, MI; Ann Arbor, MI; Grand Rapids, MI; Saginaw, MI; Greensburg, PA; Weirton, WV; Pittsburgh, PA; New Castle, PA; York, PA; Lancaster, PA

TOUR #8: October 12 – December 17, 1952

Repertoire

Schütz: Three Motets
(*Die Mit Tränen Säen, Ich Bin eine Rufende Stimme, Selig Sind die Toten*)

Schubert: *Mass in G Major*

Bloch: *Sacred Service*

Parker/Shaw, arr.: Three Spanish Folksongs
(*Hacia Belén va un Borrico, La Virgen Lava Panales, Ya Viene La Vieja*)

Brahms: *Der Abend, Nächtens, Zum Schluss*

Debussy: *Trois Chansons de Charles d'Orléans*

Strauss: Choruses from *Die Fledermaus*

Performance Locations

Oxford, OH; Urbana, IL; La Porte, IN; Glen Ellyn, IL; Goshen, IN; Chicago, IL; Des Moines, IA; Iowa City, IA; Cedar Rapids, IA; Kansas City, MO; Omaha, NE; Sioux City, IA; La Crosse, WI; Sturgeon Bay, WI; Ishpeming, MI; Wheaton, IL; Columbia, MO; St. Louis, MO; Memphis, TN; Oxford, MS; Hammond, LA; New Orleans, LA; Baton Rouge, LA; Lake Charles, LA; Shreveport, LA; Port Arthur, TX; Houston, TX; Kingsville, TX; San Antonio, TX; Austin, TX; Wichita Falls, TX; Norman, OK; Natchitoches, LA; Hattiesburg, MS; Jackson, MS; Biloxi, MS; Montgomery, AL; Mobile, AL; St. Petersburg, FL; Lakeland, FL; Thomasville, GA; Birmingham, AL; Tuscaloosa, AL; Atlanta, GA; Rome, GA; Chattanooga, TN; Nashville, TN; Knoxville, TN; Clemson, SC; Rock Hill, SC; Columbia, SC; Savannah, GA; Southern Pines, NC; Greenville, NC; Raleigh, NC; Greensboro, NC

TOUR #9: March 5 – March 27, 1953

Repertoire – See Tour #8

Performance Locations

Elmira, NY; State College, PA; Pittsburgh, PA; Indiana, PA; Westerville, OH; Holland, MI; East Lansing, MI; Detroit, MI; Canton, OH; Ithaca, NY; Syracuse, NY; Gloversville, NY; Wellesley, MA; Baltimore, MD; Salisbury, MD; Lebanon, PA; New Haven, CT; White Plains, NY; Philadelphia, PA; Montclair, NJ

TOUR #10: September 29 – December 12, 1954

Repertoire

Victoria: *O Vos Omnes*
Byrd: *Christ Rising*
Vecchi: *Fa una canzona*
Mozart: Three Psalms from *Vesperae Solennes de Confessore*
Bach: *Jesu, Meine Freude*
Brahms: *Nachthelle, Ständchen*
Avshalomov: *Tom O'Bedlam*
Strauss: Choruses from *Die Fledermaus*

Performance Locations

Sandusky, OH; Grand Rapids, MI; Kohler, WI; Freeport, IL; Decorah, IA; Omaha, NE; Kearney, NE; Cheyenne, WY; Casper, WY; Denver, CO; Boulder, CO; Colorado Springs, CO; Grand Junction, CO; Salt Lake City, UT; Idaho Falls, ID; Boise, ID; Moscow, ID; Sunnyside, WA; Aberdeen, WA; Seattle, WA; Corvallis, OR; Portland, OR; Grants Pass, OR; Coos Bay, OR; Eureka, CA; Ukiah, CA; Burlingame, CA; Berkeley, CA; Sacramento, CA; Turlock, CA; Fresno, CA; Inyokern, CA; San Luis Obispo, CA; Santa Maria, CA; Glendale, CA; Pasadena, CA; Ontario, CA; Redlands, CA; San Diego, CA; Tempe, AZ; Tucson, AZ; El Paso, TX; Roswell, NM; Lubbock, TX; Pampa, TX; Liberal, KS; Dodge City, KS; Great Bend, KS; El Dorado, KS; Kansa City, MO; Burlington,

IA; Davenport, IA; Wheaton, IL; Beverly Hills, IL; Milwaukee, WI; Chicago, IL; Ann Arbor, MI; Mt. Clemens, MI; Columbus, OH; Youngstown, OH; Jamestown, NY; Hamilton, NY, Binghamton, NY

TOUR #11: March 4 – April 3, 1955

Repertoire – See Tour #10

Performance Locations

Bridgeport, CT; Wellesley, MA; Boston, MA; Saratoga Springs, NY; Hanover, NH; Utica, NY; Hazelton, PA; Newark, DE; Cleveland, OH; Defiance, OH; Detroit, MI; Port Huron, MI; Royal Oak, MI; Benton Harbor, MI; Elmburst, IL; Wilmette, IL; Decatur, IL; Cape Girardeau, MO; Evansville, IN; Lexington, KY; Charleston, WV (TOWN?); Waynesboro, PA; Atlantic City, NJ; Baltimore, MD; Philadelphia, PA; Millburn, NJ; Worcester, MA; Quincy, MA

TOUR #12: October 2 – December 11, 1955

Repertoire

Honeggar: *King David*

Bach: *Magnificat*

Performance Locations

Parkersburg, WV; Marion, OH; Lima, OH; Bloomington, IN; Muncie, IN; Louisville, KY; Memphis, TN; El Dorado, AK; Monroe, LA; Vicksburg, MS; Alexandria, LA; Lafayette, LA; Orange, TX; Galveston, TX; Houston, TX; Beaumont, TX; College Station, TX; San Antonio, TX; Brownsville, TX; McAllen, TX; San Angelo, TX; Temple, TX; Austin, TX; Greenville, TX; Ardmore, OK; Fort Smith, AK; Fayetteville, AK; Jefferson City, MO; Carbondale, IL; St. Louis, MO; Clinton, IA; Wauwatosa, WI; Urbana, IL; Waverly, IA; Faribault, MN; Virginia, MN; Moorhead, MN; Winnipeg, Manitoba; Winona, MN; Shorewood, WI; Muskegon, MI; Battle Creek, MI; Highland Park, IL;

Chicago, IL; Kalamazoo, MI; Ann Arbor, MI; Hamilton, ON; London, ON; Toronto, ON; Buffalo, NY; Greensburg, PA; Clarksburg, WV; Gettysburg, PA; Syracuse, NY; Kingston, NY; New Haven, CT; Pittsfield, MA; Stoneham, MA; Rockland, ME; Augusta, ME; Bangor, ME

TOUR #13: February 2 – April 5, 1959

Repertoire

Handel: Suite from *Acis and Galatea*

Fauré: *Requiem*

Hindemith: "True Love" from *Five Songs on Old Texts*

Bartók: "Love Song" from *Four Hungarian Folksongs*

Schoenberg: "The Lover's Wish" from *Vier Stück*

Stravinsky: "With Air Commanding" from *The Rake's Progress*

Brahms: *Alto Rhapsody*

Offenbach: Suite from *Les Brigands*

Performance Locations

Hartford, CT; New Haven, CT; Utica, NY; Philadelphia, PA; Lansdale, PA; Washington, DC; Richmond, VA; Norfolk, VA; Charlotte, NC; Spartanburg, SC; Knoxville, TN; Atlanta, GA; Columbus, GA; Birmingham, AL; Pittsburg, KS; Kansas City, MO; Manhattan, KS; Joplin, MO; Columbia, MO; St. Joseph, MO; Lincoln, NE; Omaha, NE; Minneapolis, MN; Moorhead, MN; Madison, WI; Ames, IA; Cedar Rapids, IA; Wilmette, IL; Wheaton, IL; Chicago, IL; Canton, IL: Peoria, IL; Bloomington, IN; Indianapolis, IN; Detroit, MI; Ann Arbor, MI; East Lansing, MI; Kitchener, ON; Hamilton, ON; Hamilton, NY; Montclair, NJ; Brooklyn, NY; Allentown, PA; Corning, NY; Rochester, NY; Greensburg, PA; Uniontown, PA; Abington, PA; Wilmington, DE

TOUR #14: February 1 – March 13, 1960

Repertoire

Bach: *Mass in B Minor*

Performance Locations

Hartford, CT; New Haven, CT; Lancaster, PA; Kent, OH; Columbus, OH; Lafayette, IN; East Lansing, MI; Goshen, IN; Grand Rapids, MI; South Bend, IN; Madison, WI; Chicago, IL; Milwaukee, WI; Waverly, IA; Des Moines, IA; Iowa City, IA; Wheaton, IL; Urbana, IL; Oxford, MS; Ruston, LA; Hattiesburg, MS; Tuscaloosa, AL; Tallahassee, FL; Atlanta, GA; Nashville, TN; Johnson City, TN; Winston-Salem, NC; Durham, NC; Lynchburg, VA; Washington, DC; Philadelphia, PA; Ottawa, ON; Burlington, VT; Hanover, NH; South Hadley, MA; New York, NY; Storrs, CT

TOUR #15: January 8 – March 19, 1961

Repertoire

Bach: *Singet dem Herrn*

Haydn: *Seven Last Words*

Carissimi: *Jephte*

Britten: *Ceremony of Carols*

Performance Locations

State College, PA; Alliance, OH; Findlay, OH; Kalamazoo, MI; Ann Arbor, MI; Detroit, MI; Valparaiso, IN; Chicago, IL; River Forest, IL; Freeport, IL; Freemont, NE; Boulder, CO; Grand Junction, CO; Logan, UT; Pocatello, ID; Boise, ID; Pasco, WA; Moscow, ID; Yakima, WA; Vancouver, BC; Seattle, WA; Salem, OR; Corvallis, OR; Eureka, CA; Santa Rosa, CA; Richmond, CA; San Jose, CA; San Francisco, CA; Sacramento, CA; Fresno, CA; Burbank, CA; Ontario, CA; Hollywood, CA; Pasadena, CA; Redlands, CA; Yuma, AZ; Phoenix, AZ; Tucson, AZ; Albuquerque, NM; Roswell, NM; Midland, TX; Dallas, TX; Wichita Falls, TX; Oklahoma City, OK; Stillwater, OK; Topeka, KS;

Manhattan, KS; Alton, IL; Evansville, IL; Lexington, KY; Indianapolis, IN; Oxford, OH; Wheeling, WV; Frederick, MD; Washington, DC; Baltimore, MD; Towson, MD; West Chester, PA; Philadelphia, PA; Bridgeport, CN; Boston, MA

TOUR #16: January 29 – March 18, 1962

Repertoire

Bach: *St. John Passion*

Performance Locations

Greenville, NC; Raleigh, NC; Winston-Salem, NC; Durham, NC; Salisbury, NC; Greenville, SC; Atlanta, GA; Auburn, AL; Oxford, MI; Ruston, LA; Grambling, LA; Ruston, LA; Shreveport, LA; Fort Worth, TX; Waco, TX; Austin, TX; Houston, TX; Longview, TX; Norman, OK; Kansas City, MO; Jacksonville, IL; Milwaukee, WI; South Bend, IN; Chicago, IL; Goshen, IN; Bloomington, IN; Muncie, IN; Kent, OH; Columbus, OH; Philadelphia, PA; Hackettstown, NJ; Summit, NJ; New York City, NY; Concord, NH; Wellesley, MA; Washington, DC; Johnstown, PA; Indiana, PA; Pittsburgh, PA; Warren, OH; Houghton, NY; Rochester, NY

TOUR #17: January 3 – 27, 1963

Repertoire

Bach: *Jesu, Meine Freude*

Mozart: Three Psalms, from *Vesperae Solennes de Confessore*

Schoenberg: *Friede auf Erden*

Ives: *Harvest Home Chorales*

Ravel: *Trois Chansons*

Gershwin: *Lament for Brother Robbins,* from *Porgy and Bess*

Performance Locations

Plainfield, NJ; Lewisburg, PA; Corning, NY; Jamestown, NY; Buffalo, NY; Columbus, OH; Lexington, KY; Athens, OH; Detroit, MI; Chicago, IL; Harvey, IL; Springfield, IL; Zanesville, OH; Wilkes-Barre, PA; New York, NY; Great Neck, NY; Kingstown, NY; New Haven, CT; Worcester, MA; Philadelphia, PA; Greenwich, CT; Atlantic City, NJ; Washington, DC

TOUR #18: January 13 – March 23, 1964

Repertoire

Carissimi: *Jephthah*
Britten: *Rejoice in the Lamb,* Opus 30
Haydn: *Mass in D Minor*
Brahms: *Liebeslieder Walzer,* Opus 52

Performance Locations

Schenectady, NY; Manchester, NH; Portland, ME; Rutland, VT; Darien, CT; Manhasset, NY; Richmond, VA; Portsmouth, VA; Roanoke, VA; Asheville, NC; Columbia, SC; Rome, GA; Sarasota, FL; Tampa, FL, Fort Myers, FL; Ft. Lauderdale, FL; Miami Beach, FL; Jacksonville, FL; Atlanta, GA; Carbondale, IL; St. Louis, MO; Kansas City, MO; Manhattan, KS; Holdrege, NE; Omaha, NE; Ottumwa, IA; Waterloo IA; Rock Island, IL; Fairfield, IA; Terre Haute, IN; Urbana, IL; Rockford, IL; Platteville, WI; Madison, WI; Milwaukee, WI; Chicago, IL; Goshen, IN; De Kalb, IL; Oak Lawn, IL; Wheaton, IL; North Manchester, In; Muncie, IN; Louisville, KY; Owensboro, KY; Ft. Wayne, IN; Bowling Green, OH; Elyria, OH; Cuyahoga Falls, OH; Rochester, NY; Rome, NY; Hamilton, ON; Kitchener, ON; Haddonfield, NJ; Washington, DC; Coatesville, PA; Rye, NY; Garden City, NY; Morristown, NJ; New York, NY; Boston, MA

TOUR #19: March 31 – May 5, 1966

Repertoire

Handel: *Messiah*

Performance Locations

Cortlandt, NY; Lewisburg, PA; Huntington, NY; College Park, MD; Richmond, VA; Durham, NC; Rock Hill, SC; Atlanta, GA; Birmingham, AL; Auburn, AL; Tuscaloosa, AL; Jackson, MS; Baton Rouge, LA; Denton, TX; Muskogee, OK; Sherman, TX; Lawrence, KS; Kirksville, MO; Hopkinsville, KY; Indianapolis, IN; Lafayette, IN; Albion, MI; Goshen, IN; Green Bay, WI; Wheaton, IL; Chicago, IL, De Kalb, IL; Detroit, MI; New Kensington, PA; Rochester, NY; Amherst, MA

TOUR #20: April 3 – May 13, 1967

Repertoire

Poulenc: *Mass in G Major*

Hindemith: *Six Chansons*

Ives: *Psalm 90*

Ginastera: *Lamentations of Jeremiah*

Webern: *Entflieht auf leichten Kähnen*

Debussy: *Trois Chansons*

Schoenberg: *Friede auf Erden*

Performance Locations

Red Bank, NJ; Nashua, NH; New Haven, CT; Bethlehem, PA; Ithaca, NY; Scranton, PA; Richmond, VA; Durham, NC; Greensboro, NC; Clemson, SC; Columbia, SC; Athens, GA; Chattanooga, TN; Huntsville, AL; Owensboro, KY; Kansas City, MO; Quincy, IL; Normal, IL; Dubuque, IA; Stevens Point, WI; Appleton, WI; Kankakee, IL; Mishawaka, IN; Chicago, IL; Hinsdale, IL; Grand Rapids, MI; Kent, OH; Cumberland, MD; Washington, DC; University Park, PA; New Brunswick, NJ; Montclair, NJ; Philadelphia, PA; Waynesboro, VA; Wilmington, DE; Flushing, NY

INTERNATIONAL TOURS

TOUR OF EUROPE AND THE MIDDLE EAST:

March 16 – June 1, 1956

Repertoire

Schubert: *Mass in G Major*

Bach: *Christ lag in Todesbanden*

Mozart: *Requiem*

Lasso: *Olá! O Che Bon Eccho!*

Victoria: *O Vos Omnes*

Byrd: *Christ Rising Again*

Schütz: *Selig Sind die Toten*

Vecchi: *Fa una canzona*

Brahms: *Liebeslieder Walzer (Nos. 8-16)*

Ives: *Lord of the Harvest*

Barber: *O Thou Who Art Unchangeable*

Copland: *The Lark*

Gershwin: *Lament for Brother Robbins from Porgy and Bess*

Performance Locations

EGYPT: Cairo, Alexandria; LEBANON: Beirut; ISRAEL: Tel Aviv, Jerusalem, Haifa, En Geb, Ramat Gan; TURKEY: Istanbul, Ankara; GREECE: Athens, Salonika; YUGOSLAVIA; Belgrade, Zagreb; ITALY: Trieste, Venice, Rome; AUSTRIA: Salzburg, Innsbruck; GERMANY: Munich, Stuttgart, Cologne, Berlin, Hamburg; SWITZERLAND: Geneva, Berne; SPAIN: Madrid, Barcelona; PORTUGAL: Lisbon; FRANCE: Paris; ENGLAND: London, Liverpool, Manchester; HOLLAND: The Hague; DENMARK: Copenhagen; SWEDEN: Gothenburg, Stockholm; NORWAY: Oslo; FINLAND: Helsinki; ICELAND: Reykjavik

TOUR OF THE SOVIET UNION: September 30 – November 28, 1962

Repertoire (Program A)

Victoria: *O Vos Omnes*

Gibbons: *This Is the Record of John*

Schütz: *Selig Sind die Toten*

Vecchi: *Fa una canzona*

Lasso: *Ola! O Che Bon Eccho!*

Schubert: *Mass in G*

Schoenberg: *Friede auf Erden*

Avshalomov: *Tom O'Bedlam*

Debussy: *Trois Chansons*

Gershwin: *Lament for Brother Robbin*

Repertoire (Program B)

Bach: *Jesu, Meine Freude*

Mozart: Three Psalms from *Vesperae Solennes de Confessore*

Schoenberg: *Friede auf Erden*

Dello Joio: *Mystic Trumpeter*

Ravel: *Trois Chansons*

Ives: *Harvest Home Chorales*

Repertoire (Program C)

Bach: *Mass in B Minor*

Performance Locations

GERMANY: Berlin; YUGOSLAVIA: Belgrade, Skoplje, Sarajevo, Zagreb; SOVIET UNION: Moscow, Minsk, Leningrad, Kiev, Lvov, Chernovtsy, Kishiniev, Odessa, Yalta, Simferopol, Ryazan

TOUR OF SOUTH AMERICA: May 14 – July 23, 1964

Repertoire (Program A)

Bach: *B Minor Mass*

Repertoire (Program B)

Victoria: *O vos omnes*

Gibbons: *This Is the Record of John*

Schütz: *Selig sind die Toten*
Vecchi: *Fa una canzona*
di Lasso: *The Echo Song*
Schubert: *Mass in G*
Schoenberg: *Friede auf Erden*
Copland: *In the Beginning*
Halffter: *Ters Epitafios*
Ives: *Harvest Home Chorales*

Program (Program C)

Carissimi: *Jephthah*
Mozart: Three Psalms from *Vesperae Solennes de Confessor*
Schoenberg: *Friede auf Erden*
Schuman: *Prelude for Voices*
Barber: *Stopwatch and an Ordnance Map*
Copland: *The Lark*
Ginastera: *Lamentations of Jeremiah*
Gershwin: *Lament for Brother Robbins,* from *Porgy and Bess*
Villa Lobos: *Caboca de Cazanga*
Chivas, Carlos: *La Palemes Amul* (Boosey)

Performance Locations

COLOMBIA: Bogotá, Cali, Popayan, Pereira, Medellin
ECUADOR: Quito, Ibarra, Cuenca, Guayaquil
PERU: Lima
CHILE: Santiago, Valparaiso, Santiago
ARGENTINA: Mendoza, Cordoba, Rosario, Buenos Aires, Corrientes
URAGUAY: Montevideo
PARAGUAY: Asuncion
BRAZIL: Rio de Janeiro, Brasilia, Recife, Fortaleza, Belem

Appendix XV

Commissions and Premieres Conducted by Robert Shaw
(Compiled by Nathan Zullinger)

Composer	Work	Premiere	Forces	Date	Notes
Anderson, T. J.	*Messages*	World	ASO	1980	ASO Commission
Anderson, T. J.	*Spirituals*	World	ASO, MCGC, SCGC	1982	Commissioned by Union United Methodist Church, Boston
Avshalomov, Jacob	*Tom O'Bedlam*	World	CC	1953	CC Commission
Bacon, Ernest	*Five Fables*	World	CC	1953	
Barber, Samuel	*A Stopwatch and an Ordnance Map*	World	CC	1945	
Bernstein, Leonard	*Missa Brevis*	World	ASO/ ASOC	1988	ASO Commission
Bryant, Henry	*Desert Forests*	World	ASO	1985	ASO Commission
Copland, Aaron	*Canticle of Freedom*	World	ASO/CGA	1967	Robert Shaw Commission
Copland, Aaron	*In the Beginning*	World	RSC		
Dello Joio, Norman	*Western Star*	World	CC/WGC	1945	CC Commission
Erb, Donald	*Concerto for Orchestra*	World	ASO	1985	ASO Commission
Foss, Lukas	*The Prairie*	World	CC	1944	CC Commission
Glass, Philip	*Itaipú*	World	ASO/ ASOC	1989	ASO Commission
Gould, Morton	*Soundings*	World	ASO	1969	ASO Commission

Composer	Work	Premiere	Forces	Date	Notes
Harbison, John	*Remembering Gatsby*	World	ASO	1986	ASO Commission
Hindemith, Paul	*Apparebit repetina dies*	World	CC	1947	
Hindemith, Paul	*When lilacs last in the dooryard bloom'd: A Requiem "For those we love"*	World	CC	1946	CC Commission
Ibert, Jacques	*Tropismes pour des amours imagi-naires*	US	ASO	1977	ASO (Group Commission)
Joplin, Scott[1]	*Treemonisha*	World	ASO/ ASOC	1972	
Kay, Ulysses	*Theatre Set*	World	ASO	1968	ASO Commission
Kolb, Barbara	*The Enchanted Loom*	World	ASO	1990	ASO Commission
Lewis, John	*Tales of the Willow Tree*	World	ASO	1987	ASO Commission
MacInnis, Donald	*Intersections for Tape Recorder and Orchestra*	World	ASO		ASO Commission
Menin, Peter	*The Cycle*	World	CC	1949	CC Commission
Menotti, Gian Carlo	*For the Death of Orpheus*	World	ASO/ ASOC	1990	ASO Commission

Composer	Work	Premiere	Forces	Date	Notes
Meyerowitz, Jan	*Flemish Overture, "Homage to Pieter Breughel"*	World	CO	1959	
Parker, Alice	*Earth, Sky, Spirit*	World	YSC, ASO	1986	Young Singers of Callanwolde Commission
Parker, Alice	*Gaudete (Six Latin Hymns)*	World	ASO/ ASOC	1973	ASO Commission
Parker, Alice	*Seven Carols for Christmas*	World	ASO/ ASOC	1972	ASO Commission
Paulus, Stephen	*Concertante*	World	ASO	1989	ASO Commission
Paulus, Stephen	*Violin Concerto* [No. 1]	World	ASO William Preucil, violin	1987	ASO Commission
Poulenc, Francis	*Stabat Mater*	US	RSC	1952	
Rodrigo, Joaquín	*Concierto de Aranjuez*	US	CO	1959	
Rorem, Ned	*String Symphony*	World	ASO	1985	ASO Commission
Schumann, William	*On Freedom's Ground*	S..East US	ASOC/ ASO	1987	ASO (Group Commission)
Singleton, Alvin	*Shadows*	World	ASO	1987	ASO Commission
Smith, Russell	*Magnificat for Chorus, Soprano Solo, and Orchestra*	World	CO/COC	1969	CO 50th Anniversary Commission

Composer	Work	Premiere	Forces	Date	Notes
Taylor, Billy	*Peaceful Warrior*	World	Billy Taylor Trio, MCGC, SCGC, ASO	1984	ASO Commission
Tillis, Frederick	*In the Spirit and the Flesh*	World	MCGC, SCGC, ASO	1985	ASO Commission
White, Taylor	*Triptych for Orchestra*	World	ASO	1984	ASO Commission

INDEX

About the Author

Keith C. Burris is associate editor of *The Blade* in Toledo, Ohio. He was, for many years, editorial page editor of the *Journal Inquirer* in Manchester, Connecticut. He has written widely on politics, government, culture, and the arts for publications ranging from *Commonweal,* to *The Christian Science Monitor, The New York Times,* and *The Los Angeles Times.* He holds a PhD from the University of Pittsburgh and has taught at a number of American colleges and universities. He and his wife Amy, an artist, have three grown children, Alexander, Sophia, and William.